Sounding Out Semantics

The Limits of Philosophy

by R.J. Mott Jr.

Hermeneutic circle:
The problems in the process of interpretation that arise
when one element, for instance in a text, can only be understood in
terms of the meanings of others or of the whole text, yet understanding
these other elements, or the whole text, in turn presupposes understanding
of the original element. Each can only be understood in the light of the
others. Similarly, we may hold that the past can only be understood in the
light of the present, and the present can only be understood in the light of
the past.
The phenomenon has preoccupied German thinkers from
Schleiermacher and Dilthey through to Heidegger and Gadamer.
In Anglo-American philosophy a similar problem arises from the holism
of meaning, but is not generally felt to pose a fundamental difficulty:
as Wittgenstein said: light dawns gradually over the whole.
Oxford Dictionary of Philosophy.

Foreword

As you read this book, please keep in mind that it is a work of philosophy. A good philosopher checks his assumptions at the door. I have done so. That does not make me a good philosopher, but it's a start. I take a radical approach to many of the traditional problems of analytic philosophy. So radical in fact, that you may be inclined to dismiss the work out of hand before reading it completely. Please give it a chance. I ask you the reader to complete the hermeneutic circle that I present.

Although this book is a philosophical work, it is not meant to be a survey of Western philosophy. There are others who have written such works. However, inevitably, many of the great thinkers of occidental culture will come into play. Their impact on Western thinking and philosophy is transparent. I make no pretenses about having expertise in the nuances of each, but I do have a sense of direction and believe that I know how and why we have reached the juncture where we in analytic philosophy find ourselves.

Much of what is considered philosophy these days consists of advice, practical philosophies that do not explain, but offer platitudes meant to guide everyday living. These philosophies, while offering solace to those who need it, offer no understanding. The preachers and their followers are in full scale retreat from any attempt to explain or understand this world. Coping is the message they preach. Peace of mind, solace and hope are the ultimate objectives. So, the traditional philosophical conundrums and puzzles remain.

The contemporary revival of spiritualism is a movement in that direction. The modern-day snake oil salesmen are peddling metaphysical nostrums and potions to the gullible patients who suffer the pangs of secularism. The patients seek comfort, not understanding. Words can provide that comfort. However, I will return to reason and analysis in an attempt to provide understanding. Emotion may be a more powerful determiner of human behavior, but only reason and analysis can give us the explanations and principles that will take precedence over those emotions and save us from ourselves.

Analysis has overtaken speculation as a methodology in Western philosophy, particularly in the British/American tradition. The founding fathers of analysis had brought philosophical analysis to a point where language was at the cutting edge. They realized the significance of language in philosophical debate and had hoped to clear up the turgid thinking of previous philosophers by cleaning up the language. Language usage is the front line in the battle for clarity.

If we are to understand ourselves and our role in the universe we must have a starting point, a point on which we can all agree. Language is that point. As always, the devil is in the details.

The importance of ordinary language in doing philosophy has been acknowledged by many philosophers. Yet many other philosophers downplayed the importance of language or even dismissed it as a passing fancy. But it seems to me that understanding how we humans use language must be the cornerstone of any philosophical position. So that is where we must start.

June, 2020
Verona, WI

Contents

Chapter Three, Dualism

Chapter Four, Linguistic Puzzles

Chapter 5, Mathematics

Chapter VI, Epistemology

Chapter 00000111, The Universe

CHAPTER ONE
SEMANTICS

Introduction

Words mystify us. Humans have been using words for eons, since long before recorded history. Human speech provided the means by which we increased our dominion over nature and enabled our species to prosper far beyond what our physical abilities would allow. Words have given humans a power and reach that far exceed those of our closest relatives in the animal kingdom. Yet, with all of our linguistic sophistication, we humans have been unable to give an adequate explanation for what we do with words. Words continue to mystify us. In this book I hope to provide some new insights that might lead the way to an adequate account of what we do with words, how language works. Armed with that knowledge, we will investigate other areas of analytic philosophy.

We must begin our discussion of language by acknowledging the inherent difficulties in talking about language. The difficulties arise because we must use language to talk about language. Philosophers often refer to the object language, the one they talk about, and the meta-language, the language they use to talk about the object language. They can both be the same language, as is the case in this book. I will be using English as the meta-language and English as the object language for the most part. I must use the language I grew up in. I must add a caveat concerning this book. All of linguistics is afflicted with terminological mayhem. Any survey of linguistics will find a total lack of terminological discipline. Hundreds of terms are used in a multitude of inconsistent ways. Even basic terms such as "statement", "syntax" and "language" are redefined regularly to fit the needs of theorists. Theoretical terms such as "productive" and "inflectional" appear to be even more flexible. Nevertheless, I will be using many of these terms without defining them. In reading the book you will learn why.

In writing this book I have used a few conventions that are specific to this book. To establish and maintain the distinction between speech and written language, I use different fonts. I do so because that distinction is critical for my analysis. For the most part, when I discuss words and language, I will be discussing speech, the vocalizations humans make. As such, I will be using double quotes and a bold script font: *"the dish ran away with the spoon"* to represent speech. The readers may, of course, vocalize the words to remind themselves of the fact that I am specifically talking about the sounds. At times, I request the readers do so, just to remind them of the fact that word sounds have acoustic characteristics, not letters. Also remember that spoken words cannot be misspelled, capitalized, punctuated, or use different fonts.

When referring to the printed words on paper or the pixels on a monitor or other device, as the case may be, I will use a different bold font: **'The dish ran away with the spoon'** with inverted commas. When this font is used, I am specifically writing about the written word in any form, the visual squiggles and lines that appear on various media in various forms. The written word **'spoon'** has five letters. The spoken word *"spoon"* does not; it only has acoustic properties. I also retain the customary practice of using italics for emphasis.

The Science of Linguistics

Although *philosophers* have long discussed the nature of language, the origin of language and the childhood acquisition of language, only relatively recently have these areas of study become subjects of *empirical* enquiry. The starting point for the empirical study of language can be dated around the beginning of the 19th century when linguists attempted to reconstruct a Proto-Indo-European language and determine how it evolved into a multitude of modern European languages by tracing the changes in these languages over the centuries. Historical linguistics took root and engendered a systematic study of languages and their historical origins.

The turn of the 20th century brought about a change of direction for linguistics. Jean Aitchison provides the insight:

> "In the 20th century, the emphasis shifted from language change to language
> description. Instead of looking at how a selection of items changed in a number
> of different languages, linguists began to concentrate on describing single
> languages at one particular point in time." Aitchison (1992: 23)

The era of descriptive linguistics had begun. Linguists began to view themselves as true scientists and treated speech and writing in different languages as observable data that could be systematically recorded and analyzed for differing grammatical structures and cross-language comparisons. Rather than investigating the historical roots of European languages and the changes that were occurring, linguists began to study and describe the structural components of an increasingly diverse multitude of modern languages being discovered and used worldwide.

During the latter half of the 20th century linguistics once again changed course. In addition to recording data and analyzing it for the purpose of describing the structures of various languages, *linguists* began to speculate about how it is that humans are able to produce the speech that is observed. How is it that the human ability to speak is virtually *universal*? What sort of universal features of speech underlie this universal ability? And how is it that people are able to *generate* an infinite amount of novel speech output from finite input. What sort of system or mechanism can produce the speech behavior we humans exhibit? Led by American Noam Chomsky, many *linguists* began the quest to discover and describe a *universal generative grammar* that could explain the observed speech phenomena. This quest has produced thousands of studies and hundreds of controversies over various theories to explain the data found in these studies.

After over a century of systematic empirical study of languages by linguists we are currently left with libraries of data. Yet, nobody has provided an uncontroversial theoretical framework that can explain how humans manage to communicate via language. Nor has anyone been able to provide a conclusive or even convincing argument for any comprehensive theory that can explain how basic human verbal communication skills were first acquired by the human species or how those skills are acquired by individual humans. How and when did the human race begin to speak? How do children learn to speak? What is happening when people speak to each other?

There has been a great deal of data collected, but no generally agreed upon theories to explain the data. The speculation continues.

Nevertheless, as a result of the empirical approach to the study of language over the last two centuries, the *science* of linguistics has been compartmentalized, as are all sciences. That is the essence of Western reductionism. *Reductionism* is a methodology that *reduces* structures and processes to more fundamental components. The complex is reduced to and explained in terms of simpler components. The reductionist methodology was brought about by many historical forces, not the least of which was the sequential linear thinking brought about by written language. This reductionism in the study of language has produced the fields of *phonetics, syntax, semantics, pragmatics* and a host of sub-groupings.

In very basic terms, *phonetics* is concerned with the study of *phones*, the basic units of sound that comprise the word sounds we humans utter. *Phonemes* are categories of phones. Linguists who specialize in phonetics have developed detailed descriptions of the many acoustic variations in human speech. They have accumulated massive amounts of data from many languages and detailed the cultural differences and historical changes in word pronunciation. They continue to monitor and record the ever-changing phonetic landscape and attempt to discover the forces and processes that produce these changes in phones and phonemes.

Syntax is the study of the structure of phrases and sentences, the order in which we humans utter words. During speech, words are *non-randomly* combined into phrases and sentences. These phrases and sentences have a syntactic structure. Syntacticians attempt to determine the rules by which speakers construct grammatically correct phrases and sentences. They parse sentences, identify grammatical constituents and attempt to detail how those constituents are related in systematic ways. Syntax is said to provide the rules for building sentence meanings from word meanings. According to some theorists, syntax examines the relation of signs to signs, how the words relate to one another within a grammar.

While phonetics and syntax are of some interest to *philosophers*, they are considered to be more empirical and, as such, within the purview of descriptive linguists. The fields of semantics and pragmatics have been the primary focus of philosophers of language. *Semantics* is said to explore the relation of word symbols to their *meanings* and *referents*. Semanticists attempt to tease out the semantic content of words by isolating them from any syntactic or pragmatic considerations, i.e. how they are being used on any occasion. How speakers employ the words or what effect the words have on listeners is not relevant to a semanticist. Semanticists say that they are not interested in what a speaker is thinking or implying; they are only interested in what the words themselves say, whether written or uttered. The words carry the semantic content independently of what is going on in the speaker's mind or the context of an utterance. The job of semanticists is to take the grammatical location, the speaker, the context and any other pragmatic considerations out of the analysis and determine the lexical or literal meanings and/or the referents of words.

These independent lexical meanings and referents can then be combined syntactically to determine the semantic content of larger grammatical units such as phrases or sentences. Most semanticists claim that computing the *meaning of a sentence* requires that speakers and hearers grasp the semantic content of the individual words and the grammatical structure of the sentence. Consider the English utterances "*mary gave to bob...*" vs. "*bob gave to mary...*", for instance. Who gave to who is determined by the grammatical structure of the statement, i.e. the syntax.

Thus, by combining knowledge of the lexicon with knowledge of syntax, competent language users are able to properly interpret what these larger units of grammar mean. (In Latin, word order has no effect on a word's role as subject or object.)

In addition to the lexicon and syntax, all competent speakers must take into account the *pragmatic* elements of any utterance on each occasion of use. Each utterance or vocal production of a sentence must be analyzed separately according to pragmaticists (not pragmatists). These theorists study language *in use*. Although all languages are said to have words with lexical meanings and rules of grammar that can be isolated from their users and studied independently, speakers and writers can still utilize these elements in many different ways depending upon *pragmatic* considerations. Thus, speakers are able to use words figuratively, metaphorically, ironically, metonymically and so on, where the lexical meanings of the words used do not produce the message that the speaker is sending, e.g. the coach says: "*we Killed em*".

Pragmaticists often claim that the audience must read the speaker's intentions and consider the context of the speech to accurately interpret what *the speaker meant* by the production of any utterance. There are many such *pragmatic* considerations that must be taken into account for listeners to properly construe the message a speaker is sending, a message that differs from the literal or lexical meaning of the sentence, the semantic content. Consequently, theorists can say that there is a distinction between sentence meaning (semantics) and utterance meaning (semantics plus pragmatics).

In this book, I will attempt to show that the *semantic/pragmatic* distinction is illegitimate, and that whole enterprise of semantics is ill founded and fallacious. The conventional account of what we humans do with words is founded on an ancient analysis that has evolved and mutated, but not eliminated the basic premise that words are *signs or symbols that stand for, express, signify, represent, encode, designate, denote or refer to semantic content: their lexical meanings and referents.* I will try to provide a persuasive argument that spoken words are not signs or symbols that encode semantic content. I will try to demonstrate that this semantic premise in all of linguistic theory is fallacious and distorts all attempts to explain how words function in human behavior. I hope to persuade you that spoken words, i.e. vocal utterances, have a multitude of *uses in context*, but *no stable meanings or referents that are context neutral*. Nor do they represent or express anything in the speaker's mind. That is, human languages are not representational symbolic systems. I hope to persuade you that all human speech is conditioned verbal behavior that has consequences and is sensitive to time, location, *context* broadly construed, and the speaker's speech history.

If you accept this hypothesis, it has enormous ramifications for our understanding of the acquisition and use of language by humans. Along with the ramifications on language acquisition and use, this new hypothesis of language impacts all other areas of human knowledge and behavior.

The Historical Context
for Modern Semantics

The historical backdrop for Western philosophical analysis and the semantic theory of language is crucial to understanding the current perplexities in linguistics and philosophy of language, as well as the layman's view of what we do with words. A brief review will set the stage for critical analysis.

Philosophers have been philosophizing throughout recorded history and probably before then. They do so with words. If they philosophized with words, it was only natural to philosophize *about* words. Long ago, philosophers began to talk about their talk.

Within Occidental culture philosophizing about words was first recorded by the Greeks. Thus, we must start our historical journey with Plato who set the semantic tone for language theory in the West. As Bertrand Russell explains:

> "There is, however, something of great importance in Plato's doctrine which is not traceable to his predecessors, and that is the theory of 'ideas' or 'forms.' This theory is partly logical and partly metaphysical. ...Language cannot get along without general words such as 'cat,' and such words are evidently not meaningless. But if the word 'cat' means anything, it means something which is not this or that cat, but some kind of universal cattyness. This is the logical part of the doctrine. ... According to the metaphysical part of the doctrine, the word 'cat' stands for a certain ideal cat, *'the'* cat, created by God, and unique."
> Russell (1945: 121)

Plato fully recognized that many words were general words that could not be paired with any individual objects or *particulars*. The word sound *"cat"* did not refer to any individual cat; it referred to all cats. He concluded that the word *"cat"* must stand for or refer to an ideal cat, or a "universal cattiness". General words stood for these ideal forms by Plato's account of human word use. Spoken word symbols such as *"cat"*, *"justice"* and *"triangle"* along with their written forms had semantic referents in a parallel universe, the ideal cat, the ideal of justice, the ideal triangle and so on.[1]

After Plato, Aristotle proffered an internal mental *entity* as the semantic correlate of the word *"cat"*. General words had corresponding meanings that were mental in nature, not Platonic ideal forms in another ontological realm. The semantic correlates of many words were inside of human heads, Aristotle claimed. There was something *essential* to cats, that which makes cats cats. That essence was internalized as an impression on the soul and the meaning of the word sign *"cat"*. The meanings of general words became entities within the speaker rather than external ideal forms of Plato. Spoken words were signs or symbols that stood for, expressed, signified, represented, encoded, designated, denoted or referred to internal entities and processes: ideas, concepts, thoughts etc.

Arthur Danto cites Aristotle as he explains conventional philosophical thinking about language:

> "It happens that we have three (at least) media in which to operate. Such a view is already in Aristotle, who writes: 'Spoken words are symbols of mental experience, and written words are the symbols of spoken words.'" via Hook (1969: 126)

Since then, and in most of Western philosophy, spoken words have been considered to be signs or symbols that stand for, express, signify, represent, encode, designate, denote or refer to abstractions, thoughts, ideas, concepts and mental representations that flow through the human mind or consciousness.

Significantly, the Greeks made no distinction between words, names and nouns. Their word for all three was the same. Greek grammar was primitive at best. As Gilbert Ryle put it:

> "It was hard in Greek to even say that the Greek counterpart to our verb "is" was a word but not a noun. Greek provided Plato with no label for verbs, or for adverbs, conjunctions etc. That "is" is a word, but not a name or even a noun was a tricky thing to say in Greek... But even without this excuse people still find it natural to assimilate all words to names, and the meanings of words to be the bearers of those alleged names." Ryle via Caton (1957: 132)

Greek linguistic analysis was hobbled by a lack of sophistication about grammar. Nevertheless, Greek views about language, metaphysics, physics, mathematics, epistemology, ethics, aesthetics and government influenced every succeeding generation of thinkers in the West. Although many areas of philosophical inquiry have changed dramatically, in the field of language theory the legacy of Aristotle has remained intact: spoken words are still considered to be symbols that stand for, express etc. *mental* entities coursing through human minds.

Perhaps by taking a page out of the Greek playbook, the early Christian philosopher Augustine put his stamp on language theory as well. According to 20th-century philosopher Ludwig Wittgenstein, the naming paradigm as an explanation for language acquisition and use can be attributed to Augustine:

> "These words (Augustine, *Confessions*, I. 8.), it seems to me, give us a particular picture of the essence of human language. It is this: the individual words in language name objects—sentences are combinations of such names. —In this picture of language we find the roots of the following idea: Every word has a meaning. This meaning is correlated with the word. It is the object for which the word stands.
>
> "Augustine does not speak of there being any difference between kinds of words. If you describe the learning of a language in this way you are, I believe, thinking primarily of nouns like 'table', 'chair', 'bread', and of people's names, and only secondarily of the names of certain actions and properties; and of the remaining kinds of word as something that will take care of itself." Wittgenstein (1058a: I)

Augustine had a profound influence on succeeding generations of thinkers in Europe just as the

Greeks had. The basic Augustinian paradigm of words as names of things remained a common element in linguistic theory for over two millennia: some words, if not all words, were considered to be *names of things*.

Approximately two millennia after Aristotle, philosopher John Locke wrote:

> "Thus we may conceive how *Words*, which were by Nature so well adapted to that purpose, come to be made use of by Men, *as the Signs* of their *Ideas*: not by any natural connexion [sic], that there is between particular articulate Sounds and certain Ideas, for then there would be but one language amongst all Men; but by a voluntary Imposition, whereby such a Word is made the arbitrary Mark of such an *Idea*. The use then of Words, is to be sensible Marks of *Ideas*; and the *Ideas* they stand for, are their proper and immediate Signification.
>
> "The use Men have of these Marks, being either to record their own Thoughts for the Assistance of their own Memory: or as it were, to bring out their Ideas, and lay them before the view of others: *Words in their primary or immediate Signification, stand for nothing, but the Ideas in the Mind of him that uses them*, how imperfectly soever, or carelessly those Ideas are collected from the Things, which they are supposed to represent." John Locke, An Essay Concerning Human Understanding, 1670 (Note his capitalization of most nouns in the original treatise. The italics are his also.)

John Locke's essay set the stage for philosophical analysis of language in the modern era. How professionals in academia and the man on the street speak about language today is couched in the terms and theories that began with the original analysis of Aristotle. That view was subsequently adopted by enlightenment philosophers such as Locke and passed on to succeeding generations: words are signs that *stand for the ideas in the mind* of the speaker.

Shades of this mentalism abound in philosophers of every stripe. The Idealist philosopher Bishop Berkeley for example:

> "Words become general by being made the signs of general ideas. But it seems that a word becomes general by being made the sign, not of an abstract idea, but several particular ideas, anyone of which it indifferently suggests to the mind." The Empiricists p.141. George Berkeley (1710)

Within philosophy and linguistics, it has been routinely considered that the *representational* nature of spoken words is self-evident. The words humans use are said to *represent*, stand for, express, signify etc. what is going on inside of the speakers' minds. *Speaking* is said to transfer the thoughts, ideas and concepts from one mind to another via the word signs or symbols.

The British/American analytic tradition in philosophy was spearheaded by John Locke and Thomas Hobbes. The philosophies of Locke and Hobbes were steeped in Greek tradition and theological renditions of minds, souls and bodies that were widespread during the enlightenment. Their writings are replete with references to *God, souls, minds* and *ideas*. Although they had distanced themselves from Greek theology, their linguistic analysis was still infused with the similar metaphysics of their own era. An unmistakable *dualism* permeated the writing and the thinking these philosophers offered as explanations for the human capacity to use language. Human beings were composed of bodies *and minds*, dual entities, (hence the term "dualism.") and speech was the physical means by which these *mental* entities, such as *thoughts*, were transferred from one mind to another.

In making these claims, these philosophers accepted the fundamental Aristotelian semantic premise that words are "marks", signs or symbols which represent mental entities and tweaked it to suit their more refined grammar of the day. They made distinctions about words that the Greeks had not. They parsed sentences and created word categories: nouns, verbs, proper names, etc. Yet, they still maintained that many words were names for things. In fact, they capitalized all nouns, not just "proper names", as witnessed in the above quote from Locke's seminal essay. They did so because they considered all nouns to be names for things, e.g. "Men".

Taking up where his philosophical predecessors left off, Locke is largely responsible for the conventional view of language propounded by analytic philosophers who succeeded him. His 1690 writings on "The Signification of Words" in "An Essay Concerning Human Understanding" led philosophers down the garden path:

> "God, having designed man for a sociable creature, made him not only with an inclination, and under a necessity to have fellowship with those of his own kind, but furnished him also with language, which was to be the great instrument and common tie of society. Man, therefore, had by nature his organs so fashioned, as to be fit to frame articulate sounds, which we call words...
>
> "Besides articulate sounds, therefore, it was further necessary that he should be able to use these sounds as signs of internal conceptions; and to make them stand as marks for the ideas within his own mind, whereby they might be made known to others, and the thoughts of men's minds be conveyed from one to another."
> Nagel and Brandt (1965: 53)

For many, this analysis still rings true today. The essential presupposition in most linguistic analysis since the time of Locke has been that articulate sounds are signs of internal conceptions, thoughts or ideas that are conveyed from one speaker to another via the sounds.

Borrowing from Hobbes and Locke, John Stuart Mill began his analysis of language within a more general logical analysis nearly two centuries later. Although Mill held that most words were names of things, he tried to give an account of *word meanings* that diverged from the simple naming paradigm of many of his predecessors. He asserted that some words such as "*is*", "*often*" and "*the*" do not name anything, yet they most certainly have meanings. We English speakers use them all the time. How could we possibly use these words without understanding their *meanings*?

Mill began his semantic analysis in his pursuit of logical analysis. Since logical arguments can be made in many languages, logicians such as Mill were not concerned with the word symbols themselves; they were concerned with what the words *meant*. Gilbert Ryle explains:

> "Now for the same argument may be expressed in English or in French or in any other language; and if it is expressed in English, there may still be hosts of different ways of wording it. What the logician is exploring is intended to be indifferent to these differences of wording. He is concerned with what is said by a premises-sentence or a conclusion-sentence, not with how it is worded.
>
> "So, if not in the prosecution of his inquiry, at least in his explanations of what he is doing, he has to declare that his subject-matter consist not of the sentences and their ingredient words in which arguments are expressed, but of the propositions or judgments and their constituent terms, ideas or concepts of

which the sentences and words are the vehicles. Sometimes he may say that his subject matter consists of sentence-meanings and their constituent word-meanings or phrase-meanings…

"For our purposes it is near enough true to say that the first influential discussion of the notion of meaning given by a modern logician was that with which John Stuart Mill opens his System of Logic (1843). He acknowledges debts to both Hobbes and the Schoolmen, but we need not trace these borrowings in detail." Ryle via Caton (1957: 129)

Although Mill claimed that not all words were names, he concluded that all words and phrases must have *a meaning*. The meanings of some words could not simply be things *named* by the words and phrases. Word sounds such as "*is*", "*often*" and "*the*" must have correlated thoughts, ideas or concepts that speakers grasp when they employ the words, and the *sentences* that were uttered or written, consisting of these thoughts, ideas and concepts, must have corresponding mental entities in the speakers' minds, e.g. *propositions* (to be discussed in detail later).

Although by this time the metaphysics of Plato and Aristotle had been transformed into Cartesian mind/body dualism (to be taken up in detail in Chapter 3) the essentials of Aristotelian linguistic analysis remained constant in analytic philosophy. Words *and* sentences of different languages were said to stand for, express, signify, represent etc. *language neutral meanings*, thoughts, ideas, concepts and *propositions* in the minds of speakers. These mental entities were what interested the analytic philosophers, particularly logicians, not the various word symbols in various languages that were mere vehicles that encoded the mental entities they represented.

Mill also pointed out that descriptive phrases such as "*the prime minister*" could *denote* the same person as the *name* of the prime minister, say "*earl russell*". He then offered the theory that many words and descriptive phrases do two things; they *denote* and *connote*, further confusing the notion of *meaning*. If words and phrases could *denote* things, according to Mill, they can do it in a number of ways, often carrying differing *connotations*. Although words were still considered to be symbols that had stable core meanings, words also seemed to carry different connotations or senses when they denoted certain people, places and things. Those connotations also had to be accounted for in any explanation of *meaning*.

As a consequence of Mill's analysis, words as signs or symbols that simply name, stand for, signify, refer to or denote their meanings came into question. However, as Gilbert Ryle put it a century later:

"The notion of denotation, so far from providing the final explanation of the notion of meaning, turns out itself to be just one special branch or twig in the tree of signification. Expressions do not mean because they denote things; some expressions denote things, in one or another of several different manners, because they are significant. Meanings are not things, not even very queer things." Ryle (1949: 130)

Whatever word *meanings* were, they could not be explained within the simple naming, standing for, signifying, referring to, representing and denoting paradigms that had been used before Mill.

Nonetheless, before the 20th century and the advent of modern linguistics and behavioral science, the universally held view in Western culture was that human language was a symbolic representational system. Words were symbols that *represented* human thinking. For virtually all words and sentences there were corresponding unspoken mental entities (concepts etc.) in the speaker's mind, a mental language (mentalese or Language of Thought) that could be expressed in many different surface languages (6,000+ currently). Additionally, for many philosophers, particularly logicians, *propositions* were the complex *language neutral thoughts* in mentalese, or LOT, represented by complete indicative sentences or declarative statements which could be uttered in different forms (active, passive etc.) in any language.

Because of the prominence of these *propositions* in analytic philosophy, linguistic theory and logic, a brief explanation is called for at this time. Epistemology, or the study of knowledge, had been a field of philosophical inquiry for millennia. Within analytic philosophy all legitimate claims to knowledge, it was thought, could ultimately be reduced to these simple atomic sentences of the subject-predicate form that could be appended with "*is true*" or "*is false*", e.g. "*the tree is tall is true*", and those atomic sentences *represented* mental entities just as the individual words did; they represented *propositions*.

Propositions as the atomic units of knowledge, is received wisdom for most contemporary analytic philosophers, logicians and linguists. The way propositions are normally explained is by noting that the sentences "*the tree is tall*" and "*el arbol es alto*" are very different declarative statements or utterances, yet they both express the same thought. They represent the same *mental proposition* in the mind or consciousness of the speaker. So too, "*steel is heavier than wood*" and "*wood is lighter than steel*" are said to express the same *mental proposition*. Active and passive utterances can also represent the same proposition according to these theorists, e.g. "*jim bought a book*" and "*a book was bought by jim*" both express the same psychological proposition although they are different declarative statements. So too, if two individuals make the same statement: "*my bike is blue*" and refer to different bikes, they have uttered the same sentence but expressed different propositions. Ergo, some sentences can express or encode a virtually unlimited number of propositions depending upon who utters them.

Moreover, many logicians concluded that if statements were to have the same *meaning* they must express the same proposition. In 1940 Bertrand Russell explained:

> "When two sentences have the same meaning that is because they express the same proposition. Words are not essential to propositions. The exact psychological definition of propositions is irrelevant to logic and theory of knowledge; the only thing essential to our inquiries is that sentences signify something other than themselves, which can be the same when the sentences differ." Russell (1940: 237)

Theorists such as Russell claimed that two equivalent sentences spoken by different speakers in different languages had something in common. That commonality shared by both declarative sentences was the *same meaning*. For Russell, two sentences with the same meaning were said to represent or express the same *proposition*, an undefined psychological entity in the *mind* of both speakers. Propositions were said to be the translational constants between speakers uttering equivalent statements in different languages, the basis for shared meaning. The proposition could be expressed in any language and in different manners, such as the active or passive forms, but the proposition itself is a stable, language neutral psychological entity in the mind of the speaker according to these theorists.

Further, according to them, someone uttering *the tree is tall* (sound it out) conveyed that psychological proposition to a hearer who understood the words used by the speaker. That utterance expressed or represented a complex thought comprised of ideas and concepts that could be grasped by the speaker and hearer alike if they spoke the same language. That complex thought, the proposition, along with the constituent ideas, concepts and meanings, were transferred from one human mind to another via spoken word symbols. This analysis is consistent with the analysis of preceding Western philosophers such as John Locke and common beliefs about language held by the man on the street today.

Yet throughout the history of Western philosophy, philosophical disputes frequently ended in disputes about the words being used and their underlying propositions, ideas, concepts and *meanings*, whatever they were. Understanding word meanings became crucial to the whole enterprise of practicing philosophy in the twentieth century. Philosophers realized that if they were going to use words to state their philosophies, they needed to explain what those words *meant*. The interminable disputes about the meanings of words frustrated attempts to come to agreement on philosophical issues. Philosophers said that they needed to clean up their language if they were to reach any agreements. They needed to focus on the words, phrases and sentences they used and become much more precise about their meanings. But what were these things called *meanings*?

Indeed, *meaning* became the focal point of analytic inquiry for many philosophers and linguistic theorists. The quintessential question for these theorists became: what is the meaning of the word sound *meaning*? Presumably, all words, phrases and sentences have meanings. If so, what are these things we call meanings? Are meanings in the heads of the speakers who use words, phrases and sentences? Do they vary from speaker to speaker or are stable independent literal meanings somehow encoded in the symbols? What do people want when they ask for the meaning of a word, a phrase or a sentence? *Theory of meaning* became the core issue for many 20th century analytic philosophers.

Gradually, *meaning* also became the central focus of logicians. How could the *truth* of declarative statements and their underlying propositions be determined if the word meanings were flexible or inconsistent and varied from speaker to speaker? Constancy of meaning was an essential requirement for logicians. Consistent word meanings became a prerequisite for any logical analysis of natural language declarative sentences. Yet it seemed that word meanings were not precise or constant across speaker boundaries or the incidents of use. If meanings were in the minds of the speakers there is no guarantee that meanings would be constant from speaker to speaker. Individualized meanings in the minds of speakers allowed for variability in the truth of declarative statements. For epistemologists and logicians, this would not do.

As a result, many philosophers and logicians concluded that there had to be stable independent semantic content carried by the symbols, *their literal or lexical meanings*. These meanings were not mind dependent; they were stable across speakers and encoded in both the verbal and the written word symbols. These meanings were the essential core meanings that could be enhanced or modified by individual speakers and used in various ways depending upon context and pragmatic considerations. However, there had to be core stable semantic content of some kind carried by the words independently of any mental machinations in the head of the speaker if declarative statements were to be true or false regardless of who uttered them or when they uttered them.

As a consequence, *the proposition* represented by the utterance of an indicative sentence or declarative statement took on a life of its own. Propositions gained independent status. Propositions were no longer considered to be psychological entities in the mind of the speaker. They were said to be independent speaker-neutral entities which were not dependent upon the occasion of use, the grammatical construction, the specific language or the mental processes of the speaker. Although speakers could utter the same proposition in different languages and in the active or passive form, the proposition itself was a universal abstract entity *encoded in the symbols*. As such, its truth value remained constant from speaker to speaker and during varying incidents of its use.

Like the psychological entity Russell proposed, this abstract speaker-neutral proposition provided for a *shared meaning* between two equivalent declarative statements spoken in different languages or by different speakers or at different times. This speaker-neutral shared meaning was encoded in word symbols independently of the speakers who used them at any given time or place. It was the literal or lexical meaning shared by equivalent sentences spoken in different languages. "*the tree is tall*" and "*el arbol es alto*" share the same meaning because they share the same abstract speaker-neutral proposition.

The contention that words and sentences have shared meanings for different speakers at different times is part of a much broader semantic view of language. The semantic view purports that all words, both the spoken and the written variety, are symbols or signs which have fixed literal or lexical meanings and/or referents that are grasped independently of the speaker's speech history, the word's location in a phrase or sentence, the context of the utterance, the time of the utterance or any other pragmatic considerations. Individual words and sentences are assumed to have some sort of stable consistent meanings and/or referents that are available for all competent speakers whenever and wherever they employ the symbol. This view of individual spoken word signs and sentences with stable independent speaker neutral meanings was a tenet of the semantic faith.

Nevertheless, logicians continued to confront the vagueness and ambiguity of *meaning* and *reference* in natural languages. The logic movement in philosophy culminated in the Vienna Circle in the 1920s. Their basic unit of analysis was the proposition. Consistent with Aristotelian bivalent logic, *meaningful* propositions were either true or false as far as they were concerned. If, in principle, it was not possible to determine the truth or falsity of a proposition, a theological claim about the existence of God for example, the statement was considered *meaningless* in the sense that it was speculative, not substantive or informative. Although most logical positivists did not deny that other forms of linguistic expressions were useful, they were drawing an epistemological line in the sand. The positivists were saying that epistemic (knowledge) claims had to be expressed in the form of propositions that could be judged true or false independently of the speaker who uttered them. Those propositions encoded in the word symbols had to be independent speaker-neutral entities that did not vary from speaker to speaker or context to context. The truth of propositions had to remain constant regardless of who expressed the claims, or when, where or why they expressed them.

Moreover, many positivists claimed that to know the meaning of a statement or sentence, competent speakers must know under what conditions it could be determined to be true. The *meaning of a statement* for them became dependent upon the statement's *truth conditions*. To know what an informative sentence or statement *meant*, competent speakers must, *in principle*, be able to determine if it was true or false and, if the truth of a proposition could not possibly be established, it was nothing more than uninformative conjecture.

Underlying these positivist claims were assumptions about logic and truth that had been passed down from Aristotle. For them, propositions were true, false or substantively insignificant. This was consistent with the Aristotelian laws of logic, most notably, the law of the excluded middle. Propositions could not be somewhat true or partially true, or true at certain times and not at others. Propositions could not be true for some people and not for others. Degrees of truth, relative truth or indeterminacy of truth could not be tolerated. If knowledge claims could not be reduced to the bivalent logic of Aristotle they were not informative. Propositions were true, false or just plain speculation said the positivists.

Not only did the positivists claim that epistemic claims had to comply with Aristotelian logic, they had to be analyzable in terms of logical form and precise *reference. How* word symbols referred, designated or denoted other things became a subject of much discussion and study, and *what* words referred to, designated or denoted became a constant source of controversy. Eventually logicians and positivists concluded that every meaningful statement had to be reducible to a statement containing logical terms and precise referring terms that denoted specific observational data. They would not countenance non-empirical claims. Metaphysical or theological claims in particular were treated as speculative mumbo jumbo.

By that time *reference* had also become a critical issue in analytic philosophy, logic and linguistic theory. For thousands of years, it was accepted wisdom that names referred to other things. It was considered to be self-evident that proper names, for instance, referred to the individuals who bore them. The printed names '**Aristotle**' and '**Plato**' referred to those historic individuals, as did the spoken name sounds "*aristotle*" and "*plato*". It was also considered self-evident that words other than proper names referred to other things, e.g. '**tree**' and "*tree*" which referred to an idea, the concept of a tree or a universal ideal tree. Nevertheless, how word symbols *referred* to things and what, exactly, many words referred to presented many enigmas and paradoxes.

Not only did names and many individual words refer to things, certain phrases referred to things. During the late 1800s and the early 1900s, logicians Gottlob Frege and Bertrand Russell began a philosophical fracas on *reference* that went on for decades by posing certain logical puzzles. Definite descriptions became the focal point of heated debate for more than a century. Definite descriptions, in both the spoken and written form, were noun phrases that use the definite article "the". How did written definite descriptions such as '<u>**the** author of Waverly</u>' refer to the same individual as the written name '**Scott**', yet '**Scott**' could not be universally used as a substitute for '<u>**the** author of Waverly</u>'? One can sensibly claim that: '**Scott is the author of Waverly**'. However, it makes little sense to claim that: '**The author of Waverly is the author of Waverly**'. Moreover, how could '**the king of France**' make perfect sense, yet that definite description referred to no one? What did '**The king of France is wise.**' mean if there is no king of France, if the definite description had no referent? How could definite descriptions *mean* anything if they referred to nothing? Scholars continued to debate the merits of various theories of *meaning* and *reference* for the remainder of the 20th century.

Across the pond in America, scholars Edwin Sapir and Benjamin Whorf made a revolutionary and highly controversial claim about language in the late 1930s. After extensive field research into the culture and language of the Hopi Indians of North American, Whorf concluded that their language shaped their thinking to such an extent that it provided them with a world view quite different from people who spoke what he called "standard average European" (SAE) languages. Whorf claimed that the structure of human thought processes was non-trivially influenced by the structure of a speaker's native language. In the trivial sense, of course, people are influenced by what others say and write. That is how we humans acquire much of our knowledge. However, Whorf claimed that people who spoke different languages may see reality in quite different non-trivial ways and that those differences would have profound effects upon their very basic thought processes and their non-verbal behavior.

The Hopi, for example, had a different notion of time than SAE-speaking people, according to Whorf. How they dealt with time in their culture reflected a fundamental difference in their thinking about time which was a consequence of their language. Moreover, he wrote:

> "...It is sometimes stated that Newtonian space, time, and matter are sensed by everyone intuitively, whereupon relativity is cited as showing how mathematical analysis can prove intuition wrong....., laying the blame upon intuition for our slowness in discovering the mysteries of the Cosmos, such as relativity, is the wrong one. The right answer is: Newtonian space, time and matter are no intuitions. They are recepts from culture and language. That is where Newton got them." Whorf (1956: 152)

This claim was a direct refutation of some philosophers such as Immanuel Kant et al. who had proclaimed that all humans have the same pure intuitions about space, time, matter, causation, physical objects etc. Many modern nativists, e.g. Steven Pinker, also insist that humans have many universal innate concepts. Languages simply provide different labels for these identical intuitions or concepts that we are all born with. (Because these intuitions and concepts are considered to be native endowments of all fully functional human beings, this brand of philosophy has been dubbed "nativism".)

Although previous philosophers had written about different "thought worlds", "weltanschauungs" or "points of view" based on linguistic differences, Whorf claimed that what had previously been thought to be *universal* cognitive concepts, were, in fact, not universal. In making this claim Whorf gave birth to *the principle of linguistic relativity*. According to him, language has a profound *influence* upon our most basic thought processes, even our thoughts about space, time, matter, causation, physical objects etc. Peoples who *speak* differently about these very basic subjects will *think* differently about them. There is nothing innate or intuitive about them. He claimed that languages do not merely reflect inborn concepts; they play a constitutive role in the makeup of such concepts acquired by means of language, after birth.

Back in Europe around the mid 20th century, the very influential logician Ludwig Wittgenstein hinted that *word use* was analogous to tool use. Wittgenstein had divorced himself from the positivists because he was troubled by their insistence that *sentence meaning* could be determined via logical analysis and truth conditions. He repeatedly emphasized the functional aspects of language, that is, how it functions within a broader range of human behavior. He made a clear distinction between *the meaning* and *the use* of words and although he emphasized the pragmatic aspects of word *use* in context, he insisted that words were "signs".

For example, in his posthumously published <u>Philosophical Investigations</u> (1958) he writes:

"A definition surely serves to establish the meaning of a sign.—Well, that is done precisely by the concentration of my attention; for in this way I impress on myself the connexion [sic] between the sign and the sensation." (#258)

"Grammar does not tell us how language must be constructed in order to fulfill its purpose, in order to have such-and-such an effect on human beings. It only describes and in no way explains the use of signs." (#496)

Wittgenstein also wrote about the "concept of pain" (#282) and the "concept of order" (#345). Although he advised us not to ask for *the meaning* of a word, but its *use*, he clearly believed that words were "signs" that represent or "stand for" concepts. He assumed concepts to be mental or psychological correlates for word signs. However, he considered *the use* of words (pragmatics) to be distinct from their *meanings* (semantics) and continually emphasized pragmatic considerations in linguistic analysis; words had to be analyzed within specific contexts or *language games* as he called them.

In another posthumously publication, <u>The Blue and Brown Books</u>, he wrote about the "use of the sign" and the "meaning of a sign". He continued to make the distinction between *the use* of the words and *the meaning* of words. Although he advocated a dynamic analysis of words *in use*, it is evident that he accepted the representational view of words as signs that stand for concepts and have semantic content, their literal or lexical meanings.

Nevertheless, his writing helped initiate a sea change in linguistic theory, a movement away from the static analysis of written texts toward a dynamic analysis of *words in use*. Philosophers and linguists had begun a more extensive analysis of how people actually employed spoken words in context as opposed to the static analysis of isolated written words, phrases and sentences. *Human verbal behavior in context* became the object of their investigations rather than textual material.

The other major contribution to philosophy of language made by Wittgenstein was his analysis of word *meanings*. Many words did not appear to have any essential meanings or stable semantic content. Wittgenstein famously analyzed *the meaning* of the word "game" (1958a). He could not come up with any central or essential meaning that was captured in every use of the word. Nor were there any common features or properties for all uses of the word sound "*game*". The closest he could come to describing the ties amongst all of the uses of "*game*" was a family of *resemblances*. He claimed that there were connections among the various uses of the word sound "*game*" but no essential core *meaning* for it. He concluded that whatever *the meaning* of "*game*" was, it did not appear to be stable or consistent across all *uses* of the word.

By the mid-20th century, the old naming, meaning and reference theories of earlier philosophers had been discarded and new theories about *meaning, reference* and the *use* of words became *de rigueur* in analytic philosophy. In 1950 Peter F. Strawson published an influential paper in which he presaged the work of Wittgenstein by analyzing language in *use*. He asserted that people use words and descriptions referentially, but those words and descriptions could be used at various times for differing purposes:

"If we now consider not the whole sentence, 'The king of France is wise,' but that part of it which is the expression, 'the king of France,' it is obvious that we can make analogous, though not identical distinctions between (1) the expression, (2) a use of the expression, and (3) an utterance of the expression. The distinctions will not be identical; we obviously cannot correctly talk of the expression 'the king of France' being used to express a true or false proposition, since in general only sentences can be used truly or falsely; similarly it is only by using a sentence and not by using an expression alone, that you can talk about a particular person. Instead, we shall say in this case that you **use** the expression to **mention** or **refer** to a particular person in using the sentence to talk about him." Strawson via Martinich (1985: 232)

The logical contortions previously employed by Bertrand Russell to explain how written definite descriptions such as **'the king of France'** were perfectly sensible but referred to nothing at that time, became transparently inaccurate. After Strawson's analysis it became increasingly difficult to conclude that there were constant invariant referents for definite descriptions. Descriptions such as **'the Queen of England'** could be *used* by people to mention or refer to different people at different times; the description itself did not refer to anyone in particular. For Strawson, *reference* was taken out of the semantic realm and put squarely into the pragmatic realm. The referents of many descriptions depended on when, where and by whom they were *used*. *The semantics* of language (meanings in the individual words) began to diverge from the *pragmatics* (referential use of the words by the speaker).

Gilbert Ryle's <u>Theory of Meaning</u> in 1957 was a seminal work in the philosophy of semantics. Ryle began by separating *meaning* from the *naming* and *standing* for interpretations of words by his predecessors:

"First, if every single word were a name, then a sentence composed of five words, say 'three is a prime number' would be a list of the five objects named by those five words. But a list, like 'Plato, Aristotle, Aquinas, Locke, Berkeley' is not a sentence... So the words combined into a sentence at least do something jointly which is different from their severally naming the several things that they name if they do name things. What a sentence means is not decomposable into the set of things which the words in it stand for, if they do stand for things. So the notion of having a meaning is at least partly different from the notion of standing for." Ryle via Caton (1970:133)

As previously noted, the early analytic philosophers were heavily influenced by the Greeks and early Christian scholars. The early view held that words were names of things. They functioned like labels for the people, objects, actions, qualities and relations in our experience. The sound "*red*", for example, was the *name* for the color we see. "*dog*" was the *name* for man's best friend. Ryle was attempting to decouple *meaning* from the *naming* views of these earlier theorists. He clearly recognized that most words were not names for things and that the "notion of having a meaning" and "the notion of standing for" were, at best, muddled. Whatever *meanings* were, according to Ryle, they were not something that the word symbols *named* or *stood for*.

Ryle, like Strawson, also wanted to separate *meaning* from *denotation* and *reference*. Most of the earlier theorists had maintained that words and phrases *denoted* or *referred* to specific things, "*the queen of england*" for instance. Consistent with Strawson, Ryle claimed that the utterance "*the queen of england*" clearly has meaning, but denotes or refers to different women or no one at all depending upon when it is used. Ryle and others suggested that the *meanings* of words and phrases determined their *referents*. Yet the enigmas remained. If word symbols had meanings that could determine their referents, exactly what was the nature of these meanings? And how did these meanings determine the referents? Meaning and reference became the "occupational disease" of twentieth century analytic philosophers, as Ryle put it. Ryle ultimately concluded that the notion of meaning was not clear. He could not come up with an adequate account of word or sentence *meaning* and how it affected *reference*.

Ryle also argued, as did Mill, that proper names such as Sir Winston Churchill do not have meanings that determined their referents; they simply *referred to* or *denoted* directly to those individuals. (Names *denote*, Mills had said, but do they not *connote*.) Uttering the name "*winston churchill*", although it may conjure up images and anecdotes, tells you nothing *about* him. For a novice user the name itself has no connotations, aspects, senses, meaning or descriptive content that could help determine its referent. It seems to refer directly to that historic individual without any semantic intermediaries. The *meaning* of the name "*winston churchill*", if someone was to insist that it has a meaning, would be the individual who bears that name. (Russell argued that names were disguised or abbreviated descriptions which could differ for different speakers. That was their meaning. Consequently, speakers with different disguised descriptions would produce different propositions with identical statements, the truth of which could vary.)

One of the rarely acknowledged, yet critical insights also provided by Ryle was the recognition that *word meanings*, whatever they were, could not be isolated in some sort of one-to-one correspondence with the individual words:

> "This brings out a most important fact. Considering the meaning (or Mill's 'connotation') of an expression is considering what can be said with it, i.e. said truly or falsely, as well as asked, commanded, advised or any other sort of saying. In this, which is the normal sense of 'meaning', the meaning of a sub-expression like a word or phrase, is a functional factor of a range of possible assertions, questions, commands and the rest. It is a tributary to sayings. It is a distinguishable common locus of a range of possible tellings, askings. advisings, etc. This precisely inverts the natural assumption with which, as I said earlier, Mill and most of us start, the assumption namely that the meanings of words and phrases can be learned, discussed and classified before consideration begins of entire sayings, such as sentences. Word meanings do not stand to sentence meanings as atoms to molecules or as letters of the alphabet to the spelling of words, but more nearly as the tennis racket stands to strokes which are or may be made with it. This point which Mill's successors and predecessors half-recognized to hold for such little words as 'if', 'or', 'all', 'the' and 'not', holds good for all significant words alike. Their significances are their roles inside actual and possible sayings." Ryle via Caton (1970: 138)

At this point, Ryle reintroduced the theory of sentence primacy in determining meaning, where sentences are the minimal units of meaning and the meanings of words had to come from sentence meanings, (the primacy of sentence meaning went back at least as far as Frege.) The earlier compositional theories which claimed that the meaning of phrases and sentences could be determined if one knew the meanings of the individual words used to produce those phrases and sentences was the exact opposite of what was actually happening. In fact, individual *word meanings*, whatever they were, seemed to depend on other words and their meanings within various grammatical constructs. All meanings were interdependent. A notorious example is "*bank*", as in "*i went to the bank to make a deposit*" and "*i went to the bank to check the rivers level.*" (See frame semantics in the glossary.)

Ryle fully realized that we humans must learn to use words in combination with other words and phrases. Beginning with Ryle, many philosophers of language began to move away from the atomistic reductionism that analyzed human speech behavior in terms of individual words and their individual meanings. They claimed that human speech must be analyzed from a *holistic* perspective. There is a functional holism necessary to become a competent speaker. The work of Ryle and others complimented the work of logicians who had begun to move away from theories of individual word meanings to a meaning theory based on the truth of declarative statements. Grammatically complete sentences became the primary bearers of meaning with words being dependent secondary bearers of meaning.

Ryle also juxtaposed an atomistic *semantic* view of words with a functional *pragmatic* view of words. Are words *symbols* or *signs* that have stable speaker-neutral meanings and referents? Is speech a combination of these individual symbols with encoded lexical meanings and referents that can be enhanced or altered by pragmatic considerations of context and speaker intent? Alternatively, is speech culturally specific functional behavior that issues from human mouths and can it be pragmatically deployed in various ways? That is, are words *functional devices* that can be used in combination to get work done rather than a system of symbols representing mental entities, e.g. concepts, ideas, propositions etc.? How can we best characterize human language? Which paradigm provides us with greater explanatory power?

As a result of the work of Wittgenstein, Strawson and Ryle, the second half of the twentieth century brought about a radical shift in the focus of analytic philosophy and linguistics. J.L. Austin was point man for a growing trend toward linguistic analysis in Western philosophy. A.J. Ayer summed up Austin quite well:

> "Austin took seriously the view put forward by Wittgenstein and the Vienna Circle that philosophers had been gratuitously puzzled and in some cases led into talking nonsense by their failure to understand the workings of the language they were employing, and consequent abuses of it. Unlike Wittgenstein, however, Austin did not aim merely at the dissolution of philosophical problems through the correction of these linguistic errors. He believed that a painstaking investigation of the ways in which some set of expressions of a natural language, like English, were ordinarily used would have a positive value." Ayer (1982: 235)

Austin attempted an elucidation of *meaning* in a 1960 posthumously published work titled The Meaning of a Word. In it he attempted to deconstruct what the "meaning of a word" could possibly be. What would qualify as the meaning of a word? He concluded that:

> "… there is no simple and handy appendage of a word called 'the meaning of (the word) 'x'…
>
> "To summarize the contentions of this paper then. Firstly, the phrase 'the meaning of a word' is a spurious phrase. Secondly and consequently, a re-examination is needed of phrases like the two which I discuss, 'being part of the meaning of' and 'having the same meaning'. On these matters, dogmatists

require prodding: although history suggests that it may sometimes be better to let sleeping dogmatists lie." Austin via Caton (1970: 8,21)

Austin attributed the belief that individual words had meanings to the long-held view that all words were symbols that *stood for* things, namely, their *meanings*. He concluded, however, that this word/meaning paradigm could not account for the data, i.e. human speech.

The most radical departure from the semantic word/meaning paradigm was presented in 1957 by behaviorist B.F. Skinner in <u>Verbal Behavior</u>. Skinner rejected the traditional semantic paradigm altogether and argued for a complete functional account of human speech. The symbolic characterization of speech in all preceding semantic theories was abandoned. He wanted to establish a science of verbal behavior utilizing his stimulus-response-reinforcement (S-R-R) paradigm, rather than the traditional semantic paradigm of words with correlated literal or lexical meanings along with thoughts, ideas and concepts in the mind of the speaker. Skinner abandoned this "doctrine of ideas" and focused on human *speech* as observable behavior no different than other human behavior. He rejected the underlying dualistic claim of traditional semantic theory, i.e. verbal behavior is a system of symbols that represent *mental* entities which are transferred to and from participants in verbal exchanges.

Skinner challenged the inherent mind/body dualism of meanings and ideas in the minds of speakers:

> "Perhaps no one today is deceived by an 'idea' as an explanatory fiction. Idioms and expressions which seem to explain verbal behavior in term of ideas are so common in our language that it is impossible to avoid them, but they may be little more than moribund figures of speech. The basic formulation, however, has been preserved. The immediate successor to 'idea' was 'meaning,' and the place of the latter is being usurped by a newcomer, 'information.' These terms all have the same effect of discouraging a functional analysis and of supporting, instead, some of the practices first associated with the doctrine of ideas." Skinner (1957: 6)

He suggested the:

> "promising possibility that meanings may be kept outside the skin. They are as observable as any part of physics… Technically, meanings are to be found among the independent variables in a functional account, rather than as properties of the dependent variable." Skinner (1957: 8 & 14)

For Skinner, words, phrases and other grammatical components of speech were not reflexive units of behavior. They were units of behavior functionally dependent upon independent variables; their probability of emission varied with exposure to the independent variables and the subsequent reinforcement of the resulting behavior. Human speech, by Skinner's account, was controlled by the operant conditioning of each speaking organism. (Operants are functional units of behavior that have an effect on the speaker's social environment. Their use is determined by antecedent effects of the previous uses of such behavioral units.)[3]

Speech was a unique form of behavior exclusive to the human race, but a behavior none the less. For Skinner, there was no need to cloak the analysis of this behavior in the usual dualist garb of *thoughts, ideas*, and *concepts* in human *minds* that were encoded, represented or expressed by word symbols and then transferred to other *minds*. There were no *mental* entities or processes mentioned or implied by Skinner. Word meanings were neither in the minds of speakers nor abstract speaker-neutral entities encoded in the word symbols. "The meaning of an utterance is either some feature of the occasion upon which it is uttered or some effect upon a listener." Skinner (1969: 11.) This was a complete break from the traditional semantic assumptions about word symbols and their alleged semantic content and was quickly discounted by psychologists, linguists and philosophers alike.

Skinner gave functionalism its most thorough treatment with a complete functional analysis, abandoning semantics and its concomitant dualism altogether. Skinner put the complete control of speech behavior in the stimuli and the speech history of each human organism. He considered all verbal behavior to be a response to stimuli based on previously reinforced verbal behavior with no control exerted by the human emitting the speech. Beliefs, intentions, purposes, desires, wishes and wants as psychological forces controlling human speech behavior were eliminated along with the meanings, thoughts, ideas, concepts and propositions transferred from mind to mind.

Although Skinner's account was widely dismissed, it had one huge advantage for theorists: the observable speech behavior could be reduced to physiology, molecular biology and acoustics which could, in turn, be reduced to biochemistry and physics. Skinner's explanation could be fused with other physical explanations for the interactions of matter and energy in the universe. There was no need for the superfluous metaphysics, mentalism or psychologism that philosophical materialists railed against.

The most notable criticism of Skinner's analysis of human verbal behavior came from linguist Noam Chomsky. In 1967 Chomsky derisively criticized Skinner for the use of empirically unsound terminology such as "stimulus", "probability of emission", "deprivation", "reinforcement", "conditioning", etc. He accused Skinner of "play-acting at science" and suggested that Skinner's use of such terms was nothing more than paraphrasing in unscientific terms the traditional ways of explaining language that characterized language use in terms of "beliefs", "intentions", "wishes", "wants" and so forth. He wrote:

> "Invoking the term reinforcement has no explanatory force, and any idea that this paraphrase any new clarity or objectivity into the description of wishing, liking, etc., is a serious delusion." A Review of B.F. Skinner's Verbal Behavior p. 9; Jacobovitz & Miron, Readings in the Psychology of Language, 1967, Prentice-Hall

He further claimed:

> "In the present state of our knowledge, we must attribute an overwhelming influence on actual behavior to ill-defined factors of attention, set, volition and caprice." Ibid, p. 5

Although he recognized that mentalistic terms such as "attention", "volition" and "caprice" are "ill-defined", he insisted that they were preferable to Skinner's use of "stimulus, "reinforcement", "conditioning" etc.

Underlying the terminological fracas was a more fundamental philosophical difference. Chomsky advocated a rationalist rehabilitation using the writings of 17th century rationalist philosophers, along with 19th century linguist Wilhelm von Humboldt as springboards for his theory of universal grammar. Contemporary philosopher John Searle described Chomsky's philosophical foundation thusly:

> "The most spectacular conclusion about the nature of the human mind that Chomsky derives from his work in linguistics is that his results vindicate the claims of the seventeenth century rationalist philosophers, Descartes, Leibniz, and others, that there are innate ideas in the mind... For empiricists all knowledge comes from experience, for rationalists some knowledge is implanted innately and prior to experience. In his bluntest moods, Chomsky claims to have refuted the empiricists and vindicated the rationalists." Searle, New York Review of Books, June 29, 1972.

Previously, in 1966, Chomsky had published <u>Cartesian Linguistics: A Chapter in the History of Rationalist Thought</u>. Relying on Port-Royal Grammar [4], "in which a Cartesian approach to language is developed for the first time" (Chomsky (1966: 33), Chomsky confidently proclaimed to have:

> "...extracted from 'Cartesian Linguistics' certain characteristics and quite important doctrines regarding the nature of language and have, quite sketchily, traced their development during the period from Descartes to Humbolt. As a by-product of this study of *langue*, and against the background of rationalist theory of mind, certain views emerged as to how language is acquired and used...
>
> "The central doctrine of Cartesian linguistics is that the general features of grammatical structure are common to all languages and reflect certain fundamental properties of the mind... By attributing such principles to the mind, as an innate property, it becomes possible to account for the quite obvious fact that the speaker of a language knows a great deal that he has not learned." Chomsky (1966: 59)

In the process of re-introducing *the mind* and *mental* machinations to the debate, Chomsky re-introduced the psychological (mental) explanations that Skinner so assiduously avoided:

> "It seems to me that the most hopeful approach today is to describe the phenomena of language and of mental activity as accurately as possible, to try to develop an abstract theoretical apparatus that will as far as possible account for these phenomena and reveal the principles of their organization and functioning, without attempting, for the present, to relate the postulated mental structures and processes to any physiological mechanisms or to interpret mental function in terms of 'physical causes'." Chomsky (2006: 12)

Fully recognizing that his rationalist *mind*-based theory could not be reconciled with physiology or any other physical sciences, he wanted to press ahead and worry about such reconciliation in the future. He ultimately suggested that:

> "Linguistics, so characterized, is simply the subfield of psychology that deals with these aspects of mind." Chomsky (2006: 25)

In his 1968 lectures, Chomsky attempted to justify his insistence that human speech could not be fully explained within the non-mentalistic behaviorist's framework. He presented a number of arguments and a sleight of word:

> "But the normal use of language is not only innovative and potentially infinite in scope, but also free from the control of detectable stimuli, either external or internal. It is because of this freedom from stimulus control that language can serve as an instrument of thought and self-expression..." Chomsky (2006: 11)

All subsequent remarks about "stimulus control" deleted the "detectable". He repeatedly insisted that the human use of language was free from ambient stimulus control or internal physiological states and was subject to the *mental* machinations of the humans who use language.[5] Chomsky's arguments convinced a generation of linguists that:

> "... we must isolate and study the system of linguistic competence that underlies the behavior but that is not realized in any direct or simple way in behavior." Chomsky (2006: 4)

The "system of linguistic competence" he proposed was a "universal grammar". That "universal grammar" was an innate "schematism" (most theorists now regard it to be an innate "faculty"), the so called "deep structure" that was universally endowed to humans and transmitted via the human genome. The "universal grammar" could be "transformed" into rule-based "surface grammars" that people used when they spoke in the many languages that were witnessed worldwide. Chomsky's universal grammar was a theoretical, innate, rule-based framework (not realized in the physiology of the brain) that generated all speech behavior in humans.

The most-long lasting effect of Chomsky's lectures and writings was the search for that native endowment, universal grammar. He claimed that the behaviorist account of child language acquisition and mature language use was inadequate and that there must be a basic universal innate rule-based mental grammar that enables the acquisition and use of languages by all such genetically endowed humans. He concluded his brief critique of Skinner with the astonishing claim that:

> "...all normal children acquire essentially comparable grammars of great complexity with remarkable rapidity suggests that human beings are somehow specially designed to do this..." Review of Verbal Behavior p. 21

As a consequence of Chomsky's paper, linguists embarked on the search for a rule-based universal grammar that was "designed" and passed on through the human genome.

Kenneth MacCorquodale's 1970 response to Chomsky pointed out the many mistakes, misunderstandings and misperceptions (I am being charitable) in Chomsky's analysis of Skinner's Verbal Behavior. They are extensive and glaring. Nevertheless, the search for *innate universal rules of grammar* that would generate *well-formed sentences* has dominated linguistics for the past forty-plus years in American academia. Skinner's non-semantic functional behavior account of language acquisition and use was sidelined indefinitely. Linguists pressed on from within the traditional dualistic semantic paradigm. Human speech was considered to be mind-based volitional activity initiated by each individual organism, as opposed to Skinner's S-R-R model.

Skinner himself never responded to Chomsky other than to say that "Chomsky simply does not understand what I am talking about."[6]

Concurrently, during the mid-20th century, some philosophers and linguists began to view much speech behavior as the deployment of complex implements to get work done. *Pragmatics* or *pragmaticism* gained ascendance. J.L. Austin published a famous treatise on pragmatics in 1961. In that paper certain uses of language were described as *performative utterances*. Austin contended that the uses of many phrases and sentences were more than just representations or expressions of internal mental entities. When uttered, these speech acts performed functions. They got work done.

For example, consider this performative utterance: "*i bet you ten bucks that the Packers will win their division*". Saying: "*i bet you...*" cannot be judged true or false, or verified. It is not the expression of a psychological proposition in the mind of the speaker. Saying: "*i bet you...*" does not report an internal mental act of betting. The making of the sounds constitutes the betting. The sounds must be uttered for the act to work. That is how we English speakers often bet. If I would like to bet, I can say: "*i bet you ten bucks...*". Of course, in betting, someone must accept the bet: "*youre on*". That speech act constitutes another *performative utterance*. That speaker has accomplished something other than conveying information by uttering the sounds: "*youre on*". His speech action of saying "*youre on*" functions as an acceptance of the bet. It is verbal behavior that has consequences.

Consider other examples of performative utterances, for instance: promising when a speaker says: "*i promise to pay you on tuesday*", the speech act is the promise. The promising consists in the making of the promise, i.e. saying the words. Once again, it is verbal behavior that has consequences for the person who performs the speech act. Many times when people say: "*i hereby ...*" they are vocalizing a performative utterance, or on Thanksgiving when you politely say: "*please pass the dressing*", you are interested in the results. What matters is whether or not you get the right dish. Did the utterance function the way you intended it to? Did the utterance produce the desired results?

Many such *non-declarative* uses of words sounds were considered to be *performative utterances* or *speech acts*. Conversely, a declarative statement was not considered to be performative. Saying: "*all swans are white*" was not considered a performative speech act. It was considered to be a linguistic act that conveys information. It was an English declarative statement that expressed a proposition that is true or false regardless of who stated it in what language, or when and where they expressed it. There is a fact of the matter. If someone expresses a proposition by means of a declarative sentence, the listener can agree or disagree. However, you do not expect the listener to necessarily take action. It is not a performative utterance. So said most language theorists.

Austin recognized that the distinction between performative and what he termed "constative" utterances (declarative statements) was not always clear. Nevertheless, he maintained that "constative" utterances differed from performative utterances. (Austin via Caton 1970: 36) Declarative statements or "constative utterances" conveyed true or false propositions. Performative utterances did not.

Along with Austin, philosophers Keith Donnellan, Donald Davidson, John Searle, H. P. Grice et al. set up shop and in true reductionist fashion, began to classify performative utterances into types. Contrary to Austin and most other philosophers, a few theorists claimed that virtually all speech was performative in some respect. Paul Ziff, in his 1960 <u>Semantic Analysis</u>, defined performative speech acts much more broadly:

> "If I utter 'I waited for you', then depending on the context I may be making a statement, or giving an explanation, or offering a reason, or making an accusation, or making a complaint, or quoting, or reciting a poem, or telling a story, and so forth. (Each of these is a speech act in that the performance of each act necessitates the uttering of an utterance.) … A declarative utterance is a kind of utterance and it can be employed in the performance of many different or distinct speech acts." (Ziff 1960: 78)

According to Ziff, on some level of analysis, all speech behavior could be considered performative, including declarative propositional statements such as "I waited for you". He said that all syntactically non-deviant utterances were utilized for varying goals depending on context and speaker intent. They were shaped by speakers to produce desired responses from the listeners. The traditional static analysis of written declarative statements with stable semantic content was too limited, he thought. Context and speaker intent were critical to the interpretation of virtually any speech utterance by Ziff's account. Consistent with Ziff's account, many contemporary theorists such as James R. Hurford have claimed that "all expressions in a language can be used to carry out acts of some sort." Hurford (2007: 112)

The distinction between the performative aspects of linguistic behavior and the putative stable semantic content of words and sentences remains a fundamental dichotomy in linguistic theory. It is evidenced in the divide between pragmatics and semantics. Pragmaticists, supposedly, study the performative aspects of language *in use* where context and speaker goals are integral parts of the analysis. Semanticists, on the other hand, take the speaker and the context out of the analysis. Semanticists conduct static analyses of both written and spoken words as symbols with independent lexical/literal meanings and referents that hold constant between speakers and the circumstances in which they are written or uttered.

While disputes amongst linguists were stirring, philosophers of language proceeded apace. Following up on Russell, Wittgenstein, Strawson, Ryle and Austin, another step away from the traditional static semantic analysis of written language was provided by Keith Donnellan in 1967. His critique provided more impetus for the need to analyze language *in use*:

> "Strawson and Russell seem to me to make a common assumption here about the question of how definite descriptions function: that we can ask how a definite description functions in some sentence independently of a particular occasion upon which it is used… Just as we can speak of a function of a tool that is not at the moment performing its function, Strawson's view, I believe, allows us to speak of referential function of a definite description in a sentence even when it is not being used. This, I hope to show, is a mistake." Donnellan via Martinich (1985: 248)

Donnellan made another strong argument for the dynamic analysis of verbal behavior being used in context. Definite descriptions such as *the queen of england* had to be analyzed in action. Neither the sounds nor the static written symbols could be analyzed when not being *used by* a speaker or writer. Donnellan's analysis showed that many definite descriptions could be construed differently at different times by different people. The pragmatic elements of the utterance of a definite description had to be included in the analysis of that utterance. The static analysis of definite descriptions with independent stable lexical/literal meanings and referents that could be grasped outside of context and speaker goals was subjected to even more skepticism.

In that same year, 1967, Donald Davidson wrote an article titled "Truth and Meaning". In it he claimed:

> "On the other hand, it is now evident that a satisfactory theory of the meanings of complex expressions may not require entities as meanings of all the parts. It behooves us then to rephrase our demand on a satisfactory theory of meaning so as not to suggest that individual words must have meanings at all, in any sense that transcends the fact that they have a systematic effect on the meanings of the sentences in which they occur." Davidson via Ludlow (1987: 89)

Davidson's work continued the move away from individual words with stable independent meanings to words as variable functional components within larger grammatical constructions. *Meaning* continued to migrate from individual words to the phrases and sentences.

That shift also signaled the beginning of logical semantics or truth-conditional semantics (TCS) in which *well-formed sentences* became the units of semantic analysis. It distanced much of semantic theory from the analysis of individual words with lexical/literal meanings that could be altered pragmatically, to the analysis of *sentence meaning* with an epistemic truth test as the standard. Meanings became equated with the truth conditions of the underlying propositions represented by declarative statements. That model coincided with the tripartite division of true, false and substantively meaningless propositions proposed by the Logical Positivists decades earlier. Sentence meanings in TCS took primacy with word meanings being derived from the sentence meaning.

John R. Searle published a seminal work on *meaning and reference* in 1969. In <u>Speech Acts</u> he extended the work of J. L. Austin's insights on performative utterances:

> "The form that this hypothesis will take is that speaking a language is performing speech acts, acts such as making statements, giving commands, asking questions, making promises, and so on; and more abstractly, acts such as referring and predicating; and, secondly, that these acts are in general made possible by and are performed in accordance with certain rules for the use of linguistic elements.
>
> "The reason for concentrating on the study of speech acts is simply this: all linguistic communication involves linguistic acts. The unit of linguistic communication is not, as has generally been supposed, the symbol, word or sentence, but rather the production or issuance of the symbol or word or sentence in performance of the speech act." (Searle 1969: 16)

Searle further distanced *reference* from the word symbols by investigating reference as a speech act. Reference continued its migration away from the semantics toward pragmatics. Although he never disputed the symbolic nature of words, he forcefully argued that *reference was an act* carried out by speakers utilizing words and expressions which did not refer to anything by themselves. He re-emphasized that point by stating:

> "The term 'referring expression' is not meant to imply that expressions refer. On the contrary, as previously emphasized, reference is a speech act, and speech acts are performed by speakers uttering words, not by the words." Searle (1969: 28)

Searle reaffirmed suspicions about paradigmatic semantic analysis of written words and sentences. He called for the dynamic analysis of the speech behavior, insisting that the object of analysis should be the speaker's behavior, not the symbolic representation of that behavior, i.e. written words.

Most subsequent philosophy about language deliberately avoided characterizing words or phrases as *referring expressions*. Although most theorists maintained the long-held belief that words were signs or symbols with meanings, *reference* for many was taken out of the symbols and put into the speaker or writer. Reference became the act in which various units of speech were used by speakers to refer. *Reference* had been removed from the semantic realm and placed squarely into the pragmatic realm in much of the philosophy of language. However, the sounds that issue from human mouths were often said to stand for, represent, express, encode, denote and designate other things, their meanings, and those meanings helped determine the referents.

Searle's account of *meaning* fully recognized the importance of speaker intentions in the performance of many speech acts. He advised that *speaker meaning* was closely connected to having the desired effects on hearers and that hearers must recognize the *intentions* of the speaker for many speech acts to have their *intended* effects. In addition to understanding the lexical/literal meanings or the semantic content encoded by symbols, he asserted that listeners must recognize speakers' goals to grasp the full meaning of speech acts. Searle insisted that a combination of these elements was necessary in the analysis of human speech.

Searle followed up on the work of Austin, Donnellan and Davidson with a proposal for a dynamic analysis of "illocutionary acts". He proposed that many speech acts were performed under specified conditions. His analysis of *promising* detailed the conditions under which a non-defective promise must be made. He also analyzed the "illocutionary acts" of *requesting, asserting, questioning, thanking, advising, warning, greeting* and *congratulating*. In all cases, there were specific circumstances and presuppositions under which successful promises, requests and so on, must be made. These *illocutionary acts* could not be analyzed independently of the circumstances in which they are uttered or the presuppositions that were required for their successful performance.

However, to my knowledge, Searle gave no account of individual word meanings and declaimed that "the meaning of a sentence is determined by rules." He further asserted that:

> "The obvious explanation for the brute regularities of language (certain human made noises tend to occur in certain states of affairs or in the presence of certain stimuli) is that speakers of a language are engaging in a rule-governed form of intentional behavior. The rules account for the regularities in a game of football, and without the rules there seems no accounting for the regularities." Searle, (1969: 53)

This was a nod to Chomsky and a direct shot across the bow of Skinnerian behaviorists who had hypothesized that language was simply another form of stimulus-response-reinforcement, conditioned behavior that exhibited certain *regularities*, but was not *rule-bound*.

Searle then proceeded to explicate his axioms, principles and *rules* for speech acts. He insisted, as did Chomsky, that all speech regularities, e.g. pronunciation regularities, were *rule-based*:

> "…this is a rule and not just a regularity, as can be seen from the fact that we recognize departures as 'mispronunciations' and from the fact that the rule covers new cases, from its projective character…….It seems obvious to me that it is a rule, and that it is one which we follow without necessarily knowing (in the sense of being able to formulate) that we do." Searle (1969: 42)

These are crucial remarks because they provide justification for much linguistic research. In most modern work and theory, speech is depicted as *rule-bound* behavior consistent with "constitutive rules" that are internalized but not consciously known by speakers. Speech as rule-governed behavior has been a recurring theme in theoretical linguistics and philosophy of language for the past half century. Current research and theorizing have consistently maintained that speech is rule bound and the job of semanticists and syntacticians is to identify and explicate these rules for speech.

In 1975, H. Paul Grice introduced the term "conversational implicatures" in a paper titled "Logic and Conversation". Grice initiated the use of the general term "implicature" to cover other terms such as "imply", "suggest", "indicate", and "mean". He provided conversational scenarios where speakers *imply* something, something that is not said. For example:

> "Suppose that A and B are talking about a mutual friend C, who is now working in a bank. A asks B how C is getting on in his job, and B replies 'Oh quite well, I think; he likes his colleagues, and he hasn't been to prison yet." At this point, A might well inquire what B was implying, what he was suggesting, or even what he meant by saying the C had not yet been to prison." Grice via Martinich (1985: 166)

Grice clearly showed that in conversation, the original and primary form of human word use, there were many implications that were made with words that could not be derived from any lexical/literal meanings for the words. He also showed that conversation was a rational co-operative enterprise that required conventions and a willingness of participants to abide by those conventions to maintain a successful communicative exchange.

Grice developed a series of "conversational maxims" or rules for conversation. For conversation among people to proceed, certain conventions about co-operation had to be observed by participants: quantity, quality, relevance and manner. Grice's implicatures and conversational maxims became an entire area of inquiry in linguistics that fell outside of semantics. Implicatures are said to provide explanations for meaning that is not encoded in the symbols, meaning that is *implied*, suggested, indicated or meant, but *not said*.

In the same year, 1975, Searle expanded his analysis of speech acts by investigating what he called "indirect speech acts":

> "The hypothesis I wish to defend is simply this: In indirect speech acts the speaker communicates to the hearer more than he actually says by way of relying on their mutually shared background information, both linguistic and nonlinguistic, together with the general powers of rationality and inference on the part of the hearer. To be more specific, the apparatus necessary to explain

the indirect part of indirect speech acts, certain principles of cooperative conversation (some which have been discussed by Grice) and mutually shared factual background information of the speaker and the hearer, together with an ability on the part of the hearer to make inferences." Searle via Martinich (1985: 177)

The work of Searle, Grice et al. made explicit a view of meaning in which the literal meanings of words and sentences were divorced from their pragmatic effect. For instance, the utterance of: *could you be a little more quiet*" would ordinarily be construed as a request for more than a yes or no answer. It is a request to be quiet! The literal meaning carried by the symbols is not at all what a speaker is conveying with the employment of words in many situations. It is not what *the speaker meant*.

In 1979 Michael Reddy proposed what he called "The Conduit Metaphor - A Case of Frame Conflict in Our Language about Language" whereby words were the conduit through which ideas, thoughts, meanings and feelings "which denote internal conceptual or emotional material" were conveyed between interlocutors. The metaphor is the "frame" within which we spoke about speech. That "frame" is:

> "the assumption that human communication achieves the physical transfer of thoughts and feelings…. Naturally, if language transfers thought to others, then the logical container, or conveyer, for this thought is words, or word-groupings like phrases, sentences, paragraphs, and so on." "The Conduit Metaphor - a case of frame conflict in our language about language." via Anthony Ortony, Metaphor and Thought, Cambridge University Press. (1979: 287)

Reddy offered extensive evidence that, in English, the processes of speaking and writing were metaphorically described as systems in which the speaker inserted a feeling or thought into an external code and the listener extracted that feeling or thought from the code after it was conveyed. According to him: "A conservative estimate would thus be that, of the entire metalingual apparatus of the English language, at least seventy percent is directly, visibly, and graphically based on the conduit metaphor." Reddy via Ortony (1979: 296). He then challenged theorists to avoid the metaphor when talking about human speech.

Reddy also made the larger (and very Whorfian) claim that the conduit metaphor radically distorted our view of language and accounted for a great deal of conflict in communication theories. Of these theorists he asserted that: "The conduit metaphor has undercut them without any knowledge on their part of what was happening." Reddy via Ortony (1979: 302). He claimed that the conduit metaphor had a "biasing power" that scholars presenting theories of language and the nature of meaning had not been aware of. It forced these thinkers to make certain assumptions about language that could not be reconciled with the empirical evidence.

From the third-party *empirical* perspective what is observable (non-metaphorically) during the reception of speech is:

> "Something first happens outside your body" sound waves, alternate condensations and rarefactions of the air, cause air particles to strike repeatedly on your eardrum, so that it vibrates. The eardrum is connected by three small bones to a membrane that covers one end of a spiral tube in the inner ear. The

vibration of your eardrum is transmitted through this chain of three bones to the membrane at the end of the tube. The tube is filled with a liquid, perilymph, so that the vibration in the membrane attached to these bones causes a corresponding vibration to pass through this liquid. Inside the first tube is another one, filled with a liquid called endolymph; vibrations in the perilymph cause vibrations in the membranous wall of the inner tube and waves in the endolymph. Small hairs stick out from the membranous walls into the endolymph, which are made to vibrate by the vibrations in the endolymph. The auditory nerve is joined to the roots of these hairs. The vibration of the hairs causes impulses to pass up the auditory nerve to a part of the brain called the auditory center. Not until the auditory center is stimulated do you hear a sound. So far all the events described have been physical..." Hospers (1988: 244)

But the description of the process then differs considerably. The meta-language becomes decidedly mental because the events unfolding are not observable by third parties. Introspection becomes the observational process and the psychological language of introspection provides the descriptive content of the report:

"The entire process just described takes only a small fraction of a second; but now, when the auditory nerve has carried the stimulus to the appropriate portion of the brain, something new and different occurs: *you hear a sound*, you have an *auditory sensation*. This is "something quite new under the sun". It is something quite different from anything that went on earlier in this brief but complex process. The auditory sensation is a *mental event*, not a physical event like the preceding ones. It is an *awareness*, a state of *consciousness*. The same holds for visual sensation and all kinds of sensation: kinesthetic sensations, smell-sensations, taste, touch, heat, cold, pain, and so on; and also for states of consciousness not directly associated with the senses, such as thoughts, memories, images, emotions..." (Ibid: 245)

Indeed, a radical ontological shift has been made in the descriptive process, often unnoticed, and if noticed, unexplained. The shift takes the description from the terminology of physics to the terminology of psychology. Neither terminology can be translated into the other.

Relying on his previous paper on implicatures, Paul Grice wrote another paper of note on *meaning* in 1989. The piece was titled "Utterer's Meaning and Intentions" Ludlow (1997: 59). In it he made many distinctions about *meaning* based upon the speaker's intentions. The data he used were taken from hypothetical human discourse in which context and speaker intentions were shown to be critical to determining the meanings of words, phrases and sentences. Grice concluded that there were many different types of meaning: central meaning, timeless meaning, applied timeless meaning, occasion meaning, utterance-type occasion meaning, natural meaning and non-natural meaning.

The critical distinction Grice outlined was the difference between *saying* and *meaning*. That distinction is often pointed to as a demarcation between semantics and pragmatics. The premise is that the word symbols say one thing, the lexical/literal meaning, but the effect on listeners is an entirely different meaning, the speaker's intended meaning. A prototypical example might be: *"its cold in here"* uttered by a cold spouse. This declarative statement is not to be taken as such. Used in a certain context the cold spouse is saying he or she wants the window closed. That is what is implied, suggested, indicated or *meant* by the utterance of those words. However, that is not what he or she *said*. That distinction is a continuing theme in linguistics and entails that there is a stable lexical/literal meaning carried by the words, *what the word symbols say*. However, that lexical/literal meaning is not always *what the speaker meant*.

By analyzing hypothetical situation-based speech, Grice et al. were able to provide more evidence that the meanings of words, phrases and sentences were not fixed. Meanings often vary along with speaker goals, context, presuppositions and prosodic features of speech. Word, phrase and sentence *meanings* began to be viewed as individualized idiolectic correlates of the word and sentences in the mind of the speaker, not speaker-neutral semantic constants that were exchanged between discourse participants. In linguistic theory, consistent speaker neutral meanings became difficult to reconcile with observed speech behavior. Word and sentence meanings can vary across speakers and incidents of use it seems. Independent stable semantic content for words, phrases and sentences became even more elusive.

Many contemporary linguists and philosophers view *meaning* in this idiolectic way. Word meanings are said to be personalized thoughts, concepts and mental representations that are enhanced, or enriched versions of the core semantic content encoded by the word symbols, their lexical/literal meanings. Thus, word meanings grow, change and vary from speaker to speaker. These individualized word meanings could, in turn, produce variable meanings for identical declarative statements and variability in the truth of those statements depending upon who wrote or spoke them. Nevertheless, spoken words were still considered to be *symbols* with individual *speaker meanings*, meanings in the *minds* of the speakers.

This is completely contrary to the view held by extreme nativists. These theorists believed that the spoken words that issued from human mouths represented a stock of consistent universal concepts, meanings or mental representations that could be put together in a universal language of pure thought, LOT. According to this view, basic human cognition is the same for all people and merely dressed up, so to speak, in the variety of languages that we witness worldwide. Along with an innate grammar, some philosophers of the extreme nativist or radical innatist bent speculated that a stock inventory of identical concepts was passed along through the human genome.

Other innatists or nativists, such as Steven Pinker, proposed a more modest version of innate concepts to complement their innate grammar theories. In their view, which Pinker dubbed *conceptual semantics*, "…word meanings are represented in the mind as assemblies of basic concepts in a language of thought." Pinker (2007: 91) With appropriate credit to Kant, Pinker claimed that these basic concepts such as space, time and causation are passed on genetically and subsequently combined and enriched into more sophisticated mental representations through the process of learning. Although this theory retained the word/concept correspondence, it does allow for variation in those concepts or mental representations. Idiolectic concepts can be the result of individualized combinations or enhancements of the basic concepts. Pinker's theory has an added benefit as he says: "Conceptual semantics fits, too, with our commonsense notion that words are not the same as thoughts." Pinker (2007: 151)

Pinker's "common sense notion" about words and thoughts is reflected in one of the most critical assumptions of linguistic theorists:

"So enshrined is the Cartesian assumption that there simply is no field called 'the evolution of thought', just and for the same reason as there is no field called 'the acquisition of thought', analogously to the acquisition of language'—as if there was no such issue, and prelinguistic infants always already thought in the ways that beings do who have acquired a language. This latter assumption becomes an axiomatic one when such infants, or indeed non-human beings as well, are said to think in a 'Language of Thought' (LOT)." Hinzen and Sheehan (2013: 238)

Simultaneously, as a result of the work of Grice and others, *pragmatics* gained prominence going into the twenty-first century. Within many pragmatic theories, individualized flexible speaker concepts replaced the stable semantic content, literal or lexical meanings, encoded in word symbols. For example, pragmaticists such as Deidre Wilson and Dan Sperber focused their attention on human speech in context, as opposed to its formal structure, i.e. grammar. In 2012 they proposed an inferential view of *meaning*:

"According to the classical view, utterances are signals encoding the messages that speakers intend to convey, and comprehension is achieved by decoding the signals to obtain the associated messages. On the inferential view, utterances are not signals but pieces of evidence about a speaker's meaning, and comprehension is achieved by inferring this meaning from the evidence provided not only by the utterance but also by the context. An utterance is, of course, a linguistically coded piece of evidence, so that comprehension involves an element of decoding… However, a major development in pragmatics over the past thirty years (which has gone much further than Grice envisaged) has been to show that the explicit content of an utterance, like implicit content, is largely underdetermined by the linguistically encoded meaning, and its recovery involves a substantial element of pragmatic inference." Wilson and Sperber (2012: 23)

Going far beyond Grice's implicatures, theorists such as Wilson and Sperber have claimed that the explicit content of utterances, that which must be decoded from the symbols, must be inferentially interpreted for complete comprehension. Pragmatic inference is required at both the lexical level as well as Grice's level of implication. To them, the process of ascertaining the meanings of words must also take context into account. They contend that a "contextualist approach to semantics, combined with a relevance-oriented approach to pragmatics, can yield appropriate accounts of speaker meaning." Wilson and Sperber (2012: 23)   For traditional semanticists, who insist there is formally encoded stable meaning in the word symbols, the interpretive process begins with the determinable stable semantic content which may be enhanced by pragmatic considerations of context, presuppositions etc. However, Wilson and Sperber claimed that cannot be done because there are no *determinable stable meanings* encoded in the words. Individual word meanings must also be inferred from context just as other units of speech are: phrases, sentences, paragraphs etc.

Even more extreme are radical pragmaticists. Steven Pinker encapsulates their position:

"If you could imagine a theory that is as contrary as possible to Extreme Nativism, it might be Radical Pragmatics. Its disagreement with conceptual

> semantics is not about whether the mental representations of word meanings are innate, or whether they are atomic, but whether they exist at all. … According to Radical Pragmatics, a permanently existing conceptual structure underlying the meaning of a word is also as mythical as the Jack of Spades, because people can use a word to mean almost anything, depending upon context." Pinker (2007: 107)

Radical pragmaticists deny that anything permanent or stable is encoded in words. Words are considered to be linguistically encoded "pieces of evidence" that need to be interpreted in context. All semantic content is implicit, not explicit. Word symbols that encode stable meanings, concepts or mental representations are semantic fictions for them. Word meanings are as variable as the people who use them and the contexts in which they are used.

Whether meanings are idiolectic or stable amongst speakers and instances of use is a continuing debate. Most of current academic orthodoxy still holds that individual word symbols encode stable semantic content of some sort, their lexical/literal meanings. These consistent meanings are encoded in the symbol and grasped by all speakers. When speakers grasp these stable independent meanings encoded by word symbols, they can use the words to carry out speech acts with appropriate pragmatic considerations. They can imply, suggest, indicate or mean something other than what is literally said. But the stable literal meanings are still there, encoded in the symbol, regardless of any machinations in the mind of the speaker or pragmatic considerations. *The symbols themselves say something* by their account.

Well, after 2500 years of philosophical speculation, how much progress have we made? Are meanings in the heads of speakers or are they speaker-neutral independent entities encoded in the word symbols? Are they stable or do they vary from speaker to speaker? Do they differ for the same speaker based on context? How do words and phrases denote, designate or refer to their referents? How can any theory explain the metaphorical use of words, ironic uses, hyperbole, sarcasm, implicatures, and performative utterances and on and on? There is no agreement on how human language works. *Meaning and reference* continue to be contentious issues in linguistics and the philosophy of language. What word meanings are and how they are related to sentence meaning has yet to be determined, and how meaning and reference are related to one another is a confusion that cannot be sorted out.

The science of language, linguistics, continues to study what humans do with words. However, the theoretical foundation of that science is very much in dispute. There is an ever-expanding body of data that has been accumulated by linguists, but no one has been able to present the data in a coherent formulaic way comparable to the advances in other sciences. No theoretical model is able to account for the data. Theorists are caught up in endless debates about the meanings and referents of words, phrases and sentences.

Moreover, in spite of all the changes in theory, there is still an antiquated view in certain quarters that words are names for things. This is most likely a result of Augustine's analysis. For him the word sound *"cat"* operated on the same principles as the word sound *"augustine"*. All words are simply variants of the general principle of naming. Humans provide culturally specific names for objects and concepts. Depending upon the culture, children first learn the *names* of objects; *"ball"*, *"crib"*, *"blanky"*, etc. Eventually, they learn the names of concepts: *"father"*, *"big"*, *"mind"*, etc. *Naming* as a child-language learning-paradigm is still taught in contemporary psycholinguistics.

Although words are not said to be names in most up-to-date theories, they are nevertheless, symbols or signs. These word symbols *stand for, express, signify, represent, encode, designate, denote* or *refer to* other things. Whatever these other things are can be is a bit confusing. Do the words stand for idiolectic speaker meanings, thoughts, ideas, concepts, representations and propositions in the minds of speakers or consistent abstract speaker-neutral meanings encoded in the symbols? What does the word sound "*word*" stand for? What does the word sound "*something*" refer to or signify? What does the word sound "*it*" encode? What does the word sound "*see*" denote? What does the word sound "*difficult*" designate? What are the *meanings* of these word sounds? After all, we use them every day. They must have *meanings*, things that are somehow paired up with the word symbols so humans can use them and communicate *meaningfully*.

Modern Semantics

"**Semantics** deals with the literal meaning of words and the meaning of the way they are combined, which taken together form the core of meaning, or the starting point from which the whole of meaning of a particular utterance is constructed. Pragmatics deals with all the ways in which literal meaning must be refined, enriched or extended to arrive at an understanding of what a speaker meant in uttering a particular expression." Kate Kearns (2000: 1)

The Greeks established the theoretical foundation for modern semantics and semiotics. In fact, the word "semantic" derives from the Greek word for "sign". The word "semiotic" derives from the same source and is used to describe the science of signs and symbols. In both philosophy of language and linguistics that fundamental Greek foundation remains intact. Words are still considered to be *signs* or *symbols*. This fundamental assumption upon which semantic theory rests has not changed since the days of Plato.

Semantics, as outlined in the above epigraph from a basic semantics textbook, "deals with the literal meaning of words and the meaning of the way they are combined". Semanticists believe that they must explain the process by which speakers retrieve these *lexical or literal meanings encoded in the symbols*. They must determine how these semantic de*sign*ators (words) *stand for, express, signify, represent, encode, designate, denote* or *refer to* their semantic content, literal or lexical meanings.

Although there has been much discussion in modern semantics of speaker meaning as opposed to literal meaning, lexical meaning, explicit meaning or encoded meaning, *theories of meaning within the semantics* have continued to insist that there are timeless, placeless, speaker-neutral *meanings of some sort* invariably associated with words. These stable core meanings encoded by the words can be determined independently of the word's deployment in various contexts by various speakers. These meanings are passed from speaker to hearer, or writer to reader, and are the same for both. Theorists also assume that a competent speaker and hearer both grasp these consistent core meanings. This view frees those lexica/literal meanings from the speaker's speech history and the context of the speech. This *stable shared independent lexical/literal meaning* is a prerequisite for all of semantic theory. It is a basic assumption upon which all of semantic theory depends.

Speaker meaning in philosophy is part of a broader phenomenon of meaning, the meaning of gestures, body language, tell-tale blushing, facial expressions and numerous other prosodic features. Within communication theory, all of these elements of human communication can be used and interpreted differently by communicative participants. The recognition of linguistic speaker meaning is integrally related to recognition of non-linguistic speaker meaning. Yet within semantics, little attention is paid to the larger phenomenon of meaning and there is an assumption that lexical/literal meaning can be differentiated and separated from speaker meaning.

This lexical/literal meaning, the stable semantic content of words, is assumed to correlate inflexibly with the word sign or symbol and is grasped independently of any speaker meaning. It is *what the words say* as opposed to what the speaker or writer means.

The critical assumption that the words say something outside of their use by a speaker or writer underlies all of current semantic theory. It is the assumption that there is a consistent meaning that can be paired up with the word symbols and ascertained independently of prosodic features, speaker goals, the speaker's speech history and the context of the speech or any other pragmatic considerations. Without consistent lexical/literal meanings for word symbols, semantics loses its raison d'être. *If the word symbols say nothing* independently of their use on any given occasion, there is no need for semantics.

Puzzles in Modern Semantics

Contemporary semantics is bedeviled by puzzles. A brief review of a few of them is warranted at this point to give you a taste of the challenges faced by modern semanticists. A more detailed review will be forthcoming in Chapter 4.

One puzzle that has long baffled philosophers and semanticists is *names*. If names are words, as most theorists would agree, what do they mean? Names do not seem to have *meanings* like other words. What would the meaning of "*neil armstrong*" be other than Neil Armstrong, the person? "*neil armstrong*" must stand for, refer to, signify, encode, designate or denote the person, Neil Armstrong. The referent of the semantic designator "*neil armstrong*" must be the guy with the name Neil Armstrong. But what happens after Neil Armstrong died and was cremated? What does the sound "*neil armstrong*" now designate and what does "*neil armstrong*" mean to people unfamiliar with Neil Armstrong or his exploits? Is it a word with no meaning for them?

Morphology also presents many problems for linguists. Morphology is a subdivision of semantics in which morphemes are said to be the smallest units of meaning. The reduction of words into smaller meaningful units leads to many puzzles. Consider the morpheme "*un*" for example. Any respectable dictionary will have hundreds, if not thousands of English words that begin with that morpheme. Most have been formed by adding the "*un*" to a stem word form: "*unbiased*", "*unappreciated*", "*unhappy*" and so on and so forth. This small morphological unit seems to have a fairly consistent meaning that is not dependent upon the stem-word's meaning. The morpheme seems to add its own meaning to the word and in the process change the meaning of the stem word.

Yet, what is the meaning of "*derstand*" in "understand" or "*dulate*" in "undulate"? How is it that "*un*" seems to have an independent meaning in some words but not in others? Is it a meaningful morpheme or is it not? In addition, what is the meaning of "*ceive*" in "*conceive*", "*perceive*", "*deceive*" and "*receive*"? "*ceive*" appears to be a morphological unit, yet it has *no meaning*. Morphologists run into all sorts of problems with their morphological units of meaning because there are thousands of exceptions. "*inept*", "*remit*", and "*disgusted*" all have what would be considered morphemic prefixes: "*in*", "*re*" and "*dis*". Yet their stem morphemes: "*ept*", "*mit*" and "*gusted*" have no meanings. Where are they in the dictionary? Morphologically deconstructing words is fraught with inconsistencies.

Anaphora are other elements of grammar that present problems for semanticists and syntacticians. Anaphoric pronouns, for example, are *parts of speech* that refer back to previous referents when used in the written form, e.g. **'John looked up. He smiled.'** However, in conversation, when participants are discussing multiple third parties and Bill is the subject of conversation, someone might say: "*bill was there john looked up he smiled*" referring to Bill with the anaphoric pronoun "*he*", or was the referent John? How these pronouns are *bound* to their referents is an ongoing mystery to semanticists. How do readers and listeners determine who or what is being referred to by writers and speakers when they use anaphoric pronouns?

Anaphora are extremely common in everyday speech, particularly anaphoric pronouns such as "he", "she", "we" and "you". Every one of these words must be analyzed in terms of previous discourse and context. They are semantic and syntactic nightmares because of shifting reference. When discourse participants have a successful communicative exchange, how do they arrive at a common reference for words which have shifting reference? There is extensive literature in both semantics and syntax that tries to account for ever-changing referents of anaphora within various grammatical constructions. However, no theory has been able to explain how these parts of speech work within the constraints of the conventional semantic paradigm.

This puzzle is generally referred to as the "binding problem". There are various binding theories that suggest how anaphoric pronouns are bound to their referents. One such theory involves co-indexing multiple pronouns to their respective antecedent referents. In order to do so, semanticists must appeal to speaker intent and context, including previous discourse, elements that are not part of semantics or syntax. Invariably, to explain anaphoric pronouns, syntacticians and semanticists must go outside of syntax and semantics. Neither rules of syntax, nor rules of semantics can explain how these ubiquitous parts of speech function.

The use of "himself" in discourse presents another side of the binding problem. The meaning of "himself" seems to change based on a previous reference made in the discourse, but often it can be used quite ambiguously. One can say: "billy poked himself". The referent of "himself" in that utterance appears to be unambiguous. "himself" refers anaphorically to Billy. But what if someone says: "billy gave jimmy a picture of himself". Is the picture of Jimmy or Billy? There appears to be no way to disambiguate the meaning of this sentence without an appeal to factors outside of semantics and syntax, e.g. what did the speaker intend? There appears to be no consistent syntactic or semantic function for "himself" in that sentence, much less a *consistent meaning*.

Deixis is a phenomenon that is also difficult for semanticists to reconcile with their view that words have consistent semantic content. Deictic words are very common in both speech and writing. The *referents* of these words change with the time and place of their utterance or the person who utters them. The most common example of deixis is in the use of pronouns. The referents of the English words "i", "me", "he", "she" change with each incident of use. The use of "it" exemplifies the same phenomenon. What are *the meanings* of these deictic words? Many such words appear to have no stable semantic content whatsoever. Their referents change repeatedly, even during the most mundane conversations. Linguists have concluded that "deixis abounds in language use and marks one of the boundaries of semantics and pragmatics." Fromkin and Rodman (1998: 201)

Although they are only sometimes considered deictic phenomenon, the use of many words depends upon the speaker point of view, POV, although speaker location is generally the default setting for POV. The use of the spoken words "here", "there", "inside", "outside", "front", "back", "left", "right", "up", "down", "to", "from", "come" and "go" always presupposes a location that is relevant to the discourse participants. Consider the following statements: "i came to the party", "i went to the party", "mary told bill to come to the party", "mary told bill to go to the party". All these terms are used effortlessly by English speakers when a POV has been clearly established during discourse. But when analyzed in isolation, the necessary data to establish the *meaning* in any of these spoken words is not available. They simply cannot be used by speakers without a presupposition about POV. In the written form, POV must be established antecedently and the relevant terms used anaphorically.

The problem of *demonstratives* is closely related to anaphoric pronouns and deixis. In English, "*this*" and "*that*" can be considered demonstratives *or* anaphoric pronouns. They can be accompanied by gestures to point to subjects in occurring discourse. Someone might say: "*this dog is black*" while pointing to a dog. They refer to a specific dog with the use of "*this*". Well, what is the meaning of the sound "*this*" in this instance of use? It appears to be a deictic operator that is completely dependent upon its contemporaneous use in discourse, much like "*here*" or "*now*". Semanticists cannot capture any semantic value for demonstratives that are combined with pointing to introduce the subject into the domain of discourse. They are merely a vocal adjunct to the pointing behavior.

These demonstratives can also be used in discourse in much the same way as anaphoric pronouns. Demonstratives and pronouns adjust their reference to the circumstances of their use. Like pronouns, the use of "*that*" and "*this*" are often dependent upon previous discourse when used in the vocal form. "*this dog*" can be referred to with "*that dog*" after an initial successful reference has been made to track the subject of the conversation. In the written form 'this' and 'that' are anaphorically dependent upon previously written text. *That statement* and *this statement*, for example, depend upon the reader putting both statements into the context of *this* paragraph. These linguistic devices are used extensively and appear to be semantically void; they do not stand for or represent anything. Yet their utility makes them indispensible and widespread.

Metaphor is another phenomenon that is difficult to explain within semantic theory – for if words have a stable semantic content, how can semanticists explain the metaphoric use of words? When George Tenet told George W. Bush that finding weapons of mass destruction in Iraq was "*a slam dunk*", Bush took him to mean it was a sure thing – "*a slam dunk*" has taken on a metaphoric meaning in addition to its basketball meaning. George W. Bush and George Tenet were not talking about basketball. In conventional analysis, the metaphoric use of words is said to give different *meanings* to the words. The literal meanings of words are exchanged for *figurative meanings*. Conventional or standard meanings are swapped for non-standard meanings. The implication is that there are hidden meanings in metaphors which have to be searched for and uncovered. How does the hearer know which meanings to attach to the words? In fact, it is difficult to say that individual words have metaphoric meanings at all. Maybe phrases do, e.g. "*a slam dunk*", but it is difficult to make the case that the word sound "*slam*", taken in isolation, has a metaphoric meaning in addition to its literal meaning.

In addition to the aforementioned anaphoric pronouns, neither current semantic theory nor syntactic theory can explain the inconsistent use of *prepositions* such as those used with temporal modifiers: "*at 10 o'clock*", "*at once*", "*in june*", "*on monday*", "*by day*", "*at night*", "*over the year*", "*on the hour*", "*in a moment*", "*one month on*". Out of very specific contexts, there appear to be no consistent rules for the use of prepositions such as "*in*" and "*on*". We English speakers, for instance, can say: "*cup on the counter*", "*door on the car*" and "*paint on the ceiling*". In other languages there are often striking differences in the use of their similar parts of speech.[7] Moreover, the use of many prepositions varies from region to region for English speakers. English prepositions appear to have no stable semantic content or significance and are often used inconsistently.

Temporal indicators, likewise, appear to be totally deictic and semantically vacuous: *"earlier"*, *"ago"*, *"today"*. *"when"* is another troublesome word, as in the clause *"when i arrived the coach was already there"*. Semantic theorists are unable to explain what the semantic value is for many such constructions using temporal indicators and modifiers. Another notorious word that appears to be semantically vacuous is *"up"*. We English speakers have hundreds of expressions containing that word: *"listen up, show up, fess up, back up, catch up, keep up, man up, make up, open up, save up, shut up, clean up, give up, break up, turn up, trip up, pass up, shake up, soak up, suck up, live up to, messed up, settle up, wash up, add it up, shape up, whats up, limber up, lawyer up, mix it up, make it up, its up to you"* and so on and so forth. It has so many gratuitous and divergent uses that a meaning for *"up"* is impossible to provide.

Translation is another puzzle. Translation is often claimed to be the transfer of word, phrase and sentence *meanings* from one language to another. The constants in the translation from one language to another are said to be the *meanings*. Yet it is difficult to find any of these translational constants, these meanings. There seems to be no constant direct one-to-one relationship between the words, phrases and sentences in one language and those of another language, except in the most primitive grammatical constructions. If that were the case, electronic digital translators would be fully adequate for translation. Words, phrases and sentences with identical meanings could be swapped regardless of any machinations in the heads of the speakers or pragmatic considerations.

However, any competent translator will tell you that translation is much more than simply finding equivalent meanings in a look-up table and then making the word swap. Aside from considerable differences in syntax amongst languages, different languages present insurmountable problems in semantics. Word meanings simply do not convert from language to language. Both the lexical items and the grammatical elements of different languages vary dramatically in their theoretical semantic content and pragmatic application. Good interpreters and translators must have extensive cultural exposure and experience in *the use* of both languages to be effective. They must learn the idioms and metaphors which are ubiquitous in all languages. Trying to isolate the *literal meaning* of words, phrases and sentences from speaker intentions, contextual elements and pragmatic considerations for word swapping is a "pipe dream" for translators.

This (demonstrative) introductory brief *on* (random preposition) semantic puzzles is meant to give *you* (deictic pronoun) a *small taste* (metaphor) of the puzzles confronting both semantic and syntactic theories. There are many more. Some of *them* (anaphoric pronoun) will be detailed and analyzed later in this and other chapters. But as *you* go through *these* puzzles, I hope *you* will keep in mind the basic premises of all semantic theories.

All semantic theories, aside from the behaviorist's, assume that words are signs, symbols, or designators with stable core literal meanings and/or referents. They also assume that spoken words are expressions or representations of mental entities and processes: thoughts, ideas, concepts, and propositions in the mind of the speaker.

Truth Conditional Semantics

"The statement of the conditions under which a proposition is true is the same as the statement of its meaning, and not something different." Morris Schlick via Ayer (1933: 82)

"to know the meaning of an indicative sentence is to know what the world has to be like for the sentence to be true." Allwood, Andersson and Osten (1977: 72)

Propositions have played an extraordinary role in logic, philosophy of language and semantic theory. If you will recall my previous comments on propositions, the utterances *the tree is tall* and *el arbol es alto* are said to share a common proposition. Although propositions are not universally considered to be psychological entities, they are considered to be the common element encoded by the word symbols in equivalent indicative or declarative utterances or statements, regardless of the language used by the speaker, or the occasion of its utterance. Such equivalent utterances and/or statements are said to share a common proposition and thereby *a common meaning*.

> "A need to posit propositions… has been felt or imagined in a number of connections. Propositions or other sentence meanings have been wanted as translational constants: as things shared somehow by foreign sentences and their translations. They have been wanted likewise as constants of so-called philosophical analysis, or paraphrase: as things shared by analysanda and their analysantia. They have been wanted as truth vehicles and as objects of propositional attitudes." Willard V.O. Quine (1960: 206)

Within the field of semantics, truth-conditional semantics (TCS) had taken hold in the late 20th century because of the influence of logicians in the philosophy of language. Logicians Gottleb Frege, Bertrand Russell, Ludwig Wittgenstein and logical positivists such as Morris Schlick, had been studying the logical operators in natural language: *and*, *or*, *if*, *then* etc. They had developed symbolic systems that provided rules for logically proper deduction, implication, inference and entailment. They developed notational systems that were supposed to serve as models for logical argumentation with natural language. They asserted that logic was a means to determining the *truth* of *propositions* and thus their *meaning*. Their influence in contemporary linguistics is pervasive.

TCS is an outgrowth of logical positivism in which *the meaning* of an indicative statement or declarative statement can be known by knowing the conditions under which the statement is true. Logical positivists had asserted that all such statements were true, false or substantively *meaningless*. They had developed what they called an *empirical criterion of meaning*. If any statement could be said to have meaning, that meaning could be determined by knowing what the world would have to be like to make that statement *true*. Truth was assumed to be a fundamental concept that is grasped by native speakers. This premise comes out of a Russellian epistemology that says we must know what truth is before we can know what knowledge is. The theoretical foundation for contemporary TCS is firmly anchored in the epistemology of early 20th century analytic philosophers and logicians.

TCS asserts that indicative or declarative *statements are the basic units of meaning*, (not individual words) because only they can be true or false. TCS also assumes that every informative statement *represents a proposition* that has one and only one truth value, and therefore one and only *one lexical/literal meaning*. This analysis of natural language meaning is driven by 20th century logicians operating within the bivalent logic of Aristotle. Yet thousands of books and thousands of academicians later, logicians and positivists are no closer to a semantic theory that can explain what most ten-year olds can do with words. They can speak competently. The defects in TCS or *logical semantics* as an explanatory model are numerous and glaring.

For example, the argument for TCS seems to suffer the pain of circularity. The truth of any declarative statement, it would seem, depends on the meaning of the terms used in the statement. How can the meaning of the terms then depend upon the truth of the statement? If the relation between truth and meaning is bi-directional, we are no further ahead in our attempt to determine either the meaning or the truth of a statement. One feeds the other. Moreover, if any word such as "justice" has more than one meaning, the truth value of any statement containing it can vary and we have no way to determine either truth or meaning. Consequently, we have gained nothing from TCS other than the hypothesis that truth and meaning are somehow related.

Along with Aristotelian bivalent logic needed to propound TCS, (the shortcomings of Aristotle's bivalent logic and logical positivism are detailed in Chapter VI), current proponents employ set theory which is itself plagued by theoretical defects. In addition, TCS relies on possible world theorizing. In fact, TCS is sometimes referred to *as Possible World Semantics*. Bivalent logic, set theory, and possible world theorizing are cobbled together in a less than coherent way to provide the theoretical support for TCS. All of this theoretical support for TCS is questionable at best, and the shortcomings of TCS as a practical explanatory model of human speech are manifest. That is because TCS as a theory of *meaning* is based on a faulty premise. We will find out why in the next chapter. In the meantime, let's review a few more of the patent defects in TCS.

The basic premise of TCS asserts that to know the *meaning* of a declarative or indicative sentence is to know under what conditions it would be true. If one accepts that premise, TCS cannot produce the meaning of any expressions other than declarative statements. They are the only statements that represent the truth-bearing propositions in logical theory. As any competent linguist can tell you, declarative statements are but a small subset of a much wider universe of grammatical forms. Humans use word sounds in many ways: commanding, questioning, performative utterances etc. TCS has no way of determining the *meaning* of any these dominant verbal constructions if they have no truth value.

Not only can it not provide the meaning for any constructions other than declarative or indicative statements, it cannot provide meanings for any words or phrases used within those statements. For the past three millennia, words and phrases have been said to have *meanings*. However, within TCS, the basic unit of analysis is a statement representing a proposition. Truth conditions and thereby meaning, do not apply in any other units of grammar except derivatively. Consequently, it is not possible to explain isolated word or phrase meanings within the TCS theory. This approach to *meaning* has been inherited by universal grammar (UG) which suffers the same defect. In UG, a language is often defined as "a set of sentences".

It must be added that TCS cannot account for sentence fragments such as ellipsis which are a dominant form of discourse in many speech communities and the first things children learn. Grammatically well-formed declarative sentences have rarely been the dominant form of human discourse; quite the opposite. In all likelihood, sentence fragments were the only form of *discourse* before the advent of writing, formal grammar and its instruction via mass education. Correct grammar is a relatively recent phenomenon that has been inculcated in only a small portion of the human population, yet complete *grammatically correct* sentences are the only form of speech that both TCS semanticists and contemporary syntacticians are able to analyze within their self-proclaimed methodological limits. (The phenomena of ellipsis and sub-sentential utterances have generated a good deal of theory to explain them: as "shorthand" for complete sentences, for example. Stainton (2006) gives a good account of the debate.)

Even when sentences are grammatically correct and used by the same speaker in identical circumstances, there can be multiple interpretations. In speech, different *readings* are often disambiguated by inquiring about speaker's intent for example. *Meaning* can apparently vary with speaker intentions. That, of course, runs completely contrary to the assumptions that the meaning can be determined by analyzing the speech or text independently, isolated from pragmatic factors such as speaker intent, the speaker's speech history or context. The truth value and literal semantic content are encoded in the word symbols independently of these pragmatic considerations, there to be discovered by a decoding of the symbols alone. So say semanticists.

The *de dicto/de re* distinction is a prime example of multiple readings for the same statement based on what's going on in the speaker's head. The *de dicto* (what the words say) reading of the noun phrase "*the queen of england*" is: *whoever* is the queen of England. The speaker may say: "*the queen of england is not the head of state*" and not know the queen of England's name in this *de dicto* reading. The *de re* construal is: Elizabeth, the person who is the queen of England is not the head of state. That is, the speaker is making a declarative statement about a specific person that he can identify and possibly name. He is selecting a specific individual as the subject about whom he is making a claim in the *de re* (what the speaker meant) reading. In effect, the two readings of the identical statement made under identical circumstances seem to depend entirely upon speaker intentions and speaker knowledge.

Whether you call them different meanings or different *readings*, the net result is the same for semanticists, i.e. there is no stable semantic value in the word symbols even when the context of the utterance remains constant. For many expressions such as "*the queen of england*", there is a great deal of pragmatic variation depending upon the speaker's presuppositions and goals. That phenomenon can only be accounted for within linguistics by making appropriate pragmatic background considerations such as speaker presuppositions and intent elements of the analysis.

Scope ambiguity is another phenomenon that confounds TCS proponents. Consider the statement: "*every child should read a book*". Under the narrow scope interpretation, the statement could be rephrased: "*there is one book that every child should read*". Under the wide-scope interpretation the statement could be rephrased: "*every child should read a different book*". What does the indefinite description "*a book*" designate? A single book or different books? How can anyone determine the truth of that statement and thus its meaning (within TCS)? Without disambiguating the statement, there are two inconsistent readings that produce different truth values.

In fact, contemporary TCS literature comprises a blizzard of papers analyzing different readings of linguistic constructions that are inherently subject to multiple interpretations. Many semantics textbooks and treatises are attempts to catalogue all the circumstances in which various constructions can be used. These various *readings* detail the prosodic features, the context, the knowledge and the goals of the speaker to delineate different interpretations of the same speech act such as: "*the queen of england is not the head of state*". Scenarios are specified in which different uses for the same syntactic sequence of words will produce different results in hearers.

Yet semanticists insist that there is *a stable lexical/literal meaning* for each sentence as they analyze the text. They insist that there is one *de dicto reading*; they insist that the individual word symbols, phrases and sentences say something independently of their use by speakers. Their task, as they see it, is to determine what lexica/literal meaning is encoded in the symbols. They attempt to eliminate anything within the purview of pragmaticists but invariably end up with multiple *readings* dependent upon context, presuppositions and considerations of speaker goals. Their theories cannot provide a single *correct reading*; they provide multiple readings.

Another glaring fault with TCS is the inability to explain the inconsistent use of *logical connectives* in natural language. Logical connectives, the so-called constants used in formal logics, differ drastically from their natural language counterparts. Conjunction (and), disjunction (or), implication (if…then), negation (not) are used very differently by native speakers and logicians. This leads to a total inability to determine *meaning* of ordinary sentences if the natural language counterparts of formal logic connectives are used. Many quotidian statements containing "*and*", "*or*", "*if…then*" or "*not*" are not amenable to logical analysis and thereby TCS analysis for truth and thus meaning.

For example, with the logical connective "and": "A and B" is logically equivalent to "B and A". This logical commutative property comes from algebra, but as one philosopher pointed out, "Jane Austen died and was buried in West Minster Abbey" is not the same as "Jane Austen was buried and died in Westminster Abbey." The analysis and use of logical connectives in natural language diverges from their use in logic. Other discrepancies between logic and ordinary speech activity frustrate any attempts to determine truth value and thereby the meaning of a sentence within the TCS framework. Another example: were a speaker to say: "*i bought a book*", most listeners would conclude that that statement would be false if the speaker bought three books. That is not so according to logicians. Buying three books is logically consistent with the declaration "*I bought a book*". Where does the truth and therefore the meaning of that statement lie?

Another failure of TCS is the inability to account for natural language *proportional quantifiers*. In predicate logic, a foundational system within TCS, quantifiers such as "*all*", "*every*", "*few*", "*many*", "*most*" and "*some*" cannot be explained or represented adequately within that system. They cannot because they are all idiolectic and completely context driven. If a speaker was to say: "*most people are greedy*", what would the world have to be like to make that sentence true? Would a truth determination require a survey of every person on earth? Does "*most*" mean more than fifty percent or is the truth of that sentence indeterminate? If it is, by the standards of TCS, the speaker could not know the meaning of the sentence, because he could not know "what the world has to be like for the sentence to be true." In addition, once again, the ordinary use of these quantifiers is inconsistent with their use in logic. In logic, "*i bought some of the donuts*" does not contradict: "*i bought all the donuts*".

Neither is TCS able to explain so-called *modal terms* and *intentional operators* that are sensitive to context and speaker idiolect: "*must*", "*may*", "*can*", "*possible*", "*probable*", "*likely*". The truth value of statements such as "*rain is likely tomorrow*" cannot be determined. What would the world have to be like for that statement to be true? The use of modals such as "*likely*" precludes a determination of truth value and thereby precludes the possibility of ascertaining any literal meaning for that sentence within the TCS paradigm. These modal qualifiers do not appear to have stable independent literal meanings. Consequently, most of them are considered functional items, as opposed to lexical items with semantic content, and tossed into the pragmatics waste basket along with pronouns, demonstratives, prepositions, articles etc. The pragmatics waste basket is now overflowing with words that have no semantic content or lexical/literal value, i.e. words that have *no meanings*.

The same holds true for *quantificational adverbs*: "*never*", "*seldom*", "*occasionally*", "*sometimes*", "*often*", "*usually*", "*always*". There simply is no constant fixed semantic content that can be attributed to any of these words. Even when used by an individual speaker within specific contexts their use is highly erratic. Consequently, truth value and thereby the *meaning* of a declarative statement containing quantificational adverbs is impossible to determine within the framework of TCS. It seems *likely* that truth-conditional semanticists will *never* come up with an adequate account of what these sentences mean, and it appears that it would be *impossible* to give individual modal terms or quantificational adverbs any literal meanings.

Verb tense and *temporal modifiers* also give logicians and truth-conditional-semanticists fits. They are impossible to model within the current notational systems. A simple word such as "*yesterday*" cannot be adequately represented. It cannot because the truth of any statement using that word is time sensitive. The truth of "*mommy was working yesterday*". depends on when a speaker utters it. The analysis of tense inflections and temporal adverbs has brought about tense logic and tense semantics. About the best one can say of these new systems is that they are inconclusive. They will remain so for reasons to be explained.

This admittedly cursory outline of some flaws in TCS is simply a starting point. The problems with TCS are extensive and well-documented in the voluminous literature on the subject. That is because TCS is plagued by the scourge of formal logic. However, TCS theorists are not alone. Problems plague semantic theorists of all stripes. Although semanticists have concluded that some words such as grammatical elements have no semantic content, i.e. *no meanings*, all of semantic theory assumes that some words *do* have meanings. They believe that *content words* have encoded *lexical or literal meanings* that can be ascertained independently of the speaker's speech history and the context of their use. That assumption is simply mistaken; it is one element of the semantic fallacies.

I hope to show that TCS theorists, and all other semantic theorists, are badly mistaken. I contend that the semantic paradigm of *words* that have *lexical/literal meanings*, i.e. *semantic content*, is based on a number of mistaken assumptions. In the following chapters, I hope to outline those mistakes and show why they are mistakes. I hope to persuade you that not only is TCS a fatally flawed theory, all of semantics is fatally flawed because words have no lexical/literal meanings. I hope to persuade you that the sounds emanating from humans do not *stand for, express, signify, represent, encode, designate, denote* or *refer* to other things. I hope to persuade you that these word sounds are not signs or symbols or semantic designators and that all of traditional language theory is based on fallacies, *the semantic fallacies*, and these fallacies have extreme consequences.

Chapter One

Summary & Notes

Philosophers have been discussing human languages for millennia. However, these languages have become a subject of empirical study for only the past 200 years or so. During that time professional linguists have subdivided the science of linguistics into phonetics, syntax, pragmatics, semantics and a host of sub-groupings.

The philosophical backdrop for modern linguistics, starting with the ancient Greek philosophers, provides the theoretical support for these modern linguistic distinctions. With the maturation of linguistics as an empirical science, *semantics* became the primary concern of philosophers. The *lexical/literal meaning* or *semantic content* of words became the focus of much theorizing by philosophers and linguists alike. Most theorists both assume and assert that words are signs or symbols with lexical/literal meanings which can be determined without any consideration for the location of the word in larger grammatical constructions (phrases, sentences etc.), or the context of its use upon any specific occasion, or any machinations in the mind of the speaker/writer.

However, there are profound problems and puzzles produced by this view of meaning. Consequently, the lexical/literal meanings of words became the source of much controversy and debate amongst language theorists. Word reference also went under the empirical microscope and initiated even more controversies and debates. These debates have not abated. The philosophical foundation of semantics is as controversial today as it was three millennia ago. *Word meaning* and *word reference* continue to pose problems for philosophers and linguists alike.

Some contemporary theorists, under the influence of logicians, have attempted to establish new theoretical support for literal meaning which has migrated from individual words to sentences. For them, *the meaning of a sentence* is the same as a statement of the conditions under which that sentence is true. However, since individual words in isolation cannot be true or false, meanings for those individual words cannot be determined. Nevertheless, TCS took root in the first half of the 20th century and remains a predominant force in theoretical linguistics to this day. Yet it has produced even more problems and puzzles.

To conclude, in spite of all the effort which has been expended in attempts to explain how language works, and more narrowly, how semantics works, the jury is still out. Theorists of all kinds are awaiting a persuasive explanation of what is happening when people engage in verbal communication, and how humans come to have this ability, both phylogenetically and ontogenetically. In future chapters I will attempt to provide both the theoretical support and a broad outline for a revived non-semantic explanation of how language is acquired and used. It is radically different from what you now believe, for reasons which will become clear.

---

1. Early twentieth century philosopher Bertrand Russell declined to use the word "idea" because it had taken on multiple uses that went far beyond what the Plato had intended. He used "universals" instead: "The word 'idea' has acquired, in the course of time, many associations which are quite misleading when applied to Plato's 'ideas.' We shall therefore use the word 'universal' instead of the word 'idea,' to describe what Plato meant." Russell (1912: 64)

Russell later stated: "Seeing that nearly all the words to be found in the dictionary stand for universals, it is strange that hardly anybody except students of philosophy ever realizes that there are such entities as universals. We do not naturally dwell upon those words in a sentence which do not stand for particulars; and if we are forced to dwell upon a word which stands for a universal, we naturally think of it as standing for some one of the particulars that come under the universal." Ibid., p. 65.

Much to his credit, Russell acknowledged the Platonism at the heart of his mystical view of words: "But in each case I can only utter an instance of the word, not the word itself, which remains immovably in a Platonic heaven. Logic, and the whole conception of words and sentences as opposed to verbal and sentential utterances, is thus incurably Platonic." Russell (1940: 70)

2. Whorf was not making a claim of linguistic "determinism" whereby human thoughts are rigidly determined and limited by the language they speak. His claim was that how humans think about the world is influenced by the languages they speak.

3. Skinner's definition of an operant: "The class of responses upon which a reinforcer is contingent is called an operant." Skinner (1969: 7) "The term 'operant' distinguishes between reflexes and responses which operate directly on the environment. The alternative term, instrumental, suggests the use of tools. To say that a rat 'uses a lever to obtain food' has purposive overtones, and where nothing can be identified as an instrument, it is often said that the organism 'uses a response' to gain an effect. For example, verbal behavior is interpreted as 'the use of words,' although the implication that words exist as things apart from behavior unnecessarily complicates the analysis." Skinner (1969: 109) "An operant is a class, of which a response is an instance or a member. The usage is seldom respected. Strictly speaking, it is always instances which are counted in determining frequency, and from that frequency the probability of a *response* inferred. The probability is frequently taken, however, as the measure of the strength of an *operant*. Strength of a response has no meaning except as a property of an instance, such as its force or speed. It is always a response upon which a given reinforcement is contingent, but it is contingent upon properties which define membership in an operant. Thus, a set of contingencies defines an operant." Skinner (1969: 131) "*The action of the stimuli*. Operant reinforcement not only strengthens a given response; it brings the response under the control of a stimulus. But the stimulus does not elicit the response as in a reflex; it merely sets the occasion upon which the response is more likely to occur. The ethologists' 'releaser' also simply sets an occasion. Like the discriminative stimulus, it increases the probability of occurrence of a unit of behavior but does not force it. The principal difference between a reflex and an instinct is not in the complexity of the response but in, respectively, the eliciting and releasing actions of the stimulus." Skinner (1969: 175)

4. In Chomsky's words: "Summarizing the Port-Royal theory in its major outlines, a sentence has an inner mental aspect (a deep structure that conveys its meaning) and an outer, physical aspect as a sound sequence. Its surface analysis into phrases may not indicate the significant connections of the deep structure by any formal mark or the actual arrangement of words. The deep structure is, however, represented in the mind as the physical utterance is produced. The deep structure consists of a system of propositions, organized in various ways. The elementary propositions that constitute the deep structure are of the subject-predicate form, with simple subjects and predicates (i.e. categories instead of more complex phrases). Many of these elementary objects can be independently realized as sentence." Chomsky (1966: 40) "Notice that the theory of deep and surface structures as developed in the Port-Royal linguistic studies implicitly contains recursive devices and thus provides for infinite use of the finite means that it disposes, as any adequate theory of language must." (Chomsky1966:

41.) "The Port-Royal grammar is apparently the first to develop the notion of phrase structure in any fairly clear way." Chomsky (1966: 42) "… the undifferentiated thought expressed by the sentence is derived directly from this underlying representation, which is regarded, throughout, as common to all languages (and typically corresponding to the usual order of French…) Chomsky (1966: 49)

5.   Chomsky's theory relied on Cartesian dualism which he considered to be obvious and not worth discussing: "Descartes is therefore pointing out that, just as in its normal use "verbal behavior" is free of the identifiable external stimuli or internal physiological states, so it is evidently not developed in the individual by conditioning. He does not elaborate on this, regarding it perhaps as too obvious to merit discussion. It is noteworthy that modern behaviorist speculation about human learning denies these truisms." Chomsky (1966: 80)

6.   In Randy Allen Harris's The Linguistics Wars he cites a letter from Skinner to Stephen O. Murray dated September 6, 1977 as the source of this quote.

7.   From Stephen C. Levenson: "Still, however rich the rest of the semantic distinctions, it could be that every language encodes a notion precisely like English *on* and *in*. Not so: many languages fractionate these notions and indeed have much more specific notions, like 'in a hemispherical container' versus 'in a cylindrical container'. Tzeltal makes many such distinctions in spatial predicates (Brown, 1994). But perhaps we simply need to qualify the claim: if a language encodes spatial relations in prepositions (or postpositions), then every such language encodes a notion like English *on* or *in*. This is not remotely true either. In current work, Sergio Meira and I have mapped adpositions (prepositions or postpositions) of a dozen languages of different stocks onto exactly the same set of 70 spatial scenes, each scene depicting a subtype of topological relation. What emerges quite clearly is that there is no basic agreement on what constitutes an 'in' scene, a spatial relation of containment, or any other basic topological relation. It is simply an empirical matter that spatial categories are almost never the same across languages, even when they are as closely related as English and Dutch." Language and Mind: Let's Get the Issues Straight! (2003: 31)

A Story

An indigenous group called the Munduruku, who live in isolated villages in several Brazilian states in the Amazon jungles, have no words in their language for square, rectangle, triangle or any other geometric shape except circles.

The members use no measuring instruments or compasses, they have no maps, and their words for directions are limited to sunrise, sunset, upstream and downstream. The Munduruku language has few words for numbers beyond five except 'few' and 'many,' and even those words are not used consistently.

Yet researchers have discovered, they appear to understand many principles of geometry as well as American children do, and in some cases almost as well as American adults. An article describing the findings appears in the Jan. 20 issue of Science.

'Across cultures that live extremely different lives, we see common foundational sets of abilities,' said Elizabeth Spelke, a co-author of the paper and a professor of psychology at Harvard, 'and they are not just low-level kinds of abilities that humans share with other animals, but abilities that are at the center of human thinking at its highest reaches.'

To test their understanding of geometry, the researchers presented 44 members of a Munduruku group and 54 Americans with a series of slides illustrating various geometric concepts. Each slide had six images. Five of them were examples of the concept; one was not.

The Munduruku subjects, tested by a native speaker of Munduruku working with a linguist, were asked to identify the image that was 'weird' or 'ugly.' For example, to test the concept of right angles, a slide shows five right triangles and one isosceles triangle. The isosceles triangle is the correct answer.

In data that do not appear in the article but were presented by e-mail from the authors, Munduruku children scored the same as American children—64 percent right—while Munduruku adults scored 83 percent compared with 86 percent for the American adults.

The researchers also tested the Munduruku with maps, demonstrating that people who had never seen a map before could use one correctly to orient themselves in space and to locate objects previously hidden in containers laid out on the ground.

The indigenous people were able to use the maps to find the objects, even when they were presented with the maps at varying angles so that they had to turn them mentally to match the pattern on the ground in front of them. Dr. Spelke found this particularly significant.

'The Munduruku, who aren't themselves in a culture that relies on symbols of any kind, when they were presented with maps were able to spontaneously extract the geometric information in them,' she said.

The idea that an understanding of geometry may be a universal quality of the human mind dates back at least as far as Plato. In the Meno dialogue by Plato, written about 380 B.C., he describes Socrates as he elicited correct answers to geometric puzzles from a young slave who had never studied the subject.

Do these findings among the Munduruku confirm Socrates' contention that concepts or geometry are innate? Stanislas Dehaene, another co-author and a professor of psychology at the College of France, is not willing to go quite that far. People learn things, after all, just by living in the world.

'In our article we do not use the word 'innate,' he said in an e-mail message. 'We do not know whether this core knowledge is present very early on – the youngest subjects we tested were 5 years old – or to what extent it is learned. The Munduruku, like all of us, do interact with 3-D objects, navigate in a complex environment, and so on.'

Instead, Dr. Dehaene described an innate ability, rather than an innate knowledge. 'Our current thinking is that the human brain has been predisposed by millions of years of evolution to 'internalize,' either very early on or through very fast learning, various mental representations of space, time and number,' he explained.

I have proposed that such representations provide a universal foundation for the cultural constructions of mathematics,' he added.

Dr. Spelke sees in these results evidence of the universality of human thought processes. 'Geometry is central to the development of science and the arts,' she said. The profile of abilities that the Munduruku show is qualitatively very similar to what we see in our own culture. This suggests that we are finding some common ground at the center of human knowledge.

By Nicholas Bakalar
The New York Times, Tuesday, January 24, 2006

CHAPTER TWO
THE SEMANTIC FALLACIES

Origins

"As early Sumerian writing functioned as a device to record commercial and bureaucratic transactions, the written language of that time is very restricted. Falkenstein (1964) calls it a 'sentenceless language'. This is not to be understood as a language that fails to reproduce the sentences of the spoken language, but rather as the absence of segments larger than a word or lexeme. Early Sumerian writing can thus be considered word writing in the sense that graphs represented words and words only... The expressive power of pure word writing is obviously very limited. In the beginning only concrete visible objects were represented with pictograms." Coulmas (1989: 77)

The history of writing provides some critical insights necessary for the proper analysis of human speech. As Florian Coulmas notes above, the first known *written* word symbols were non-arbitrary pictograms. They were developed by functionaries of the state as a means of keeping records. The pictograms or icons represented word *sounds*. The word sounds that were first represented were those used to refer to "concrete visible objects" and thereby easy to represent with pictograms. For example, ☼ could have been used to *represent* the Sumerian equivalent of the English word sound "*sun*". "Pure word writing" was a simple graphic system for representing some individual word sounds.

However, many word sounds used by early Sumerians were not used to refer to "concrete visible objects" and thus were difficult to represent iconically. The representations of some of these sounds were evidenced in later versions of Sumerian iconic writing systems as Roger Brown points out:

"The Sumerians used the word *ti* for life but had no written sign for this idea. It is difficult to represent. As it happened, the spoken form *ti* had two meanings in Sumerian. *Ti* was a homophone meaning *arrow* as well as *life*. The arrow is easily represented as '→'. At some point it occurred to the Sumerians to use this same sign '→' to designate life. This is a shift to the phonetic principle in writing... The written form is generalized along a dimension of sound rather than meaning and so becomes a derivative form speech." Brown (1958: 63)

Indeed, writing has always been a derivative form of speech. Writing has always represented the sounds produced by humans, not "concrete visible objects" or "ideas". It has been and still is a way to record speech.

Eventually, iconic symbols gave way to non-iconic symbols that stood for, expressed, signified, represented, encoded, designated, denoted, or referred to sound units. The most prominent sound units were individual spoken words. Coulmas traces this further development of Sumerian writing:

"The Sumerian ideograms, for example, were reduced to abstract symbols as early as 2500 BC, almost all of them having lost their iconic features. To the extent that visual iconicity was reduced, the relation of the sign to its linguistic form attained equal weight. Gradually the graphical sign thus came to stand for a sound unit. Initially this unit was a word, and the words which could thus be visualized were restricted to those having a concrete referent, such as *ox, grain, fish, mat, bird, donkey*, etc. For the most important practical purposes of writing this was quite enough. But words with more abstract meanings, such as *brother, go* or *dear* were still impossible to write. Generally speaking, properties, movements, states of affairs, events and relations could not be represented easily by means of pictorial sign... phonetization coupled with graphical abstraction opened the path to a solution of this problem too. As the relation between graphical sign and phonic word form became more stable and prominent, it became conceivable to use graphical marks for sound configurations only, irrespective of their meanings, because the meanings were no longer self-evident by the icon." Coulmas (1989:29)

As Coulmas details, phonetization and the loss of iconic features gradually led to a system of graphical marks for sound configurations in Sumerian graphology (he considered some meanings *abstract* because images could not be used to capture these (so called meanings.) The written word symbols were *phonetically* linked to the spoken words. This critical advancement enabled ancient writers to use graphical marks for all sound configurations, not just those "with a concrete referent". It allowed literate people to record all of their speech behavior.

Future technological advancements eventually allowed people to use devices that reproduce the sound for us, such as a digital recorder. However, we can still use written symbols for the sounds that allow readers to reproduce the sounds themselves. Such written text *is* representational; *it represents speech behavior*. The symbolic record of the activity, a series of written words represent speech acts, nothing more. For example, the written sentence **"The tree is tall"**, is a recording of a speech act utilized by someone at some time, either vocally or sub-vocally; *it does not represent meanings*.

Written word symbols, whether iconic or phonetic, have never stood for, expressed, signified, represented, encoded, designated, denoted or referred to anything other than sounds produced by humans, their verbal behavior, whether silent or aloud. Putting a so called "meaning" in the written symbol was a bit more understandable when iconic systems were prevalent and the symbols could be linked to the sound by virtue of their iconicity. After all, it took very little learning or imagination to understand that the written symbol ☼ represented a functional equivalent of the English word sound "sun". However, the *meanings* that were coupled with *phonetically* based written word symbols were not even determinable from the symbols alone, much less obvious. As Coulmas says, those *meanings* were not "self-evident". (There is much iconicity remaining in sign languages, e.g. ASL)

In fact, *meanings* for graphical representations of sounds were never self-evident; they were never there at all. Written words, whether they are iconically based or phonetically based, are transcriptions of vocal speech or sub-vocal speech. There is no reason to believe that these written symbols encode *meanings*, whatever meanings might be. To say that written words stand for meanings is akin to saying that the optical codes on CDs stand for meanings. Both the optical code and written words of any kind record sounds, sounds with functional roles to play in the behavior of the human speakers who use them.

In addition to the history of writing, the history of reading provides some critical insights for linguists. Reading is a skill based on speech. Readers first learn to read out loud. Readers make the sounds. They speak the words. In fact, silent reading was very rare until the 10th century. With the addition of punctuation marks in the 15th century, comprehension of text became easier and more widespread. The act of reading also became predominantly private. Nowadays, there is an entire industry devoted to teaching sustained silent reading in our school systems. Most of us take silent reading for granted, but it is a relatively recent phenomenon and it takes a good deal of training to avoid the natural inclination to produce the sounds from which the functionality of written words is derived.

For competent readers, the written symbols that represent the sounds ultimately become functionally autonomous. Within the literate English-speaking community for example, the written symbol **"sun"** will function much the same as the word sound *"sun"* for a well-trained reader and speaker. Florian Coulmas puts it this way:

> "Indeed, mature alphabetic orthographies encode morphological and lexical information in addition to phonetic information; and mature readers make use of this information more than they do of letter-sound correspondences."
> Coulmas (1989:230)

Within the semantic paradigm where meanings or semantic information are associated with spoken word symbols, linguists recognize the functional transference from sound to symbol by saying the written word symbols have lexical information independent of the sound production. They do not. There is no lexical information or semantic content in either the sounds or the symbols for those sounds.

There are, however, functional values for phonetic units such as words, abbreviations, clauses, phrases, idioms, acronyms and complete sentences when used in context with relevant presuppositions. The written symbols themselves can perform the functional roles of their corresponding acoustic units when used by a properly trained writer or reader. The written symbols **'is'**, **'sun'** and **'he'** can be employed in the same way that the sounds *"is"*, *"sun"* and *"he"* are for those who can read and utilize the original sounds. However, there is no literal information in those sounds or any other sounds. The sounds are *functional devices*, not signs or symbols with *meanings*.

When literate people become accomplished readers, the sounds and the symbols for those sounds perform the same *function*. When they see the symbol **'he'**, for example, they recognize an anaphoric reference to a previously identified male subject. The written symbol can be an alphabetized symbol, a logograph, a pictogram or any other symbol for the original sound. If they can read silently, symbols of many kinds become functionally autonomous for users who no longer need to process the intermediate functional sounds upon which the symbols were based. The written symbol **'he'** has a functional value based on the sound it represents. There is no need to introduce something called the meaning of **'he'** into the analysis.[1]

The functional roles of human speech were lost with the formalization of speech that accompanied writing. Normative grammar and semantics are based on *written* language. The standards are established by writers, linguists and grammarians. The static structural analysis and the theoretical underpinnings of modern linguistic theory are based on standardized rule-based writing, not conversation. As a result, linguists and grammarians talk about written word and sentence *meanings*, as if they had independent fixed semantic content outside of their use by humans. In Coulmas' terms:

> "The interpretation of a spoken utterance is first and foremost the interpretation of the speakers intended meaning. The focal question is *what* **the speaker** *means by the utterance*. Once the words are engraved in stone or clay tablets, inscribed on parchment and paper and thus given a stable physical presence, the focal question about their interpretation becomes *what do the words mean*. The meaning no longer resides in the speaker but in the text… However, it can hardly be doubted that strategies for interpreting written and spoken utterances differ on several counts. Written words possess meaning by virtue of the conventional relationship between linguistic forms and meanings. This is, of course, also true of spoken words. But their interpretation depends to a much greater extent on both context of situation and the assumed intentions of the speaker. Speech is bound to the 'here' and 'now' and 'I' (that is, to a specific deictic center, relative to which it is to be interpreted). The written word, on the other hand, is subsequently detached from the 'here', 'now' and 'I' of its production. In order to be fully interpretable, it must therefore be self-sufficient and explicit. All information that can be inferred from reference to common deictic field in speech has to be made explicit in writing. Reification thus means that a linguistic message becomes interpretable as detached from, and independent of, its conceiver. It also means the code itself becomes an object."
> Coulmas (1989:13)

In spite of the ambiguous use of "mean" and his semantic orientation, Coulmas makes a salient point about written words.

With the advent of writing, philosophers began to put an enduring, writer-neutral, stable and independent *meaning in the text*. Contrary to spoken language, written language has permanence. The written words are stable, enduring and the same for all readers. This allowed for a theoretical relationship between a stable written symbol and a stable enduring theoretical entity, *its meaning*. This fundamental assumption allowed philosophers, linguists, teachers and truck drivers to say when they see a printed word: *"what does that word mean"*. An independent stable *meaning* is thought to be encoded in the written word symbols regardless of who produced the symbols or the context of that production, including previous discourse. The printed words themselves are claimed to *say something*.

Furthermore, because theorists associated the *written word symbols* with stable independent meanings after the advent of writing, they also began to associate *spoken words* with stable independent meanings. The analysis of written words and sentences has led philosophers and linguists to the absurd conclusion that the sounds that issue from human mouths are signs or symbols that have speaker neutral, independent meanings just as the written symbols supposedly do. They attached stable consistent semantic content to the word sounds issuing from human mouths that is indifferent to the speaker's speech history, the speaker's goals and the context of the utterance. The word *symbols*, both the written and the spoken varieties, were said to have timeless, placeless, stable literal or lexical meanings encoded in them. This is the genesis of the first semantic fallacy, i.e. words of either kind have consistent *literal or lexical meanings* that are identical for all speakers.

Since the time of Plato, philosophers and linguists have treated all words, both the spoken and the written varieties, as signs or symbols with stable independent semantic content. If we take their bait we inevitably end up in their camp. If we accept the contention that either written words or spoken words are *symbols* that have consistent *meanings*, we have lost the argument. We get caught up in their semantic world. We then accept their contention that the word symbols themselves *say* something independently of any speaker. i.e. word symbols have a *de dicto* reading in addition to their *de re* reading. When we do, we have crossed the Rubicon.

However, if theorists do not assume that spoken words are symbols, these theorists can still ask: what is the speaker trying to accomplish? They can also ask what the functional value of this acoustic device is for this speaker in this context. They can describe speech and analyze it in terms of a specific context, presuppositions, speaker goals and the functional role that the various grammatical devices play in a complex web of that human's communication behavior. They need not have independent literal or lexical meanings associated with each word sound. Nor do they need speaker meanings in the minds of the speakers. If words are not considered symbols, *meanings* of any kind can be taken out of the analysis.

Theorists *must* concentrate on *speaking* as one element within an array of communication behavior and not the inherently incomplete symbolic representations of word sound use, viz. written language. If they do so they may succeed in developing a theory that avoids the semantic trap which has plagued philosophers and linguists since antiquity. They must always remember that speaking is vocal behavior performed in coordination with other communication behavior at some time and place in response to some stimuli. It is action. Words sounds that are emitted from human mouths can only be interpreted accurately when they are *used* by someone at some time in conjunction with other behavior and an entire milieu of context and presuppositions.

The formalism begun with writing has led language theorists down the garden path of semantics. Never-the-less, to make the semantic claim that words have *literal* or *lexical meanings* which are separate and distinct from their use in context is unsupported by the data, i.e. human speech. In fact, all human speech is behavior conducted by a human with a history of word-sound use that affects any future speech behavior with acoustic devices conducted at a time and place with innumerable presuppositions and contextual elements that are indispensable to interpretation of the behavior.

As a consequence of writing and the breakdown of speech into grammatical units considered to be signs or symbols, *reference* was also put into the symbols. Many words are said to stand for, signify, denote or designate, refer to specific objects, concepts and so on. "Proper names" for instance, are said to refer to the people who bear the name. Robert J. Mott Jr. is my name. Both the script **'Robert J. Mott Jr.'** and the sound "*robert j mott jr*" are said to be word symbols that refer directly to me, the person writing this manuscript. Words and other units of speech such as the inscription **'the Queen of England'** or the utterance "*the queen of england*" are said to refer to other people as well. Reference was put into the symbols along with meanings. *Reference* is the second of the semantic fallacies and will be critiqued in due course.

Human speech has also been characterized as representational activity. Speech supposedly, consists of symbols that *represent*, express or encode mental activity. Speakers are said to have mental or psychological correlates for the word symbols in their minds or consciousness. Every theory of language that has been proposed since the time of Aristotle, other than that of the behaviorists', has taken the *representational* nature of spoken words to be a given. Spoken words are claimed to be symbols or signs that represent or express mental experience, the thoughts in the mind or consciousness of the humans who utter and write them. This is the third of the semantic fallacies and will be critiqued as well.

As a corollary of this representational characterization of human speech, semanticists commit themselves to *dualism* of one sort or another. The individual word sounds and sentential utterances are claimed to represent mental or psychological entities, not brain components, i.e. axons, dendrites and synapses. If the word sounds that issue from human mouths represent thoughts, ideas, concepts, speaker meanings, mental representations, propositions etc., speakers must have minds or a consciousness to contain these mental or psychological entities that are correlated with the word symbols. A mind/body or consciousness/body dualism is a necessary corollary to the representational characterization of human speech behavior. A full-blown philosophical critique of *dualism* is presented in the next chapter.

I hope to show that all three of these semantic posits *meaning, reference* and *representation,* are erroneous and lead to the innumerable puzzles and problems in contemporary philosophy of language and linguistic theory. As skeptical as you may be, I hope to persuade you that human speech is not a symbolic activity. That being the case, spoken words do not have meanings of any sort; they have no semantic content. Nor do words refer to anything. The words do not make reference. Nor do they represent or express mental content, e.g. ideas, concepts, propositions etc. These three posits are pervasive and pernicious within both philosophy of language and linguistic theory. They are the bedrock foundations upon which all of current semantic theorizing rests. They are wrong. These three errors can be summed up as *the semantic fallacies.*

The non-semantic perspective I am proposing rejects all three of these semantic assumptions and the concomitant dualism necessary for semantic theory to succeed. In spite of the widespread belief that the *symbolic* nature of human speech behavior is obvious, theorists are making a huge and fateful error with this claim. It is neither obvious nor self-evident that human vocal behavior is a system of signs or symbols with consistent speaker-neutral lexical meanings and referents, or that speaking represents peculiar non-physical entities and processes in the speaker's head. In fact, spoken words, phrases and sentences are gerrymandered units of grammar, some of which have variable independent functionality when used by various speakers at various times in various contexts.

Words and Meanings

"Words sit uneasily at the boundary between morphology and syntax. In some languages 'isolating' languages, such as Vietnamese—they are plainly low-level units, with little or no internal structure. In others—'polysynthetic' languages, such as Eskimo-word-like units are highly complex forms, equivalent to whole sentences. The concept of 'word' thus ranges from such single sounds as English *a* to *palyamunurringkutjamunurtu* ('he/she definitely did not become bad') in the Western Desert language of Australia.

"Words are usually the easiest units to identify, in the written language. In most writing systems, they are the entities that have spaces on either side... Because a literate society exposes all its members to these units from early childhood, we all know where to put the spaces...

"It is more difficult to decide what words are in the stream of speech, especially in a language that has never been written down. But there are problems, even in languages like English or French. Certainly, it is possible to read a sentence aloud slowly, so that we can 'hear' the spaces between the words; but this is an artificial exercise. In natural speech, pauses do not occur between each word, as can be seen from any acoustic record of the way people talk. Even in very hesitant speech, pauses come at intervals—usually between major grammatical units, such as phrases or clauses. So if there are no audible 'spaces', how do we know what the words are? Linguists have spent a great deal of time trying to devise satisfactory criteria—none of which is entirely successful. The Cambridge Encyclopedia of Language (1997: 91)

The use of the English word sound **"word"** or its equivalent in other languages came about as a result of the development of writing systems and the parsing of vocal behavior into units that could be represented graphically. The graphical representations for these parsed sounds, as well as the sounds themselves, came to be known as *words*. That grammatically prescribed unit of writing and speech, the word, could then be paired or correlated with a distinct and consistent independent meaning or meanings. This is the conventional semantic view of words and meanings espoused by philosophers, linguists, grammarians, lexicologists, philologists and the man in the street, and it has come about as a direct consequence of the linguistic formalism brought about by writing, grammar and phonetic spelling conventions.

However, there are profound problems with this view. For a start, dissecting human speech into words is an inexact enterprise. As David Crystal points out in the epigraph, there are clean delineations of independent words with visible breaks and boundaries in the written form. Yet, linguists have discovered that these breaks and boundaries do not necessarily coincide with speech breaks and boundaries. It seems that the dividing line between *spoken* words, phrases and sentences is often quite blurry. In fact, theorists are discovering that they need not carve speech into *words*. Most theorists these days talk about "lexemes" with meanings or "form/meaning

61

pairs".

Daniel L. Everett provides us with humorous anecdotal evidence for what may or may not constitute *a word* when analyzing speech:

> "Let us say it is about noon and you are hungry. You speak southern Californian English. So you turn to your friend or spouse or class and you say 'Squeat!' Everyone understands you, except the occasional foreigner in your midst. What the hell is 'Squeat'? Said more slowly it becomes 'Let's go eat.' Say it as fast as we normally do in American English and it comes out 'Squeat', even though we hear it differently, as 'Let's go eat,' which is itself a reduced form of 'Let us go and eat.' Sounds like one word but it is really four." Everett (2012:141)

Is the sound "*squeat*" really four words? Not everyone will agree that it is. Such sloppy diction, acronyms and abbreviations present insurmountable problems for semantic theorists. Consider this vocal speech behavior: "*the operation was fubar as nato commander in this sector um i want that report asap*" How many words did that speaker use? What about: "*huh i voted for that sob lbj*"? How about "*i aint gonna make that mistake again*". Consider the written forms as well. The point is simply: what constitutes a word is controversial, even when limited to the written form.

In normal discourse words often meld into one another. Not surprisingly, language learners often have difficulty picking out individual *words* within a stream of speech. They learn how to use combinations of phonemes but do not know which parts of speech are words. Recognition of the words is only apparent after they parse the written forms in grammar school where some gaps in speech are formalized with the separation of words in grammatically correct sentences. Why some sound units are called words and others called acronyms, abbreviations, morphemes, phrases, idioms or sentences can be quite mysterious. Among beginning grammar school students and illiterate humans, whether they are children or adults, the whole notion of *words* is suspect.

When children learn speech behavior in their community, they make no distinctions about what a word, a phrase or a sentence is; they simply use the phonetic combinations of various sorts and syntax as devices to get their linguistic work done:

> "Also from the perspective of language acquisition, Wray and Grace (2007, p. 561) summarize a similar view: '(Children) apply a pattern-recognition procedure to linguistic input, but are not naturally predisposed to select a consistent unit size (Peters 1983). They home in on phonological forms associated with effects that they need to achieve,… The units of the lexicon are, thus, variously, what the formal linguist would characterize as morpheme-, word-, clause-, and text size (Wray 2002b)'." Hurford (2012:270)

While an English-speaking child says: "*give it to me*" (a sentence), a Spanish speaking child says: "*damelo*" (a word). The sounds have an effect; they induce action on the part of the hearers. They are acoustic devices that get work done no matter how grammarians might categorize them in their parts-of-speech taxonomy.

Many speech communities have no formal systems for learning preferred speech behavior. They have no grammarians to teach grammatical distinctions and rules. Yet their children learn to speak just as their parents speak. They learn to speak the way their parents do because they are learning the functional value of the acoustic devices that their parents produce, whether that noise is "*give it to me*" or "*damelo*", whether that phonetic device has been labeled a morpheme, a word, a name, a phrase, a clause, an idiom, a holophrase, an acronym, a contraction, a sentence, a lexeme or a linguistic gestalt. Learning to speak does not require dictionaries, reading and writing skills, grammarians or their parts of speech or their rules.

Nevertheless, (three words or one?), in learning proper grammar and spelling conventions *nowadays*, (three words or one?) students are consistently and incessantly told that they are speaking and writing with individual *words* that have meanings. As they become grammatically correct speakers they are conditioned to ask for or look up the meanings of words as if there is some stable semantic content that can be attached to words regardless of context or the speaker's speech history. They are led to believe that there is a "more or less fixed" meaning encoded in the symbol, whether it is a spoken word or a written word. We can blame philosophers, linguists, grammarians, lexicologists, philologists and teachers for this word/meaning model which is pervasive and pernicious.

Moreover, even if philosophers, linguists, grammarians, lexicologists, philologists and teachers can agree on some unit of speech being a *word* that has a *meaning*, further classification of that word into a verb, noun, auxiliary etc. is problematic. This classification of various *parts of speech* cannot be based on any theoretical semantic value or meaning for individual words. Consider the following speech act: "*the yinkish dripner blorked quastofically into the nindin with the pidibs*". Mature English speakers who have had grammatical training will all agree on the nouns, adjectives, verbs, adverbs in that nonsense sentence. However, the mythical meanings of individual *words* play no part in this grammatical categorization.

Additionally, the grammatical categories of words are not precise or exhaustive. Guy Deutscher chronicles the transition of the word sound "*gonna*" from its original use in referring to the action of going, indicating movement, or "*going to*", to its use as a grammatical element, as in "*I am gonna try*", which has the same use as "*i will try*". He concludes that:

> "So if you discover that a word like 'gonna' won't fit neatly under either of your labels, then you should remember that what's problematic is not the word itself, but your labels." Deutscher (2005: 281)

As it turns out, the parsing and categorizing of human speech components is an inexact science at best, even the formal variety of speech that follows all the conventions imposed by grammarians. Many words defy the conventional grammatical *parts of speech* classification altogether, such as "*altogether*".

The category into which grammarians put many words is often *position based*, as in *pre*-positions, in spite of the fact that word order is not universal, fixed or stable. The history of English has shown many changes in the conventions of speech syntax. Worldwide, other languages show many different syntactic structures with and without parts of speech comparable to English. Nouns, verbs, auxiliaries, prepositions, etc. often have morphological regularities that give clues to a word's function within any syntactically conforming construction. But those morphological regularities have many exceptions and outliers as well. Theorizing about what is a noun, a verb, an adjective, an auxiliary, a preposition etc., as it turns out, is plagued with inconsistencies, exceptions and huge theoretical potholes that should give grammarians doubt about their entire enterprise.

The parsing of human speech into words, phrases, sentences etc. is a tedious but necessary task that is required to produce the impoverished written recordings of speech behavior. However, it is not necessary to speak effectively. Speakers learn the functional value of acoustic devices and syntax from others in their speech community. What counts as a word, a phrase, a clause or a sentence makes no difference whatsoever to an infant learning to speak or an accomplished speaker in a preliterate society. The functional value of the acoustic devices "*damelo*" and "*give it to me*" are identical. These sound implements may have different etymological origins and different grammatical categories, but from a functional standpoint, there is no distinction to be made.

The fundamental problem in semantics is the word/meaning relationship brought about by the characterization of verbal behavior as system of individual spoken word symbols with individual meanings. The current semantic orthodoxy still holds that there is a context-invariant lexical or literal meaning encoded in each spoken word that is stable and grasped by all competent speakers. This is simply not the case. What both literate and illiterate speakers recognize when they use acoustic devices within specific syntactic constructions is the functional roles the devices play within those constructions. They recognize *how* they can implement these various devices in various syntactic constructions to point, connect, displace in time and space, indicate the direction of the action, and so on and so forth.

In fact, if you insist that verbal utterances carry *meaning*, syntax itself could also be said to carry *meaning*. Syntax in the form of grammatical constructions carries useful information independent of the words in the construction. Michael Tomasello makes the point:

> "Thus if I say to you 'The dax got mibbed by the gazzer,' you know—without knowing the meaning of a single content word—that the gazzer did something (called mibbing) to the dax (and we have entered that event from the perspective of the dax, as patient). Indeed, the Gestalt properties of constructions can even 'override' individual word meanings in many cases. For example, the grammar books will say that the verb *sneeze* is an intransitive verb, used with a single actor, the one who sneezes. But I can say something like 'He sneezed her the tennis ball' and you will concoct a scene in which his sneezing caused a ball to go from him to her. That movement is not communicated by the verb sneeze, but rather by the construction as a whole (the ditransitive construction). It is thus not an exaggeration to say that the construction itself—the abstract pattern—is a linguistic symbol, albeit a complex one with internal structure (Goldberg 1995). This means that just as linguistic communities pass along particular words in their vocabulary, they also create and pass along grammatical constructions."
> Tomasello (2008:298)

Linguistic communities pass along syntactic regularities because they are critical to comprehension. Speech must flow in a certain way; some elements must precede others. They often provide critical information about the scene or activity the speaker is trying to describe. Most theorists have concluded that they carry meaning, *grammatical meaning* as opposed to the *lexical meaning* of the individual words.

Information about the direction of the action, for instance, is indicated in the use of many verbs, e.g. *"john gave mary the glass"* The temporal order in which the sounds *"john"* and *"mary"* are made within that grammatical construction indicates the direction of the act of giving, who gave to whom. The temporal asymmetry of speech can be used as a functional device just as the word sounds are. The syntax has functional value as do the acoustic devices that were used in the production of that syntactic sequence. Other languages use other devices, e.g. tone languages.

The erroneous word/meaning paradigm has produced a litany of theories of meaning. For example, philosophers and linguists often attempt to explain the mythical *meanings* of word sounds by saying those words have *semantic features*. The meaning of the word sounds *"leopard"*, *"lion"*, *"panther"*, *"tiger"* and *"kitty"*, it is claimed, have the feature of being feline. The analysis of a zoologist might conclude that, but a child can use all of those words competently without any idea that they have anything to do with being feline. In fact, children competently use sounds all the time without knowing that they have semantic features, much less knowing what those features are.

Similarly, other theorists have claimed that word meanings have *properties*, or that concepts embody properties, or that words have combinations of properties. For example, the meaning of the word *"father"* or the concept of father has the *property of* being a parent. That property distinguishes the word *"father"* from the words *"uncle"* or *"bachelor"*, which share the property of male and adult. One such view holds that word meanings are clusters of these properties. However, it is quite clear that when children use the sound *"father"*, they do not need to know how to use the sounds *"male"* or *"adult"* or recognize the properties of being male and adult. Kids use *"father"* or *"papa"* or *"dad"* long before they learn how to use *"adult"* or *"male"*. They have no idea that the word *"father"* has the *properties* of being an adult male parent.

After the fact, philosophers, grammarians, philologists, and lexicologists attempt to classify a word such as *"father"*. How many features or properties could they give it? Adult, male, animal, has offspring, biologically related, legally related? By which state laws? Theorists head down a slippery slope with features and properties. Speaker *uses* of the phonetic device *"father"*, as it turns out, are no more precise than the uses of *"adult"* or *"kitty"*. Giving words properties and features is not required if you acknowledge that word sounds have functional roles to play in situational human communication behavior. The sound *"father"*, for instance, can sometimes be used by a child to point to the big guy next to her.[2]

Nor are speakers required to have *facts* about words to determine the mythical semantic content, not even core facts: the fact that an adult must be 18 years old, for instance. Or is it 19, or 21 or 16? The word sound *"adult"* has no core facts that are paired up with it by children acquiring English as a primary language; the sound has uses in context, often conflicting and disparate uses. When children use sounds such as *"father"*, *"adult"*, *or "kitty"* they know nothing about words, meanings, properties, features or facts. Nevertheless, they learn the functional value of vocal instruments, no matter how the grammarians classify and explain them.

In spite of the inability to explain human speech within the word/meaning paradigm, many intellectuals insist that a word must have an *essential* meaning. As intellectuals are wont to do, they have labeled those who subscribe to that theory as *essentialists*. These philosophers claim that word sounds have core meanings that we humans can abstract from the various uses of the word. They claim that words such as *"father"*, *"parent"*, *"adult"*, *"kitty"*, *"game"* and *"furniture"* can be precisely delimited by reducing them to stable core meanings. And after speakers grasp these essential meanings they can competently use the words and enhance the essential meanings in various ways. This essentialism has been handed down from the Greeks and should be given the same credence that we give the ancient Greek view of the cosmos.

Just as an exercise, try to determine the *essential meaning* of *"furniture"*. Try to delimit the use of that word. Try to list the necessary and sufficient properties, features, facts or conditions for the competent use of the word sound *"furniture"*. Which of the following would you say are furniture: a bean bag chair, a stove, a school desk, the old bar stool next to your work bench, a portable work bench, a table-top television, a console TV, a foldable TV table/tray, a nicely designed humidifier, faux plants, a large sculpture (how large?), built-in bookshelves, a Murphy bed, a bed frame, a reading lamp, a table, a pool table, a card table, a cable spool being used as a table, a filing cabinet, an easel, a pillow, and so on? What features, facts or properties do all of these items have in common? What is essential to all of these items? What boundary separates furniture from non-furniture?

As it turns out, sometimes the word *"furniture"* seems appropriate to describe the above items and at other times it does not. In between there are times when our linguistic intuitions are in doubt. However, these intuitions about the use of the sound *"furniture"* are not based on meanings, essential or otherwise. The use of the word sound *"furniture"* in different situations generates intuitions about future use. Have other people you know routinely said that bean bag chairs are furniture? If they have, you will consider the use of the word sound *"furniture"* to be appropriate when talking about bean bag chairs. The point is, there are simply no universal or essential properties, features, facts or conditions that can be associated with word sounds which would enable you to definitively determine what is or is not furniture.

To suggest that there are stable speaker neutral definitions or meanings for all words, even essential meanings, is simply unsupportable by the linguistic data. Words with multiple, flexible, shifting or nonexistent meanings abound: pronouns such as *"he"*, *"she"*, *"it"*, *"we"*, *"you"*, *"them"*, prepositions such as *"if"*, *"of"*, *"on"*, demonstratives such as *"this"*, *"that"*, locatives such as *"here"*, *"there"*, articles such as *"the"*, *"a"*, speaker/hearer centric phrases such as *"my bike"*, *"your dog"*, temporal indicators such as *"today"*, *"tomorrow"*, *"now"*, *"then"*, quantifiers such as *"some"*, *"most"*, *"every"*. None of these words has anything that might qualify as a stable meaning or definition.

Many times the supposed meanings for individual words are completely ignored. Idioms such as *"kicked the bucket"* and *"spill the beans"* provide examples of speakers using words without regard for the lexical meanings or definitions of the individual words. Only when word sounds are utilized in combination are listeners able to determine if they have been implemented in their most common use or in figurative or metaphorical or ironic or poetic or rhetorical uses, or a multitude of other ways. Listeners must make an uptake of speaker presuppositions and context to determine how individual words are being utilized on any occasion of use.

Furthermore, the literal vs. figurative meaning is a distinction that works for various grammatical constructions, such as idioms. But it does not work for individual word sounds. Word sounds must be used in conjunction with other word sounds and a lifetime of speaker experience to properly construct an effective message. Isolating a word sound and claiming that it has a fixed core meaning is simply not consistent with the linguistic data, i.e. human vocal behavior. There are no fixed, core meanings, referents or definitions that can be correlated with human word sound use, even if there was agreement on what constitutes a word.

As exemplified previously, polysemy is a recurring nightmare for semanticists. Word sounds with multiple *meanings* abound in all languages. Speakers use these like sounding words effortlessly and often. Take the word sound *"play"*. What is common to playing: baseball, soccer, ping pong, chess, cards, a record, a person, a movie, a violin, a flute, a drum or a piano? In English any given use of that speech sound is governed completely by pragmatic consideration of context, presuppositions and speaker goals. What it means to *play* varies dramatically. There is simply no way in which semanticists can isolate that word sound and determine a meaning for it outside of its pragmatic employment within a specific frame of reference.[3]

It is also said that *definitions* are word meanings; the meaning of a word is its definition. There are some circles in which it is believed that word definitions are in the heads of speakers. Perhaps you have a mental dictionary in your mind, one with definitions for every word you can use? After all, if you don't know the definition of a word, how could you use it? Well, as a matter of fact, competent speakers use many word sounds every day that they would find impossible to define, or give an accurate *meaning* for, e.g. *"adult"*, *"take"* and *"number"*. I use these word sounds every day without being able to adequately define them.

I use *"adult"* repeatedly when talking to my grandchildren. Fortunately, they never ask me to define it. My dictionary has 107 definitions for *"take"*. I can't remember one of them. I am also able to utilize the word sound *"number"* quite competently without being able to define it. It took Bertrand Russell and Alfred North Whitehead two years to define *"number"* in Principia Mathematica. The rest of us need not do so. We are able to use these acoustic devices competently without being able to give an adequate definition or a meaning for the words because our ability to deploy words in various contexts is based on their functional value, not *definitions or meanings*.

Definitions and meanings for words, like so many other aspects of languages and our attitude toward them, are a consequence of writing and books, viz. dictionaries. Humans used words long before lexicologists began to give us words with their definitions and meanings. Speakers adopt the use of acoustic devices without knowing their definitions or meanings because they are conditioned to use them in context based on their utility. By observing and adopting the vocal behavior of their care givers, young speakers establish behavioral patterns which will guide their future use of these devices.

Analogously, the fact that the function of a screwdriver can be described in terms of torque and inclined planes, does not entail that competent screwdriver users must be able to explain screwdrivers in terms of torque and inclined planes. Humans use linguistic devices of many kinds, without the ability to describe or explain how they use them. Nevertheless, they are able to demonstrate their skill to others and adjust it as circumstances warrant based on a complete history of their interactions with linguistic devices used in context with innumerable presuppositions.

Not long ago my daughter came over for a visit. As is our custom, we consumed a couple of delicious brewskies from the Capital Brewing Co. As I opened her bottle she began talking. Not wanting to interrupt her, I grabbed a glass from the cupboard and extended it toward her in an offering gesture. I simply went through the motions after I decided to offer her a glass.

Similarly, had I said: *"would you like a glass"*, I would not have combined the meanings of "*would*", "*you*", "*like*", "*a*" and "*glass*" in my head to make the offer. After I had determined my objective, I would have simply uttered the words. They would have come out with no cognitive effort. Humans often use words without forethought or planning. The sounds just flow out of our mouths in response to stimuli. They are conditioned responses to the situational stimuli. In this case, my goal could have been achieved with either of the communication devices at my disposal, the gesture or the speech act. Either action would have had the same effect. The only difference was the choice of *behavior*.

We humans utilize various communication devices to get the response we want from our audience. Speakers understand the functional value of various acoustic devices just as they understand the functional value of facial expressions, prosody, gestures, syntax etc., and apply them to accomplish their communicative tasks. These instruments are used to generate effects on other humans. In the scenario above, many body parts were put into action to make gestures. In the second option, vocalization muscles did the work.

The same sounds that issue from a human mouth can be used in a multitude of widely varying functions, depending upon context, speaker goals and the occasion of use. Even the most common verbs are found to be highly ambiguous by contemporary semantic theorists. Thus they come up with layers of meaning in addition to the literal meaning: pragmatic meaning, truth-functional meaning, lexical meaning, structural meaning et al. The nature of *meaning* is as mysterious now as it was 2500 years ago. It is so, because word sounds and their derivative symbols *have no meanings*, literal or otherwise. All sounds used by humans have communicative functional values that are shaped by a broad array of cultural, historical and contextual elements.

Unfortunately, the semantic paradigm has been a huge impediment to a functional analysis of human speech behavior. That is not the case with non-human animal communication:

> "A number of scholars have recently cautioned against using human language as an interpretive framework for non-human primate communications (Owings and Morton 1998; Owren and Rendall 2001). According to these theorists, non-human primate communicative signals are not used to convey meaning or to convey information or to refer to things or to direct the attention of others, but rather to affect the behavior of others directly. If this interpretation is correct—and it is certainly consistent with the facts outlined above—the the evolutionary foundations of human language lie in the attempts of individuals to influence the behavior of conspecifics, not their mental states." Tomasello via Morten Christiansen & Simon Kirby (2003:101)

Indeed the "interpretive framework" for human communication is the problem. The proper framework should be the same for all primates. Neither human nor non-human communication is used to convey meaning or information, but rather to affect the behavior of others, including their future verbal behavior. Any "information conveyed" requires a change in verbal behavior about the world, not changes in so called "mental states".

In the final analysis, words and their meanings are totally unnecessary for the use and comprehension of human vocal behavior. *Words* and *meanings* are artificial constructs that obfuscate an accurate account of the acquisition and use of vocal behavior by humans, phylogenetically and ontogenetically. You assume that words have *meanings* because you have been thoroughly conditioned to do so from your earliest introduction to language. That inherited word/meaning paradigm is thoroughly embedded in your speech behavior about speech. You have been misled.

If spoken words are not considered to be symbols, they need not be associated with any *meanings*. There need not be semantic content, lexical meanings or literal meanings associated with word sounds. Phonetic units, whether grammarians call them morphemes, acronyms, words, contractions, phrases, clauses, idioms, sentences, lexemes or linguistic gestalts, can all be analyzed in terms of their communicative function and its consequences on their audience. One can ask: What is the functional role this phonetic device performs within the totality of the communicative behavior of this speaker under specific circumstances? Is it a device used to point to people, objects, actions, events, kind-sortals, states of affairs etc.?[4] Alternatively, is it a speech element of another type: a marker, displacement indicator, a logical operator etc.? How does the use of this device meet the needs of speakers in the context of their overall communicative performance?

Meanings give certain *words* semantic content in formal semantic theories, but they are inexplicable and completely superfluous in the analysis of human verbal behavior. So, let us join J.L. Austin, Donald Davidson, Willard V.O. Quine, B.F. Skinner, the radical pragmaticists et al., and dispense with individual word meanings altogether.[5]

The Meaning of "*meaning*"

"… As Quine has long urged, we should abandon the notion of meaning altogether. With the exception of Quine, most verificationists have found this course unattractive. Thus they were caught in a serious dilemma—caught between their desire to continue talking about meaning in something like the traditional way, and their adherence to the network theory of meaning which taken seriously implies that nothing can be made of the notion of linguistic meaning." Putnam (1975: ix)

"Quite simply, Wittgenstein holds that philosophers come to their tasks with a certain conception of how things must be. This picture lies in the background, unexamined, and dictates questions asked and specifies the form the answers will take. One such picture concerns the essence of language: Words stand for things—these things being their meanings—a sentence is a combination of such words." Fogelin (1976: 109)

"The current state of knowledge about meaning phenomena is very patchy: some areas are relatively well charted compared with others. But in all domains, serious black holes of ignorance abound. Many of the fields of uncertainty involve very fundamental issues… " Cruse (2015: 448)

Old philosophies die hard. The prevailing wisdom amongst most philosophers and laymen alike still claims that words are symbols that encode *meanings*. People persistently ask: "*what is the meaning of that word*". It is assumed that words are symbols that stand for, express, signify, represent, encode, designate, denote or refer to those meanings. Words are thought to have stable semantic content of some sort, lexical or literal meanings and these meanings are something other than the uses of word sounds by various people at various times in various contexts.

Prevailing wisdom also holds that speakers must know *the meaning* of a word in order to *use* it. *Meaning* and *use* are said to be two different areas of research and theory. Semantics proper is concerned with the lexical or literal word *meanings*, the semantic content of words. Pragmatics, on the other hand, is the study of the *use* of the word symbols for various purposes once their literal meanings have been grasped by competent speakers, i.e. how the words are employed in various ways: implicatures, sarcasm, irony, hyperbole, metaphors, metonyms etc. Thus the same word with the same meaning can be used differently on different occasions; so say philosophers, linguists, teachers and truck drivers.

This characterization of words is a mistake. As skeptical as you may be, one of the aims of this thesis is to persuade you that words do not have literal meanings, lexical meanings or meanings of any kind; they have no semantic content. I will attempt to demonstrate that the semantic paradigm is an incorrect view of language. In order to do so, we must talk about the pragmatics of "*meaning*". We must talk about the *uses* of the word sound "*meaning*". We will be pulling ourselves up by our bootstraps.

Our first step in talking about the *uses* of "*meaning*" is to analyze how speakers deploy "*meaning*", the word sound, so that we may be clear about some of its uses and make some necessary distinctions. Lexicologists will all acknowledge that the spoken word "*meaning*" has multiple uses. For example, in some instances competent speakers use the word sound in lieu of "*significance*" or "*importance*". The sound "*meaning*" can share their functional value.

Consider this sentence: "*dis foto of mi muther has deap meening fer me*". (Sound it out.) The word sound "*meening*" in this context has no similarities to its use in lexical contexts. The *meaning* of the photo has nothing to with the semantic content of the photo. In this instance, the picture has sentimental value to the speaker. We can conclude that "*meaning*" can often be used by speakers as the functional equivalent of the word sounds "*significance*", "*importance*" or "*sentimental value*".

In other non-lexical contexts, the use of the word sound "*meaning*" can be translated as intention. We may ask about the motives for someone's actions: "*what was your meaning in saying that*". Translated: "*what was your intention or purpose why did you say that*". This use of the spoken word "*meaning*" is a request for an explanation as to why the speaker said what they said and/or a more comprehensible translation of what was said. The derivation of this use of the word is "to have in mind", purpose, design or intent. It is used in context to request the motives for the action of the speaker or writer and an interpretation of what was said.

There is also what is sometimes called *the causal theory of meaning*. We often say things like: "dark clouds, lightning, and thunder approaching *mean* it will soon be raining," or certain symptoms appearing in a patient mean that they have cancer. "Meaning" used in this sense can be used to foretell certain consequences which are caused by observable signs extant at the time of the claim made by a speaker.

However, in linguistic contexts, when we ask for the meanings of words, we are asking for something that is linked to or associated with the individual word symbols. We ask what the words stand for, express, signify, represent, encode, designate, denote or refer to. We assume that both spoken words and written words are *symbols*. We assume they are tokens or proxies for something else, their *meanings*. This is the *semantic use* of the spoken word "*meaning*".

Such requests for the meaning of symbols are found throughout society and are the subject matter for the field of *semiotics*. For instance, one can ask: "*what is the meaning of that wheelchair symbol on that sign*". This is not a request for the sentimental value of the icon or the intentions of the person who posted it. Nor is it a request for the consequences of posting the sign. Within a semiotic context it could be construed as: How am I to interpret the symbol? What should I associate with the symbol? The symbol is a proxy for what? What does the symbol *stand for* or *mean*?

Likewise, if theorists assume that spoken words are *symbols*, they conclude that when people ask for the meaning of a word they are asking for an explanation of the semiotic kind, one that requires an association or relation between the spoken word symbol and something called its meaning. They put semantic content in the vocal symbol or sign. They assume that there is something aside from the word sound's idiolectic functional value in the speaker's individual human speech behavior that can invariably be associated with the word symbol. They make an assumption that is unwarranted.

To sum up this brief introduction, adding to the difficulties in explaining what we humans do with word sounds are the multiple ways we English speakers use the word sounds "*mean*" and "*meaning*". One use is clearly tied to *lexical* or *literal meaning* and is an illegitimate offspring of linguistic theorists. Alternatively, if theorists acknowledge that speech is behavior, not symbol manipulation, there is nothing other than the speaker's speech history, encyclopedic knowledge and contemporaneous context, along with the variable functional value of word sounds within a broad spectrum of individual human communication behavior, available to explain the employment of word sounds and their derivative written symbols. Spoken words need not be tied to semantic content if we do not treat them as signs, symbols or semantic de*sign*ators. Words can be linked to neurological events in the brains of speakers and the contingencies of reinforcement. In doing so, we can join Michael Reddy in rejecting the conduit metaphor and begin to appreciate Willard V.O. Quine's plea to abandon the notion of meaning altogether.

Spoken Words vs. Written Words

"For the explicit codification of lexical conventions and grammatical rules sets standards against which utterances may be judged more or less correct or linguistically well-formed, standards which—to varying degrees—may be emulated or enforced. That is to say, language has acquired the status of an institution. Children not only learn to speak, as they have always and everywhere done, through immersion in an environment of vocally accomplished caregivers, they also receive formal schooling in the principles of language, as formulated by those appointed by society to act as its guardians—the grammarians and dictionary-makers. Above all, they are taught to *write*. The influence of writing on modern ideas and practices of language cannot be overestimated... For writing is not simply the equivalent of speech in an alternate medium. It is rather a kind of reconstructed, as if speech: as if the verbal utterance were fully amenable to systematic analysis in terms of syntactical rules; as if the tone of voice and pronunciation were entirely dispensable to meaning; as if the utterance had an existence in its own right, independently of the context of its production.

"None of these things are actually true of speech, except perhaps for some kinds of 'reading aloud'. Yet modern linguists have operated largely on the assumption that they are. Thus it turns out that the prototypical instance of the linguistic utterance, a rule-governed, context-independent proposition delivered without expression or affect, is that artifact so familiar to us but unknown to non-literate societies: the sentence of writing." Gibson and Ingold (1993: 458)

Kathleen R. Gibson's and Tim Ingold's points in the above quote are well taken. The effect of writing systems and formalized grammars on human vocal behavior cannot be overstated. The breakdown of speech into grammatical units of words, phrases, sentences, nouns, verbs, etc. is a direct consequence of writing. These units of grammar derived from the analysis of written language, along with *rules* for the formation of grammatically correct written sentences, have been institutionalized and passed on from literate speakers and writers to their progeny. These grammatically correct written sentences, in consequence, have had a profound effect upon human speech behavior by establishing recommended speech patterns.[6]

This *rule-bound* recommended speech behavior has been taught to generations of literate human speakers. Thus, many of the regularities witnessed in various speech communities are a result of these *prescriptive rules* which are inculcated in speakers and passed on from generation to generation. Even so, there are numerous speech communities which have no prescriptive rules, or the rules are ignored. Much of their speech behavior is fragmentary or elliptical, i.e. structurally incomplete according to grammarians. Sentence fragments and deviant speech patterns form an overwhelming portion of the speech behavior in some speech communities. Most of their speech is *unruly*.

The more salient point for my purpose is that writing is a "… kind of reconstructed, as if speech." The use of spoken words and the use of written words are interrelated, but there are profound differences between them that must be accounted for in linguistic theory. Unfortunately, the analyses of grammatically well-formed *written* sentences that are said to designate fixed semantic content had become the hallmark of analytic philosophers, logicians and linguists in the twentieth century. Yet their analysis of grammatically well-formed written sentences had not been able to solve paradoxes, puzzles and contradictions that have been around for millennia.

In an attempt to solve these language mysteries a clear distinction will be made in this thesis. To reiterate and reemphasize, I will make it a point to talk about *spoken words* represented by this script font: *"thees spokin wurds"* (sound it out). For the most part, I will be discussing *human speech*, the phonetic units that are emitted from human mouths. These units are not misspelled or punctuated: they have no letters or spaces. They are fleeting physical phenomena with acoustic properties. Yet they must be the units of analysis for all language theories. When necessary, I will talk about written words using this font: **'these written words'**. These units of writing have visual properties, not acoustic properties.

To begin, speaking requires humans to produce sounds. *"these spoken words"* (sound it out) have a temporary quality. Spoken words have an *occasion of use* because they are actions, vocal behavior that occurs at a time and a location. Every occasion of spoken word use is unique. In ordinary conversation, the original and primary use of human language, of speech behavior, requires the speaker and the hearer to have spatial-temporal proximity. Writing, telephones, the internet etc. have extended these dimensions of human discourse. However, before the advent of writing and modern technology, normal human discourse had a location and occasion of use that was shared by all participants and was critical to comprehension.

These sounds produced by humans not only have an occasion of use, they are goal-oriented actions. They are multi-use vocal implements utilized at various times for various human goals. Consequently, all speech behavior has conditions under which it is effective in reaching the goals of the speaker, and conditions under which it is not effective. To analyze the symbolic written representations of speech behavior, i.e. text, out of context, is a fool's errand. It is a fool's errand in which philosophers and linguists have been engaged for millennia. Language scientists and theorists alike must *listen* to the data *in context*. The *vocal behavior* is the subject to be studied, not written recordings of such behavior outside of any context.

The limitations of analyzing written language cannot be overstated. Even semanticists acknowledge that written language is a greatly impoverished version of spoken language. Linguists refer to the intonation, pace, volume, spacing, stretching, rhythm, pitch etc. as the *prosodic features of speech*. These prosodic features are rarely represented in written words, phrases and sentences, yet they are more often than not, critical to the proper interpretation of the speaker's intended message. Neither can the written word symbols do justice to all the accompanying gestures, facial expressions and body language. The introduction of emoticons and emojis of late, is an attempt to reintroduce some of these contextual features into the static written representations of speech behavior. Yet, even with some of these prosodic and contextual features spelled out by means of punctuation, font variation, emoticons, emojis etc., written sentences simply cannot fully represent human speech.

For instance, according to much research, gestures are not simply an add-on to human speech.

They are an essential part of the overall communication effort on the part of speakers. Michael C. Corballis reports on psychologist David McNeill's research:

> "… He has shown on the contrary, that the gestures we use when we speak are in fact precisely synchronized with the speech, suggesting that speech and gesture together form a single, integrated system… More importantly perhaps, nearly all of these gestures are made during speech, indicating that gesturing is not an alternative to speech or a compensation for an inability to find words. Iconic gestures, in particular, are an integral part of the language process." Corballis (2002:101)

In addition to the prosodic features and accompanying gestures etc. that differ on each occasion of use, there are innumerable cultural, social, philosophical, and historical *presuppositions* involved in speaking. These presuppositions are essential components of mature competent speech in any language community. The same word sounds may be used quite differently depending on this encyclopedic background information and the goals of the speaker. The instances of failed speech communication because of mistaken interpretation of any of these elements of discourse are legend. The probability of miscommunication expands geometrically with textual representations of speech activity when many of the writer's presuppositions are not shared by readers, reading Shakespeare for instance.

All of the presuppositions required to speak competently can be considered elements of *context*. Although the word "context" is often used in linguistic theory and communication theory, definitions vary. Michael Tomasello provides a broad construal:

> "Instead, in the current view, a large part of the explanation for human's uniquely complex ways of communication gesturally is that 'context' for humans means something very special. For humans the communicative context is not simply everything in the immediate environment, from the temperature of the room to the sounds of birds in the background, but rather the communicative context is what is 'relevant' to the social interaction, that is, what each participant sees as relevant as well—and knows that the other knows this as well, and so on, potentially ad infinitum. This kind of shared, intersubjective context is what we may call, following Clark (1996), common ground or, sometimes (when we wish to emphasize the shared perceptual context), the joint attentional frame. Common ground includes everything we both know (and know that we both know, etc.), from facts about the world, to the way that rational people act in certain situations, to what people typically find salient and interesting (Levenson 1995)." Tomasello (2008: 74)

Although he was discussing gestural communications, the elements of context for gestural communication hold constant for most vocal communications. I will be using "context" in this sense, synonymously with "common ground". The "shared, intersubjective context" or "common ground" Tomasello refers to includes innumerable presuppositions about human physiology and how humans interact with other humans, implements, artifacts, animals, plants, natural features of the environment and so forth. Such knowledge about how humans interact with other humans, artifacts, implements etc. underlies all human behavior, including speech.

For example, if someone introduces the word sound *"car"* into the domain of discourse, there are an incredible number of presuppositions about car structure and operation by humans that enter the discourse as well. If a speaker was to say: *"the car was headed for the ditch so i grabbed the wheel from the driver and kept it on the road"* listeners with car familiarity would not conclude that the speaker removed the steering wheel from the column. Listeners would correctly conclude that the passenger took control of the steering wheel to guide the car away from the ditch. These presuppositions gained through experience with cars are necessary for the effective use of the English word sound *"car"*. It is "intersubjective context" or "common ground" or "background". Take virtually any word you want and your experience in the world informs you about its use. It is what some linguists call "encyclopedic knowledge" gained from a lifetime of experience. It is *context*, broadly construed.

Even children with limited real-life experience and fewer presuppositions than adult speakers develop a probable world strategy to interpret sentences for their most probable meanings, sentences such as: "Jim gave his dog a bath yesterday and his cat last week." (did Jim bathe the cat or feed it to the dog?) The sentence is grammatically correct, yet it yields at least two interpretations. Hearers who are trying to find the correct meaning of that statement use the most plausible one, even language learners who have had limited experience with pet owners and their animals. That plausibility comes as part of their encyclopedic knowledge.

The phenomenon of polysemy (the same word with many meanings) provides extensive evidence for the effect of this common-ground or encyclopedic knowledge on speech. Polysemous words abound and present innumerable examples of speech data that do not fit the individual word/meaning semantic paradigm. Speakers use polysemous words extensively and effortlessly, navigating through a thicket of multiple interpretations for the same word sound. The word *"open"* is a case in point. Opening a car door, a bottle, a store, an envelope, a window, a line of credit, a hole in the defensive line, etc. are very different things. There are innumerable ways to use the word sound *"open"* and the interpretation of the word in each case depends on what is being opened. Relevant experience with car doors, bottles, store openings, envelopes, windows etc. is critical to understanding the use of *"open"* on every occasion of use. In many cases, only the non-linguistic context can determine how to construe *"open"*. For instance, saying *"would you open it"* as you hand a bottle of wine to your host.[7]

In fact, some radical pragmaticists insist that the context only provides *some of the relevant evidence* necessary for a proper construal of a sentence such as *"open the bottle"*:

> "Suppose Mary says to Peter: Open the bottle. In most situations, she would be understood as asking him to uncork or uncap the bottle. One way of accounting for this would be to suggest that the general meaning of the verb 'open' gets specified by the properties of the direct object: thus, opening a corked bottle may be the standard way of opening it, but another way is to saw off the bottom, and on some occasion, this might be what Mary was asking Peter to do. Or suppose Mary says to Peter: Open the washing machine. In most situations, she would be asking him to open the lid of the machine. However, if Peter is a plumber, she might be asking him to unscrew the back; in other situations, she might be asking him to blow the machine open, or whatever…

"The general point of these examples is that a word like 'open' can be used to convey indefinitely many concepts. It is impossible for all of these to be listed in the lexicon. Nor can they be generated at a purely linguistic level by taking the linguistic context, and in particular the direct object, into account. It seems reasonable to conclude that a word like 'open' is often used to convey a concept that is encoded neither by the word itself nor by the verb phrase 'open X'."
Wilson and Sperber (2012: 33)

Context also includes innumerable presuppositions about cultural norms and rational human behavior. If someone was to say: *"bill repairs cars"* hearers would not conclude that Bill is in his shop 24-7 under the hoods of cars and that is the only thing in life that Bill does. They would also assume that Bill uses tools, not magic, to repair cars. Most folks would rightly conclude that Bill has a skill that he uses on occasion, either in pursuit of a hobby or an occupation, but none of this information is carried by the word sounds: *"bill repairs cars"*. It is all shared, intersubjective context or common ground that is learned through experience within a specific culture by interacting with other rational humans and human artifacts.

These presuppositions may vary, dramatically, from speaker to speaker. Even with the introduction of the simple word *"car"*, the number of presuppositions would vary with each participant and their relevant experience with cars. A mechanic may have many presuppositions about cars that a college professor would not. Discourse participants bring a lifetime of experience, an encyclopedic knowledge, to their speaking behavior and rely on it for relevant presuppositions that are not encoded in the words and can differ from speaker to speaker. These independently learned but shared presuppositions are essential to any effective discourse.

Shared presuppositions may often come from previous discourse. In fact, as a result of discourse deixis, almost every verbal utterance changes the context and therefore the interpretation of all succeeding utterances. Obvious examples are anaphoric pronouns such as *"we"* or the temporal indicator *"then"*. The relativized *"we"* is controlled wholly by presuppositions from previous discourse about whom "we" includes. The word sound *"then"* is also inherently context driven and ultimately anchored to the discourse time. Even traditional linguists will admit that there are many words that must be analyzed within the context of the previous discourse. They claim that "meaning crosses sentence boundaries". We have many words that help us do precisely that:

> "To return to straightforward issues in discourse deixis, there are many words and phrases in English, and no doubt most languages, that indicate the relationship between an utterance and the prior discourse. Examples are utterance-initial usages of *but, therefore, in conclusion, to the contrary, still, however, anyway, well, besides, actually, all in all, so, after all*, and so on." Levinson (1983: 87)

Word location within a phrase, sentence, paragraph or book can also vary the interpretation of many terms. For example: contrast *"i went to the bank to make a deposit"* with: *"i went to the bank to check the river level"*. The placement of the word in a grammatical context changes the interpretation of the word. Thus many semanticists have parted company with literal or lexical semanticists who insist that words encode stable core meanings outside of any grammatical context. Along with radical pragmaticists they view all context, including occurring discourse as pieces of evidence that when combined, can provide an accurate determination of word function on that occasion of use.

Presuppositions about the speaker can also modify the interpretation of any speech produced by that speaker. Previous experience with the speaker, his reputation or his so- called personality affects the interpretation process for listeners. For example, if someone has a dry sense of humor listeners must be on the lookout for puns and clever remarks that are not intended to be taken seriously. Neither can sarcastic people be taken "at their word". So too, the speech of temperamental people must be construed differently on each occasion. They produce understated and overstated claims. Some speakers are ironic, using irony extensively. Competent speakers in any culture must adjust their interpretation of speech behavior for the person doing the speaking and his or her personality or mood.

Furthermore, within various social circumstances people familiar with each other, say a husband and wife, make numerous assumptions about each other's habits and beliefs that affect their conversation. If one spouse says "*i am going to the club*" the other spouse makes certain assumptions about which club "*the club*" is. The club to which the speaker is going is assumed because of previous habits and the belief that the speaker will continue to do as he has in the past. Shared intersubjective context can be specific to certain discourse participants and is often critical to accurate comprehension.

The same holds true for entire cultures where cultural norms are assumed by all discourse participants. Only deviations from normal patterns of behavior are required to be expressly stated. As Daniel L. Everett puts it after an explanation of a Wari story:

> "Once again the background of culture is most clearly seen in what people do *not* say. Culture is thus found throughout discourse, in what is said and what is not said, the latter being what I call the 'dark cognitive and cultural matter' of discourse." Everett, (2012: 198)

For an example that is a little closer to home, suppose an adult American says: "*i haven't had a drink in two months*". A non-native English speaker who is not familiar with Western culture might be inclined to ask: "How can you possibly survive that long without liquids?" Of course, adult Americans would recognize that the speaker was referring to alcoholic beverages because of previous behavior, verbal or non-verbal, even though that is not what they said.

Culture is reflected in all human behavior, including speech behavior. In close-knit, small speech communities much is not said because it is assumed by all discourse participants. In large, diverse speech communities, effective discourse requires speakers to explicitly provide more information to hearers. Nevertheless, much information about cultural norms, such as the operation of automobile or alcohol consumption, is assumed by all discourse participants.

In addition to the "dark cognitive and cultural matter of discourse" that are assumed by all, there are other matters, for one reason or another, which cannot be stated. There are often prohibitions against certain speech because it may be considered sacrilegious, profane, offensive, or just inappropriate. Polite conversation in American culture, for example, does not allow small talk about personal hygiene, personal sexual activity or personal finances. As Otto Jespersen wrote:

"But learning a language implies other things, learning what you may not say in the language, even though no reasonable ground can be given for the prohibition." Jespersen (1964: 139)

Much speech behavior is also bound by unstated and unique conventions for maintaining propriety and civil discourse.

Another one of the critical presuppositions in human discourse is honesty. Honesty is the default setting for most conversation. Listeners assume the speaker is being straightforward unless there is an uptake that indicates otherwise. There are many linguistic and non-linguistic clues that inform listeners that a speaker is being ironic, sarcastic, hyperbolic, deceitful or mocking, but the presupposition of straightforward truthful communication is generally the starting point. This presupposition is rarely questioned by semanticists who routinely treat all discourse samples and their derivative textual representations as straightforward honest declarative statements.

All human discourse requires non-speaking experience, innumerable presuppositions and expectations about human behavior. Under this broader construal of *context*, all this information is necessary for the proper utilization and interpretation of the word sounds. Although speakers do not have every presupposition about the word *"car"*, *"open"* or *"drink"* in mind when they use the words, based on previous uses within a variety of situations, all competent speakers have some relevant experience, presuppositions and expectations that affect such speech. They have many pieces of evidence.

If there is a lack of experience or failure of presupposition discourse breaks down. Saying: *"i grabbed the wheel from the driver"*, *"open this bottle"* or *"no drinking this week"* would make no sense whatsoever to a Munduruku tribesman, a newly arriving alien or a 15th century peasant time-traveling to the 21st century, none of whom would have the relevant experience and presuppositions about cars, bottles and alcohol, or how modern people use them.

The evidence is incontrovertible. The human use of vocal behavior is inextricably tied to a huge web of presuppositions. Yet, philosophers and linguists are notorious for analyzing the impoverished transcriptions of discourse, the "as if" speech. They parse symbolic representations of grammatically correct speech, a written text, and attempt to recreate the actual conditions under which the speech behavior could be used to reach various goals by adding back novelty conditions, felicity conditions, familiarity conditions etc. The conditions and presuppositions must be added back to make the "as if" speech amenable to a comprehensive analysis.

Even so, the common ground reconstructions are never complete. The prosodic features, gestures, facial expressions and numerous mutually shared presuppositions that induce correct listener uptake of the speaker's *meaning* are not reconstructed. No matter how many conditions and presuppositions analysts try to recreate, the textual recordings of speech simply do not carry the information necessary for an adequate interpretation of the human speech behavior they represent.

Of course, written words have occasions of use as well: when we write them and when we read them. They have multiple occasions of use because they can be used at many times in many places by many people. However, they also have a life of their own. These written symbols for the sounds remain after each occasion of use; they are enduring stable entities. Between uses, they lie dormant until a skilled person uses them again, and when a skilled person learns to read the word symbols, they resurrect the action, the verbal behavior, though they cannot resurrect the speaker's goals and presuppositions or the context of the original utterance. The present point is that philosophers and linguists simply *must* analyze each speech act with all of its prosodic features, presuppositions and contextual elements to determine how it is being used on each occasion of use. They cannot analyze a written recording of a speech act, a written sentence, in isolation. They must *listen* to the data in context (broadly construed).

A Non-semantic Proposal
Acoustic Devices

"From a more functional point of view, children are hearing and producing whole utterances, and their task is to break down an utterance into its constituent parts and so to understand what functional role is being played by each of those parts in the utterance as a whole. When they produce holophrases, children have simply assigned the function of the utterance to a single linguistic unit (perhaps with an associated intonation contour), and so in the future they will have to attend to other linguistic units in similar utterances and in this way fill out their linguistic expression to fit the adult-like conventions." Tomasello (2003: 40)

The human use of language begins with noise production. Language learners must first sort out and limit their noise production. They must learn to produce phonemes. Linguists have categorized over 150 phonemes. Yet, in any given speech community only a fraction of those 150+ are used. Learning infants acquire the phonemes that their caregivers use, and the evidence clearly shows that the rapidity of that acquisition is strongly correlated to the frequency of use by the caregivers. After acquisition, novice speakers combine these phonemes into functional units, holophrases, words, idioms, acronyms, abbreviations, etc., using the same prosodic features that others in their speech community use.

This functional interpretation of language acquisition in children is completely contrary to the current compositionality or lexical syntax theories where the *meaning* of a complex expression is determined by *the meanings* of its constituent words and their grammatical relationships. Such lexical syntax theories are after the fact reconstructions presupposing grammatically correct complete sentences composed of words with stable consistent lexical meanings. But these theories cannot be reconciled with the observed speech behavior of humans. Human speech simply cannot be deconstructed into *words with meanings*; it must be parsed into multipurpose acoustic devices of many kinds based on their functional value when all contextual elements, including relevant presuppositions and the speaker's speech history are recognized and accounted for.

Among competent adult speakers, counterexamples to lexical syntax theories are too numerous to count. Consider the much-used idiom, *"Kicked the bucket"*. (Sound it out.) In contemporary America the use of that utterance is not dependent upon knowing the theoretical meanings of the sounds *"Kicked"*, *"the"* or *"bucket"*. Even non-English speakers can learn to use the idiom when and if they have heard it used in context in lieu of the word sound *"died"*. They can learn how to use that holistic three-word lexeme and utilize it without regard for the dictionary meanings of its constituent terms or the grammar of the English language.

There are many such idioms that have *uses* totally unrelated to the individual words. There are innumerable other "dead metaphors". They have lost their metaphorical connection, yet they remain in common use because speakers within certain speech communities know how to employ these acoustic units without having any knowledge whatsoever about their metaphorical origins. Etymology may reveal their historical roots, but that knowledge is not required to utilize them effectively. Dead or alive, metaphors are holistic functional devices with a host of presuppositions and contextual elements necessary for their successful deployment, while familiarity with the mythical meanings or functional values of their constituent terms is unnecessary.

Semanticists have come up with a dodge to account for this holistic word use phenomenon. They say that our speech is composed of *meaningful units* called *lexemes*. Morphemes, words, phrases, idioms, dead metaphors, even complete sentences can all be lexemes. "*Kicked the bucket*" as a lexeme, supposedly has a meaning that is not dependent upon its constituent words. Well, what happened to the individual word meanings? How do competent speakers know when to attach so-called semantic content to the individual words and when not to? What rules allow speakers to use the multiword holistic lexeme as a single unit and ignore the constituent terms? In fact, these "lexemes" are holistic devices just as their constituent words may be on other occasions of use.

Of late, many linguists have come to express the lexeme/meaning relationship as a "form/meaning pair". They say that words, as well as other grammatical *forms* such as idioms, have *meanings*. Linguists are driven to this form/meaning dodge through their inability to tie individual meanings to individual words or other units of grammar, in many cases. However, they need not do so because neither words nor idioms, nor any other grammatical forms, have meanings. Various combinations of phonemes have various functional values when used in various contexts, regardless of whether grammarians call these linguistic units morphemes, words, phrases, idioms, dead metaphors, lexemes or grammatical forms.

The semantic content of so-called lexemes is a recurring theme in *philosophy of mind*. Philosophers like to discuss the phenomenology of speech, the what-it's-like feel of speech activity. They attribute the phenomenal feel of vocal behavior to the semantic content of the activity. Terrence Horgan and John Tienson for example, discuss the phenomenal aspects of word use, "the what-it's-likeness of intentionality." They acknowledge that we often speech-think with words, and that when we use words, they are accompanied by "auditory imagery". Via Chalmers (2002: 523) (Speech-thinking is simply silent or covert speech, only accessible to the speaker.)

They then relate Galen Strawson's comparison between two people who listen to speech in a language familiar to one and foreign to the other. Imagine yourself (if you are a monolingual English speaker) at the UN listening to the Chinese representative speak in his native language. The phenomenal what-it's-like feel of this speech would be totally different for you as opposed to a native Chinese speaker. These philosophers would attribute this difference to the *content* of the speech activity, that is, listeners do or do not know the *meanings* of the words. (Ibid 522.)

Alternatively, I would suggest that the different what-it's-like feel of the speech is a result of listeners recognizing or not recognizing, the functional value of the acoustic devices being used. One listener recognizes what the speaker is *doing*; the other does not. Speakers and hearers must know *how* to use so-called lexemes and use them the same way, in the same context. They must recognize and appreciate the *utility* of each acoustic device which is engulfed in a lifetime of Chinese-speaking behavior, not the mythical meanings of the word symbols and other lexemes. At times, this recognition of utility also gives listeners the phenomenal what-its-like feel of speech behavior in their native tongue at times. This sudden comprehension of speech or writing presents listeners and readers with an "Aha, now I get it!" moment.

Consider the following example from Horgan and Tienson:

> "Consider, as a similar example for a single speaker, first hearing 'Dogs dogs dog dog dogs,' without realizing that it is an English sentence, and then hearing it as the sentence of English that it is. The phenomenal difference between the experiences is palpable. (If you do not grasp the sentencehood of the 'dogs' sentence, recall that 'dog' is a verb in English, and compare, 'Cats dogs chase catch mice.')" Via Chalmers (2002: 523)

Even if we vocalize these sounds as we read them, we may not immediately grasp the *use* of these word sounds. The grammatical construction of the sentence is unclear as are our intuitions about the functional roles of the sounds. Ordinarily, the syntax, morphology, prosody and context give listeners clues as to the roles the words play. However, in this instance they are opaque.

In the above quote, which words are being used as devices to refer to animals and which ones are being used to refer to the action of dogging something, as would a doggedly determined detective? When hearers do recognize the functional roles the components play, the phenomenal experience changes, not because they become aware of the *content* of the words, but rather because they realize how the writer was employing the words.

We recognize that the speaker is referring variously to animals, a characteristic about them and an action they perform. That is the phenomenal feel that hits us at the "aha!" moment; we finally recognize what the speaker is attempting to accomplish with the words. He is making a statement about dogs that can be dogged by other dogs. Those dogs, in turn, can dog other dogs. We have all experienced many such "aha" moments when we recognize what someone else *is doing and how*: recognizing how an elegant computer program will function, or how a solution to an engineering problem works. We recognize *utility not meaning*.

Much similar recognition is an integral part of the socialization process. From contemporary social rituals to tool use, observers familiar with modern societies are able to appreciate the utility of much of their behavior. On the other hand, Munduruku tribesmen, a newly arriving alien or a 15th century peasant time traveling to the 21st century would be baffled by our language, social customs and use of modern technology because they lack the requisite encyclopedic knowledge. They simply would not understand the functional value of much of our behavior, including our vocal behavior. However, upon recognizing the utility of such behaviors they would have "aha" moments when a light goes on and they say "now I get it". They could then adopt the behavior and utilize it in the proper context.

The point is, linguists should not ask for the *meaning* of words, because they have none. We must follow the lead of the radical pragmaticists. Linguists can only ask what the functional role of any acoustic device is in a given situation for an individual speaker. Learning what we can do with these acoustic devices comes from others in our speech community. It is conditioned behavior that has been acquired by a human organism by means of lifelong iterated learning. Glib speakers have a whole bag of holistic utterances ready and waiting for an occasion of use, from morphemes to complete sentences such as: "*yahearwhatiamsayin*". Speakers learn the functional role of these utterances within their linguistic communities and within specific contexts; they then ad lib.

They can improvise because the implementation of acoustic devices is not limited to the ways they have been used in the past. Speakers can originate novel speech behavior just as they can create other novel behavior because they recognize the utility of such behavior. They can create new vocal combinations because they have learned *how* to use morphemes, idioms, metaphors, metonyms etc., not because they know their mythical meanings. For instance, they learn *how* they can embed phrases such as *"your dog"* in a multitude of syntactic sequences. It is recursive verbal behavior comparable to much other human behavior where small units of behavior are nested within other larger units of behavior.[8]

The combinations of phonemes that originate in human mouths may differ from culture to culture, but the functional value is often the same because human needs are often the same. For instance, speakers are able to get what they want by producing the sounds *"give it to me"* or *"damelo"*, depending upon where they grow up. A phonetic device of that type, no matter what its grammatical form, will be found in almost every language *because it is useful*. Humans were making use of such culturally distinct phonetic combinations long before philosophers, linguists, grammarians and lexicologists began to parse, speak and write about words and meanings.

Do humans need acoustic devices that are larger than individual words? *"youbetcha"*. Is that combination of phonemes a word, a sentence, a phrase, an idiom or a lexeme? None of the above! Does it have meaning or semantic content? No! Is it an acoustic device with a history and a function? Yes! It can be used in lieu of *"you're welcome"* and *"de nada"* to acknowledge a *"thank you"* from someone. In colloquial America, with appropriate prosody, facial expressions etc., it can also be used as a forceful affirmation or agreement indicator. In that case it is an acoustic device that has the same functional value as demonstrably nodding your head in agreement. Either form of *behavior* has the same effect on discourse participants. Will a competent speaker of American English know when, where, why and how to employ it? You bet cha!

Reference

"There is support for such a pragmatic concept of reference in Strawson's (1950) claim that 'referring' is not something an expression does; it is something that someone can use an expression to do"; and in Searle's view that "in the sense in which speakers refer, expressions do not refer any more than they make promises or give orders" (1979: 155).

"Thus, in discourse analysis, reference is treated as an action on the part of the speaker/writer." Brown and Yule (1983: 28)

Apart from the difficulties of explaining *words* and their so-called *meanings*, semantic theorists find it impossible to explain *reference*. Some grammatical units are said to *refer*. In addition to their meanings, or by virtue of their meanings, spoken words and phrases are often said to refer to people, objects, actions, events etc. For example, the spoken name "*winston churchill*" and the spoken definite description "*the prime minister of england during the latter part of world war two*" are said to *refer to* a specific man. Other examples: the word sound "*sun*" is supposed to *refer to* the astronomical body we see in the sky, the word sound "*money*" is supposed to *refer to* the paper and coins of the realm that are used in commercial transactions, the word sound "*reading*" is said to *refer to* the behavior you are engaged in now. We have been led by philosophers and linguists to believe that, because words are signs or symbols, the words and phrases do the referring, *whether they are spoken or written*.

Reference is a core issue in semantic theory, and throughout the history of semantics, the multiple uses of the word sounds "*refer*" and "*reference*" have caused a great deal of confusion. As a result other word sounds such as "*signify*", "*designate*" and "*denote*" have gone in and out of favor, but the basic idea is the same. Both spoken and the written words and phrases are said to direct the attention of listeners and readers to other things. The reference, *sig*nification, de*sign*ation or denotation is made by the signs or symbols independently of the speaker or writer who might use them. The relationship proposed is a relationship between the word symbols and *their* referents. *The reference is put in the symbols.* This characterization of both written and spoken words is widespread and pernicious. It is another of the semantic fallacies.

Of course, the acoustic devices "*refer*" and "*reference*" have no *meaning*. They have multiple *uses*, none of them precise. These uses tend to get conflated when philosophers and linguists talk about human word sound use. Philosophers P. F. Strawson and John Searle, per the above epigraph, have attempted to disambiguate the uses of "*refer*" by saying that word symbols signify, designate, denote, stand for, etc. while speakers *use those symbols to refer*. They attempted to split *reference* from signification, designation, denotation, standing for etc., because they discovered that certain words and phrases, whether written or spoken, could be *used to refer* to different things on different occasions; the putative referents are not stable. These theorists attempted to take the *reference* out of the symbols and put it in the speaker or writer, taking reference out of the semantic realm and putting it squarely in the pragmatics realm. However, this distinction is not widely acknowledged in linguistic theory and practice. Most philosophers and linguists still talk about the *referents* of words and phrases.

Even if it had taken root, it simply changes the historic puzzles concerning *reference* into puzzles about standing for, signification, designation and denotation. Be-that-as-it-may, if someone asks for the referent of a word sound, we must say that there is none. Contrary to the claims of philosophers and linguists, acoustic devices used in referring acts by speakers, do not stand for, signify, designate, denote or refer to anything because they are not signs or symbols. They are acoustic units that have functional values when utilized by competent speakers in appropriate circumstances. As part of a vocal repertoire, some are devices that can be used to refer. At times, under certain conditions with appropriate considerations for context and presuppositions, speakers can perform referring acts with some acoustic devices and their derivative symbols. However, the reference does not lie in the grammatical unit, whether that unit is a name, a word, a phrase, a description or any other category grammarians prescribe; the reference lies in the behavior of the speaker.

The Referring Act

"In the months around their first birthdays, and before they begin acquiring language in earnest, most infants in Western culture begin pointing, with some evidence that this is a widespread, if not universal, pattern cross-culturally (Butterworth 2003)." Tomasello (2008: 111)

"Young children do not learn their initial linguistic conventions by simply associating or mapping arbitrary sounds onto recurrent experiences in an individualistic manner. Rather, they acquire their initial linguistic conventions by attempting to understand how others are using particular sounds to direct their attention within the space of their current common ground..." Tomasello (2008: 161)

"When we observe the child in action, however, it becomes obvious that it is not only the word mama which means, say, 'Mama, put me in the chair,' but the child's whole behavior at that moment (his reaching out toward the chair, trying to hold on to it, etc.). ... the only correct translation of mama, or of any other early words, is the pointing gesture. The word, at first, is a conventional substitute for the gesture; it appears long before the child's crucial 'discovery of language' and before he is capable of logical operations." Vigotsky (1962: 30)

As I mentioned previously, humans do many things with language: we command, pray, cajole, lie, question, entreat, joke, beckon, exclaim, promise etc. We use word sounds for many reasons without performing *a referring act*. If a speaker was to say to a child: *"come here"*, for instance, the speaker would not have performed a referring act. This utterance may be directed at the child, but *the speaker has referred to* nothing. The speaker is not making a claim or a declaration *about* anything. The utterance is a command or directive that initiates a response from the listeners. That is its functional value. It is vocal behavior that moves a child in some way. Many such speech acts do not include a referring act. They have no subject matter. They are not about anything. Linguist James R. Hurford et al., have classified such acts as "dyadic" because they only involve a speaker and listeners. Hurford (2007: 167)

However, speech behavior that does have subject matter: questions, declarative statements et al., generally includes acts of reference because the speech is about something, a subject. This vocal behavior is "triadic" because it involves a speaker, listeners and *a subject*. Referring to the subject of conversation is called "topicalization" by many linguists. It is the process of fixing the subject of the conversation by *pointing with sounds*. One of the most fundamental thing we humans do with words, the thing we must know how to do in order to establish the subjects of our discourse, is to point with sounds. We must learn how to connect to the world with acoustic devices of many kinds.[9]

Ordinarily, speakers introduce the subject matter into a conversation with an initial referring act. I could ask about a dog, for instance, by using a deictic vocal device: "*what breed is that*" and point my finger to a nearby dog at the same time. In a PowerPoint presentation, while the audience is focused on the screen, I could flash a picture of a dog and say: "*this dog*", thereby establishing the subject of discussion with another deictic vocal pointing device. At times, presuppositions and contextual elements of discourse will lead to assumptions about the subject of the discourse by discourse participants. Two people could be viewing the neighbor's dog romping through their yards and one could ask the other: "*what breed is he*". The subject of the conversation is implied by the context of the utterance and a possible nod or a glance. The referent of "*he*" has been fixed by contextual elements of the conversation.

However, speakers often want to talk *about* something, or someone, displaced in time or space. Under appropriate circumstances and with correct presuppositions, a speaker could say: "*what breed is your dog*" even though the dog is not present. They are using the phonetic device "your dog" in a referring act. They are fixing the subject of discourse by means of a deictic referring act performed with sounds, (diectic because "*your dog*" is listener-centric). For a competent mature English speaker who hears these sounds in the proper context, the phonetic device "*your dog*" will have an effect. It will focus the listener's attention on a specific dog, even if the subject dog is displaced in time and/or space.

Speakers can also establish the subject of discourse by the use of speaker-centric (deictic) descriptions, as in: "*my neighbor jims german shepherd*" Speakers can use proper names to perform referring acts as well, by themselves or in combination with descriptions, as in: "*jim smiths dog*". There are many ways to fix the subject of the discourse by performing referring acts with various acoustic devices. The salient point being, that much of human speech requires topicalization or establishing a subject. Such vocal behavior often includes *acts of reference* with acoustic devices to draw the attention of other humans to the target of their discourse.

There are many ways to establish the subject of a conversation, but once it has been established, speakers must *track* the subject somehow in continuing discourse about it. Once the subject of discourse is established, speakers perform subsequent acts of reference during the production of declarative sentences or questions. Subsequent referring acts can be abbreviated. Instead of saying: "*my neighbor jims german shepherd*" each time, the speaker can say: "*jims dog*" or "*the dog*". Speakers can use the definite article in subsequent referring acts because the subject of conversation has already been established. The present point is, after the subject has been established, speakers maintain focus on the subject by means of their word-use skills, by performing subsequent referring acts with the definite article, pronouns etc. Discourse participants can thereby keep *track* of the subject.

Such linguistic referring acts establish and maintain focus on the subject of the discourse and allow speakers to continue saying things *about* the subject. The referring acts give conversations the aboutness that they have. Performing an act by stating "*jims dog*" produces a result in hearers. It is conditioned human behavior that generates behavior in other similarly conditioned humans. These acts of reference are performed with culturally specific phonetic combinations by competent speakers within any language community, and to reemphasize, *the behavior constitutes the reference, not the acoustic device employed in the act*. It is a fundamental form of human behavior performed with functional acoustic units; it is not symbol manipulation.

Analogously, in context, humans are able to connect to their targets with fingers, pointers, laser beams, sticks, eyes, their chin and feet. All of these can be used as devices in acts of reference. In all cases, *reference* is the relation between the person and the target of their pointing. The device used is incidental. None of the devices has any independent connection to the target, be they fingers or words (for reasons that will become apparent, the relation between certain phonetic units and the world will be discussed in much greater detail in the next chapter. For now, the *act* of reference is the focus.)

Unfortunately, because of one semantic fallacy, theorists often say that the sentence itself, either the written words or the spoken words, has aboutness or "intentionality" in the jargon of many philosophers. In this view, the vocal devices are said to be about something. For example, the vocal utterance: *"jims dog ran away"*. The reference, the "intentionality" or the aboutness of the utterance is put in the words, not in the behavior of the speaker. The relationship of reference is said to be between the word symbols and the target, not between the speaker and the target. It is a fundamentally flawed characterization of linguistic reference that has toxic ramifications.

Referring acts are fundamental forms of *human behavior*. They are some of the first things human infants learn. Referring acts in children begin as gestures:

> "The ontogenetic origins of pointing are less clear than for other gestural categories (Lock et. al., 1990), but it appears to be a gesture with universally similar form.
>
> "In addition to these physical gestures, the infant develops vocal counterparts to them…Common to these systems are the views that these vocalizations are not truly symbolic, are very tied to specific contexts, and are not phonetically structured. The complementarity between these vocalizations and the gestures that are used alongside them is apparent in the empirical findings of Bates et. al. (1979), who concluded these systems are equivalent… Grieve & Hoogenraad (1979) have characterized these early forms as a means of *sharing* experiences rather than *meanings*; that is, they are not fully referential. This shift to the referential, symbolic domain is accomplished in the next stage… The transition to symbolic, referential communications is poorly understood. It involves the establishment of vocalizations as names. Vocalizations become less tied to contexts, and, apparently, more to objects. A 'naming explosion' has often been reported, and is taken as evidence that a child has gained the insight into the general principle that things have names." Gibson and Ingold (1993: 280)

The medieval analysis that words are names for things will not go away. It leads to untold confusion, as we shall see. What linguists mis-name the "naming explosion" is not naming at all. Children do not learn that things have names. Children learn that they can connect to things in the world with acoustic devices as well as their fingers. After they begin their pointing behavior with fingers, the maturation of the nervous system in children times the onset of vocal pointing. They then learn vocal behavior that compliments and ultimately replaces their fingers.

There is considerable clinical and neurological evidence to support this conclusion. One piece of evidence is the fact that linguistic impairments tend to correlate with gestural impairments. For instance:

The present study has not shown that gesture and language are inseparable, but rather that in at least one clinical population, gesture and one aspect of language—the lexicon—are impaired in parallel manner." Gibson and Ingold (1993: 211)

"For over a hundred years clinical observation has suggested that aphasia and ideomotor apraxia, more often than not, co-occur... Despite different methods of assessment and different subject selection criteria, researchers have consistently found significant correlations between gesture and language disturbance. This is particularly true for referential gestures, transitive actions used in the recognition or labeling of common objects." (Gibson and Ingold 1993: 194)

Humans learn how to point with sounds just as they point with their fingers. They are not learning unique names for unique items. They are not "labeling common objects". Theorists must simply wake from their dogmatic slumbers. The erroneous semantic word/referent paradigm for human vocal behavior that has dominated philosophy and linguistics corrupts all further analysis.

Much psychological research reveals equivalence between gestures and speech in early childhood communicative behavior. The utterance of the sound *"blanky"* is substituted for and combined with pointing gestures. However, that behavior does not establish a **meaning** for the word sound *"blanky"*. Nor does it establish a *name* or *label* for an object or a *referent* for the word sound. It establishes a *functional value* for the sound. Children replace fingers with sounds as instruments for pointing and ultimately learn that the vocalizations used by competent speakers to do their pointing are far superior to fingers, because they can point to much more than objects in the here and now. They can point to things displaced in time and space.

Based on such research, James R. Hurford recently put it: "Displaced reference in language starts its evolutionary trajectory with an intuition of object permanence." Hurford (2007: 41) It is a well-established fact that, early on, children learn that the objects of their perception do not go out of existence when they are not perceived. "The intuition of object permanence" enables children to point to objects displace in time and space. Not only can a child make his *"blanky"* the subject of dad's attention when it falls on the floor next to the crib, he can point to the *"blanky"* out of view in the hall with a word sound. Dad dutifully responds to the *"blanky"* request regardless of whether the blanky is next to the crib or unseen in the hallway.

In any case, the vital point here is that the functional nature of human speech is apparent from the start. Initial human word sound use is egocentric. Children must be able to direct the hearer's attention to the object of their desire. Using sounds, they get what they want. The critical element in language learning is utility. Does the vocal behavior get the desired results? Does the child get his blanket when he says *"blanky"*? The sound *"blanky"* is functional behavior that is reinforced by the consequences of using it in context.

When humans learn how to point with their fingers or point to with sounds, they initially start with basic objects. They begin to learn *how* to direct the attention of caregivers to the ball, the blanket or the dog by pointing or uttering, the words: *"ball"*, *"blanky"*, and *"dog"*. If word sounds are considered to be signs or symbols, it is easy to believe that the word sounds refer to, stand for, *sign*ify, de*sign*ate, denote, name or label the objects. This is what philosophers have been assuming since antiquity. Bertrand Russell makes the claim explicit in the mid-twentieth century:

> "…'object words' are defined, logically, as words having meaning in isolation, and, psychologically, as words which have been learnt without its being necessary to have previously learnt any other words." Russell (1940: 80)

He and other logicians established their "object language" as the most fundamental in a hierarchy of languages.[10] To Russell the primary language was an "object language" or language of objects, the lowest type and the first one an infant learns. According to Russell and many other theorists, children first learn the *referents* of object words, such as *"ball"* and *"crib"* in their language acquisition process. This process of learning the referents of object words first supposedly accounts for what is called "the noun bias" in language acquisition by native speakers. That thoroughly debunked theory alleges that infants begin their language acquisition by learning the *meanings* or *referents* of the grammatical noun-class words first.

However, that theory is not even close to being accurate. Some children first learn to use word sounds as social lubricants or aids for influencing the behavior of others. Michael Tomasello points out that this aspect of language acquisition is often ignored:

> "And quite often the first words children learn are not nouns but personal-social words such as hello, goodbye, please, no, and thank you. Because these words are performatives, and not referential at all, they are largely ignored in discussions of children's first words. But the important point is that the nature of the referent involved cannot be the only factor determining whether children do or do not learn a word because they learn some words that lack a concrete referent." Tomasello (2003: 47)

The salient point here is that children learn *how* to use the vocal devices to achieve their goals. The word sounds do not have referents, concrete or otherwise. Word sounds have functional value. Some have value as social lubricants. Some can be used in performative speech acts: *"i promise to be good dad"*. Others have value as devices for pointing. There is no need to posit meanings and referents for words or any other gerrymandered grammatical units; and to say that children learn to name things is positively medieval, or worse.

Once their referring skills improve, children can connect to more than the objects of their desire. They can point to the running of the dog, not just the dog. A caregiver points to a running dog by saying *"the dog is running"*. The running of the dog is similar to the running of the cat. The children distill that similarity out of the flux of experience with the help of the referring acts of others. They recognize that they can point to the action of running with sounds. They learn the functional value of basic verbs. They learn to point to the running, the walking and so on. They engage in iterated learning.

Nouns and verbs are often used to point to objects and actions. Not incidentally, nouns and verbs are the two grammatical classes of word sounds that appear to be universal, depending on how you define nouns and verbs of course.[11] Later on, modifiers such as adjectives and adverbs are utilized in pointing to the *black* dog running *down* the driveway, although adjectives and adverbs are not present in some languages. Children initially learn to use sounds to point to objects, then actions, events, directions, kind-sortals, etc. that their caregivers connect with via language, even when displaced in time and space. All of these functional acoustic devices become part of a child's vocal repertoire.

Children also learn that pointing with specific phonetic combinations is much more precise than pointing with fingers. Pointing with fingers is confusing because hearers cannot be sure what in the child's field of vision they are pointing to. If a child were to point to a running black dog with their finger and say "*flibix*", how does anyone know what they are pointing at? The finger goes out and the sound "*flibix*" comes out of the child's mouth. The hearer does not know if the child is pointing at the dog, the dog's leg, the color of the dog, or the dog's running. They cannot use her finger to point at the blackness as something distinct from the dog's running or the dog's leg. Only after the child learns how to use culturally specific word sounds can they point to the color of the subject, the shape of the subject, or the action of the subject.

Fingers are used to point, but what they are being used to point at can be quite confusing. Ludwig Wittgenstein clearly recognized the problems with gestural pointing:

> "Point to a piece of paper. And now point to its shape—now to its color—now to its number... How did you do it?" Wittgenstein (1958a#33):

What prevented Wittgenstein from recognizing the pointing use of sounds was his conviction that words are symbols that refer to, stand for, represent, encode, signify, designate or denote other things. However, the phonetic units a child uses are not symbols; they are devices that have functional values based on the speech history of the child. The functional value of these various devices is stored in the form of 3-D neurological structures within *the brain*.

Human infants learn how to perform referring acts with sounds. However, unlike finger pointing and because of the ability to point at things displaced in time and space, speakers can point to inferred entities with phonetic units. If a hearer has complete contextual congruence and a mutually shared history of word sound use, the speaker can point to angels, demons, spirits, minds, mojo, centers of gravity, point-particles, the concepts of prosperity, disappointment and infinity. Such referring acts often go unexamined because we are accustomed to this vocal behavior. But when we do reflect upon them, not surprisingly, the response is often "*what are you talking about*".

When we humans talk *about* many "things" we have the desire to objectify them and make existential claims about these things. We have a tendency to say that when we put a word in the subject position of a sentence and talk about *it*, there must *be* something that we are talking about, e.g. disappointment. Whatever the subject matter is, it must have existence, physical, metaphysical or mental.

Alfred Bloom wrote extensively on this "entification" process for English speakers. (he claimed that traditional Chinese speakers do not "entify"):

> "But when an English speaker adds '-ity,'-ness', '-ance,' '-tion,'-ment,' '-age' to talk of 'sincerity,' 'redness,' 'importance' and 'abstraction,' of 'the committee's 'acceptance' of that proposal,' of 'John's 'discovery' of that ancient theory,' of 'the proliferation' of nuclear arms,' or of 'Joan's 'generalization' of the argument from one context to another,' he talks of properties and actions as if they were things; he converts in effect what are his baseline model of reality characteristics of things and acts into things in themselves—and by means of such entification,

ascends to a more conceptually detached way of dividing up the world." Bloom (1981: 37)

Other theorists have been led to the same conclusion about the English language. Michael Tomasello states:

> "Langacker (1987b) notes that the discourse function of identifying the participants in events and states of affairs requires language users to construe whatever they wish to talk about as a 'thing,' so it can be referred to, no matter what its 'true' ontological status. And the major characteristic of a 'thing' is that it is bounded often spatially, but sometimes only conceptually (as in *The disappointment lasted all night*) in a time-stable manner. (Givon, 1979) Tomasello (2003: 197)

These theorists can be forgiven for their lapses into mentalism with the use of "conceptually" detached or bounded. What they explain as conceptually detached or bounded is accurately explained as behaviorally detached or bounded. What induces this entification of grammatical subjects is the behavioral intuitions inculcated through the previous uses of word sounds to point to objects which do exist.

Because of our vocal acts of reference, we speakers *infer* sincerity, redness, importance, acceptance, disappointment, gods, demons, animal spirits, gravitational fields, non-extended point particles, and on and on, to give order and stability to what we sense. These inferences get us into inextricable philosophical perplexities, as we shall see. However, the universe does not change because of human utterances. Nothing of ontological significance results from the noises coming out of human mouths. We speaking humans should not be misled by our entification.

Nevertheless, because of this entification process, many philosophers and linguists have come to talk a certain way about their use of word sounds. They say that there must *be* something referred to by a word sound or phrase. Thus, if they use the word sound "*chair*" in a generic way not referring to any specific chair as in: "*bring a chair with you*", they claim that there must *be* something referred to by the word sound "*chair*". They claim that the word stands for, represents or refers to a universal or an abstraction or the concept of a chair. Au contraire, the word "*chair*" stands for, represents and refers to nothing. That phonetic device is not a symbol. However, it does have a functional value within the speech repertoire of a competent English speaker.

In this instance "*a chair*" is used to indicate an unknown or unspecified subject of a certain kind; it is used as a placeholder or variable. That is its functional value. "*a chair*" functions as a place holder or variable just like "A" does in: A + 7 = 12. Words often function as placeholders until speakers get the specific identifiable people, objects, actions, events, kind-sortals, etc. as subjects of discussion. Indefinite descriptions, used as variables, such as "*a chair*" or "*any dog*" and terms such as "*somebody*", "*anytime*", "*something*" are ubiquitous in our linguistic behavior. These variables allow mature speakers to speak about unknown or unspecified subjects until they can make a more specific reference.

For example: "*anybody can come*", "*whenever you get there*", "*something for nothing*", "*the whatchamacallit is here*". Speakers learn to use various culturally specific phonetic units as variables to make claims about unspecified people, places, objects and so on.

When a speaker abuses linguistic variables, it baffles the listeners. *Someone* can say: "*a man is something*". It has the correct grammatical form but seems vacuous because there is no referring act performed. "*a man*" and "*something*" are used as variables until a specific man and a specific kind-sortal can be selected. In this case, both the subject and the predicate are indeterminate. A hearer doesn't know quite what to make of such statements because there is no subject of discourse. There is nothing for the statement to be *about*.

Another example is "*a man is a man*". That utterance seems to be egregiously vacuous. It is an obvious tautology. Most English speakers know the functional value of the phonetic device "*a man*" and realize that it is being used as a variable. No acts of reference have been performed with that utterance. The statement is not about anyone. The question should be: what use could possibly be made of that utterance? What human goals could be furthered through the use of the utterance "*a man is a man*"? A speech act used in this way is often pointless blather. Competent speakers recognize that fact.

Nevertheless, someone may use "*a man is a man*" sensibly. Using the prosodic features of speech in context, with that utterance a speaker may imply that men and women are different and that a man who is the subject of the conversation is indeed acting like a man in these circumstances. The conventional explanation of this phenomenon would distinguish between what is said and what is implied. We are told that it is not what the words mean but what the speaker means with the words. In context with appropriate presuppositions, prosody and speaker goals, a competent speaker can employ the utterance "*a man is a man*" to perform an implicature, though, most often, the phonetic device "*a man*" is simply *used* as a variable.

Many phonetic units can be utilized as variables or referring-use expressions based on speaker goals and context. For example, a speaker may use "*the president*" as a variable, intending to refer to the man who occupies the Oval Office, whoever that might be. He could say: "*the president needs to be experienced in foreign policy matters*", not intending to refer to the current president specifically, but to any person who is president. This is the aforementioned *de dicto* reading of "*the president*" as opposed to the *de re* reading in which that phrase is used in context to refer to a specific president, say Donald Trump.

A speaker may *use* that definite description as a variable, *or* in a referring act depending upon context and speaker goals. If theorists believe that the phrase itself refers to, stands for, signifies, designates or denotes a specific individual their analysis falters. One such theorist is Philosopher Keith Donnellan who sets up one puzzle this way:

> "If someone said, for example, in 1960 before he had any idea that Mr. Goldwater would be the Republican nominee in 1964, "The Republican candidate for president in 1964 will be a conservative"… the definite description here would denote Mr. Goldwater. But would we wish to say that the speaker had referred to, mentioned, or talked about Mr. Goldwater? I feel that these terms would be out of place. Yet if we identify referring and denoting, it ought to be possible for it to turn out (after the Republican Convention) that the speaker had, unknown to himself, referred in 1960 to Mr. Goldwater. On my view, however, while the definite description used did denote Mr. Goldwater (using Russell's definition) the speaker used it *attributively* and did not *refer* to Mr. Goldwater." Donnellan via Martinich (1985: 253)

The correct analysis of Donnellan's scenario is that before the Republican convention, whoever used the phonetic device "*the republican candidate for president in 1964*" would have been speaking about an indeterminate person and attributing something to him, whoever he might be. The definite description was being used as a variable. After the nominating convention, when the Republican candidate had been established, the specific individual (Barry Goldwater) could be referred to with that acoustic device. In one incident of use the subject is not known, in the other he is.

Speakers deploy various linguistic devices to perform their referring tasks depending upon many presuppositions and other contextual elements, including the time of the utterance. Donnellan's example clearly demonstrates that the reference does not lie in the acoustic device. The initial definite description "*the republican candidate for president in 1964*" used prematurely refers to no one. Nor does it denote anyone. It can be used as a variable or used to refer to someone in particular, depending upon the circumstances. Competent speakers recognize that the utility of these descriptions varies and effortlessly adopt the various uses.

Regarding "definite descriptions", Donnellan also asserted that if a speaker believes that nothing fits the description, "it is likely that he is not using it referentially." even though he says:

> "it is possible for a definite description to be used referentially where the speaker believes that nothing fits the description." He claims that "there is a presumption that the speaker believes something fits the description – namely, that to which he refers." (Ibid: 253)

We should not make such presumptions. Speakers can utilize "definite descriptions" and "denoting phrases" in many ways. Mocking is one of them. For example, a speaker could have mockingly referred to Nicolas Sarkozy through the use of the description "*the King of france*" even though they are fully aware of the fact that there is no king of France.

The use of denoting phrases or definite descriptions for referring acts is fraught with possible misinterpretations. The fact that the phrases themselves, both the utterances and the written recordings of those utterances, *can be used* to refer to different things has been amply demonstrated by many theoreticians. The same grammatical unit can have varying functional values depending upon a multitude of contextual elements that speakers must recognize to employ the terms effectively. Speakers can assert, imply, mock etc. with the same grammatical units, depending upon the circumstances.

The successful use of referential linguistic devices, no matter what they are called by grammarians and philosophers, is always context dependent. In Donnellan's example there are multiple scenarios where the referring act fails. Suppose the hearer knows nothing about American politics. Suppose the hearer knows nothing about history. The hearer may be a perfectly competent English speaker without the requisite background knowledge for the reference to succeed. The referring act by the speaker simply fails to produce the desired results. Sometimes definite descriptions are utilized successfully, sometimes not, depending upon a multitude of factors that competent speakers must recognize and consider when they deploy these devices.

The form of the speech act often gives clues to what the speaker is trying to accomplish, but much more is needed to properly construe an act of reference. The listeners must detect and consider the observable elements accompanying the speech: prosody, gestures, expressions, previous discourse, and innumerable presuppositions along with the immediate context. Their previous vocal experiences enable competent listeners to rapidly interpret all these elements of context and accurately recognize the vocal behavior as a referring act most of the time.

Sometimes, the referring act is successful despite the inappropriate use of a linguistic device. For example, a speaker may be intending to refer to a *presumptive nominee* before the Republican convention, not the candidate. He may have used the denoting phrase "*the republican candidate for president in 1964*" inappropriately, i.e. before the presumptive nominee was actually nominated at the convention. Nevertheless, listeners could recognize the speaker's goals and focus their attention, accurately, on the person who is the presumptive nominee but not yet the candidate. From the speaker's standpoint, his referring act was successful, in spite of the fact that he used an inappropriate linguistic device.

A speaker can also be mistaken about the target of his referring act. One of the most famous examples from Bertrand Russell is "*the present King of france*". Someone may say: "*the present King of france is bald*" and make perfect sense, even though there is no present king of France. To a minimally informed person, the speaker's referring act simply failed. The hearers do not know about whom the speaker is talking. Listeners recognize the goal of the speaker and the reference he was attempting, *but the referring act failed*. The speaker's behavior failed, not the words. Had he used the words in other circumstances his behavior may have succeeded. Moreover, he could be using that definite description mockingly as in the case mentioned above.

Listeners might realize that a speaker is performing a referring act by virtue of the form, yet the act itself is unsuccessful. Without knowing the speaker's objectives, listeners have no idea if their referring act was successful or not. Only the speaker can determine that. If the speaker and his listeners are talking about the same subject, their referring act has been successful. However, all referring acts are subject to failure, whether they are done with fingers, laser beams or other devices such as names, demonstratives, definite descriptions, denoting phrases, etc.

When denoting phrases or definite descriptions are recorded symbolically in the written form, readers recognize the writer's reference by virtue of the speech act that has been recorded. The text only transcribes the speech act of the writer; it records the acoustic devices utilized by the writer, either silently or aloud, within a communicative background of encyclopedic knowledge. These written references still require all the presuppositions and contextual elements that vocal references do. The point is, the textual recording still does not refer to anything other than the functional behavior it records, and that behavior is what does the work.

On a practical level, we are able to perform referring acts with spoken words in many ways. We can use proper names such as: "*george washington*". We can use definite descriptions such as: "*the father of our country*". We can refer by position in space or time: "*the man on the far right in the painting*", or "*the man who preceded thomas jefferson as president*". People who are adept speakers are able to refer to the same thing in myriad ways. The more one knows about something, the more ways one can refer to it. I can say "*william jefferson clinton bill clinton the 42nd us president hillary clinton's husband the last president to be impeached*," etc.,etc. And by so altering our method of referring, we can spin the referring act with *affective* language use.

In addition to their referring-use functional role, most referring-use acoustic devices have an affective functional role in human behavior. That is not to say that words have *emotional meanings*. It just means that different words and combinations of words have different emotional effects. Words with an affective role to play in the use of language serve to evoke emotions, express feelings, and inspire action. Words produce visceral responses.[12] Many words are "fightin' words". Other words are verbal palliatives to facilitate civil exchanges and prevent them from becoming heated. This affective force is an essential element in all speech behavior, including acts of reference. After all, "It is not what you say, but how you say it."

Referring acts are not sterile. Proper names come closest to isolating the referring role from the affective role of the behavior. Proper names, supposedly, have no senses or connotations. In spite of that, many parents take extraordinary care in naming their children, fully recognizing the effects of naming a son *"sue"* or *"rover"*. This affective role of various acoustic devices cannot be minimized or ignored in analyzing human speech. Nor can philosophers, logicians or linguists use the graphical representations for the sounds, i.e. text, as a medium of analysis and expect to find context-indifferent and affectively sterile *meanings* for the words used in referring acts.

The referential role and the affective role of acoustic units vary with each use and user. People use sounds in the way they have been conditioned to use them. Some may have little or no referential value for them; others may have little or no affective value. However, the functional roles the acoustic devices play within human speech behavior are not separated or contradictory, they are complementary. Referring acts conducted with sounds or their derivative written symbols almost invariably have an affective component that mature speakers recognize and account for in a judicious selection of words and phrases with which they perform their acts of reference.

The affective functional role of referring use expressions is scalar, with *"this"*, *"that"* and proper names at one end of the scale, and *"the omniscient supreme leader"* at the other. This affective functional role of words and expressions drove Bertrand Russell to the conclusion that *"this"* and *"that"* were the only logically proper names, "names" with no connotations or senses. The sounds *"this"* and *"that"* have a shared egocentricity when used by a speaker with a demonstrative point of a finger in a referring act near the hearer. So, the referential efficacy is great, and the affective force is near zero, under these circumstances. (Prosody could still add affective force.) At the other end of the scale, the definite description *"the omniscient supreme leader"* seems to have a great deal of affective force, enough to inspire humans to kill each other. Words have that power and competent speakers know it.

Of course, many philosophers recognize that much speech behavior is used affectively. There is nothing revolutionary about this hypothesis. J. S. Mill spoke of connotations and denotations. Gottlob Frege spoke of sense and reference (sinn and bedeutung). J. L. Austin characterized the affective use of language as: "...the second kind of 'meaning', or the force, of an expression." Caton (1970: 43) Yet many philosophers and linguists, under the influence of logicians, have chosen to ignore this functional role of human speech in their search for invariant sterile meanings and referents encoded in the symbols. Gilbert Ryle, for instance, wrote: "Differences in stylistic elegance, rhetorical persuasiveness, and social propriety need to be considered, but not, save *per accidens*, by philosophers." Caton (1970: 126) Ryle recognized the different functional roles of verbal behavior, yet, he wanted to ignore the affective use of words in the search for the core invariant semantic content which could provide the stable truth value for propositions. That ignoramus didn't know what he was talking about.

Prosody provides another avenue for the affective use of speech behavior. There is a great deal of cross language evidence that the prosodic features of speech are the first thing infants pick up on. They react to the tone, rhythm, volume, etc. before they react to any of the theoretical semantic content. These prosodic features of speech often do far more to inform listeners about the emotional state and the goals of the speaker than the words themselves. How speakers alter their prosody reveals a great deal about their purpose and their strategy. Politicians and pundits regularly shape their referring acts with prosody as well as word selection to appeal to their audiences.

In addition to the prosodic features of speech, there are innumerable clues that accompany speech behavior. There are multiple uses for word sounds depending upon gestures, body language, facial expressions etc. that contribute to the affective force of speech. A lifted eyebrow, a wink, a curled lip: all sorts of clues tell us that the speaker is conducting a referring act in a disparaging way for instance. Listeners assess speech in this context. The semantic paradigm that allows for the analysis of words and phrases devoid of affective force should be thoroughly discredited. The paradigmatic straightforward grammatically well-formed declarative sentence delivered without any affective force is beloved by philosophers and linguists, but it represents a minute fraction of actual human speech behavior.

Antonio R. Damasio (1994) argues persuasively that this emotive aspect of language use has its roots in neurophysiology. These feelings generated by words are an integral part of our decision making and cannot be separated from the reasoning process. We rarely have all the information necessary to make completely rational decisions relying on reasoning with emotionless indicative statements. We often rely on what he calls "somatic markers". Yet this theory cannot be reconciled with current semantic theory or logic. Completely neutral referential acts without any affective force are still pipe dreams for linguists and logicians.

There is also a reciprocal role for referring acts in human emotions. The words speakers employ say as much about the speaker as they do about the subject of their speech. People judge other people based on their word use. They guesstimate a speaker's status, sophistication, intelligence, education etc. based on his or her speech. The highbrow British accents heard on television in England and America are widely regarded as evidence of superior standing in all these areas compared to the lowbrow chatter heard on sitcoms and talk shows. The performance of referring acts with style and elegance is a finely-honed skill that pays many dividends for those who perfect it.

When speakers assess the impact of their referring acts, they also recognize that the act may have an attributive role; they can attribute characteristics to the subject of their reference through their choice of referring devices. This functional role is a complement to the referential role and the affective role of a referential speech act. For instance, someone could say: *"jfk was a great president"*. The attribution of greatness is done with a predicate. The moniker *"jfk"* can be used referentially without much attributive or affective force. The response could be: *"that sob led us into viet nam"*. The referring act is carried out through the use of *"that sob"* which also has a great deal of affective and attributive force. We have attributed certain traits to JFK by tracking him through the use of *"that sob"*.

Attributing characteristics to the subject of reference via the referring act has confused semantic theorists for centuries. Gottlob Frege, for example, confronted this issue in the 19th century. He was perplexed by the paradox of reference. How can two expressions *that refer* to the same object have different *meanings*? By his analysis, the phrases *"the morning star"* and *"the evening star"* both designate the same object, the planet Venus. Yet, he concluded they have very different *senses*. His analysis produced a complicated and implausible solution that began with the distinction between sense and reference (sinn und bedeutung). In his words with his parentheses:

> "Now it is plausible to connect with a sign (name, word combination, expression) not only the designated object, which may be called the nominatum of the sign, but also the sense (connotation, meaning) of the sign in which is contained the manner and the context of the presentation…We let a sign express its sense and designate its nominatum." Frege via Martinich (1985: 200)

Frege made the same fundamental error that others did. He treated spoken words as symbols; "signs" in his terminology. Because he considered spoken words to be signs that de*sign*ate, the reference and the connotation was in the "sign" not the speaker's act. He failed to recognize that *the referring acts*, done with acoustic devices, have attributive and affective components. *It is the behavior that must be analyzed*, behavior with many functional roles in human communication.

Referring use words and descriptions can be *used* attributively and affectively. Clearly, speakers can spin a referring act in many ways. Philosophers might say that words and phrases have different "senses" or "connotations". However, this is nothing more than saying that the words and phrases have multiple roles to play in the communicative behavior humans acquire from their caregivers. The attributive and affective roles that words play in human vocal behavior cannot be separated from their roles as referring devices.

Moreover, there is no mental entity that is expressed or represented by a finger-pointing gesture. Nor is there any mental entity expressed or represented when you point with referential acoustic devices. Speakers are stimulated internally or externally and point to their target with eyes, their chin, fingers, laser beams or word sounds. They are engaging in behavior that generates a response in similarly skilled humans. Saying; *"the dog"*, *"the running"* or *"the blackness"* have an effect. They focus the hearer's attention. No immaterial thoughts, ideas or concepts are necessary to implement or explain the use of these devices.

Unfortunately, neither pointing with fingers nor the use of acoustic devices are precise acts. This indeterminacy of reference has been a bugaboo of empiricists, logicians and logical positivists. Truth value is the Holy Grail for them, but the truth of indicative or declarative statements depended upon precise reference. There could be no disputes about what vocal word symbols referred to if these theorists were to determine the truth value of their propositions. Yet, the referents of word symbols (within their semantic paradigm) were imprecise. To this day, they search for word symbols, both written and vocal, with precise referents. They look for "rigid designators" and "natural kind terms" with unambiguous semantic referents, to no avail.

The point here is that the indeterminacy of reference is *not* due to the indeterminacy of word sounds because the word sounds do not refer to anything. Indeterminacy is due to inadequate skill of the speaker or the improper use of that skill. Accomplished speakers can make more precise reference than those with fewer words at their disposal. Their repertoire of acoustic devices and the ability to combine them is a skill that enables more precise reference, but not perfect reference. Referring acts are still subject to failure. If the hearer's attention is not directed to the speaker's target, the referential act fails, no matter what word sounds or other pointing devices they use.

The salient feature of language learning is functional value. Learners may get reinforcement from their speech acts. Does the phonetic device get the work done? Does baby get the right blanket when he says "*blue blanky*". Babies learn to point more or less precisely with various word combinations and get the appropriate responses from their listeners. They learn to point to the "*blue blanky... now*". At this stage of development language learners know nothing about truth, falsity or how to produce a declarative statement that is true or false. Language learners, however, are not affirming the truth or falsity of propositions when they first learn to speak complete indicative sentences. They are learning how to point and connect with acoustic devices in a multiplicity of situations.

Learning this referring-with-sound skill is a *precondition* to propositional speech about the world. Without the ability to perform referring acts with sounds us humans cannot say much about the world. We cannot produce declarative statements. Talking about anything requires fixing and tracking the subject matter of our discourse. We must be able to point to the subject (the dog), the actions (the running dog) and the kind-sortal (the black dog), and we perform these acts with culturally specific natural language words. To talk *about* anything in the world, to engage in declarative speech, humans must be able to point with acoustic devices of many kinds.

The incorrect analysis of the referring acts of children has led linguists to many category mistakes. One such mistake is the distinction linguists make between content words and *grammatical elements*. The word sounds "*dog*", "*running*" and "*black*" would be examples of content words, words with hypothetical semantic content. Grammatical elements or grammatical items, on the other hand, are functional operators without any semantic content: conjunctions, determiners, complementizers, adjuncts et al. All these grammatical elements have functional regularities which contribute to the meaning of a phrase or sentence within a grammar it is said, but have no independent meaning or semantic content according to linguists.

This content/function dichotomy is also realized by linguists in the distinction between *categorematic* and *syncategorematic* expressions. The former are said to have independent content or meanings. The latter do not:

> "Categorematic expressions, which include the vast majority of words, are the descriptive words such as nouns, adjectives and verbs. These words are termed categorematic because their descriptive content, or sense, provides a basis for categorization… Syncategorematic words are all the rest, including the examples here… *as, some, because, for, to although, if, since, and most, all* …What syncategorematic words have in common is that they do not have independent, easily paraphrasable meanings on their own, and we can only describe their meanings by placing them in context. Unlike the categorematic words, they are not themselves descriptive of reality, do not denote parts of reality. Rather, they serve to modify categorematic expressions…" Kearns (2000: 5)

Language theorists are forced into this content/function bifurcation because of the semantic fallacies. While they fully recognize that some words, viz. grammatical elements or syncategorematic words, are functional components of speech and have no independent semantic content or meanings, they insist that other words do have meanings.

However, these so called "content words" contain nothing and refer to nothing. They have no meanings, no semantic content and no referents. What linguists refer to as "content words" or "categorematic expressions" are acoustic devices that have functional values just as their non-content words do. Such words and expressions are functional devices because they produce effects in hearers. They are used by humans to point, deliver affective force, attribute characteristics to the referent of the act and a host of other functions. They move people in some way. The semantic fallacies lead theorists to the content/function divide when, in fact, there was and still is no divide.

Although the sounds may vary from language to language and occurrence to occurrence, the functional role of many of these phonetic units is apparent. By using word sounds in many different grammatical categories humans are able to affect their listeners in ways they desire. All word sounds do work. Contemporary anthropologist Michael Tomasello is a leading proponent of a functional interpretation of language acquisition and use. His work has led him to the following conclusion about many so-called "referring expressions":

> "...what is typically called a noun phrase may be constituted by anything from a proper name to a pronoun to a common noun with a determiner and a relative clause hanging off it. But for many syntactic purposes these may all be treated as the same kind of unit. How can this be—given very different surface forms? The only reasonable answer is that they are treated as units of the same type because they all do the same job in utterances: they identify a referent playing some role in the scene being depicted. Indeed, given the very different forms of the different nominals involved, it is difficult to even think of an alternative to this functionally based account." Tomasello (2003: 302)

Moreover, just as humans can direct a listener's attention to the "*red ball rolling down the driveway*", we can direct the listener's attention to our own speech. We humans can refer to our use of word sounds just as we can refer to our other behavior. Our speech can be reflexive. By using the proper acoustic devices in referring acts we speakers can refer to the processes of speaking. We talk about talking. However, do not be deceived. We are *not* talking about the *words with meanings and referents*. We are talking about observable behavior. There is no need to invent speaker meanings, ideas, propositions, thoughts or concepts in the mind of the speaker or independent speaker-neutral literal meanings and referents. All of the philosophical and linguistic discussions about meaning and reference are a result of the semantic fallacies and the dualism inherent in such speech about speech.

Some philosophers have insisted that reference is in the act, not in the word symbols, e.g. John Searle. In spite of their efforts, word/referent is still the paradigmatic model used in contemporary semantics. The process of metaphoric extension in linguistic theory, for example, is said to give a word a new referent which has something in common with the old referent. Metonymic extension is said to give words new referents as well. This sort of analysis is completely misguided by the semantic fallacies. It is high time that philosophers and linguists acknowledge this fact and get on with the analysis of referring acts conducted by humans with the various linguistic devices at their disposal. Linguistic reference is conditioned human *behavior* performed in response to stimuli as a result of previous reinforcement.

Representation

"Besides articulate sounds, therefore, it was further necessary that he should be able to use these sounds as signs of internal conceptions; and to make them stand as marks for the ideas within his own mind, whereby they might be made known to others, and the thoughts of men's minds be conveyed from one to another."

"Of Words" John Locke, 1690

Let me begin this part of my disquisition with a disclaimer. I must use the language I was brought up in. Consequently, it is not possible for me to avoid using mental terms when discussing language theory. We modern English speakers, much like John Locke, regularly talk about *minds* containing *thoughts, ideas, conceptions* which are conveyed to other minds by means of language. (The conduit metaphor.) Many such mental terms will remain useful elements when I write about English speech behavior. However, just as saying: "*oh my god*" does not stake out a theological position, saying: "*i have an idea*" does not put me in the dualist camp. This is how I have been conditioned to use words. That being said, let's discuss *representation* and *mind/body dualism* in both linguistic theory and English speech about speech. (Dualism will be taken up in the next chapter.)

Most conventional semantic theories suggest that speech is a dual-track process taking place in a dualistic universe. Speakers are said to have thoughts, ideas, concepts and propositions followed by or accompanied simultaneously by the verbal expression of those thoughts etc. The thoughts, ideas, concepts and propositions are *mental* in nature while the speaking behavior is allocated to the *physical* world. According to this theory these unobservable non-physical entities in the speaker's mind or consciousness are said to be expressed or represented by the word sounds that are projected by the speaker's physical speech organs. Mind/body dualism of one form or other is required to maintain this characterization of human speech.

Imagine a child who has already learned to use the sounds "*cat*" and "*dog*" in a referring way. The child watches a black dog running, then a white cat running. The English-speaking parent says: "*running dog*", then: "*running cat*". At some point, the child realizes that the sound "*running*" can be used to pick out the recurrent characteristic of running displayed by both animals. He recognizes running, the action. He has made a kind-sortal of running as opposed to walking. Philosophers and linguists contend that an ethereal thought, idea, concept, meaning or mental representation of [RUNNING] is created in that child's *mind*.

Alternatively, the child connects a word sound to a pre-existing mental entity, the nativists' option. The third option is a non-mind-dwelling universal or abstraction which is designated by the word sound "*running*" and enjoys a third ontological status outside of dualism, e.g. subsistence (Frege). However, why do we need to create these various non-physical correlates for human speech behavior? We do because our symbolic representational characterization of spoken words and our conditioned English speech about speech *demand* it.

This dualistic *representational* explanation for human speech was popularized by philosophers, such as Locke in the above epigraph, and has since become a part of everyday English discourse. As English speakers, this ontological divide is now embedded in our linguistic behavior about our linguistic behavior. This is how we English-speaking humans talk about our talk. We have been conditioned to say that we have mind-dwelling entities as the semantic correlates for the word sounds and other grammatical units projected by our vocal system. Yet there is no empirical evidence whatsoever to support this speech behavior about our speech behavior and, upon critical analysis, even the theoretical foundation is shaky at best.

Theories that posit *mental phenomena* as necessary precursors or accompaniments to speech behavior are hard to square with the linguistic evidence and present innumerable puzzles. Consider *concepts*. The need for these mind-dwelling phenomena in linguistic analysis has been promoted by means of the following argument. The acoustic device "*a dog*", as in "*i want a dog*" cannot stand for, signify, designate, denote, express, represent or refer to a particular dog, say Fido or Rover. The indefinite phrase "*a dog*" must stand for or represent a universal dog, the idea of dog or the *concept* of dog. Many general words, it is asserted, must represent general concepts in the mind of the speaker. Plato had his ideal dog as the correlate for the word "*dog*". Aristotle had his dog impression on the soul. Succeeding theorists such as John Locke have ensconced thoughts, ideas and "internal conceptions" in the mind of the speaker as *mental* correlates for words such as "*dog*". This semantic paradigm of word sounds as symbols representing occult entities within human heads is as old as occidental philosophy and entirely misguided. It is the third of the semantic fallacies, i.e. r*epresentation*.

A word about etymology is in order here. Etymology is history, the history of linguistic tools. It is a history of how acoustic devices have been utilized. Like definitions, the etymology of a word's use is informative but unnecessary for the successful deployment of the word. Speakers grasp the functional value of acoustic devices, regardless of the historical backdrop or the dictionary definitions. However, that functional value which is handed down from generation to generation operates in a metaphysical milieu. That metaphysical background is presupposed in the word's use and is often revealed in its etymology. In the case of the word sound "*concept*", the etymology clearly indicates that it is a child of metaphysics.

The etymological origin of "*concept*" is Latin. It is an artifact of medieval scholars and their metaphysics. As Brand Blandshard points out:

> "As to the four words just noted by Professor Ryle as especially deceptive, three—'conception', 'idea' and 'judgement' – have been pointed out by Professor Passmore to be words not originating in common usage at all, but coined by philosophers." Blanshard (1962: 352)

For centuries, Western philosophers have needed occult mental entities as the correlates of word symbols in their dual-track universe. The use of these philosophical terms has since trickled down to linguists, teachers and truck drivers, along with the mind/body dualism their use requires. These thoughts, ideas, concepts, etc. are all philosophical straw men that have infiltrated the greater public domain.

Down through the years, various philosophers have attempted to explain just what *concepts* are. Ludwig Wittgenstein famously analyzed the "concept of game". He could not come up with anything common to all *uses* of the word sound *"game"*. He found a "family of resemblances" amongst the various uses of the word *"game"*, but no core concept or necessary and sufficient criteria by which someone can determine whether an activity belongs in the category of *game*:

> "And the result of this examination is: we see a complicated network of similarities overlapping and criss-crossing: sometimes overall similarities, sometimes similarities of detail." Wittgenstein, (1958a: #66)

Well, you say there must be something essential which you take away from games to make them not-games. You say there must be an essential criterion for the use of the word sound *"game"*, as the Greeks thought, that which makes something a game. However, there is no need to have essential criteria, meanings or concepts for word sounds if you do not claim that speech is a representational system of signs or symbols. Many times we English speakers cannot decide whether something is a game or not. Our intuition (conditioning) gives us clues, but no definitive answer.[13]

Are jigsaw puzzles games? Some of us may be convinced by reasoned argument that they are games. Others may not. There is no fact of the matter. Try to delimit the use of *"game"* and you will come up empty handed. Consider the following: archery, darts, baseball, bridge, snooker, ice dancing, Frisbee, love, small-game hunting, duck duck goose, shooting craps, soccer, rowing or crew, mountain climbing, sudoku, drag racing, ice fishing, yoga, jazzercise, roller skating, sledding, cheerleading, synchronized swimming, solitaire, *Wii*, ring around the rosy, sailing, bird watching, wrestling, professional "wrassling", boxing, ultimate fighting, playing catch, cricket fighting (very big in China), cock fighting, dog fighting, bull fighting. What do they have in common? What distinguishes a game from a sport? As it turns out, the various uses of *"game"* or *"sport"* do not have to satisfy any essential criteria for things to be called games or sports. There simply are no necessary and sufficient features of activities that can be applied to determine the proper uses of these words.

As a result of theorizing by Wittgenstein et al., some contemporary theorists have proposed the "Prototype Theory" in which "conceptual categories" are based on best exemplars, or prototypes, for the category, e.g. bridge is a very good exemplar of a game and wrestling is a very poor exemplar of a game. Thus, there are central and peripheral members of a category, i.e. varying degrees of membership in the category. The exemplars or prototypes such as bridge have 100% membership in the category *game* and wrestling has 5% (??) membership. However, there are many problems with this theory, not the least of which is: category boundaries are very fuzzy or non-existent. As linguist Alan Cruse put it:

> "One of the most serious shortcomings of the standard prototype view is that no category boundary is recognized... Yet a category without a boundary is virtually useless: a primary function of a category is to discriminate between things which are in it and things which are not in it." Cruse (2011: 65)

Another prominent problem appears once again. In <u>Philosophical Investigations</u> Wittgenstein claimed that "You learn the concept of pain when you learned language" (#384). Contrary to many contemporary theorists, he insisted that there is no concept of pain that can precede the use of the sound "*pain*". According to Wittgenstien, without using language, you would not have the concept of pain.

Brand Blanshard responded:

> "There are philosophers of our day who discuss the problem of universals as if it were simply a problem of how words are used, or should be used, of whether abstract nouns, for example, are to be classified as proper names. But the problem is not one of how words are used, or might or should be used, for it has nothing essentially to do with words at all. You learned the *concept* of pain when you learned language,' says Wittgenstein. That is to exalt words absurdly. The use of universals both antedates the use of words and is presupposed by it; one could not use the word 'cat' in one's recognition of cats unless one already recognized the mark or the sound 'cat' as itself an instance of the word." Blanshard B. (1962: 391). ("The problem of universals" will be taken up in due course.)

Wittgenstein's and Blanshard's comments reflect the chicken and egg puzzle about concepts that has baffled philosophers for millennia. If you insist that spoken words express, encode, or represent concepts in the human mind, which come first in the speech acquisition process for individual speakers? Must we have concepts in order to use words or do concepts come into existence simultaneously with the first word sound use? Maybe the second word use? Maybe the hundredth? Did you have the "concept of pain" before you knew how to use the word "*pain*" or must you use the word sound "*pain*" many times to develop the concept of pain?[14]

Some contemporary philosophers still maintain that there is a complete language of concepts, etc., viz. mentalese or LOT (language of thought) that is represented or expressed by public languages. By their account, all languages are translatable, where identical non-symbolic concepts are clothed in the various symbols of public speech and, in effect, childhood language acquisition is learning a second language, the first language being mentalese, or LOT. These philosophers then subdivide the conceptual language into fully-fledged concepts, ad hoc concepts, lexicological concepts, concept templates, mini-concepts, complex concepts, proto-concepts etc., in a futile attempt to account for human vocal behavior within this representational concept/word model.

However, postulating a menagerie of mentalese concepts which can be represented by the thousands of different word sounds in thousands of different languages gets us no closer to understanding human language use. It simply hypothesizes a host of mental (non-physical) entities as accessories to verbal behavior. Contemporary philosopher Robyn Carston recognized the problem of the proliferation of concepts within linguistic analysis. She said: "the introduction of a whole additional population of mental entities... is not to be taken lightly." Carston (2002: 71) In fact, it begs the question at issue. Why do we need concepts or any other *mental* entities to explain human verbal behavior?[15]

The word "*concept*" has gained wide currency in philosophical speculation and linguistics without much agreement on its use. Of course, whatever concepts might be, there seems to be a consensus that we can't observe them in any empirical manner, and the way most philosophers try to explain their *concepts* is by analyzing verbal behavior or written transcripts of such verbal behavior. "Conceptual analysis" by utilizing and analyzing verbal behavior is taken to be the road to "conceptual clarity", though, once again, this begs the question. Why do they insist that there are *mind or consciousness* dwelling correlates associated with human word usage when all they are able to observe and analyze is *speech behavior* or its derivative written text?

In Hilary Putnam's disquisition on "The Meaning of 'Meaning'" he tackles the issue of mental concepts. He reports on the attempts by Gottleb Frege and Rudolph Carnap to reject the mental interpretation of concepts:

> "Most traditional philosophers thought of concepts as something mental. Thus the doctrine that the meaning of a term (the meaning 'in the sense of intension,' that is) is a concept carried the implication that meanings are mental entities. Frege and more recently Carnap and his followers, however, rebelled against this 'psychologism,' as they termed it. Feeling that meanings are *public* property—that the *same* meaning can be 'grasped' by more than one person and by persons at different times—they identified concepts (and hence 'intensions' or meanings) with abstract entities rather than mental entities. However, grasping these abstract entities was still an individual psychological act. None of these philosophers doubted that understanding a word (knowing its intension) was just a matter of being in a certain psychological state…" Putnam via Chalmers (2002: 582)

As Putnam correctly points out, the contrived ploy used by Frege and Carnap to avoid "psychologism" was to create a third ontological status for concepts outside of the mind/body paradigm, just as they created *abstract* propositions as translational constants and stable meaning bearers for logical theory. Nevertheless, "grasping" the meaning of a word was considered by all of them to be a psychological (mental) act. They simply could not avoid the mind/body dualism inherent in their use of SAE languages.

When an English-speaking child learns to use the sound "*big*", is there any moment when they grasp the *concept* of the sound "*big*" or the meaning of the sound "*big*"? At what point? After they learn that a big dog is still smaller than a big house? You say big and small are relative terms. Well, how does a child learn that? They learn it by using the word sounds in context. This child learned that "*big*" and "*small*" have functional roles as comparative evaluators that are very much determined by the objects to which they are applied.

Linguists fully recognize that the use of proportional quantifiers such as "*big*" and "*small*" require discourse familiarity and are totally dependent upon presuppositions and the context in which they are deployed. English-speaking children have learned how to make the distinction between big and small in reference to dogs, more or less. They can point to the distinction with the word sounds "*big dog*" or "*small dog*". They remember their functional roles as comparative proportional quantifiers that must be used within a specific frame of reference. (See "frame semantics" in the glossary.)

However, you might say that the word sound "*dog*" is different. You say you cannot use "*big*" or "*small*" isolated from a specific context, but when someone says the word "*dog*" you can imagine a dog outside of context. To be sure, when someone says the word "*dog*", you can conjure up an image of a dog. But that is not what you do every time you use the word "*dog*". Your use of the acoustic device "*dog*" does not require an image any more than your use of pliers does.

And if you were to say: "*i would like to have a dog*", you may imagine a German

Shepherd. The hearer may conjure up an image of a poodle. In this case, how could you claim that both hearer's and speaker's minds have the same concept or the same meaning? You both have very different images. Nevertheless, you have made a linguistic connection and, in most cases, your task has been accomplished. You say the word "*dog*" and the hearer understands what you say, with or without images, because the hearer understands the functional role of the sounds "*i would like to have a dog*" in the English language. The speech is a performative act, not a representational act. It generates a response in a listener, not a train of meanings and concepts chugging through their noggins.

Moreover, if you imagine a dog, it is a specific dog. It has four legs, ears, eyes, a tail, etc. It may not be an identifiable breed. It may be rather generic but it must be a dog of some sort. However, you do not imagine the concept of dog. From the first-person perspective looking inward you will find nothing that might be considered *the concept of dog*. The point I am driving at is: there is no *introspective evidence* for the mental or psychological entities that are hypothesized as correlates for the words humans speak, and at no time in the process of child language acquisition does a child have access to *other speaker's* purported mental entities, mental processes or psychological states. At no time is a child able to observe the alleged thoughts, ideas, concepts, speaker meanings etc. that competent speakers are supposed to have.

What is publicly accessible to the child is the vocal behavior of competent speakers used in context with a host of other accompanying communicative behavior. That is what the infant adopts. The child can observe context and hear how a word sound is being utilized in that context with the encyclopedic knowledge they have so far gained. The child can thereby emulate this functional behavior. They can engage in observational learning. Language learners only need to observe how the sounds are being employed within an array of human communicative behaviors and context. There is nothing else for them to observe and learn from.

What's more, if spoken words are symbols that stand for, signify, represent or express mental entities, what does the sound "*it*" stand for? What is your concept of "*it*"? In fact, "*it*", the sound, stands for nothing. The sound "*it*" has a linguistic function; it is a deictic pronoun that is completely context-dependent and is often used to point to an anaphoric subject. There are many such officially recognized "non-content" words in any language. What semanticists fail to recognize is that no word sounds have content; they stand for, signify, represent or express nothing in the mind of the speaker or anywhere else. They are all elements of speech behavior that have utility and fall within a broader range of human communication behavior.

The sound "*infinity*" is no different from "*it*". What does "infinity" represent? What is your concept of infinity? In fact, that sound has a precise use for mathematicians and an imprecise use for the rest of us. We have learned how to use the sound "*infinity*" by transforming "*infinite*" into a noun and putting it in the subject slot within our English syntax. "*infinite*" is used in place of "*without end*" or some other such construction. "*without end*" grew out of "*with*" and "*out*" and "*end*", very basic sounds with very basic functions. The functional role of all these word sounds has evolved from more-primitive units of speech. We all have foundational word sounds upon which we build an array of useful verbal expressions. *Concepts* are not needed to explain such vocal behavior.

New words work their way, daily, into our speech behavior. We also get updated regularly on how to use old words by confronting new contexts at every turn. Novel contexts require novel word use. Routine contexts produce routine word use. When we offer someone a drink, for example, we say: *"would you like a drink"*. The words simply come out in response to social stimuli. So called "small talk" is riddled with mind- numbing-clichés that require little or no thinking. There is no evidence of a concatenation of mental entities parading through our heads before or during this speech behavior. We simply use the acoustic devices (a whole question in this case) as we have been conditioned to use them, in routine or novel circumstances.

The acquisition of these acoustic devices is an accretive process. Buzzwords enter language on a daily basis: *"downsizing"*, *"digitizing"*, *"offshoring"*, *"delayering"*. We are not developing new ideas, concepts or mental representations to correspond to each new word. We simply learn how to employ the new words in lieu of more complex linguistic expressions. In context, we can say *"delayering"* in place of *"managers are being fired"*, just as we say *"potable"* instead of *"clean enough to drink"*. In the process new neural connections are being made to guide future deployment of the new verbal devices. But to say that speakers have acquired new thoughts, ideas or concepts is as vestigial as our coccyx. It is outdated verbal behavior about verbal behavior.

David Crystal describes the process of word use acquisition:

> "When we acquire a new lexical item, we do not simply tack it on to the end of a list of already-learned items. Rather, the new item had to find its place within the lexicon we have already acquired. Let us imagine we encounter the item sponsorship for the first time: this becomes part of the set of items we already have for types of money-giving, such as *donation, award, grant, fee, endorsement, gift, scholarship, honorarium, subsidy,* and *annuity.* It does not become part of the items we already know for types of fruit or types of vehicle. And in joining the relevant set, it has to elbow its way in: we may have to change our mind about the sense of other items already there. *They're offering us a sponsorship*, we might say, then learn that what we have been offered is really a *donation*, because of the different tax implications, and thereafter the meaning of *donation* is narrower for us than it was before we learned *sponsorship*. When we learn a new lexeme we always make at least two gains in precision…
>
> "In the real, psycholinguistic world, a definition is not learned all at once; it is learned bit by bit, by adding features of meaning to the account. We must not expect total accuracy the first time." Crystal (2005: 198)

Despite Crystal's semantic orientation and his use of standard semantic terms such as "lexeme", "meaning", and "definition", his analysis is spot on. Learning how to employ words is a give-and-take process. We refine our *use* of a new word sound and other words related to it in our linguistic arsenal. Gradually we refine our use and become more precise about when and where the new word will be useful. Our verbal behavior changes as we adapt to the use of a new linguistic device.

This give-and-take process of word use refinement is a lifelong process. Speakers constantly adjust and modify their word usage. At no point can you say that a speaker has finally acquired the essential or complete *meaning* of the word. At no point in the process of speech acquisition and refinement can you say that a speaker has finally gotten the unadulterated complete *concept*. The use of *"sponsorship"* does not at some point become perfected. Speakers' uses for the word sound "*sponsorship*" vary and grow. People who are dependent upon such things as sponsorships and grants make very fine distinctions that the rest of us do not. However, at no point is their use of any term final and invariant.

In his analysis of ostensive definitions and private symbols, H.H. Price laid out a hypothetical case of new word use. He describes someone who:

> "…suddenly begins to use the sound 'squongle' for objects with bristles on them, such as hairbrushes, tooth brushes and hedgehogs. He had never heard other people utter this sound in the presence of bristly objects; indeed he has never heard them utter this sound at all. Yet he proceeds to use this sound, understandingly in his own thought and discourse. It is what is sometimes called a 'private' symbol not because other people cannot hear him utter it, nor yet because they cannot discover what he means by it (they could, by noticing carefully the circumstances in which he utters it), but because he has *given* it the meaning which it has for him." Price, (1953: 225)

Let us assume that our hero begins to use this sound in discourse and others learn how to use it as well. They can use the phonetic device "*squongle*" in lieu of "*bristly objects*". They can make public acts of reference to bristly objects with that sound. They can focus their attention and that of others on squongles (bristly objects) by using the sound. That being said, Price's characters have gained no new cognitive ability. After they started using "*squongle*", there was no new distinction or *concept* that they gained. They had always been able to discern bristly objects from non-bristly objects, more or less. They have gained nothing other than a new sound with the equivalent functional value of "*bristly objects*" in their speech behavior. That behavior changed and nothing else.

Furthermore, if our hero wanted to make more distinctions, he could distinguish blue, green, red, and yellow bristly objects: "*squongles*", "*squingles*", "*squangles*" and "*squengles*". This would not require new concepts or cognitive abilities. It would require new sounds to use in his pointing behavior. He will have combined the use of "*blue*", "*bristly*" and "*objects*" into the use of one sound, "*squongles*". His new speaking would be more efficient than if he used "*blue bristly objects*". He gains a new sound to more efficiently point to an old distinction though he has gained no new concepts, and no new mental entities. That is my point.

Well then, what is the meaning of the word sound "*concept*"? What does the word "*concept*" represent? Does the spoken word "*concept*" stand for something? No doubt, a formal semanticist would insist that it does: the word sound "*concept*" stands for the concept of concept. This then brings us to Frege's paradox: if the word sound "*horse*" stands for the concept of horse, what does "*the concept of horse*" stand for? *Mutatis mutandis*, what does the concept of concept stand for? Concepts, as mental entities represented by word symbols, bring on such insoluble philosophical puzzles.

Regrettably, because of their symbolic characterization of language, Locke, Wittgenstein, Ryle, Blanshard, Putnam, Frege, Carnap, Carston and all other Western language theorists were driven by a perceived need to correlate mental or abstract entities with word sounds. On the other hand, if word sounds are characterized as conditioned vocal behavior generated in response to stimuli there is no need for the sounds that issue from human mouths to be correlated with anything other than occurring stimuli, the previous operant conditioning of the organism and neurological events in the *brain* of the speaker.

In the field of linguistics, the use of the term "idiolects" in recent years is evidence of a trend toward *meanings* as being personal rather than identical speaker-neutral correlates. In this idiolectic view, word meanings are personalized by individual speakers. These individual meanings are dependent upon the speech history of the speaker and the presuppositions that are produced by their entire life experience. This recognition of individualized learning and use of word sounds presents an alternative to the semanticist's theorizing about fixed semantic content that is consistent from speaker to speaker. It is a step in the right direction because it recognizes the personalized use of word sounds. However, it does not eliminate the dualism. It maintains the semantic fallacy of words as symbols that are somehow tethered to transcendental entities in the human mind, viz. *speaker meanings*.

The *existence* of speaker meanings, ideas, concepts and other such mental entities and states has been dogmatically assumed by generations of philosophers and linguists, and all attempts to explain these entities with the use of mental or psychological terminology beg the question. The conventional wisdom and theoretical talk about mental entities existing in the human mind or consciousness is pernicious and totally misguided. The alternative is to eliminate them and the entire semantic paradigm that philosophers and linguists have relied upon to explain human speech behavior for generations.

In an attempt to eliminate the "doctrine of ideas", behaviorist B. F. Skinner tried to explain away concepts by putting them in the world as observable phenomenon. "A concept is simply a feature of a set of contingencies which exist in the world." Skinner (1974: 105). However, there is no need for concepts, or any other correlate for a word, if we acknowledge that speaking is not symbolic representational activity; if we acknowledge that human speech is vocal behavior that is controlled by the contingencies of reinforcement to which the speaker has been previously exposed.

Unfortunately, dualism of one sort or another and the verbal behavior we English speakers utilize are inextricably linked. They form a symbiotic relationship. We cannot use a language which has evolved in a metaphysical milieu containing ethereal minds, thoughts, ideas, concepts and mental representations to explain language evolution, acquisition and use. *"if you think you can i hope to change your mind that thing that contains your thoughts ideas and concepts no not your brain you cant change your brain your mind that thing that endures through time but is not extended in space that thing in your head where the conscious ideas form before they are expressed in your speech"*. This is how we English-speaking humans are conditioned to speak about ourselves and our vocal behavior. It is mistaken.

However, that mind/body dichotomy is firmly implanted in our vocal behavior and our cognitive processes. The embedded dualism accounts for our instinct or intuition about some uses of words. We do not sense that the use of a word is inappropriate because the *meaning* is inappropriate; we simply sense that its *use* is inappropriate. It is unacceptable behavior for us. We cannot use physical terms such as *"color"* and *"shape"* to describe minds, thoughts, ideas, concepts and mental representations. They are mental things. Nor can we ascribe concepts and thoughts to thermostats or amoeba. *"concepts"* and *"thoughts"* are mental terms, reserved for people with minds.

As Benjamin Whorf implied, you think about language the way you do because you speak about language the way you do. Your thinking and your intuitions about word usage are governed by mind/body dualism. So, you cannot simply declare an end to dualism and go about using the same words you have been using. If you are to explain how language works, you must change your word usage as well as the theoretical foundations of linguistic analysis. To break the grip of semantics and dualism *you must change your verbal behavior about your verbal behavior.*

The neurological theory and science relating word sound use to brain function is still in its infancy. Nevertheless, there is considerable evidence that the *dualist* explanations laden with thoughts, ideas, concepts, speaker meanings, etc. which theorists now use to explain what humans do with word sounds, is in fact superfluous. I will take the liberty of quoting Antonio Damasio at length in his explanation of how word sound use is tied to brain function, as opposed to *mental correlates*:

> "The brain forms memories in a highly distributed manner. Take for instance, the memory of a hammer. There is no single place of our brain where we will find an entry with the word hammer followed by a neat dictionary definition of what a hammer is. Instead, as current evidence suggests, there are a number of records in our brain that correspond to different aspects of our past interaction with hammers: their shape, the typical movement with which we use them, the hand shape and the hand motion required to manipulate the hammer, the result of the action, the word that designated it in whatever many languages we know. These records are dormant dispositional, and implicit, and they are based on separate neural sites located in separate high-order cortices…
>
> "If I give you the word *hammer* and ask you to tell me what 'hammer' means, you come up with a workable definition of the thing, without any difficulty, in no time at all. One basis for the definition is the rapid deployment of a number of explicit mental patterns concerning these varied aspects. Although memory of separate aspects of our interaction with hammers are kept in separate parts of the brain, in dormant fashion, those different parts are coordinated in terms of their circuitries such that the dormant and implicit records can be turned explicit sketchy images, rapidly and in close temporal proximity. The availability of those images allows us, in turn, to create a verbal description of the entity and that serves as a base for the definition." Damasio (1999: 220)

Damasio's account is a precursor to a complete description of word sound function explained in neurological terms. When the account is complete, there will be no more need for all of the *mental* paraphernalia now invoked to explain the human use of noises to do work. Human interactions with hammers and the word sound "*hammer*" leave interdependent neurological patterns in the brain that can be used at a later date. Nothing needs to be said about ethereal entities inside your head, i.e. "explicit mental patterns."

Unfortunately, some contemporary writers in philosophy of language and linguistic theory have added another use for the word sound "*representation*" and its written derivative **'representation'**. They write about "mental representations", asserting that there are new non-physical correlates in the human mind or consciousness, not thoughts, ideas, concepts etc., but rather "mental representations". The mental representation for the word sound "*dog*", for

111

example, is DOG, an as of yet undescribed, undefined and unexplained non-physical entity. Theorists claim that these mental representations are useful posits in spite of the fact that they cannot be described, defined or explained. However, they present the same philosophical puzzles that *concepts* and *ideas* do, e.g. the chicken and egg puzzle. Which comes first, the word use, or the mental representation?

Other theorists have had the good sense to claim that words and/or phrases are correlated with representations in the brain.[16] The representations are described as neural states or neural events. For example, the word sound "*dog*" is "represented" by a certain neural condition in the brain. In what way these neural states or events "represent" the word or phrase is difficult to explain. Derek Bickerton attempts to do so:

> "All you have in there are trains of electrochemical impulses: they may *represent* other things, but they do not *constitute* those other things, yet they are all you have to think with." Bickerton, (1995: 24)

Do the "trains of electrochemical impulses" represent the word sound "*dog*" emitted from the speaker's mouth or the dog? How does an electrochemical impulse *represent* anything? Nevertheless, we must give credit where credit is due. These theorists have moved beyond the psychologism and dualism implicit in talk about *mental representations*. However, there is no need to talk about *representations of any kind* if theorists would jettison the semantic paradigm.

Without a doubt, there are networks of neurons firing when acoustic devices are being used, just as there are neurons firing when pliers and pianos are being used by humans. All these devices are used in context to achieve goals when humans are properly stimulated. In response to the stimuli the brain generates the behavior by means of neural activity, though there is no defensible point in saying that behavior of any kind is *represented* in the brain, much less the *mind*. That kind of talk simply muddles the fact that human verbal behavior, when correctly framed in a non-semantic paradigm, can be correlated with neural activity in *the brain*. *Representations* are not necessary to make this point.

In the non-representational paradigm I am proposing, there are no thoughts, ideas, concepts or mental representations of any kind correlated with word sounds, neither before nor after their introduction into the speaker's vocal behavior. That vocal behavior is determined by the functional roles that acoustic devices play when utilized by individual speakers in varied contexts. For instance, the word "*game*" plays many roles. Some roles are quite clear, "*the game of bridge*". Others are not so clear cut, Wittgenstein's own "*language games*", for example. Do we really want to talk about our speech behavior as a collection of games? We do not know if that use of "*game*" is appropriate, not because we have a fuzzy or unbounded *speaker meaning, idea* or *concept* of "*game*", but because we have never used the sound "*game*" in that way and our linguistic intuitions about its use in that way are not firm. We must be convinced that it is an appropriate use of "*game*". A person using "*game*" in this new way must show us how this use of "*game*" is similar or analogous to the other uses of "*game*". How does it *resemble* other uses of that word? If they succeed in convincing us that use is appropriate, our concept of game hasn't changed; we have added another functional role for the word sound "*game*" to one English language game.

Imagine a foreign national coming to America with little knowledge of our language habits, an Englishman for example. He asks you what the difference is between a sport and a game. After all he says: "*they are completely different concepts*". If he tries to explain the difference between the concepts he will be doomed to failure. Ultimately, he will be forced to concede that we Americans call some activities sports, others we call games. Some we call either games or sports, and some activities can be called neither. The Englishman will just have to get used to how we use these word sounds here in America. Importantly however, he will not have to change any concepts. He has none. He will solely have to change his verbal behavior while here in America.[17]

An alternative line of questioning might be: When did the word sound "*game*" come into *use*? Answer: possibly when we needed to make the distinction between work and play and point to it with a sound. Nothing is different until it makes a difference. When we humans need to make a distinction, we do so and point to that new kind sortal with some sort of acoustic device. The fact is we learn a new use for "*game*" in the same way that we learn the uses for "*dog*". Someone else uses it a certain way. We adopt his behavior. For a child learning a language, the new sound "*game*" starts out as a relatively simple distinction and ultimately ends up being a word that cannot be precisely defined.

The overarching theme in this section is that thoughts, ideas, concepts, speaker meanings and mental representations are artifacts inherited from philosophers, grammarians and linguists. In fact, there is no empirical or introspective evidence of any kind that speakers have non-physical entities in their heads to pair up with the word sounds coming out of their mouths. These hypothesized mental and psychological correlates for the word sounds are unnecessary excursions into metaphysics. This way of speaking about speech is ultimately rooted in Greek mysticism. It is unacceptable vocal behavior about vocal behavior that has dire consequences.

Starting with Aristotle, the semantic template has been one of *representation*: grammatical units tethered to mental entities. With that template came the various forms of *dualism* and all the concomitant problems with linguistic analysis and theory. If you allow the semanticists this representational view of language you will be carried into their dualistic universe (another bad option is abstract entities that enjoy a third ontological status outside of mind/body dualism: subsistence, abstract space etc.).

Gottlob Frege and Bertrand Russell joined the parade down the primrose path, led by Aristotle, Augustine, Descartes, Locke, Berkeley and Kant. Wittgenstein, Austin, Strawson, Donnellan, Davidson, Searle, and Grice et al. followed in lockstep. Platonic dualism, Aristotelian dualism, Cartesian dualism, or more nuanced versions of contemporary dualisms are built into their analysis of language when they claim that spoken words represent, encode or express thoughts, ideas, concepts, speaker meanings or mental representations in the mind or consciousness of the speaker.

This implicit dualism in semantic theory cannot be reconciled with contemporary physiology or physics. Talk about thoughts, ideas, concepts, speaker meanings and psychological propositions cannot be reduced to talk about axons, dendrites and synapses. For physical scientists the question becomes: Can we explain language use without resorting to these ethereal entities, be they the metaphysical entities of Plato, the mental entities of Aristotle and Descartes, the psychological entities of Russell, Wittgenstein, Chomsky, Pinker or the abstract entities of Frege and Carnap, et al.? Yes, we can, but only if we do what B.F. Skinner did and say goodbye to the language we grew up in.

Universals

> "Seeing that nearly all the words to be found in the dictionary stand for universals, it is strange that hardly anybody except students of philosophy ever realizes that there are such entities as universals." Bertrand Russell (1912: 65)

The problem of *universals* is part and parcel of theory of language debates and the many philosophical perplexities surrounding these debates. Unfortunately, there are multiple uses for the term *"universals"* which confuse the matter. Linguists and laymen alike often use that word to discuss features that all languages might have, or features which all humans are capable of learning. They speak about so-called *language universals* such as nouns, questions, negative utterances, recursion etc.[18] These putative language universals have become contentious. As Jean Aitchison points out:

> "Many linguists hope to find language universals—features common to all languages....Absolute linguistic universals, features common to all languages, are rare, unless one takes an over-broad view of the word 'universal'. Even when apparently found, they differ in details from language to language." Aitchison (1996: 185)

Nevertheless, the work of many descriptive linguists over the past half century has been directed at finding these language universals. Theoretically, when they are found and catalogued they will provide evidence for a *Universal Grammar*.

However, within philosophy, *universals* are taken to be something quite different. They have an extensive and distinguished pedigree. The philosophical use of *"universals"* comes from the Greeks.

Quoting H.H. Price:

> "Characteristics, we say, are of at least two different types, qualities and relations. What has been said so far then comes to this: there are *recurrent characteristics* in the world. Which repeat themselves over and over again in many different contexts... Now these recurrent characteristics have been called by some philosophers *universals*. And the line of thought we have been pursuing leads very naturally to the traditional Aristotelian doctrine of *universalia in rebus*, universals in things... the Platonic doctrine of *universalia ante rem*, 'universals anterior to (or independent of) things'." Price (1953: 10)

Plato believed that universals existed independently of things, *"ante rem"*. Aristotle believed that universals existed in things, *"in rebus"*. Regardless, within philosophy, universals became the general things which general words referred to, signified, designated, denoted or stood for within the semantic paradigm. As Bertrand Russell confidently proclaimed in the epigraph to this section, "nearly all the words in the dictionary *stand for* universals", but only philosophers know that.

Historically, universals have been juxtaposed with *particulars*. Russell, in a critique of Plato, presents the contrast this way:

> "The absolute minimum of what remains, even in the view of those most hostile to Plato, is this: that we cannot express ourselves in a language composed wholly of proper names, but must have also general words such as 'man,' 'dog,' 'cat'; or, if not these, then relational words such as 'similar,' 'before,' and so on. Such words are not meaningless noises, and it is difficult to see how they can have meaning if the world consists entirely of particular things, such as are designated by proper names. There may be ways of getting round this argument, but at any rate it affords a *prima facie* case in favour of universals." Russell (1945: 126)

Universals were the wellspring of Platonism and have been a solid footing in semantic theory ever since. The semantic view of language requires universals as the referents for general words. For example, the word symbol "*dog*" does not stand for any specific dog such as Rover or Spot; it refers to or stands for a *universal* dog. This strain of talking about human cognition and human vocal behavior runs down through the history of philosophy and manifests itself in many variations. Contemporary philosophers Mark C. Baker and Stewart Goetz frame the distinction this way:

> "Particulars are things that can be identical to one another in all their properties without being the same thing. For example, there are different cars and different shades of red. But two cars could have all the same physical properties—size, shape, color, etc.—and still be different cars. In contrast, two shades of red could not be identical in every respect and still be two distinct shades of red. So a car is a particular, whereas a specific shade of red is a universal." Baker & Goetz (2011: 12)

Other philosophers have opposed universals with *simples, individuals* or *objects*. These "objects" were "primary elements" according to Wittgenstein (1958a#46). No matter what they were called, these simples, individuals or objects were things that could be individually identified and often named. They were the same as particulars and contrasted with *general things* that general words stood for, i.e. *universals*.

H. H. Price's position, however, differs from some assumptions about universals:

> "The doctrine of *universalia in rebus* may, of course, be mistaken, or gravely misleading. … But I cannot see that it is in the least absurd or silly, as the most approved thinkers nowadays seem to suppose. Nor can I see that it arises entirely from erroneous views about language, as the same thinkers seem to suppose; for example, from the superstition that all words are names, from which it would follow that general or abstract words must be names of general or abstract entities. On the contrary, this philosophy seems to me to be the result, and the very natural result, of certain *ontological* reflections. It seems to me to arise from reflections about the world; from consideration of what things are, and not—or certainly not merely—from consideration of the way we talk about them. On the contrary, it could be argued that we talk in the way we do, using general

terms and abstract terms, because of what we find the world to be; because we find or notice *recurrences* in it." Price (1953: 10)

Price dismisses the Greek and medieval view that words are names for things. He then reiterates his critical point that "we find or notice recurrent characteristics in the world" and makes an ontological claim; these recurrences *exist* in some sense. More to the point here, he claims that this recognition process is extra-linguistic:

> "Recognition of recurrences is a *pre-verbal* process in the sense that it is not dependent on the use of words." Price (1953: 37)

It occurs in pre-speech infants and many non-human creatures that recognize recurrent characteristics and categorize them. They perform cognitive kind-sortals of many kinds… or sorts. For example, both you and your pet beagle can recognize dogs as dogs, as opposed to cats. In a widely reported story, a family dog, Chaser, was taught to perform kind-sortals on common objects such as balls and Frisbees:

> "The 1,022 words in Chaser's vocabulary are all proper nouns. Dr. Pilley also found that Chaser could be trained to recognize categories, in other words, common nouns. She correctly follows the command "Fetch a Frisbee" or "Fetch a ball." She can also learn by exclusion, as children do. If she is asked to fetch a new toy with a word she does not know, she will pick it out from ones that are familiar." NYT, Jan 17, 2011

Animals of many species recognize the sameness of two triangles when they are presented simultaneously. They recognize and categorize smells, sounds, colors, shapes and so on and so forth. Recognition of recurrent characteristics and categorizing them has been observed in many creatures.[19] Most non-human animals adjust their behavior based on this recognition and categorization. It is a survival mechanism widely observed in nature and most highly developed in humans.

The ability to recognize and categorize recurrent characteristics of objects, actions, events, properties and distinctions has also been observed and reported in pre-speech children:

> "Children's constructions of temporary object groupings serve to promote classificatory and logico-mathematical skills. Thus children may compose sets of like objects (as, for instance, placing blue objects in one grouping and red in another)… Multiple groupings can result in classificatory sorting of objects." Gibson and Ingold (1993: 254)

There is nothing controversial about these findings.[20] In humans this ability to sort and classify is demonstrably facilitated by mature language users. Caregivers can point out classifications or *sorts* for objects, etc. that they find salient. From Susan Carey:

> "There is striking evidence that language might play some role in the developments we see at the end of the first year of life. The emerging capacity to individuate objects on the basis of kind distinctions is closely tied to linguistic competence…

"In a new set of studies, Xu (2002) has shown that labeling the objects during the trials themselves facilitates individuation in this paradigm... Infants were provided verbal labels for the objects... The negative finding with all of these nonlexical contrasts suggests that perhaps language in the form of labeling plays a specific role in signaling object kind-sortals for the infants." Carey (2009: 270)

In spite of Carey's use of the term "labeling" and "labels", her research and that of others indicates that the vocal behavior of mature speakers affects the sorting process of infants, and contrary to Price's assertion, we humans do not merely recognize what is already there. As Derek Bickerton put it:

"But the categories into which we divide nature are not in nature, they emerge solely through the interactions between nature and ourselves." Bickerton (1990: 53)

The influence of mature speakers within any culture accounts for many of the differences in kind sortals made in different languages and cultures.

For example, James R. Hurford reports on a kind-sortal routinely made by Korean speakers that is not normally made by English speakers:

"English has only one word for 'containment', namely in, whereas Korean distinguishes two different types of containment, tight (Korean *kkita*), and loose (*nehta*). In Korean these are verbs, meaning roughly put in; *kkita* would be used for putting a peg tightly into a hole, whereas *nehta* would be used for putting a knife in a drawer. By watching how the babies switched attention between different scenes presented on video, the experimenters were able to tell what differences between scenes were salient for the babies. The babies distinguished between scenes with tight insertion and those with loose insertion... Of course, English speakers can distinguish between tight insertion and loose insertion, but this distinction is not reflected in their habitual fast categorization of observed scenes. There is a growing consensus that although the Sapir-Whorf hypothesis does not hold in its strong form, vocabulary and other features of particular languages can influence the habitual processes of their speakers." Hurford (2012: 159)

Edward Munnich and Barbara Landau report another difference in routine spatial kind-sortals between Korean and English:

"As is the case in Japanese, the Korean basic lexicon does not distinguish obligatorily between relationships of contact and noncontact along the reference object's axial extensions. Observing arrays such as a ball ON a table as opposed to a ball ABOVE a table would surely elicit the lexical distinction among English speakers, but not Korean speakers...

"... All English speakers consistently invoked the *on/above* distinction. In contrast, only half of the Korean speakers ever mentioned contact in their descriptions of scenes that portrayed contact. In addition, those who used contact terms did so only occasionally. That is, the contact/noncontact distinction is not carried by the basic lexicon: although it can, of course, be encoded by Korean, it is not mandatory. In contrast, the distinction is mandatory in English: it would be ungrammatical to use the term *above* for a ball located ON a table, or the term *on* for a ball floating in the air ABOVE a table." Munnich and Landau via Gentner and Goldin-Meadow (2003: 132)

There can be little doubt that what English speakers habitually notice and think about is different than what Korean speakers habitually notice and think about. The language people are brought up in influences how they carve up their world. Many kind sortals become mandatory components of speech and force speakers to attend to different aspects of their physical and social environment, e.g. in English, a ball is either on or above the table. That is not the case for Korean speakers.

This phenomenon is widespread. For instance, the Matses tribe in the Amazon mandates that speakers distinguish different degrees of pastness with their tense devices. Guy Deutscher informs us:

"...there are three degrees of pastness in Matses: you cannot just say that someone 'someone passed by there'; you have to specify with different verbal endings whether this action took place in the recent past (roughly up to a month), distant past (roughly from a month to fifty years), or remote past (more than fifty years ago). In addition, the verb has a system of distinctions that linguists call 'evidentiality,' and as it happens, the Matses system of evidentiality is the most elaborate that has ever been reported for any language. Whenever Matses speakers use a verb, they are obliged to specify—like the finickiest of lawyers—exactly how they came to know about the facts they are reporting." Deutscher (2010: 153)

For reasons that could be determined by further investigation, the Matses have found it to be of significant utility to make distinctions about degrees of pastness. Obligatory tense devices have evolved within their language to point out this distinction whenever they report an action or event. Thus, their vocal behavior habituates them to recognize these distinctions and point them out in their discourse.

Some languages lack a grammatical tense system altogether. Others have as many as seven. The Washo language spoken in Nevada has four past and three future tenses marked by the following suffixes:

-leg	earlier today or last night
-ay?	yesterday or a little earlier
-gul	within the speaker's lifetime
-lul	before the speaker was born
-asha?	in the immediate future, for up to a few hours from now
-ti?	more than a few distant, but still within today
-gab	tomorrow or any time later

This obligatory tense system forces speakers to make distinctions that we English speaker can make but are not obligated to make in our everyday speech. M.W. Dixon (2016: 87)

The same is true of evidentiality in the Matses language and the Parahã language. Both have an obligatory evidentiality distinction for declarative assertions of fact. Speakers *must* make a category distinction about the source of their information. Was the information a result of direct observation, hearsay or determined by means of evidence? This characteristic of verbal assertions has become habituated into the cognitive processes of these speakers. They *must* perform a kind-sortal about evidentiality and report this distinction by means of tense devices when making declarative speech claims. Everett (2012: 89)

In addition to degrees of pastness and evidentiality in John B Carroll's <u>Language Thought and Reality</u> he reports on another obligatory aspect of a language unfamiliar to English speakers:

> "...the Chichewa verb system, which is extremely sensitive to the causative aspects of acts. For example, there are several past tenses, use of which depends not only on the remoteness of the past time being referred to (before or since last night) but also on whether the act continues to have an influence on the present." Whorf (1956: 80)

Such verbal behavior results in obligatory cognitive behavior. Kind-sortals about the causative effects of past actions are required of Chichewa speakers. They must make distinctions about which past actions have effects on the current state of affairs they confront, and which don't.

Far ahead of his time, Benjamin Whorf documented distinctive kind-sortals in the native Shawnee and Coeur d'Alene languages of North America seventy-plus years ago. That research led him to his *principle of linguistic relativity*. For example:

> "Or take the Coeur d'Alene language, spoken by the small Indian tribe of that name in Idaho. Instead of our simple concept of 'cause,' founded on our simple 'makes him do so,' the Coeur d'Alene grammar requires its speakers to discriminate (which of course they do automatically) among three causal processes, denoted by three causal verb-forms: (1) growth, or maturation of an inherent cause, (2) addition or accretion from without, (3) secondary addition i.e., of something affected by process 2. Thus, to say 'it has been made sweet' they would use form 1 for a plum sweetened by ripening, form 2 for a cup of coffee sweetened by dissolving sugar in it, and form 3 for griddle cakes sweetened by syrup made by dissolving sugar." Whorf (1956: 266)

Speakers are forced to make a triadic distinction regarding causality that English speakers are not obligated to make. It is a habitual sorting of their causal interactions with the world engendered by their habitual speech behavior.

Language learning is an accretive two-way process. These obligatory language devices force speakers to attend to certain aspects of their physical and social environment. However, the physical and social environments also force cultures to develop linguistic devices such as tense, aspect, etc. to provide them with the ability to point out the salient features they find critical to cultural cohesion. The Matses and Parahã find the evidentiality aspect of knowledge claims critical to social cohesion; English-speaking cultures do not. Perhaps we English speakers have something to learn from the Matses and the Parahã.

The "aspectual" nature of the English language, although it is often not obligatory, is exhibited in many ways not relevant to other speech communities. With English verbs, for instance, speakers are able to point out distinctions about activities, states of affairs, the duration of events, iterations of events, the homogeneity of events and more. From Steven Pinker:

> "Aspect, recall, is about the shape of an event, and one's *viewpoint* on it. By 'shape' I mean how an action unfolds in time. Linguists sort verbs into classes, each called an *Aktionsart*, German for 'action type,' based on their temporal contour. The deepest divide is between 'states,' in which nothing changes, like knowing the answer or being in Michigan, and 'events,' in which something happens. Events in turn divide into those that can go on indefinitely, like *running around* or *brushing your hair*, and those that culminate in an endpoint, like *winning a race* or *drawing a circle*." Pinker (2007: 197)

There are many other classes of verbs in English that are sorted along aspectual lines.[21] All of this so-called "aspectual" nature of Chichewa, English, Korean, Matses and Parahá is a result of different cultural evolutions. Aspectual semantics has become a broad field of study within the linguistics discipline and clearly shows culturally distinct linguistically conditioned ways of speaking about the same objects, activities, events, and states of affairs.

Whorf reported on another very different aspectual worldviews of some Native Americans created by their languages:

> "In the Hopi language, 'lightning, wave, flame, meteor, puff of smoke, pulsation' are verbs—events of necessarily brief duration cannot be anything but verbs. 'Cloud' and 'storm' are at about the lower limit of duration for nouns. Hopi, you see, actually has a classification of events (or linguistic isolates) by duration type, something strange to our mode of thought. On the other hand, in Nootka, a language of Vancouver Island, all words seem to us to be verbs, but really there are no classes 1 and 2; we have, as it were, a monistic view of nature that gives us only one class of words for all kinds of events. 'A house occurs' or 'it houses' is the way of saying 'house,' exactly like 'a flame occurs' or 'it burns.' These terms seem to us like verbs because they are inflected for duration and temporal nuances, so that the suffixes of the word for house event make it mean long-lasting house, temporary house, future house, house that used to be, what started out as a house, and so on." Whorf (1956) p. 215.

Contrary to English speakers, the Hopi view lightning, waves, flames etc. as events not objects. The Nootka view houses as events. This aspectual nature of human speech behavior reflects a classificatory sorting of physical and cultural phenomena that can vary considerably and produce widely diverging views of the same basic activities, events and states of affairs. Although the Sapir-Whorf principle of relativity is still controversial, it has recently enjoyed a noteworthy revival.

Whorf's theory had drawn much criticism. The most damning was that there was no non-linguistic evidence to support it. That is, critics claim that the only evidence for linguistic behavior having Whorfian effects is other linguistic behavior.[22] However, recent psycholinguistic research has provided much evidence in other cognitive domains according to people such as Elizabeth Bates, Lera Boroditsky and Stephen C. Levinson. According to a fact sheet issued by Boroditsky on the internet:

"Beyond showing that speakers of different languages think differently, these results suggest that linguistic processes are pervasive in most fundamental domains of thought. That is, it appears that what we normally call 'thinking' is in fact a complex set of collaborations between linguistic and non-linguistic representations and processes. Unbeknownst to us, linguistic processes meddle in and subconsciously influence our thinking from the very basics of perception to the loftiest abstract notions and the most major life decisions. Language is central to our experience of being human and the languages we speak profoundly shape the way we think, the way we see the world, and the way we live our lives."

There has been extensive research into both verbal and non-verbal behavior of non-English speakers which clearly indicates that many kind-sortals are linguistically determined. Different languages force their speakers to carve the world up differently, resulting in cognitive processes different than speakers of Whorf's SAE languages.[23] Those cognitive verbal processes, in turn, influence non-verbal behaviors.

Many cross-cultural communication difficulties can be attributed to this principle of linguistic relativity. Many people do not speak or speech-think the way you do because they attend to different kind-sortals or aspects of their experience.[24] They have an inclination, if not an obligation, to point them out, and you do not. Matses and Parahá, for instance, must tell English speakers that their speech behavior requires a determination of evidentiality when making a declarative assertion of fact. English speakers can then become conditioned to speaking *and thinking* as the Matses and Parahá do.

Human cognitive growth is the story of more and more kind-sortals being recognized and referred to with language. For most inquisitive people, classificatory sorting is a life-long learning process. More and different *sorts* continue in an ever-expanding classificatory sorting of objects, actions, events, properties, distinctions etc. Eventually English speakers familiar with business can distinguish among different *sorts* of labor cost reductions: delayering, outsourcing and offshoring, for instance.

This life-long speech determined kind-sortal process for mature speakers is hierarchical. Derek Bickerton makes the argument:

"…the lexicon is hierarchically structured, that is marked by levels of ascending generality, like *spaniel-dog-mammal*, with each term in it being superordinate to some terms and/or subordinate to others…

"Note that this hierarchical structuring extends throughout the lexicon. Take any word, say *anger; anger* includes a range of other words like *fury, annoyance, rage, irritation*, and so on, but at the same time is itself a member of a set that includes *love, envy, gratitude*, and *disappointment*, all of which in turn fall under emotion. What this means is that any word in any language is not merely intertranslatable – that is to say, capable of being converted into a string of other words in the same language – but falls into its place in an intricately patterned structure of words that forms, as it were, a universal filing system allowing for rapid retrieval and comprehension…" Bickerton (1990: 43)

Bickerton goes on to describe this filing system and how language serves as a "classificatory mechanism". Language helps speakers make the kind-sortal distinctions and arrange them in a useful hierarchy, starting with the most basic functional units such as "*dog*".[25]

> "This hierarchical organization is critical to the comprehension and use of the terms. For mature competent English speakers the utilization of the word "irritation", for example, can be optimized by understanding its relationship with other related terms such as "annoyance" or "anger". The relationships within the hierarchy determine whether the use of any term is appropriate or optimal. It should also be noted that the definitions of words are often given in terms of related words within the hierarchy. The definition of word sound "dog", for instance, is given by explaining that it is a species of mammal with certain features different from other mammals. And spaniels would be one type of dog. In fact, from within the semantic paradigm, some theorists claim that all word meanings "can be expressed in terms of the logical relationships with other words" Aitchison (1992: 86)

Some kind-sortals, although not mandatory, or even rational, become institutionalized in languages. For instance, many languages have the male/female gender distinction codified as a noun class marker, e.g. masculine, and feminine nouns. (In fact, 'gender' derives etymologically from Latin *genus*, via Old French *gendre*, and originally meant 'kind' or 'sort'.") Corbett (1991: 01) Others have the distinction between edible/inedible objects codified in their verbal behavior. Others have animate/inanimate distinction markers for the noun class. These distinctions become part of their habitual vocal behavior in spite of the fact that they may be inconsistent or even contradict the original *raison d'être*. For instance, the word for "bottle" is feminine in German and the word for "girl" is neuter.

The current point is that humans have the ability to do classificatory sorting of objects, actions, events and their features based on many criteria. Non-human animals can do so as well. However, non-humans cannot connect to a category such as tight containment because they cannot engage in a verbal referring act. Humans have that ability, but different people have a different verbal upbringing, which leads to different habitual cognitive processes. However, nowhere in acquisition of language, any language, do they acquire *universals*, abstractions, thoughts, ideas, concepts or mental representations that can be paired up with word sounds.

To behaviorist B.F. Skinner the verbally enhanced sorting process can be completely explained and described within his stimulus-response-reinforcement paradigm:

> "Any property of a stimulus present when a verbal response is reinforced acquires some degree of control over that response, and this control continues to be exerted when the property appears in other combinations. If this process of extension were unchecked, chaos would result, since every stimulus shares properties with many other stimuli and should therefore control a great variety of responses...
>
> "The verbal community deals with this problem by resorting to another behavioral process which sharpens stimulus control and opposes the process of extension. It reinforces responses in the presence of a chosen stimulus property and fails to reinforce, or perhaps even punishes, responses evoked by unspecified properties... Suppose, for example, that the community repeatedly reinforces a verbal response in the presence of a small red pyramid... If the response is to be

of practical use, it must be pinned down to perhaps one property—let us say shape. The community refrains from reinforcing responses emitted in the presence of red or small objects which are not pyramidal. It continues to reinforce the response, however, whenever any pyramid is present regardless of color, size, or other property. The resulting verbal operant would traditionally be called 'the name of the shape of a pyramid' and classified as abstract." Skinner, (1957: 107)

Within the dualist paradigm, this process is said to give rise to a *mental* entity in the mind of a speaker who can competently use the word sound *"pyramid"*: an abstraction, concept, idea, thought, mental representation, etc. That sound is also claimed by some, e.g. Russell, to refer to, stand for, signify, designate, or denote a universal, as did the Greeks. However, our recognition of recurrent characteristics and the process of making kind-sortals do not create universals, speaker meanings, abstractions, mental representations, thoughts, ideas, or concepts; philosophers and semanticists do. They continue to insist that these occult non-physical entities are created in their heads and paired up with the noises coming out of their mouths.

That way of speaking about our speech is linguistic behavior inherited from the Greeks, medieval meta-physicians and modern linguists. Unfortunately, that verbal conditioning shapes the speech-thinking of contemporary semantic theorists. English speakers are forced to slice the world into the mental and the physical when they speak. In consequence, this conditioned speech behavior has a profound influence upon how they speech-think about themselves and their linguistic behavior. They think and write about "thoughts", "thinking", "representations", "abstract notions" and "languages" the way they do because their speech conditioning compels them to do so. In fact, nothing more than verbal operants are created.

Children begin their linguistic odyssey by pointing to the kind-sortals they recognize in their experience. They then begin pointing to sorts about size: big, small, tiny; sorts about shape: round, square, straight; sorts about color: black, blue, red, green, sorts about texture and density: rough, smooth, liquid, solid, mushy and so on and so forth. Eventually, they will be able to make sorts about locations: below, in, at, next to; sorts about time; before, during, tense indicators; sorts about relative possibility: may, might, could: sorts about contingency: because, unless, until; sorts about necessity: must, may, have to, etc. They learn what culturally specific salient features of the world are important enough within their cultures to point out with sounds.

Eventually, we adult human speakers are able to connect with many features we recognize and *sort* from our environment by means of linguistic devices. Humans are able to draw the attention of other humans to kind-sortals about the time of an action, the place of an action, the stage of completion of an action, the direction of an action, the gender of the participants in an action, whether or not the speaker has personally witnessed an action or obtained the information about an action by hearsay. Many of these kind-sortals are connected to by means of specific word sounds, e.g. *"run"*, *"ran"*, *"here"*, *"there"*, *"running"*, *"to"*, *"from"*, *"he"*, *"her"* so on.

However, the words themselves are only one device among many by which humans can direct the attention of other humans to the kind-sortals they find salient or important. Speakers employ other linguistic devices to do some of their connecting to kind-sortals. In some languages, morphology such as word endings are used, as are tense indicators in English that reveal when the action occurred relative to the time of the utterance or from the point of view of the subject. In other languages, prosodic features such as pitch, tone or stress may be the devices used to point out the same classifications about the time of the action. Whatever the means by which the connecting is done, the function and the results are the same: the attention of listeners is drawn to the features of an action or event that the speaker finds salient or important.

Moreover, the kind-sortal classification process is not precise. Speakers become more precise when the demands of a profession, hobby or the context require it. When English speakers learn to use "white" we do not put all things into the white or non-white categories. Some things are definitely white, and some are definitely not white, and some are neither. Our speaking, and therefore our thinking, is not bivalent. We learn how to use *"white"*, *"adult"*, and *"big"* in context. We find that the use of a word sound is appropriate at some time and at other times it is not. It is not that the *concepts or mental representations* are flexible or fuzzy. It is simply that our use of word sounds is situational and flexible depending upon speaker needs. Often, there are situations where we don't know if a word should be used or not. Is the paint actually white? Is that person an adult? Does that dog qualify as a big dog?

When forced to make a decision about word use, the criteria by which we categorize things are imprecise. Our word use reflects that. When we use a term we do not use it in a bivalent manner. We do not think everyone is either bald or not bald. When we use a word such as *"bald"*, as Bertrand Russell famously did, how do we know whether someone is bald or not? Exactly how many hairs must one lose before becoming bald? There are all sorts of functional qualifiers we use: thinning, balding, somewhat bald, partially bald, receding hairline, male pattern baldness, etc. There is lot of wiggle room, not in the concept but in the deployment of the words. In everyday usage there is no need to determine precisely who is bald and who is not bald. If there was a need, we could not do it. *"the bald guy"* will work perfectly if every other person is the room has a full head of hair. At the hair loss clinic, that acoustic device will not be of much use.

The Greeks confronted the imprecision of kind-sortals such as *bald* with the paradox of the *sorites* or the paradox of the heap, *"heap"* being the English functional equivalent of the Greek word *"sorites"*. Premise one of this logical argument states that 1,000,000 grains of wheat is a heap. Premise two says that 1,000,000 grains minus 1 grain is still a heap. Repeated reductions of the heap by 1 grain, eventually leads to 1 grain of wheat being called a heap. At no precise point during these reductions does the heap of wheat become not-a-heap. Yet surely, one must say that a single grain of wheat is not a heap of wheat. The paradox simply points out that word use is fuzzy and judgmental. When humans classify things as being bald, or a heap, they use judgment and skill in determining their choice of words depending on the circumstances.

In addition to sorting and classifying imprecisely, we humans reason imprecisely with words. Fuzzy logic attempts to quantify the imprecise reasoning we do with natural language. Fuzzy logic is reasoning with fuzzy sets. Instead of Aristotelian bivalent logic where every proposition is either true or false and word use is assumed to be precise, fuzzy logic tries to account for the fact that word use is never that clear cut. It mathematically represents fuzzy word use with fuzzy sets and multivalent logic. Propositions that are somewhat true can be digitized within that system.

Although fuzzy logicians still consider words to be symbols that stand for concepts, they recognize and try to account for the "vagueness of the concepts" by saying that words can be represented by fuzzy sets. They give mathematical "meanings" to words such as *"cool"*, *"slow"* and *"bald"*. They contend that they can represent our fuzzy concepts with fuzzy sets and thereby produce artificial intelligence which more closely approximates human reasoning processes. They do so because they realize that human reasoning processes do not coincide with the bivalent logic of Aristotle. Traditional bivalent logic had polar opposites, true and false. However, natural language statements are rarely true or false with complete certainty because kind-sortals are never precise. Kosko (1993)

Some antonyms such as *"up"* and *"down"*, *"male"* and *"female"*, *"in"* and *"out"*, *"alive"* and *"dead"* may appear to be polar opposites and thereby amenable to bivalent logical analysis, despite the fact there will always be situations in which it is not clear whether someone or something is up, male, out or alive. Truth value in natural language statements, when they are used in a straightforward manner, is fuzzy and totally dependent upon the context of use and the speaker needs. While fuzzy logicians would say that *the concept or the meaning* of *"bald"* is fuzzy or imprecise, they should say that the use of the word *"bald"* is clearly appropriate at times, clearly inappropriate at other times, and much of the time it is neither. The point is, all natural language *usage is fuzzy*. Any analysis of these word sounds in use will find variation, ambiguity and imprecision based on individual variations in kind-sortal categorization and the circumstantial need for precision.

In Brand Blandshard's stout defense of <u>Reason and Analysis</u>, he recounts the Aristotelian belief in man as the rational animal, and elaborates on the Greek beliefs about the differences between humans and other members of the animal kingdom. He attributes the difference to our ability to "abstract". Blanshard makes two crucial errors that others have made when he says:

> "Most words –'red', 'run', 'roof'—are tags for abstractions. If animals fail to invent them, it is not because they lack usable tags, but because they lack the baggage to tag them with. A man who does not have baggage in abundance is less than normal. 'I see a horse,' said Antisthenes to Plato, 'but not horseness.' 'That,' said Plato with more candor than tact, 'is because you have eyes but no intelligence.'" Blanshard (1962: 51)

Blanshard assumes that the process of abstracting creates a transcendental entity, an abstraction. He also assumes that some spoken words are "tags for abstractions", as did the Greeks. However, word sounds are not tags for abstractions. These sounds are *not tags, nor labels, nor names* for things (horseness). They are sounds that have a function in human behavior. Blanshard, Plato and Aristotle are all mistaken. There is nothing created or brought forth in the ideal heavens or human *minds* by the human use of sounds. Human brains, however, do change the verbal behavior of the organism.

Abstracting, if you insist on using the term, is the ability to make kind-sortal distinctions. Abstracting is a neurological process observed in many creatures. Many creatures can distinguish red things from blue things. They can distinguish running from walking. They can distinguish roofs from walls. Humans have the most advanced "abstracting" ability. We humans exercise that ability to detect similarities, differences and relationships with our limited perceptual tools. That does not entail that the word sounds *"red"*, *"run"* or *"roof"* have abstractions associated with them anymore than *"hello"* or *"this"* have abstractions linked to them.

H.H. Price also goes off track when he claims that:

> "Finally, words themselves have to be recognized. If I am to speak or listen understandingly, to write or to read, I have to *recognize* the sounds or the black

marks as being the words they are. I have to recognize this visible mark or noise as a sensible 'token' of a certain 'type'—word. Otherwise it will not function for me as a word at all; it will be a curious sound or mark and nothing more." Price (1953: 38)

Price claims that language learners must recognize the sounds as "words" or "tokens". Quite the contrary; humans need not recognize the sounds as "tokens" or "words". They only need to adopt acoustic units as functional implements, as a means to an end. Children need to know nothing about tokens, words, symbols, semantics or grammar. Children must be able to distinguish among the many combinations of phonemes available and apply each distinct combination in the functional role that it has within the communicative behavior of their linguistic community.

One functional role infants come to recognize and adopt is the referential value of connecting to the world with acoustic devices. Getting baby's blanky is of the utmost importance to the infant. They need to know how and when to say *"blanky"*. They learn this by doing it and seeing what kind of response they get. Their use of these sounds is shaped by the feedback they receive.[26] The behavior of others is the arbiter of their linguistic competence. The child points to their blanket with the sound and gets the response they want. Their behavior is reinforced. They need not recognize the sound *"blanky"* as a token, a word, a symbol or a sign.

A concluding word about the Sapir-Whorf hypothesis is in order here. As we have discussed, the hypothesis asserts that how we perceive and categorize things in the world is influenced by our habitual linguistic behavior. A. P. Martinich objects:

> "The first view is sometimes called the Sapir-Whorf hypothesis, after Edward Sapir and Benjamin Whorf, sometimes the thesis of linguistic relativity, and sometimes that of linguistic determinism... The reason it is absent from standard philosophical handbooks is a combination of two things: either the explanation of it is self-contradictory or it is inconsequential. In its inconsequential form, the hypothesis asserts that the vocabulary for some languages divides the world differently from the way the vocabulary of some other languages does. So there is no exact single word equivalent in Spanish for 'brown' in English; and Eskimos have words for, say, seventeen kinds of snow, whereas English has only one. There is no doubt that each language has many words for which there is no existing word in some other language. It would be strange if this were not the case, given the diversity of histories accompanying the use of language. However, this thesis is inconsequential because it is consistent with the following two facts: all the distinctions that are made in one language can be made in another language either by using phrases, 'powdered snow', 'wet snow'... or by enriching the language with new words, often some form of the semantically elusive word. That's how words like 'espresso', 'mauve', 'taupe', and thousands of others got into English.
>
> "The contradictory version of the hypothesis is something to the effect that languages determine how people perceive reality. And because of this linguistic relativity or determinism, people of one language group or culture conceptualize the world so differently from people of another language group or culture that one cannot understand the other. The incoherence of this hypothesis emerges

as soon as its proponent provides evidence for it. For the evidence consists of explaining in the proponent's own language the very differences that are supposed to be impossible for him and his audience to understand about the world." Martinich (1985: 23)

Many philosophers such as Martinich dismiss the principle of linguistic relativity because, however various human languages may be limited by vocabulary, people can make the same distinctions and exercise the same thought processes by utilizing the existing vocabulary in different ways. However, there is evidence that not everything expressed in any given language can be expressed in all other languages. People do, in fact, have cognitive limitations resulting from their habitual verbal behavior.

For instance, Douglas Hofstadter and Immanuel Sander recently (2013) gave us an insight into the effect that speaking Russian has on Russian cognition:

"We might point out here that where English has two most basic conjunctions ('and' and 'but'), Russian has three—'И' ('and'), 'HO' ('but'), and 'a' (whose meaning floats somewhere between 'and' and 'but'). This means that Russian speakers and English speakers have slightly different category systems concerning very basic, extremely frequent phenomena that take place in discourse space. Picking up the subtleties of when to use 'a' instead of 'И' or 'HO' takes a long time." Hofstadter and Sander (2013: 74)

Simply put, how could this difference between Russian and English not have an effect on the cognitive processes of these speakers? Much of the time what one can sensibly think is dictated by what one can sensibly say.

Also, recent reporting by anthropologist/linguist Daniel L. Everett suggests that the Pirahã people in Brazil are incapable of expressing some things that English speakers do with ease.

"… Pirahã has no perfect tense… The Pirahãs lack this kind of tense because all their references to time are relative to the present, not to hypothetical events in the past or the future.

"The absence of Pirahã perfect tense indicates not merely the absence of a special tense word or suffix, but a much deeper lacuna. There is no way to convey a perfect tense meaning ever in Pirahã. In fact, Pirahã has very few words for time, period… But there is no controversy to the assertion that the Pirahãs do not need a wide array of time words. These words have no work to do in a society in which members sleep, eat, hunt, fish, and gather, without regard for the time of day, day of the week, week of the month, or month of the year." Everett (2012: 269)

"Can anything at all be translated from any language to any other language,' the answer seems to be, 'No'. Different languages might have different expressive powers for different kinds of information.'" (Everett 2012: 294)

The jury is still out for many. But recent research seems to confirm the principle of linguistic relativity, *not linguistic determinism.*[27] Habitual speech behavior has dramatic effects on human cognition, both speech-thinking and non-speech-thinking alike. Although many languages may have enough flexibility to enable non-habitual speaking to interpret almost any foreign expression, the habitual verbal behavior is still very influential in determining habitual thinking about various matters.

Propositions

"When two sentences have the same meaning that is because they express the same proposition. Words are not essential to propositions. The exact psychological definition of propositions is irrelevant to logic and theory of knowledge; the only thing essential to our inquiries is that sentences signify something other than themselves, which can be the same when the sentences differ." Russell (1940: 237)

Because of the prominence of *propositions* in analytic epistemology, logic, philosophy of language and truth conditional semantics I must return to them and present an alternative to the standard doctrine espoused by analytic philosophers, logicians and theoretical linguists. Certain assumptions about propositions are misleading and infect much contemporary linguistic theory. An alternative view of propositions is crucial to making any headway in philosophy of language, logic and linguistic theory. So, without further ado, let's take a look at propositions from a non-semantic perspective.

Various uses of language are recognized by philosophers. The use of language that is of particular importance to analytic philosophers is stating facts or making epistemic claims to knowledge in the form of declarative or indicative statements. These epistemic claims are often said to *represent or express* psychological propositions. Bertrand Russell, in the epigraph to this section, described propositions as the undefined psychological entities that the statements signify. Likewise, in much of epistemology, philosophy of language, theory of logic, and truth-conditional semantics, propositions are considered to be the identical underlying *language neutral thoughts* shared by speakers who make equivalent statements in different languages, active/passive etc.

According to this theory, when two speakers utter "*the tree is tall*" and "*el arbol es alto*", for example, they are expressing the *same proposition*. These verbal utterances are very different, but both utterances represent a language-neutral undefined psychological entity, a common thought in the mind of the speakers. This common psychological entity that is *sign*ified, de*sign*ated, represented, expressed or encoded by the two statements gives them the *same meaning* according to Russell and others. That shared meaning is a result of the shared proposition, the *same thought* in the minds of the speakers.

Philosophers such as Russell posit these psychological propositions because they have long regarded the use of spoken sentences as physical activity that signifies, designates, represents, expresses, encodes or stands for mental activity. Although the proposition underlying the sentential utterance might not have an "exact psychological definition", there is no doubt that it is psychological, that is *mental*, not physical. This psychological view of human speech entails some form of dualism, both at the individual word level and the sentential level. Without this mind/body dualist assumption, they cannot postulate mental or psychological correlates such as propositions for sentences.

Not surprisingly, problems arise with this view. For instance, how can theorist be sure that the underlying psychological propositions in the minds of two speakers are identical, even if they speak the same language? If these propositions are not identical there can be variability in the meaning and thus the truth of the propositions in various speakers' minds. The identical statement out of one speaker's mouth could be true, and out of another speaker's mouth false if the underlying proposition is not a language-neutral, speaker-neutral, context-neutral entity.

Consequently, many theorists attempted to avoid the "psychologism" and the implicit truth variability in declarative statements that this view of propositions engenders. They hypothesized *abstract propositions*. In this theory, propositions are considered to be *speaker-neutral* abstract entities that are signified, designated, represented, expressed or encoded by the verbal symbols used in the statement. They are *what the words say*. These speaker-neutral abstract propositions give statements both the *same meaning* and thereby the same truth value, in spite of any language differences, different thought processes in the head of any individual speaker, or the context of the utterance.

This theoretical view also allows theorists to consider both the oral assertion: "*the tree is tall*" and the written assertion: '**The tree is tall**' to be semantically equivalent. Both statements represent an identical speaker-neutral abstract proposition that is encoded in the symbols, be they vocal or written. By eliminating the personalized psychological proposition and hypothesizing an *abstract proposition*, the same stable *literal meaning* can be carried by the written symbols as well as the vocal symbols. This, in turn, enabled grammarians and linguists to conduct static analyses of the written statements for semantic content, rather than dynamic analyses of vocal behavior with all its dynamic contextual elements of prosody, presuppositions, previous discourse, etc.

It is quite evident that these propositions, both the psychological and the abstract, were invented by philosophers to complete semantic theories of language and logic. They needed theoretical entities to account for a *common meaning* that was supposedly shared by different speakers who uttered the same statements in one language, or comparable statements in different languages. Common meaning would provide a common stable truth value to propositional statements no matter who uttered them or when and how they did so. However, few of these hypothetical speaker-neutral, context-neutral, timeless statements with unvarying propositional content have been found.

Linguists, philosophers and logicians continue the search for immutable declarative propositional statements that have fixed meanings that hold constant no matter what the circumstances or who uses them. They search for a stable independent meaning encoded in the symbols, both written and spoken, that can be ferreted out and exposed for all to see and agree upon. The literature in philosophy of language and linguistics is a constant back and forth between theorists with different "readings" of statements caused by different contextual and background considerations. Statement meanings that remain fixed regardless of context are difficult to find.

Let's start over. If we do not take spoken words to be symbols, saying "*the tree is tall*" (sound it out) is an act; it is vocal behavior; it is human sound production. The utterance "*the tree is tall*" signifies nothing. It designates nothing. It represents nothing. It expresses nothing. It encodes nothing. It stands for nothing. It signifies nothing. It is not composed of symbols. That utterance is vocal behavior which has different effects on different hearers based on context, the hearer's speech history, the incident of use, etc.

If theorists are willing to jettison the semantic analysis of language, they can dispense both with the psychological propositions supposedly represented by the utterance of a declarative sentence and the fixed abstract propositions supposedly encoded in the symbols. Rather, what is common to both Spanish and English declarative sentential utterances is the functional value of the phonetic units, somewhat idiosyncratically learned through their repeated deployment. The spoken words are functional behavior performed in response to stimuli which produces feedback.

Each assertion is not a "constative utterance", in J.L. Austin's terminology; it is a performative utterance. It is not an expression of a psychological proposition or a speaker-neutral abstract proposition. The entire vocal effort is behavior, it is a performance. If it is a straightforward declarative utterance, it begs assent or dissent, depending upon a host of considerations, straight forward honesty being the most obvious. If the hearer recognizes the functional value of the sounds and assumes the speaker is being honest, they will make the same judgment and agree or disagree based on their construal of *"tall"* relative to trees and the context of the utterance, etc. Other utterances of that statement are similar performances, all relativized to context, speaker goals, prosodic features and other communicative clues which might lead listeners to believe that the speaker is being truthful, poetic, sarcastic, comedic, etc.

Consider a marriage proposal. In a romantic context, if a man proposes to a woman, is there a mental proposition that corresponds to the proposal? Is a marriage proposal a representation of some mental act that the suitor has performed (he may have rehearsed it, but we wouldn't call his fifty rehearsals "proposals")? No, his verbal action is the proposal. The man is not reporting a mental proposal by proposing verbally. The proposal is performed through the use of words. A marriage proposal is clearly a performative speech act, not a representational act. The speaker hopes to elicit certain behavior from the hearer.

Through parallel analysis, *a declarative proposition is the act*, not something signified, designated, represented, expressed, encoded by the act. The proposition is carried out with words, the sounds. To say that someone has stated or asserted a proposition is to say nothing more than that the person has performed a speech act. Assuming that the speech act is a straightforward honest assertion, the speaker is conditioned to expect a response of some sort (the response may be a neural connection in the listener's brain and a nod of agreement.) A declarative sentence is no less a performative utterance than is a marriage proposal. Neither form of vocal behavior signifies, designates, represents, expresses, encodes, or stands for a psychological or abstract proposition.

A proposition, a performative speech act, is done by formula. We have learned a method of doing it with the acoustic devices at our disposal, just as we learn a method of proposing marriage. We have learned *how* to do something and adjust the behavior to fit the circumstances; it is utilitarian like our other behaviors. In addition, there is nothing cognitively unique or distinctive about the productivity of propositional speech behavior. It is utilitarian combinatorial human behavior in response to stimuli that has consequences.

Spoken language is action. It is a sequence of phonemes and gaps. We hear the action instead of seeing it. However, we English speakers *think* it is unique because dualist philosophers, logicians, and theoretical linguists have informed us that it is representational symbolic activity. Theorists have concocted an alternative universe full of propositions, thoughts, ideas and concepts to pair up with words and sentences. As a result, English speakers have been thoroughly conditioned to talk about words, sentences, phrases, idioms and all the other grammatical units as representing or expressing these *mental entities*. In our day to day talk about our talk we use expressions such as: *"get your thoughts across better"*, *"putting thoughts into someone's mind"*, *"exchange ideas"*. It is impossible to avoid such talk. That semantic paradigm of words carrying mental entities from one human head to another, the conduit metaphor, has become enshrined in our speech about speech.

From the non-semantic perspective, when a speaker performs propositions such as *"the tree is tall"* they are making a judgment about the height of the tree. They are making a kind-sortal. They are categorizing the height of the tree relativized to the circumstances with many presuppositions. They then propose that categorization to the hearer in an effort to get his or her assent or acknowledgement. The proposition is a proposal, a straightforward declarative speech act, a judgmental act performed to elicit agreement or possibly inform someone who has come to rely on the speaker about the size of trees.

Consider the following. While gesturing toward a cloud, a speaker says only *"that cloud"* to another person. The hearer would probably respond: *"yes what about that cloud"* or *"what are you trying to tell me"*. The hearer recognizes the speaker's act of reference but expects more. A referring act, no matter what the method, is a hollow gesture. Speakers are expected to say something about the subjects of their verbal referring acts. Even cavemen had to say *"cloud black"* to make much use of their limited acoustic devices.

Speakers going as far back as the Stone Age were able to refer and *connect*. They often made a connection with a basic propositional utterance; they would *predicate*. Reference and predication allow us to form a distinctive kind of knowledge. To predicate with words in modern English, we use the semantically vacuous copula *"is"*, or another form of it adjusted for tense, person and plurality. The sound *"is"* functions as the verbal connector. Some languages, such as Russian, operate without a copula. The connection is implied by word order, e.g. *"cloud black"*. In modern English we perform a propositional act of predication by utilizing the copula and saying: *"that cloud is black"*.[28]

This linguistic predication is verbal behavior described by B. F. Skinner:

> "Predication is effected by a relational autoclitic to which has been added an autoclitic of assertion. Let us say that a single object evokes the two tacts *chocolate* and *good*... The common source of the two responses, the fact that they are made to the same object, can be indicated by the relational autoclitic of order. Good chocolate is appropriate only to a single type of situation; it is a response to good chocolate. It shows neither assertion nor predication. *The chocolate is good* shows a relational autoclitic of ordering and grouping and it contains an autoclitic of assertion. Taken together these make it a predication." Skinner (1957: 334-335)

When speakers make these statements, they stimulate listeners to perform the same propositional speech act consisting of the same functional units of verbal behavior. The hearer makes the same predication, more or less, depending upon their conditioned speech skills. They follow the speaker's direction. Their attention is directed to the same objects, actions, events, etc. The same sorting and connecting is performed though neither the speakers nor the listeners are connecting concepts or ideas in their minds; they are attending to kind-sortals and making neural connections in their brains that are retained for future use.

These basic propositional acts, consisting of basic autoclitics become more and more complex as speakers develop their speaking skills. As they become more complex, multiple interpretations for propositional speech acts are possible, depending upon speaker conditioning and the usual considerations of context, prosody etc. That makes the analysis of any vocal behavior in isolation fruitless. Consequently, when the analysis is limited to a written recording of vocal behavior the functional value of that behavior often becomes even more opaque. As a result, the classic analysis of static textual verbal behavior within the semantic paradigm has thoroughly confounded linguists by creating paradoxes and puzzles that are insoluble.

For example, there has been much philosophical wrangling for the past forty years over the written statement: **'Water is H₂0'**. Some philosophers claim that the word **'water'** and the word **'H₂0'** de*sign*ate the same *referent*. They are often called "rigid designators". It is further claimed that that this written statement is an eternal sentence, one which *means* the same thing in all possible worlds, forever. On the contrary, these written words have no fixed meanings or referents, and the written statement **'Water is H₂0'** can be construed many ways. It is the recording of a propositional speech act that depends upon all the contextual elements of speech for multiple interpretations.

For instance, a writer could be using that recorded speech act to make a claim about the chemical composition of the clear liquid substance we English speakers can refer to with the sound *"water"*. Or, a writer could be using that the assertion to make a claim about the way he will use those terms. Speakers can be talking about their talk, not the substance water. Maybe they are just saying that's how they would define the word *"water"*. They could also use that assertion to make a stipulative definition for certain purposes, i.e. while in the chemistry lab they will use both terms interchangeably. If we take the speech act to other possible worlds, as philosophers have done, the possible interpretations multiply.[29]

All of this confusion is exacerbated by the ambiguous use of *"is"* within English propositional speech acts. Russell clearly recognized the problem in <u>Descriptions</u>:

> "The *is* of "Socrates is human" expresses the relation of subject and predicate; the is of 'Socrates is a man' expresses identity. It is a disgrace to the human race that it has chosen to employ the same word *'is'* for these two entirely different ideas—a disgrace which a symbolic logical language of course remedies."

Correctly analyzed, *"is"* is an operator; it has two connecting functions. It connects the subject to the predicate when it is used by the speaker as a copula, as in: *"the cloud is white"*. Alternatively, when the speaker intends to use *"is"* as the functional equivalent of "equals" it connects two subjects in an identity relationship. For example: *"mark twain is samuel clemens"*. The word sound *"is"* has at least two roles to play in the verbal behavior of English speakers. In Russell's dualistic semiotic world, *"is"* is employed to "express" two entirely different "ideas". What could these "ideas" be?

The story of the English copula *"is"* provides revealing insights into language acquisition and use, along with the functional value of propositional speech acts. Guy Deutscher relates an interesting linguistic fact about the English copula *"is"*:

"But many languages, such as Russian, don't need such a copula, and simply say the equivalent of 'stone sharp'. (In fact, copulas like 'is' are usually of a secondary origin, and often ultimately come from some marker of emphasis which with time and frequent repetition loses its force and becomes obligatory.)" Deutscher (2005: 239)

This insight becomes highly significant in understanding the development of language. The connection we English speakers make with "*is*" probably originated with a simple juxtaposition of an object and a kind-sortal that we gleaned from our experience and pointed to with the word sounds "*stone*" and "*sharp*". The connection, made originally by means of word order (syntax) "*stone sharp*", was formally enshrined with the copula "*is*" because it clarifies the speaker's goal and makes the propositional act more obvious.

Unfortunately, the obligatory marker origins of "*is*" in English have since metamorphosed into an existential function within certain contexts:

"It is clear that syntax will not be needed by symbol using creatures until their form of symbolic communication becomes complex enough to generate more than a single noun and a single verb. For example, consider the sequence, modifier –noun –verb. Does the modifier modify the noun or the verb? In most cases this is solved semantically, without recourse to rules of organization because the same type of things in the real world usually cannot modify both verbs and nouns. For example, a ball can be green, but 'pushes' are not green. However, this is not true for all nouns and verbs. 'Kicks can be up or down, for example, and trees can be up or down as well.

"In this case the problem of ambiguity is typically solved by introducing the special verb, 'to be', as in 'The tree *is* down', so that 'down' becomes a comment on the state of the tree. Here, 'down' cannot be a comment on the state of the verb, because actions have no states, they are processes. Thus, whenever the 'to be' verb is used with a modifier, the modifier is directed to the noun simply because the 'to be' verb cannot be modified. The purpose of the copula is not one of semantic content, but rather to permit the typical noun-verb format to occur in expressions where the only action is one of existence. This is necessary because the act of formally noting existence cannot in and of itself be modified and still retain its status as a denotator (not semantic) of existence." Gibson and Ingold (1993: 105)

"*to be or not to be*" Let us not be fooled by this existential function of "*is*" into thinking that our use of that word sound has any impact on the nature of the universe and what *exists*. This existential function of "*is*" has been transformed into "being" and hideously abused by some philosophers of the existential tradition. When philosophers produce existential imperatives by declaring that something has "*being*", they are simply abusing a perfectly useful word.

"*is*" has functional origins and functional values. The sound "*is*" has no referent and no meaning. It *is* not a sign, a symbol or a semantic designator. It *is* a word sound with multiple functions that have gradually evolved over an extended history of its use. In that respect it *is* the same as any other word. It should also be noted that the use of "*is*" *is* context dependent. "*is*", "*was*" and "*will be*" are all context dependent. They are time sensitive. The ordinary use of these word sounds in discourse cannot be taken out of a time context.

In any case, the overall thrust of this section is a claim that propositions are not mental or abstract entities; they are actions, they are human behavior. They are not psychological entities that can be represented or expressed by public languages. They are not psychological entities which serve as translational constants and truth bearers. They are not abstract entities with stable, independent, semantic content and stable truth values. Propositions are speech acts, and, as is the case with any speech act, they can be used and construed in many ways.

Proposing is one of the things we humans do with word sounds. The proposition, as a mental entity or an abstract speaker-neutral entity, are fictions created by philosophers for a variety of reasons. Do not be duped into thinking that your speech acts represent, signify, designate, denote, encode, or stand for anything. All speech is behavior in response to stimuli that has consequences which may, or may not reinforce the behavior.

The Use of the Word "*comprehension*"

> "Comprehension, the process of understanding an utterance, requires the ability
> to access the mental lexicon to match the words in the utterance we are listening
> to with their meanings." Fromkin and Rodman (1998: 389)

This quote exemplifies the "dictionary in the head" theory of semantics. It also exemplifies the use of the word sound "*comprehension*" and its derivative text version '**comprehension**' in modern linguistics. Listeners are said to match the meanings in their "*mental lexicon*" with the utterances that issue from speaker's mouths. *Comprehension* is claimed to be this mental feat of matching mental meanings with words. Although there is no evidence whatsoever for this peculiar explanation of human verbal behavior, it is accepted because philosophers, linguists and grammarians are working within the semantic frame and an implicit mind/body dualism which is embedded in their SAE verbal behavior. However, there is no warrant for talking this way about our talk. Philosophers, linguists and grammarians should simply say that speakers learn *how* to use various linguistic devices within language specific syntaxes. Thus, when speakers learn *how* to use these various linguistic devices, they also become listeners who know how the devices are being used by others.

That vocal behavior becomes structured as a result of the architecture of the human brain and other commonalities of human anatomy which produce common behavior, as well as the linguistic environment in which children are raised. Comprehension of anything is *knowing how* to perform, whether the performance is tying a bow knot, playing a musical instrument, or writing the next great American novel. There is no need to inject supernatural *mental* entities and processes into the analysis if you do not start by assuming the dualistic semantic paradigm.

Chapter Two

Summary & Notes

With the advent of the written word, the semantic theory of human sound production and utilization began its ascent. Functional units of sound were recorded graphically and parsed into words, phrases, sentences, etc. The individual word symbols were then said to have meanings that could be associated with them, whether they were vocal symbols or written symbols. Literal or lexical meanings were said to be carried by both the written symbols and the vocal symbols as they were transmitted from person to person. These fixed, independent meanings were said to be encoded in the symbols and stable across all speakers and for every occasion of use. The pairing of words and these stable meanings became the paradigmatic model for the human acquisition and use of speech.

Along with this stable, independent, semantic content, semanticists put stable, independent reference into the words and other units of grammar. The words and phrases, as symbols, were said to refer to, signify, designate, or denote their referents. *Reference* became a relation between the symbols and things in the world that held regardless of the verbal upbringing of the speaker or the context of their verbal behavior. Three millennia of philosophers and linguists have worked within this erroneous paradigm of words and phrases with meanings and referents.

Additionally, word symbols were said to *represent* or express other activity, mental activity. Spoken symbols were said to express speaker meanings, thoughts, ideas, concepts, *mental representations* and propositions in the minds of speakers. This is the third of the semantic fallacies: *representation*.

To make these claims, theorists had to embrace *dualism* of one kind or another. The mind/body dichotomy which is now embedded in our SAE verbal behavior and our derivative thought processes, is a prerequisite for this explanation for human speech behavior. Unfortunately, mind/body dualism, mainly in the form of folk psychology, is conditioned into contemporary English verbal behavior about that verbal behavior. All explanations for human speech currently on offer, other than behaviorism, are couched in dualistic psychological or mental terms.

The way we humans currently talk about our talk is a product of ancient metaphysics and three millennia of misguided philosophy. The presumed mind/body dichotomy and the symbolic nature of sounds that are emitted from our mouths are outgrowths of ancient philosophical speculation and the advent of writing systems that record the sounds. That talk about our talk, based on thousands of years of philosophical speculation, obfuscates the proper analysis of human verbal behavior.

Theorists must eliminate their presuppositions and assumptions about the nature of language and the nature of humans if they wish to correctly analyze human speech behavior. We do not need the metaphysics of Plato, or the mentalism of Aristotle and Descartes, or the psychologism of much contemporary theory, to explain how language works. The empirical and introspective evidence supporting such semantic theorizing about human speech is non-existent. In fact, the data (verbal behavior) indicate quite the contrary. Those data indicate that humans use acoustic devices and syntax in coordination with other conditioned, communicative behavior in response to various stimuli. All of that verbal behavior is performative action, including asserting or proposing by means of declarative statements.

Linguists and philosophers have been whittling away at semantics and dualism for the last century, freeing many word sounds from their semantic constraints, e.g. grammatical elements. Yet, semantic theorizing about what word symbols *mean, stand for, signify, designate, denote, encode, refer to, represent,* or *express,* persists. It is time to entirely dispose of the semantic paradigm. It is time to recognize that human speech is S-R-R conditioned behavior that can be explained within the behaviorist paradigm. B. F. Skinner gave a broad account of speech in behaviorist terms. A fine-grained behaviorist account can be had if the current semantic paradigm is jettisoned. Human speech behavior can then be reduced to physiology, acoustics, molecular biology and, ultimately, to physics and chemistry.

Theorists must reject talk about words as signs, symbols and semantic designators. They must reject talk about humans with minds and mental phenomena. Theorists must change their speech behavior about themselves and their speech, eliminating the idealism, the mentalism, the psychologism, and the semantics. Because every time speakers use these mental or psychological terms, they reinforce the dualism implicit in their use. When philosophers, scientists, and linguists change their speech about themselves and their speech behavior, others will as well. The bad behavior must stop. Theorists must lead the way.

Adapting to this new approach will require a complete reorientation in analysis. Semantics in all its manifestations must go. Theorists must view speech in the same way that we view other human behaviors. It is a different type of behavior, but behavior none the less. Human verbal behavior can be explained by observing it and the physiology of the body emitting it. Moreover, we must observe the action, not the impoverished representations of the action. We simply cannot analyze the static representations of vocal behavior, i.e. written symbols. All linguistic analysis must be based on discourse function. Theorists must *listen* to the data.

Should we not use the word sounds "sunrise" or "sunset"? As we all know, the sun does not actually rise up in the morning nor set at night. The earth rotates in a solar orbit which creates the illusions of sunrise and sunset. Yet, "sunrise" and "sunset", although misleading, are perfectly useful word sounds. In the same vein, we can utilize word sounds such as "mind", "concept", "idea", and their derivative symbols. However, we must realize that these words, and others like them, must be used with provisos. They are shorthand methods of explaining complex human behavior and its origins. They are part of our linguistic heritage and folk psychology that has, for millennia, played a role in explaining human speech, but they are unsupported by any evidence.

The philosophical perplexities and the poor science that come from the wobbly foundations of semantics and dualism are manifold. I hope to expose them in the following chapters of this book. First though, I will confront the mind/body problem head on. Then, I will present evidence for the acceptance of a non-semantic approach to linguistic analysis and theory, starting with solutions to traditional puzzles in linguistic theory. From there I will proceed to a new look at the philosophy of mathematics from a behaviorist standpoint. Following that I will review traditional problems in epistemology from the same non-semantic perspective. I will then take a look at physics and philosophy of science from the non-semantic perspective. Gordian knots will be untied.

1. Empirical evidence for the functional autonomy of written text for literate humans appears as phonological dyslexia. David Crystal reports that: "…people lose their ability to convert isolated letters into sounds; they are unable to pronounce even simple nonsense words, e.g. *pob*). But they are able to read real words, showing a non-phonological route from print to meaning must exist." Crystal (1997: 213)

The route does not take them to *meaning*; it takes them to *function*. Mature readers are able to independently glean the functional value of the symbols without going through the intermediate sounds. They know the functional value of the sounds "*is*", "*sun*" and "*he*" and adopt that function for the written symbols for those sounds as well.

2. No doubt semanticists will object to this characterization of this behavior because the relation between the sounds and the items pointed at has not been explained. However, B. F. Skinner went to great pains to show how phonetic units are associated with objects, actions, events, etc. through operant conditioning. Novice speakers learn to associate the sound "*blanky*" with the object, and the sound "*blue*" with the color of the object. This association was called a "tact" by Skinner for reasons to be explained later. Until then, I will continue to use the word "point".

3. Languages vary dramatically in the use of such polysemous words. In Mandarin, for example, speakers have four distinct verbs to indicate "*playing*" four broad types of musical instruments: stringed instruments, wind instruments, plucked instruments, banged instruments. There is no generic form of the English word sound as in; "*playing a musical instrument*". Speakers must use distinct words for "*playing*" different types of instruments. Each group of instruments is a different frame of reference using different terms for the generic "*play*" in English. Hofstadter and Sander (2013: 12)

M.W. Dixon reports on the same lack of generic terms in other languages: "…shared (One might say, universal) concepts can—most of the time---fairly easily be translated between languages. However things can get a little tricky when two languages differ in specificity. Language A may have a general verb 'carry', to which can be added an optional specification such as 'in the hand'. In contrast, language B lacks a general verb 'carry', having instead an array of (unanalysable) specific verbs: 'carry on the head', 'carry over the shoulder', 'carry against the belly', 'carry on the hip', 'carry in the hand', and perhaps more. In order to translate into language B a sentence from language A such as 'Father carried the consignments into the house', more information is required—how did he carry it?" Dixon (2016: 147)

4. The difficulty with neatly categorizing our experience is hereby acknowledged. I might add that it is one more indication of the futility of using grammatical categories of nouns and verbs to categorize things humans perceive as objects, actions, events, kind-sortals and the state of affairs. Benjamin Whorf laid out the problem: "Let us consider a few examples. In English we divide most of our words into two classes, which have different grammatical and logical properties. Class 1 we call nouns, e.g., 'house, man'; class 2, verbs, e.g., 'hit, run.' Many words of one class can act secondarily as of the other class e.g., 'a hit, a run,' or 'to man (the boat),' but, on the primary level the division between the classes is absolute. Our language thus gives us a bipolar division of nature. But nature herself is not thus polarized. If it be said that 'strike, turn, run,' are verbs because they denote temporary short-lasting events, i.e. actions, why then is 'fist' a noun? It is also a temporary event. Why are 'lightning, spark, wave, eddy, pulsation, flame, storm, phase, cycle spasm, noise, emotion' nouns? They are temporary events. …It will be found that an "event" to us means "what our language classes

as a verb" or something analogized therefrom. And it will be found that it is not possible to define 'event, thing, object, relationship,' and so on, from nature, but that to define them always involves a circuitous return to the grammatical categories of the definer's language.

In the Hopi language, 'lightning, wave, flame, meteor, puff of smoke, pulsation' are verbs—events of necessarily brief duration cannot be anything but verbs. 'Cloud' and 'storm' are at about the lower limit of duration for nouns. Hopi you see has a classification of events (or linguistic isolates) by duration type, something strange to our modes of thought. On the other hand, in Nootka, a language of Vancouver Island, all words seem to us to be verbs, but really there are no classes 1 and 2; we have, as it were, a monistic view of nature that gives us only one class of words for all kinds of events. 'A house occurs' or 'it houses' is the way of saying 'house,' exactly like 'a flame occurs' or 'it burns.' These terms seem to us like verbs because they are inflected for duration and temporal nuances, so that the suffixes of the word for house event make it mean long-lasting home, temporary house, future house, house that used to be, what started out to be a house, and so on." Whorf (1956: 215)

5. Skinner's take on meanings: "To say that the behaviors have different "meanings" is only another way of saying that they are controlled by different variables" Skinner (1969:156)

6. "A well-known set of reinforcing contingencies is a language. For thousands of years men spoke without benefit of codified rules. Some sequences of words were effective; others were less so or not at all. The discovery of grammar was the discovery of the fairly stable properties of the contingencies maintained by a community. The discovery may have been made first in a kind of personal problem solving, but a description of the contingencies in the form of rules of grammar permitted men to speak correctly by applying rules rather than through long exposure to the contingencies. The same rules became helpful in instruction and in maintaining verbal behavior in conformity with the usages of the community." Skinner (1969: 141)

7. Because they lack the encyclopedic knowledge required for the proper construal of "open" in English, first language learners often make errors in the application of the word: "Typical are examples from a child who used open between about 16 and 21 months not only for canonical actions on doors, windows, boxes, and the like, but also for separating two Frisbees, unscrewing a plastic stake from a block, spreading the handles of nail scissors apart, taking the stem off an apple, a piece out of a jigsaw puzzle, a handle off a riding toy, and a shoe off a foot, and also for turning on an electric typewriter, a light, and a water faucet. Bowerman and Choi (2003: 113) Space Under Construction: Language-Specific Spatial Categorization in First Language Acquisition.

8. As Derek Bickerton writes: "Syntax is not serially but hierarchically arranged, with structures nesting inside other structures." Bickerton (1990: 139). The much-ballyhooed recursion in human vocal behavior is employed routinely by inserting functional units such as phrases into larger constructions. Recursion is widely evidenced in sentences such as: "*jimmy told the teacher that he heard mary say give it to me*". Functional units from individual words to complete sentences are nested within larger constructions.

9. Although he is entirely misled by the semantic fallacies, Michael Tomasello provides an account of the ontogenetic origins of triadic acts of reference: "… Six-month-old infants interact dyadically with objects, grasping and manipulating them, and they interact dyadically with other people, expressing emotions back-and-forth in a turn-taking sequence. If people are around when they are

manipulating objects, the infants mostly ignore the objects. If objects are around when they are interacting with people, they mostly ignore them. But at around 9-12 months of age a new set of behaviours, begins to emerge that are not dyadic, like these early behaviours, but triadic in the sense that they involve infants coordinating their interactions with objects and people, resulting in a referential triangle of child, adult, and the object or event to which they share attention. Most often the term 'joint attention' has been used to characterize this whole complex of social skills and interactions (see Moore and Dunham 1995). Most prototypically, it is at this age that infants for the first time begin flexibly and reliably to look where adults are looking (gaze following), to engage with them in relatively extended bouts of social interaction mediated by an object (joint engagement), to use adults as social reference points (social referencing), and to act on objects in the way adults are acting on them (imitative learning). In short, it is at this age than infants for the first time begin to 'tune in' to the attention and behaviour of adults on outside entities.

Not unrelated, at around this same age infants also begin actively to direct adult attention and behaviour to outside entities using deictic gestures such as pointing or holding up an object to show it to someone. These communicative behaviours represent infants' attempts to get adults to tune in to their attention and interest to some outside entity. Also important is the fact that among these early deictic gestures are both imperatives, attempts to get the adult to do something with respect to an object or event, and declaratives, attempts to get adults simply to share attention to some object or event." Tomasello via Christianson, Morten & , Kirby, Simon (2003: 95)

10. Taking his clues from Tarski, Russell established a hierarchy of languages: "Tarski... has shown that the words 'true' and 'false,' as applied to the sentences of a given language, always require another language, of higher order, for their adequate definition….The arguments for the necessity of a hierarchy of languages are overwhelming, and I shall henceforth assume their validity." Russell (1940: 75)

From Russell's standpoint, logical operators such as "and" and "or" are constituents of a higher order language of logic which also happens to bear truth and falsity in the form of propositions. The indelible stamp of logicians and their search for truth was applied to linguistic analysis. It generated a hypothetical hierarchy of languages.

11. Jean Aitchison writes in <u>The Seeds of Speech</u>: "The class of adjectives is a notorious swing-category in languages', it has been said. The border-line between nouns and adjectives, and between adjectives and verbs, often seem arbitrary. Some adjectives seem more like nouns, *as in a* **gold** *watch, a* **tin** *tray*, others more like verbs, as in *a* **lasting** *peace, a* **whistling** *kettle*. As one researcher notes: 'It is, of course, no accident that the lexical class 'adjective' has remained problematic, exhibiting even within the same language some 'more noun-like' properties and some 'more verb-like' ones.[I]

I. Givon 1979: 14. Aitchison (1996: 133)

Once again, the speech data should give grammarians pause about the whole enterprise of parsing language into grammatical parts-of-speech.

12. Consider these examples of affective speech, (authors unknown): *"he was indifferent" "he didnt mind" "he didnt care at all" "he didnt give a hoot" "he didnt give a darn" "he didnt give a damn" "he didnt give a tinkers damn" "he didnt give a good god damn" "he didnt give a flying fuck"*

13. B.F Skinner defended behaviorisms use of intuitions: "It has been said that 'under behaviorist

assumptions, which insisted that language was behavior, such concepts as intuition were regarded as being as unfit for scientific study as ghosts or dreams,' but behaving intuitively, in the sense of behaving as the effect of unanalyzed contingencies, is the very starting point of a behavioristic analysis. A person is said to behave intuitively when he does not use reason. Instinct is sometimes a synonym: it is said to be a mistake to 'attribute to logical design what is a result of blind instinct,' but the reference is simply to behavior shaped by unanalyzed contingencies of reinforcement." Skinner (1974: 146)

Intuitions, instincts or what many contemporary writers refer to as "common sense notions" are a result of conditioned verbal behavior. These "common sense notions", instincts or intuitions about language use are a consequence of previous verbal behavior and the contingencies of reinforcement to which that behavior was exposed.

14. The chicken and egg enigma is also realized in the ongoing debate amongst theorists about the origins of language. Nativists such as Steven Pinker believe that human thought of a rudimentary kind with limited concepts precedes the human use of words. Bickerton et al., hold the opposing position that rudimentary language preceded the human ability to think the way that we do: "Eventually, language and human cognition did coevolve. But first, the first words had to trigger the first concepts and the brain had to provide those concepts with permanent neural addresses. Only then could the creation of concepts enable the mind to roam freely over past and future, the real and the imaginary, just as we can do nowadays in our talking and writing. In other words, before typically human ways of thinking could grow, language itself had to grow." Bickerton (2009:210)

15. A proliferation of concepts plagued Bertrand Russell as well: "It is not hard to see why Russell might have found these consequences of the theory of denoting concepts implausible. To begin with, the infinite hierarchy of denoting concepts is completely *ad hoc*: apart from the exigencies of the theory of denoting concepts, there is no reason at all to accept it. The existence of such an infinite hierarchy may seem, at the least, implausible… Worse, the infinite regress which generates the hierarchy appears to be vicious." Hylton, (1990: 251)

Russell's problem derives from the same source that Carston's does: the semantic theory of language and the belief that spoken words *represent* something in a "human mind".

16. James R. Hurford, for instance: "A problem that lurks behind quarrels over the term 'representation' is that in ordinary language usage, representations are static and relatively permanent, like pictures in an art gallery (which are iconic) or letters in a printed book (which are symbolic). The formulae to be developed in Chapter 5 are intended as snapshots of partial transient states of a dynamic neural system at some point in time. The formulae above bear the same general kind of relation to neural activity in the animal's brain as the chemical formula $H2SO4$ bears to the state of some liquid in a flask at a particular time…

In the notation to be developed, the capitalized terms are more like theoretical, and so far non-explanatory, place-holders: ROCK stands for whatever goes on in an animal's brain when it recognizes, or thinks about, things roughly coextensive with what we would call a rock." Hurford (2007: 14). For Hurford, as is the case for most theorists, human speakers are simply the latest and greatest in a long line of hominids.

17. From the Wall Street Journal: "Brighton, England—There is little doubt that bridge is a mentally challenging card game known to generate fierce passions—and even end in acrimony.

But does that make it a sport? A British judge is set to rule on the question this week, a decision that English bridge aficionados hope will finally accord them the same respect given to snooker and darts, both which are recognized as sports in the U.K.

Leading the charge is Ian Payn, vice chairman of the English Bridge Union and a serial contestant on some of the U.K.'s more cerebral television quiz shows. His group has taken the U.K.'s main sports administration body to court after it refused to accept bridge as a legitimate sport. …The international Olympic committee has long recognized the card game as a sport, even if it hasn't yet admitted it to the Olympic Games…"

18. "Languages may or may not have morphology, that is, inflection or derivation. Languages may or may not use constituent structure (as in the familiar tree-diagrams) to encode fundamental grammatical relations (Austin and Bresnan 1996; Levinson 1987). Thus, they may or may not have syntactic constraints on word or phrase order. Languages may or may not make use of such basic word class distinctions as adjective, adverb, or even arguably, noun and verb (Mithun 1999, 60-67). If they do, the kind of denotation assigned to each may be alien from an English point of view. Languages force quite different sets of conceptual distinctions in almost every sentence: some languages express aspect, others don't; some have seven tenses, some have none; some force marking of visibility or honorific status of each noun phrase in a sentence, others don't; and so on and so forth. Linguists talk so often about universals that nonlinguists may be forgiven for thinking that they have a huge list of absolute universals in the bag; but in fact they have hardly any that have even been tested against all of the 5%-10% of languages for which we have good descriptions. Almost every new language that is studied falsifies some existing generalization—the serious comparative study of languages, and especially their semantic structures, is unfortunately still in its infancy." Levinson (2003: 29)

19. James R. Hurford outlines some of the scientific literature on animal recognition in The Origins of Meaning, pp.49-60. He quotes studies by Damasio (1989), Kemmerer (2006), Bickerton (1995), Barsalou (1999), et al. There is much scientific evidence that animal recognition (including humans) is correlated with neural patterns in the brain. Unfortunately, because of the dualism they inherited in their verbal behavior, these theorists often get caught up in talk about ideas, concepts, mental representations, conceptual representations and so forth. There is no need to do so. A great example would be: "Bickerton (1995) also mentions Damasio's convergence zones, in particular cross-modal ones. He discusses the idea of a *mental* 'holistic cat', unifying all the auditory, visual, olfactory, and tactile properties of cats into a single *concept*. Bickerton suggests, however, that it is only with the advent of linguistic labels that such cross-modal 'holistic' *concepts* get built: 'there are at least a few reasons for thinking that the only holistic cat is the linguistic cat—or in other words that it takes some kind of arbitrary symbol to tie together all the representations of all the attributes that make up our *idea* of 'cat" (p. 24). Bickerton is correct that the advent of public linguistic labels influences *private representations*; but unified cross-modal *concepts* do exist before language, in animals and in babies." Hurford (2007: 55)

There is no empirical evidence whatsoever for universals, abstractions, ideas, concepts, mental representations, conceptual representations, private representations etc. It is totally unscientific to discuss anything other than the neural activities in the brain. Much of what is written and said about the use of such word sounds is metaphysical speculation, nothing more.

20. It should also be noted, as did Michael Tomasello: "Classical views of categorization focus on the perceptual features of items in the world, but Nelson (1974, 1985, 1996; see also Mandler, 2000) has shown that early in development categories are formed on the basis of function. Thus, for a young

child a ball is something one can act on in certain ways and that does certain things; its function derives from the role it plays in activities and events." Tomasello (2003: 124)

As was the case with Tomasello's description of the neural connections made when the word "hammer" is used, the use of the word "ball" is based on some neural connections made because of the way the balls are used, not just their observable features.

21. For a brief sample of aspectual semantics pertaining to English verbs, I will further quote Steven Pinker: "...why can an English speaker *throw someone a box* ('cause him to have it by throwing it to him') but not *lift him the box* ('cause him to have it by lifting it to him')? Why can you *tell him the news* but not *mutter him the news*?

"Verbs of giving go both ways, logically enough: feed, give, hand, lend, loan, pay, sell serve, trade. So do verbs that indicate imparting force to and object instantaneously, sending in on a trajectory to a recipient, as in *Lafleur slapped him the puck*: bash, bat, bounce, bunt, chuck, flick, fling, flip, heave, hit, hurl, kick, lob, pass, pitch, punt, roll, shoot, shove, slam, slap, slide, sling, throw, tip, toss. But with locative alteration, physics matters. Verbs that indicate the continuous application of force to an object to keep it moving, rather than one quick fillip to send it on its way, don't like the double-object construction nearly as much. That's why it's odd to talk about lifting him the crate, and other drawn-out maneuvers: carry, drag, haul, hoist, lift, lower, lug, pull, push, schlep, tote, tow, tug...

"The distinction between events that are construed as instantaneous, like throwing, and events that are construed as protracted in time, like lugging, matters a lot in language. Linguists call this general realm of meaning---how states and events are distributed in time----'aspect' (not to be confused with the other timekeeper in language, tense)." Pinker (2007: 60)

The key point is that "physics matters". Languages reflect many *aspects* of our physical and cultural environment. However, they do not reflect all the same aspects.

22. Paradoxically, the claim that there are no non-linguistic behaviors that can be shown to be a result of the Whorfian effect is itself a result of the Whorfian effect: "Second, comparing studies conducted in different languages poses a deeper problem: there is simply no way to be certain that the stimuli and instructions are truly the same in both languages. This problem remains even if the verbal instructions are minimal. For example, even if the task is nonlinguistic, and participants are asked simply their language's equivalent of 'which one is the same?', one cannot be sure that the words used for 'same' mean the same thing in both languages. If in one language the word for 'same' is closer in meaning to 'identical,' while in the other language it is closer to 'relationally similar,' speakers of different languages may behave differently, but only because of the difference in instructions, not because of any interesting difference in thought. There is no sure way to guard against this possibility when tasks are translated into different languages. Since there is no way to know that participants tested in different languages are performing the same task, it is difficult to deem the comparisons meaningful." Boroditsky via Gentner and Goldin-Meadow --Language and Mind (2003: 67)

These researchers appear to be asserting that because cross-language verbal instructions may result in different behavior, all such studies looking for such different behavior as a result of differences in language, must be disregarded. However, if the difference in behavior is a result of the differences in the interpretation of verbal instructions, is that not evidence in favor of Whorf's principle of linguistic relativity?

23. I use the term SAE languages in this book although it was coined by Whorf and is an inexact term. I use it for lack of a better term. Indo-European is too broad and West Germanic is too narrow. I leave it to linguists to decide which languages are related to one another and which ones incorporate

the same distinctions embedded in the English language.

24. I use the term "speech-think" here although it is not detailed until Chapter Three. Language is a necessary component of our speech-thinking. No doubt we do non-linguistic thinking as well, but language expands our thinking ability. When we do much of our thinking, we are necessarily doing it with words. Speech-thinking makes us unique. However, there is no reason to interject mental entities into the analysis, e.g. naked thoughts that are translated into public language. We do our speech-thinking with public words. People who have no language skills are cognitively limited. Moreover, speech-thinking is not mental activity conducted in *the mind*; it is physical activity produced by neural connections in the brain.

25. According to Bickerton and Aitchison: "Moreover, there is considerable structural, cross-linguistic, and historical evidence that even in languages that exist today, what are claimed to be the oldest nouns among those referring to other life-forms, do so at the approximate level of the species (that is, words like dog were used earlier than words like spaniel or mammal). Bickerton (1990: 44)

It should be noted that the definitions of words are often given in terms of related words. The definition of word sound "*dog*", for instance, is given by explaining that it is a species of mammal with certain features different from other mammals and spaniels would be one type of dog." Aitchison (1992: 86)

26. Overt direct feedback utilized to shape verbal behavior is limited. However, as Terrence Deacon put it: "Children's language experiences are embedded in a rich and intricate social context, which provides them with multiple routes to pragmatic social feedback. Moreover, the language interactions that young children engage in are often simplified by the adults, and certain features are exaggerated to make them more salient." Deacon (1997: 105)

27. "Since Pinker's (1994) 'obituary,' Whorfian research has experienced a renaissance. Experimental evidence has reopened debate about the extent to which language influences nonlinguistic cognition in domains such as space (Levinson, 1996; Li & Gleitman, 2002; Majid, Bowermand, Kita, Haun, & Levinson (2004). color (Gilbert, Regier, Kay, & Ivry, 2006; Kay & Kempton, 1984; Roberson, Davies, & Davidoff, 2000; Witthoft, et al., 2003), number (Casasanto, 2005a; Gordon, 2004; Gelman & Gallistel, 2004; Miller, Major, Shu, & Zhang, 2000; Pica, Lemer, Izard, & Dehaene, 2004; Spelke & Tsivkin, 2001), and time (Boroditsky, 2001; Casasanto et al., 2004; Chen, 2007; January & Kako, 2007; Nunez & Sweester, 2006). One obstacle to resolving this controversy has been devising truly nonlinguistic tests to evaluate how speakers of different languages perceive or remember their experiences, particularly in the more abstract conceptual domains such as time.

Across languages, people use the same words to talk about time that they use to talk about space (Alverson, 1994; Clark, 1973; Gruber, 1965; Haspelmath, 1997; Jackendoff, 1983; Lakoff & Johnson, 1980; Traugott, 1978). For example. English speakers might talk about a *long* vacation or a *long* line and moving *forward* or moving a truck *forward*. Evidence from, behavioral experiments suggests that people not only talk about time using spatial language, they also think about time using mental representations of space (Boroditsky, 2000, 2001; Boroditsky & Ramscar, 2002, Casasanto, 2005b, in press; Casasanto & Boroditsky, 2003, 2008; Casasanto et al., 2004; Cohen, 1967; Gentner, 2001; Nunez & Sweester, 2006; piaget, 1927/1969: Torralbo, Santiago, & Lupianez, 2006: Tversky, Kugelmass, & Winter, 1991). Although using spatial metaphors for time may be universal (Alverson,

1994; cf. Silva, Sinha, Zinken, Sampaio, 2008), the particular mapping from space to time vary across languages. For instance, depending on the language, speakers might talk about the future as if it lies ahead of us (in English), behind us (in Aymara), or below us (in Mandarin Chinese). Behavioral studies suggest that speakers of the languages that use different spatiotemporal metaphors may indeed think about time differently (Boroditsky, 2001: Nunez & Sweester, 2006)." Daniel Casasanto, Language Learning 58: Suppl. 1, December 2008 pp. 63-79.

28. There are indications that during our "inner speech", as Lev Vigotsky called it, the propositional form may be abbreviated to pure predication because the subject of the predication is already in the speaker's crosshairs. "Our experiments convinced us that inner speech must be regarded, not as speech minus sound, but as an entirely separate speech function. Compare with external speech, inner speech appears disconnected and incomplete…

"We applied this method and found that as egocentric speech develops it shows a tendency toward an altogether specific form of abbreviation: namely, omitting the subject of a sentence and all words connected with it, while preserving the predicate. This tendency toward predication appears in all our experiments with such regularity that we must assume it to be the basic syntactic form of inner speech." Vigotsky (1962:139)

Inner speaking may often be condensed, and thus, seem to be different from and independent of the external speech behavior. Surprisingly:

"Our Indian languages show that with a suitable grammar we may have intelligent sentences that cannot be broken into subjects and predicates. Any attempted breakup is a breakup of some English translation or paraphrase of the sentence, not of the Indian sentence itself… When we come to Nootka, the sentence without subject or predicate is the only type. The term "predication" is used, but it means "sentence". Nootka has no parts of speech: the simplest utterance is a sentence, treating of some event or event-complex." Whorf (1956: 242)

29. Hilary Putnam does so in his paper entitle: "Meaning and Reference". "For the purposes of the following science-fiction examples, we shall suppose that somewhere there is a planet we shall call Twin Earth… One of the peculiarities of Twin Earth is that the liquid called "water" is not H_2O but a different liquid whose chemical formula is very long and complicated… If a space ship from Earth ever visits Twin Earth…etc." Martinich (1985: 289).

My point is simply that by utilizing different possible world scenarios, as Putnam did, theorists can concoct quite a number of uses for the written declarative statement **'Water is H_2O'**.

CHAPTER 3

DUALISM

Introduction

"It is assumed that there are two different kinds of existence or status. What exists or happens may have the status of physical existence, or it may have the status of mental existence... It is a necessary feature of what has physical existence that it is in space and time, it is a necessary feature of what has mental existence that it is in time but not in space. What has physical existence is composed of matter, or else is a function of matter; what has mental existence consists of consciousness, or else is a function of consciousness." Ryle (1949:13)

This dualism in its many forms has been a critical component of European American (EA)[1] speech and thinking for centuries. The human *body* has been variously juxtaposed with the spirit, the soul, the mind, the self, the psyche, or subtle variations of these immaterial entities which reside in human bodies yet are distinct from the bodies. They are distinct and separate components of humans which enjoy a different type of existence; mental existence. The prominence of this mind/body dualism or one of its permutations in Western thought over the past centuries is undeniable. It has been a source of controversy and puzzlement for philosophers of every generation since its inauguration. Of course other non-EA cultures have their own versions of this mind/body distinction. The distinction is pervasive and corruptive.

The mind/body distinction in the West derives from the soul/body distinction:

"The distinction between mind and matter, which has become a commonplace in philosophy and science and popular thought, has a religious origin, and began as a distinction of soul and body. The Orphic, as we saw, proclaims himself the child of the earth and of the starry heaven: from earth comes the body, from heaven the soul. It is this theory that Plato seeks to express in the language of philosophy." Russell (1945: 134)

Minds, in their modern guise, entered the world via the Greeks. However, as Bertrand Russell noted about Anaxagoras:

"He differed from his predecessors in regarding mind (nous) as a substance which enters into the composition of living things, and distinguishes them from dead matter.....Both Aristotle and the Platonic Socrates complain that Anaxagoras, after introducing mind, makes very little use of it" Russell(1945: 62)

Future generations of Christians reverted back to souls or spirits as accompaniments to the physical body:

"The dualism of the kingdom of God and the kingdoms of this world is found in the New Testament, but was systematized in Saint Augustine's *City of God*. The dualism of the spirit and the flesh is to be found in Plato, and was emphasized by the Neoplatonists; it is important in the teaching of Saint Paul; and it dominated the Christian asceticism of the fourth and fifth centuries." Russell (1945: 302)

Renaissance philosopher Rene Descartes formalized the distinction between minds and bodies for secular EA theorists with his substance dualism. He argued for the existence of minds within humans, claiming that they consisted of res cogitans (thinking substance) as opposed to the physical body which consisted of *res extensia* (extended substance or matter).

Although the Greeks had no word comparable to our English word "consciousness", in recent years, as a result of historical forces such as the rise of science, the spirits, souls and minds of yesteryear have been replaced by a more modern and less-controversial immaterial entity within human bodies, viz. *consciousness*. In contemporary philosophy of mind, it is said that consciousness is the crux of the mind/body problem. The simplistic mind/body substance dualism of Anaxagoras and Descartes has been updated to *consciousness*/body dualism in the current argot. Consciousness is juxtaposed with the physical body wherein lies consciousness according to much modern philosophy and EA folk psychology.

Consciousness is said to be the medium in which private *mental entities exist*, e.g thoughts, ideas, concepts etc., and *mental activities*, e.g. thinking, believing and knowing etc., take place. Moreover, the consciousness itself is said to be ontologically unique; it cannot be reduced to observable physical phenomena or accounted for with current physical laws. Rather than outdated spirits, souls, or minds, consciousness is now said to *exist* within the human body.

However, while consciousness is described, it is also said to contain or consist of other *mental* phenomena: the raw feel of pain, the experience of sunset red, the taste of broccoli, the sound of high C, the smell of a rose. These are all said to be personal, subjective, existentially unique, irreducible private sensations. They are elementary *sense data* or *qualia* that are insubstantial yet exist in consciousness, consist of consciousness, or are functions of consciousness:

> "Sense-data. Much of the controversy surrounding phenomenalism has to do with exactly what it is that we see, hear, and so on, in perception. You might say 'We see trees, tables and so on.' True enough; but what exactly is it that we are immediately aware of, without any element of inference? Locke and Berkeley said 'ideas,' used in a very broad sense of the word; Hume said 'impressions'; Mill said 'sensations.' But all these terms are confusing." Hospers (1988: 75)

G.E. Moore then introduced the term 'sense-data', which was subsequently adopted by Bertrand Russell and many others. They claim that without human consciousness these sense data cannot *exist*. Consciousness and its sense data are the difference makers, allowing contemporary philosophers to distinguish between humans and automatons. Humans have consciousness and its constituents. Automatons do not, nor does any other non-sentient entity or artifact.

Additionally, these elementary sense data, as constituents of consciousness along with the thoughts and thinking, are only privately accessible to the person experiencing them. Critically, they are not subject to third-party observation or measurement. Although scientists can observe the neurobiological events that are correlated with consciousness and its constituents, (neurobiological consciousness correlates or NCCs), they cannot observe the consciousness itself;

only the person in whom the consciousness exists can detect its presence by means of *introspection* it is claimed.[2] Introspection, supposedly, provides each of us with the observational evidence for qualitatively and ontologically unique consciousness and its constituents, although the consciousness is not a necessary component or concomitant of all mental activity.[3] However when English-speaking humans introspect, what they claim to observe is a personal unified consciousness that engages in the mental activity and experiences the sensations. This consciousness and its constituents have an intrinsic "qualitative, unified subjectivity" and "first-person ontology".

Curiously, as Gilbert Ryle pointed out in the above epigraph, consciousness does not exist in physical space. Consciousness and its constituents have no physical dimensions, yet they persist through time and interact with the physical body which contains them. Well, how can consciousness exist without any spatial dimension, yet have duration, i.e. temporal extension? Additionally, how does non-physical conscious mental activity produce physical activity in the body? Curious stuff this consciousness, in many ways!

Consciousness of the Self

"Socrates' point in the (*Phaedo*) may be put like this: It would be grotesque to say that his body decided to remain in prison and accept the death penalty; obviously it was *he*, Socrates, who decided and was responsible for his sitting in the jail awaiting his end. Socrates' body was simply executing the orders of Socrates, the person self-housed in or somehow connected with that body. A person or self is certainly not identical with the body in which it lives, according to Socrates, since our bodies obviously do not ponder alternatives and make decisions; on the contrary, it is we, conceived as persons or selves somehow more or other than our bodies, who weigh and pick from among the alternatives manifesting our decisions in the way we move our bodies. Traditionally, that aspect or part of a person which ponders, decides, and initiates changes in that person's body has been known as 'the self'. What we mean by a 'person' or 'human being' must therefore include more than a human body; a human body is not human until a 'self' has been added." Myers(1969: 14)

We often hear people discuss *self consciousness* in the prosaic sense of being unable to focus on the task at hand because of worry about oneself and how one appears to others. Obsessive self consciousness is said to be a psychological problem within EA folk psychology and is dealt with therapeutically. We also hear talk about *consciousness of the self*, or self awareness. Socrates, St. Augustine, Descartes and many of their philosophical progeny concluded that humans are more than just bodies. Humans have an internal agent in addition to their bodies, the self. That self ponders, decides, and initiates changes in the behavior of the body. This consciousness of the self is what we are concerned with in this section, not the so-called psychological problem of self-consciousness.

To this day, many people say they are conscious of their *selves*. These selves are the seats of consciousness and *mental* activity. They are said to exist in each human for the duration of each human's live bodily existence, and possibly beyond. These conscious selves direct the intentional behavior of each fully functional human organism. Without conscious selves, humans are not human, they would not have the mental attributes that they supposedly have. They would be mere automatons or zombies, theoretically indistinguishable from normal humans but bereft of any inner life.[4]

The history of *the self* in its various forms has deep roots in theology, philosophy, and EA folk psychology. Some of the history is rather colorful. At one point, the self was described as a homunculus (small person) within a human body who controlled that body. At that point in history, sperm were considered to be the carriers of the homunculi. That is how humans reproduced. The homunculus was passed from male to female during fertilization. Interesting questions arose. Did the homunculus have a homunculus within its tiny little body? If not, what would direct the action of the homunculus? Did the homunculus have a mind or a self, or was the homunculus a mindless mini-body? Well, that would explain a great deal of human activity. However, I digress, or I should say infinitely regress.

More plausible versions of *the self* have been proposed by Western theologians, philosophers, and psychologists throughout recorded history. The self has variously been reported to be the spirit, the soul, the mind, the ego, the psyche; all are non-physical entities enduring through time but not extended in space, yet all are located within the human body. The self, in all its EA transformations has always been a non-physical entity of some sort *existing* in human bodies and consisting of conscious thoughts, knowledge, beliefs, ideas, concepts, intentions, sense data, etc. This self that provides the container or the medium for these constituents is inside a human body but has no physical existence; it has mental existence. This conscious self, or its constituents, do not have physical attributes; they have mental attributes.

The second consistent premise in arguments for the *existence* of this non-physical self inside the body has been that each human is directly aware of his or her self by means of *introspection*. Because the self is non-physical, it cannot be observed by third parties. However, each fully functional human being has privileged access to his or her self, the self that experiences the sensations and does the thinking, the deciding and the intending. Introspection is said to be the method by which a person can detect his or her immaterial conscious self. Immanuel Kant's analysis is typical:

> "By means of outer experience I am conscious of the actuality of bodies as external appearances in space, in the same manner as by means of the inner experience I am conscious of the existence of my soul in time…" Kant (Prolegomena 1783 p.84)

The variations on this theme are many, e.g. Descartes famous dictum: "*Cogito ergo sum.*" In each case, the variations on the arguments for a self inside the human body consistently maintain that we humans are aware of our inner self and consciousness by means of "inner experience" or *introspection*. Alternatively, in the words of Colin McGinn, a third eye provides each of us with a unique internal view of our selves by means of "mindsight". McGinn (2004)

The third consistent theme in discussions about the EA self is the self as the director in control of its corporeal container. Human bodies are the receptacles wherein the self resides, if only on a temporary basis for many, and that self is the agent that controls its physical embodiment. As Socrates argued in the *Phaedo*, the self is the seat of personal responsibility and moral accountability where decisions are made regarding the body's behavior. It is the initiator of human action, the causal origin of most human behavior. The self, not the body, is the seat of free will. The self decides what to do and drives the intentional behavior of every fully functional human.

The self, as the psychological agent, is in charge of the body. It plays the executive role, performing the command and control functions when the body is conscious. When a human falls asleep or gets knocked out, however, it loses this sense of control, even though the body's autonomic nervous system still controls the basic functioning of the body. When the human body loses consciousness, the executive in charge, the self, calls it a day. However, when the consciousness comes back, the inner agent gets back to work and takes control. That resurrected self is aware of its actions and its surroundings. That self is observing things, then deciding what the next course of action will be for the body.

This command and control function of the conscious internal self provokes one of the most baffling questions in all of philosophy: how can this immaterial conscious entity, the self, interact with the material body? How does the human spirit, the soul, the mind, the ego, the psyche, or the self control the human body? For instance, my self decides to move my right leg right now and, *voila!* It moves. One can describe all the physical processes of nerve endings, electrical impulses, synapses in the brain, etc., but that does not tell me how my conscious self, that non-physical agent within my body, controls my very physical leg. What I want to know is how my thoughts and ideas and intentions, mental things residing in consciousness, get my leg to move?

How can we bridge this causal barrier between consciousness and the body? If you assume that you have a soul, a spirit, a psyche, an ego, a mind, or a conscious self, how do you explain the control that it has over your body? If physics is causally complete, i.e. all physical effects have physical causes, how can a non-physical agent be the cause of physical effects? How can you explain the interaction of two types of entities and processes existing in two different ontological realms? Something has to give.

If the self does wield such control over the body, moreover, then the physical universe is *not* causally complete and physicists will never fully account for all physical effects with physical causes. If the conscious intentional mental activity of a self has physical effects, physics cannot provide a complete explanation for all the physical phenomena physicists observe. Perhaps the forces of nature described by physicists do not really account for all physical phenomena. Perhaps spoons can be bent by thinking hard enough.

Contrarily, if selves are *unable* to control bodily activity, how can humans be responsible for their behavior? These selves, the internal agents, must have influence over their corporeal containers if humans are to be morally responsible for their actions. As Socrates made clear in the <u>Phaedo</u>, the body does not make moral decisions; the self does. Each self must decide what is right or wrong and be held accountable for the resulting action. The internal executive in charge makes decisions of its own free will. If this is not the case, we humans are no more responsible for our actions than are the mosquitoes that bite us.

Do not be beguiled by my use of words, although I have not used them in any non-traditional way within the EA folk-psychology paradigm. This is how we English- speaking humans, particularly EA philosophers, use language. If you accept mind/body or consciousness/body dualism in any form, along with the traditional semantic paradigm of language, my questions will remain unanswered. When humans use words this way we cross into the bifurcated English speaking world of physical human bodies and the non-physical entities contained in those bodies: souls, minds, conscious selves, thoughts, beliefs, ideas, concepts, intentions, qualia, and things that go bump in the night.

As it turns out, humans have the ability to infer many things because we can point with sounds. Human animals are able to point inwardly and outwardly with word sounds. The inward pointing enables humans to postulate internal, non-empirical processes and entities that have a peculiar non-physical *existence*. They endure through time but are not extended in space. They cannot be observed by third parties but have causal interactions with physical entities and processes that are observable by third parties. It would seem that we English speaking humans utilize our verbal skills to infer many mystic entities wherever and whenever we need them to make our causally connected yet ontologically divided universe minimally coherent.

Socrates, along with the Western philosophers and theologians who followed him (as well as many before them), accepted this bifurcated universe and formalized it. Methods and habits of pointing to non-physical entities and processes located inside the skin became embedded in much human linguistic behavior. We now use word sounds to point to this alternative world of non-physical entities that provide explanatory heft when we find other explanations complicated, unsatisfying, or downright hostile to our preconceived beliefs about ourselves and the world we inhabit. As a result, we English-speaking humans talk the way we do and confront endless conundrums about minds, bodies, consciousness, and the self.

A Non-semantic Proposal
for the Self

"Descartes and St. Augustine share not only the argument *Cogito ergo sum*—in Augustine *Si fallor, sum*—but also the corollary argument claiming to prove that the *mind* (Augustine) or, as Descartes puts it, *this I*, is not any kind of body. 'I could suppose I had no body.' wrote Descartes, 'but not that I was not', and inferred that 'this I' is not a body. Augustine says 'The mind knows itself to think', and 'it knows its own substance': hence 'it is certain of being that alone, which alone it is certain of being.'...In these writers there is the assumption that when one says 'I' or 'the mind', one is naming something such that the knowledge of its existence, which is knowledge of itself as thinking in the various modes, determines what it is that is known to exist." Anscome via Rosenthal (1974: 71)

The peculiar problem of the indexical "I" has plagued philosophers since antiquity. According to philosopher Elizabeth Anscombe: "Whether 'I' is a name or a demonstrative, there is the same need of a *'conception'* through which it attaches to the object." (Ibid: 76) The challenge for Anscombe and others has been to explain this *conception* of "I". After all, it is a word symbol. So, within the *semantic paradigm* the sound "*i*", as well as the printed '*I*', must express or encode something: a speaker meaning, an idea, a concept, or a mental representation; *something* within the speaker's mind or consciousness must be represented by the word sound "*i*".

Sadly, that is not the case. You cannot attach a conception, an idea, a speaker meaning, or a mental representation to the word sound "*i*" any more than you can attach such mental entities to "*here*" or "*that*". If you try you will fail. Neither is there an abstract semantic entity designated by the sounds "*i*", "*here*" or "*that*". That is because all of these word sounds are functional acoustic devices. English-speaking humans use these linguistic devices in many ways. Subsequently, what is important to the understanding of such human verbal behavior is not the hypothetical internal machinations of conceptions, ideas, speaker meanings or mental representations postulated by psychologists and philosophers, it is the previous history of the speaking organism and that speech behavior which has been reinforced.

The word sounds "*i*", "*me*", and "*my*" are often used to point inwardly to the non-corporeal entity that supposedly inhabits fully functional human bodies. Habitually saying "*i moved my leg*" or "*my body tells me that i need a rest*" or other such phrases, conditions people to infer that there is an internal agent within their bodies. In English the acoustic devices "*i*", "*me*" and "*my*" often become convenient linguistic tools for pointing, not to their body, but to the self, the volitional agent who makes decisions and determines the fate of the organism. The use of "*i*", "*me*" and "*my*" enables each organism to sense that it is more than what others observe; it

156

is an organism with a hidden internal agent who has unified personal identity and a personal history. *That psychological or spiritual entity that people infer inside their bodies results from their verbal behavior.*

Prior to the use of those word sounds there is no intuition, sense, or awareness of a self because there is no way to point to the self, the gathering point of all the sensory data, the unified conscious agent that controls the body. Humans can point a finger at their feet, at their heads, at their arms, their stomachs, but they cannot point a finger at *their selves*. They need word sounds to do that, and from the habitual use of these pointing sounds, humans develop intuitions about their selves and grand theories about the causal powers of the internal agent that controls the behavior of the body.

When English-speaking infants learn how to employ *"i"*, *"me"*, and *"my"*, their non-corporeal self comes into being. When infants learn to point with these acoustic devices, they become more than just an organism; they become an organism with a psychological agent that does the thinking, experiences the sensations and controls the body. The linguistic pointing to a singular self within the ever-changing organism and ever-changing sensory input creates the illusion of unity and continuity in a personal identity. The sense of a singular enduring self develops as the organism repeatedly refers to its *self* with *"i"*, *"me"* and *"my"*.

In fact, the only constant for an ever-changing English-speaking human organism is the repeated use of the sounds *"i"*, *"me"*, and *"my"*, which enables it to coalesce its sensations and its history into a single self. *"i"* sentences are autobiographical. That is the functional role the sound *"i"* plays. *"i"* creates the self, the first person, as the focal point of that organism's history. The autobiographical *"i"* begins its story. *"i"* is the protagonist in the life drama of each English-speaking human.

What's more, every time an English-speaking human body emits the sounds *"i"*, *"me"*, and *"my"*, the sense of self is enhanced. The intuitive feeling that that human body possesses an enduring stable internal agent is reinforced. The sense of a unified personal identity and the continuity of consciousness are "common sense" intuitive feelings resulting from the repeated use of the sounds *"i"*, *"me"*, and *"my"* by English-speaking humans, or their functional equivalents in other languages.

"self" is another sound that humans who speak English are able to use in a number of ways that may or may not reinforce consciousness/body dualism. Speakers can combine it with the sound *"my"* into what grammarians and lexicographers call a word, *"myself"*. In normal conversation, if a speaker was to say: *"i was there by myself"*, they are not reinforcing dualism with the use of *"myself"*. They could just as well have said: *"i was there alone"*. Their goal is to let the hearer know that no other person was with them. Or, in context, it could simply be restated as: *"i was not accompanied by anyone i knew"*. The present point is that there are multiple uses for the statement *"i was there by myself"* and the word sound *"myself"*.

At other times when speakers use the sounds *"my self"*, what grammarians and lexicographers call two words, the speaker is focusing the hearer's attention on *the self*, the non-corporeal entity captured inside the corporeal frame, the singular self that does the thinking and experiences the sensations. In doing so they are reinforcing dualism.

Although he is not alone in doing so, Daniel Dennett brilliantly makes an insightful point about the fiction of the single, unified self inside the human body:

"...Multiple Personality Disorder (MPD), in which a single human body seems to be shared by several selves, each, typically, with a proper name and an autobiography. The idea of MPD strikes many people as too outlandish and metaphysically bizarre to believe – a 'paranormal' phenomenon to discard along with ESP, close encounters of a third kind, and witches on broomsticks. I suspect that some of these people have made a simple arithmetic mistake: they have failed to notice that two or three or seventeen selves per body is really no more metaphysically extravagant that one self per body. One is bad enough."
Dennett (1991: 419)

As a rule, what we English speakers attribute to most humans is a complex of knowledge, beliefs, memories, imaginings, emotions, dispositions, and continuing sensations that constitute the one unified conscious self. This picture invites many philosophical questions. Is the self located in the head? The entire body? Do humans have the same self through the lifetime of the body? Why is one self more acceptable than multiple selves, or no self at all?

Although modern science has de-homunculized, de-souled, de-spirited, and de-minded humans in favor of more contemporary versions of immaterial entities, states and processes inside their bodies, the self and consciousness serve as vestigial reminders of our metaphysical heritage. Additionally, in spite of its questionable lineage, the single immaterial personal self with ideas, desires, beliefs, intentions, etc. still has explanatory power for many, though it is difficult to square with the behavioral and neurological evidence. It also produces enigmas and puzzles in profusion.

For instance, the problem of *other minds* has been a bugaboo for legions of philosophers that has been ongoing for millennia. In brief, how can people justify their claims to know that other people have minds or internal selves? I know that I have a mind supposedly because of the introspective evidence. However, other minds and their constituents are simply unknowable for me because they are undetectable by me. What I observe about other people are their bodies and their behavior, not their minds or the mental processes. Even though other people talk about their own minds and mental activity within those minds, they could be zombies. There is absolutely no direct evidence available to me that people, other than me, have minds.

Within psycholinguistics, other minds have been prominent subject matter for researchers for the past 40 years or so. Early theorists concluded that the inference of other minds inside other human bodies is a necessary accompaniment to mature verbal communication. According to this theory, competent speakers must infer psychological agents in others to facilitate effective communication. Theorists often write about the "mind reading" ability of listeners. This is part of their "social intelligence", often missing in autistic humans. The comprehension of the verbal behavior of others, it is said, requires the inference of a mind in the speaker along with all the mental states and processes, thinking, believing, knowing and wanting things.

As a consequence, much psycholinguistic research was done regarding the acquisition of a *theory of mind* by children.[6] Once again, psycholinguists are theorizing about how children acquire a theory, the theory that other people have minds just like their own, with all the thoughts, ideas, desires, beliefs, intentions, etc. These children have no direct evidence of other minds in other people, yet they, with some exceptions, ultimately presume that other humans have minds like their own. The early research confirmed that, as human children mature, they *infer* that *mental* entities, states, and processes are the causes of everyone's bodily behavior. Other people go to the fridge for milk because they *want* milk, or they *know, believe,* or *think* that milk is in the fridge. Susan Carey tells us:

> "From the earliest ages (less than age 2) children used desire and goal language mentalistically, in sentences such as; 'He likes chocolate ice cream; I like vanilla,' 'He wants to go to the zoo.' In contrast, no uses of mentalistic language expressing epistemic states emerged until age 3 or so (as in 'I thought my socks were in the drawer, but they were under the bed)'… Karen Bartsch and Henry Wellman (1995) showed that children command the linguistic structures needed to use epistemic language, and that they talk about mental states a lot, and that their input contains as much talk about epistemic mental states as desires, preferences and so on." Carey (2011: 206)

The data showed that the inference of such causal epistemic mental states in themselves and other people was strongly correlated with the development of more mature speech behavior in children.

Subsequent research to investigate the impact of child language acquisition on child theory of mind acquisition was inconclusive about the causal role of speech behavior in theory of mind development for children. Although, there were some strong indicators that language played a role. For example:

> "If language acquisition plays a central role in theory-of-mind development, then deaf children with delayed language will experience corresponding delays in their understanding and reasoning about mental states. Several studies of deaf children have reported just such effects:
> 1. Deaf children with language delay (oral or signing) show a delay of up to several years in their reasoning about the cognitive states (thoughts, beliefs, and knowledge) of others." De Villers and de Villiers in Gentner and Goldin-Meadow (2003: 344)

Nevertheless, up until that time, there were a number of competing theories to account for the empirical evidence, but the data were sparse, and the interpretations of the data could and did vary. According to de Villiers and de Villiers the question had become whether language proficiency was "prerequisite rather than a reflection of cognitive change." (Ibid: 343)

In 2003, Michael Tomasello summarized the research to that point:

> "Empirical research on the relationship between language and theory of mind has not progressed to a state where we can choose among all these different theoretical alternatives, but the research does seem to indicate fairly clearly that the acquisition of a language either facilitates or enables children's appreciation that other persons are psychological agents with their own mental lives." Tomasello (2003: 279)

To my knowledge, no research since then has produced any countervailing evidence. However, the acquisition of language does not "facilitate or enable" children's appreciation that other persons are psychological agents. The childhood acquisition of the English language *creates* other minds and their constituents out of whole cloth.

As it turns out, the verbal behavior of many speaking humans creates and sustains the ethereal minds in other humans as well as their own. The use of "I", "me" and "my" by other speakers, as well as a vast vocabulary of psychological terms that postulate mental processes and states within these speaking organisms, lead English language learners to infer that these other speakers have minds and mental activity just as they themselves supposedly do. The influence of this vocal behavior begins at birth and is pervasive.

These other minds are the intentional agents that direct the behavior of the other bodies. These other minds have the knowledge, the beliefs, the false beliefs, the desires and the intentions which cause the observed behavior of their bodies. These other minds experience the sensations. They exercise free will and decide what their bodies will do next. All of these inferences about humans and their behavior are a result of conditioned English verbal behavior and its foundations in the mind/body dichotomy. Dualist assumptions about other bodies with other minds and free will arise because the habitual verbal behavior of English speakers has incorporated those assumptions.

Unfortunately, the basic framing of the issue as "theory of mind" research couched in the usual mentalistic terms such as "beliefs", "false beliefs", "mental states" skews the data unalterably toward a dualistic interpretation of the data. Mind/body dualism is baked into the linguistic cake and accepted by researchers uncritically, including theorists who study the behavior of children for signs that they "believe other people have minds." But when researchers endow mice with false beliefs (de Villiers and de Villiers 2003) a gigantic philosophical red flag should be waved regarding interpretations of the study data.

Most humans also assume that other creatures without language skills are sentient; they have consciousness. They assume that some other creatures have some sort of awareness of themselves because they can distinguish themselves from other creatures and inanimate objects. Yet, human word use is not precise, and questions arise about whether or not animals might have the same awareness of *a self* that humans have. Do they infer inner psychological agents like we do? Do they believe that they have spirits, souls, minds, egos, psyches, or conscious selves?

The research available on our nearest relatives in the animal kingdom indicates that no such inferences can be clearly demonstrated:

> "A survey of empirical studies of imitation, self-recognition, social relationships, deception, role-taking, and perspective-taking suggests that in every case where non-human primate behavior has been interpreted as a sign of theory of mind, it could instead have occurred by chance or as a product of nonmentalistic processes such as associative learning or inferences based on nonmental categories. Arguments to the effect that, in spite of this, the theory of mind hypothesis (among non-human animals) should be accepted because it is more parsimonious than alternatives or because it is supported by the evidence, are not compelling." Heyes via Hurford (2007: 308)

This quote sums up the research to that point. Non-speaking animals make no inferences about other minds, or their own mind for that matter, because they cannot speak. My pet beagle and other animals recognize the difference between themselves and their immediate environment. However, my beagle does not infer a volitional agent in himself or others. He can say nothing about his self because he cannot point to his self; he cannot use "*i*", or "*me*", or "*my*", in pointing behavior. He cannot say: "*i moved my leg*", or "*my body tells me*". Because he lacks this ability he has no sense of self identity or personal agency. He is merely a stimulus/response reflexive organism.

Because of the mind/body dualism infused in their vocal behavior, SAE (Standard Average European) speakers have come to characterize all human behavior, both their own and that of others, with all sorts of mental adjectives: smart, cautious, considerate, benevolent and malicious and so on and so forth. The originator of the "ghost in the machine" metaphor, Gilbert Ryle, frames the issue in these terms:

> "In unconscious reliance upon this dogma theorists and laymen alike constantly construe the adjectives by which we characterize performances as ingenious, wise, methodical, careful, witty, etc. as signalizing the occurrence in someone's hidden stream of consciousness of special processes functioning as ghostly harbingers or more specifically as occult causes of the performances so characterized. They postulate an internal shadow performance to be the real carrier of the intelligence ordinarily ascribed to the overt act, and think that in this way they explain what makes the overt act a manifestation of intelligence. They have described the overt act as an effect of a mental happening..." Ryle (1949: 50)

English-speaking humans have ways of accounting for their behavior that rely on the ghost in the machine as opposed to God, demonic possession, dead ancestors, etc. If a person says that he or she behaved a certain way because he or she *knew, believed* or *thought* such and such, he or she is attributing the observable behavior to a mental entity, state or "happening" that preceded the action and *caused* the behavior. English-speaking humans have concocted an alternate ontological universe of mental entities, states and "happenings" to explain their actions. The linguistic confection of the unified ethereal self as a causal agent with epistemic states and processes such as intending, wanting, desiring, knowing, believing, thinking, wondering, expecting and so forth is a critical component in the modern verbal behavior of SAE-speaking cultures. The continued use of that verbal behavior with its mentalistic repertoire then reinforces the dualistic mind/body paradigm required for its success.

However, the view that mental entities, states and processes within all of us are causal forces is not a universal world view. There are many linguistic cultures which allow for other causes. Angeline Lillard (1998) reported:

> "Some contemporary cultures also highlight gods' or spirits' roles in human actions. For example, the Newar of Nepal see behavior as being caused by a god rather than by a persons' self (Parish, 1991, 1994), although they locate this god within one's own heart rather than externally as did the ancient Greeks. For Tibetan Buddhists, behavior is motivated, not by the mind or rational part of a person (*rigs pa*) but by the *sem* (combining mind with soul, anima, or lifeforce; (Paul, 1995). Hence, although the mind is still behind the action, it is a different sort of mind than EAs think of. The Tallensi of Africa, according to Fortes (1987), assign ultimate responsibility for the affairs of their own lives to dead ancestors who are thought to live among them. Although the Tallensi live their lives as though they were in control (Fortes, 1987, p. 202), the final credit for

161

their deeds goes to the ancestors. The Baining appear to accept it as a matter of course that on occasion, ghosts take over one's body and make one do strange things (Fajans, 1985). For the Micronesian Ifaluk as well, behavior can be caused by a spirit entering one's body and taking over (Lutz, 1985). Many more examples of such thinking exist (see Mageo & Howard, 1996, for a few). Lillard (1998) Psychological Bulletin Vol. 123, No I, 3-32

The point is, people brought up in non-SAE linguistic environments do not always view personal *mental* phenomena or states as the causes of their behavior.

Nevertheless, within the SAE-speaking world, modern psychology has developed whole catalogues of mental diseases and terminology: angst, neurosis, obsessive, compulsive, etc. That terminology has joined the common vernacular which has a superabundance of mental terms to explain human behavior: wise, intelligent, wish, strive, know, believe, hope, intend, want, fear etc. This panoply of vocabulary supports the ghost in the machine myth. In consequence, English-speaking humans have a parallel universe that their vocal behavior creates and sustains along with incorrigible intuitions about human bodies with internal non-corporeal mental phenomena with causal efficacy.

Properly viewed, the mind/body problem is not an empirical problem or a conceptual problem; it is a *verbal behavior problem*. All the talk about human mental attributes and abilities reaffirms the dualist paradigm of the conscious self/body dichotomy, the psychological agent within the body that does the thinking, believing, knowing, and intending. With word sounds humans can point to all manner of hypothetical mental states and processes within themselves and others as causal forces. They cannot determine the physical causes of behavior because of the complexity. Ergo, they accept ghostly *mental causes*.

The metaphysics of Plato, Socrates, Augustine, Descartes, et al. provided the philosophical foundation for the dualism embedded in current SAE verbal behavior. Succeeding theorists then used language as it was given to them by the previous theorists, dutifully stringing words together in ways that sustained and enhanced the myth of the ghost in the machine, the autonomous self directing the body by wanting, believing, hoping, deciding and intending to do things. Today's folk psychology, professional psychology, and semantic theory are all grounded in verbal behavior infused with the myth of the ghost in the machine. Consequently, the myth is difficult to eliminate if the debate is conducted with conventional SAE verbal behavior.

The introspective view of the self and its epistemic causal states is a fiction built of verbal gossamer. When the metaphysics, the mentalism, and the psychologism are abandoned, the inward pointing reveals nothing but sensations, somatic feedback from the organism's proprioceptive, exteroceptive, and interoceptive nerve systems. Once the dualistic verbal behavior is eliminated there is no empirical evidence whatsoever for a unified internal psychological agent with ghostly wants, desires, knowledge, hopes, true beliefs, false beliefs, intentions etc. to motivate the behavior of the organism.

Descartes doubted everything, but he never questioned his verbal behavior. He never doubted that the word sound "*i*" was a symbol that referred to a self or soul. He never entertained the possibility that the internal psychological agent in himself and others was a product of his verbal behavior. Had he done so, he would have concluded that *cogito per lacuna ergo sum*: I think with words, therefore I am. Descartes could not have imagined himself as a soul without a body unless he could use word sounds. The self and its causally efficacious epistemic states would not have been available.

As the self's progenitor and a quaint theological artifact, the soul still provides interesting fodder for philosophical analogies. Daniel Dennett (1991), for instance, compares the soul to the center of gravity. Like the center of gravity, the soul or the self is has a theoretical location. Yet it has no extension in space. If you disassemble the lunar lander you will not find the center of gravity, yet it has one. The center of gravity *causes* the lunar lander to react to gravitational forces in predictable ways. Like the center of gravity, the self *causes* the body to act, in somewhat predictable ways.

According to Dennett the self is *a concept, an idea, an abstraction*. He allows these metaphysical camels' noses into the ontological tent. Nevertheless, the basic comparison is well taken; the soul or the self are analogous to the center of gravity. They are inferred entities with causal powers. They are theoretical posits that have great explanatory utility in EA cultures. So too, much like centers of gravity, *the self* and its mental contents are useful fictions within a dualistic, yet causally connected, model of the human animal and its behavior.

However, there is an alternative to the self as the central location of each human's cognitive capacity and causal powers. From B.F. Skinner's perspective:

> "There is no place in the scientific position for a self as a true originator or initiator of action." Skinner (1974: 248)

> "The machine a man builds and instructs continues to operate when he is no longer in contact with it, but we 'give him credit' for what it does. He is responsible for its behavior. Similarly, the phylogenic and ontogenic contingencies of which the behavior of a man is a function pass into history while the man is still behaving, but we must 'give them credit' for what he does. They are responsible for his achievements. We do not look for ultimate responsibility in a machine, nor should we look for it in man. And this applies as well to the behavior of building and instructing machines. All human behavior, including the behavior of the machines which man builds to behave in his place, is ultimately to be accounted for in terms of the phylogenic contingencies of survival which have produced man as a species and ontogenic contingencies of reinforcement which have produced him as an individual." Skinner (1969: 296)

His alternative view is consistent with the other explanations within the behaviorist paradigm:

> "Verbal behavior presumably arose under contingencies involving practical social interactions, but the individual who becomes both a speaker and a listener is in possession of a repertoire of extraordinary scope and power, which he may use by himself. Parts of that repertoire are concerned with self-knowledge and self-control which, as we shall see …are social products even though they are usually misrepresented as intensely individual and private things." Skinner (1971: 117)

Skinner's attempts to eliminate the internal controlling agent were greeted with more than skepticism. They were summarily rejected because the single unified self as the originator of human behavior has been institutionalized in so many ways.

Skinner's behaviorism tried to dispossess man of his humanity, yet humans stubbornly refuse to let go of it. They cling to souls, selves, minds, consciousness and mental causation in a desperate attempt to retain their exclusive perch atop the evolutionary pyramid and their claim to immortality. They desperately want to believe that there is more to them than mere bodies. They want to make sure that they do not lose their *selves* and their free will. That fictional perspective may salve your ego, but there is no empirical evidence to support it. Without the dualistic assumptions, a careful analysis of verbal behavior will reveal that the *self* and *mental causation* are useful fictions, but fictions none the less.

In summary, the self and its causally efficacious mental states and processes came into existence, not because of any creative, emergent, or generative physical processes, rather because of *verbal behavior*. The non-corporeal self arose with the evolution of human verbal behavior. It gained stature and became respectable in the West with the metaphysics of philosophers such as Plato, Aristotle, Augustine, Descartes et al. Now, it should be in full-scale retreat as an accurate assessment of language reveals that the self has no being, neither physical nor metaphysical.

The soul, the mind or the self must be recognized for what they are, metaphysical inferences derived from using word sounds the way we SAE-speaking humans currently do. These inferences are then reinforced with some brand of dualism: substance dualism, feature dualism, parallelism, epiphenomenalism, phenomenal dualism, emergence dualism, conceptual dualism, dual aspect theory, et cetera. We then persist in speaking the way we do, reinforcing the dualism and the myth of the ghost in the machine.

It is highly unlikely that we English speakers will stop using the sound *"i"*, *"me"*, or *"my"*, because they have immense functional value. Additionally, the illusion of the internal agent with epistemic states and causal powers has immense emotional appeal and institutionalized explanatory acceptance. That being the case, the verbal behavior of many people will continue to create and sustain the mind/body model of human animals. Nevertheless, each SAE-speaking organism must realize that its verbal behavior is what produces the "common sense" intuition that there is an agent inside of its body with various mental states and mental powers.

Consciousness

"Consciousness is the umbrella term for the mental phenomena that permit the strange confection of you as observer or knower of the things observed, of you as owner of thoughts formed in your perspective, of you as potential agent on the scene. Consciousness is a part of your mental process rather than external to it. Individual perspective, individual ownership of thought and individual agency are the critical riches that core consciousness contributes to the mental process now unfolding in your organism. The essence of core consciousness is the very thought of you—the very feeling of you—as an individual being involved in the process of knowing of your own existence and of the existence of others. Never mind, for the moment, that knowing and self, which are real mental entities, will turn out to be, biologically speaking, perfectly real but quite different from what our intuitions might lead us to imagine." Damasio (1999: 127)

The word sounds "*mind*" and "*mental*" are used by philosophers, scientists, teachers and truck drivers with abandon. They are used in all manner of explanations and descriptions of human beings and their behavior. Let us not *assume* that they are symbols that have any *meanings or referents*. These sounds are used by various people in various contexts at various times in response to various stimuli.

In addition to these words, over the past few centuries, the word sound "*consciousness*" has gained currency. *Consciousness* has been paraded front and center in philosophy of mind and cognition over the past three centuries. It has become the focal point of philosophical debates regarding human bodies that are more than mere biological organisms. Throughout these debates, it has been assumed that the word sound "*consciousness*" has a meaning and a referent; that assumption is not warranted.

Nevertheless, when speakers use the word sound "*consciousness*", *they* often appear to *be referring to something*. Some have said that consciousness is what humans lose when they go to sleep, although others say that dreams are another *form* of consciousness. McGinn (1999) In spite of those disagreements most will agree that there is a present awareness of surroundings and bodily sensations that is apparent when humans are awake. That awareness disappears when they sleep, although it will reappear if they receive stimuli powerful enough to penetrate their unconsciousness. When someone is knocked unconscious or is in a coma, the consciousness is even more remote.

People have conscious moments and unconscious moments. In conscious moments they are sporadically *conscious of* things: trees, hunger, sadness, and their own consciousness. This directed consciousness has been described by some philosophers as *transient consciousness* as opposed to *state consciousness,* or *creature consciousness.* Much philosophical and scientific debate has been devoted to consciousness. It has been defined, redefined, divided and subdivided. Yet all this writing and research has failed to produce agreement on just what consciousness *is*, and how to account for it.

When comparing themselves to other species, humans tend to shrink the executive role as they move down the biological chain. With humans at the top of the evolutionary pyramid, they exert the maximum command and control autonomy. The internal agent is the decider who has free will and is responsible for the behavior of the body. Further down the evolutionary pyramid, pet beagles may have certain autonomous functions, yet most humans refuse to assign any moral responsibility to them. Beagles do not decide what is right or wrong. Nevertheless, they do decide some things. They decide to play with their owners, for instance. Or do they?

Even further down the phylogenetic scale, insects are merely stimulus-response mechanisms incapable of the executive role and consciousness. Insects do not decide; they do not have free will. Mosquitoes do not decide to bite after determining that it is the right thing to do. They just reflexively bite. It is also obvious to humans that sunflowers do not decide; they follow the sun's track across the sky, not because they want to, rather because they are reflexively responding to the solar radiation; they are not sentient, conscious creatures. That is clear. Or is it?

This expansion of the executive role as organisms move up the scale is evidenced in human linguistic behavior, yet that behavior is decidedly erratic. Do they really want to say that a dog *decides* to play with them? In one sense, yes… Then, in another sense, no. Does the dog have an executive in charge? After all, it must be conscious. It regularly decides to play with its owner. Are those conscious decisions? In one sense… then again? As a general rule, humans are more inclined to assign responsibility and agency to creatures that have consciousness that they think is similar to human consciousness. The more primitive an organism is, the less likely they are to attribute responsibility or agency to it because the consciousness must be primitive too, if it exists at all.

Nevertheless, the linguistic intuitions about the use of *"Know"*, *"decide"*, and *"intend"*, et al. created by English verbal behavior do not always yield a clear verdict about consciousness and its constituents in other creatures. In <u>Thoughtless Brutes</u> Norman Malcolm confronts the subject of consciousness in animals:

> "When readers of Descartes first come upon his theme that animals are automatons, lacking consciousness, they are astonished… The doctrine of the automatism of animals was a topic of much controversy for a century and a half after Descartes death." Malcolm via Rosenthal (1991: 454)

Descartes had theological reasons for his position. For him, the seat of human consciousness was the human soul. Having a soul was a precondition for consciousness. To admit that animals had consciousness was to admit that they had souls. To admit they had souls was to admit that they had access to God's kingdom of souls. This was heresy.

However, most 21st century EA people have trouble accepting dogs as automatons. Although animal *souls* have been discredited by most of today's thinkers, animal consciousness is an accepted fact. People routinely attribute consciousness to some animals, such as dogs, without compunction. Dogs cannot be treated like machines or beetles. That is because they are conscious creatures with sensations, feelings, and some primitive cognitive ability. Yet, attributing consciousness to a beetle raises eyebrows. To this day, the philosophical issue of consciousness in various creatures is controversial.

English-speaking people don't know quite when to ascribe consciousness and its constituents to various other organisms, or to what degree. People routinely talk about certain conscious animals knowing, deciding, and intending things. Attributing these epistemic states to dogs is said to be anthropomorphizing, by some philosophers. However, for many people, it is difficult to accept the alternative. The confusion about the role of consciousness and mental attributes in other creatures and the counterintuitive character of Descartes thesis is realized in daily SAE speech.

Descartes also wanted to separate *life* and *consciousness*, thereby freeing the conscious soul from the dead body. This separation was a theological necessity. Gareth B. Mathews explains:

> " '...But I, perceiving that the principle by which we are nourished is wholly distinct from that by means of which we think, have declared that the name soul when used for both is equivocal... I consider the mind not as part of the soul, but as the whole of that soul which thinks.'
>
> "Descartes makes clear elsewhere that he wants to give an account of something's being alive in terms of its having in it warm blood...The mind, of course, has no blood in it... and therefore is not alive. Yet the mind thinks, is conscious. Thus it does not follow from that fact that something is conscious that it is alive. Indeed, although the person made up of body and mind can presumably both be said to be alive and to be conscious. Descartes understands the person to be alive because the body is alive and conscious because the mind is conscious." Mathews via Rosenthal (1991A: 65)

For Descartes, the mind was the container in which consciousness resides. These consciousness containers were not dependent upon the live corporeal human body for their existence. Thus, these non-physical containers of consciousness could survive the loss of life by the material human body and maintain a non-earthly existence.

Unlike Descartes however, most of today's theorists will attribute consciousness to many *live* organisms. However, they will not attribute consciousness to mechanical devices: robots, cyborgs, computers, etc. Supposedly, *inanimate* physical objects do not have mental content or consciousness. *Animate* objects do, at least some of them do. Humans for sure. What about dogs? Amoeba? Coral? Polyps? Beetles? Sunflowers? Which live organisms are conscious? Which ones are *animate*? Which ones are sentient?

Again, what about beagles? Well, most people get confused about their pets. Human intuitions, based on the linguistic behavior children have learned from their caregivers, produce mixed signals. How should they use words such as *"mind"* and *"consciousness"* in regard to their dearly beloved faithful canine companions? They want to make *him* or *her* out to be more than an automaton. Maybe he or she is conscious but has no mind or soul. Does he or she think, know, and believe things or have intentions? Riddles abound. The use of the English word sounds *"he"*, *"she"*, and *"it"* confuse the issue even more by personifying *him* or *her* and de-humanizing *it*.

Nevertheless, there is no doubt that humans have consciousness. Of that they are sure. Humans relish their consciousness. Consciousness is what they hope to retain when they die. Although religions acknowledge the deterioration, death and eventual dissolution of human bodies, conscious souls and minds are granted metaphysical status which permits them to *exist* after the death of the physical body. These mysterious non-spatial entities populate the heavenly orbs and give humans a glimmer of hope that they may experience the joys of life in the afterlife. After all, what fun would the afterlife be if humans were not conscious of it? Humans must retain their consciousness at all costs.

Consciousness in its present form, containing the knowledge, beliefs, desires, ideas, concepts and intentions, still enjoys a non-physical status, and the causal connection between the physical world and the non-physical world of consciousness is uncritically accepted by most people. With the advent of psychotropic drugs, lobotomies, electroshock, even confirmed materialists routinely talk about the effects of physical processes upon mental processes and consciousness, ignoring the philosophical problem of physical/mental interaction.

Conversely, it is said that mind over matter can serve to heal the sick and overcome adversity. People believe in the power of positive thinking. The dual world ontology of conscious minds and physical matter is often bridged in ordinary conversation and practical experience. Yet the theoretical underpinning for such talk and action is still missing. Mental/physical dualism or consciousness/body dualism still poses a philosophical dilemma for theorists who have been unable to close the *causal gap* between consciousness and physical bodies. How can mental states and processes cause changes in physical states and processes, or vice versa?

Moreover, while trying to explain the causal gap, the *explanatory gap* arises. The explanatory gap arises because consciousness cannot be *explained* by physics. Science cannot explain how human brains produce the non-physical subjective conscious experiences of pains, visual sensations, thoughts, beliefs, intentions, knowledge, etc. The terminology used to describe mental experiences cannot be reduced to physical terms. Scientists can detail all the brain parts, subparts and processes down to the subatomic level, but they still cannot explain how the brain produces the inherently subjective conscious experiences of pains, visual sensations, thoughts, beliefs, intentions, knowledge, etc. from neural processes.

Neither ordinary language, nor the language of physics, can explain or describe *what it is like* to feel happiness, see redness, or taste a tomato to someone who hasn't experienced those sensations. That is because people use elemental terms such as *"bright"* and *"red"* to do their describing and explaining. They can describe the sunset as a bright-red round ball of light on the horizon by means of their verbal skills, though they cannot describe or explain the personal experience of brightness or the redness in any more basic terms. They cannot reduce these terms to anything more fundamental without shifting to third-person physical terminology, e.g. EM radiation, etc.

The adherents of this argument claim that no matter how a person *explains* their own sensations, those explanations will not allow listeners to adequately understand the sensations, as if the sensing is the understanding. In reality there is simply no way that one body can give your body that body's sensations. Words cannot do that work. However, the understanding does not lie in the sensations; it lies in the ability to produce statements about the sensations.

Of course, philosophers have remained busy trying to close these gaps in their theories. One way is to *eliminate* consciousness by using various arguments to make the claim that those conscious states and processes *do not exist*. Others claim that consciousness and mental events can be *reduced* to physical states and events. One group is trying to eliminate the causal and explanatory gaps; the other is trying to bridge them by reducing mental terminology to physical terminology. Not surprisingly, they are called *eliminativists* and *reductionists*. Most of these theorists try various analogical strategies to explain away the gaps. Some of the arguments used are quite ingenious.

Some philosophers, for example, have declared consciousness to be an *emergent* phenomenon, one that does not exist in individual neurons of the brain, but emerges when neurons combine. Much like life force or sentience, consciousness comes into being when the proper atoms, molecules, or chemicals combine. William Hasker provides a concise and lucid explanation of *emergentism*:

> "Take a mathematical equation of a certain sort, plot it onto a set of coordinates, and a fractal pattern appears—complex, unexpected, and sometimes stunningly beautiful. Dissolve some chemicals in water, let the solution stand for a while under the right conditions, and regular, highly organized crystals are formed. When the right numbers and kinds of chemical molecules are arranged in a particular complex structure, we have something new—a living cell. And given a sufficient number of the right kinds of cells, properly organized, there is the wonder of awareness, involving sensation, emotion, and rational thought. In each case, what "emerges" is something qualitatively new—a fractal pattern, a crystalline structure, life, consciousness. But if you view these phenomena in the light of emergence, you will not think of this new element as something "added from the outside"' but as arising somehow out of the original constituents of the situation." Hasker via Baker & Goetz (2011: 212)

Under this emergentist theory, consciousness emerges at some level of organization. However, it can still be *reduced*, through chemistry, to molecules and atoms. Questions are begged: If consciousness emerges from physical entities, why can't it emerge from computer bits just as it emerges from human brains? At what point in the development of human brains does it emerge? Which other brains does it emerge from? Beetle brains? Exactly what is it that is emerging and where does it fit in the ontological landscape?

Other modern philosophers have likened consciousness to a computer program. The human body is the computer, while the *mind* provides the software to run the brain and thus the body. *Mental* states and processes are merely computational states of the brain. This view was dubbed *computer functionalism* or strong artificial intelligence. Hilary Putnam explicates his version:

> "According to functionalism, the behavior of, say, a computing machine is not explained by the physics and the chemistry of the computing machine. It is explained by the machine's program. Of course, that program is realized in a particular physics and chemistry, and could, perhaps, be deduced from that physics and chemistry. But that does not make the program a physical or chemical property of the machine; it is an abstract property of the machine... Understanding why the machine, say, computes the decimal expansion of π, may require reference to the abstract of functional properties of the machine, to the machine's program and not to its physical and chemical makeup." Putnam (1975: xiii)

Putnam's functionalism admits to the possibility of a physical reduction of a program ("be deduced"). But the devil is in the details. Nevertheless, it is the most promising of such functional accounts and might ultimately lead to an explanation of human verbal behavior in terms of the physical and chemical states of the human brain which precede or accompany such speech.

Another of the contemporary adherents of computer functionalism is Steven Pinker. He proposes that beliefs, desires and knowledge, three of the so-called *propositional attitudes*, are information composed of symbolic configurations.

> "The symbols are the physical states of bits of matter, like chips in a computer or neurons in the brain. They symbolize things in the world because they are triggered by those things via our sense organs, and because of what they do once they are triggered. If bits of matter, that constitute a symbol are arranged to bump into the bits of matter constituting another symbol just the right way, the symbols corresponding to our belief can give rise to new symbols corresponding to another belief logically related to it. Eventually, bits of matter constituting a symbol bump into bits of matter connected to muscles, and behavior happens. The computational theory thus allows us to keep beliefs and desires in our explanation of behavior while planting them squarely in the physical universe. It allows meaning to cause and be caused." Pinker (1997: 25)

Here again, the supposed symbolic nature of language confuses the issue. Why not simply say that patterns of verbal behavior in humans can be encoded in organic matter, much like many other animal behaviors? Configurations of cells can react behaviorally if stimulated. In any case, the computer hardware/software (brain/mind) analogy is ubiquitous in contemporary academia.

However, simply declaring that the mind is a "system of organs", as Pinker has done, or declaring that he has placed beliefs, desires, and knowledge "squarely in the physical universe" are not supported by his arguments. Pinker's writing is emblematic of a great deal of writing by psychologists, neurosurgeons, et al. They ascribe mental entities and processes to the brain, an organ. Such meat-based mentalism is widespread in the works of eminent writers and has been roundly criticized.

In <u>Neuroscience and Philosophy</u>, a number of philosophers and eminent neuroscientists debate the attribution of psychological states and processes to the human brain, criticizing many other neuroscientists for writing that brains know things, reason, pose questions, construct hypotheses, understand, compare, decide, etc. These writers exhibit a profound philosophical indifference if not obtuseness. M.R. Bennett and P.M.S. Hacker claim that these ascriptions of *mental* processes to an organ are a "degenerate form of Cartesianism". They call it a conceptual error and have dubbed it the mereological fallacy:

> "The mereological fallacy manifests itself in different ways. It is transparent when one suggests that the birthday cake was cut by efferent nerves exiting from cervical levels 5-8 of the spinal cord." Bennett, Maxwell et al (2007: 188)

However, it is not so transparent when neuroscientists talk about one hemisphere of the brain "communicating" with the other hemisphere or the brain "deciding" matters. Bennett and Hacker conclude:

> "Neuroscientists are understandably eager to communicate the knowledge they have attained over the past decades about the functioning of the brain and to share with the educated public some of the excitement they feel about their

subject. That is evident from the flood of books written by numerous distinguished members of the profession. But by speaking about the brain's thinking and reasoning, about one hemisphere's knowing something and not informing the other, about the brain's making decisions without the person's knowing, about rotating mental images in mental space, and so forth, neuroscientists are fostering a form of mystification and cultivating a neuro-mythology that is altogether deplorable..." Bennett, Maxwell et al. (2007: 47)

"Moreover, these are not metaphorical uses. They are not bold extensions of terms, introducing new meanings for theoretical purposes. They are simply misuses of the common psychological (and semantic) vocabulary—misuses that lead to incoherence and various forms of nonsense..." Bennett, Maxwell et al. (2007: 156)

In <u>The Soul Hypothesis</u> Mark C. Baker and Stewart Goetz also complain about the disregard of the dualist dichotomy in much contemporary brain science literature:

"Habitual in this literature is the ascription of psychological predicates to biological tissue. On this account, it is the brain that (somehow) thinks, perceives, plans, feels, and otherwise lives a life more or less accidentally surrounded by the rest of the body and that fictive entity, the *person*, whose life this presumably is. Bennett and Hacker have drawn attention to all this in a closely argued treatise on the philosophical errors and misapprehensions now so common in cognitive neuroscience." Baker & Goetz (2011: 62)

Indeed, some scientists now utilize new non-psychological terminology such as "information processing" in lieu of "thinking". They refuse to use terms that are inherently psychological.

Of course, these deviant forms of speech which attribute psychological entities and processes to brains are not a result of conceptual errors. They are violations of habitual speech thinking which precludes brains from thinking and minds from bleeding. Perhaps such deviant word usage will have a salutary effect upon the dualist dogma engrained in out speech patterns, eventually eliminating the misleading verbal behavior and our "common sense" understanding about minds and their inhabitants in another "mode of existence."

Usage patterns will eventually change in any case. People now have *smart* phones, *smart* appliances, etc. They may not be *intelligent*, but they are smart. This author recently encountered a clerk at a local home improvement store who, in providing an explanation for a delay, said that the checkout computer was *thinking*. After being asked if the computer had a mind to do the thinking, she recanted. The present point is simply that speech behavior often deviates from habituated patterns that embody certain philosophical distinctions. When those conflicts are explicitly stated, speakers will reconsider their speech behavior because there are certain limits beyond which they will not go at this point in our verbal history, e.g. attributing a *mind* to a computer.

Other thinkers have declared consciousness to be an *epiphenomenon*, a form of *parallelism*. The analogy for these thinkers was the humming of the computer, which is an epiphenomenon of the hardware in operation. Likewise, mental states and processes are epiphenomenal side effects of organic processes, despite the fact these epiphenomenal mental processes *cannot interact* causally with physical phenomenon. As John Searle said: "they just go along for the ride". Humans experience physical phenomena and epiphenomena. Epiphenomena such as consciousness are simply the parallel effects of certain physical processes occurring within the organism and have no peculiar existential status or causal powers.

However, analogs of these mental epiphenomena, such as the humming of a computer or the whistle of a train, are subject to third-party observation and verification. Human consciousness as experienced by a human organism, is not. No one can directly verify consciousness in another human, NCCs yes – consciousness no. This epiphenomena explanation seems to be a ploy to put mental phenomena and consciousness outside of the materialist's matter and energy paradigm without admitting to body/consciousness dualism. Consciousness is neither matter nor energy. Nor is it the mental phenomenon these theorists claim; it is an epiphenomenon which cannot interact with the human body, although it is dependent upon the human body. Hmmm…!

Other theorists have rallied round the *supervenience* theory. This theory says the consciousness supervenes on the brain. (Philosophers love to make up new words.) That is, the phenomenon of consciousness is dependent upon the brain, or is related to the brain. Any changes in states of consciousness will be accompanied by changes in brain states because they are the same phenomena *described* differently. They are different *levels of description* for the same basic processes, much like air pressure and molecular motion are descriptions of the same process at different levels. Lower levels of brain processes produce upper-level consciousness. This theory has attracted many counter arguments which need not be detailed here.

Other philosophers, *identity* theorists, have declared consciousness to be identical to brain states. Much like the discovery that lightning was identical to an electrical discharge or water was identical to H2O, consciousness has been discovered to be identical to brain states. Various aspects of consciousness were described in terms of neural correlates of consciousness (NCCs). Other writers, however, claimed that correlates are just that. They are correlative, not identical. There is no identity relationship between neurons and consciousness. They say that the properties of brain states and consciousness are conspicuously different. Pains, itches, beliefs, intentions, hopes, and dreams have different phenomenal characteristics to neurons, axons, dendrites and synapses. These mental phenomena have irreducibly mental properties.

This led to a philosophical fraternity of *property* or *feature dualists*. These philosophers contend that consciousness is a *property* or *feature* of brains, an introspectively perceptible yet non-empirical property or feature. These properties or features are undetectable by anyone other than the person in whose brain they exist. Of course, third parties can detect the NCCs associated with the properties or features, but not the properties or features themselves. Questions arise. Is it a property or feature of all brains, or just human brains? Sleeping brains? Flat-line brains? Dead brains? Well no, *conscious* brains! Well… *live* brains to be sure.

However, as is the case with consciousness, modern biologists have difficulty defining or explaining *life*. What constitutes a living organism? Is a virus a living organism? What do living organisms have that non-living organisms do not? Is life an emerging phenomenon too? Once again, the speech intuitions of competent English speakers are not clear because the use of the word sound "*life*" is not precisely specified. The distinction between life and non-life is not clear cut. Well then, how can these theorists determine with certainty whether creature brains are alive or not and, consequently, whether they have the property or feature of consciousness?

Among the *eliminativists,* some *physicalists* may simply deny that there are any such things as

172

mental phenomena or consciousness. They contrive various arguments to exclude what are said to be mental phenomena and consciousness from their discussions. They variously claim that there is nothing over and above human "reactive states", or that there is no central location in the brain where humans can find the neural correlates associated with phenomenal experiences or consciousness. Hence, humans do not experience redness, or the taste of a ripe tomato or consciousness. These eliminativists claim that consciousness is merely an illusion.

Reductionists, on the other hand, have tried to shift the perspective to the third person, describing consciousness in observational terms. They attempt to frame the talk about consciousness and its constituents in empirically based language. Yet, these reductionist approaches to bridging the ontological divide seem to be unsatisfactory because the experience of consciousness seems to be inherently subjective. Their non-subjective empirical talk does little to satisfy the need for gap closure.

Other philosophers, such as Daniel Dennett, insist that consciousness is subject to scientific methodology. He has dubbed his methodology "heterophenomenology"[8]. He hedges that strategy by stating:

> "Heterophenomenology is the beginning of a science of consciousness, not the end. It is the organization of the data, a catalog of what must be explained, not itself an explanation." Dennett (2005: 40)

He then argues:

> "There are many properties of conscious states that can and should be subjected to further scientific investigation right now, and once we get accounts of them in place, we may well find what satisfies us as an explanation of what consciousness is. After all, this is what has happened in the case of the erstwhile mystery of what life is. Vitalism—the insistence that there is some big, mysterious extra ingredient in all living things—turns out to have been not a deep insight but a failure of imagination. Inspired by that happy success story, we can proceed with our scientific exploration of consciousness. If the day arrives when all these acknowledged debts are paid and we plainly see that something big is missing (it should stick out like a sore thumb as some point, if it is really important) those with the unshakable hunch will get to say they told us so. In the meantime, they can worry about how to fend off the diagnosis that they, like the vitalists before them, have been misled by an illusion." Dennett (2005: 178)

Indeed, people may all be misled by the illusion that they have phenomenal experience that is inherently subjective and existentially unique. So, what is the source of this illusion and why have more than three millennia of philosophers been so misled?

As a result of these stubborn age-old disagreements, another group of philosophers, *mysterians*, have proclaimed consciousness/body dualism to be an unsolvable mystery. As such, they say that philosophers must simply admit their ignorance and move on. Colin McGinn explains this theory:

> "In this book I argue that the bond between the mind and the brain is a deep mystery. Moreover, it is an ultimate mystery, a mystery that human intelligence

will never unravel. Consciousness indubitably exists, and it is connected to the brain in some intelligible way, but the nature of this connection necessarily eludes us." McGinn (1999: 05)

"The problem is not lack of evidence; it is lack of concepts, of conceptual framework. We are facing a problem that points to an enormous hole in our conceptual resources, a theoretical blindspot of epic proportions. This is why I refer to the problem as a mystery" McGinn (1999: 62)

He goes on to suggest that admitting our ignorance is never a bad thing and that it is much preferable to invoking other theories (including God) to account for the "mystery". And so it goes. The *mystery* of consciousness/body dualism is still with us, and will remain so, according to many contemporary thinkers.

These contemporary philosophers have dispensed with souls, spirits, and minds for the most part, yet *consciousness* and its constituents stubbornly refuse to go away. Philosophers, scientists and linguists *talk and write* extensively about consciousness and mental phenomena using the SAE languages that they inherited, trying to bridge or eliminate the causal gap and the explanatory gap. In the process they use part of their language to describe and explain some of their experience from the first-person perspective. That language cannot be reconciled with the language they use to describe and explain their experience from the third-person perspective of science. That reconciliation will not happen because the use of that conditioned verbal behavior *is* the problem.

English speakers have a complete arsenal of mental and intentional terminology that applies to the internal world of consciousness: "*concepts*", "*conscious*", "*consciousness*", "*intentionality*", "*phenomena*", "*sensation*", "*think*", "*mental content*", "*knowledge*", "*belief*", "*understanding*", "*attention*", "*introspection*", "*free will*", etc. What concepts do these word sounds represent? What do these terms refer to? What do these terms mean? What do these words designate? By now you should know the answer to these questions if you do not assume the semantic view of language. In fact, these word sounds represent nothing, they refer to nothing, they mean nothing and they designate nothing. They are not symbols; they are vocal devices in the repertoire of competent English speakers, and they inherit a divided behavioral history.

A Non-semantic Proposal for Consciousness

The language used in writing about mind and consciousness, even when used in an empirical setting, is laden with metaphysical freight. It is unavoidable, given the history and function of many word sounds within conditioned SAE verbal behavior. Human speech has evolved from humble beginnings in simple pointing behavior to complicated metaphysical theorizing about the *existence* of spirits, souls, minds and consciousness within the human body. For at least the last two and a half millennia, much human speech has evolved in a philosophical milieu of mind/body dualism or a variation thereof. Because of that history, dualism, in one form or other, remains firmly embedded in the verbal behavior of most humans and although dualism, as a philosophical issue, has a long history, the mind/body dichotomy, as a *linguistic* phenomenon, has only been the subject of philosophical inquiry for a century or so. It is time to reconsider such an inquiry with the semantic fallacies clearly in focus.

In 1949, Gilbert Ryle began the serious assault on the vexing mind/body problem as a linguistic issue in <u>The Concept of Mind</u>. He began by describing common beliefs about consciousness and mental activity as the "dogma of the ghost in the machine." Ryle attributed the distinction between the mental and the physical to "a category-mistake"[9]. He attempted to demonstrate that mental terms and physical terms are different logical types. Ryle did not deny that people have *mental* processes or *mental* content. His claim was that they were *logically* distinct.

Ryle provided analogies to buttress his claim:

> "A foreigner visiting Oxford or Cambridge for the first time is shown a number of colleges, libraries, playing fields, museums, scientific departments and administrative offices. He then asks 'But where is the university? I have seen where the members of the Colleges live, where the Registrar works, where the scientists experiment and the rest. But I have not yet seen the University... His mistake lay in his innocent assumption that it was correct to speak of Christ Church, the Bodleian Library, the Ashmolean Museum *and* the University, to speak, that is, as if 'the University' stood for an extra member of the class of which these other units are members. He was mistakenly allocating the University to the same category as that to which the other institutions belong."
> Ryle (1949: 16)

Regrettably, because of the semantic fallacies, he considered his effort a *conceptual analysis* of mind and consciousness. He used words, e.g. **'concepts'**, as others have used them, precluding the possibility of a materialist reduction. Brilliant though he was, he mistakenly adopted the semantic paradigm's representational characterization of human verbal behavior. He assumed that spoken words were symbols that represented concepts and "stood for" other things, "an extra member of the class, etc." You may agree with Ryle that mental terms and physical terms are different logical types, but that analysis left the mind/body rift intact. That ontological barrier was firmly ensconced in his speech and his writing.

In spite of that, he initiated a movement in the philosophy of mind toward linguistic analysis that attempted to analyze the mind/body conundrums by looking carefully at how people utilize language. Yet, the officially sanctioned concept/word semantic relationship derived from the mind/body dichotomy was never dispelled. The semantic myth of words as symbols representing mental entities was never questioned. The linguistic behavior Ryle inherited and used embodies the very dichotomy he tried to dispel.

SAE-speaking philosophers of all stripes need to confront the semantic fallacies directly by recognizing that the semantic view of words and dualism are bundled. If you buy into one, you automatically get the other. For instance, contemporary philosopher David Papineau (2002) has introduced a theory he calls *conceptual dualism* in which he claims that humans have a special set of *concepts* for thinking about conscious states and a compelling "intuition of distinctness" about conscious states. He asserts that there is a "dualist compulsion" pulling people to the conclusions they reach about an ontologically distinct consciousness and that:

> "A successful materialism must explain the compelling intuition that the mind
> is ontologically distinct from the material world. This anti-materialist intuition
> comes so naturally to us that we are unlikely to become persuaded of materialism
> simply by *arguments*." Papineau (2002: 3)

However, Papineau fails to consider that his intuitions and compulsions about ontologically distinct conscious states could be a result of his verbal behavior. In fact, there are no special concepts for thinking about conscious states; there are no concepts, period. However, there is a distinct repertoire of conditioned SAE vocal behavior used to talk about inferred mental states and processes, e.g. *"conceptual"*. In addition, the continued use of that repertoire creates the dualist compulsions.

Parenthetically, when theorists do confront any philosophical issue, they should bear in mind that many philosophers' views are informed by what one can sensibly say. When these theorists attempt to support their philosophical position by asserting that one can or cannot intelligibly say such and such, or that it makes no sense to say such and such, they are making such claims based on their conditioned normative verbal behavior, most likely English. That behavior limits their speech and thought about verbal behavior, or any other philosophical issue. People with other speaking traditions may not agree to what can sensibly or intelligibly be said or thought. The functional value of their units of speech may allow them to say and think things that English speakers are incapable of, and vice versa.

Another philosopher, John Searle, wrote <u>Rediscovery of Mind</u> (1992) in which he re-presents an argument that consciousness is not a Cartesian mental *substance*, but rather a *feature* of brains, much as liquidity is a feature of water. He reintroduces *feature dualism*:

> "I see the human brain as an organ like any other, as a biological system. Its
> special feature, as far as the mind is concerned, the feature in which it differs
> remarkably from other biological organs, is its capacity to produce and sustain
> all of the enormous variety of our conscious life. By consciousness I do not mean
> the passive subjectivity of the Cartesian tradition, but all of the forms of our
> conscious life—from the famous 'four f's' of fighting, fleeing, feeding and

fornicating to driving cars, writing books, and scratching our itches. All of the processes that we think of as especially mental—whether perception, learning, inference, decision making, problem solving, the emotions, etc.—are in one way or another crucially related to consciousness. Furthermore, all of those great features that philosophers have thought of as special to the mind are similarly dependent on consciousness: subjectivity, intentionality, rationality, free will (if there is such a thing), and mental causation." Searle (1992: 227)

While Searle rejects substance dualism and laments the vocabulary inherited from his philosophical predecessors, he maintains that the *mental features* of human experience are intrinsically different from *physical features* and that consciousness and its constituents have a different *mode of existence*. However, in spite of lamenting the terminology he is forced to use, he speaks and writes the way other SAE-speaking philosophers do, and he fails to recognize the role of his S-R-R conditioned verbal behavior in his speech about himself and his *feature* of consciousness.

Further questions regarding *feature dualism* arose: are concepts, ideas and thoughts also features of brains? Are they features in addition to the consciousness? Or are they constituents of the feature of consciousness? And why are these features only detectable through introspection? Any human can detect the feature of liquidity in water by observing it? However, only Searle can detect the feature of his brain he calls consciousness. By examining it, people other than Searle have no reason whatsoever to believe that his brain has the feature of being conscious. Humans could observe the behavior of his body and suggest that he is alive and conscious, yet this says nothing about an empirically observable feature of consciousness in his brain. (Once again NCCs yes... consciousness no.) So, when he goes to sleep, why does the feature of consciousness disappear? Questions proliferate.

In fact, no one can dispel the mind/body myth by using word sounds such as *"consciousness"*, *"mental"*, *"think"*, *"conceptual"*, *belief*, *"intentional"*, *"free will"*, *"thought"*, *and "modes of existence"* as they have traditionally been used. The use of these word sounds has evolved in a metaphysical milieu that conditions their users to speech-think with these word sounds in dualistic terms. They can only be used on one side or other of the ontological ledger. All analyses of the mind/body dichotomy using conventional English verbal behavior inherit the intrinsic dualism and semantic fallacies inherent in that behavior. They will fail on that account.

To emphasize this point consider this quote from a 1999 philosophy of mind article by Ned Block and Robert Stalnaker:

> "Recall that, for Chalmers, a concept is something like a mental word —a syntactic or quasi-syntactic object. It is not a meaning, but something that has a meaning. But of course a word (or a concept, in this sense) will 'pick out' or refer to something in a world only in virtue of its semantic properties—its meaning. So when we consider how a concept from our own world applies in other worlds, we are considering the interpreted concept—the concept with its actual meaning. On the interpretation of primary intensions that Chalmers is rejecting, the meaning used to 'pick out' an extension for the concept in a given possible world was the meaning that it had in that world. On Chalmers' intended interpretation, we 'retain' the meaning the concept has in the actual

world, asking what extension it determined in a given counterfactual possible world 'considered as actual.' But now we can see a dilemma: to get the primary intension, we carry our concept around from world to world, taking its actual meaning with it, to see what it picks out... So this answer is of no help in explaining what the primary intension of a concept is. All that is being said is that the primary intension of a concept is the function that yields, for each possible world, the value of its primary intension for that world." Block and Stalnaker via Chalmers (2002: 391)

Part of the background for this quote is an unwarranted and totally misleading distinction made by Rudolf Carnap in the mid-twentieth century. Carnap introduced new terminology whereby he tried to make a distinction between the intensional-with-an-s component of word symbols (their meanings), and their *extensional component*, i.e. what they pick out, (their referents). The *extensions* for words were the members of a set that were selected by the *intensions* of the word. The *intensions* for words were the selection criteria. For example, the *intension* of the word sound "*dog*" would be the criteria, e.g. hairy, loyal, tail-wagging, domesticated etc., that would qualify something as a dog. What the word sound "*dog*" picks out are beagles, collies, dachshunds, all those creatures out there in the world that English-speaking humans call dogs, the *extensions* of "*dog*" by his account.

Relying on the age-old semantic paradigm, Carnap mistakenly took spoken words to be symbols with meaning, (their intensions), as well as referents, (their extensions). Both the meaning and the reference were put in the word. This Carnapian distinction has led to an entirely misguided contemporary analysis that words have intensions (meanings) and those intensions (not intentions), in turn, *determine* word extensions (referents). It has also led to much confusion about intensionality-with-an-s and intentionality-with-a-t, the psychological force that provides the impetus for much human behavior within dualist explanations for that behavior.

That being said, the Block/Stalnaker quote is a morass due to their use of the English language in the way that philosophers do. If philosophers would not begin with the assumption that words are signs, symbols or semantic designators, there would be no need to hypothesize fanciful word sounds full of meanings, referents, concepts, semantic contents, intensions or extensions. Philosophers cannot do conceptual analysis of the sort Ryle, Block and Stalnaker attempt because there are no *concepts* to analyze, only word sound usage, i.e. *verbal behavior* that is part of a broad spectrum of human communicative techniques. And that *verbal behavior is the culprit*.

Word sounds have functional values that humans recognize and adopt the same way they recognize and adopt tools for various uses. Humans use these sounds and their derivative symbols to do many things. There is no need to propose "mental words", "quasi syntactic objects", "primary intensions of concepts", "intensional concepts", "logical concepts", "phenomenal concepts", or concepts of any sort, if they would not treat word sounds as symbols. If philosophers would jettison the semantics and acknowledge that language is conditioned human behavior, they will not get caught up in this sophistry about minds, meanings, intensions, intentions, concepts, mental phenomena, and consciousness. Their new analysis of dualism should begin by looking at verbal behavior, how English-speaking people use the words "*conscious*", and "*consciousness*".

The Use of the Words
"conscious" and *"consciousness"*

"Similarly wise are the Greeks from 500 B.C. onward, as well as the writers and protagonists of Genesis, the authors of the Mahabharata, and the *shi* who collected the Tao-te Ching. But none of them deal with the notion of consciousness that preoccupy us now. It is not just that the word for consciousness is not to be found in Plato or Aristotle, neither ***nous*** nor ***psyche*** being equivalents. The concept is not there either. (Psyche did refer to some aspects of an organism that I believe are critical for the appearance of what we now call consciousness (breath; blood) or that are closely related (mind, soul), but did not correspond to the same concept. The preoccupation with what we call consciousness now is recent—three and a half centuries perhaps—and has only come to the fore late in the twentieth century.

"The coinage of the words by which we denote the 'phenomena of consciousness' in the languages that carried Western thought to us also suggests that curiosity about and the understanding of these phenomena probably marched in reverse order of their complexity. In the history of the English language, for instance, the Middle English word related to consciousness is ***inwit*** a superb construction blending the notion of interior (***in***) with that of mind (***wit***). The word ***conscience*** (from the Latin ***con*** and ***scientia***, which suggests the gathering of knowledge) has been in usage since the thirteenth century, while the words consciousness and conscious only appear in the first half of the seventeenth century..." Damasio (1999: 231)

Antonio Damasio, in his marvelous account of consciousness from a neurological perspective, <u>The Feeling of What Happens</u>, gave us that brief etymology of the word sound *"consciousness"*. The Greeks had no equivalent term. Damasio explains: the origins of the *"consciousness"* can be traced back to the Christian seat of moral values and knowledge, the human *conscience*. Twists and turns of fate have transformed that seat of moral values into a container that has replaced souls and minds as the receptacle for thoughts, sensations, and other mental phenomena in the post-modern era.

Damasio of course, uses language the way he has been conditioned to use it. So, analysts must consider the dualistic semantic paradigm implicit in his writings. Let us not assume that there is a *concept* of consciousness or that the word has a literal *meaning*. The sound *"consciousness"*, and its derivative symbol **'consciousness'** have many and varied uses within the verbal behavior of English-speaking people. With this caveat concerning the semantic fallacies clearly in focus; let us elaborate on the current uses of the sound *"consciousness"*.

"*consciousness*" is a useful sound. Some of the uses of this sound by philosophers are quite disingenuous. They conflate the use of "consciousness" with the use of "*intelligence*", "*selfconsciousness*", or "*attention*". Let us attempt to sort through this thicket of linguistic behavior while remaining focused on the truly problematic use of "*consciousness*", the referring use of the word whereby SAE-speaking people point to something in their experience, the difference between humans and rocks, that which they lose when they go to sleep.

Although Damasio and others have attempted to refine the uses of words such as "*conscious*", "*aware*", and "*wakeful*", the word sounds "*conscious*" and "*aware*" can be used similarly. To be aware of something is to be conscious of it. Imagine what it would be like to be conscious of something yet not aware of it, or vice versa! The dictionary definitions of these words have a symbiotic relationship; each is defined in terms of the other. You can throw "*cognizant*" into the mix as well. English-speaking humans use it similarly. They also use "*consciousness*", "*awareness*", and "*cognizance*" similarly. (Significantly, the nominalized form of "*conscious*", viz. "*consciousness*" is no longer used in most areas of human psychology.) However the current point is that the use of these words is not clearly delineated in philosophy, science, psychology or everyday language, although some theorists have tried. They are intermixed and matched on a completely ad hoc basis.

Be that as it may, in philosophical discussions, science, psychology, and ordinary conversation, these word sounds are often used to point out a distinction that humans can make. Humans often make a distinction between conscious moments and unconscious moments; then they talk about that distinction. The distinction becomes the subject of conversation, but that does not entail the *existence* of an entity pointed to with the sound "*consciousness*" any more than talking about their happiness entails the *existence* of happiness inside of their bodies.

At times, "*consciousness*" is used to point to the sum total of a speaker's sensory input. SAE-speaking humans tend to objectify this continuing process of sensory reception and talk about it as if it was located in their heads. However, the use of this word sound has no ontological ramifications whatsoever. As with happiness, hunger, redness, and liquidity, consciousness need not *exist*. There need not *be* a chunk of something called happiness, hunger, redness, liquidity or consciousness located somewhere. Nominalizing word forms does not require speakers to objectify what they are talking about and give it a location.

Moreover, if Western philosophers insist that consciousness *exists*, why should they locate it in the human head? (historically speaking, many did not, including many Eastern philosophers.) Enigmas about the location of consciousness are many. How is it that when humans experience a pain in a knee, the pain is in the knee, but the consciousness of the pain is in not in the knee? Is the pain distinct from the consciousness of the pain, the pain being in the body and the consciousness of the pain in consciousness? Or does consciousness have "the status of mental existence" throughout the entire body? Words fail English-speaking humans when they begin to make existential claims about consciousness and try to locate it. The sounds "*where*" and "*exist*" are perfectly useful *in context* for English speakers. They should not be asked to do more than they can do.

Humans say things such as: "*my pain is in my knee my taste of ale is in my mouth my hunger is in my stomach my love is in my heart*" Words have functional values that permit them to do certain work. Philosophers often expect them to do more work than they are capable of doing. Is the sweetness in the sugar or, in your tongue, or in consciousness? Is sweetness a primary or a secondary property? Is sweetness a feature of consciousness or a phenom, a qualia, a sense datum? None of the above! When English speakers nominalize words such as *sweetness*, *happiness*, *redness*, and *consciousness*, then infer that the *referents* designated by these words must exist somewhere, they rely on age-old superstitions about minds and bodies and word symbols, with meanings and referents.

When humans are not willing, wishing, deciding, and intending in their consciousness, they somehow manage to behave. *Unconscious* forces mysteriously take over the organism. One wonders if these unconscious forces are located in human unconsciousness.[10] Where is the *unconsciousness* located?

> "The behaviorist is often asked 'What about the unconscious?' as if it presented an especially difficult problem, but the only problem is consciousness. All behavior is basically unconscious in the sense that it is shaped and maintained by contingencies which are effective even though they are not observed or otherwise analyzed." Skinner (1969: 246)

Humans also talk about *subconscious* events, things happening out of the glare of the spotlight, so to speak. *Subconsciousness*, supposedly, is beneath consciousness. It too must be filled with subconscious entities and forces and located in the head. These attempts to *locate* non-spatial entities inevitably bring about enigmas that won't go away. Today's thinkers have a tendency to use spatial analogies to mask their ignorance with distinctions about low-level properties, higher-order concepts, first-order qualities, level-one cognition, subconscious, surface grammar, deep structure, etc. Theorists love to play boxology, but that game does nothing to bridge the causal gap or the explanatory gap. The *consciousness/body* dichotomy is not a feature of brains; it is a feature of poor speech habits engendered by philosophers, EA folk psychology and the pseudoscience founded thereupon.[11] The reason many human creatures say that there is something in their body called *consciousness* is because of their word usage, not their experiences. Do not allow your conditioned verbal behavior to dictate your ontology.

The Use of the Word "*intentionality*"

> "The standard philosophical term for aboutness is intentionality, and according to Elizabeth Anscombe (1965) it 'comes by metaphor' from the Latin, ***intendere arcum in***, which means to aim a bow and arrow at (something). This image of aiming or directedness is central in most philosophical discussions of intentionality… the processes that are actually involved in keeping a mind in enough contact with the things in the world so that they can be effectively thought about: the process of attending to, keeping in touch with, tracking and trailing…. The actual business of aiming at something, 'keeping in the crosshairs,' involves making a series of adjustments and compensations over time, under 'feedback control'… Locking on to a target long enough to identify it is an achievement that calls for more than a single, momentary informational transaction." Dennett (1991: 333)

"*intentionality*" is a word sound that is frequently bandied about in philosophy of mind. Intentionality is often said to be a property of the mind, the ability of the mind to be aimed or directed. The modern use of the word was popularized by Franz Brentano who adopted it from Middle Age scholastics in the late nineteenth century:

> "The property of intentionality is described as the reference to an object, the direction toward an object. For example, when one is thinking of a number, the psychical phenomenon of thinking has the essential property of directing itself to something different than itself, an object. Thus no physical phenomenon has this property… In summary, all psychical phenomena refer intentionally to an object, while no physical phenomena have this property." Velarde-Mayol (2000: 30)

Brentano claimed that intentionality was "the mark of the mental". By Brentano's account, Human minds were aimed at or directed at things, most particularly, psychological attitudes such as, desiring, believing, knowing, suspecting, etc. which are directed at *propositions*, e.g. *believing* that "the moon is made of green cheese". Brentano was attempting "to clarify the meaning of the two terms 'physical phenomenon' and 'mental phenomenon,' removing all misunderstanding and confusion… clarify the concepts…" Chalmers (2002: Brentano: 479). Since then, "*intentionality*" is often used in this way and has become part of the philosophical and psychological jargon of the modern era.

Brentano's analysis preceded Rudolph Carnap's distinction about the *intensions* and the *extensions* of words. In any case, largely because of Brentano and Carnap, the use of **'intentionality'** with-a-t and **'intensionality'** with-an-s, is widespread in philosophy. For example, John Searle writes:

"Intentionality-with-a-t, as we have seen, is that property of the mind by which it is directed at or about or of objects and states of affairs in the world independent of itself. Intensionality-with-an-s is opposed to extensionality. It is a property of certain sentences, statements, and other linguistic entities by which they fail to meet certain tests for extensionality." Searle (2004: 122)

To confuse matters even more, at one point Daniel C. Dennet made a distinction between intentionality-with-a-t, intensionality-with-an-s, and Intentionality-with-a-capital-I.

'Intentionality'-with-a-capital-I was also a property of sentences. He claimed that declarative statements, both the utterances and their textual recordings, are *about* things; they are directed at their subjects. They have "aboutness" or Intentionality–with-a-capital-I, independently of their deployment and use by speakers and writers, according to Dennett. He also claimed that a good rule of thumb would be to substitute "aboutness" for "Intentionality" any time you see it used this way. Nevertheless, they markedly confuse matters, particularly when the distinction is not made in a philosopher's vocal behavior.

Ignoring these confusing side shows, this dissertation will be covering what many philosophers would say is the capacity of humans to have *intentions* and act on them. In Brentano's writing, psychological theory, folk psychology, and common parlance, it is said that humans exhibit *intentionality*. Humans are said to *intend* to do things. The perceived aim or directedness of human behavior is said to be a result of *intentions*, which are mental states of human consciousness. Philosophers continue to debate the nature and role of these mental states which are said to be the causes of much observable human behavior.

It must be said at the outset that humans, at times, recognize intentional action in non-human animals, plants and machines. For instance, while watching a robot at the auto factory you realize that the purpose of the machine is to tighten lug nuts. If you see your dog dutifully retrieving the stick you threw you may assume the dog has an intentional mental state that precedes the behavior. If you witness a sunflower turning toward the sun, you could infer the sunflower intends to follow the sun, much as people did five hundred years ago. People recognize why machines, animals and plants do what they do, that their actions are aimed or directed.

Dennett gives John Searle credit for making a distinction about such uses of "intentionality":

"I am encouraging readers to ignore a crack in the foundation, indeed a yawning chasm in the middle of my discussion of intentionality: the problem of *original* intentionality. John Searle (1980) coined the term, and the sharp distinction he draws between *original* and *derived* intentionality is on the face of it intuitively satisfying, and even deeply compelling. The doctrine of original intentionality is the claim that whereas some of our artifacts may have a kind of intentionality derived from us—our books and movies, our computers and signposts, for instance—we have original (or intrinsic) intentionality, utterly underived." Dennett (2013: 157)

As a matter of philosophy, clinical psychology, folk psychology and law, human behavior is partitioned into intentional and non-intentional. People are said to be intentional creatures, not just complex machines or reflexive stimulus-response organisms. In fact, attributing intentions to machines, animals, or plants is often considered anthropomorphizing, i.e. attributing human traits or qualities to non-humans. Humans are very different from machines, dogs, and plants.

They are after all, human. They are conscious *intentional* agents who control their own destiny. They have underived intentionality according to Searle et al.

In the Occident, this intentionality, as contrasted with divine control, astrology, animism of various kinds, or demonic possession, only became fully accepted as an explanation for human behavior in the 17th century Searle (2002: 127). The history of the English language provides certain insights into the creation of *the intentional stance* more than four hundred years ago. The nominalization of verbs, for instance, has produced many of these hypothetical mental states. Purposes and intentions are two such entities. The word sound "purpose", for example, was once a verb used much like English speakers currently use *"will"*: *"i purpose to walk home"* (not *"propose"*). Today's English speakers say: *"i will walk home"* or *"it is my intention to walk home"* After nominalization, *purposes* and *intentions* became mental states, like the power of *the will*.

Since then, the *intentional explanation* for human behavior has been institutionalized in philosophy, social sciences, psychology, law, and most importantly, in SAE languages. Humans are said to exhibit intentional behavior, yet *this intentionality as a mark of the mental leads* to all sorts of puzzles and questions. Don't dogs intend to do things? Do they have intentionality? Thus, the most puzzling of all philosophical questions reappears. How can these non-physical intentional states motivate human behavior? What possible force could bridge this causal gap between these mental intentions and a body's physical behavior?

Of course, this most profound puzzle about intentionality, properly framed, is how to reconcile the physical sciences with the human sciences. The physical sciences analyze nature from a non-intentional paradigm. For physicists, chemists, biologists, etc., the natural world has natural processes occurring in an orderly physical law- governed way regardless of human or godly intentions. They postulate a clockwork universe unaffected by intentionality of any sort from any source. Neither sunflowers nor humans act intentionally. The behavior of all organisms is explained within a *mechanical/functional paradigm*. Sunflowers follow the sun because of chemical reactions, etc. with no reasons, beliefs, knowledge, nor intentionality stated or implied. A mechanical/functional explanation for the behavior of all sentient creatures outside of humans is accepted as adequate.

On the other hand, economics, political science, sociology, and psychology, do not use the same non-intentional paradigm of matter, energy and forces in their explanations for human behavior, either as individuals or groups. Humans as intentional agents are at the root of every human science. The *reason clauses* in the soft sciences and psychology can only be reduced to human intentions, either collectively or individually. Humans are not mere automatons; they are rational agents with reasons for doing what they do. They reason, and then intentionally carry out their desires because of their reasons. Unlike the physical sciences, human sciences are deeply rooted in human rationality, intentionality and the causal efficacy of epistemic mental states such as knowledge, beliefs, desires, and *reasons*.

This intentionality is also a critical component in much contemporary semantic theory. The intentions of the speaker are said to be critical to the interpretation of speech by listeners. The listeners must know the speaker's *intended meaning* when they use word sounds. When there are multiple interpretations for a verbal behavior the hearers must uptake the contextual features of the discourse and the speaker's intentions to properly construe much conversation, implicatures for instance. Reading the *speaker's intentions* to properly interpret his or her speech behavior is considered a pragmatic consideration that must be taken into account when analyzing human discourse within the semantic paradigm.

This intentionality has been a standard component of philosophy, psychology, social sciences and linguistic theory for hundreds of years. Daniel Dennett defends the legitimacy of this interpretation for human behavior, that is: "… the patterns in human behavior that are describable from the intentional stance, and only from that stance." via Chalmers (2002: 562).

Dennett and many other philosophers maintain that the intentional stance is the correct *strategy* for interpreting human behavior:

> "First I will describe the strategy, which I call the intentional strategy or adopting the intentional stance. To a first approximation, the intentional strategy consists of treating the object whose behavior you want to predict as a rational agent with beliefs and desires and other mental stages exhibiting what Brentano and others call intentionality." Dennett (1987: 15)

Dennett insisted that the intentional strategy can "reliably and voluminously" predict the behavior of any "intentional system".

> "Here is how it works: first you decide to treat the object whose behavior is to be predicted as a rational agent; then you figure out what beliefs that agent ought to have, given its place in the world and its purpose. Then you figure out what desires it ought to have, on the same considerations, and finally you predict that this rational agent will act to further its goals in the light of its beliefs. A little practical reasoning from the chosen set of beliefs and desires will in many—but not all—instances yield a decision about what the agent ought to do; that is what you predict the agent will do." Dennett (1987: 17)

Dennett claimed that, as a strategy, intentionality is effective in predicting the behavior of humans, non-human animals, and even plants. Other philosophers have suggested that Dennett has done nothing more than formalize folk psychology as a legitimate "strategy" for whatever that is worth.

While acknowledging the Skinnerian S-R-R account of human behavior, many philosophers insist that the intentional stance is more than a strategy; it is a better *explanation* of that behavior. Daniel Dennett clarifies:

> "A Skinnerian behaviorist, for instance, would say that the strategy works because its imputation of beliefs and desires are shorthand, in effect, for as yet unimaginably complex descriptions of the effects of prior histories of response and reinforcement. To say that someone wants some ice cream is to say that in the past the ingestion of ice cream has been reinforced in him by the results, creating a propensity under certain background conditions (also too complex to describe) to engage in ice-cream-acquiring behavior. In the absence of detailed knowledge of those historical facts we can nevertheless make shrewd guesses on inductive grounds; these guesses are embodied in our intentional stance claims. Even if all this were true, it would tell us very little about the way such propensities were regulated by the internal machinery". via Chalmers (2002: 566)

Let us not be so hasty in dismissing the behaviorist account. Physicists cannot predict which way an American football will bounce. That does not give them license to abandon the principles of physics. So too, the fact that humans cannot yet precisely predict all of the actions of other humans with behaviorist principles, nor describe the internal operations of their bodies in fine-grained physical detail, does not warrant the abandonment of the principles of behaviorism and biomechanics in favor of the metaphysics and the psychobabble of intentionality.

Skinner succinctly sums up the behaviorist's rejection of the intentional stance as an explanation:

> "The words *intend, propose* (as a synonym for *purpose* as a verb), *expect, believe, think,* and *know* often seem to be concerned with the future. They are all used idiomatically with an infinitive or dependent clause describing action, as in *I intend to go, I propose to go,* or *I think that I shall go.* Such expressions suggest that the speaker will go, but they do not identify the past consequences which account for the probability that he will do so." Skinner (1969: 125)

The reason someone will go somewhere lies in the past behavior of the person and the reinforcement that behavior generated: the type, the strength, the frequency etc.

Of equal importance, Dennett et al. fail to realize that they are captives of their own verbal behavior. The verbal behavior they inherited and utilize still gives them the intuitions they have about humans with the knowledge, beliefs, desires and intentions that sunflowers lack. That conditioned speech behavior, infused with dualism, has a firm grip on their thinking. That speech conditioning gives them the intuitions and "common sense" understanding about the intentional capacity of humans that was not there four hundred years ago. They are caught up in a mental world of reasons, knowledge, beliefs, desires, intentions and purposes, totally non-empirical posits. They cannot bring themselves to think that humans are no more than complicated sunflowers, because their conditioned verbal behavior will not allow it.

Intentionality has become woven into the fabric of SAE-speech behavior.[12] There are thousands of terms in English that characterize human beings from the intentional stance. Various *mental or psychological* states such as intentions are said to be the reasons for the behavior of the organism. It is impossible to avoid such characterizations when using English. Pointing to inferred *intentions* as causes of behavior enables SAE speakers to fill a huge gap in the picture of a predictable, ordered and causally complete universe. When the organic machinery and the behavioral history of people are too complex to invoke the forces of bio-chemistry, physics and the stimulus-response-reinforcement (S-R-R) paradigm, modern SAE-speaking humans invoke mental or psychological *intentions* as causes of, or the reasons for their observed behavior, not the antiquated alignment of the planets, ghostly ancestors, demons, spirits, or gods.

Before Darwin, the intentional stance played the major role in Creationism. An intentional agent, God, created the universe and the creatures in it. It was not an unintentional accident. It was designed and created by the will of God. Darwin came along and provided impersonal and non-intentional explanations for the origin of species. He theorized that natural selection and sexual selection were the purely physical ratcheting mechanisms that provided for the descent with variation of all species including Homo sapiens. These non-teleological explanations are consistent with empirical evidence thus far observed and the other physical explanations in the physical sciences, including attempts to explain the origin of the universe in non-intentional terms, e.g. The Big Bang Theory.[13]

On the other hand, explanations for human behavior within the soft sciences and psychology currently rely on totally underived intentions (Searle), those internal mental causes that motivate humans but not machines, animals, or plants. However, these explanations *are not consistent* with natural selection, which relies on empirically observable states and processes, not hypothetical and unobservable internal *mental* states and processes. Yet, these intentional explanations in the soft sciences and psychology are consistent with English verbal behavior and the common-sense intuitions it produces. Because of that fact, they are currently accepted as plausible.

Still, the intentional stance gives humans the same unreliable predictions about their behavior that the alignment of the planets, ghostly ancestors, demons, spirits, or gods gave them prior to the advent of intentional explanations. That is because they are all ill-founded. Without assuming all the metaphysical accoutrements required by intentionality and the intentional stance, human beings are controlled by amazingly complex internal physical processes and a history of interactions with the environment. The fact that intentional explanations are much more economical and widely used is not sufficient grounds for accepting them as adequate explanations. And the theoretical background required to justify these intentional explanations is brimming with paradoxes.

On the other hand, J.B. Watson and B.F. Skinner, provided the framework for non-teleological, non-intentional explanations for all animal behavior, including human verbal behavior. Their non-teleological explanation is consistent with Darwin's theory of descent with modification and the empirical evidence thus far discovered.[14] It relies on stimulus-response-reinforcement (S-R-R), molecular biology and ultimately physics to explain the behavior of all organisms. It is an historical explanation, as is evolution, in which the entire history of an organism's reinforcement and punishment explain future behavior. It should not be abandoned in favor of metaphysical speculation about contemporaneous mental or psychological states and processes as the causes of human behavior.[15]

In spite of that, you say you have *intentional experience*, the experience of voluntary action. It is a "common sense" intuition about your behavior. You *feel* that you are in control. You make up your mind. You initiate volitional action. You exercise your free will when you engage in intentional behavior. If you speak English you speech-think this way because you have been conditioned to speech-think this way. Thus all the talk about you controlling your destiny, deciding, intending and so on, produces the "common sense" intuitions that *you* are in charge. Your vocal behavior misleads you.

If you speak English, you have used thousands of word sounds grounded in the intentional stance. Your *feelings, senses,* and *intuitions* about your intentional experience are a result of your speech about your *self* and its causal powers. Your feelings, senses, and intuitions about self control allow you to point inwardly with the sound "*intentions*" and attribute your behavior to these ethereal entities within you. Your feelings, senses, and intuitions, generated by your speech behavior, mask an organism controlled by the same interactions that control a beagle, a sunflower, a thermostat, and evolution, i.e. purely physical interactions.

Because humans are able to perform linguistic referring acts, they are able to *infer*. Some vocal behavior enables humans to point to unobservable entities and forces as the causes of their behavior. Because they *infer* these mysterious entities and forces within themselves, and talk about them, they develop feelings, intuitions, and "common sense" beliefs about these entities and forces. They *feel* that they have an internal self with knowledge, beliefs, intentions, and purposes. They have *intuitions* that they are in charge. Their *common-sense* tells them that they are masters of their destiny. They have free will. However, if humans were to alter their verbal behavior and eliminate the use of personal pronouns, personal possessives, mental and intentional terminology, those senses, intuitions and common-sense beliefs about their intentionality, would fade away.

Intentional Acts

"Communicative displays are prototypically physical characteristics that in some way affect the behavior of others, such as large horns which deter competitors or bright colors which attract mates. Functionally we may also group with displays reflexive behaviors that are invariably evoked by particular stimuli or emotional states and over which the individual has no voluntary control. Such inflexible physical and behavioral displays, created and controlled by evolutionary processes, characterize the vast majority of communication in the biological world. In sharp contrast are communicative signals that are chosen and produced by individual organisms flexibly and strategically for particular social goals, adjusted in various ways for particular circumstances. These signals are intentional in the sense that the individual controls their use flexibly toward the goal of influencing others. Intentional signals are extremely rare in the biological world, perhaps confined to primates or even great apes." Tomasello (2008: 14)

Spoken words can be used to do many things. Speakers can use them to pray, command, commend, exhort, inspire, affirm, deny, describe, explain, plead, mock, console, refer, cajole, exclaim, sing, query, joke, insult, et cetera. However, neither the-spoken words nor the written words *do* anything by themselves; *words do not behave*. Humans behave with them. *Words say nothing*. They are communal devices that humans learn to *use* by mimicking someone else in their linguistic community. Utilizing these devices, by most accounts, requires an *intentional* agent. Experts claim that the vast majority of human communication is *intentional*, controlled by individuals and used "flexibly toward the goal of influencing others".

When humans use acoustic devices, they are often said to be using them intentionally. When humans perform various speech acts, they are said to have a purpose. Their vocal behavior is said to consist of goal-oriented, volitional acts. It is said that speakers are willfully *trying* to use their language skills to influence the behavior of listeners, by imparting information to them, requesting information from them, coaxing behavior from them, et cetera. Most theorists say that human speech is purpose-driven intentional behavior. Philosophers, psychologists, teachers, truck drivers, and linguists speak about human speech from the intentional stance, e.g. people *trying* to use their verbal skills to produce *desired* outcomes.[16]

Within philosophy of language there is extensive literature on joint communicative *intentions*, conversational implicatures, and conversational maxims. John Searle, H.P. Grice and Michael Tomasello are leading theorists who have provided cases where they claim that parties to a conversation must recognize the communicative intentions of a speaker. *Meaning*, it is said, cannot be carried by the words alone. In addition to being a semantic phenomenon, meaning is claimed to be a pragmatic phenomenon. Language theorists claim that when hearers only determine the lexical meaning and ignore a speaker's intentions, the result is ambiguity or simply misunderstanding.

For instance, note the ambiguity in the use of this sentence by a speaker: *"visiting relatives can be boring"*. Does the speaker *intend* to make the claim that relatives visiting him are boring or that him visiting the relatives is boring? It is said that reading the communicative intentions of speakers is critical to the correct comprehension of this speech act. Sometimes, speaker intentions are clearly recognized. At other times they are vague or completely opaque. When they are not clear, ambiguity and bafflement creep in; so it is claimed.

Consider the speech act: *"i will be forced to respond"*. Would you construe that as advice, a threat, a promise, a warning? That speech act can be used in many circumstances, but the context and the incident of use, may not give a clear indication how the speaker is using the utterance. Listeners must determine what the speaker *intended* to say, not just what the words supposedly said. Listeners must determine what the speaker meant to say. Correct uptake of speaker *intentions* is said to be the determining factor in how listeners correctly interpret this speech act. Volitions, purposes, and intentions are part and parcel of theories about human discourse.

In conversation, listeners are often forced to inquire about the speaker's intentions, *"what do you mean"*. They are not asking about the dictionary meanings of the word sounds. They are asking about the speaker's intentions. How is he or she using the word sounds in this incident of use? What is he or she trying to accomplish? Where is he or she going with this speech act? The speaker must then paraphrase the original speech act or explain it to make their intention more transparent because listeners have been unable to read their communicative intentions; so *say* the experts.

Listeners often recognize what someone is trying to say, even if they have not said it correctly. They recognize an inappropriate word or phrase use and find it humorous. Such malapropisms are a quite common. This body recently heard someone say: *"it juggled my memory"*. A common explanation would be: He intended to say: *"it jogged my memory"*. This malapropos phenomenon is familiar. It can be described in many ways, yet listeners sometimes know what a speaker is getting at no matter how what they say is stated or mis-stated. Listeners know what was meant in spite of any error. They somehow read the speaker's intentions; the experts tell us.

Speech behavior without intentions appears to be pointless. No credence is put in the utterances of a parrot because the parrot has no intentions. It is not using the acoustic devices for any purpose. People recognize that it is not trying to accomplish anything with the sounds that are emitted from its beak. *"parrot"* has now entered the popular lexicon as a verb because of that. People now can say that someone is parroting someone else if the speaker is just mouthing words. That person is not employing the words in an intentional meaningful way.

According to many theorists including Michael Tomasello in the preceding epigraph, recognizing speaker intentions and theory of mind are often claimed to be a baseline assumption in human communication that is lacking in non-human communication. It is a requirement for becoming a competent speaker that is not apparent in most non-human animals. Non-human animals fail to recognize speaker intentions or minds in attempts by humans to communicate with them. Consequently, according to these theorists, animal-to-human speech communication is a pipe dream:

> "... both Michael Tomasello, an expert on primate social cognition, and Paul Bloom, a psychologist whose principal interest is how human children learn words, have contrasted chimpanzee's apparent ineptness in understanding the goals and intentions of others with the human children's relative facility for such things... Bloom wrote, 'The failure to appreciate the representational intentions of other people... is so extreme (in chimpanzees) that it entirely precludes word learning.'" Marcus (2004: 137)

Even if researchers determine that some non-human primate vocalizations are employed flexibly and strategically, indicating intentionality-with-a-small-i-and-three-ts, it is suggested that their communicative intentions are different from ours. Listeners would have to view their vocal behavior from their intentional perspective, not the human intentional perspective. Wild chimpanzees, for example, have three dozen vocalizations used flexibly and strategically. Calvin (1996: 66) Researchers could attribute *intentionality* to the chimps just as they do for human primates. Presumably, these unobservable chimp intentions would be different than human intentions.

In any case, all of these characterizations of human communication behavior, other than those made by strict behaviorists, are made using an intentional strategy. Humans are said to have intentions when they carry out most of their behavior, including speech. It is reasoned, rational, volitional behavior motivated by intentions or purpose. English speakers routinely make a distinction between intentional behavior and unintentional behavior such as accidents or coerced behavior. In fact, *they make a distinction that is not warranted*.

Please consider an alternative view of intentions. B.F. Skinner has described intentionality thusly:

> "A person acts intentionally, as we have seen, not in the sense that he possesses an intention which he then carries out, but in the sense that his behavior has been strengthened by consequences." Skinner (1971: 103)

> "What a person 'intends to do' depends upon what he has done in the past and what has then happened. A person does not act because he 'feels angry'; he acts and feels angry for a common reason, not specified." Skinner (1971: 68)

Skinner claimed that human verbal behavior could be explained within the stimulus-response-reinforcement paradigm of behaviorism. People could infer whatever they wanted about psychological states and forces within the human organism. The only data available are the history of the organism, the stimuli, the response of the organism, and the reinforcement or lack thereof, and that is enough to explain the behavior, any behavior.

To have an intention, or purpose, need not be framed within the usual dualistic psychological paradigm. Intentions can be framed as predilections to act in a certain way based on genetic inheritance, a history of previous S-R-R conditioning, and the stimuli to which an organism is exposed. All the future behavior of an organism, including verbal behavior, is shaped by the previously reinforced behavior. The behavior evolves over the history of an organism. Skinner explicates:

> "The primate hand evolved *in order that* things might be successfully manipulated, but its purpose is to be found not in a prior design but rather in

the process of selection. Similarly, in operant conditioning the purpose of a skilled movement of the hand is to be found in the consequences which follow it. A pianist neither acquires nor executes the behavior of playing a scale smoothly because of a prior intention of doing so. Smoothly played scales are reinforcing for many reasons, and they select skilled movements. In neither the evolution of the human hand nor in the acquired use of the hand is any prior intention or purpose at issue." Skinner (1971: 195)

Like Darwin's non-teleological explanation for the origin of species, Skinner provided a non-teleological, impersonal, non-intentional explanation for human verbal behavior which is consistent with observable data and physical science's picture of a causally closed universe.

Speaking is no different than playing the piano. Intentions and purposes as mental forces that motivate human speech behavior or piano playing are another moribund fiction of philosophers, psychologists, linguists, teachers, and truck drivers. Humans are not different in kind from other creatures. Humans are more complex, but are S-R-R creatures nonetheless. Their complex behaviors, and explanations for those behaviors, often obscure the fact that all of their behaviors are a result of genetics, a history of operant conditioning, and occurrent stimuli. If theorists jettison the mentalistic language habits, all human behavior can be analyzed using the same methods used in analyzing other animal behavior.

Another way of looking at the matter is summed up by B. F. Skinner:

"...expressions involving goals and purposes are abbreviations. Very often we attribute purpose to behavior as another way of describing its biological adaptability...In both operant conditioning and the evolutionary selection of behavioral characteristics, consequences alter future probability. Reflexes and other innate patterns of behavior evolve because they increase the chances of survival of the *species*. Operants grow strong because they are followed by important consequences in the life of the individual." Skinner (1953: 90)

Charles Darwin eliminated the anthropomorphized divine intentionality from the history of the universe and the descent of man. Natural selection and sexual selection became the impersonal non-intentional, non-teleological ratcheting mechanisms by which species survived and prospered or became extinct. Those same selection mechanisms are at work in the life-or-death struggle of each individual human animal and his or her progeny. Language skills provide a huge advantage to the humans who master them and pass them on to their offspring. Verbal behavior helps promote the survival of each individual and the species.

To be sure, natural selection does produce favorable outcomes for organisms which are better suited to their environmental niche as a result of their genetic inheritance, long-necked giraffes for instance. Natural selection also favors individual organisms because of their *behavior*. That behavior may be inborn (the running ability of a wildebeest) or it may be conditioned by their caregivers through reinforcement, as is the case with the hunting by lions and human verbal behavior. In the case of human organisms, modern verbal behavior provides a monumental behavioral advantage in the survival rates of individuals' and the species as a whole.

Explaining human behavior from the intentional stance is no better than Creationism as an explanation for the origin of the universe, the species therein and their behavior. However, that does not mean that speakers must immediately abandon the use of mental terms such as *"mind"*, *"intention"*, *"purpose"*, etc. as strategic implements. They are useful fictions. They are simplistic and marginally effective ways of describing and controlling human behavior, much easier than describing the complex interactions that have transpired throughout the history of each human organism and combine with occurrent stimuli to produce the responsive behavior of the organism.

However, theorists *must* "keep in mind" that this mentalistic talk is totally unsupported by any empirical evidence and leads us to incorrect conclusions about the forces that cause human behavior. When word sounds such as *"mind"*, *"intention"*, and *"purpose"* are used to explain human behavior, including speech, they lead us down the garden path of mind/body dualism and all of its philosophical absurdities. On the other hand, although it is extremely complex, the case for the behaviorist's account of human behavior which eliminates the "doctrine of ideas" along with minds, concepts, intentions, purposes, wants, wishes, and reasons is consistent with natural selection, sexual selection, and a causally closed physical universe. That being the case, it is the explanation most likely to succeed in the final analysis.

Mark C Baker and Stewart Goetz will have the last word in this section:

> "Darwin demystified and despiritualized biology, by showing that biological species are created by the same forces of descent with variation and natural selection that had been familiar to breeders of domestic animals for years. What then remains for more recent generations to demystify and despiritualized? One obvious answer is the (human) mind. If explanatory categories like spirit/soul, purpose, and agency can be expunged even from this domain—if one can remove crucially mental concepts ever from our understanding of the mind— that would be the final frontier for this image of a reductionist naturalized science." Baker & Goetz (2011: 248)

The Use of the Word *"point"*

You, no doubt, have noticed the author's prominent use of the symbols **'point'** and **'pointing'** in this book. They represent the word sounds *"point"* and *"pointing"*. The use of both of these sounds and their derivative symbols within conventional English speech and writing assumes that an internal agent does the pointing, the agent that controls the bodily behavior. The intentional stance, as a part of folk psychology and its derivative conditioned speech behavior generates this presupposition about our human pointing activity. Pointing, within the paradigmatic mind/body intentional stance, is bodily activity directed by the ghost in the machine.

So, because of the English language the author has been conditioned to use, the author has often written as if humans are intentional creatures that utilize word sounds as implements to do their pointing. However, *humans do not originate behavior of any kind. Stimuli do.* Human organisms, based on their genetic inheritance and their previous conditioning, *respond to* both internal physiological states and external stimuli. From a behaviorist's perspective, human pointing and referring behavior are controlled by stimuli and the *contingencies of reinforcement.*[17] Any *intentional* explanations, regardless of their effectiveness as a *strategy*, are simply mistaken.

Often, the stimuli that govern human behavior are not apparent, so humans mask their ignorance of these stimuli with the intentional stance and mystical mental motivators controlled by the inferred agent. Since most of them are not willing to accept demonic possession, divine intervention or animal spirits as causes for human behavior, mysterious non-physical *intentions* within the body are regarded as reasonable explanations. These *intentions*, these inferred mental causes are utilitarian. Without them theorists could not produce acceptable explanations for the behavior of humans in today's intellectual climate.

However, the origin of the pointing behavior of human organisms is genetic. It is a response to stimuli. That *procedural* behavior is passed on by the genes. It is then reinforced under certain circumstances by responses from other humans when it appears early on in childhood. The reinforcement of gestural pointing behavior ultimately leads to pointing-with-sound behavior in most humans. The pointing-with-sound referring acts witnessed in human verbal behavior are conditioned *responses*. Human organisms do not *intend* to point. They respond to stimuli and a history of reinforcement when they point with sounds.

The *intentionality* posited in most analysis of speech behavior is not there. Humans are conditioned to respond to certain speech acts with other speech acts. The difference between statements, commands, promises, requests, questions, and so on are not the unobservable intentions of the speaker that are "read" by listeners; these speech acts are functionally distinct because of their circumstantial orientation and the reinforcement of previous such speech acts. The circumstances of each act provide numerous clues about what speech act will produce the results previously reinforced, not the results that are *intended, desired or wanted*. The intentions, desires, wants and other such mystical causes of human speech behavior are nowhere to be found, much less "read" by listeners.

Moreover, *speaker meaning* is an intentional term. Understanding speaker meaning is not a matter of recognizing speaker intentions; it is a matter of producing the conditioned response the speaker has previously received as reinforcement for his or her verbal behavior based on context and the conditioning of the responder. The speaker is then reinforced by the consequences of his or her action. For example, the responder notices the rabbit's leg and comments on it. That confirms the speaker's reference which was a product of the speaker's previous conditioning and rabbit leg stimulus. The speaker attended to the leg of the rabbit and performed a referring act, bringing the rabbit's leg to the hearer's attention. The verbal give-and-take *about* the rabbit's leg is complimentary reinforcement that helps track the subject of conversation. Theorists need not insert mysterious *speaker meanings* into the analysis.

In fact, they need not use "*reference*" or "*pointing*" to describe this verbal behavior. Both of these terms are among the 10,000 such terms in English assuming the intentional stance, inferring an intentional agent who controls the reference or the pointing. To avoid such implications, B. F. Skinner invented the term "tact". While it would be unwieldy to attempt a synopsis of Skinner's <u>Verbal Behavior</u>, a few salient points about "tacts" are critical to understanding the non-semantic analysis of language he offered:

> "In all verbal behavior under stimulus control there are three important events to be taken into account: a stimulus, a response, and a reinforcement... (S-R-R. Remember, the interrelationship among these events are the contingencies of reinforcement. My comment)

> "There are two important types of controlling stimuli which are usually non-verbal. One of these already mentioned: an audience characteristically controls a large group of responses ... The other is nothing less than the whole of the physical environment—the world of things and events which a speaker is said to 'talk about.' Verbal behavior under the control of such stimuli is so important that it is often dealt with exclusively in the study of language and in theories of meaning.

> "The three-term contingency in this type of operant is exemplified when, in the presence of a doll, a child frequently achieves some sort of generalized reinforcement by saying *doll*... There is no suitable term for this type of operant. 'Sign', 'symbol', and more technical terms from logic and semantics commit us to special schemes of reference and stress the verbal response itself rather than the controlling relationship. The invented term 'tact' will be used here. The term carries the mnemonic suggestion of behavior which 'makes contact with' the physical world. A tact may be defined as a verbal operant in which a response of a given form is evoked (or at least strengthened) by a particular object or event or property of an object or event. We account for the strength by showing that in the presence of the object or event a response of that form is characteristically reinforced in a given verbal community.

> "...The only useful functional relation is expressed in the statement that the presence of a given stimulus raises the probability of occurrence of a given form of response. This is also the essence of a tact." Skinner (1957: 81)

At a very early stage in each human organism's linguistic odyssey, that organism is conditioned to verbally respond to environmental stimuli, such as a doll with the utterance *"doll"*, in an English-speaking culture. The connection between the stimulus and the utterance need not be characterized as *reference or pointing*. The utterance is simply a conditioned response to a stimulus which is incorporated into the child's verbal behavior. It is speech behavior in response to a stimulus which is reinforced in many ways by the speaker's speech community. It is one of the first things a child learns. He or she can connect to the world by means of tacts. There is no need to couch the connection in *intentional* terms such as *"reference"* or *"pointing"*. What's more, all other human speech behavior can be couched in such non-intentional terms.

Of course, some humans have learned to tact with putative immaterial states they claim to observe within their bodies. English speakers do so with a plethora of *psychological* terms: love, hate, fear, belief, knowledge, ideas, concepts, reasons, and thoughts in minds and consciousness. Thousands of terms are used to tact with various inferred mental or emotional entities, states and processes. Consequently, the way many humans talk about the experiences from the perspective of the inferred "ghost" looking inward is strikingly different than the way they *talk* about the experiences from perspective of an outside agent where they cannot observe any of the alleged internal entities, states and processes. The third-person perspective only observes the body and its behavior. Thus, first-person reports do not agree with the third-person reports because the contextually specific *use* of language from either ontological perspective excludes the use of the other.

Although much theory in many fields presumes that human beings have intentions, the analysis of B.F. Skinner was spot on. There is no need to frame the vocal tacting behavior of humans in intentional terms. Initially, human organisms respond to salient stimuli by tacting with their fingers. Later, those same stimuli provoke tacting-with-sounds, i.e verbal behavior in properly conditioned organisms. Still later, many stimuli from inside and outside the organism generate more complex verbal behavior.[18] However, at no time is there an immaterial internal agent in control, directing the tacting or the more complex verbal behavior. Verbal behavior is not controlled by the inferred agent with *intentions*; rather it is controlled by the complex hidden results of prior S-R-R conditioning and the occurring stimuli.

Human Tacting

As a consequence of their perceptual apparatus, many creatures have the ability to zoom in on salient features of their idiosyncratic global scene. Hawks, for instance, have the ability to focus on a rabbit's size, the rabbit's color or the rabbit's leg if that feature grabs their attention. By virtue of their genetic inheritance and operant conditioning, creatures focus on the features that are necessary for their survival and respond to them in a manner that enhances their chances for survival. However, most non-human creatures cannot direct the attention of other creatures to these features because they cannot tact with sounds. They cannot tact with the size, the color or the leg of the rabbit. They cannot bring those features of the global scene to another animal's attention. They can only respond to the features they notice as a result of their own alertness or a generalized alarm signal.

More to the point here, these creatures are not missing mythical abstractions, ideas, concepts or meanings in consciousness; most creatures are simply missing the ability to tact with sounds. Many of them can make the distinctions between black and white, running and sitting, cats and dogs. They can make many of the same kind-sortals that humans do. Some have even been conditioned to tact with them. "A grey parrot has learned… a 70-word vocabulary that includes thirty object names, seven colors, five shape adjectives, and a variety of other 'words' – and can make requests with some of them." Calvin (1996: 67) What most non-human animals are lacking is the skill that humans learn at approximately 12 months of age, vocal tacting with kind-sortals they have been taught to notice. Without this vocal tacting ability, humans would be reduced to dog status. They could only tact with onechubbywhitesittingrabbit by means of a finger.

Like other creatures, the human perceptual system presents the world to them in a certain way, a way that promotes their survival as a species. There is a century's worth of unequivocal data now proving that what humans *see* cannot be constructed from the raw data received through the optical system. The brain fills in many parts of a panoramic scene from a limited amount of input. The flux of sensory experience received by human sense receptors is modulated by the brain, which then presents the augmented experience for kind-sortal categorization.

As maturing human infants begin to notice faces, objects, actions, features etc., they begin the kind-sortal process and eventually tact with these kind-sortals. Moreover, the most recent research unsurprisingly reveals that this kind-sortal process is influenced by the languages people are brought up in. For example, some Japanese and Pirahã speakers make no distinction between blue and green; both colors (in English) are categorized as the same color and tacted with by means of the same color word. In neither language are speakers mandated to make a distinction between green and blue, although they are quite capable of doing so. They just say and think the equivalent of: *"that shirt is grue"* for either a blue or a green shirt to an EA's way of thinking.[19]

Russian speakers, on the other hand, are obligated by their language to make a distinction between light blue (*"goluboy"*) and dark blue (*"siniy"*). A Russian speaker *cannot say or think* the Russian equivalent of: *"my favorite color is blue"*. That would be like an English speaker

197

saying: *"my favorite color is blue and green"*. This is not to say that their perceptions or sensations differ; their vocal tacting behavior and their thought processes are different. Much of the most recent research indicates the color spectrum is continuous, though color categories are discrete, and the discretization appears to be largely a function of language.

So too, there are multiple languages, e.g. Tzetal in Mexico, in which speakers cannot say *"take the next right turn"*. Bloom and Keil (2001: 357). They simply do not make the body-centric left/right distinction. As a result, not only can these speakers not say it, they cannot think it. Spatial distinctions, whenever they are stated or thought about, are framed in compass directions: north, south, east and west. Their spatial cognitive abilities are not up to the task of thinking *"take the next right turn"*.

Furthermore, such language-specific directional thinking has direct consequences on other forms of thinking and behavior, even in people utilizing closely related languages:

> "… In one study, four toy animals were placed on a table in a random order—such as, in left-to-right order (and North to South order): cow, pig, horse, sheep. Subjects were asked to remember the array, were rotated 180 degrees to face another table, and were asked to recreate the array 'exactly as it was'. Dutch speakers tended to preserve relative order; they would put on the table, in left-to-right order: cow, pig, horse, sheep. The Tenjapans tended to do the opposite, putting the animals on the table in left-to-right order, sheep, horse, pig, cow, violating relative order but preserving absolute location." Bloom & Keil (2001: 357)

Since these groundbreaking studies, there have been many others (Boroditsky, 2001; Nunez & Sweetser, 2006; Casasanto & Boroditsky, 2003, 2008) that demonstrate a connection between cognitive linguistic behavior and cognitive non-linguistic behavior. These studies consistently indicate that different frames of reference and spatiotemporal metaphors in various languages produce different thinking about time and space. There is no longer any doubt that the use of any language has effects in non-linguistic cognitive domains. The question now is: *How much* language affects non-linguistic thinking and behavior?

In summary, the fundamental human act of tacting by means of word sounds is a skill humans learn early on. It begins a linguistic odyssey that enables humans to distinguish themselves and prosper as a species. However, the species-specific receptor organs limit the use of that skill. In addition, the language they are brought up in constrains their verbal tacting and thus, their thinking. Nevertheless, after they learn the basic tacting skill they set out on a life-long journey, tacting by means of various acoustic devices. Without these devices humans would be reduced to dreaming and barking at the moon.

The Use of the Word Sounds
"phenomena" and *"sensations"*

"Physical objects, according to phenomenalists, are inferences from sense-data. This assertion goes contrary to the way we ordinarily speak…"

"For the phenomenalist, sense data constitute the very *foundation of empirical knowledge*. From sense-data we get to physical objects; without sense-data this would be impossible. The structure of our knowledge of the world has sense-data as its ground floor, or foundation." Hospers, (1988: 76)

The etymology of *"phenomena"* provides more revealing insights into the philosophical debates regarding mind/body dualism, consciousness and epistemology. The Greek source of the English word is *"phenomai"*, to *appear*. The use of the sound *"phenomena"* and the symbol **'phenomena'** within English literature and philosophical writing dates to the early Middle Ages. The use of *"phenomena"* within philosophy and science is often related to *appearances* or perceptions produced by the human visual system. Its use has expanded to include just about any sensation given to human bodies by their receptor organs or somatic feedback systems. These days, in philosophical literature, tastes, noises, smells, pains, itches, tactual sensations, feelings of joy or fear, inner speech, imaginings and memories are now included under the umbrella term *"mental phenomena"*.

Historically, meta-physicians in the form of religious authorities, developed elaborate theological systems to provide for an afterlife in an alternative universe where human souls could live their eternal lives in a blissful disembodied *existence*. This *non-physical* world was populated with varying assortments of gods, angels, harps, royal servants, animals etc. where these disembodied souls would enjoy a different "mode of existence". In the West this theological dualism was secularized by the substance dualism of Descartes, which in turn, was supplanted by the *phenomenal dualism* for many 20th century philosophers.

In addition to the ordinary physical phenomena which can be observed by third parties and which can have physical dimensions, phenomenal dualism asserts that there are a plethora of *mental phenomena*: thoughts, ideas, concepts, dreams, imaginings, raw feels, quale, qualia, sense data and so forth; *non-physical* phenomena *existing* inside human bodies and only detectable by the body experiencing them. Although these mental phenomena are extended in time; they are not extended in space. Consequently, they are granted a separate ontological status or "mode of existence", from physical objects and events, the argument being that they would not *exist* if there were no creatures to witness them. However, they do not exist in the same sense that stars, trees, cups etc. exist, i.e. extended in time *and space*.

Much of this philosophical thinking about *mental phenomena* hinges on the appearances vs.

reality contrast. This traditional contradistinction was introduced by the pre-Socratic philosopher Democritus and was memorialized by Plato in The Republic. Plato created the allegory of the cave for a number of arguments which need not concern us here. In it he relates a story about prisoners chained to a wall with their heads immobilized, only able to see shadows on the wall in front of them. As such, they never see reality; they only see the shadowy effects of the reality behind them. For them, reality consists of the shadows or appearances on the wall in front of them. So too, many philosophers argue that humans are not seeing reality with their normal senses; they only see *appearances*. Reality is filtered and distorted by our rose-colored perception, so to speak.

Plato insisted that the appearances, although they merely represent reality, *exist*. According to Bertrand Russell:

> "I come now to existence, on which Plato lays great stress, We have, he says, as regards sound and colour, a thought which includes both at once, namely that they exist. Existence belongs to everything, and is among the things that the mind apprehends by itself; without reaching existence, it is impossible to reach truth." Russell (1945: 154)

Indeed, the *existence* of appearances or phenomena in the minds of men has been a continuing theme in the corpus of Western philosophy for 2500 years. Philosophers of all stripes have conjured up spirits, souls, minds, consciousness and its habitués and given them *an existence* that endures through time but is not extended in space.

Long after Plato, analytic philosopher John Locke (1632-1704) distinguished between primary and secondary qualities such as colors, sounds and smells provided by human sensory apparatus. He stated that these secondary qualities *exist in the perceiver*, because without the sensory apparatus that most creatures enjoy, there would be no colors, sounds, or smells; they would not exist. Locke objectified these sense impressions and located them within the human mind. He originated the building-block approach to philosophical analysis of perception. It is an atomistic reduction of perception to the smallest components of that perception, today's sense data, "phenom", or "sense impressions"...

Locke's position is usually called "representative realism". He claimed that "our knowledge of the physical world comes via sense-impressions, and it is only these sense-impressions of which we have direct knowledge." Hospers (1988: 63). These sense-impressions may represent reality. Then again, they may not represent anything in the so-called physical world. Contemporary philosopher John Hospers concludes:

> "Doesn't it seem as if the representative theory of perception, starting with commonsense beliefs shared by almost everyone, leads us into an utter skepticism about the existence of nature, of a physical world?" Hospers (1988: 63)

Fifty years after Locke British Philosopher Bishop George Berkeley (1685-1753) argued just that: "that we do not perceive material things, but only colours, sounds etc., and that these are 'mental' or 'in the mind'." Russell (1945: 651) Berkeley brought about a century of *Idealism*. The central claim of this brand of philosophy was that humans could indubitably know only our own *ideas*. It was an epistemological position which held that not only was knowledge of the external world not possible: the very existence of an external world could be denied. The appearances given to us by our senses are all we have and all we can indubitably know.

According to Hospers:

> "Berkeley attempted to solve the problem [of the reliability of perception] by getting rid of the world-out-there, No such world exists, he said, and we could have no knowledge of if it did; all we have knowledge of is our sense-impressions. Berkeley, like Locke, called these "ideas"; hence the term for his theory is "idealism"—taken not from the word "ideal" but from "idea." And so we are easily led to Berkeley's main conclusion: *All that exists is minds and their ideas, not merely all we can know, but all that exists.*" Hospers (1988: 164)

Just after Berkeley's death, Immanuel Kant published his <u>Critique of Pure Reason</u> in which he institutionalized the use of "phenomena". He contrasted phenomena with "noumena" or "things-in-themselves" which could not be apprehended. The phenomena were given to people by means of perception, but the "noumena" were imperceptible to us. Much like sub-atomic particles, the ultimate constituents of physical objects are beyond our ken. Humans simply cannot know what reality is like. They can only know various *appearances* of reality according to this analysis.

This theme of juxtaposing appearances with reality continued unabated into the twentieth century as philosophers of all types developed *theories of perception*. The exceptionally influential philosopher Bertrand Russell grabbed the "mental phenomena" baton in the early twentieth century and ran with it. <u>In the Problems of Philosophy</u> (1912) he tried to justify our "knowledge of the external world". He began by grounding such knowledge in "knowledge by acquaintance", or direct perception:

> "… for him acquaintance is the only fundamental epistemological relation. All knowledge, if it is to be worthy of the name, must be based upon direct and unmediated contact between the mind and the object which is known… ultimately always knowledge of an object, rather than propositional in character…" Hylton (1990: 364)

For Russell, the objects of perception were "sense data" (from Moore). They were the basis of all knowledge of the external world and they were not true or false, as are propositions about them. Theories of perception such as Russell's were juxtaposed with Naïve Realism or Direct Realism which claimed that the *physical objects* are sensed directly, not the *appearances* of physical objects which could be broken down into "sense data". Realists claimed that physical objects were not *inferred* from the sense data as the idealists claimed; they were directly observed.

Later, Positivists accepted the sense data canard or similar theories of perception to complete their epistemology and ground it in the senses. They needed all the theoretical terms of the sciences reducible to observational terms, e.g. "red" and "round". Since then, analytic philosophers have routinely accepted similar analyses of perception and gone on to create a complete menagerie of sense impressions, sense data, quale, qualia, phenom etc. that play out in the theater of the mind or consciousness. According to these reductionists, these items "inhabit our conscious experience". They *exist* in consciousness. This theme of an external physical world juxtaposed with an internal mental world of conscious experience that enjoys a separate status of existence is still a prominent component of modern philosophical analysis.[20]

Contemporary philosopher Daniel Dennett's catalog of "phenom" is in abbreviated form. Others could add to his inventory, yet his initial analysis is representative of much contemporary philosophical discussion about distinctive mental phenomena *existing* in consciousness. He refers to:

> "… items – the fauna and flora, you might say – that inhabit our conscious experience: thoughts, smells, itches, pains, imagined purple cows, hunches and all the rest… Our phenom is divided into three parts: (1) experiences of the 'external' world, such as sights, sounds, smells… (2) experiences of the purely 'internal' world, such as fantasy images… daydreaming, talking to yourself, recollections, bright ideas…(3) experiences of emotion or 'affect'… ranging from bodily pains, tickles, and 'sensations' of hunger and thirst, through intermediate emotional storms of anger, joy, hatred…" Dennett (1991: 44)

The phenomenal raw feels: the sights, sounds, smells, pains, tickles etc. provided by the sense organs, are then the subject of philosophical debate. Inevitably, when discussing philosophical issues concerning consciousness, these *mental* phenomena or "phenom" surface.

Modern philosophers have fallen for this *representational theory of perception* hook, line and sinker. They assert that humans do not *directly* perceive *external* objects; they perceive *representations* of objects, i.e. internal *mental* images. These internal images *represent* the external objects which normally cause them. The images can then be decomposed into more elemental data: phenom, qualia or sense data such as the color red. Western philosophers have produced many arcane and incomprehensible theories based on this representational theory of perception.

This phenomenal atomism is driven by the same reductionist forces that produced logical atomism and linguistic atomism. What humans perceive is broken down into the smallest features of perception, such as the color red, that can be tacted with by means of words. These features are then claimed to be items in their phenomenal inventory. So say many philosophers, including (no surprise here) phenomenalists who claim that human experiences can be reduced to these mental phenomena which are all we can indubitably know. Philosophers have sliced and diced the sensations produced by human nervous systems based on their verbal tacting ability (the redness, the taste and the smell of the tomato). They then draw the conclusion that these features of the objects they perceive *exist* in their consciousness in the form of *mental phenomena*.

Much of the credibility of this reductionism within philosophy of perception is a result of modern physics. Science has demonstrated that electromagnetic waves of a certain magnitude strike an object, say an apple, and reflect to the receptors in human eyes which, in turn, convert the light waves into another electromagnetic phenomenon which is interpreted by the brain as the experience of the color red. But it is suggested the color red is not in the apple or in the light waves or in sense organs or in the brain; the redness, the taste and the smell are mental phenomena *existing in human consciousness*. Thus, any *physical* explanation cannot account for the human experience of seeing red. As a result, the phenomenal atomism account of perception seems plausible.

The traditional *philosophical* arguments for appearance vs. reality are many. Russell, for example, asserted that the perceptual image of a coin is only circular when people view it from directly overhead. The color of the coin also changes with perspective and lighting conditions. Thus, they never see the *real* coin; what they see are different appearances of the coin, different shapes and colors. The real coin is beyond their ken. What they *directly perceive* are the mental phenomena in their consciousness and those phenomena could not *exist* without the perceiver.

Other arguments from illusion are numerous, the infamous bent stick for example. When a straight stick is partially submerged in water, it appears to be bent. In reality it is straight. Consequently, the perceiver does not perceive the actual stick; they perceive phenom, qualia or sense data produced by the stick and the water in their visual field. Not to belabor the point, but hallucinations of desert oases, dreams, imaginings etc. all produce these mental phenomena or phenomena that exist in consciousness without any corresponding physical objects. So, what humans directly perceive are sense impressions, sense data, phenom, qualia etc., the minimal constituents of perception that *exist* in the mind or consciousness, not coins and sticks and desert oases.

This explanation, to be sure, must be made within a dualist paradigm: the external world of physical entities and processes contrasted with the internal world of mind-dwelling entities and processes. By means of dualistic language, philosophers have drawn this picture of an external world of physical objects *existing* in physical space and an internal world of phenomenal objects *existing* outside of physical space. Lately however, because *the mind* is not chic, in most contemporary theories the physical ontological realm is contrasted with *consciousness*. The qualia, along with other mental entities, "inhabit our conscious experience".

There are a number of recent arguments for phenomena in consciousness enjoying the status of mental existence. Most are variations of *the absent qualia argument*. They are discussed in Chapter VI as *epistemic arguments* where philosophers argue that people do not "*know* what it's like" to be a bat, or that certain people may not "*know* what it's like" to see red. These same arguments are viewed as *ontological* arguments by many who conclude that these qualia (a red spot) which are absent in the consciousness of blind people, come into existence when they first appear in these same people.

One of the most famous and ingenious arguments originated by philosopher Frank Jackson is entitled "What Mary didn't know". In this tale Mary, a world-renowned neurologist who knows everything there is to know about the human brain, has never been outside of a black, white and gray room. She has never experienced color perception. Once released from the room, it is claimed that she learns "what it is like to see red". As an epistemic argument, Mary finally "*knows* what it is like" to see red. As an ontological argument, Mary finally realizes "what red *is*". She realizes that the color red *exists*. This tale supposedly lends credence to the view that mental phenomena in consciousness are unique in character and *exist* in consciousness, thereby justifying consciousness/body dualism.

However, the ontological interpretation fails for many of the same reasons the epistemic interpretation fails. First, now that Mary has experienced color perception, she can no doubt dream in color as well. She can have dreams of vivid red sunsets while she is an unconscious state, i.e. sleeping. While having these dreams, where are the red sense data? Do these sense data enjoy yet another separate "mode of existence" in her unconsciousness? How many modes of existence are there? Mary also has many sensations derived from her digestive and intestinal tract. Do they *exist* in her consciousness? You can be the judge of that.

It can also be supposed that Mary has led a deprived childhood. Mary was depressed and unhappy for her entire childhood and adolescence. She had never experienced happiness. Then Mary met Tom. Mary fell head over heels in love with Tom. Mary experienced happiness for the first time in her life. Mary finally knew what it was like to be happy. Mary's love for Tom made her happy during every waking moment. So where is Mary's happiness? By parallel argument it should be concluded that Mary's happiness *exists* in her consciousness. So too for Mary's loneliness, her pigheadedness, etc. Is there any limit to what *exists* in Mary's consciousness, unconsciousness or subconsciousness?

By means of arguments which rely on the normal verbal instincts and rational ability of competent speakers, philosophers have made sense data, qualia, phenom etc. respectable theoretical posits. However there are a great many objections to this picture theory of perception and its supposed incorrigibility. Most of this atomistic reduction of perception is a totally misguided analysis based on equivocation, ambiguity and imprecision in the use of the word sounds *"see"*, *"perceive"*, *"know"* et al. Behaviorists such as B.F. Skinner have proposed alternative explanations for consciousness inhabiting sense data.[21]

Radical behaviorist William M. Baum discusses seeing at length. Like Skinner, he argues:

> "The relationship between seeing and the thing seen becomes clearer still when we examine instances of what Skinner called 'seeing without a thing seen.' If I dream of a wolf, is a wolf present? If I imagine my childhood home, is my home there? Probably one reason copy theory exists is to try to explain such instances. Supposedly if I am seeing, something must be there to see; since there is neither a wolf nor a house, a copy must be held up somehow to my vision (not my eyes!). Copy theory used this way is a form of mentalism; the apparent explanation is no explanation at all. Where is the ghostly mental copy, what is it made of, and how can it be seen? Whereas before we had an action of seeing to explain, now we have the same action plus a mysterious copy with a mysterious relationship to the action." Baum (2005: 53)

Philosophical talk about mental copies and their "existence in another mode" is perilous and uncalled for. When philosophers attempt to make such claims about their sensations, their reports are subject to all the vagaries, ambiguities and metaphysical absurdities inherent in the use of human languages.

It must also be noted that, consistent with Whorf's principle of linguistic relativity, not all people would talk about perception as English-speaking philosophers do. While some English-speaking philosophers would say that trees, clouds, mesons, adult mayflies and humans are *physical objects that exist*, some Native Americans would have said they are *events that happen*. There is no non-relative fact of the matter. So too, many English-speaking philosophers may insist that imaginary tomatoes, pains, itches and other mental phenomena exist in consciousness. People who speak other languages may disagree and insist that they are events that happen and they are not happening in their heads. There is simply no language-neutral fact of the matter about what exists and what occurs or where they exist and where they occur.

Here are a few more points regarding sensations and language about them. This body has an array of acoustic devices used to tact with its sensations and infers that others have similar sensations. However, the sensations could be totally idiosyncratic. When someone tacts to the red of a ball, their receptor organs may be producing a sensation unique to them. It may be body specific. This is detailed in the famous inverted spectrum tale.[22] However, that makes no difference in their use of the word *"red"*. As long as that body can distinguish that specific section of the light spectrum from other frequencies, it will be able to tact with that distinction by using the word "red". It will be able to detect red things from blue things, regardless of its unique sensations. That body will be able to say: "that is red". Another body with a different sensations but the same ability to discriminate, will agree.

Some people have synesthesia or overlapping senses. Visual, auditory, tactile, gustatory and olfactory sensations are experienced when most humans would not experience them.[23] People see numbers and letters as having colors, or they see the sound of a drum as a three-dimensional shape. In cases such as these, it is possible to imagine what it would be like to have similar sensations because the descriptions of their sensations still rely on normal sensations and perceptual abilities common to most humans. Synesthesia is a blending of normal human sense perceptions, not a distinctive unique sensation such as echolocation in bats. In any case, synesthetes have the same ability to make the same distinctions as non-synesthetes. Consequently, synesthetes become competent speakers in spite of their unique sensory experience. The point is simply that idiosyncratically experienced sensations are not barriers to the competent use of language.

What is the *concept of red?* Normally sighted people *can* distinguish between red, blue, green, etc., regardless of their language. However, they *do* make color distinctions based on their cultural and individual needs and tact with them by means of word sounds. (Do you need to distinguish mauve?) For English speakers "red" is a sound that can be used in various ways. Most often it is a device used to tact. By means of tacting with the sound "red" a competent English speaker can connect a characteristic with an object by means of a linguistic proposition, e.g. "the ball is red". A speaker can make that declarative knowledge claim. However, *no concept of red* is required to do so. It is an act of discrimination and tacting which even pigeons can be taught to do. No "sensory concept" is created in the organism's mind or consciousness. Moreover, there is no feat of abstraction required to speak about any sensations produced by the human nervous system.

What's more, any talk about the correctness or accuracy of perception is also misguided. How can anyone's perception count as "veridical" or correct or accurate? Is this body's uncorrected 20/80 vision a veridical perception of the world? How about this body's corrected 20/20 vision? Why not 20/15 vision? Within certain norms, variations in eyesight do not prevent humans from tacting with the roundness, redness and number of marbles. Most humans are able to tact with the same distinctions made in spite of variations in the underlying perception. The point being, there are no true or accurate or correct or veridical perceptions of the world. Perception varies and there is no need or ability to find one which is the *veridical*.

Neither are people's sensations true or false. They are simply had. Scientists are notorious for conflating the subjective first-person experience of sensations, with *the reports* about those sensations. Daniel Dennett (2005: 44) credits Joseph Levine (1994), who claimed that "conscious experiences themselves, not merely our verbal judgments about them, are the primary data to which a theory must answer." Indeed, the "primary data" are the sensations. The reports are declarative verbal claims; the sensations are not. Listeners may judge those claims to be true or false, though the truth or falsity only comes with the claim. Human sensations are no truer than are chemical reactions.

Of course, humans may doubt the cause of their sensations. They may say that the pink elephants their friend is seeing were caused by the six margaritas they had consumed, not by real elephants dancing in the hotel suite, but the sensations are simply had. When philosophers say that experiences are veridical they may be saying that the experiences are what they would normally expect a human with normal sensory perception to have, idiosyncratic as that might be, given the normal cause-and-effect relationship of physical processes and human sensations. However, sensations are just that, regardless of what humans think are the causes or locations. Sensations are neurological occurrences within human bodies as experienced by that body. Organisms of all sorts have sensations. What causes these sensations varies.

Moreover, if it is agreed that many other creatures have sensations, few organisms would be likely to have the same range of sensations and somatic states that humans experience because they have very different physiology. It is unlikely that humans have the same sensations that sharks, snakes, bees or bats do. For example, some animals can sense ultraviolet radiation. Humans cannot. Sensations are likely to be species specific. The point being, if theorists grant that qualia *exist* in human consciousness, it seems they should grant the *existence* of qualia of other kinds in other species' consciousnesses. And, as a practical matter people do. Nobody wants animals to experience pain.

In any case, theorists can be sure that other sentient creatures, no matter how their sensations differ from ours, will not agree that they have phenom, qualia or sense data that enjoy a "separate mode of existence in consciousness", and they will not be conscious of their consciousness. They will distinguish between their conscious states and their unconscious states, though they cannot tact with that kind-sortal distinction or speech-think anything about it. Their pain, their happiness and their consciousness simply come and go. At times the organic material that composes their bodies reacts to certain stimuli; at other times it does not. You see, only verbally conditioned English-speaking philosophers can come up with absent qualia arguments for the "*existence* of human consciousness and its inhabitants in a separate mode."

An alternative view of such "mental phenomena" might start like this: By means of functional acoustic devices, humans are able to tact with "attributes", "properties", "qualities" or "features" of the objects of their holistic perception, e.g. kind-sortals of color. With word sounds they can tact outwardly at the so-called "primary qualities": size, shape, number etc. With other word sounds they can tact inwardly to the so-called "secondary qualities" colors, smells, tastes etc. When the theorists wax philosophical they say they want these features of their experience explained to them. Please explain these *phenomena*. Tell us what they consist of and where they are located, if not consciousness? The question is begged. What are the phenomenologists asking for? What would constitute an adequate explanation?

Normal people *see* trees, cups, stars, people etc. within a visual scene, i.e. naïve realists. Although the brain helps coalesce these physical objects, they are not inferred. They are *seen*. What human receptor organs and intermediary physical processes present to them is a scene, not *phenomena*, qualia or sense data, not the individuated properties or features of objects of their perception. Humans are presented with a panorama out of which they notice or attend to specifics based on the contingencies of reinforcement. Psychologists like to make a distinction between global attention and local attention. Humans see the forest before the trees. They can then zoom in, as it were. After seeing the forest, smaller details are attended to. They notice a red flower in the foreground.

After zooming in on the flower, people can notice or attend to various features of the objects of their perception, their colors, shape, size, smell etc., just as other creatures do. Organisms of all sorts notice salient features that are critical to their survival, often developing super sensitivity to particular colors, shapes, smells etc. Nevertheless, what organisms originally perceive are not the objects or more elemental features of the objects; they perceive the global scene, then notice or attend to various objects and their salient features such as the redness. That noticing or attention to salient features is not driven by an internal agent in humans or non-humans. In all species it is driven by heritable genes, the previous contingencies of reinforcement to which the organism has been exposed.

Ultimately, mature humans notice many things which are of utmost importance to their survival, such as the red in the light at the intersection. They also develop specialized noticing skills. The artist may notice many different hues of green in a tree. The botanist may notice the shape of the leaves or the stage of development. The sawyer may notice the curve in the trunk. They notice all of these features of the tree because they are conditioned to notice them by means of word sounds used by others.

Tacting by means of word sounds is a fundamental human ability that expands exponentially with competent linguistic behavior. When philosophers tact with the color of the dog, the sound of the bird, the smell of the rose, the hunger in their stomach, the pain in their leg they must be aware of what they are doing and recognize that this is not possible without conditioned verbal behavior. Humans cannot tact with these so-called phenomenal sense data produced by their sense receptors without such acoustic devices. However, the ability to tact with the features and distinctions that any specific language recognizes should not be used to justify ontological claims about sense data that enjoy "the status of mental existence."

Each organism generates sensations that have a unique subjective feel about them, such as the sensations produced by your digestive tract or your circulatory system. The subjective feel of the sensations is merely an acknowledgement that the sensations are coming from inside the skin. The inward tacting with the sensations does not create an alternative universe of mental phenomena or conscious experience that endures through time but is not extended in space. There is no supportable reason to believe that there is anything red or tasty *existing* inside your eyeballs, or your tongue, or in your brain, or your consciousnesses.

Unfortunately, the evolution of human speech behavior over previous millennia has created and maintained an alternate ontological state for human sensations, memories, imaginings etc. Philosophers have explained such products of their internal organs by creating the two-world ontology that included souls, minds, selves, and consciousnesses full of *mental* phenomena. Thus those explanations are unwarranted and incoherent under careful scrutiny.

Humans could and should talk about the red, their pain, their hunger and their happiness as perfectly normal organic processes that each human experiences internally. Reports about human sensations need not comport with the consciousness/matter dogma. Human talk about sensations, phenomena, qualia, and sense data located in consciousness is just that, talk. It is conditioned human linguistic behavior, begot by Plato, Aristotle, Augustine, Descartes and analytic philosophers such as Locke, Moore and Russell.

The use of the word sound "*sensation*" does not carry all the metaphysical baggage that "*thought*", "*concept*", and "*mind*" do for philosophers. That being said, they have pushed it in that direction with their specious arguments for phenom, qualia, and sense data located in consciousness. Phenom, qualia, and sense data in consciousness are the modern-day creations of philosophers to replace the time-worn and discredited souls and minds of yesteryear. For phenomenal dualists, rather than souls and minds, *phenomena* are the things *existing* inside human skin but are not subject to third-party observation. Like souls and minds, they have *existence* in time but not space.

All the contemporary speech behavior about phenomenal entities and occurrences sets up a peculiar ontological status outside the standard physics paradigm. It is metaphysics worthy of Plato, Aristotle, Augustine, Descartes, Locke, Moore and Russell. Let us not make grand pronouncements about the order and nature of the universe based on our speech behavior. Let us recognize the origin and function of human speech and dispose of the mind/matter dichotomy once and for all. Life, consciousness, sentience, sapience and sensations—can all be reduced to known processes with paradigmatic scientific explanations. These processes will describe and explain what is happening within the limits of human explanation, i.e. the limits of human language.

Utilizing word sounds such as "*mental phenomena*", "*consciousness*", "*qualia*", "*sense data*" "*sensations*", "*phenom*", "*existence*" et al. as they are currently being used and producing new philosophical arguments will not breach the ontological barrier. The use of these word sounds creates and sustains the ontological barrier. The change required of philosophers is a change in their verbal behavior. They must stop using words that have the embedded mind/body dualism or some alternative third ontological status implied or inferred. Philosophers' intuitions and their thinking will change with the change in their verbal behavior. The mythical *mental* phenomena, consciousness, qualia, sense data, phenom etc. will disappear when theologians, philosophers, psychologists, teachers and truck drivers stop speaking about themselves the way they currently do.

Reductionist sense datum theories of perception proposed by philosophers are stinky red herrings. When philosophers say they have sensations, phenomena, qualia or sense data located in their consciousness, they are simply mistaken. Humans have the ability to discriminate by means of their receptor organs and their somatic feedback systems. There is no reason whatsoever to conclude that when humans make these distinctions about their sense experience and tact with them by means of word sounds, they are talking about ethereal mental phenomena or phenomena that *exist* in consciousness. It is all part of the ghost in the machine myth. It is a misguided and pernicious result of metaphysical speculation and the English speech that derives there from.

One Use of the Word "*think*"

This sound "*think*" that originates in the mouths of English speakers is said to be a word. Within the English-speaking community, people use the word "*think*" to tact with many putative *mental* activities: remembering, imagining, wondering, daydreaming, calculating, covert speech, etc. Within the EA dualist paradigm, all these activities require a mind or consciousness to do the thinking. This folk psychology, based on thousands of years of increasingly complex verbal behavior leading up to modern English, says that human heads contain minds which do the thinking for human bodies. When humans are thinking they are said to be engaging in something other than physical activity; they are engaging in *mental* activity.

The mental activity supposedly represented by vocal speech or covert speech is *mentalese* or *language of thought (LOT)*, a language of pure unexpressed thought. Mentalese or LOT is claimed to be a cognitive language which is common to all speakers and *represented* in myriad surface languages. In addition to the theoretical problems with this paradigm mentioned in Chapter One, it produces various puzzles, e.g. could a person not think in mentalese/LOT without the need for translation into natural languages when speaking to himself covertly?

Ludwig Wittgenstein asks us to conduct an experiment regarding the need for a language of pure thought which presumably accompanies or precedes verbal behavior:

> "Suppose I tried, deliberately, to speak without thinking; - what in fact would I do? I might read out a sentence from a book, trying to read it automatically, that is, trying to prevent myself from following the sentence with images and sensations which otherwise it would produce. A way of doing this would be to concentrate my attention on something else while I was speaking the sentence, e.g., by pinching my skin hard while I was speaking.—put it this way: speaking a sentence without thinking consists in switching on speech and switching off certain accompaniments of speech. Now ask yourself: Does thinking the sentence without speaking it consist in turning over the switch (switching on what we previously switched off and vice versa); that is: does thinking the sentence without speaking it now simply consist in keeping on what accompanied the words but leaving out the words? Try to think the thoughts of a sentence without the sentence and see whether this happens." Wittgenstein (1958a: #43)

Can you generate the pure ideas, concepts or thoughts after switching off the speech? No, because, contrary to theories arguing for a language of pure thought behind the public languages, both covert speech and public speech are verbal behaviors that require operant conditioning. Without conditioned speech behavior, such covert thinking is not possible. Humans simply cannot produce covert speech without having the experience of public speaking. Speech-enabled people utilize the same verbal instruments in either case. Silent speakers must be capable of recognizing the functional value of word sounds and employing them appropriately. Then they learn to suppress the phoneme production and say that they are *thinking*, engaging in a *mental* process, but they cannot generate pure unverbalized ideas, concepts or thoughts that supposedly lie behind the verbalized ideas, concepts, or thoughts. Wittgenstein's switch cannot produce naked thoughts, mentalese, or LOT.

The point is, there is *no evidence*, observational or introspective, for a sequential ordering of naked, unexpressed thoughts, ideas, concepts, representations, or "notions" in a language of *mentalese* or LOT prior to using words silently or aloud. Silent speaking does not require concepts, ideas, thoughts, or any other mental entities to precede or accompany it. It requires the proper stimulation from within the organism, or from the environment and the capacity to covertly implement acoustic devices. Each human organism has a history of reinforcement for its previous verbal behavior that combined with occurring internal or external stimuli, produces the occurring verbal behavior, vocally or sub-vocally, with no need for an underlying naked language of thought, the so called *mentalese* or LOT.

Contrary to theories of human speech which rely on mentalese, there is evidence for a simple suppression of vocal behavior in humans. The Wikipedia entry for sub-vocal speech is:

> "During normal speech, air is forced pass the larynx and the tongue. Words are then formed by the articulator muscles in the mouth and jaw. These muscles go into action regardless of whether air is sent past them. Electric signals from the brain are sent to these speech muscles even when one is just saying words to themselves."

When humans remember how to employ an acoustic device they remember muscle movements, just as they remember how to play *Beethoven's Fifth* or how to tie their shoelaces or how to drive a car. Speaking, vocally or sub-vocally, requires speech muscle memory. Humans learn how to produce the sounds. They also learn when and how to use them based on their functional value. They can produce the words vocally, or sub-vocally. Of course sub-vocal speech need not be depicted as a peculiar *non-physical, mental* activity. Nor does it require any such *non-physical mental* activity during or prior to the sub-vocal speech.

Our English verbal behavior about our sub-vocal speech does not fit the facts. Humans accept the dual-track (words expressing naked thoughts) explanation of word use for multiple reasons, not the least of which is, no third parties can observe their silent speech. But suppose someone could observe human sub-vocal speech, maybe not hear the speech, but monitor it in such a way as to detect what speakers are saying in spite of the fact that they are doing it silently. Would you still say that say that silent speech is an occult *mental* activity called *thinking*?

Scientists are on the verge of monitoring covert speech. On March 18, 2004 NASA issued a press release in which they claimed to have:

> "...come close to reading thoughts not yet spoken, by analyzing nerve commands to the throat... (Charles) Jorgensen's team found that sensors under the chin and one on each side of the Adam's apple pick up the brain's commands to the speech organs, allowing the subauditory, or 'silent speech' to be captured... Biological signals arise when reading or speaking to oneself, with or without actual lip or facial movement."

If these scientists could capture the silent speech, would they be capturing the subject's thoughts, detecting the naked concepts and ideas that are correlated with his words? Would they be reading his mind?

Humans are able to remember vocal muscle movements and repeat them to accomplish the linguistic work that they have been conditioned to perform. The links between muscle memory and speech are evidenced in clinical studies. The same brain area that controls other motor functions controls the speech function. Humans produce countless novel combinations of muscle movements to reach their goals. Opening a door poses no great mystery for theorists. They do not require ideas, concepts and thoughts to precede or accompany each muscle movement in the sequence required to unlock and open a door. Why do they insist that the noises produced by muscle movements are symbols that represent or express some other mysterious non-physical "thoughts"?

Not surprisingly, neurological research reveals many similarities between tool use and word use. Katherine R. Gibson and Tim Ingold have reported extensively on the relationship between tool use and word use:

> "Quite apart from sharing similar neurological, cognitive, and structural substrates, language and tool-use may have mutual feedback and facilitative relationships... These works must all be seen as preliminary, however, because our understanding of the relationships between behavioral domains remains weak." Gibson and Ingold (1993: 10)

The evidence is not yet conclusive. Even so, there appears to be a very strong correlation between human linguistic behavior and tool use. Humans learn *how* to use word sounds and material tools, *how* to make them do their bidding. Humans rely on mutual goals, observational learning and social reinforcement to utilize many tools to do so. Those devices include sounds that are emitted from human mouths. Speaking with words vs. thinking with words, what is the difference? One is vocal; the other is sub-vocal. The process is the same. In either case humans must use their brains to manipulate the acoustic devices.

Moreover, much of our non-linguistic thought is governed and guided by linguistic thought:

> "... it is not true that we build up a picture of the world and then dress it out in language. Rather, language builds a picture of the world that we use for thinking and communicating..." Bickerton (1995: 23)

Contrary to much current theorizing in the evolution of verbal behavior, Derek Bickerton, argues that: "... language came first and enabled human thinking" Bickerton (2009: 191) and that: "... language is by now the main engine of thought." (Ibid: 185). He is one of many philosophers and linguists who are beginning to acknowledge that humans cannot think the way they do without verbal conditioning. That conditioning gives people the cognitive tools necessary to do the thinking that they do in multiple domains. As Bickerton argues, language enabled a unique human form of cognition that expanded and evolved along with the human brain. While much research has yet to be done in this area, it has become increasingly recognized that humans gain much of their cognitive superiority in the animal kingdom by virtue of their ability to use language. That superior cognitive power is observed in non-linguistic domains as well, where the influence of language is pervasive.[24] Unless you are an academic with an axe to grind it is difficult to think otherwise.

Granted, not all thinking requires words. For instance, people like to say that they *think* before making a chess move or performing a mathematical calculation. Thinking is presumed to occur in pre-speech infants, deaf isolates and most non-human creatures. English speakers use the term "thinking" in many non-linguistic contexts where cognitive processes are assumed to precede the behavior of an organism. So, just as intentions have become acceptable explanations for much human behavior, thinking, as a non-physical and unobservable *mental* activity, has become an acceptable explanation for much of the observed behavior of human organisms.

Unfortunately, because of thousands of years of philosophy and its resultant speech history in the West, this thinking process in humans is characterized as uniquely human and ontologically distinct. Philosophical problems then arise because these unobservable *mental* processes are hypothetical posits that cannot be supported philosophically or empirically. Rather, people should say that certain as yet unexplained neural processes in the brain precede behavior of all sorts. *Thinking is a physical process*, the results of which are observed in many creatures.

When asked whether he thought with words or pictures, John Maynard Keynes, under the spell of dualism, famously said that he did his *thinking* with *thoughts*. If you agree with Keynes and insist that you think with thoughts, you will also, no doubt, insist that you have intentions, beliefs, knowledge and reasons which affect your thinking. You will also insist that there are thoughts, ideas, concepts and mental representations correlated with the noises issuing from your mouth. That is because your sub-vocal verbal behavior is firmly in the grip of your conditioned vocal behavior which insists that your thinking consists of manipulating thoughts in your mind.

.

The Use of the Words
"belief" and "Knowledge"

Some philosophers want to subdivide consciousness. One such subsidiary domain is *state consciousness* or *creature consciousness* as opposed to *transient consciousness*. At times SAE-speaking people with EA folk psychological traditions are said to be in a continuous believing or knowing state of consciousness, believing or knowing, for example, that all swans are white.[25] That belief or knowledge has duration, i.e. it is extended through time. The belief or knowledge is said to be retained in some form in the mind and can be brought to a transient conscious state by a volitional act of the person having that state of belief or knowledge about swans.

Other philosophers suggest that believing and knowing are more like *transient consciousness*, consciousness that is temporary and directed. This is the Intentionality-with-a-capital-I previously alluded to. These forms of transient consciousness are directed at declarative propositional claims such as: "*all swans are white*". They are claimed to be forms of consciousness that reflect cognitive relations between humans and psychological *propositions*. These *propositional attitudes* of believing and knowing propositional content are expressed by saying: "*i Know*" or "*i believe that all swans are white*". Rather than continuous states of consciousness, the believing and knowing are different types of short-lived transient conscious *attitudes* directed at propositional content.[26]

Linguistically, this dichotomy of state consciousness and transient conscious attitudes is often reflected in and sustained by the dual status for the verbs "know" and "believe". Within English, they are said to have a *stative aspect* and a *dynamic aspect*. In the stative aspect the beliefs and knowledge are assumed to be long-lasting and continuous mental states retained in the human memory even though people may not be expressing them or remembering them at any given time. In the dynamic aspect the beliefs and knowledge are transient propositional attitudes only held when they are expressed. The belief or knowledge is not a long-lasting state of consciousness. Both of these *aspects* of "know" and "believe" are incorporated in the conditioned use of these English verbs and drive the theories about such knowledge and beliefs.[27]

The upshot is simply: if English-speaking philosophers conduct their analysis by using the terms "*Know*", "*believe*", "*Knowledge*", and "*belief*" as they ordinarily do (in both stative and dynamic aspects) in such discussions, any efforts to bridge or eliminate the ontological gap will fail spectacularly. The ontological divide and all of its inherent contradictions and absurdities is built into such conditioned *aspectual* English speech behavior about beliefs and knowledge.

Do humans have mental content and mental states? Do humans have beliefs and knowledge stored in their memories and brought forth to a state of transient consciousness? Do humans have psychological propositions in their minds? Do humans have the propositional attitudes of belief or knowledge toward these propositions? They only do if philosophers and scientists start with some form of mental/physical dualism and they want to explain human behavior from this traditional folk psychology perspective. Thus, these unobservable "inhabitants of conscious experience", i.e. our knowledge and beliefs, join intentions as motivating forces for the observed behavior of each human organism. They are the *mental activity or mental states* that make human behavior more than random actions. They are the *reasons* for what we do within the dualistic paradigm rather than behavior which has previously been reinforced to varying degrees in the behavioristic paradigm.

Without assuming dualism, do humans have tendencies to behave as they have been conditioned to behave? Yes, whether that behavior is speaking, playing the piano or using a pair of pliers. Do they have an inclination to make declarative propositional statements as their parents and peers do? Yes! Does this behavior require certain states of enduring consciousness, transient consciousness or propositional attitudes of belief or knowledge toward psychological propositions in their minds or consciousness? No! Declarative propositional statements are a result of conditioned behavior every bit as much as playing the piano. Humans do not have beliefs or knowledge in the form of propositions in their heads any more than they have music in their heads. What they have in their bodies is conditioned speech muscle movement controlled by a brain with correlated *neural states* and *neural events*.

Human perception *presents* the universe to us in such a way that objects and events are positioned within a space and time framework. Humans are continually orienting themselves within this spatial-temporal background that they remember in a non-linguistic form, just as other organisms do. There is nothing controversial about this. Most sentient organisms routinely mark their location in time and space by means of neural connections and effortlessly navigate through space and time, without attending to these states of affairs or saying anything about them. However, if stimulated, humans have the ability to tact with these states of affairs linguistically. That speech behavior brings these states of affairs to the foreground in the form of a linguistic proposition.

For example, if a human organism remembers there is milk in the fridge, it could simply respond to a stimulus for milk by getting up and going to the fridge. Or it might be stimulated to say: "*the milk is in the fridge*". The organism's inclination to make this declarative statement is based on its S-S-R history and the stimuli by which it is currently influenced. In either case, the organism's behavior is dependent upon its neurology and the stimulation it receives, not a *state of consciousness* or *mental content* that it totes around in its head. The *belief* that the milk is in the fridge is simply background information recorded in the neurology of the organism's brain that does not come to the foreground until the human is stimulated to act upon it.

Retaining background information about states of affairs, or *remembering*, is not unique to the human species. Organisms that keep a record of where they have been and what they have sensed are ubiquitous within the animal kingdom. Even bees have pretty good memories. Do they have minds to hold their memories? Do they have beliefs about the location of the pollen? Do they have states of consciousness regarding the location of the pollen? No! But then neither do people. Bees make neurological connections just as humans do to note their orientation within the states of affairs they encounter. They then engage in behavior, including communicative behavior about these states of affairs, e.g. to guide other bees to the pollen.

All creatures, including humans, engage in behavior because of neural connections. At times, these neural connections mislead them. Humans have fallible recall about the actual state of affairs. For example, the author recently *believed* that he had left his reading glasses at home. Rather than go back home to get the glasses, he simply bought a cheap pair. After purchasing the new pair, the author found the old pair inside his jacket pocket. He was simply wrong about his original *belief* about his circumstances. He made a faulty assessment of the state of affairs based on neural confusion or lapse. His memory was defective.

However, at no point did the author put any of the neural connections in linguistic form. He did not stop and articulate the belief: "*i left my reading glasses at home*" either silently or aloud. The author's *belief* in the state of affairs and his reaction to the believed state of affairs consisted of nothing more than mechanical behavior in response to the remembered state of affairs stored in its neurons, what he *believed* to be an accurate assessment of the situation. Human and non-human animal activity is often guided by these non-linguistic memories about states of affairs. However, there is no reason to conclude that these thoughts are supernatural events taking place in the brains of the participants, be they mice or men.

Sometimes these so-called beliefs about states of affairs in the world influence human behavior; sometimes they do not. It depends on how strongly the neural connections are linked to stimuli. For instance, the human belief that the sun is a star rarely influences their behavior and thus, it rarely comes to the fore. It stays in the background. The belief that the milk is in the fridge, is a background neural connection that often influences this author's behavior regardless of whether the author articulates that belief or not. It often comes to the foreground because it is more useful on a daily basis. It is articulated much more often because it is useful to others as well. However, that belief is not a mythical mental state, state of consciousness or a propositional attitude that is stored in this organism's *mind or consciousness*. It is background information about objects, events, and distinctions that this organism has recorded in its neurology and utilizes in response to stimuli.

Within the mechanical/functional explanation, beliefs and knowledge can be construed as neurologically recordings of objects, events, distinctions, states of affairs etc. Unlike most other species, however, humans can make these states of affairs explicit and useful to other humans by utilizing tacts and syntax to make the relative location of objects, events and so on a matter of discussion. This is one of the things that humans have learned to do with word sounds. In that regard human animals are unique on their planet. However, it leads theorists to many faulty conclusions and philosophical conundrums.

For example, the legend of humans toting mental content, i.e. knowledge, beliefs, and desires around in their minds causes consternation for animal lovers. As Donald Davidson commented:

> "And there is Norman Malcolm's dog who, having chased a squirrel into the woods, barks up the wrong tree. It is hard not to credit the dog with the belief that the squirrel is in that tree." Davidson via Rosenthal (1991: 363)

Just as humans do, animals position themselves relative to objects and events in time and space and adjust their behavior accordingly based on their innate or conditioned behavior. They also make many distinctions about number, color, size, shape, and so on. The apparent goal-oriented behavior of these non-human creatures can be made coherent within the current dualist paradigm by attributing knowledge and beliefs to them in the same way humans attribute knowledge and beliefs to themselves. They should feel no compunction about doing so. It is just as plausible to attribute knowledge and beliefs to dogs and squirrels as it is to attribute them to humans.

However, they open up a large philosophical can of worms if they allow dogs, squirrels and rats to have *beliefs*.

One of the reasons that human animals are reluctant to attribute beliefs to Malcolm's dog is because the dog cannot speak. In non-human animals the neural connections have no potential for becoming an expressed belief. Malcolm's dog cannot convert his neural recordings of the states of affairs into declarative knowledge or beliefs. He cannot assert anything because he cannot utilize functional acoustic devices. So, humans are reluctant to say that dogs, squirrels and rats have beliefs. If they were to attribute beliefs to dogs, squirrels and rats they might be forced to endow them with minds or souls. The next thing you know, God would be allowing dogs, squirrels and rats into the City of God.

Human organisms have many of these standing neural connections that govern their behavior. Those that speak have the ability to tact with the states of affairs that are retained in the form of these neural connections, making a connection audible: *"the milk is in the fridge"*. *Within the dualist paradigm* this declaration leads theorists to conclude that a *psychological entity* corresponding to the speech behavior *exists* in the mind or consciousness. The *belief* is said to be a state of consciousness or a mental attitude toward a proposition. The ability to express the belief is then said to be evidence for that state of consciousness or mental attitude. This picture is a misguided attempt to explain human speech behavior based on thousands of years of bad philosophy and the bad speech behavior it has engendered.

Propositions are linguistic acts, not psychological entities floating around in human minds as Intentional objects. Humans have innumerable inclinations to behave vocally, including utterances of declarative propositional statements based on neural recordings of the states of affairs they observe and remember. "Mental content", "propositional attitudes" and "psychological propositions" themselves are entirely misleading characterizations of what all animals, both human and non-human, have in their heads. Unfortunately, the way SAE speakers talk about these hypothetical epistemic states of believing, knowing, hoping, doubting etc. easily leads some philosophers to assert that the stored forms of such beliefs, knowledge must be propositional. The consequence of this characterization is, as Daniel Dennett said: "… one can easily be misled into thinking that it is *obvious* that beliefs and desires are rather like sentences stored in the head." Chalmers (2002: 559 Dennett)

Dennett then expounds on "serious belief attribution" to distinguish those systems that "really" have beliefs and desires. He makes the distinction when there is none to be made. If you presuppose dualism and utilize current English speech behavior, you will think that some organisms "really have beliefs and desires" while others do not. Then the debate begins over what things "really have beliefs and desires". Does Norman Malcolm's dog really have *beliefs*? What about desires? What about the industrious squirrel running away from the dog? Does it really have a *belief* that the nuts are where he hid them? What about that tick clinging to the squirrel's tail? Does it really *believe* that the squirrel has blood? What about that rat stuck in the maze? Does it have a false *belief* about the location of the cheese? What about your calculator? Does it *believe* that 2 +2 = 4?

Some people attribute knowledge, beliefs and desires to pet beagles and other complex organisms. Their word use is flexible enough to allow that move in some contexts for some purposes. However, at what point in the continuum between thermostats and humans do people endow systems with *mental content* such as knowledge, beliefs and desires? It depends on whom they ask. Once again, the inherent dualism in their speech behavior is the culprit. There is no clear-cut answer. Their habituated verbal behavior gives them intuitions about such mental content, but no clear cut answers. People use the English stative and dynamic aspect word sounds about the putative mental content of any animal when they feel that it can provide an acceptable explanation, and they can get away with it.

People use word sounds such as *"Know"* and *"believe"* anyway they want in spite of what philosophers, grammarians and logicians write. People attribute knowledge, beliefs and desires to people, dogs, bees, calculators, lightning, thermostats, etc.

Some people may object that lightning does not *know* the best way to the ground. Other people may object that the thermostat does not really *know* when to shut the furnace off. A person may object that bees really don't *believe* there is pollen in the clover field. Nor do rats believe, wrongly, that the cheese is in another location. Endowing inanimate objects and simple S-S-R organisms with epistemic states such as beliefs and knowledge stretches credulity at some point, based on the intuitions generated by the interlocutor's previous use of S-R-R conditioned linguistic behavior.

There is an alternative functional/mechanical explanation like the one for sunflowers following the sun across the sky. That alternative functional/mechanical explanation is available for machines and lesser organisms. But the limits of the paradigmatic folk psychology explanations are different for different people.

Daniel Dennett began to zero in on the problem:

> "What do we learn beliefs are when we learn how to use the words 'believe' and 'belief'? The first point to make is that we do not really learn what beliefs are when we learn how to use these words. Certainly no one *tells* us what beliefs are, or if someone does, or if we happen to speculate on the topic our own, the answer we come to, wise or foolish, will figure only weakly in our habits of thought about what people believe. We learn to *use* folk psychology as a vernacular social technology, a craft; but we don't learn it self-consciously as a theory—we learn no meta-theory—and in this regard our knowledge of folk psychology is like our knowledge of the grammar of our native tongue." Dennett (1987: 47)

True enough, we English speakers learn how to use the word sound *"belief"* (and *"Knowledge"*) within a dualistic milieu of folk psychology and English grammar. We do so without any theoretical underpinnings. However, our knowledge of folk psychology is not only "like our knowledge of the grammar" in that we require no formal theory or special training to acquire such folk psychology. It is part and parcel of our English speech behavior. As such, it is impossible to speak the language competently without adopting the folk psychology intrinsic to its use.

When English-speaking humans *use* the sounds *"belief"* and *"Knowledge"* they are responding to stimuli with a tact. That tact is a verbal operant evoked by other verbal operants produced internally by the organism or produced externally by other discourse participants. It is verbal behavior that has evolved in a speech environment that infers many undetectable entities: intentions, beliefs, and knowledge located in ethereal human minds. If philosophers tell you that beliefs consist of states of consciousness, transient consciousness, propositional attitudes, Intentional objects or mental states with propositional content, tell them that you don't believe them.

The Use of the Word *"understanding"*

> "To motivate the discussion, let us start with the question: what does understanding a sentence (as opposed to knowing whether it true or false) involve? On the traditional view, it would seem that *understanding* a sentence must involve something like this: knowing in which *possible* worlds the sentence *would* be true. This suggests: there must be a natural 'correspondence' between sentences in a language, on the one hand, and sets of possible worlds on the other." Putnam (1975: 73)

Here, once again, we see a renowned philosopher using possible world theorizing along with a notoriously difficult "correspondence" in an attempt to explain what *understanding* a sentence might mean. Such theorizing is an entirely misguided attempt to explicate the use of the word "understanding" in both philosophy and ordinary usage. It is misguided because "knowing in which possible worlds a sentence would be true" is limited to declarative or indicative sentences and is completely counter to our ordinary use of the word "understanding". If someone was to say: "Get me a hammer", any competent English speaker would *understand* that speech act even if it has no truth value and cannot be verified by any possible world theorizing.

We should broach this vexing issue from another perspective because *understanding* is one of the most widespread and insidious *mental states* that is commonly believed to somehow support or accompany the production of much human behavior. The performance of mathematical operations, for example, is said to rely on the *understanding* or comprehension of mathematics. Theorists in every field of human endeavor claim that once one *understands*, say calculus, the equations of physics or the Chinese language, one can successfully utilize calculus, the equations of physics or the Chinese language.

When humans say that they *understand* something they are often claiming that this putative cognitive state is responsible for their successful performance. Theorists in many, if not all fields assert that there is a stable mental state of understanding, somewhat like a mental state of knowledge, which underlies each performance. That mental state is not lost after each performance. Like knowledge, the understanding remains in the human mind over time (in SAE-speaking cultures). It is said that people understand *how* to ride a bike, *how* to write cursive, *how* to play the piano, *how* to dance the waltz or drive a car. Theorists require a special long-lasting state of mind called "understanding" to precede or support these efforts?

However, there is no external evidence at all for mental states or processes of understanding being prerequisites for these performances. One of the difficulties in trying to explain what *the understanding* consists of was made more perspicuous by Wittgenstein:

> "We are trying to get hold of the mental process of understanding which seems to be hidden behind those coarser and therefore more readily visible

accompaniments. But we do not succeed; or, rather, it does not get as far as a real attempt. For even supposing I had found something that happened in all those cases of understanding—why should it be understanding? And how can the process of understanding have been hidden, when I said "Now I understand" *because* I understood?! And if I say it is hidden—then how do I know what I have to look for? I am in a muddle." Wittgenstein (1958a: #153)

Indeed, how would one look for the "mental process of *understanding*"? Ex hypothesis, it is not empirically observable because it is a mental state. Yet introspectively, how would a mental state or process of understanding be recognized? One might possibly say that a level of confidence about one's performance might be felt or reached prior to the behavior, but that is no guarantee of a successful performance. Without performing in one fashion or another it seems that there is absolutely no evidence for this mental state or process of understanding. The only evidence for the understanding is in a successful performance.

Does the dancing bear understand dancing? Does the bee understand where the nectar is? Does the oyster understand that it is out of the water? What does the sunflower understand or the thermostat? With the word sound *"understand"* English speakers head down the same slippery slope that they do when they use *"Know"* and *"believe"*. In fact, understanding *how*, i.e. *procedural* knowledge, is the only understanding required for any human behavior. That knowledge is not a cognitive state however; it is the ability to produce certain behavior which is a result of a history of previous positive reinforcement or lack thereof.

Unwittingly, Wittgenstein's analysis of the "mental process of understanding" reveals how deeply the mind/body dichotomy is rooted in SAE languages. Looking for a *mental* process or state that "stands under" behavior is driven by your habitual speech behavior. "Understanding" like "comprehension" is just another of the 10,000+ words in the English language that promotes the myth of the ghost in the machine, the ghost that has concepts, ideas, thoughts, intentions and the understanding. If a human can produce the behavior known as calculus, the equations of physics or Chinese speech, it needs no *mental* process, state, structure or apparatus to support that performance. It only needs years of operant conditioning.

The Use of the Word *"attention"*

Humans can be conscious, yet not conscious *of* anything at any specific moment in time. At other times they are both conscious and conscious *of things*. Within analytic philosophy, consciousness of things has been called transient or transitive consciousness as opposed to state consciousness, creature consciousness, or intransitive consciousness. This directedness or focus that consciousness can have is spoken of as attention, attending to or noticing. The spotlight metaphor is ubiquitous. The internal director can focus the spotlight of *attention* on whatever is most important to the person at any given moment. This is the way English-speaking humans *talk* about their internal agent and, at times, its ability to control the focus of their consciousness. They say things like: *"i focused on the task at hand"* or *"i paid attention"*. The inferred self takes control and directs the consciousness of the organism.

Alternatively, stimuli grab the attention of humans. At times, it is *said*, the attention is given over to outside forces such as the rabbit in the hedgerow ahead or the itch in an embarrassing spot that gets a person's attention. When human attention is not directed by the internal agent, it is left to wander about or be commandeered by internal or external stimuli which attract it. However, at some point the internal agent once again gains control and directs the transient consciousness. Attention becomes controllable until another stimulus steals it away from the controller.

At other times, consciousness is *said* to give in to the demands of *subconscious* forces. All sensory input is ignored and the person's attention is directed by these subconscious forces, even though she or he is conscious. It seems that the executive in charge often cedes his command to other unnoticed mental entities and forces in the background. The transient consciousness is there but it is directed by subliminal unnoticed forces working behind the curtain to control the attention of that organism.

Annaka Harris, after reviewing much of the recent science of consciousness, reports:

> "With so many behind-the-scenes forces at work---from the essential neurological processes we previously examined to bacterial infections and parasites---it's hard to see how our behavior, preferences, and even choices could be under control of our conscious will in any real sense. It seems much more accurate to say that consciousness is along for the ride – watching the show, rather than creating or controlling it. In theory, we can go as far as to say that few (if any) of our behaviors need consciousness in order to be carried out."
> Harris (2019:41)

Humans also *say* that their attention is sequential. They are aware of, or attend to, one thing after another. They *say* that this constitutes their stream of consciousness or train of thought. People say that they have varying attention spans. Some people are more focused than others. Not only do we notice or attend to things, unlike other creatures, we notice that we notice and talk about that noticing or attention.

SAE-speaking humans have uncountable ways of expressing their beliefs about consciousness and attention using metaphors and analogies which lend themselves to talk about consciousness that may not, in fact, be an accurate portrayal of their experience. This is not to say that their experiences can somehow be veridical, accurate, or true. It is simply saying that the way they talk about their experience may be inaccurate reportage. The science of attention and consciousness is often at odds with the verbal behavior about consciousness SAE-speaking humans have become accustomed to using. The point is, SAE-speaking people have a huge repertoire of questionable verbal behavior built around the fable of a unified singular self that controls the mind's attention and insists that it is consciously doing so. However, this is not the only view. An alternative view of this directedness of human attention is expressed by B. F. Skinner:

> "A person responds only to a small part of the stimuli impinging upon him. The traditional view is that he himself determines which stimuli are to be effective by 'paying attention' to them. Some kind of inner gatekeeper is said to allow some stimuli to enter and to keep others out. A sudden or strong stimulus may break through and 'attract' attention, but the person himself seems otherwise to be in control. An analysis of the environmental circumstances reverses the relation. The kinds of stimuli which break through by 'attracting attention' do so because they have been associated in the evolutionary history of the species or the personal history of the individual with important—e.g., dangerous—things…The inner gatekeeper is replaced by the contingencies to which the organism has been exposed and which select the stimuli to which it reacts."
> Skinner (1971: 177)

In spite of their thinking to the contrary, human attention is not controlled by an inferred internal agent. Each human organism's behavior is controlled ultimately by its genes and "the contingencies to which the organism has been exposed". The transponder inside of each of them continually processes internal and external stimuli and then observes the organism's cognitive resources being deployed.

The Use of the Word *"introspection"*

"Philosophers have often thought that knowing oneself involves knowing one's mental and bodily states as they succeed one another. And that this requires introspection. But philosophers have also concluded that, as it is often conceived, introspection cannot or does not exist. They have argued that one difficulty is as follows: Suppose you have a pain; to have a pain is to be aware of it; then, to introspect that means that you must be aware of being aware that you have the pain. But, they claim, you never find that, besides the pain, you are also aware of something called awareness of the pain. If you insist that you did make such a finding, they would ask if you can be aware of being aware of being aware of the pain. How many awarenesses can you be simultaneously be aware of?" Myers (1969: 124)

Philosophers often discuss the process of *introspection* whereby humans supposedly become *conscious of their consciousness*. During the process of introspection, the internal agent takes control and directs transient consciousness toward state consciousness or creature consciousness. The inferred self supposedly detects the consciousness in all of its forms plus the constituents of consciousness: thoughts, ideas, concepts, qualia etc. This process of introspection has been an occupational hazard for philosophers since antiquity. It has also been a matter of contention.

The above epigraph, for instance, is burdened with the usual metaphysical freight and philosophical enigmas. What would it be to *know* one-self? How do philosophers *conceive* of introspection? Nevertheless, Myers' point is well taken. Can philosophers be conscious of their consciousness of consciousness of consciousness? Talk about consciousness of consciousness leads to vicious regress.

Philosophical explanations of *introspection* are muddled and filled with enigmas. Many have suggested that philosophers use *"retrospection"* instead of *"introspection"*. Any attempts at introspection by a person inevitably end with that person being aware of something that they previously experienced milli-seconds ago. Moreover, if that body, so to speak, looks back at its previous vision of a red ball, it is not *seeing* anything. A memory is not the same as a visual sensation. That body is remembering the seeing and, much as David Hume reported, it remembers nothing in addition to the perception. It remembers having a perception but it remembers nothing in addition that could be referred to as consciousness of the perception.

No matter how consciousness is defined, humans have conscious moments that differ from unconscious moments. They recognize that difference just as other sentient creatures presumably do, but when English-speaking people think about this kind-sortal, consciousness vs. unconsciousness, they must tact with the kind-sortal by means of the word sound *"consciousness"*. They do not have to say it aloud, but they must have the capacity to recognize the functional value of that word and use it to tact to the distinction between their conscious moments and their non-conscious ones.

Humans can tact with dogs and trees by means of their fingers, but they cannot tact with happiness, loneliness, or their consciousness without word sounds. Each SAE-speaking human organism must tact with the happiness, the loneliness or the consciousness by means of word sounds, otherwise, its attention flits from one thing to another, subject to its prioritized sensory input and innate reflexes. The significant concern of this section is that *the act of introspection* is a linguistic act. Even though it is result of stimuli, there is no other way for people to direct their attention to consciousness or its putative contents.

At times, when humans talk about the difference between their conscious states and their unconscious states, they recall that they were aware of a difference. They say they were experiencing consciousness... or was it awareness? Or cognizance? Or life? Or vital spirits? Any unbiased report from extraterrestrials will conclude that humans are simply products of an astonishingly complex history of conditioned responses and genetic predispositions played out within their bodies and producing immediate somatic feedback with which they can tact by means of the word sound *"consciousness"*. SAE-speaking humans can talk about this somatic feedback as consciousness and remember it when they use the word sound *"consciousness"* to direct their attention to the feedback. They then refer to this process as introspection.

From an intelligent, non-human perspective, each human organism monitors its own performance and issues feedback. The internal feedback gives the organism the qualitative subjective feel because it happens within the organism. Some feedback is termed physical: the qualitative, subjective somatic feedback associated with digestion and the intestinal tract, for example. However, the same organism tacts to the qualitative, subjective feedback associated with vision or silent speech and insists that it is mental in nature. All this tacting via speech to somatic feedback within the body leads to much misguided talk about the nature and location of what is being tacted with. The myth of the unified ghost in the machine shining the spotlight of introspection on an occult non-physical consciousness is a product of this misguided talk.

For the most part, this body can distinguish between conscious vs. unconscious moments because of somatic feedback. This body is simply conscious at times and conscious of things at times. It is also aware at times and aware of things at times. It is cognizant at times and cognizant of things at times. At times it is consciously processing sensory input; at other times it is not. This is how English-speaking humans use these word sounds. This linguistic behavior does not entail that consciousness, awareness, and cognizance *exist* inside human heads. Conscious vs. unconscious is simply a distinction English-speaking human make about their somatic feedback, or lack thereof, and tact with, by means of the word sounds *"conscious"* and *"unconscious"*.

Introspection through the "mind's eye", supposedly, yields the semantic referent for the sound *"consciousness"*, what it denotes or designates. However, the sound *"consciousness"* has no semantic referent. It denotes or designates nothing. It has uses. *"consciousness"* can be *used* to tact with various sensations within the skin, but this linguistic process of tacting with various somatic sensations within the human body yields no evidence for the *existence* of an internal agent or a non-physical consciousness which is home to constituents in another ontological realm. It yields feedback from the proprioceptive, exteroceptive and interoceptive nerve systems.

The Use of the Words *"free will"*

Contemporary humans have conditioned verbal responses about their selves, their consciousness, their intentions, their purposes and their *free will*. Within the current dualist paradigm the internal conscious self is the source of intentions, decisions, choices and free will. The buck stops there. The ghost in the machine sees alternative courses of action and exercises its free will by choosing a course of action. English speech behavior abets this dualistic view of human beings that has been promulgated by philosophers for millennia. English-speaking people sanctimoniously use words such as *"decide"*, *"choose"* and *free will"* to preserve the unique status they grant themselves.

Whereas dumb machines can exhibit purposeful behavior, i.e. humans can see the purpose of the machines, humans refuse to allow them purpose or intentionality. In the robotic assembly of autos, for example, the output of robots is dictated by the input and the architectural design of the robots. The decision making is not in the machines; it has been put there by their human designers. As mentioned previously, John Searle dubbed it "derived intentionality" as opposed to the "original intentionality" in people. The machines do not really *decide* amongst different courses of action. The human-derived if-then architecture of machines along with the contemporaneous input from the assembly line enables the robots to select which of the diverging branches of action to utilize. *This is the same ability humans have and refer to as free will.*

In the case of human free will, of course, there is no architect. The heritable capacities and initial behavior passed on by the genes are then shaped by the contingencies of reinforcement each human is exposed to during their history. As the organism matures and is increasingly exposed to more contingencies, the probability of any course of action increases or decreases because of the previous history of the organism, i.e. numerous encounters with its physical and social environment along with the positive or negative reinforcement those encounters generate.

Nevertheless, much English speech behavior about intentionality and free will tacts with an ostensible constituent of the mind, *the will*. Volitional human behavior is subject to the will. You say you will do such and such and then you will it to happen. Because of their *free will*, people voluntarily do things if they have *the will* to do them. Free people can do things *at will*. Their action is deliberate and *willful*. *Willpower*, or lack thereof, is often claimed by the determining factor in your ability to proceed, succeed or even live. If your desires are strong enough your willpower strengthens and carries you through to your objective. All manner of human behavior is subject to *the will* of the person who carries out the behavior. So say all manner of theorists.

There is nothing extraordinary about such talk. Nevertheless, it is all fantasy based on the thousands of words and idioms used in support of the inferred internal agent with mystical properties and powers such as *willpower*. Still, I repeat, human behavior is not subject to a human *will*; it is subject to the organism's inherited genes, the previous contingencies of reinforcement to which the organism was subjected and the strength of the internally or externally originating stimuli to which it is contemporaneously exposed. To suppose otherwise is to suppose Darwin was wrong and Descartes was correct. That is, human organisms really do have immaterial minds with ideas, concepts, intentions, and *a free will* by which they control their own destiny.

In spite of such widespread beliefs, no less than robots, the basic architectural design of humans is provided by the genes and altered by environmental influences during maturation. The flexibility in the basic design provides for multiple mature architectures based on the conditions the organism encounters during maturation. Based on different mature architectures and differential reinforcement for incredibly diverse behavior, human organisms produce different outcomes. *Decisions* in human lives are not *made* by the autonomous individual, the internal agent controlling the free will. They simply occur based on the mature architecture, the previous history of the organism and whatever contemporaneous stimulus input the organism is subjected to.

Yet, this way of explaining human behavior won't make humans feel good. Other explanations are more *satisfying and hopeful* (two more of the 10,000+ words promoting the intentional stance). The inferred self is said to be the decision maker, the executive in charge, the internal agent that controls the destiny of the organism. The ghost in the machine exercises its free will. It decides and chooses the future behavior of the human body in which it is ensconced. However, all this talk is self-indulgent sophistry. Without the self, *who* could be making the choices and decisions? Those choices are a necessary fiction for social order in contemporary human society. It is all part of the weltanschauung of poets, pundits and political theorists. However, this confection is no less a creation of language and dualism than the self, consciousness and intentions. Like "*consciousness*", "*introspection*", "*attention*", "*intention*" etc., "*decide*", "*choose*" and "*free will*" are word sounds that depend upon and promote the dualist paradigm. They are part of the SAE linguistic heritage. That erroneous linguistic behavior produces some good social behavior. Humans have been talking about themselves this way for thousands of years. They have been wrong. Without the ghost in the machine, there is no one to make the decisions and choices by exercising their free will.

The Use of the Word "*rule*"

There is a long history of philosophical debate about what rules are and what it is for humans to adopt rules, obey rules, enforce rules, conform to rules, flout rules and so on. Much human behavior is claimed to be rule governed, including speech. In spite of the fact that few people can recite or explain the rules of speech, these rules are said to be internalized somehow and subsequently govern the speech behavior of all competent speakers. Yet, few of these subconscious rules of speech (not just regularities) have been found to be universal. Invariably, any putative rules have many exceptions and omissions. That makes them highly suspect.

On the other hand, within philosophy and science, there is little serious debate about non-human animals adopting, enforcing, obeying or flouting rules. These creatures have no *choice* about their behavior. They have no idea if they are flouting rules or not. They are captives of the reflexive behavior they inherit and the conditioned responses that their previous history produces. Non-human organisms of all sorts are said to behave the way they do oblivious to any rules. They are not volitional agents. They do not make, understand, follow, flout or recognize rules of any sort. They are quite different than humans; they do not have internal agents to exercise their free will.

Many human rules which can be recited and explained, e.g. driving rules, are used to explain human behavior. People are said to have reasons for creating these rules and reasons for *choosing* to obey or flout them, depending upon their *intentions*. It is said that if they understand them, humans *decide* whether they will obey rules or flout them. The rule flouting must be *intentional* for humans to be culpable. The point is, for humans, using *rules* as an explanation for behavior requires the intentional stance and the dualistic internal self who has the understanding, and the free will to follow or flout rules.

Without free will, rules and the intentional stance, humans become nothing more than stimulus-response "protein robots" in the words of Daniel C. Dennett. Human societies, built upon rules, have a huge stake in free will, rules and the intentional stance. They are part and parcel of our social and political philosophies and are deeply imbedded in our speech behavior. In spite of that, it is all part of the ghost in the machine legend. What will it take to give up dualism, the intentional stance and the myth of the internal agent with free will who chooses whether or not to obey *rules*? It will take an epiphany on the scale of that of Copernicus', Newton's, Darwin's, Einstein's, Whorf's, and Skinner's.

The Science of Consciousness

In <u>Consciousness Explained</u> (1991) philosopher Daniel C. Dennett tries to "compose a scientific theory of consciousness". He tries to integrate the latest brain science and philosophy. It is an intriguing look at consciousness, using English while trying to eliminate the distinctions that are an integral part of that conditioned English verbal behavior. The goal is admirable, but not achievable because the challenges are not scientific or philosophical they are behavioral. The challenge is to recognize the mentalism inherent in the use of word sounds such as "*conscious*", "*consciousness*", "*intentionality*", "*phenomena*", "*sensation*", "*think*", "*mental content*", "*Knowledge*", "*belief*", "*attention*", "*introspection*", "*free will*" and 10,000 more dualism-based words by restricting the use of these words to quotidian discourse. These words have practical value in everyday conversation, but they have no place in the scientific or philosophical explanations of human beings.

Dennett recognizes dualism as "a boring dodge enshrined in the concept of a "*deux a machina*". Dennett (1991: 25). Yet his attempt to eliminate the *deux* and retain the *machina* is doomed to failure if he uses words the way most English-speaking humans do. He fails to recognize how deeply embedded dualism is in that verbal behavior. If anyone tries to "compose a scientific theory of consciousness" utilizing contemporary English speech behavior they will fail because that linguistic behavior is anchored in dualism, lock, stock and barrel.

Dennett recognizes the dualism embedded in human speech:

> "The idea that a self (or a person, or, for that matter, a soul) is distinct from a brain or a body is deeply rooted in our ways of speaking, and hence in our ways of thinking." Dennett (1991: 29)

Nevertheless, he continues to use the linguistic behavior that he inherited from Plato, Aristotle, Augustine, Descartes, Russell, Ryle et al. and has since trickled down to teachers and truck drivers. Dennett uses word sounds and their derivative symbols more or less in the way that those philosophers used them. For example:

> "On the view of consciousness I will develop in this book, it turns out that consciousness, like love and money, is a phenomenon that does indeed depend to a surprising extent on its associated concepts." Dennett (1991: 24)

The view of consciousness that SAE-speaking humans have, depends not on concepts, but on their habituated speech behavior and the concomitant speech-thinking that they do with the words. The use of word sounds such as "*consciousness*" and "*concepts*" are all loaded with metaphysical freight; they presuppose a mind/body disconnect. Whatever other methodological objections one might have to Dennett's effort are beside the point. Without using the dualistic language, the human body simply processes input and converts it to output. Input and output to a body have collateral somatic consequences. Nothing needs to be said about hypothetical beliefs, desires, intentions, concepts, mental events etc. in a scientific explanation of humans and their behavior.

The challenge as Dennett sees it "is to construct a theory of mental events using data that scientific method permits. Such a theory will have to be constructed from the third-person point of view, since all science is constructed from that perspective." Dennett (1991: 71) However dualism has been fully incorporated into the third-person perspective of science as well as the first-person introspective account. The third-person language scientists use is replete with *"beliefs"*, *"intentions"*, *"concepts"*, *"mental content"* etc. Yet there is no observational data from the third-person perspective to back up any of the claims that humans have beliefs, desires, intentions, concepts, or mental content of any kind within their bodies. Hence, there is no reason to give any credence to the claims or analysis utilizing the speech behavior that incorporates such terminology, be it first-person or third-person terminology.

Aside from the verbal behavior issues, Dennett, Antonio Damasio and others have pointed to numerous experiments which should give SAE-speaking humans doubt about the way they think about consciousness. Human assumptions about consciousness based on first-person reports may be at odds with the test data gathered in third-person empirical reports. For example, everyday talk about "stream of consciousness", the flowing stream metaphor, may not be warranted. Dennett reports:

> "One of the most striking features of consciousness is its discontinuity—as revealed in the blind spot, and saccadic gaps, to take the simplest examples. The discontinuity of consciousness is striking because of the **apparent** continuity of consciousness. Neumann (1990) points out that consciousness may in general be a gappy phenomenon, and as long as the temporal edges of the gaps are not positively perceived, there will be no sense of the gappiness in the 'stream' of consciousness." Dennett (1991: 356)

Kristof Koch updates the research on saccadic suppression in his 2019 book The Feeling of Life Itself:

> "Given that you make more than 100,000 daily saccades, each one lasting between 20 and 100 milliseconds, saccadic and blink suppression adds up to more than an hour a day during which you are effectively blind! Yet until scientists started studying eye movements, no one was aware of this remarkable fact." Koch, (2019: 20)

Utilizing the spotlight of language after they have been stimulated to do so, humans *introspect* and talk about what they "see". They then use faulty analogies claiming that their experiences are like a flowing stream or a movie in the theater of the mind. The theater of the mind metaphor has *mental* movies showing on a *mental* screen with *mental* surround sound, *mental* smell-o-vision etc. There are many reasons and much evidence to suggest that conscious experience is not at all like a flowing stream or a movie playing on a theater screen in the head. Unfortunately, the faulty analogies have helped create the metaphorical entities required to make the analogies seem plausible. The fault is not with the experience; it is with the analogies and the conditioned verbal behavior used in the thinking and the reporting about the experience.

Consider more evidence from James R. Hurford who sums up research on the limits of human ability to make the temporal distinctions necessary for the "stream of consciousness" metaphors to succeed:

> "... something is also known about the temporal 'size' of perceived events, in humans, and it seems likely that the facts are not very different for closely related primates. The lower limit is about 30 milliseconds. 'Sensory data picked up within 30ms are treated as cotemporal, that is, a relationship of separate stimuli with respect to the before-after dimension cannot be established (Poppel, 1997). Temporal order threshold being identical in different sensory modalities (Hirsh and Sherrick, 1961), thus, also indicates a lower limit for event identification. 'A low-frequency mechanism... binds successive events up to approximately 3 seconds into perceptual and actions units... Metaphorically, the brain asks every 3 seconds 'what is new?'" Hurford (2007: 96)

Indeed, the temporal order of the events in our "stream of consciousness" may not be what people perceive it to be. What they perceive as co-temporal events may in fact be sequential. These sequential events are often bundled by their brains.

The well-known cases of so-called "blindsight" provide more experimental evidence that confutes human thinking about their conscious experience. Colin McGinn summarizes the experimental results and conclusions:

> "... This is the peculiar syndrome, by now quite well known, in which a person (or animal) suffers damage to certain regions of the visual cortex, as a result of which sensations of sight disappear, but not everything visual goes. Such a person reports himself as blind, and indeed he behaves in normal circumstances indistinguishably from a blind person; after all, he lacks visual experiences. But if an experimenter requests that the patient try to make a guess about various objects placed before his eyes, then it turns out that the patient performs above the level predicted by chance. He can, for example, guess the shapes of presented objects to an impressive degree of accuracy, even though he reports himself as shooting in the dark. There are no conscious experiences to back up his guesses, but somehow the information is getting in. The environment is still feeding into his ability to make judgments about what is around him, despite his visual blankness. Thus there is a sense in which he is sighted and a sense in which he is blind. Hence the label "blindsight," an oxymoron if there ever was one...

> "What does blindsight show about the inner structure of consciousness? It shows, I think, that in normal vision there is a component of that experience that is not subject to introspection... The reasoning here is as follows: (1) In normal vision we make judgments about the environment on the basis of the information contained in our experience; but (2) in blindsight some of these judgments are left intact, despite the fact that no experience is subject to introspection; so (3) it must be the case that in normal vision there is visual processing that is not given to introspection." McGinn (1999: 147)

Given these results and appreciably more clinical research, the conclusion can be drawn that human introspection is not a reliable source of evidence for what is occurring in people's conscious moments. It appears that information about the world seeps into human memory in various ways that are not given to introspection.

Brie Gertler and Lawrence Shapiro made another significant observation about the relation between introspection, language and consciousness in cognitive science:

> "Now consider the use of introspective reports in the study of consciousness. I focus on the use of such reports to determine whether or not a subject has a conscious state of a specified type. Three widely discussed domains of consciousness research are blindsight, implicit memory and prosopagnosia. In all three domains, subjects with neurological deficits are said to lack conscious informational states of a normal sort, but they are also found to possess related information in nonconscious form. Blindsight subjects lack conscious visual experience in a portion of their field of view (their scotoma), but nonetheless show signs of having visually obtained information about objects in the unseen area...
>
> "How do cognitive scientists determine in all these cases that consciousness is present or absent in their subjects' states? The answer is fairly straightforward. Subject to some qualification, consciousness researchers rely on their subjects' introspective reports. To test for scotoma, as in the case of Weiskrantz's (1986) patient DB, the patient is asked to report what is seen when stimuli are presented to different points in the visual field. DB did not report seeing stimuli falling anywhere in the region... Hence it was concluded that DB lacked conscious vision in those areas. But asked to guess about certain stimuli in those areas, DB's performance revealed some kind on information-bearing state. Since he denied having (visual) information of this sort, however, this state was declared to be nonconscious. Thus the ability or inability to report a state is taken as a criterion of its being conscious or unconscious." Gertler and Shapiro (2007: 68)

It seems that the only criterion for consciousness consists in the ability to report it, though that reporting is often unreliable.

Antonio Damasio has provided a comprehensive look at consciousness from a neurological point of view. His extraordinary work with brain-damaged patients provides him with extensive insights on the relationship between neuroscience and what he refers to as "levels of consciousness". Damasio approaches consciousness from a biological perspective, consciousness as a biological phenomenon not a non-physical entity existing in human heads.

> "In short, core consciousness is a simple, biological phenomenon: it has one single level of organization; it is stable across the lifetime of the organism; it is not exclusively human; and it is not dependent on conventional memory, working memory, reasoning, or language. On the other hand, extended consciousness is a complex biological phenomenon; it has several levels of organization; and it evolves across the lifetime of the organism." Damasio (1999: 16)

He details the biology of consciousness and makes distinctions about awareness, wakefulness, emotions, feelings, core consciousness and extended consciousness. Damasio provides a look at the neurological basis for the machinery of consciousness in all its forms. Emotion, attention, feelings etc. can all be mapped to structures within the brain.[28]

As he makes clear, consciousness is not monolithic. The neurological uses for the sound *"consciousness"* cover a lot of ground. Damasio argues quite persuasively that the phenomenon of consciousness, when observed under the empirical microscope, is anything but a single internal process. What humans say about themselves using the umbrella term of *"consciousness"* is quite varied. However, the most fundamental point he makes is that the third-person perspective provided by science can account for all of what humans ordinarily call consciousness. Neuroscience can provide a perfectly adequate explanation for what is occurring inside of each living human organism.

Some of that science, in recent years, has turned the consciousness paradigm upside down:

> "…using EEG, researchers can reliably detect cortical activity signaling these impending movements about a half a second before subjects feel they made the decision to move… We now have reason to believe that with access to certain activity inside your brain, another person can know what you're going to do before you do." Harris A. (2019:27)

With evidence such as this, scientists should not feel compelled to engage in the philosophical debate about consciousness and mental activities. They need not be dualists, idealists, physicalists, materialists, panpsychists or mysterians. These are artificial choices imposed by the linguistic behavior they have inherited from philosophers. Committed scientists must eliminate all traces of dualism from their scientific speech behavior because it is not scientific. But if you insist that humans have non-physical entities inside their heads when they speak you have already wandered into the bifurcated English-speaking universe of traditional semantic theory. That dualistic paradigm of word use is both a consequence of, and a constant affirmation of mind/body dualism, though you need not take that first step.

Arrangements of organic matter often produce experiential sensations within human bodies. Those sensations need not have a container other than the body. Humans no longer need the metaphysical excrescences of Plato, Aristotle, Augustine, Descartes, Russell, Chomsky or Pinker to explain how they function. There is no need for minds, consciousness, concepts, intention, et cetera, to explain how humans function. These mysterious non-corporeal entities and processes are products of their verbal behavior not products of Mother Nature.

In summary, it seems safe to conclude that much of human talk about consciousness is based on unreliable introspective evidence, shaky methodology, and consists of outdated verbal behavior with all its inherent metaphysical absurdities. If such talk is eliminated the absurdities will be eliminated as well. It must be added that Whorf's principle of linguistic relativity comes into play here. That is, not all humans talk and think about their conscious experience the way English-speaking philosophers do, e.g. claims for the *existence* of consciousness in another mode.

Yet, there seems to be something distinctly different about consciousness, you say. It surely cannot be a matter of speech behavior, you say. Somehow, with words, humans should be able to explain or describe consciousness. So, to be philosophically informative and satisfying, they must breach the ontological barrier. But, just suppose that the author is correct in claiming that human verbal behavior *creates* the ontological barrier? Suppose the linguistic conditioning that

SAE-speaking humans undergo establishes fuzzy but-absolute boundaries beyond which they cannot speak or think. Just suppose that vocal behavior creates the "intuition of distinctness" and the "dualist compulsion" that Papineau reports (2002). OK, you begrudgingly admit that language may be part of the problem, but not *the* problem. You are not alone.

While some prominent philosophers such as John Searle acknowledge that vocabulary is *part* of the problem (2004: pg.75), no one has proposed an accurate assessment of the consciousness/body problem from a non-semantic perspective. No one has said that SAE speech behavior leads them to sense that they have internal agents, selves and unified consciousness inside their skulls that they can point to with "*i*", "*me*", "*my consciousness*" and "*my self*". No one has said that because of their verbal behavior humans *assume* that they have an internal director who can direct their attention to a consciousness and its putative constituents. Until now, no one has said that *such speech behavior is the problem*. Well, I do. And the empirical evidence thus far supports me.

Humans make distinctions about their sensations and experiences. Some are caused by things outside their bodies; some are caused by things inside their bodies. The totality of sensory input seems to be what they are pointing to most often when they use "*consciousness*". When that input disappears, so does the consciousness. Where did it go? Where was it? The *consciousness* was nowhere, but the body was processing input and generating somatic output. Beyond that, talk about sensations in consciousness is not science; it is bad verbal behavior based on years of previous bad verbal behavior.

Artificial Intelligence

Given human hubris, it is not surprising that for many of them the standard for artificial intelligence (AI) is claimed to be the ability of a computer to think as a human would think. *The Turing Test* is often said to be a test for AI. Computer engineers would build a Turing machine in a room and have someone ask it questions. That person could also ask questions of a human in the same room. If the inquirer could not determine whether the answers are from the machine or from the human, theorists must grant that the machine in the room is *intelligent*.

Reasonable follow-up questions might be: if the machine is intelligent, does it believe certain things and *know* other things? Can it truly *think*? Would humans endow the computer with a thinking *mind*? The answers to these philosophical questions are quite simple. No, machines are not intelligent. They do not believe or know things. Nor do they engage in mental activity or have minds, not because of the limits of current technology, but rather because of the limits of current conditioned English verbal behavior which has the ontological barrier firmly in place. If you are a competent English speaker, you will not say or think that machines can believe or know things or engage in mental activity. You will refuse to say or think that machines can have minds or consciousness existing in them.

However, if you are a competent English speaker, you will say and think that humans have beliefs and knowledge stored in a supernatural container existing behind their eyes called a mind or consciousness. You will also be firmly convinced that you engage in a non-physical activity called thinking with thoughts in that same supernatural location that has no physical dimensions and cannot be observed by any means. Along with the thoughts, you will be firmly convinced by your speech behavior that you have a mind that controls your body, a mind that understands, decides, intends, and wills thing to happen for the bodily machine.

Unobservable egos, spirits, souls, selves, minds and consciousness are the locations for the unobservable mental activity that supposedly takes place between your ears. These non-physical containers warehouse non-physical entities and processes in which EA-speaking humans have invested 3000+ years of folk psychology, philosophical speculation, and linguistic habituation. They are antiquated artifacts that once served useful purposes; they provided acceptable explanations for human behavior. They still do for the man on the street. For sophisticated thinkers, they no longer do.

In spite of that, most philosophers are still constrained by their habituated speech intuitions. John R. Searle's intuitions, for instance, corrupt his famous Chinese room experiment in which he dismisses the possibility of a Turing machine that "understands" language. It will prove instructive to analyze Searle's 1983 *gedankenexperiment* in light of our previous discussions:

> "Imagine that a bunch of computer programmers have written a program that will enable a computer to simulate the understanding of Chinese. So, for example, if the computer's given a question in Chinese, it will match the question against its memory, or data base, and produce appropriate answers to

the questions in Chinese. Suppose for the sake of argument that the computer's answers are as good as those of a native Chinese speaker. Now then, does the computer, on the basis of this, understand Chinese, does it literally understand Chinese, in the way that Chinese speakers understand Chinese? Well, imagine that you are locked in a room, and in this room are several baskets full of Chinese symbols. Imagine that you (like me) do not understand a word of Chinese, but that you are given a rule book in English for manipulating these symbols. The rules specify the manipulations of the symbols purely formally, in terms of their syntax, not their semantics. So the rule might say: 'Take a squiggle-squiggle sign out of basket number one and put it next to a squiggle-squoggle sign from basket number two.' Now suppose that some other Chinese symbols are passed into the room, and that you are given further rules for passing back Chinese symbols out of the room. Suppose that unknown to you the symbols passed into the room are called 'questions' by the people outside the room, and the symbols you pass back out of the room are called 'answers to the questions.' Suppose, furthermore, that the programmers are so good at designing the programs and that you are so good at manipulating the symbols, that very soon your answers are indistinguishable from those of a native Chinese speaker. There you are locked in your room shuffling your Chinese symbols and passing out Chinese symbols in response to incoming Chinese symbols. On the basis of the situation as I have described it, there is no way you could learn any Chinese by manipulating these formal symbols.

"Now the point of the story is simply this: by virtue of implementing a formal computer program from the view of the outside observer, you behave exactly as if you understood Chinese, but all the same you don't understand a word of Chinese... If you don't understand Chinese, then no computer could understand Chinese because no digital computer, just by virtue of running a program, has anything that you don't have. All the computer has is a formal program for manipulation uninterpreted Chinese symbols. To repeat, a computer has syntax, but no semantics. The whole point of the parable of the Chinese room is to remind us of the fact that we knew all along. Understanding language, or indeed, having mental states at all, involves more that just having a bunch of formal symbols. It involves having an interpretation, or a meaning attached to those symbols." Searle via Chalmers 1983: 671)

One might criticize Searle's argument based on the first premise, which states that "a bunch of computer programmers have written a program that will enable a computer to simulate the understanding of Chinese". Because of the influence of universal grammarians, Searle assumes that speech is rule bound, hence programmable. It is not. The ability to use acoustic devices in context is not rule-bound behavior; (one also wonders what the difference is between "simulated understanding" and understanding. Possibly the computer just nods in agreement and frequently says "exactly") In any case, no computer will ever simulate the understanding of Chinese, or any other language, for a whole host of reasons mentioned in the previous chapters, e.g. présuppositions about human interactions with their natural environment, human artifacts, etc.

In his thought experiment, Searle recognizes the impossibility of a computer duplicating Chinese speech behavior, but for the wrong reasons. He gets much closer to the correct reason in the following witty Searle story, compliments of one of his students Daniel L. Everett:

> "A man went into a restaurant and ordered a hamburger. When the hamburger arrived it was burnt to a crisp, and the man stormed out of the restaurant angrily, without paying for the burger or leaving a tip.
>
> The computer scientist then asks the computer, 'Did the man eat the hamburger?' To this the computer answers, 'No.'
>
> Searle then asked if he could put a question to the computer after this display: 'Did the man put the hamburger in his ear?' The computer answered, 'I don't know.'
>
> Now, that is surprising. If the computer had learned about humans and their cultural activities, shouldn't it know that we don't stick food in our ears, by and large? All humans know this. Somehow the computer was not learning things that all humans know as a matter of course. And Searle claimed that it was incapable of doing so, even in principle. Searle called this information, the background." Everett (2002: 163)

In this exchange Searle hints at the point I made in Chapter Two. AI will only be possible when machines can duplicate all of human sensory experience, including the emotional responses produced by their limbic system and the historical interactions with other humans and their environment that condition people to behave verbally as they do. These artificially intelligent machines must also be able to tell bad jokes, use sarcasm, brag about themselves, grieve at the loss of humans, and remember how people interact with other people, implements, and their environment. These machines must also process information by using analogies and metaphors, and if machines come along that are able to duplicate all of human behavior, they will be as unique and unpredictable as each human being is. Human intelligence is nothing to brag about. Trying to duplicate it in machines is highly unlikely and totally unnecessary.

Humans learn many things about other humans and their behavior in relation to food, tools, weapons, and language, by being members of a culture. They observe others and adapt the behavior appropriate to their surroundings. There is nothing controversial about this. However, the communicative ability of a computer cannot duplicate a human's unless it has had the same relevant experiences which produce verbal behavior in humans. It must be the functional equivalent of a human being who has undergone many years of iterated learning regarding the natural environment, human artifacts, the behavior of other people, etc. Neither computers nor humans can duplicate human speech ability with formal procedures. There is no system of rules by which either can become competent speakers.

Searle also mistakenly assumes the semantic stance, that words are symbols with "meaning attached". However, word sounds are not simply interchangeable units of *meaning*. Word sounds and combinations of sounds are acoustic devices whose use has been previously reinforced. In fact, computers cannot mimic human word sound use, not because the computer would be missing *semantic content*, but rather because word sound use is individual behavior idiosyncratically conditioned into each human organism over the lifetime of that organism and its interactions with the natural environment, human artifacts, the behavior of other people etc.

However, the crux of the problem is, once again, our speech behavior. SAE-speaking humans would have to change their verbal behavior to accommodate computers that believe, know, think and understand. These speakers might currently allow them to be smart, but *mental* activity still cannot be attributed to machines, no matter how smart they are. In SAE languages, mental processes and mental states cannot occur in non-sentient artifacts. The ontological divide is firmly embedded in your long-entrenched verbal behavior about mechanical devices. Computers will never believe, know, think or understand because your habituated verbal behavior will not allow them to.

Searle uses language as he has been conditioned to use it. He assumes the intentional stance and the dualism implicit in his use of ordinary words such as: **'understand', 'knew', 'mental states', 'meaning',** and **'symbols'.** He fails to take into account his own use of the English language and the underlying assumptions inherent in that verbal behavior and its derivative symbolic recordings. He assumes that there is a *mental state of understanding* that supports human verbal behavior. Many philosophers such as Searle continue to insist that there is something more than physical matter inside humans; there are mental states and processes. They are what distinguish man from machine.

In fact, philosophers, scientists and AI engineers should eliminate the verbal behavior that characterizes humans as having *intelligence, minds, consciousness* and *mental* capacity. They should eliminate dualism and the intentional stance from their scientific speech behavior. They can characterize humans as fuzzy adaptive systems governed by the same forces that govern non-human creatures and machines. When they do, there will be nowhere to store the beliefs, knowledge, concepts and thoughts that word symbols supposedly represent. The understanding will also disappear. In the process, semantics will fall by the wayside as well. So too will the pipe dream of a Turing machine.

Chapter Three

Summary & Notes

Why are humans left with the duality of physical entities and processes juxtaposed with mental entities and processes? Why have humans so characterized themselves? They do so because it gives them a monumental dollop of survival value. Not that they intended to do it. They have no intentions. The same impersonal non-intentional natural selection process that brought about the evolution of species also brought about the evolution of human speech and all the philosophical perplexities therein.

The habituated use of "*I*", "*me*," and "*my*" by English speakers leads them to a sense that they have an internal agent that directs their behavior. As a result of their verbal behavior, these humans say that the central location of the continuing receipt of sensory input within the organism is some-thing called the soul, the self, the mind, or consciousness. They infer that there is a singular, enduring, non-physical agent inside their bodies that is receiving the input and controlling the bodily behavior. That agent is also said to be the repository for all sorts of *mental* states and *mental* processes used to explain human behavior: free will, understanding, knowledge, beliefs, ideas, concepts, intentions, thoughts and thinking.

English-speaking people use the words sounds "*free will*", *understand*", "*Know*", "*believe*", "*ideas*", "*concepts*" "*intentions*", "*thoughts*", and "*thinking*" because they have functional value within the consciousness/body paradigm. They help create acceptable explanations for much of their behavior. Free will, understanding, etc. are all jumbled in an inconsistent hodgepodge of mental and emotional explanations for humans doing what they do. These non-physical causes are whatever philosophers and contemporary psychologists deem them to be, and whatever they can dupe folks into accepting as satisfactory explanations for their behavior.

Humans have two sources of stimuli. Some are somatic feedback from within the organism and some are received from outside of the organism. The organism *responds* to both stimuli with tacting behavior. When humans began tacting with sounds they began a process which categorized the stimuli based on the putative location of the stimuli. Ultimately, some humans inferred that there were mysterious non-physical processes and entities located within their bodies to account for the observed behavior of the organism. A host of verbal behavior coalesced around these non-physical processes and entities as well as the non-physical containers that held them. People began to talk about souls, selves, minds, consciousness and all the occult states and happenings therein.

That verbal behavior also creates powerful intuitions and "common sense" beliefs about those mental entities and processes etc. that are corroborated with dualistic philosophies of one form or other. Human awareness of the self and its conscious mental activity is a product of the historic metaphysical picture painted by Plato, Aristotle, Augustine, Descartes, Russell et al. and the resultant verbal behavior. To say or think that mental activity is *essentially* different than physical activity is brought about by such linguistic behavior. The language practices and the myth of the ghost in the machine with paranormal abilities are mutually reinforcing.

"Consciousness" is a word sound people use to tact with a distinction they make about their experience. Whether that distinction is justified or not, there need not *be* anything to which it refers. There is no need for a supernatural entity, consciousness, as a referent for the sound "consciousness" anymore than there is a need for a referent for "non-sleeping" or "redness." Humans make distinctions and tact with them by means of sounds. There are no ontological implications whatsoever. Saying: "I am conscious" is saying not much more than: "this body is not sleeping".

From the third-party perspective of science, a human body receives input that lights up certain receptors in eyes, ears, tongues, noses and skin. As do millions of other organisms, human organisms respond. There is no reason to suppose that humans are unique in this regard. However, in addition, humans have learned to use noises in tacting with many objects, actions, events and distinctions they perceive. They have also inferred many others based on their tacting skills, e.g. forces, causes, intentions, minds, spirits, selves, happiness and consciousness. That speech behavior makes them unique. However, making existential claims about those inferred entities and processes is ontological hubris that needs to be halted. There is no supportable reason to believe that there is an alternative ontological realm called consciousness ensconced in human bodies.

Consciousness, like life, is a biological phenomenon. As such, it should be viewed, not as a miraculous inexplicable chasm between men and machines, but rather a normal progression in the evolutionary history of organic matter. Humans lose nothing when they "lose consciousness". Their bodies cease certain somatic functions, and when those somatic functions cease permanently, the body dies due to mechanical failure. The interface of input and output becomes inoperative. The life-sustaining sensations and the chemical reactions of the organism cease. Other chemical processes begin. No *thing* is lost. No things called consciousness or life were there to begin with.

Humans can account for their subjective experience from the third-party perspective by acknowledging that their use of word sounds enables them to tact and infer free will, knowledge, beliefs, ideas, concepts, intentions, thoughts, thinking, and all the assorted flora and fauna of the self, the self that can be conscious or unconscious, happy or sad. Without these sounds produced by their bodies, along with the tacting skill, they could neither say nor think anything about consciousness, minds, selves, or mental entities of any kind. The ontological speculation would not be possible and the implicit dualism in much of their speech behavior would not have developed.

The philosophical challenge of many modern-day theorists has been to either reduce minds to physical entities, or eliminate minds, both by means of argument. But, neither reductionists nor eliminativists can reduce or eliminate consciousness if they retain the consciousness/body, meaning/word dualism embedded in their verbal behavior. That mind-matter paradigm will only be changed by changing their verbal behavior. Theorists must stop the philosophical gibberish about free will, knowledge, beliefs, ideas, concepts, intentions, thoughts and thinking. They must restrict their verbal behavior to talk about other behavior and neurological states.

Charles Darwin, through The Origin of Species, described to the world the process of natural selection. In doing so he freed our cosmogony from the intentional stance, dualism and metaphysics. A new perspective on our linguistic behavior can free all of science and philosophy from the intentional stance, dualism, and metaphysics.

---

1. "A definitional matter must be addressed initially. It should be noted that European American (EA) is used here to refer to what is commonly termed Western because the Western hemisphere is not as culturally homogeneous as the European American portion. EAs, as used here, refers to adult upper- and middle-income Americans of European descent, the majority of whom are thought to hold the naïve folk psychology described or implied by the late 20th century academic literature on psychology and philosophy of mind. Reflecting the European origins of this theory (back to Ancient Greece), many elements are probably shared by Europeans as well, and many non-EAs also share much of the theory." Lillard (1998) Ethnopsychologies: Cultural Variations in Theories of Mind, Psychological Bulletin1998, vol. 123, No. I, 3-32

EA folk psychology includes many beliefs about people and their mental constituents. For example, people are said to have knowledge and beliefs about themselves and others as rational agents who are responsible for their own behavior. For the most part, EAs do not fault the gods, demons, witches, the alignment of the planets or their dead ancestors who have temporarily seized control of their bodies when held to account for their actions. They say that *the reason* they do things is because they have certain *knowledge and beliefs*. For instance, the *reason* people seek medical care rather than consulting a witch doctor is because they *believe* in modern medicine. The mind is the location of these various mental entities, states and processes such as beliefs which determine the behavior of the organism. This theory is also known as the European American Social Science (EASSM) theory of mind.

2. Let us agree that all human sensations are personal and non-transferable, i.e. this body's sensations happen to it and no one else. Each human's sensations are a result of their internal neurochemistry and each human has privileged access to its sensations. There is no outside confirmation possible. There may be corroborating third-party evidence that a sensation has occurred, e.g. NCCs etc., but not direct confirmation from third parties.

3. "Curiously enough, part of the answer was supplied by the psychoanalysts, who insisted that, although a man might be able to see some of his mental life, he could not see all of it. The kind of thoughts Freud called "unconscious' took place without the knowledge of the thinker. From an association, verbal slip, or dream it could be shown that a person must have responded to a passing stimulus although he could not tell you that he had done so. More complex thought processes, including problem solving and verbal play, could also go on without the thinker's knowledge. Freud had devised, and never abandoned faith in, one of the most elaborate mental apparatuses of all time. He nevertheless contributed to the behavioristic argument by showing that mental activity did not, at least, require consciousness. His proofs that thinking had occurred without introspective recognition were, indeed, clearly in the spirit of Lloyd Morgan. They were operational analyses of mental life— even though, for Freud, only the unconscious part of it. Experimental evidence pointing in the same direction soon began to accumulate." Skinner (1969: 225)

4. Insensate unthinking human zombies are philosophical posits taken seriously by many philosophers. They are hypothesized to act just like humans, but are not human because they lack consciousness. Philosopher Daniel Dennet explains: "…by definition, a zombie behaves indistinguishably from a conscious being—in all possible tests, including not only answers to questions (as in the Turing test) but psychophysical tests, neuro-physiological test—all tests than any 'third person' science can devise." Dennet (2005: 15)

"What is it like to be a zombie? By definition: nothing." Dennet (2005: 38) Dennett however, is not an adherent of what he calls the zombic hunch: "I have long claimed that this conceivability is only apparent; some misguided philosophers think they can conceive of a zombie, but they are badly mistaken." (Ibid: 15)

5. Reserved.

6. "Premack and Woodruff (1978) introduced the term theory of mind to refer to a tendency to impute mental states to oneself and others." Lillard (1998) Ethnopsychologies: Cultural Variations in Theories of Mind, Psychological Bulletin1998, vol. 123, No. I, 3-

7. Reserved.

8. "Heterophenomenology is explicitly not a first-person methodology (as its name makes clear) but it is also not directly about "brain processes and the like": it is a reasoned, objective extrapolation from patterns discernible in the behavior of the subjects, including their text-producing or communicative behavior, and as such it is about precisely the higher-level dispositions, both cognitive and emotional, that convince us that our fellow human beings are conscious." Dennett (2005:149

9. Wittgenstein makes a similar point about category mistakes in The Blue Book and attributes it to confusion caused by our language use which can bring about what we clearly recognize as nonsense: "…On the other hand the problem here arises which could be expressed by the question: 'Is it possible for a machine to think?... And the trouble which is expressed in this question is not really that we don't yet know a machine which could do the job. The question is not analogous to that which someone might have asked a hundred years ago: 'Can a machine liquefy a gas?' The trouble is rather that the sentence, 'A machine thinks (perceives, wishes)': seems somehow nonsensical. It is as though we had asked 'Has the number 3 a colour?'…
We are up against trouble caused by our way of expression." Wittgenstein (1958a: #47)

10. "It is often said, particularly by psychoanalysts, that behaviorism cannot deal with the unconscious. The fact is that, to begin with, it deals with nothing else. The controlling relations between behavior and genetic and environmental variables are all unconscious so long as they are not observed, and it was Freud who emphasized that they need not be observed (that is, conscious) to be effective. It requires a special verbal environment to impose consciousness on behavior by inducing a person to respond to his own body while he is behaving. If consciousness seems to have a causal effect, it is the effect of the special environment which induces self-observation." Skinner (1974: 169)

11. Psychiatric talk about egos, consciousness, subconsciousness, alternate consciousnesses, mental causation, ad nauseam, is an extension of folk psychology and its foundation in Greek metaphysics. Such unreflective psychobabble is said to be "science" but there are no psychological laws comparable to the laws of physics or chemistry. Psychiatry cannot predict anything with precision or certitude. Psychiatry is no more a science than is astrology or voodoo. It is based on the mysterious process of introspection, not observational evidence that can be confirmed by third parties. It is based on a language with occult entities and forces occupying an occult container within the human body. Talk about conscious, unconscious, subconsciousness and other paranormal forces that control human behavior is useful mythology, but mythology none the less. No less so than demonic possession.

12. From the introduction to Whorf's <u>Language, Thought, and Reality</u> by John B. Carroll: Intentions as motivating mental forces may not be a universal speech phenomenon. Linguist Harry Hoijer, who researched the Navaho language and culture and claimed that the Navaho, because of their language, had a much more passive view: "Hoijer claims to have found a suggestion of a correlation between the world view implied by the Navaho verb system (that people only 'participate' or 'get involved' in acts rather than initiate them) and the passivity on general restlessness or fatefulness of Navaho mythology." Whorf (1956:28).

13. Skinner gives all due credit to Edward L. Thorndike for his work which preceded Skinner's and laid the foundation for a non-teleological explanation of any organism's behavior, including humans: "We are interested in the behavior of an organism because of its effect on the environment. (One effect on the social environment is, of course, the arousal of our interest.) Some effects seem to throw light on the behavior which produces them, but their explanatory role has been clouded by the fact that they follow the behavior and therefore raise the specter of teleology.

An attempt has been made to solve the problem by creating a prior surrogate of a given effect. A quality or property of purpose is assigned to behavior to bring 'what the organism is behaving for' into the effective present; or the organism is said to behave in a given way because it intends to achieve, or expects to have, a given effect; or its behavior is characterized as possessing utility to the extent that it maximizes or minimizes certain effects. The teleological problem is, of course, not solved until we have answered certain questions: what gives an action its purpose, what leads an organism to expect to have an effect, how is utility represented in behavior? "The answers to such questions are eventually to be found in past instances in which similar behavior has been effective. The original problem can be solved directly in the same way. Thorndike's <u>Law of Effect</u> was a step in that direction: the approximately simultaneous occurrence of a response and certain environmental events, (usually generated by it) changes the responding organism, increasing the probability that responses of the same sort will occur again. The response itself has passed into history and is not altered. By emphasizing a change in the organism, Thorndike's principle made it possible to include the effects of action among the causes of future action without using concepts like purpose, intention, expectancy, or utility. Up to that time the only demonstrable causes of behavior had been antecedent stimuli... The <u>Law of Effect</u> added an important new class of variables of which behavior could be shown to be a function." Skinner (1969: 105)

14. Evolution is descent with modification. Darwin did not originate the theory of evolution. Nor did Darwin call his theory a theory of "evolution". Darwin called his theory the "a theory of descent". These days, it is commonly referred to as the theory of natural selection. The full title of his first book was: "On the Origin of Species by Means of Natural Selection, or the Preservation of Favoured Races in the Struggle for Life". As he noted in that book, the Greeks had hypothesized a teleological theory of natural selection over 2000 years earlier: "Aristotle, in his 'Physicae Auscultationes', after remarking that rain does not fall in order to make the corn grow, any more that it falls to spoil the farmer's corn when threshed out of doors, applies the same argument to organization: and adds 'So what hinders the different parts (of the body) from having this merely accidental relation in nature? As the teeth, for example, grow by necessity, the front ones sharp, adapted for dividing, and the grinders flat, and serviceable for masticating the food; since they were not made for the sake of this, but it was the result of accident. And in like manner as to the other parts in which there appears to exist an adaptation to an end. Wheresoever, therefore, all things together (that is all the parts of one whole) happened as if they were made for the sake of

something, these were preserved, having been appropriately constituted by an internal spontaneity; and whatsoever things were not thus constituted, perished, and still perish.' We here see the principle of natural selection shadowed forth, but how little Aristotle fully comprehended the principle, is shown by his remarks on the formation of teeth." Darwin (1859: 527) Origin of Species, Everyman's library.

Subsequent to Aristotle, many others, most notably Lamarck, had proposed evolutionary theories: "But where Lamarck arrived at his end directly, by having the organism adapt itself, as by an act of will, to its environment, Darwin arrived at it circuitously, by engaging the organism in competition with its neighbors so that only the best adapted survived." Himmelfarb (1959: 317)

For thousands of years, there were theories of evolution, whereby descendant species varied from their progenitors. Darwin's theory eventually won out largely because, as Gertrude Himmelfarb explained: "More important, however, than any assets which Darwin's theory might be thought to possess was the bankruptcy of his opponents. The only serious rival, as a general theory, was creation." Himmelfarb (1959: 351)

In any case, Darwin's theory of descent provided the non-teleological non-intentional explanations of the physical processes of natural selection and sexual selection within species which produced new species and the incredible diversity of life forms on earth. It has now been accepted as fact.

15. To couch the matter in the behaviorist paradigm: "At the moment we must content ourselves, as the methodological behaviorist insists, with a person's genetic and environmental histories. *What are introspectively observed are certain collateral products of those histories.*" Skinner (1974:19) (My emphasis added.) "An adequate science of behavior must consider events taking place within the skin of the organism, not as physiological mediators of behavior, but as part of the behavior itself. It can deal with these events without assuming that they have any special nature or must be known in any special way. The skin is not that important as a boundary. Private and public events have the same kinds of physical dimensions." Skinner (1969: 228)

16. "Trying" is one of the 10,000+ English words immersed in the dualism of the English language. However, there is an alternative explanation for *trying* by any organism: "'Try' implies that a response has already been affected by relevant consequences. A cat is 'trying to escape' if it engages in behavior which either has been selected in the evolution of the species because it has brought escape from dangerous situations or has been reinforced by escape from dangerous situations or has been reinforced by escape from aversive stimulation elsewhere during the life of the cat." Skinner (1969: 134)

17. "An adequate formulation of the interaction between and organism and its environment must always specify three things: 1) The occasion upon which the response occurs 2) the response itself 3) The reinforcing consequences. The interrelationship among them are the 'contingencies of reinforcement'." Skinner (1969: 7) "A stimulus is no longer merely the conspicuous onset or termination of an energy exchange, as in reflex physiology; it is any part of the occasion on which a response is emitted and reinforced. Reinforcement is much more than 'being rewarded'; a prevailing probability of reinforcement, particularly under various intermittent schedules, is the important variable. In other words we no longer look at behavior and environments as separate things or events but at the interrelations among them. We look at the contingencies of reinforcement. We can then interpret behavior more successfully." Skinner, (1969: 10)

18. "It is the contingencies which prevail in a given verbal community which 'generate sentences.'

They shape and maintain the phonemic and syntactical properties of verbal behavior and account for a wide range of functional characteristics—from poetry to logic. They do so without the help of the *mind* of the speaker or listener." Skinner (1969:12) The human brain provides any help needed.

19. Also, recent (2012) reporting by anthropologist/linguist Daniel L. Everett suggests that the Pirahã people in Brazil are incapable of expressing some things that English speakers do with ease. Given the immense differences in their physical and social environment, it would be odd if this were not the case. "…Pirahã has no perfect tense… The Pirahãs lack this kind of tense because all their references to time are relative to the present, not to hypothetical events in the past or the future.

The absence of Pirahã perfect tense indicates not merely the absence of a special tense word or suffix, but a much deeper lacuna. There is no way to convey a perfect tense meaning ever in Pirahã. In fact, Pirahã has very few words for time, period… But there is no controversy to the assertion that the Pirahãs do not need a wide array of time words. These words have no work to do in a society in which members sleep, eat, hunt, fish, and gather, without regard for the time of day, day of the week, week of the month, or month of the year." Everett, D (2012: 269)

"'Can anything at all be translated from any language to any other language,' the answer seems to be, 'No'. Different languages might have different expressive powers for different kinds of information.'" Everett, D (2012: 269)

20. In the <u>Blue and Brown Books</u>, Ludwig Wittgenstein takes great pains to disabuse theorists of the belief that they can locate a visual field of qualia in their heads. He attributes such beliefs to a "grammatical misunderstanding". Ludlow (1997: 38)

See McGinn's <u>Mindsight</u> (2004: 63) for a brief synopsis of philosophical objections to what he calls the picture theory of perception.

See Dennett's <u>Sweet Dreams</u> (2005) in which he describes an experiment which reveals the phenomenon of "change blindness". Philosophically sophisticated subjects are shown two nearly identical pictures alternatively in millisecond intervals: "Subjects often study these alternating pictures for twenty or thirty seconds, with the change displayed dozens of times before their very eyes, before being able to spot the change." (2005: 83)

They were then queried about their phenomenal experience, put in the uncomfortable position of choosing among three answers: "…All three answers have their problems. If you are inclined to answer Yes, you are constrained to admit that swift and enormous changes in your qualia can occur without your knowledge. You must countenance the possibility that you often, even typically, are oblivious to large sudden shifts in your qualia. This would undermine the standard presumption that you are authoritative or even incorrigible about them…

"So perhaps you are therefore inclined to answer No. Then you can retain your authority about your qualia by claiming that since you noticed no shift, your qualia didn't shift, no matter what else in your brain shifted… This claim, however, threatens to trivialize qualia as just logically constituted by your judgments or noticings, an abandonment of the other cannonical requirement for qualia: that they be 'intrinsic' properties."

"Let's turn to option C then. If, confronted with this problem, you decide that you don't know whether your qualia were shifting before you noticed the change, you put qualia in the curious position of being beyond the horizon of both third-person objective science and first-person subjective experience. I have found, in fact, that people confronted with these three choices don't agree; all three answers find supporters who are, moreover, typically surprised to find that the other two answers have any takers at all. This informal finding supports my long-standing claim (Dennett 1988) that philosophers actually don't know what they are talking about when they talk about qualia." Dennett

(2005: 83)

Dennett sets his task early on in the footnotes: "The task of explaining away 'qualia'–based intuitive objections to materialism is what in large part I have undertaken in this book." (Dennett (2005: 23) This task, he admits, is daunting. "Yes, it is indeed difficult to deny that there are qualia. I've been working on the task for years, with scant progress!" Dennett (2005: 29)

21. B.F. Skinner attacked what he called the "copy theory" of perception: "What are the private events to which, at least in a limited way, a man may come to respond in ways we call 'perceiving' or 'knowing'? Let us begin with the oldest, and in many ways the most difficult kind represented by 'the stubborn fact of consciousness.' What is happening when a person observes the conscious content of his mind, when he 'looks at his sensations or images'? Western philosophy and science have been handicapped in answering these questions by an unfortunate metaphor. The Greeks could not explain how a man could have knowledge of something with which he was not in immediate contact. How could he know an object on the other side of the room, for example? Did he reach out and touch it with some sort of invisible probe? Or did he never actually come in contact with the object at all but only with a copy of it inside his body? Plato supported the copy theory with his metaphor of the cave. Perhaps a man never sees the real world at all but only shadows of it on the wall of the cave in which he is imprisoned. Copies of the real world projected into the body could compose the experience which a man directly knows. A similar theory could also explain how one can see objects which are 'not really there,' as in hallucinations, after images, and memories. Neither explanation is, of course, satisfactory. How a copy may arise at a distance is at least as puzzling as how a man may know an object at a distance. Seeing things which are not really there is no harder to explain than the occurrence of copies of things not there to be copied.

…It adds nothing to an explanation of how an organism reacts to a stimulus to trace the pattern or the stimulus into the body. It is most convenient, for both the organism and psychophysiologist, if the external world is never copied—if the world we know is simply the world around us. The same may be said of theories according to which the brain interprets signals sent to it and in some sense reconstructs external stimuli. If the real world is, indeed, scrambled in transmission but later reconstructed in the brain, we must then start all over again and explain how the organism sees the reconstruction.

…It took man a long time to understand that when he dreamed of a wolf, no wolf was actually there. It has taken him much longer to understand that not even a representation of a wolf is there.

The heart of the behavioristic position on conscious experience may be summed up in this way: seeing does not imply something seen. We acquire the behavior of seeing under stimulation from actual objects, but it may occur in the absence of these objects under the control of other variables. (So far as the world within the skin is concerned, it always occurs in the absence of such objects.) We also acquire the behavior of seeing-that-we-are-seeing when we are seeing actual objects, but it may also occur in their absence." Skinner (1969: 230-235)

22. Dean Zimmerman gives us a good version of the tale: "Suppose goggles were constructed that would systematically shift one's experiences of shades of color. Whenever one would normally have an experience as of something red, the goggles cause an experience as of something violet; whenever one would normally experience orange, the goggles cause an experience of indigo; and so on, inverting the entire spectrum of experienced colors (except for one lone shade of green, in the middle, which the goggles leave alone). Someone fitted from birth would learn to use color words in the same circumstances as the rest of us and would discriminate shades just as finely as the rest of us, but her experiences would be radically different, phenomenally, from ours—as she would discover when the

goggles were finally removed." Zimmerman via Baker & Goetz (2011: 180)

23. "… there is considerable agreement among experts today that it is not correct to refer to our 'five senses', since proprioception, thermoception, and nociception (among others) would be left out of such a roll call, there remains a major blur about what our senses really are. Since the experts can't even agree on how many senses we have, let alone on what they all are, they often talk about 'our five main senses.'" Hofstadter & Sander (2013) p.60.

24. Lev Vigotsky detected the effects of verbal behavior on non-verbal behavior a half century ago: "Vigotsky (1962) observed that young children would often give themselves instructions overtly. For example, a two-year-old might say, 'pick it up' while picking up a block. At this age, the verbalization tends to guide and control the action. By producing a verbalization that describes an action, the child sets up a resonant connection between vocalization and action. Later, Vygotsky argues, these overt instructions become inner speech and continue to guide our cognition." Tomasello and Slobin, Beyond Nature-Nuture, p.100.

In the 21st century there has been more and more research done on the relation between language and human cognition. Except for few holdouts, it is generally conceded that language does influence other cognitive domains. The debate is about the extent to which it does.

25. Not all cultures portray people as having enduring mental content such as knowledge, beliefs and reasons which are stored in the mind: "Vinden and Astington (2000) review some evidence from non-Western cultures like those of Samoa and the Baining people of Papua New Guinea in which external causes of behavior are invoked in place of internal causes specific to an individual. Vinden (1996) points also to the lack in internal state descriptions among speakers of Junin Quechua in Peru, one of several Quechua languages that have no separate words for mental states like belief; instead of a word corresponding to believe, they use the Junin Quechua counterpart of "say" (Adelaar 1977). Vinden also contends that little conversation in the culture concerns intentions, desires, and beliefs, and that the speakers of Junin Quechua may operate in daily life in the landscape of events that Bruner (1986) describes as prior to the landscape of consciousness in Western children's narrative thought. Vinden's work among the Junin Quechua suggests a significant delay in the acquisition of false-belief understanding. A majority of the children were still failing the (culturally modified) classic false-belief tasks (unexpected contents) at 8 years old…" Gentner and Meadow (2003: 372 de Villers and de Villers)

Indeed, having knowledge, beliefs and reasons for doing the things we do is part of our linguistic heritage. This requires the support of the dualistic mind/body philosophical paradigm where the internal contents of the mind, i.e. knowledge, beliefs and reasons, are invoked to explain the behavior of an organism (as opposed to external causes). This view is not universal, even within EA-speaking cultures. B.F. Skinner, for instance, suggests that: "…The 'reasons' which govern the behavior of the rational man describe his relations between the occasions on which he behaves, his behavior, and its consequences…We insist, with Freud, that the reasons men give in explaining their actions should be accurate accounts of the contingencies of reinforcement which were responsible for their behavior." Skinner (1969: 152)

26. While I do not wish to digress into an exposition of Skinner's Verbal Behavior, suffice it to say at this point that Skinner called these propositional attitudes "autoclitics". They are units of verbal behavior that are "based upon or depend upon other verbal behavior". Skinner (1957: 315) Such

autoclitics as: "*i believe that, i Know that, i am reminded that, i surmise that, i hesitate to say that, i suppose that, i think that*", et cetera, are all followed by more systematic verbal behavior, i.e. declarative propositional statements: "*the moon is made of green cheese*" for example. These autoclitics are used in response to stimuli based on previous verbal conditioning and do not express or represent a distinctive state of consciousness or cognition.

27. A revealing fact about languages gives theorists another insight into how linguistic conditioning affects the zeitgeist of speakers. The *aspectual* classification of beliefs and knowledge that is found in English is not universal among languages. Some languages have no stative aspects for their comparable terms, only the dynamic aspect. For speakers who use these languages, they believe or know something only when they remember it and express it. The belief or knowledge is in the physical event of stating the knowledge and not assumed to be long lasting and continuously stored in the memory. If one is not stating the belief or knowledge, one does not have the unexpressed belief or knowledge at that time. The belief or knowledge is not assumed to endure in the speaker's mind unexpressed and available for recall.

28. William M. Baum explicates *feelings* from a behaviorist's perspective: "Seen in the light of public circumstances, the feelings and the statements about them arise from history with similar circumstances… Sometimes feelings arise simply because of genetic programming. We need no special training to find standing on the tip of a cliff frightening or to find sexual stimulation enjoyable. Most of the time, however, feelings arise in a situation because that situation has been correlated with some phylogenetically important event—a reinforcer, punisher, or unconditional stimulus. In other words, feelings and statements about feelings arise because of respondent conditioning that occurs along with operant conditioning.

English includes a rich vocabulary for talking about the feelings that accompany situations in which reinforcement and punishment have occurred in the past. Since feelings arise from the same history of reinforcement and punishment that accounts for apparently purposive behavior, feelings are by-products, rather than causes, of the behavior." Baum (2005: 103)

CHAPTER FOUR

LINGUISTIC PUZZLES

Introduction

The fundamental challenge faced by today's philosophers is accounting for the human animal's use of sounds. Thus far, the puzzles in philosophy of language and linguistic theory have precluded any consensus about how this system of sounds works, let alone consensus in other fields of philosophy, e.g. philosophy of mind. So, let us investigate some of the traditional puzzles posed by the conventional semantic analysis of language and look at them in a new light, the non-semantic perspective. Please keep in mind that the author is attempting to pull himself up by the bootstraps. I must use the English language as it was given to me.

The purpose in recording this sub-vocal speech in this chapter is to make comparisons between conventional philosophical thinking about word use as symbolic representational activity, and an alternative way of looking at word use as non-semantic functional behavior with acoustic devices, action with consequences. The hope is that the contrast will persuade you that the orthodox semantic views are not adequate to the task of explaining what humans do with word sounds and their derivative symbols. With that in mind, let's take a look at some the traditional problems in philosophy of language and compare the semantic theory with the non-semantic behaviorist theory.

The Origin of Language

"Human language seems to have emerged within a relatively short space of time, perhaps as recently as 30,000 years ago. But that still leaves a gap of over 20,000 years before the first unequivocal evidence of written language." Crystal (1997: 293)

"The profoundest thinker on these problems in the eighteenth century was Johan Gottfried Herder, who, though he did little or nothing in the way of scientific research, yet prepared the rise of linguistic science. In his prize essay on the Origin of Language (1772) Herder first vigorously and successfully attacks the orthodox view of his age...that language could not have been invented by man, but was a direct gift of God." Jespersen (1964: 27)

The meaning/use distinction or semantics/pragmatics distinction is at the core of the semantic fallacies. The author has been laboring to point out, in as many ways as he can, that the distinction is unwarranted. It is result of the semantic view of spoken words. If humans eliminate the characterization of spoken words as symbols or signs, they can eliminate meanings and referents and the whole enterprise of semantics. They can focus on human speech as functional behavior, a different frame of reference. One way to dispel the semantic fantasy is to look at the development of our current spoken word usage. The author will be quoting extensively from Professor Guy Deutscher's erudite and fascinating 2005 book, The Unfolding of Language.

The overall thrust of Deutscher's book is that language could have begun with very basic verbal components and grown into the complex structure that it is today:

"Setting off from an early prehistoric age, when our ancestors only had names for some simple objects and actions, and only knew how to combine them into primitive utterances like 'bring water' or 'throw spear', we will trace the emergence of linguistic complexity and see how the extraordinary sophistication of today's languages could gradually have evolved." Deutscher (2005: 8)

Deutscher takes the semantic view of language as a given and uses the same terminology and the same justification for that view:

"Somewhat later, after 40,000 years ago, European cave paintings provide even more striking signs of artistic creativity. According to some linguists, it is only when there is evidence of such symbolic artifacts (and not just functional tools) that the use of 'human language' can be inferred, for after all, the quintessential quality of language is its symbolic nature, the communications with signs that mean something only by convention, not because they really sound like the object they refer to." Deutscher (2005: 14)

Unfortunately the semantic fallacies lead Deutscher to believe that the word sounds utilized in tacting with the actions of bringing and throwing, as well as objects such as water and spears, were "names" for those actions and objects. It also leads him to describe this unfolding as a process of changing the meanings of signs. What his absorbing book actually reveals is the expansion in the use of *acoustic devices*, not changes in the *meanings of signs or symbols*. In the course of human cultural evolution the expansion of word utility and tool utility went hand in hand. The same cognitive progress underlies both evolutionary histories. Tool use and word use have unfolded within parallel culturally specific histories with analogy and metaphor providing new uses for tools and words in an ever-expanding functional migration from one frame of reference to another.

Deutscher provides numerous insights on the origins and evolution of word sound function in many languages. He presents this unfolding process as a pervasive metaphorical movement whereby acoustic units make transitions from very down-to-earth concrete applications to more general uses. This analogical or metaphorical process is quite simple. Humans recognize the functional value of physical tools and acoustic devices. They then use the same tools and acoustic devices to do new work in a new frame of reference. Humans see *how* something works and they transfer that utility to a novel arena. This one-way path toward expanding utility is evident in tool use and word use everywhere. It continues unabated.

Deutscher explains the role of metaphoric thinking in this generalization process:

> "Far from being a rare spark of poetic genius, the marvelous gift of a precious few, metaphor is an indispensable element in the thought-processes of every one of us. As will soon become apparent, we use metaphors not because of any literary leanings or artistic ambitions, but quite simply because metaphor is the chief mechanism through which we can describe and even grasp abstraction." (Deutscher 2005: 117)

The word sound "*metaphor*" comes from the Greek "*meta-phora*", "to carry across". In Latin, the equivalent would be "*trans-fer*". When we humans use metaphoric thinking, we carry across or transfer the utility of various devices from one domain to another. We recognize operational similarities and deploy our utilitarian devices to do work in new domains. Humans engage in metaphorical or analogical thinking with implements of many types, including words.[1]

Deutscher chronicles the transitions of many words from their use in specific physical situations to more generalized use outside their original concrete realm. This functional migration from the concrete to the general is widespread and revealing. It reveals the process by which humans have taken word sounds of limited use within a specific physical domain, where they were grounded in human sense experience, and expanded their use far beyond these origins. This functional transition is a constant theme within word histories and reflects a basic one-directional flow of word function from specific and concrete, to general and abstract.

This metaphoric transformation is not just exemplified in poetic or sophisticated speech; it is part and parcel of our everyday discourse. The English sound "*have*" is a case in point:

> "Take the word 'have' for instance. By anyone's standards, 'have' is not some fancy optional extra, but an indispensable component of the hard-core of language. We 'have' hands and legs and eyes, we 'have' relatives and friends, we

'have' clothes and houses, we 'have' dandruff and the flu, and it's difficult to imagine having even the simplest conversation without having 'having' at the tip of one's tongue. And yet, even though 'have' is the bread-and-butter of the vernacular, it is nevertheless a fairly abstract notion, quite unlike physical activities such as 'kicking' something or 'putting' it somewhere. Think about it this way: what do you actually do when you 'have' something? (Not much, probably, if what you 'have' is a third-cousin-twice-removed in Oklahoma with whom you've lost all contact.) ...many languages today (most, in fact) don't have a verb that corresponds to the English 'have', and so they use other ways of expressing possession... Russian, Turkish and Irish all opt for the strategy of using physical proximity as a metaphor for the notion of possession... 'position is possession'... In addition to physical proximity, there are also various other sources speakers can draw on to express the notion of 'having' something. (The languages below) all use another common image, that of 'target' or 'goal'. The idea here is that if something is intended *for* you, or destined *to* you, it is yours..." (Deutscher 2005: 130)

Deutscher goes on to elucidate the "notion of possession" in various languages and how "*have*" "...ultimately derives from a Proto-Indo-European stem "kap", which meant "*seize*"". Originally, the word sound "*have*" was utilized in claiming possession. Its function was extended to uses far removed from its origins, i.e. the seizing of objects or the location of objects where proximity equaled ownership. Metaphorical thinking then enabled a more general use of the word to make claims about *having* tools, goats and wives regardless of proximity.

The point Deutscher convincingly makes is that our use of the English word sound "*have*" comes from primitive pedestrian sources regarding ownership and proximity. Eventually, English-speaking humans claimed to *have* third cousins, real estate, aches, minds, and ideas. As the needs in developing societies changed, word function changed via metaphorical thinking. These days, a man might claim to *have* a wife. If he does, ownership and proximity are not part of that claim.

The origin of "*decide*" is reported by Deutscher as well. It comes about in English from the Latin verb used to refer to the act of cutting off, in Swahili: *cut matter*, in Indonesian: *sever*. The use of the English sound "*decide*" has origins in an everyday activity common to many cultures: cutting off or severing. The function of the word then transitions to more general use, moving from the specific, observable physical action of severing to action we purport to make in our minds, deciding, i.e. cutting off other alternatives in favor of one. This functional migration of word sounds is observed over and over in our everyday language.

Today's children learn that they have "*choices*" and they have to "*decide*". They learn how to use these word sounds in a context. Today, that context includes a philosophical milieu created by Plato, Aristotle, Augustine, et al. that includes minds, free will, intentions, and other such mental entities. Consequently, contemporary English-speaking people say that they have the *free will* to *decide* based on their *intentions* and *desires*. However, 30,000 years ago, children didn't *decide* things in their *minds* or make *choices*; they cut off chunks of meat. "*Decide*", as we use it today, has a decidedly different functional value.

This metaphorical process is evidenced in the transition of many so-called content words to grammatical elements. Grammatical elements, (or grammatical words, or grammatical items, depending on your choice of terminology) such as prepositions: "*from*", "*about*", "*around*", were originally used to tact with spatial distinctions. They started out as content words, as linguists are inclined to say. "*from*", "*about*", and "*around*" were sounds used to tact with directions and spatial relationships, observable everyday distinctions. They were subsequently generalized to other domains such as time: "*a week from tomorrow about noon or around two-ish*". Further generalization removed them even further from their origins in the spatial dimensions, such that: "*we now speak from our experience and our learning about language and then have debates centered around the penumbral aspects of meaning*". This functional migration moved these sounds from referring-use words based on the spatial, directional or action images at their origins, to the purely functional elements of present-day English grammar.

Some of these prepositions originated as *displacement* indicators, one of the defining characteristics of human linguistic communication. Time and place displacement are critical to human social organization. By means of certain sounds, humans can direct each other's attention to objects and events outside of the here and now. We can converse about objects and events in distant places at other times. Our positioning within time and space begins with simple distinctions about "*here*", "*there*", "*from*", "*to*", "*sundown*", "*sunup*", and ultimately leads to the ability to locate our subject matter in a framework of infinite space and time.[2]

Deutscher continues in this vein and traces the transition of so-called content words to functional components of speech. This functional transition allowed our hominid ancestors to provide other information, such as the direction of the action: "*zug have spear sunup throw spear at mastodon*". However, during the course of this functional transition from content words to grammatical elements, semantic content did not disappear or erode as semanticists are inclined to say. Semantic content was not there to begin with. The transition from content words to structural components, or grammatical elements, was a sublime advancement in the use of acoustic devices, not symbols with and then without semantic content. Beginning as everyday referring-use sounds, these sounds changed their uses as they became more generalized.

Another contemporary linguistic transition illustrates this change in *use* as opposed change in *meaning*. "Marking" is said to be one process of losing meaning. I'll let Deutscher explain:

> "… in Britain these days, one is often asked something like 'would you like a bag at all?'… But why 'at all'? …The answer must be that we are witnessing a change in the making, where what started out as an emphatic intensifier, meaning something like 'would you like anything whatsoever?', is now going down the path of attrition, losing that emphasis, and becoming just a kind of extended question marker… But with repeated use, 'at all' is losing its distinctiveness and becoming conventionalized as a marker of a polite question."
> (Deutscher 2005: 99)

With all due respect and admiration for Professor Deutscher, the change is purely functional. The function of "*at all*" changed from an emphatic intensifier to a marker for a polite question. The origins of many markers and grammatical elements were in referring-use word sounds, common nouns, and verbs. There is no point in attributing meanings or semantic referents to such words unless you say they are symbols. Of course, we can speculate about the use of other words that will provide the functional equivalent of *"at all"* in these circumstances by paraphrasing, but what possible meanings could we attribute to *"at"* and *"all"* in either use?

These functional transitions are repeatedly evidenced in other areas of human endeavor. We humans have the ability to use words and tools for purposes other than their original purpose. We transfer utility from one frame of reference to the next. We recognize how to utilize words and tools in novel ways. Within language, these functional word transitions are ubiquitous:

> "A simple experiment suffices to demonstrate that there is no way of getting around a concrete-to-abstract metaphor. Try choosing at random a few of the most abstract of abstractions you can imagine, and then tracing their ultimate origin. As long as their pedigree is known, chances are they will go back to some simple words from the physical world. The word 'abstract' itself is one such example, for what could be more abstract than that? Today 'abstract' may be the fare of philosophers, a word to refer to concepts that are removed from physical reality. But the origins of 'abstract' are much more earthly, as 'abstract' comes from the Latin verb which simply meant 'draw away' (abstrahere)." (Deutscher 2005: 128)

This passage from Deutscher is pregnant with philosophical offspring. Indeed, "abstract" is a term that originated with philosophers. It is part of the same metaphysical musings that utilize "concepts" and "physical reality". So, take the metaphysics with a healthy grain of salty skepticism. This functional transition of the sound *"abstract"* has not moved anything from physical reality to conceptual status. Abstractions and concepts in human minds are not created; human applications for word sounds are broadened. The metaphorical transition of sounds is a functional phenomenon that is explainable without resorting to such metaphysical musing.

Deutscher also offers a fascinating review of the forces of erosion in language. One of these well-documented changes concerns word pronunciations that change as a result of indolence, e.g. the consonantal drop in the past tense verb ending, -ed, (hopped instead of hop-ped). He goes on to debunk the commonly held belief that this erosion is a one-way trip to linguistic anarchy. Deutscher also details what he refers to as the erosion in meaning:

> "Alas, it seems that meaning is just as prone to attrition as sounds. And ironically, the decay in meaning seems to be set off not by any indolent desire to save effort, but rather by almost the precise opposite: the wish to enhance expressiveness. Speakers sometimes go to great lengths to intensify the effect of their utterances in order to lend their speech more force and emphasis, and in doing so they tend to go for words with ever more muscular meanings. In the short term, this method may achieve the intended result, but in the long run, the strategy is self-defeating, simply because it is inflationary… the purists have a point, since their factual description of the process is spot-on: the strength of meaning of a particular word depends on its distinctiveness, so the more often we hear a word, and in less discriminating contexts, the less powerful the impression it makes. When certain intensifiers are used more and more often, it is only natural that an inflationary process will ensue, resulting in attrition of meaning." (Deutscher 2005: 97)

My bone to pick with Deutscher is not that we go for more *muscular* meanings, but rather that there are meanings at all, much less the muscular variety. Some words have more force by virtue of their novelty, emphasis or metaphorical attributes, not their meanings.

The emphatic power of expression is a functional characteristic of speech marked by novelty, pronunciation, volume etc. Consider superlatives in the size dimension: *"big"*, *"large"*, *"huge"*, *"massive"*, *"titanic"*, *"gargantuan"*, *"mammoth"*, *"colossal"*, *"enormous"*, *"monumental"*, *"gigantic"*, *"ginormous"*, et cetera. This consistent striving for ever more emphatic ways of expressing the larger proportions of oil tankers and offensive football tackles is a consequence of speaker goals. Speakers want to emphasize the outsized portions of the subject of conversation. As some words become common-place, their capacity to lend intensity to a statement diminishes. The ability to produce the desired effects diminishes. The desire to produce forceful expressions of proportion will continue with novel expressions in the future, e.g. *"giga-tankers"*. These new word sounds will replace and have the same use that *"gigantic"*, *"colossal"* and *"gargantuan"* once had. They will be functional equivalents. They will give speakers the ability to tact with and emphasize dimensions in a new way.

The crucial point in the foregoing examples is the repeated functional transition in the *use* of words. In many cases, the transition is from the realm of concrete observable actions and spatial relations to more widespread general use. What is said to be "the flow toward abstraction", as a rule, developed in four stages. The word use began with body parts, moved to space and time, then on to the mental realm, the non-physical realm created and maintained by philosophers of all stripes.

> "These examples illustrate four stages of the flow towards abstraction, the last three of which should by now be thoroughly familiar, as they go from space (behind) to time (after), and from there, to the abstract domain of mental faculties. But Ewe shows that the spatial term 'behind' is itself a product of metaphor, and reveals the ultimate origin of the word megbe: a solid noun, part of the human body." (Deutscher 2005: 139)

What Deutscher points out in these transitions is a constant change in function from the specific to the more general. This natural selection of words sounds is based on utility. Words become more useful as the areas of application grow. The broader the applications, the more useful it is and thus the more it is used. Its staying power is enhanced. The culmination in this process, the final transition to the "domain of mental faculties", required metaphysical support. Plato, Aristotle, Augustine, et al. provided it. *"deciding"* went from cutting meat to the exercise of your free will.

Let us start near a beginning:

> "girl fruit pick turn mammoth see
> girl run tree reach climb mammoth tree shake
> girl yell yell father run spear throw
> father stone take meat cut girl give
> girl eat finish sleep" (Deutscher 2005: 210)

Get the picture? Even with this primitive speech behavior a speaker could recreate a scene. In context with appropriate presuppositions, there could have been nothing more than simple nouns and verbs to complete a description of an event. It is pure tacting behavior with temporal sequencing as the only unifying element. No grammatical elements, no inflections, no recursion, no predication, no propositional content, not even syntax would have been necessary.

The functional value of syntax, no doubt, led to the evolution of consistent syntactic behavior. Regularities in the order of the words sounds were adopted because they had utility. For example, word order in English became useful in reporting the direction of actions performed by the subjects of discourse. According to Kathleen Gibson and Tim Ingold:

> "The form of symbolic communication becomes complex enough to generate more than a single noun and a single verb... The quintessential situation which causes a need for syntactical rules arises when there is more than one noun and the verb itself is insufficient to specify the direction of this relationship, as in 'put the hat in the box'. 'Put hat in box' is ambiguous because it can be enacted in a number of different ways. In a sentence containing words such as 'put', 'hat', and 'box,' the relational problem can be solved by assigning words to all possible positional relationships between hat and box (in, on, under, etc.). However, in "Tickle Jane Sue' the number of potential spatial relations that can be assumed between Jane and Sue is too numerous to specify what it is the speaker intends to have occur during a tickling bout. Some means is needed to specify agent recipient and role reversal of these classes. In English, the chosen device is word order. In Latin, the chosen device is a case system in which nouns take on different endings indicating their grammatical roles in the sentence. In other languages, devices such as pitch may be used to accomplish the same goal.
> Gibson and Ingold (1993: 104-105)

Syntax developed as one method of pointing out the direction of the action. It is not a "rule" however. It is a convention of the English language. It is a convention that evolved, one of many possible conventions to indicate the roles of individuals and objects in reports about their interactions.

A conventional linguistic interpretation would be forced to conclude that the syntax gave the utterance some meaning or semantic content. Linguists, in fact, do conclude that. In addition to lexical meaning supposedly encoded in the individual words, word order gives *structural meaning* or *grammatical meaning* to a complex expression. It does not. There is no meaning in the syntax when speakers indicate the direction of action. The functional value of syntax, in this use of English, is much the same as pointing with a finger. Syntax is one way English speakers point out who did what to whom; they utilize syntax to indicate the direction of the action.

In other languages, speakers are able to indicate the direction of the action when reporting events by the use of word cases or prosodic features such as pitch. Different languages have adopted different devices to point out the direction of an action. Speakers learn to capture the temporal asymmetry of events and actions by utilizing the devices their languages offer. Although these utilitarian developments did not produce the same devices across all languages, the devices all served to further similar human goals.

All primitive languages expanded beyond the basic tacting function of nouns and verbs. Eventually, the English language evolved such that speakers can now use grammatically complete sentences: "*the mammoth shook a tree*" which indicates who did the shaking and when they did it (past tense). "*the*" indicates that a particular mammoth that has already been introduced, as the subject of discussion. "*a tree*" is used as a variable referring to some tree, an as-yet unspecified tree. Our expanding use of word sounds enables us to perform much more exacting work by using grammatically complete sentences, although sub-sentential speech is still a substantial portion of our speech acts.

Humans began their linguistic behavioral history combining phonemes to provide themselves with a broad range of sounds to tact with a broad range of objects and actions: "*throw*", "*spear*", "*mammoth*". They combined these basic acoustic devices with prosodic features and developed syntactic combinations. They combined the uses of the sounds with other speech elements to create complex functional communication behavior. They moved from simple word use to more complex word use just as they moved from simple gross motor skills to texting and driving. In the process, they became the ultimate teachers and learners within the animal kingdom.

Although children are very adept at observational or iterated learning because of their genetic heritage, they could not do it without their caregivers to imitate.[3] Word sound use is individual behavior learned from others within the speech community. However, the observational or iterated learning process which provides for the transmission of language from one generation to the next requires no intention or design. It happens because of natural selection, the "invisible hand". Larger and larger speech communities grew as the survival value of some cultural components, such as language, proved superior to others.

That process continues today as languages within certain cultures with superior economic and technological underpinnings succeed, and others fail.[4] Of course, some speech communities are helped enormously by formalizing and standardizing their speech behavior, often aided by the written form. It produces speech varieties that are more stable, more functional, and which can be spread more easily. However, it all began with family units where infants imitated their caregivers to produce utilitarian vocal behavior in their struggle to survive.

The basic questions in linguistic theory these days are not so much whether language evolved, but *how* it evolved, and whether a more generalized improvement in intelligence produced speech, or vice versa. (See <u>Language Evolution</u> by Morton H. Christiansen and Simon Kirby.) The field of language evolution has produced some remarkable research in an attempt to answer these questions. Researchers from many disciplines have contributed, but there is no consensus on how human speech evolved. Yet there seems to be agreement that three adaptive systems contributed to the adoption and growth of human verbal behavior: individual learning, cultural transmission and biological evolution.

Of course, the development of such language theorizing has created schisms. For instance, certain features of human communication are lacking in animal communication. Some theorists have concluded that this apparent gap between animal communication and human communication must be bridged if they are to prove that human languages could have evolved. Some try to account for the gap by producing theories of gradual transition. Others speculate about a sudden mutation in the human brain which allowed for the use of a protolanguage. The work of Bickerton, Carey, Desalles, Deutscher, Hurford and many others are part of the ongoing dispute between *continuity theorists* and *discontinuity theorists*. (Darwin was a continuity theorist, 1859) In spite of this academic kerfuffle, evolution is the only way to explain the development of language, unless one accepts the creationist's account of the origins of human language or treats it "… as if it had sprung from Jove's brow—one, entire, unique and indivisible", as Bickerton (1995: 50) put it. Treating speech as conditioned behavior would greatly ease theorist's efforts in doing so.

Child Language Acquisition

"The human brain is unique in having the necessary hardware for mastering a human language—that much is uncontroversial. But the truism that we are innately equipped with what it takes to learn language doesn't say very much beyond just that. Certainly, it does not reveal whether the specifics of grammar are already coded in the genes, or whether all that is innate is a very general ground-plan of cognition... readers outside the field of linguistics need to form a healthy disrespect for the arguments advanced on all sides of the debate."
Deutscher (2005: 17)

We do many things with language: we question, we entreat, we report, we lie, we joke, we pray, we insult, we exclaim our joy, and so on and so forth. We do all these things in the way our caregivers have done them, in a language peculiar to our little corner of the world, with words, idioms and accents as different as our faces.[5] The process of learning a language has been experienced by all of us. Many of us have also witnessed the process in our children as they grow older. Yet explaining this process has proven to be exceptionally difficult. For millennia, philosophers and linguists have been speculating and debating about our ability to learn our native languages. The philosophy and the science of language have yet to reach any conclusions about how individual human children acquire this unique ability to use noises in productive ways.

Compounding the confusions are the varied uses of the word "*language*". Once again, there is no *concept* or *meaning* that can be associated with the sound "*language*". Nor is there an officially sanctioned *definition* for what constitutes a language. There is a saying amongst linguists that a language is a dialect with an army and a navy. Others say:

> "A language, for linguists, is a system of representations and rules in the mind of a person. If the person ceases to exist, that particular person's language ceases to exist. In other words, we have been talking about the Samoan language and the Warlpiri language, but we have been doing so informally. From a linguistic perspective, each Warlpiri speaker and each Samoan speaker has his or her own sent of symbols and rules, what we call his or her own mental grammar, his or her own I-language." Isac and Reiss (2013:15)[6]

So, let us not be duped into thinking that we know what *a language is* or what *language in general is*. The spoken word "*language*" has multiple uses. Many of those uses have been shaped by caregivers, acquaintances and teachers who promulgate the officially sanctioned methods of speech, while their uses are not exhaustive or uncontroversial.

At any rate, the acquisition of language by children has been one of the most contentious and befuddling areas in linguistics. It is so because of the erroneous theoretical framework within which the linguists conduct their investigations. They hold that most spoken words are symbols that have semantic content, literal or lexical meanings. They also contend that words are symbols that stand for, signify, encode, designate, denote or refer to other things. They also think that spoken words are symbols that represent abstractions, thoughts, ideas, concepts, meanings, mental representations, propositions, and all the rest of the mental flora and fauna that purportedly *exist* in human *minds*. Language theorists of all stripes retain the ancient semantic paradigm and its concomitant mind/body dualism when they try to explain how humans acquire the ability to use sounds.

In the current child language acquisition debate, speech is characterized as symbolic activity by all theorists, save for the behaviorists. Language theorists of the nativist variety, such as Noam Chomsky and Steven Pinker, claim that the acquisition of human speech behavior cannot be entirely accounted for by behaviorists. They claim that operant conditioning alone or iterated learning cannot be responsible for certain observed linguistic phenomena. These nativists have concluded that humans have more than a general cognitive ability that can manifest itself in the ability to use language. This group of Neo-Platonists or Neo-Rationalists, if you prefer, suggest that there is a language domain-specific innate *Universal Grammar* that every person is born with. This universal grammar underlies the variety of surface grammars acquired by people worldwide.

However, after more than four decades of extensive research and theorizing, a universal grammar has yet to be described or discovered. A rule-based system that captures all of the observed phenomena of the multitude of surface grammars has not been produced. After a half century of research, *the evidence* for a rule-based universal grammar or "deep structure" is non-existent. In fact, most of the evidence has suggested just the opposite. For example, the childhood acquisition of irregular verbs and plurals in English has been shown to be a simple matter of rote learning. There is no system of *rules* which can account for their acquisition and use.

Grammars are as diverse and pliable as phonemes, morphemes, lexemes and all the other grammatical units of human speech that have been parsed by linguists. And *the arguments* against any such universal grammar provided by the human genome are manifold. The leading proponent of the innate Universal Grammar (UG) theory is Noam Chomsky. His central argument for a UG is that language is generative, i.e. people can *generate* an infinite number of possible sentences from the limited sample of sentences they hear. He proposes:

> "...that in every human language surface structures are generated from structures of a more abstract sort, which I will refer to as 'deep structures,' by certain formal operations of a very special kind generally called 'grammatical transformations.' ...Thus a set of base rules defining an infinite class of deep structures and a set of grammatical transformations can serve to generate the surface structures." Hook (1969: 53)

This theoretical *rule-based* UG is the offspring of rule-based speech theory in philosophy of language. It assumes that some grammatical rules are innate, and some are learned or "internalized". (This sounds suspiciously like operant conditioning.) Moreover, none of these rules are said to be conscious rules. Competent, mature speakers are unable to articulate these rules, yet they adhere to these rules in the formulation of grammatically well-formed sentences.

This view has brought about considerable debate about what a *rule* is. On that there is no consensus because the word sound *"rule"* has no fixed literal meaning either. John Searle, who did a great deal of philosophical work supporting UG, put considerable effort into analyzing our use of the English word sound *"rule"*. Searle (1969) He tried to distinguish rules from laws, conventions, norms, mores etc. What common thread runs through the rules of chess, the rules of etiquette, the rules for driving, the rules of geometry, the rules for fishing, the rules of baseball, the rules of grammar etc.? In what way are all these *rules* the same? By what means do we know what constitutes a rule and what is a not a rule. He came to roughly the same conclusion that Wittgenstein did regarding the word *"game"*.[7] English speakers have wildly different uses for the word sound *"rule"*. Although there may be some etymological thread amongst those uses, there is no stable or core semantic content that can be associated with every use of the word sound *"rule"*. There are no universal properties, features or facts that can be associated with all uses of that word. The uses of that word have a *family of resemblances*, to use Wittgenstein's analogy.

This lack of precision about the word sound *"rule"* reduces any explanatory power it might have. In fact, the word sound *"regularity"* has appreciably more explanatory clout. In many regulated events, say a football game, regularities are accounted for by the rules. However, in much unregulated human behavior regularities are a result of custom, habit or simple operant conditioning. There are many cultural regularities exhibited in gesturing for example. Would we say that the regularities observed in culturally specific gestures are *rule* bound?

There are many other cultural regularities in all sorts of human behavior: eating, courting, worshipping, et cetera. Regularities also appear in nature quite regularly: E=MC2, geese fly south, chemicals react the same way and birds build nests. Would you want to call E=MC2 a rule, or say that geese fly south because they are following a rule, or say that trees consume CO_2 or birds build nests because they are following rules? Following a rule, at a minimum it would seem, would require knowledge of the rule. Yet, competent speakers are, more often than not, unable to articulate any grammatical rules. The distinction between rules and regularities is a recurring theme in criticisms of UG.

In addition to the objection that *"rule"* is difficult to define narrowly enough to know what would constitute a grammatical rule, after we humans supposedly learn or internalize the rules of grammar, we break them with regularity and impunity. As Paul Ziff put it in his attempt to analyze and explain semantic theory:

> "If one were forced to choose one fact about language and say of it that it was
> the most important fact of all then it might be this: that one can generally in fact
> deviate from syntactic or semantic regularities." Ziff (1960: 25)

The evidence for deviations from well-formed grammatically correct speech in everyday life is obvious and overwhelming. Many languages have *prescriptive* rules that are routinely ignored by the large proportions of its speakers. It requires an army of grammar police in academia to maintain any semblance of conformity with the rules that these self-appointed grammar police establish.

Moreover, through reconstruction, historical linguists also have provided overwhelming evidence for diachronic shifts in word use: grammar, morphology, phonology, and syntax in every language where such research has been done. For example, in the early 16th century, Middle English words like *"can"*, *"must"*, and *"may"* began to be used, not as verbs, but as a new inflectional category. Lightfoot, Westergaard (2007)

Because of such changes in grammar, much of Early and Middle English is incomprehensible to modern English speakers. However, because of widespread grammatical indoctrination in English-speaking cultures, speech and writing have stabilized somewhat over the past few centuries.

Grammar school learning of language skills consists of learning the formalizing general patterns of linguistic behavior, learning these *prescriptive rules*. Students conjugate verbs and learn all the exceptions to the rules, irregular verbs in English for example. Students learn how to parse sentences and identify sentence constituents: nouns, verbs, prepositions etc. They learn to form grammatically correct complete sentences and are strongly encouraged, if not forced, to comply with the prescriptive rules of grammar as promulgated by the guardians of standardized grammar. All of this history leads one to believe that *rule-bound* grammatical skills are a result of grammarians and linguists, not something encoded in the genes.

One should add that the parsing of grammatical units that are supposed to adhere to the rules of grammar is beset with problems. Modern linguists have developed constituency tests to determine the categories for the elements of grammar. However, those tests have proven to be completely unreliable. Most categories of words are position based, positioned within *grammatically well-formed sentences*, e.g. *pre*positions. Of course, invariably there are borderline cases where the categorization of a part of speech relies on appeals to pragmatic considerations or context. It has been impossible so far, for researchers to come up with a systematic foolproof categorization scheme for sentence parts in the surface languages, much less a reliable diagrammatic system for their syntactic interactions. *Rule-based grammar* fails at the constituent level as well as the sentential level.

Consider gender. For those of us who speak English, few words have gender. (Pronouns do.) So, if you think you know what gender is, you are probably mistaken. There are some languages with no gender and others with ten or more genders. Linguists say that gender is a noun class with an assignment system. (Have a linguist explain what a noun is.) Gendered nouns must agree with other parts of speech. Yet the systems are inexact at best. Classifying many nouns based on gender is haphazard. There may be guidelines, but there are hundreds of exceptions to the guidelines that make no sense whatsoever. All attempts to explain these systems based on gender assignment *rules* have been unsuccessful. Nevertheless, speakers who use gender-based languages are matching the gender of different parts of speech long before they are told what gender is.

So, how do speakers match genders? Certainly not by following rules which they have not yet been taught and cannot explain. In fact, there are no underlying universal *rules* to the gender classification of words in any language, but there are many *regularities* with many, many exceptions. Native language learners hear how others in their linguistic community combine the words and use them in the same way. Their linguistic behavior is shaped by observational or iterated learning. First language learners remember the conjunction of sounds with other sounds through repetition. Second language learners must simply memorize the noun genders and drill the sound combinations into their behavior.

Although linguists are reluctant to admit that gender classification is based on operant conditioning, there is striking evidence of that fact:

> "Deaf children who learn to speak French do not learn to assign nouns to gender (Tucker, Lambert & Rigault 1977: 59); the reason is that they cannot hear the language and so cannot discover the assignment rules." Corbett (1991: 61)

Rules, schmules! Deaf children cannot assign gender because they have not been conditioned to use the sounds in the way others use them. Gender classification occurs in most non-impaired speakers long before any rules for it are introduced.

In spite of the theoretical difficulties, most theorists nowadays still claim that the human use of language consists of words and rules, i.e. lexicon and syntax. Syntactic rules are supposed to determine the structure of phrases and sentences. Yet you will often hear these same language theorists appealing to their ears as the arbiter of linguistic disputes about *proper* (rule-governed) syntax. They will say that *something* "*doesn't sound right*" or it "*sounds odd*". However, these appeals to the sound of a phrase or sentence cannot be appeals to syntactic rules because syntactic rules are not there, much less sound based. If *sounding odd* is to be the standard for incorrect usage, we would have no need for grammarians or their rules.

In fact, we don't. Based on previous word sound use which has been gained by iterated learning, competent language users can determine if a phrase or sentence has the right ring to it. Based on their previous conditioning, competent first-language users are often able to converge on what is *proper* usage. In fact, most linguists insist on using native speakers for the so-called *Grammatical Judgment Task (GJT)*. It is a common practice in academic circles for experts, who may be non-native speakers of a language but know all the so-called *rules* of that language and can articulate them, to defer to native speakers when determining the "well-formedness" of phrases or sentences, even though the native speakers cannot articulate the rules they are supposedly following. Much like phonetic rules whereby non-native speakers will never sound like a native speaker, it appears that the rules of grammar for second-language learners are just too much for mature human brains to accommodate. The rules can only be learned by children it seems if expert non-native speakers must defer to non-expert native speakers for a GJT.

An alternative explanation for the phenomena is that early childhood conditioning sets phonetic, syntactic, and functional *regularities* in human speech behavior. Those conditioned regularities govern mature speech in spite of any rules of grammar. Often mature speakers suspect something is ungrammatical. Yet they cannot determine which, if any, rule has been broken. We know something is awry because someone's speech behavior just doesn't *sound* right. This happens not because they broke a rule, but because the offending speech behavior is counter intuitive, and those intuitions are the result of our linguistic conditioning.

Indeed, proper rule-based grammar may sound odd to many speakers, depending upon their idiolect and their era. For example: "*joe understood not my book*" sounds odd to my ear, yet it was grammatically correct and perfectly good to the ear of an earlier Englishman. Word sound use changes over time, including syntax and the prosodic features of speech, i.e. intonation, stress patterns, temporal spacing, etc. If one is to appeal to sound as the arbiter, one can only be appealing to conditioning. What else could account for something *sounding odd* to the ear of a native speaker but not an accomplished non-native speaker who knows all the rules? Linguists and grammarians love their rules, but we speaking humans don't need no stinking rules!

Children first learning to use language have no intuitions at all about language and frequently make use of word sounds in ways that adults find comical. They have no idea that what they said broke a rule. They learn quickly though. In terms of fuzzy logic, children are adaptive fuzzy systems with observed behavior as input and functional behavior as output. Data flows into the neural system and, gradually, fuzzy regularities evolve. Children imitate what they see and hear, then adjust such behavior based on feedback.

Furthermore, if learning a first language was a matter of learning rules and vocabulary, we should be able to program computers to talk just as we have programmed them to do mathematics. Not only has that not been done, it is impossible, in principle, to do it. It is impossible because there can never be enough rules to cover all the functional variations and the limitless situations in which words must function. Theorists can no more make enough rules to explain all the uses of language than they can make enough rules to explain all the uses of tools. Humans are an inventive lot and, because of their ability to think analogically and metaphorically, they will continue to use words sounds in novel ways for novel objectives. Rules go out the window if novel circumstances require novel word use. Humans are not restricted by rules when they need to get the job done, whether the job is accomplished with hammers, pliers or linguistic devices.

Rule-based speech behavior is simply another misguided attempt to explain such behavior. As Hilary Putnam said in his criticism of Paul Feyerbend:

> "It is evident that Feyerbend is misusing the term 'meaning'. He is not alone in such misuse: in the last thirty years, misusing the term 'meaning' has been one of the most common, if least successful, ways of 'establishing' philosophical positions. But how did this distressing state of affairs come to be?'
>
> …What is curious is that Feyerbend does not follow this course. Indeed, many of his purposes would have been better served had he chosen to follow Quine in repudiating the theory of meaning altogether. He wishes to show that linguistic philosophy is irrelevant and misguided; clearly, if it all rests on a mistaken notion, that there are such things as rules of language, then it is badly misguided." Putnam (1975: 122)

Rule-based theories of language use by humans simply cannot explain the observed data, i.e. all of human speech behavior.

Another alleged justification for a rule-based (UG) is the "poverty of stimulus" argument. It is claimed that the (S-R-R) behaviorist model of child language acquisition cannot account for all the novel sentences that children produce. Adult care givers, as accomplished native speakers, only give language learners a small sample of the grammatically correct sentences they will ultimately produce. That small input sample cannot account for all of the sentences the learner will produce in the coming years; it is said. However, the same can be said of any human behavior. We humans generate all sorts of novel behavior that we have never observed in other humans.

The poverty of stimulus argument for a genetically carried UG is regularly combined with the claim that human speech is generative. Hence, there is alternative appellation for UG, *Generative Grammar* (GG). The GG "schematism" is supposed to *generate* the multiple and diverse surface grammars witnessed worldwide from a more basic UG. That is, an innate GG can generate an infinite number of well-formed sentences in the surface grammars from a more basic system by means of techniques such as recursion. This generative capacity of human speech and the poverty of stimulus are given as evidence for the existence of an innate GG.

However, the productive or generative capacity of speech is merely a statistical fact. As any statistician will tell you, the number of possible permutations for any set of words will be a function of the number of words available and the number of syntactic regularities. The generative or combinatorial possibilities with words are virtually endless because we have a large number of words available to use. Although the syntax for any language restricts the possibilities, (we English speakers cannot say: "*a the bit man dog*") given the extraordinary number of words in the English language with their multiple context-dependent uses, the possible combinations are practically limitless. The combinatorial power and productivity of a language is on a par with many other productive, combinatorial, generative, human behaviors. It is simply a matter of sequencing and embedding many functional units together to get work done.

The sequencing and embedding of behavioral atoms and molecules are evidenced in young children in their early months as they learn gross motor skills. Children start out with the very smallest of motor movements, which are eventually sequenced, often recursively, into larger molecules of motor behavior. They gradually go from undifferentiated, random arm motions and leg kicks to reaching and grasping. They learn to control the limbs and then the digits, coordinating them with eye movements. Ultimately, by combining smaller bio-mechanical movements, they develop gross motor skills that allow them to drop a coin in their piggy bank or throw a ball. The entire development of motor skills is a process of recursively sequencing small units of learned behavior into larger functional units, and then even larger functional units. There are infinite combinations of such behavior.

Writing about the subject-verb-object structure of English, William Calvin says:

> "The SVO declarative sentence of English is only one of the six permutations of those units, and each permutation is found in some human language. Some word orders are more frequently found than others, but the variety suggests that word order is a cultural convention rather than a biological imperative in the manner proposed for Universal Grammar." Calvin (1996: 72)

Calvin also notes that "chaining" words together is consistent with other human behavior: combining notes into melodies and steps into dances. There is nothing unique or unusual about stringing functional sounds into novel sequences. Humans can sequence many basic behavioral units in novel chains to achieve the goals they are stimulated to seek.

Moreover, this chaining ability is not unique among humans. It is a *not* a difference *in kind* from non-human animals. It is a difference in degree.

> "Chomsky argued that a 'generative grammar' was uniquely human. A generative grammar is one that can produce an infinite number of grammatical utterances, and this underwrites the complexity of human language. …However, although these examples indicate that simple—and even generative—grammars can be found in non-human animals, there is an enormous gap between these grammars and the syntax of human speech." Gibson and Ingold (1993: 114-115)

The ability to generate different sequences of sounds, gestures, or dance steps is not unique to humankind. Birds chirp in different sequences for different purposes. Other animals display all sorts of combinatorial abilities. The fact that there is an enormous gap between human and non-human animals is of little consequence. The limitations on the combinatorial power of any behavior depends on the number of basic building blocks, the useful combinations, and the generative capacity of the organism's neural machinery. The extensive generative capacity of human languages is a consequence of us developing many more building blocks and combinatorial regularities over the eons, and the highly evolved generative capacity of the human brain.

Generative grammarians will counter that language use is more than just chaining words together. They claim that *recursion*, by means of embedded clauses, is unique to human language. ("*recursion*" comes from the Latin for "run again") Aitchison (1996: 151). Recursion is said to enable the productivity and the creativity of language, the ability to generate rule-governed sentences of infinite length and novel sentences that have never been heard by the speaker. However, the claim that recursion is limited to speech is pure piffle. Recursion in other forms of human behavior is ubiquitous. Recursion is evidenced in music, dance, and tool use et cetera, where small units of behavior are embedded in larger units of behavior. (it should be noted that there has been recent research that suggests recursion is not a universal feature of languages. See Everett 2012.)

As a practical matter, recursion in language by means of embedded clauses has limits. Infinite sentences run up against the human ability to remember embedded clauses. After three or four embedded clauses, speakers cannot remember what they were talking about. Moreover, as a result of a recent academic dispute, "...even recursion, Chomsky's syntactic holy-of-holies, had non-human origins. Chomsky was willing to accept the possibility that recursion had developed in some non-human species..." Bickerton (2009: 173) Recursion, although it has been redefined numerous times to fit the theory, is not unique to humans. Nor is it unique to human language. Many parts of speech are units of behavior that can be used recursively just as many other small units of behavior can be used recursively, by humans and non-humans alike.

Many human behavior patterns entail sequential order of some sort. We learn to mix and match to get the results we want. We recognize function and utility, whether it is with implements, dance steps, or acoustic devices. We can then synthesize novel combinations when we recognize how the functional units work. It is all learned behavior, learned by the reinforcement of stimulated responses. Sequencing and embedding of vocal muscle movements in novel ways should be no more mysterious than sequencing and embedding finger, hand, and arm movements to unlock the door at your new apartment or performing brain surgery. It is all conditioned behavioral units which can be recombined in novel ways.

Neurological evidence indicates that language sequencing and non-language sequencing originate in the same area of the brain. This, in turn, indicates that sequencing of behavior is a core function of the brain that is exemplified in many ways.

> "There are two major lines of evidence that suggest the lateral language area above the left ear also has a lot to do with nonlanguage sequencing. The Canadian neuropsychologist Doreen Kimura and her co-workers showed that left-lateral stroke patients with language difficulties (aphasia) also have considerable difficulty executing hand and arm movement sequences of a novel sort, a condition known as apraxia...
>
> "The Seattle neurosurgeon George Ojemann and his coworkers further showed, using electrical stimulation of the brain during epilepsy operations, that much of the left-lateral language specialization is involved with listening to sound sequences... The big surprise was that these exact same areas seem heavily involved in oral-facial movement sequences—even nonlanguage ones, such as mimicking a series of facial expressions.

> "One of the hazards of naming things in the brain is that we expect something called the language cortex to be devoted to language. But data such as Ojemann's show that, at its core, the cortical specialization is far more generalized, concerned with novel sequences of various kinds: hand as well as mouth, sensation as well as movement, mimicry as well as narrative." Calvin (1996: 100-101)

Sequencing is a core capability of our neural machinery, and our neural machinery is a consequence of evolution and genetics. This much is uncontroversial. However, the human ability to use functional acoustic devices is. It is controversial because of the semantic fallacies. In fact, our genetic makeup enables us to speak because speaking is generative behavior consistent with other generative behaviors which have evolved through the primate line. The neural machinery that we have inherited from our ancestors enables us to engage in many kinds of generative and combinatorial activity. The human ability to produce a plethora of unique sound sequences that generate responses in other human organisms is just one result of this neural machinery.

Humans are able to articulate a much broader range of sounds than other creatures. We use a combinatorial system of phonemes to produce this vast array of functional acoustic devices that grammarians categorize as words, phrases, idioms, acronyms etc. The human ability to combine phonemes into innumerable combinations with functional values and recombine those sounds into larger functional units should not be greeted as a miraculous inexplicable transition from grunts to speech. It is a progressive series of steps in a natural selection for behavior that has promoted the advancement of humans as individuals and a species. As our vocalizations became more complex, we increased our chances for survival. These verbal survival skills are then passed on by human caregivers via observational or iterated learning.

Chomsky's thesis that there is a rule bound "innate schematism" that regulates human vocal behavior has been refuted by numerous thinkers. One of the most compelling has been presented by Reuben Abel:

> "For Chomsky's 'explanation' is suspiciously ad hoc. Language is not in fact unique in the spectrum of human capacities. Consider, for example, the enormous gamut of nonverbal social intercourse. This ranges from religious ritual, and etiquette at a formal banquet, to how you behave in a subway crowd…The contingencies are novel, unbounded, and unpredictable; the 'rules' are (presumably) finite and recursive; your unreflective awareness of appropriate conduct in new social contexts is formally identical with our intuitive sense of grammatical usage… Shall we postulate an array of 'innate schematisms' to 'explain' these abilities.
>
> "No Chomsky's solution is too facile. Linguistic competence is not unique, but is continuous with other human capacities. Let us not so readily abandon Occam's razor." Hook (1969:121)

People learned how to use acoustic devices long before there were grammarians, linguists, or rules. It is grammarians who formalized descriptive regularities into prescriptive rules. It is linguists who then proclaimed that there must be some universal rules of grammar passed on through the human genome to account for child language acquisition. But there is no evidence whatsoever supporting that theory.

An alternative explanation for the child language acquisition phenomena is that conditioning establishes the sequential regularities in functional acoustic devices for each speaking organism. B.F. Skinner was on the right track:

> "The transformational rules which generate sentences acceptable to a listener may be of interest, but even so it is a mistake to suppose that vocal behavior is generated by them. Thus, we may analyze the behavior of small children and discover that, for example, part of their speech consists of a small class of 'modifiers' and a larger class 'nouns.' It does not follow that the child 'forms a noun phrase of a given type' by 'selecting first one word from the small class of modifiers and selecting second one word from the large class of nouns.' This is a linguist's reconstruction after the fact." Skinner (1974: 110)

Moreover, the evidence clearly indicates that humans acquire their diverse language behaviors the same way they learn other diverse behaviors. As Daniel L. Everett recently wrote:

> "In fact, the evidence is overwhelming that language is learned, rather than 'grown' homogeneously by all normal members of the species. Language in every society requires years of experience and exposure to data for any child to reach adult levels of fluency. These are hallmarks of learning, not genetic determinism." Everett (2012: 99)

Genetic influence on animal behavior is a given. To say that humans have the potential to learn language based on our genetic makeup (98% of which is shared with birds and chimps) is not enlightening. Once again, Everett clarifies the debate:

> "But finding genetic support for language is not the issue, though debates about nativism often make it appear as though it were. Rather, the question is whether or not there is anything exclusively dedicated to language learning or language form in our genotype. The answer is that we currently know of no such thing, aside from the shape and development of the human vocal tract." Everett (2012: 88)

Moreover, there is no *language gene*, in spite of some claims that there is, FOXP2. As Gary Marcus says:

> "Although the media often talk about the 'genes for language," most of the genes that are involved in language won't be unique to language... researchers will find that most of what makes up the gift for gab is a product of roughly the same kinds of neural tissue that support other mental functions." Marcus (2004: 143)

Furthermore, whatever Chomsky might be referring to through the use of "schematism", it cannot be a schematic of the sort that electricians use whereby the outcome of the design is predetermined. Modern geneticists point out that genes operate more like algorithms in that there are many if-then decision points in the genetic process that trigger cascades of effects based on environmental factors. Genes are sculpted by behavior and vice versa. There is no blueprint or schematic that predetermines the end product of the process. All genes employ feedback mechanisms that change outcomes. Consequently, there is immense variability in behavior allowed by our genetic makeup.

The doctrine of innate ideas goes back to the Stoics and gets resurrected whenever human behavior cannot be explained adequately by contemporary science. The nature/nurture controversy pops up repeatedly with innate ideas being invoked to explain everything from mathematics to the existence of God. Now Neo-Platonists have revived it to account for their inability to explain how humans learn to use sounds within the semantic paradigm. Unfortunately, these nativists start their analysis with a basic misunderstanding about what we humans do with word sounds. If they treated speech as behavior consistent with other human behavior they might not need an innate UG.

Opposing the Neo-Platonist's theory of child language acquisition espoused by Chomsky is a school of thought led by Michael Tomasello, co-director of the Max Planck Institute for Evolutionary Anthropology in Leipzig, Germany. Tomasello is a leading advocate for the *usage-based* theory of child language acquisition. Although his analysis is infused with dualism and the semantic fallacies, his work can be consistent with behaviorism if the semantics and dualism are eliminated. In Tomasello's words:

> "Generative grammarians believe that the human species evolved a genetically based universal grammar common to all peoples and that the variability in modern languages is basically on the surface only. There are a number of accounts from this perspective, ranging from Chomsky's (1986) single-mutation account to Bickerton's (1984) two-stage account to Pinker and Bloom's (1992) gradualist account. But in all these variants the basic idea is the same: that the fundamental grammatical categories and relations underlying all of the world's languages come from a biological adaptation (or set of adaptations) in the form of universal grammar.
>
> "The alternative is the usage-based view, in which there is no need to posit a specific genetic adaptation for grammar because processes of grammaticalization and syntacticization can actually create grammatical structures out of concrete utterances—and grammaticalization and syntacticization are cultural-historical processes, not biological ones. Thus it is a historical fact that the specific items and constructions of a given language are not invented all at once, but rather they emerge, evolve, and accumulate modifications over historical time as human beings use them with one another and adapt them to changing communicative circumstances." Tomasello (2003: 13)

Tomasello et al. have provided research over the past few decades which has presented compelling evidence for this usage-based view. Even so, the theoretical backdrop for Tomasello's work and the work of the others will prevent them from providing a complete behaviorist account. Tomasello's work is couched in familiar semantic terminology. He speaks of "linguistic symbols", "naming objects", "word meanings", "novel labels for novel objects", "lexical representations", and so forth. The semantic fallacies and mind/body dualism pervade and corrupt his analysis of the research results. Nevertheless, those results provide compelling evidence that human speech is a result of conditioning not an innate universal grammar which is transmitted genetically.

The challenge Tomasello and the others face is behavioral. The fundamental reason Tomasello, Chomsky, Pinker, Bickerton, Hurford and the others come to the conclusions they do is because they believe that language is a representational symbolic system. They take their clues from Plato, Aristotle, Augustine, Descartes, Locke, Mill, Frege, Russell, Wittgenstein, Austin, Strawson, Kripke et al.[8]. Contemporary linguistic theorists have inherited their speech behavior and its inherent dualism, along with the semantic fallacies from their philosophical predecessors. These elements corrupt all further analyses.

At times, Tomasello confronts some of the problems with semantic theory, but he fails to resolve them. Examples from Constructing a Language (2003):

> "At the moment, the issue of how best to characterize children's early word meanings is unresolved." Tomasello (2003: 58)

> "An even deeper problem with garden-variety learning theory as an account of word learning is that the theory does not even acknowledge that linguistic symbols are special. The theory implicitly holds that a linguistic symbol is simply a sound (or possibly a hand sign) that 'stands for' something in the world. What it means for one thing to stand for another is never really addressed." Tomasello (2003: 84)

These problems will disappear if linguists will jettison the semantic paradigm and the mentalism that underpins their theorizing. Once they acknowledge that words are not symbols that "'stand for' something in the world" and that they do not have "meanings", the accuracy of the usage-based theory of child language acquisition will become obvious. Tomasello acknowledges the functional nature of word sound production. He recognizes that what we do with word sounds is functionally driven, yet he is unable to break free of the semantic paradigm and dualism embedded in his use of an SAE language. His theorizing is misguided by his habitual verbal behavior.

Whatever universal features linguists might eventually find in the 6000+ modern human languages it would be difficult to attribute them to the human genome. A much more likely conclusion can be drawn. As B.F. Skinner said:

> "Universal features of language do not imply a universal innate endowment, because the contingencies of reinforcement arranged by verbal communities have universal features." Skinner (1974: 48)

Universal human goals beget universal linguistic features. Survival is the ultimate human goal, both as individuals and cultures. A natural selection process provided the mechanism whereby the use of noises by humans of all cultures would have developed universal features. The species developed both mechanical devices such as wheels and bows along with verbal devices for tacting, connecting, indicating direction etc. All of these devices enhanced the survival chances of individuals and groups.

To learn a language is to learn a skill. When a child first learns to use phonemes, they learn functional behavior, not rules or meanings. From David Crystal:

> "For example, one child used the word *dada* in three different ways: as she heard someone approach outside, she said *Dada?*, with a rising intonation; as she saw that it was indeed daddy, she said *Dada*, with a triumphant, falling intonation; and then she said *Da-da!*, with an insistent, level, intonation, with her arms

outstretched. At a later stage in development, these three functions would be called *question, statement,* and *command.* At this stage, these utterances do not have a distinctive grammatical form, but the use of prosody and gesture convey the force of these sentence types nonetheless." Crystal (2005: 254)

What is the meaning of the sound "*dada*"? It has no meaning and never will. However, that utterance has uses, many uses. How and when to produce variations on that sound in combination with gestures and eye movement to get the results the child wanted is what they learned when they learned to speak. These variations were positively reinforced. Thus, they become more likely to be emitted in the future with the proper stimulation. The child has gained no abstractions, concepts, ideas or meanings. They have gained the ability of use the acoustic device "*dada*" in three different ways. They have learned behavior. They have undergone operant conditioning to produce phonemes with the prosody and gesture that get them the results they expect. They will continue to do so for the rest of their lives. This process explains all of human language acquisition.

So, what do we know when we say that we have acquired a language? Do we become human dictionaries full of word meanings? Do we acquire unconscious rules? Do we inherit a collection of concepts to which we can attach words? Do we learn to use symbols? *None of the above!* What we humans acquire is an ability to use acoustic devices to do many things. We acquire vocal instruments to do our bidding. We acquire a skill. We have *know-how.* We learn *how* to produce useless phonemes and combine them into useful phonetic units. We then sequence these sounds into words, phrases, sentences etc., to stimulate responses in other organisms. If the other organisms are human and able to do approximately equivalent things with the same functional phonetic units; we say they share our language. They have acquired the same ability to use the same noises with appropriate prosody, gesture etc.

Language is heritable, not genetically, but behaviorally, and when we inherit a language from our predecessors, we inherit their phonetics, their grammatical constructions, their metaphors, their idioms, etc. We also inherit the metaphysics built into the use of their language. The metaphysics of our forebears has deep footings in the intellectual edifice of Occidental thinking and word sound usage in the Western world. The linguistic behavior of SAE-speaking people has an intrinsic mind/body dichotomy that manifests itself whenever we use that verbal behavior to discuss our verbal behavior. However, there is *no evidence* to support the contention that word sounds *stand for* non-physical entities that are located in a non-physical container in your head, *none.* Nor is there any evidence that your head contains a rule based Universal Grammar.

Naming and Descriptions

"How do words refer to sensations? –There doesn't seem to be any problem here; don't we talk about sensations every day, and give them names? But how is the connexion [sic] between the name and the thing being named set up? This question is the same as: how does a human being learn the meaning of the names of sensations? – of the word 'pain' for example." Wittgenstein (1958a: #244)

Down through the ages, one school of thought held that all words were names. The arbitrary sounds that humans are said to *call* things, were the *names* of those things. For example, the sound *"tree"* in English and the sound *"arbol"* in Spanish were the names of the large plants in the forest. As Wittgenstein suggested the word sound *"pain"* was the name of a sensation you feel. This paradigm held that humans gave names to many things, much as we give names to our children. Words of both varieties, written and spoken, functioned like labels for things. It was commonly believed that common nouns stood for, represented, *sign*ified, de*sign*ated, denoted, or referred to the things named, just as *proper names* stand for, represent, *sign*ify, de*sign*ate, denote, or refer to the unique people, places and things they name. These common names for common objects, actions etc. were then handed down from generation to generation. To learn the meanings of words was to learn the *names* for objects, actions etc., what those things were *called*.

This tradition started with the Greeks and was passed on to early Christian scholars. It was easy for them to jump to the conclusion that all words came about as a result of the naming principle, i.e. arbitrary sounds being used as labels or names for things. Remember, for the ancient Greeks our modern grammatical distinctions between proper names and common nouns would have been extremely difficult to make. Because of the primitive nature of their grammatical distinctions, names, nouns, and words were considered one and the same for all intents and purposes. Recognizing *proper names* as a unique category of nouns, and nouns as a unique category of words, came about much later in history with the formalization of grammar.

Nevertheless, the view that all words are names for things presented puzzles for these ancient philosophers. Many words are general words that do not name specific objects. The word sound *"chair"*, for instance, does not name any *particular* chair. It is a general word that applies to any chair. If *"chair"* is a name, what does it name? There are many chairs and many types of chairs. How could one word be a name for many different chairs? The word *"chair"* must name an ideal chair or a *universal* chair or the essence of chairness, that which makes chairs chairs. This line of thought led to different conclusions.

Plato needed to meld his metaphysical views with this naming principle. Thus, for Plato, the Greek equivalent of the word sound *"triangle"* could not name any *particular* triangle because there were no perfect triangles in the world. There were only flawed replicas of an ideal triangle. The Greek equivalent of the word sound *"triangle"* was the name of that perfect triangle in the Platonic heaven. That ideal triangle, the pure form, was not a part of the physical realm. It joined the ideal chair in the Platonic heavens, the *ideal* chair named by the Greek equivalent of the word sound "*chair*".

More in line with contemporary thinking, Aristotle held that words did not name metaphysical entities in the heavens; rather they named entities within the human body although they were not part of that body. The word sound "*triangle*" was the name of an impression on the human soul. The paradigmatic naming process people use for children, cities, pets etc. (*particulars*), was still thought to be the way we humans developed all words in any language. Most ancient philosophers considered most words, no matter how we parse them today, to have come about as a result of the human naming process. Most, if not all, words were arbitrary sounds that named things. Consequently, the Greeks needed *universals*, ideal forms, essences, and impressions on the soul to be the things named by general words such as "*triangle*", "*chair*", or "*dog*", as opposed to "*rover*" as a name for a *particular* dog.

However, problems with the naming principle arose. For instance, if all words are names for things, how could philosophers explain the diversity of languages? If all words are names, how is it that different languages have such different names for the same things? How is it that we humans have thousands of different names in thousands of languages that name the same object, "*tree*" and "*arbol*" for example? Yet, it is clear that there are still some unique names that do not differ from language to language. Aristotle is Aristotle in both Greek and English. Actual names of people and places, the ones we currently capitalize, are still considered *proper names*, as opposed to all words as names. They remain the same in all languages.

Over the course of history, there was a gradual transition away from the naming paradigm as an explanatory model for all words. The theory that all words were names presented insoluble problems for language theorists and was gradually replaced by the semantic paradigm. General words were no longer said to name things. (What does "*not*" name?) Rather than being names for things, most general words were said to be *symbols* that stood for, signified, designated, denoted, or referred to general things, *universals* as opposed to particulars. They also expressed or represented concepts, meanings, or abstractions and so on. Yet, actual *proper names* still presented philosophical perplexities because they did not require universals, concepts, meanings, or abstractions for them to function as they did within human speech.

Many theorists suggested that proper names directly represent, signify, designate, denote, or refer to specific people, places, etc. There does not appear to be any mental correlate or semantic content necessary to determine the referent of a name. In Carnapian jargon, proper names have extensions but no intensions. The name sound "*neil armstrong*" must refer directly to Neil Armstrong, the first man on the Moon, without any mediating concept or meaning that determines its referent, Neil Armstrong. In fact it seems odd to say that the name "*neil armstrong*" has a *meaning* or that speakers have a *concept* of Neil Armstrong. If we look in the dictionary, there is no definition of Neil Armstrong; there is a picture of one Neil Armstrong out of many and his exploits. What could be simpler?

Then again, if proper names have referents, it could be that speakers have mental correlates of some sort that determine the referents. Perhaps the sounds "*hamlet*", "*neil armstrong*" and "*beelzebub*" have associated meanings or concepts in speakers' minds that determine the referents of the names. After all, how could speakers correctly use the name sounds "*hamlet*", *neil armstrong*" and "*beelzebub*" if they don't have mental correlates in their minds, e.g. his exploits? Speakers don't just go about mindlessly spouting *"hamlet"*, *"neil armstrong"* and *"beelzebub"* at random. These names must have speaker meanings, associated concepts, or semantic content of some sort.

Well then, we are back to square one. What could be in the speaker's mind when he uses the name Neil Armstrong? An image of a guy in a space suit? The memory of Neil Armstrong? The concept of Neil Armstrong? A cluster of properties, features or facts about Neil Armstrong? As you can see, theorists have a very difficult time explaining difference between the spoken words *"neil armstrong"* and *"chair"*. It is difficult to maintain that proper names have correlated speaker meanings, concepts or literal meanings and what they would be. Unlike general words, names seem to be inherently definite and tied to specific people, places, and things.

In the modern era, John Stuart Mill began the erroneous analysis of proper names in the *Year of Our Lord 1881*. He stated:

> "Proper names are not connotative; they denote individuals who are called by
> them, but they do not indicate or imply any attributes as belonging to those
> individuals. When we name a child by the name of Paul or a dog by the name
> of Caesar, then the names are simply the marks used to enable those individuals
> to be made subjects of discourse." Of Names via, (Martinich: 266)

Mill theorized that names are not "connotative" and claimed that they are strictly denotative; they have no "attributes" associated with their use because nothing can be learned about the person, place, etc. by using a name. However, he still thought of them as symbols or "marks", both the spoken and the written varieties. His analysis came up with three "great divisions of names" to account for the use of names, though in the final analysis, he could not give a satisfactory account for the use of names. He was later joined by Russell, Frege and succeeding language theorists who entered into a philosophical fray over names.

The crux of the fray can best be presented in this way: the Greeks had a name for the morning star, *"hesperus"*. They also had a name for the evening star, *"phosphorus"*. According to them both names referred to objects seen in the sky during the morning and the evening respectively. But lo and behold, when it was discovered that Hesperus and Phosphorus were one and the same thing, viz. the planet Venus, something significant had been discovered. That discovery was a discovery about astronomy, not a discovery about words. As it turns out, both names referred to the same object within the semantic paradigm, and if both names referred to the same object, they should be interchangeable. They clearly were not. For thousands of years, people used these names in much different ways. This became known as the paradox of reference because these co-referring expressions could not be freely substituted for each other. They were *proper names* with the same referent but different *meanings*, it seemed.

Gottleb Frege wrote a seminal piece, "On Sense and Reference", about that time. In it he proclaimed that:

> "A proper name (word, sign, sign combination, expression) *expresses* its sense,
> stands for or designates its reference. By means of a sign we express its sense and
> designate its reference." Frege via Ludlow (1997: 567)

For Frege, proper names had senses and referents. Frege surmised that names designated their referents by virtue of their sense. 'Hesperus' and 'Phosphorus' clearly had different senses (*sinn*) but the same referent (*bedeutung*). Although the referent for both these names was the same astronomical body, the names had different senses which led speakers and hearers to the referent. The sense of a name helped determine its *referent* according to Frege.

Subsequently, Bertrand Russell, because of considerations for his theory of logic, suggested that names were *disguised or abbreviated descriptions*. According to Russell, the name "*hesperus*" was, in effect, shorthand for "*the evening star*" or some other definite description that could be used to designate the planet Venus, such as "*the second planet from the sun*". Frege had claimed that people could competently use the name "*hesperus*" by virtue of its *sense*, whereas Russell claimed the competent use would come about by virtue of definite descriptions which could be replaced by the name. "*hesperus*" was a disguised form of the definite descriptions: "*the second planet from the sun*" or "*the evening star*", both of which helped determine the referent.

Frege's and Russell's analyses began a line of thought about names in which certain *properties, features,* or *facts* were associated with names and the competent use of the name was dependent upon those properties, features, or facts being known by the speaker who used the name. For example, both the name "*aristotle*" in the spoken form, and the name '**Aristotle**' in the written form, would bring to mind the properties: teacher of Alexander the Great, pupil of Plato, etc. The name "*hesperus*" would bring to mind; the morning star and the second planet from the sun. All of these properties, features and facts associated with the names would lead speakers to the competent use of names. Names, in essence, had descriptive content by virtue of the definite descriptions, properties, features and facts associated with them.

Some philosophers claimed that competent speakers had to know at least one essential property, feature, or fact about the named person, place, or thing. For instance, a speaker had to know at least one essential core fact about Aristotle to use the name competently, e.g. he was a Greek philosopher. Decades later, philosophers such as John Searle provided *cluster theories* for names. For a speaker to competently use a name there had to be a minimum number of properties, features, or facts that they could associate with the name. The debate raged on over how it was that proper names referred to specific individuals, places, etc.

Logician Saul Kripke came along in 1972 and turned these theories on their head. Much like Mill, he claimed that any descriptive content a speaker associated with a name did not determine the referent of that name. Kripke claimed that names did not de*sign*ate by virtue of the properties, features, or facts associated with what they named. He claimed that there was nothing in the mind of the speaker which determined the referent of a name. Names were "rigid designators" that designated their referents in any language without regard to what was in the speaker's mind. These "rigid designators" were inaugurated by an initial linguistic "baptism", and then handed down from speaker to speaker through their social interactions.

This most celebrated example of misguided analysis is Kripke's "Naming and Necessity". Kripke makes the critical error in the first paragraph: "If we want a common term to cover names and descriptions, we may use the term 'de*sign*ator'." Kripke via Martinich (1985: 272) He begins by lumping names and descriptions together because he clearly recognized that names and definite descriptions can be used to do the same work, that they are functionally equivalent. However, he got caught up in the semantic world by saying they are semantic de*sign*ators. He assumes that names and descriptions de*sign*ate rigidly regardless of any mental content in the mind of the speaker, any context, presuppositions, or speaker goals. He makes no distinction between the spoken name and the written name and asserts that they both are symbols that *rigidly designate* people, places, etc. He put the denotation, the reference, or the *designation in the symbols*, both the written and the spoken varieties. The assumption that names are signs or symbols is his jumping off point.

His analysis continued by separating definite descriptions and names. "I'm just going to use the term 'referent of the description' to mean the object uniquely satisfying the conditions in the definite description." Kripke via Martinich (1985: 275). Kripke realized, of course, that descriptions can establish precise reference by establishing enough unique conditions, e.g. "*the tall dark haired man with the hat and the goatee sitting in the second seat of the third row tonight*". The name "*joe schmoe*" does not work that way. Kripke realized that names differed from descriptions in that they did not put forth conditions for their use and he wanted to distance himself from the descriptivist views of theorists such as Russell who claimed that, at the least, some conditions, properties, features or facts had to be in the mind of the speaker for the competent use of a name.

Kripke introduced his main thesis and admits to its origins: "One of the intuitive theses I will maintain in these talks is that names are rigid designators." (Ibid p. 278) Unfortunately, he relied on his intuition, which is nothing more than his inclination to use words in a certain way based on the operant conditioning he had undergone to produce his verbal behavior. In any case, Kripke attempted to clarify his murky intuitions:

> "To clear up one thing which some people have asked me: When I say that a designator is rigid and designates the same thing in all possible worlds, I mean that, as used in *our* language, it stands for that thing, when we talk about counterfactual situations. I don't mean, of course, that there mightn't be counterfactual situations in which in the other possible worlds people actually spoke a different language. One doesn't say that "two plus two equals four" is contingent because people might have spoken a language in which "two plus two equals four" meant that seven is even. Similarly, when we speak of a counterfactual situation we speak of it in English, even if it is part of the description of that counterfactual situation that we were all speaking German in that counterfactual situation. We say, "suppose we had all been speaking German" or "suppose we had been using English in a nonstandard way." Then we are describing a possible world or counterfactual situation in which people, including ourselves, did speak in a certain way different from the way we speak. But still, in describing that world, we use *English* with *our* meanings and *our* references. It is in this sense that I speak of a rigid designator as having the same reference in all possible worlds. I also don't mean to imply that the thing designated exists in all possible worlds, just that the name refers rigidly to that thing. If you say "suppose Hitler had never been born" then "Hitler" refers here, still rigidly, to something that would not exist in the counterfactual situation described." Kripke via Martinich (1985: 282)

Here Kripke introduces a heuristic device commonly used by contemporary philosophers, possible worlds. Possible worlds are now used extensively in logic and Truth-Conditional

Semantics. Possible worlds are used as a means of setting up hypothetical situations and counterfactuals. They facilitate the making of distinctions between *contingent truths* and *logically necessary truths*. Possible worlds allow us to imagine a world in which things may be quite different from our world. For example, we can imagine the earth suddenly veering out of its orbit without being acted upon by some outside force. That scenario contravenes the laws of physics, but it is not *logically* impossible. Hence, the fact that the earth maintains its orbit is a contingent truth, contingent upon the laws of physics in this galaxy, but there may be galaxies with different laws of physics or laws that lapse at times. With that in mind, Kripke claimed that the name "Hitler" would designate the same individual in all possible worlds. Kripke's theory can be condensed to the following:

> "In general our reference depends not just on what we think ourselves, but on the other people in the community, the history of how the name reached one, and things like that. It is by following such a history that one gets to the reference...

> "A rough statement of a theory might be the following: An initial 'baptism' takes place. Here the object may be named by ostension, or the reference of the name may be fixed by a description. When the name is 'passed from link to link,' the receiver of the name must, I think, intend when he learns it to use it with the same reference as the man from whom he heard it...." Kripke via Martinich (1985: 288)

Kripke posited that an initial "baptism" confers the name on some individual person, place, etc. That link between the name and its referent, once established, is handed down from speaker to speaker. According to Kripke, names name people, places, etc. without any ideas, concepts, meanings, properties, features, or facts to guide speakers. Proper names are "rigid designators" because they do not differ from language to language and designate the same people, places, etc. regardless of language, the occasion of use or any pragmatic considerations. Names rigidly designate their referents in all possible worlds without regard to what is going on in the speaker's head or any other possible world. On the other hand, definite descriptions such as "*the most famous pupil of plato*" are non-rigid designators because they are contingent facts about people that could vary in other possible worlds.

Kripke's theory has been a source of much controversy amongst philosophers. However, the problem here is deeper than the difference between names and other words. The problem is the semantic paradigm. The problem is in thinking that names, or any word sounds, are semantic designators. Making distinctions between names and other words will not solve the semantic puzzles about names or any other words. Only the elimination of semantics will accomplish that. As long as words and names are treated as signs, symbols, or semantic designators, names will remain a mystery. *The reference must be taken out of the symbol and given back to the speaker.*

However, names do give us an insight into how we use all words. We use acoustic devices of all sorts, including names, to perform referring acts. Names do not represent anything in human heads. Nor do they have meanings or semantic referents. Names, like descriptions, are acoustic devices that can be used in specific contexts to tact with specific people, places, times, events, etc. Humans can focus the attention of a hearer on a specific subject of conversation by performing a referring act with a name sound, a unique utterance utilized to refer to a unique individual, town, date, historical event etc. if employed in the proper context with all the necessary presuppositions and prosodic features of speech and correct listener uptakes.

Because humans keep bringing offspring into the world, we have ritualized ceremonies to give newborns names. We say that we *name* them. People are baptized and given unique names; sounds utilized in *calling* them in for supper. It is much easier than calling out: "*will the second son of the barber who works in a shop on the street that runs parallel to the river that runs north and south through the town we live in come home for supper*". Names are convenient because speakers can introduce unique individuals as subjects of discussion without the use of definite descriptions. They are the functional equivalents to these definite descriptions, but much more efficient.

Naming is an efficient way of pointing at other humans who can be uniquely identified, a hard wired-human capability. There is indisputable evidence that facial recognition processes are located in a specific brain area and can be impaired or eliminated by damage to that area. Although you may not remember his name, out of 40,000 people at the ballpark you can recognize someone you met three years ago at a wedding. Facial recognition is an evolutionary adaptation that allows humans to use proper names for other humans. The same facial recognition ability is evidenced in other species which can uniquely identify individuals of their own species (penguins for example) although we humans cannot identify individuals of other species without a great deal of effort.[9]

Other proper names are acquired in one way or another for the same reason; they can be *used* to tact with unique countries, cities, celestial bodies, boats, horses, dogs etc. They are custom-made tacting devices. They are not symbols or signs that stand for, represent, signify, denote, designate or refer to anything. Names are very useful *behavior*; they are vocal action that induces a behavioral response in listeners who are familiar with the name sound. Their use brings the target of the speaker's tacting behavior to the attention of listeners who have the appropriate speech conditioning and familiarity with the target in one way or another.

Proper names such as "*socrates*", "*adolph hitler*", "*neil armstrong*", "*salem ma.*" and "*world war two*" (sound them out) have no referents. Nor do other sounds. Spoken names are no more symbols or signs than are other spoken words. The utterance of a proper name by a speaker in context enables humans to efficiently tact with specific people, places etc. If speakers do not want to describe a person every time they want make them the subject of discourse, they use their name. The written "marks" for those proper name sounds, although phonetically imprecise, represent the spoken name. To suggest that spoken names are labels for things or semantic de*sign*ators, rather than implements *used* to tact with things, leads analysts astray. Once again, the tacting is done by the speaker or writer, not the sound.

As discussed earlier, children begin their language acquisition by learning that sounds can be used as devices to pick out objects and actions in their environment. They do not name things. There is no *naming explosion*. (The naming explosion is what many linguists call this process of rapid acquisition of referring-use sounds.) They use sounds to direct attention. They perform referring acts with sounds such as "*blanky*", "*mommy*", and "*billy*". At some point they learn how to use what grammarians call proper names. These name sounds have the same behavioral function as many other sounds do; they direct the listener's attention to the desired locus when used appropriately.

However, names have functional value only when they can be uniquely used. That is determined by the context and the discourse participant's familiarity with the name. A name that you are unfamiliar with is of no use. If you recognize it as a proper name you will realize its function, but you will not be able to use it. (One of the reasons we capitalize proper names is to recognize their function in the written form.) History is littered with names. The logs at Ellis Island are brimming with names. There are many names you will have no use for. You will not use them because you do not need them. You will never be required to make those individuals the subjects of conversation.

Moreover, context and presuppositions are all important in proper name use, just as they are with other words. In 1922, if an American had said: "*suppose hitler had never been born*", the likely response would have been: "*who*". I can also imagine a couple of street dwellers in modern day America in conversation, one of whom has a passing knowledge of WWII and the other is clueless. One says: "*suppose adolf hitler had never been born*". The other says: "*who*". The reference simply fails if we assume the speaker is trying to pick out Adolph Hitler, the fuehrer, the leader of the Third Reich. The speaker's goal, the appropriate use of the name, the cultural context, were all there (you would think), yet the reference can fail without the proper background information for the hearer. Proper names have a unique functional value that competent speakers recognize. However, they must use them in context with many presuppositions on every occasion of use.

The use of names is subject to the same success or failure as are our other methods of referring. If we recognize the speaker's goal, that they are trying to designate a person by using a name, we may still not be familiar with the name and have no idea who the speaker is trying to make the subject of their conversation. Most of us have experienced the failure of a name reference at some time or other. For example: "*joe schmoe*" is coming tonight" "*who*" "*oh i guess you dont know joe schmoe*". We mistakenly thought the hearer was familiar with Joe Schmoe and knew his name. The scenarios for failed referring acts with proper names are innumerable.

The act of reference using a *definite description* might also fail for many reasons. A hearer's cluster of beliefs about the subject of discourse may be entirely different from the speaker's, or limited to the one specific relevant description, e.g. "*the first man to stand on the moon*". If I utter: "*the first man to stand on the moon*" to a reasonably knowledgeable person, I will expect that phrase to do the same work that "*neil armstrong*" does. Yet, the hearer may know nothing else about Neil Armstrong, the astronaut. Whether the reference is successful or not would be determined by further discourse although there is no guarantee that the deployment of the definite description "*the first man to stand on the moon*" will meet the speaker's objectives.

In fact, we often use multiple referring acts in order to insure correct reference. For instance: "*the 2000 democrat presidential candidate al gore was seen boarding his personal jet today*". The definite description and the name serve the same function, i.e. tacting with the unique individual, Al Gore. The duplication of effort serves to increase the chances of success, but it is no guarantee. Someone unfamiliar with American politics may have no idea who the speaker is referring to. The reference can fail. The hearer will be unable to put a face with the name, though, as I pointed out earlier, that does not preclude the hearer from talking about "*the 2000 democrat presidential candidate*" even though they may not know it was Al Gore. The definite description can be used as a variable, an unknown person, depending upon the speaker's background knowledge. However, the utility lies in the act, not the sound or the symbol for the sound.

The relevant point is that the referring use of definite descriptions and proper names can fail for the same reasons. Speaker goals, the cultural and contextual congruence of discourse participants, and linguistic competence determine the success or failure of any referring act. Definite descriptions and names are used at various times for various purposes by various people to make unique people, places, events, etc. the subjects of discourse. The success or failure of a referring act depends on the goals of the speaker. Did the act accomplish his objectives? Did the use of the name or definite description focus the listener's attention on the proper subject?

In spite of Kripke's contention that proper names are "rigid de*sign*ators", speakers often have the same names for different people and places. *"james jones"* and *"salem"* are examples. When speakers use proper names in a referring way, they can become more specific if they need to. The level of specificity is determined by the speaker during each occasion of use, depending on the hearer's presumed background knowledge and the speaker's goals. The speaker may not need to say: *"salem oregon"* if she is in Oregon, near Salem and wishes to refer to that unique town while speaking with an acquaintance. She may simply say: *"let us go to salem"*. However, if she is in Massachusetts near Salem with the same friend, she could use emphasis and specify *"salem oregon"* if she wishes to make the same reference. The occasion of use, the listener's presuppositions, and the speaker's goals determine how the referring act is to be done successfully. In spite of claims to the contrary, proper names are context dependent. They require background familiarity and contextual clues to be used effectively.

Human cultures have adapted various systems to maintain personal identity distinctions amidst an increasing population and wider social contacts. In most Western societies, we have adopted a first name, middle name, surname system. At the family level of interaction, the first name or a nickname will suffice for a referring act. *"come here jimmy"*. In class, the teacher can refer to one of multiple Jims by intoning *"jim jones is absent"*. As James Jones' career advances, he makes sure that people know he is James E. Jones, or James Earl Jones, and in some circumstances, the name must be supplemented with a description. The individual must be referred to as *"james earl jones the actor"*. The presuppositions, context, and the speaker's goals dictate the level of specificity in the performance of a referring act done with a name or a description. In some circles this phenomenon is referred to as "rigidifying" the name or description, clearly as a result of Kripke's inaccurate analysis.

In conversation, after the initial introduction with names, e.g. John Smith or WWII, the pronoun *"he"* or *"the war"* will keep the focus where it belongs. Those sounds (in English) will keep the listener's attention focused on the correct subject. That is a functional value of anaphoric pronouns such as *"he"*, *"she"* and *"it"*, in discourse. They are abbreviated ways of tracking the subjects introduced through the use of names and definite descriptions. Of course, these pronouns are not bound to anaphor by any semantic or syntactic rules of grammar. They are bound by the pragmatics of the discourse. If the speaker has successfully made some male the subject of a conversation they may utter the pronoun *"he"* in an appropriate use and maintain that male as the subject of discourse.

There is one major difference between other words and proper names. People's names are not determined by conventional usage. We are free to use whatever sounds we want when naming someone, i.e. finding a unique sound to use as a device in tacting with unique individuals. We can design our own implements for this referring job. To be sure, there are traditional names, but we mix and match with other sounds to reduce the number of *john smiths*. We take even greater liberties when spelling proper names. The phonology often does not match up with the orthography, yet we deal with this quite nicely because the average individual rarely needs to know the spelling of others' names.

The artist formerly known as Prince took the process one step further by creating a unique, non-phonetic symbol which he used to refer to himself in print. This, of course, would not work. In his case, the symbol represented no sound, so readers had no clue how to use his name symbol in speech acts. Without a name sound to match up with the symbol, it could not be used in a vocal referring act. Whatever his name was, speakers were reduced to using a definite description, in conversation *the artist formerly known as prince*, to direct the listener's attention to that unique individual.

The history of linguistic analysis has taken us from all words as names for things, to the contemporary semantic view of words as symbols that have semantic content and referents. However, proper names continue to pose problems for semantic theorists. If theorists begin their analysis with the belief that all word sounds, including names, are signs, symbols or semantic designators, they must explain what their semantic referents are. Any semantic explanation of proper names will present enigmas because semantics is the problem.

However, if theorists acknowledge the functional role of acoustic devices in human behavior, the perplexities disappear. Some grammatical units can be used to tact with specific people, places and things if used with due consideration for all presuppositions, context and speaker goals. We mark these sounds in various ways to recognize their role in our behavior. The phonetic unit we use in English to tact with these special functional sounds is *proper names*.

Most competent theorists have abandoned the ancient theory that general words are names for things and acknowledge that proper names have no meaning or semantic content. Now, they must move beyond the view that any words have semantic referents or semantic content and acknowledge that acoustic devices have functional roles in our human behavior. Neither proper names, nor any other words, have *meanings* or *referents*; they are sounds that have uses for properly conditioned humans.

Deixis

"In all languages there are many words and expressions whose reference relies entirely on the situational context of the utterance and can only be understood in light of these circumstances. This aspect of pragmatics is called deixis (pronounced 'dike-sis'). Fromkin and Rodman (1998: 199)

"Deixis abounds in language use and marks one of the boundaries of semantics and pragmatics. The pronoun *I* certainly has a meaning independent of context—its semantic meaning, which is "the speaker"; but context is necessary to know who the speaker is, hence what "I" refers to." Fromkin and Rodman (1998: 201)

"But the general conclusion must be that most aspects of discourse deixis, and perhaps all aspects of social deixis is therefore not reducible in its entirety, and perhaps all aspects of social deixis, lie beyond the scope of a truth-conditional semantics. Deixis is therefore not reducible in its entirety, and perhaps hardly at all, to matters of truth-conditional semantics." Levinson (1983: 96)

"The facts of deixis should act as a constant reminder to theoretical linguists of the simple but immensely important fact that natural languages are primarily designed, so to speak, for use in face-to-face interaction, and thus there are limits to the extent to which they can be analysed without taking this into account." Levinson (1983: 54)

The word "deixis" derives from the Greek word for "pointing". Within descriptive linguistics, deixis is a pragmatic phenomenon considered to be outside the purview of semantics. Linguists claim that many word sounds stand for, represent, encode, signify, denote, designate or refer to different things depending upon the circumstance in which they are uttered. It does not appear that these words have a literal content or constant semantic referents. The meanings and/or referents of these word sounds vary with the speaker and the time and place of their utterance. Deixis within linguistics establishes a boundary between semantics and pragmatics, between words with fixed referents supposedly, and those with shifting referents depending upon the circumstances in which they are used. The referents of word sounds such as *"i"*, *"here"*, *"it"*, *"tomorrow"*, *"these days"*, *"ours"*, *"my dog"*, for example, are completely context dependent and speaker centric. There are no stable lexical meanings for these words.

In an effort to sort through the deixis phenomenon, linguists have categorized deictic words and expressions in many languages. Many deictic word sounds are dependent upon who is the speaker, for example: *"i"*, *"me"*, *"mine"*, and *"we"* in English. It is said that the referents of those words shift with the speakers who utter them.

Linguists have suggested *place deixis* and *time deixis* as two more categories of deictic words. Examples of place deixis would be: *"from here"*, *"this house"*, *"yonder mountains"*, *"over there"*. In effect, what the word *symbols* are supposedly *pointing to* (remember the origins of "deixis") changes with the speaker and his location at the time of the speech act or another deictic center previously established. The word symbols *"come"* and *"go"* are a place deictic linguistic phenomenon of the latter kind. Their use is always relative to a previously established location, the dietic center of the discourse, which may be the location of the discourse or another location assumed by the discourse participants. Statements such as *"will you come to the party"* as opposed to *"will you go to the party"* depend upon a speaker-centric deictic location or point of view (POV). The asymmetry or directionality of actions and events is reflected in the use of many English verbs as place deixis.

Time deixis abounds in virtually all languages. In English, the *meaning* of word sounds such as *"then"*, *"now"*, *"today"*, *"yesterday"*, *"within the hour"*, are all grounded in the time of the utterance. The interpretation of these words is entirely dependent upon the time of their utterance or a deictic time previously established. Time deixis brings to mind a sign I used to see, on a daily basis on the marquee of a local saloon: **'Free beer tomorrow!'** In semantic theory, the time of the utterance, or the time of the reading of a sign in this case, determine the *meanings* of all these time-deictic words and phrases.

Verb tenses are also considered to be time deictic by many analysts because their *meanings* are sensitive to a temporal point of reference. From either the time of the discourse utterance, or the projected point of view of the speaker, all tense indicators derive their point of reference. Any further time references are anaphorically dependent. For example: *"i was running"*, *"i am running"*, *"i will run"*, *"i was about to run"*, *"i will have run"*, *"i will have been running"*. In all of these constructions the use of tense indicators for time are relative to the time of the utterance or a time point of view (POV) previously established by the speaker.

In addition, linguists have categorized the use of different pronouns for different people as *social deixis*. Many cultures and languages have honorific or social status related titles to be used when addressing people of differing social status or in differing economic circumstances. For example, a professor may use informal first names with students in class. Most often, the reverse would be considered a breach of etiquette. Professors must be addressed as Professor Smith, for example. Formal and informal versions of *"you"* are common in European languages. They are socially deictic. Social deixis in many languages is apparent in many settings and governs the use of names as well as pronouns: employer/employee, teacher/student, male/female, parent/child and so on.

The phenomenon of deixis is widespread in all languages and presents an insurmountable problem for semanticists in their notational systems. Even linguists acknowledge the lack of stable meaning and reference; they recognize the functional value of deictic words and phrases. They realize that these words are devices, though they err in supposing that these words are different from other words. They assume that there is a distinction between words with stable, independent, lexical meanings, and deictic words. They assume that there is a boundary between semantics and the pragmatic deixis phenomenon. In fact, there is no distinction to be made. No word sounds are semantic designators with stable literal meanings or semantic referents of any sort.

If you accept the fact that all word sounds have context-dependent behavioral functions, not *meanings and referents*, deictic words are only the most obvious examples of words that have no stable semantic content and are used to tact with various things depending upon the speaker and the time and location of their utterance. For example, if one hundred speakers all uttered the same sentence: "*i purchased a new blue bike today*", each utterance would be semantically identical, but pragmatically distinct because each speaker would be referring to a different bike. Consequently, the truth would have to be assigned to each utterance and not the sentence everyone used in its performance.

Consider the word sound "*seal*" (sound it out), for example. It has roughly thirty definitions according to my dictionary. Every production of that specific word sound is identical. It is said to be homophonically ambiguous. Yet, English speakers are able to determine how a speaker is using that word sound, at least in part, by locating the sound within grammatical constructions. Is it being used as a noun or a verb? We might say that the word sound is *grammatically deictic*. That is, the interpretation of the sound is at least partially dependent upon its location within the grammatical form being uttered.

Other presuppositions and discourse elements will determine if that sound is being used to tact with animals, emblems, impressions, marks, gaskets, assurance, binding, concluding (seal the deal) etc. The word sound "*seal*" has many and diverse uses. The use of that sound is driven totally by presuppositions, sentence context, etc. No consistent core meaning can be correlated with the sound, yet speakers are not changing the *meaning* or *referent of a symbol*; they are changing the functional value of a sound, depending upon a host of contextual elements including their conditioned objectives and their personal speech history.

As pointed out earlier, even the sounds "*james jones*" and "*salem*" can be used to tact with diverse people and places depending upon context, speaker goals, and occasion of use. There are very few, if any, acoustic devices that are used exclusively for one purpose, and, if there are any, they can be changed in about 30 seconds by an accomplished speaker who will utilize the sounds in a novel way to get their work done. To say that some words are deictic, and others are not, is to say that some words have literal/lexical meanings and stable referents while others do not. However, linguists must come to realize, that all acoustic devices are deictic and have functional values that must be determined with a pragmatic (vs. semantic) behavioral analysis. They must come to realize ultimately, that they must consider the time, place, the grammatical location and personal speech history of the speaker for them to correctly analyze *any* speech act or written representations of such speech acts. They must come to realize that the noises coming out of human mouths are not symbols with stable consistent semantic content that can be analyzed out of context.

The Morphology Myth

> "The study of the internal structure of words, and of the rules by which words are formed, is called **morphology**. This word itself consists of two morphemes, *morph* + *ology*. The morphemic suffix *–ology* means "science of" or "branch of knowledge concerning." Thus the meaning of morphology is "the science of word form."
>
> "Knowing a language implies knowing its morphology. Like most linguistic knowledge, this is generally unconscious knowledge." Fromkin and Rodman (1998: 69)

Morphology, the study of word formation, is one branch of *semantics*. Many words consist of two or more morphemes. Morphemes are considered minimal linguistic signs, grammatical units where a connection between sound and meaning can be made. The word sound *"undesirable"* is claimed to have two morphemes, or units of meaning, *"un"* and *"desirable"*. *"un"* also appears in numerous other words and has similar morphemic meaning for each of them it is claimed: *"unlikely"*, *"unhappy"*, *"unbelievable"*. *"un"* has a meaning that modifies the meaning of the stem word. So we are told by linguists.

Likewise, the morpheme *"phon"* in *"phonetic"*, *"symphony"*, *"telephone"*, *"euphonius"*, is said to have the same meaning. Many polymorphemic words are said to be composed of smaller meaningful units like *"phon"*. Becoming a proficient speaker of any language is said to consist in part, in learning its morphology, in being able to deconstruct the meaning of larger words into smaller units or vice versa. Having this ability supposedly enables proficient word users to construe *word meanings* from *morpheme meanings*, and amazingly, we can do this unconsciously, according to experts.

Linguists say that some morphemes are useful by themselves and function independently, *free morphemes* such as *"like"*. Others appear only with free morphemes or stem words and serve to modify that stem word in some way, such as *"un"* and *"ly"* in *"unlikely"*. They are called *fixes*: suffixes, prefixes, infixes and circumfixes. They are bound morphemes, bound to the free morphemes or stem words. These *bound morphemes* do not appear independently, but they are said to have independent meaning.

However, this morphological analysis of words presents some puzzles:

> "A morpheme was defined as the basic element of meaning, a phonological form that is arbitrarily united with a particular meaning and that cannot be analyzed into simpler elements. This definition has presented problems for linguistic analysis for many years, although it holds true for most morphemes of a language. Consider words like *cranberry, huckleberry,* and *boysenberry.* The *berry* part is no problem, but *huckle* and *boysen* occur only with berry, as did *cran* until

cranapple juice came on the market... Bound forms like huckle-, boysen-... require a redefinition of the concept of morpheme. Some morphemes have no meaning in isolation but acquire meaning only in combination with other specific morphemes....Just as there are some morphemes that occur in a single word (combined with another morpheme), there are other morphemes that occur in many words, but seem to lack a constant meaning from one word to another." Fromkin and Rodman (1998: 73)

The problems presented by this analysis of morphemes parallel the entire enterprise of semantics and the mistaken view that words are symbols that have *meanings*. Morphologists run into all sorts of problems with these minimal units of meaning because there are thousands of exceptions. "*inept*", "*remit*", "*disgusted*", for example, all have what would be considered prefixes: "*in*", "*re*" and "*dis*". Yet their stem morphemes: "*ept*", "*mit*" and "*gusted*" have no meanings.

No doubt, at times, when speakers use morphemes, they can change the functional value of words. Morphemes can be used as functional acoustic units. As *un*believable as this may sound to semanticists, the "*un*" fix has a functional behavioral value that speakers *can* utilize in routine or novel combinations. Some of these morphemes have become standard parts of habituated vocal behavior and are accepted as functional units that can be attached to stem words to perform standardized functions, often relying on placement to be recognized as a functional unit. e.g. "unfollow". Think Facebook.

We English speakers, for instance, cannot say: "*followun*", "*likelyun*", or "*believableun*". However, there is no *rule* that limits the placement of the sound "*un*". The functional morpheme "*un*" is restricted to prefixation because of habituation. After "*un*"'s introduction, it became useful in many novel morphemic conversions. Many of these conversions became officially sanctioned, acceptable, and grammatical. Check your dictionary for officially sanctioned "*un*" words. Other "*un*" words are *un*sanctioned and *un*grammatical. Nevertheless, they become useful speech behavior when employed in an *un*normal context and might ultimately become *un*unacceptable. They will become normalized as a consequence of historical processes and the utilitarian results they offer.

For example, the function of the suffix "*able*", in English, can be used to convert verbs into adjectives, thereby permitting English speakers to place those sounds in different locations within grammatical constructions and thereby change the functional value of the original sound. It has etymological ties to "*enable*", "*ability*" and not surprisingly, *the word* "*able*". However, when speakers use "*treatable*", "*scalable*", "*drinkable*", or "*actionable*", there are no new entities created in their minds. What is new is the function of the new word sound within English grammar. It is a function that listeners will grasp because they appreciate that this is one use of the morpheme "*able*", not because "*able*", as a word or a morpheme, has a semantic content. They may have never used the word sound "*able*" in their lives or be able to make any etymological connection, but they are perfectly able to use the suffix "*able*" because they have become habituated to its use as part of their English speech behavior.

We learn acoustic devices as children and general*ize* their functions. There are many exceptions, but first we must general*ize*. Children, as part of their language acquisition, are said to acquire morphological rules of word formation based on units of *meanings*. However, children are not learning meanings or rules; they are learning how to use acoustic devices within conforming temporal sequences. They are learning the utility of phonetic combinations. They are learning behavior. They learn that talking in English about two blankets requires the addition of a plural "s" to the sound "blanket". They generalize the functional role of the sound "s" for plurals. Later on, they learn a plethora of exceptions.[10]

Word formation has history. There are some regularities, more or less, with many exceptions and anomalies but there are no hard and fast-rules; it is not rule governed. We English speakers have "in-sufficient", "in-accurate" and "in-attentive". We also have "un-attractive", "un-becoming" and "un-available". Some words we are not quite sure about. Is that action "unadvisable" or "inadvisable"? Are those rights "in-alienable" or "un-alienable"? Is that evidence "in-disputable" or "un-disputable"? We are unsure because morphology is, at best, inexact. Or is it unexact?

Indeed, English-speaking children generalize many regularities of word formation. They generalize the methods of constructing past tense verbs and plural nouns. First, they recognize the general functional roles of "ed" and "s", the morphemes used in the formation of past tense verbs and plural nouns. Then they are said to over-generalize. Children routinely go through a stage whereby they incorrectly regularize verb tenses and noun plurals. They say things such as, "bringed", "haved", "runned", "foots", "gooses" and "sheeps". This phenomenon has nothing to do with *meanings or rules*. The tense functional "ed" and the plural "s" have no meanings. They have *uses*, uses that children recognize and regularize based on their conditioning, exceptions included.

This over-generalization is often taken to be an argument against language as conditioned vocal behavior because the children have never heard their caregivers produce *un*grammatical English forms such as "bringed". Thus, they could not be imitating them. However, learning language is not imitating the exact sentences and phrases that caregivers produce. It is learning the functional roles of phonetic units. It is learning a system with regularities that can be discovered by repetition and feedback and, because of various linguistic evolutionary forces, most languages have many exceptions to their morphemic regularities. Thus, English-speaking students spend an inordinate amount of time and effort learning such things as irregular verbs and irregular plural nouns. Nevertheless, by age ten, most children have had enough exposure to the morphological irregularities in their native languages to routinely use them. They are conditioned to do so by then.

After children learn the function of a spoon, knife and fork, they produce a great deal of novel behavior. Their movements with these instruments do not precisely imitate their parents. Neither should we expect their every use of word sounds to replicate what a caregiver has said at one time or another. When children learn how to use sounds they become more than parrots mimicking what they hear. They learn a skill which will serve them in many ways *un*imagined by their parents. They realize that there are generalities and similarities in our grammaticalization and regularize their vocal behavior accordingly. Eventually, some become philosophers and linguists who invent new words such as "realizeability" on an *ad hoc* basis, using morphological generalization.

The original tacting acts with sounds create free morphemes. Children begin their linguistic odyssey by learning to tact utilizing free morphemes, word sounds such as "doggie", "blanky" and "blue". The so-called bound morphemes are learned later because they change free morphemes. They must have something to modify. They are fixes. The functional role may be reversing the free morpheme as in *"unwinding"*, *"unavailable"*, or *"unbelievable"*. It should be noted that this process has nothing to do with *meanings or rules*. The *functional roles* of bound morphemes become generalized, standardized, normalized and regularized.

As adults we routinely change word function by adding bound morphemes or fixes. We take *"real"* and create: *"unreal"*, *"realize"*, *"realization"*, *"unrealizable"*, *"realizability"*, etc. This enables us to move sounds around in our grammatical constructions. However, there are no new mental entities created. We simply change the functional role of the sounds. We take a *real* word sound that is *really* useful and *realize* that we can use it as the subject of conversation. That *realization* is not an *"aha"* moment whereby there is a sudden burst of cognition. No light bulb goes on. We simply adapt the functional role of many morphemes and begin to utilize them in our verbal behavior.

I have no need to consult a dictionary or a morphologist to use a nonce-word I heard recently: *"ugli-fication"*. The latest attempt at beautification by local civic leaders resulted in the "ugli-fication" of a city landmark. I recognized the functional role of the morpheme *"fication"*, as in *"beautification"*. Some writer combined that functional value with the functional value of the stem word "ugly" and came up a very usable word sound. Like children learning irregular verbs, adults must navigate the turbulent seas of language. We must learn what is considered standard English, *standard* being determined by a committee deep within the bowels of academia. They say that morphemes have *meanings*. They say that they know the *rules* of word formation with morphemes. They have deluded themselves, although I don't know when they became luded.

Metaphor
"No man is an island"

Explaining metaphors has been a formidable obstacle in the path to discovering how language works. Metaphor, metonym, hyperbole, understatement, satire, irony and euphemism are all recognized as word uses that flout *literal meanings*. They are tropes (figures of speech) that prove useful. Yet when linguists analyze these uses of language, they cannot reconcile *meaning* with *use*, semantics with pragmatics. How is it that speakers and writers can take words that *mean* one thing and *use* them to *mean* something different? Regarding the above epigraph, obviously, no man is an island. But that is not what the speaker *meant* in the that metaphor. Well then, how do we know what the speaker *meant* if he's not using the words' ordinary *meanings*?

In conventional analysis there are a number of theories which try to explain the metaphorical use of words: the comparison theory, the interaction theory, the substitution theory and the network theory. Other than the network theory, they all assume that there is a stable literal meaning encoded in words and a computational process whereby speakers and listeners determine the *figurative meaning* being used in the metaphor. The insinuation is that there are hidden meanings in metaphors which can be determined by following certain procedures. However, there is little if any evidence to suggest that language learners or well-educated speakers go through any computational process to learn and use metaphors. On the other hand, the network theory proponents and the radical pragmaticists propose that we give up on the notion of meaning altogether, including figurative meanings.

In 1978 Donald Davidson had an explanation for metaphors:

> "Generally it is only when a sentence is taken to be false that we accept it as a metaphor and start to hunt out the hidden implication. It is probable for this reason that most metaphorical sentences are patently false, just as all similes are trivially true." Davidson via Martinich (2001: 440)

By Davidson's analysis, hearers realize that the utterance *"no man is an island"* is false. Hence the hearer "hunts out the hidden implication". Saddled (one of many uses) as he was with semantics and literal meanings for words, Davidson developed a convoluted explanation in an attempt to salvage the semantic connection of word sounds to "ordinary" lexical or literal meanings.

> "I depend on the distinction between what words mean and what they are used to do. I think metaphor belongs exclusively to the domain of use. It is something brought off by the imaginative employment of words and sentences and depends on the ordinary meanings of those words and hence the ordinary meanings of the sentences they comprise." Davidson via Martinich (2001: 436)

Davidson attempts to explain metaphors as pragmatic phenomena but he refuses to abandon semantics. He denies that metaphors have any special meaning or special semantic content. He insists on retaining "ordinary meanings" for all the words and sentences in a metaphor, whatever they might be. Yet he maintains that these words with their "ordinary meanings" can be used to do queer things totally unrelated to these ordinary meanings.

> "There is a simple way out of the impasse. We must give up the idea that a metaphor carries a message, that it has a content or meaning (except of course, its literal meaning). The various theories we have been considering mistake their goal. Where they think they provide a method for deciphering an encoded content, they actually tell us (or try to tell us) something about the effects metaphors have on us… No doubt metaphors often make us notice aspects of things we did not notice before." Davidson via Martinich (2001: 444)

The semantic/pragmatic divide forces this ruse. While he acknowledges that metaphors produce effects in hearers or readers, Davidson denies that they have a *figurative meaning*. He retains word and sentence *literal* meanings, the "encoded content". He insists that the words used in metaphors retain their original semantic content, yet, they somehow make listeners or readers "notice aspects of things". Davidson acknowledges the fact that metaphors force behavioral changes in listeners. They have a pragmatic effect unrelated to the supposed semantic content of the words. He recognizes the functional role of metaphor, yet he tries to retain literal meanings for the words used in the metaphor.

Other theorists suggest that there is no clear distinction between literal meanings for words and their metaphorical meanings. Words have multiple meanings that are flexible and completely driven by previous speech or writing which provide a grammatical context, other context (broadly construed) or other pragmatic considerations. The claim that words have stable, ordinary, or literal meanings is abandoned. Somehow, speakers size up the situation they are in and look up the appropriate meaning in their mental dictionary. They then attach the appropriate meaning to the word sound in that incident of use. (The hearer does the same thing one would assume.) Nevertheless, multiple meanings are retained in the *mind* of the speaker and brought to bear on the interpretation process on an ad hoc basis. The question is begged: If word sound use is completely determined by pragmatic considerations etc., do we need semantics and literal word meanings of any sort?

Through the use of metaphors at times, like similes, speakers are able to direct listeners' attention to similarities. Similes (using *"like"* as in: *"the church is like a hippopotamus"*) are frontal assaults on similarity, going directly at the target, whereas, metaphors (*"no man is an island"*) head to the target with a tangential attack. The functional role of most metaphors, in context, is to call attention to similarities or differences. Most competent mature speakers recognize the goals of a speaker when they use words metaphorically, metonomously, satirically, ironically, etc. even if the listeners cannot identify which trope is being used. They do so because of their extensive history of word use. As David Rumelhart reports:

> " … far from being a special aspect of language, which perhaps develops only after children have full control of literal language, figurative language appears in children's speech from the very beginning." Ortony (1979: 79)

Language learners, be they children or second-language learners, have great difficulty with metaphors because they are told that the speaker or writer is not using the ordinary *meanings* of the words (within the semantic paradigm), they are using *figurative meanings*. It takes some time, patience, and effort for speakers to learn that word use is quite pliable, that word *meanings* are difficult to get a handle on, though they ultimately learn that word sounds can be used to do many different things depending upon the frame of reference, presuppositions, etc.

Metaphor in language is ubiquitous and competent speakers *must learn to use them as the holistic functional devices that they are*. <u>Surfaces and Essences</u>, by Douglas Hofstadter and Emmanuel Sander, is a veritable catalogue of linguistic data listing thousands of word phrases, idioms, and sentences with analogical origins, demonstrating that human speaking is analogical or metaphoric at its roots. (Metaphor and analogy are distinct but closely related phenomena. Some analogies are non-metaphoric). By thinking analogically with language, human speakers categorize just about everything they can attend to. This categorization then facilitates more analogous thinking and makes it easier for thinkers to make intuitive leaps of discovery or creativity and produce even more analogies. These analogical leaps are at the core of human cognition. Hofstadter and Sander make the case that:

> "You feel that you are deliberately creating an analogy to advance a certain point of view, but actually it's the other way around: your point of view comes from a myriad of hidden analogies that have given you a certain perspective on things."
> Hofstadter and Sander (2013: 383)

Many writers have detailed the analogical or metaphorical origins of many, if not most, tropes. Analogies and metaphors continue to dominate creative speaking and writing. This process has taken us from monosyllabic grunts used to tact with objects, actions, distinctions, and kind-sortals, to complex constructions that orient us in time, space, family relationships, causal relationships, ownership, and on and on. This process has been possible because we recognize the situationally derived functional value of holistic acoustic devices, not *the literal and figurative meanings of words*. We then transfer these functional values from one domain to another.

For instance, in this section's epigraph, the use of "island" to refer to an isolated piece of land is transferred to the realm of human social interaction. A man cannot be isolated. He must have other people. Hence: "No man is an island." Meanings have not been swapped. Within our verbal behavior, we humans recognize functionality and readily transfer it from one acoustic device to another. Once it is transferred, speakers adopt the utilitarian verbal behavior, no matter how grammarians might categorize that behavior.

Moreover, even highly educated competent speakers will use many metaphors, including "dead metaphors", without knowing their origins. Competent speakers only need to know the functional value of these holistic parts of speech. For example, the source of "he kicked the bucket" is known by few in spite of its widespread use. (The squeamish details are in footnote 11.) When a useful new metaphor comes along, they will adopt it, completely disregarding the origins. Nor do they need to categorize the trope as a metaphor, metonym, simile, or whatever. When poker players wear their "*Full Tilt Poker*" hats, how many of them realize that the use of the metaphor "*full tilt*" originated in medieval jousts? In fact, to use it, they have no need to know that, or even know that it is a metaphor.

Translation

"Thousands of other instances could be provided showing the difficulties of translation between languages which relate to markedly different cultures. But this sample is sufficient to incontrovertibly demonstrate the false nature of the adage 'everything can be said in every language'. In summary, languages differ in what must be said and also what can be said in them." Dixon (2016: 187)

The process of translating words from one language to another is often characterized as a process of converting words with equivalent *meanings*. Identical or near identical semantic content is said to be the translational constant between equivalent words in different languages. However, a simple process of looking up equivalent words with equivalent meanings, when possible, does not enable translators to convert messages from one language to another. Any polyglot will confirm that proficient translation requires much more than learning the so-called meanings of words in the disparate languages.

Moreover, official doctrine now recognizes that some grammatical elements have no semantic content. They are purely functional elements of speech. For instance, what would be the semantic content of *"that"*, *"she"* or *"here"*? What are the *meanings* of *"that"*, *"she"*, or *"here"* that are carried over from one language to another? If these are words without meanings, what would be their translational constants? How can polyglots translate these words without meanings? In fact, they do it with all words, because none of them have meanings, but they all have uses. Translators must recognize the functional value of acoustic devices in context. A good translator will get the point across, regardless of what the individual words are supposed to *mean*.

The competent use of any language is a constant learning process. Individual words, idioms, phrases, and other acoustic devices have changeable functional values that vary depending upon the varying needs of each speech community. Competent translators must recognize all these factors, along with culture, history, tradition, and many conversational maxims. They must constantly update their speech behavior in multiple languages because languages change. As they do update themselves, translators must learn the *uses* for new words, idioms etc., because the translational constant between languages is utility, not meaning.

Why is it that people learning a new language have no intuitions about the use of new words? They are given a list of foreign words and what the purported equivalent words in their native tongue. They then think in their native language and convert that thinking to what is supposedly the foreign equivalent. They use the new foreign words in context to get a feel for their use. Only after an extended period do they become competent speakers of the new language. Then they begin to think in the new language rather than think in their native language and convert it. They also begin to dream in the new language. New intuitions come with the new thinking and the new dreaming. The new thinking, dreaming and intuitions come about due to their competent *use of new verbal behavior in context*, not as a result of attaching new symbols to old meanings.

Synonymy and Substitution

"*Synonymy*   This is a relationship of 'sameness' of meaning, e.g. *kingly / royal / regal, pavement / sidewalk, youth / youngster.* The search for synonyms is a longstanding pedagogical exercise, but it is as well to remember that lexemes rarely (if ever) have *exactly* the same meaning. There are usually stylistic, regional, emotional, or other differences to consider. And context must be taken into account. Two lexemes might be synonymous in one sentence but different in another: *range* and *selection* are synonyms *in What a nice ---- of furnishings*, but not in *There's the mountain ----*." Cambridge Encyclopedia of Language, pg 105

"In English, and in other languages, there are no absolutely exact synonyms. Two words may have similar meanings but they are never substitutable, one for the other, in every circumstance." Dixon (2016: 164)

Etymologically, the word sound "*synonymous*" originally applied to names. The theory that words were names of things enabled this use of the word sound "*synonymous*", i.e. same name. Synonymous proper names designated the same person, e.g. "*mark twain*" and "*samuel clemens*", or "*clark Kent*" and "*superman*". The naming model of word acquisition and use was the basis for the original use of the sound "*synonymous*" and applied to all word sounds. Operating like names in this antiquated theory, other synonymous words had the *same meaning*: "kingly/royal/regal". Synonymous words also *sign*ify the same things: "pavement/sidewalk".

Synonymy is a feature we often hear about in discussions of language. Lexicologists talk about the identity of *meaning* between two lexemes. Lexemes are said to be synonymous if they *mean* the same thing, but what does "mean the same thing" mean? Does that mean that the semantic content associated with two synonymous lexemes is identical on all occasions of use? How can we determine if the meanings of two lexemes are identical if we cannot determine what the meanings are outside of their use within specific sentences, as in the above examples for the word sounds "*range*" and "*selection*"? It appears that *meanings* for most word sounds are variable and depend upon a number of factors, including their relationship to other word sounds in various grammatical constructions.

The explanations for synonymy get caught up in a tangle of meanings, semantic content, semantic referents, definitions, concepts and such, if we say that spoken words are symbols that have stable meanings and referents. Analysts inevitably confront the vagueness and ambiguity in the various uses for the word sounds "*meaning*", "*significance*", "*reference*", etc. They must ultimately admit that the meaning of the phrase "*mean the same thing*" is not clear or consistent and the use of the word sound "*synonymous*" is just as muddled.

In 1953, Willard Quine demonstrated that the "notion of synonymy" is anything but clear. He was attempting to draw a fine line between analytic statements and synthetic statements. (they will be discussed in Chapter VI.) He pointed out that the *definition* of "synonymy" is tied to *meaning*, i.e. words are synonymous if they have the same meaning. Yet, meaning is often *defined* in terms of synonymy, i.e. words have the same meaning if they are *synonymous*. He also claimed that synonymy cannot be explained in terms of definitions:

> "Recognizing then that the notion of definition does not hold the key to synonymy and analyticity, let us look further into synonymy and say no more of definition." Quine via Martinich (2001: 50)

He, of course, realized that lexical definitions are *descriptive*. Lexicologists are empiricists who observe the data. They base their definitions on their observations of native speakers and how they *use* words. Consequently, these lexical definitions change along with the changes in usage. Definitions are not fixed. How could synonymy be determined by means of definitions if the definitions change with the times?

Furthermore, many supposedly synonymous words seem to have different affective values, different senses, or different "connotations". However, *within logic* the affective force of words is to be ignored. The semantic content residing in the symbols must be separated from their affective force. Synonymy resides in the semantic content, the lexical or literal *meaning*. Consequently, Quine, a logician by trade, attempted to do so.

> "Now let us be clear that we are not concerned here with synonymy in the sense of complete identity in psychological associations or poetic quality; indeed no two expressions are synonymous in such a sense. We are concerned with what may be called cognitive synonymy." Quine via Martinich (2001: 55)

By making the affective/cognitive bifurcation, Quine was able to retain a "cognitive synonymy". His "cognitive synonymy" hinged on stable independent semantic content carried by symbols and interchangeable salva veritate. As Quine saw it, for the interchanged constituents of a proposition to be synonymous, the truth value of the proposition had to be maintained. However, Quine's cognitive/affective bifurcation is founded on the premise that words have an invariant semantic content attached to them and that this literal meaning can be separated from the emotive effects of the word's use. It presupposes a dichotomy between a literal semantic content that is *cognitive* and the affective force of words.

To the contrary, words cannot be sterilized, as it were. The affective functional component of word sounds cannot be ignored when comparing them for synonymy; it is an essential part of their use. Synonymy, or substitution, is an equivalence of functional value in natural language that must incorporate all functional features of word sound use. Sometimes acoustic devices are used synonymously. At other times the same word sounds are *used* differently, depending on sentence structure, context, the speaker's speech history, presuppositions, prosodic features, etc. If speakers substitute one word for another and it gets the job done, it is synonymous on that occasion of use.

Talk about synonymy and substitution in semantics is misguided. We speakers learn how to use acoustic devices from others. In order for them to do the work we expect of them, we must recognize their utility in context. We often have more than one device that will do the work we want done, depending upon circumstances. Yet, to say that two words function precisely the same in all circumstances, at all times, regardless of speaker's speech history, is a fable. It is a fable founded on another fable: word sounds are symbols with stable, independent, semantic content, their literal or lexical meanings.

The functional equivalence of names and definite descriptions is a case in point. They can be used synonymously. If a proper name can replace a definite description it is synonymous in that incident of use. In context, "*george washington*" can be synonymous with "*the first american president*". They are functionally equivalent in their linguistic roles as referring-use terms. A speaker *could use them* to do the same work, i.e. making the first American president, George Washington, the subject of a conversation for people who are familiar with American history.

So too, idioms can be used as functional equivalents for other words. "*Kicked the bucket*" can be used as the functional equivalent of "*died*" in certain circumstances. "*slam dunk*" can be used instead of "*sure thing*". Words with metaphorical connections enter the English language daily as functional equivalents.For instance, these days, "*delayering*" can be used in place of "*firing people*". Additionally, many words become popular simply because they are more efficient functional equivalents, e.g. "*potable*" in lieu of "*clean enough to drink*". Synonymy is a result of functional equivalence and is totally circumstantial and idiosyncratic. Sometimes two words are synonymous, sometimes not.

Within our speech behavior, the acoustic devices we use enjoy a great deal of plasticity. We twist them and shape them to fit our needs. Clever speakers can substitute word sounds in ways that no one has ever done before.Creative speaking is novel behavior, one of many novel behaviors we humans display. It is consistent with other behaviors that are adapted to meet changing circumstances. The field of historical linguistics has documented innumerable shifts in word function (lexical change) driven by utility. Variations in word use become popular and succeed based on the need for the functionality in novel environments. It is all part of the analogical or metaphorical cognitive capacity of human beings that is evidenced in behavior of all sorts. We humans are a creative bunch.

Ultimately, all word use is idiosyncratic within conventional boundaries. People substitute words based on their utility, the store of words they have available, and the precision with which their linguistic work needs to be done. A horse breeder, for instance, has to make much finer distinctions about a horse's gait than I do. He can refer to trotting, galloping, running, cantering, prancing (?) etc. I cannot make those distinctions and have no need to. I can substitute "*galloping*" for "*running*" in my speech behavior without consequence when I talk about horses. Those words are synonymous for my purposes. I need not be as precise in my ordinary conversation about horses as a horse breeder needs to be. The salient point is that the functional equivalence depends on the linguistic ability of the speaker *and* the listener.

Some articulate speakers can use tens of thousands of words. Some people get by with a few thousand words. Less-refined speakers and writers have more limited vocabularies. They may not make the finer distinctions that more sophisticated speakers do. For instance, nowadays, we often hear speakers using "*less*", when "*fewer*" is appropriate. Those speakers do not make the distinction that brought about the use of two different noun classes in English, i.e. measurable things vs. countable things, as in *count nouns* and *mass nouns*. They think that distinction is unnecessary in many circumstances. (This was formerly a kind-sortal mandated by the English language and marked by the many/much and fewer/less distinction.)

These same speakers will still use "*much*" and "*many*" in that regard, as in "*much time before thanksgiving*" and "*many days before thanksgiving*". They would never say "*much days before thanksgiving*" or "*many time before thanksgiving*". Yet, they will not mark that distinction when they say "*less time before thanksgiving*" and "*less days before thanksgiving*". "*less*" is substituted for "*fewer*" without regard for the distinction between measurable time and countable days. The substitution of "*less*" for "*fewer*" is accepted and functionally equivalent for them.

Successfully substituting one word for another is based on utility. If a speaker were to substitute one word sound for another, only they can judge the success or failure of the substitution based on their linguistic goals. Did the speech act accomplish those goals? Did the hearers get the message with the appropriate affective force, the right uptake and the desired appraisal of the speaker's linguistic competence and intelligence? If it was, their substitution was successful. They used the word synonymously. Others may agree or disagree with the speaker. There is no fact of the matter.

Furthermore, no philosopher, linguist or grammarian can dictate how precisely our linguistic work must be done. Along with multiple roles played by acoustic devices in our behavior, our speech acts are inherently imprecise. We make them as precise as we think we need to make them. Whatever the effects of those sounds coming out of human heads are, the humans using them will still act like the human animals that they are. Some are sloppy and imprecise; others are meticulous and precise in their speech. Some speakers will consider "*less*" and "*fewer*" synonymous in certain contexts, others will not.

That does not mean that speakers can use words willy-nilly if they expect to do any work. Speakers do have conventional uses for words sounds. Competent speakers learn how to use sounds, first in their family, then in the larger speech community. Yet, that learning does not lock in or fix the use of the word sounds. It is a beginner's lesson. Speakers hear and see what others do with words. Then they improvise to achieve their goals. If they have all the elements necessary for an effective speech act in place, they can slip in a new word or a new use for a word. The hearer or reader will recognize a linguistic goal and the new use for the word. The *realizability* of the goal through novel word use will be proven and that word will have a new role to play in the behavior of the discourse participants. That role may be the same role played by another word sound in those circumstances. If so, that new word has been *used* synonymously.

Fixed semantic content, literal meanings and synonymy of meaning for words are semanticists' folly. Philosophers, logicians, and semanticists come up with their opacity puzzles and their paradoxes because they think that the synonymy of words and phrases is dependent upon the mythical, fixed, semantic content. They put the literal meaning in the word symbols and search for that constant literal meaning that will enable free substitution of synonymous words in all contexts for all speakers. However, synonymy is not in the word or the phrase; it is in the speaker's speech history.

Vagueness and Ambiguity

"... is a natural consequence of the basic mechanism of word learning... the learning process being an implicit induction on the subject's part regarding society's usage, the penumbral cases are the cases for which that induction is most inconclusive for want of evidence. The evidence is not there to be gathered, society's members having themselves had to accept similarly fuzzy edges when they were learning. Such is the inevitability of vagueness on the part of terms learned in the primitive way: and it tends to carry over to the terms defined on the basis of these." Willard V.O. Quine (1960: 125)

We tend to think that words are vague and ambiguous. However, it is not the word sounds or the symbols for those sounds that are vague or ambiguous. As the eminent logician and philosopher Willard V.O. Quine noted, the *vagueness* is a result of "society's *usage*". Ordinarily, if phonetic combinations are within cultural norms for pronunciation, competent speakers have little difficulty determining what words are being used by other speakers. Recognizing the sounds and the symbols for those sounds is not the problem. Our conditioned linguistic behavior, however, leaves a great deal of flexibility in the use of these multipurpose acoustic devices and their derivative symbols.

Even at the most fundamental level of word usage, learners find that a word's use is an inexact enterprise. The use of the word *"green"*, for example, covers a lot more ground at an early age. Children make such very basic kind-sortals. When they grow older and do some interior decorating *"green"* is virtually *useless* because adults make much finer distinctions and green comes in many varieties. *"green"* is much too vague for many adult contexts. We should not conclude from this that the word sound *"green"* has a vague or fuzzy *concept* associated with it. Nor should we conclude that the meaning is vague or fuzzy. But we can conclude that the deployment of that term is flexible not fixed.

When speakers learn the use of words such as *"green"*, the context most often determines its appropriate use. If our speech role models do not make many distinctions about the color green, we will not make them either. Our vocabulary of color words will reflect that. That says nothing about our *ability* to discriminate colors. It says something about our *need* to discriminate colors. Circumstances dictate how precise speakers need to be in their use of the sound *"green"* and all its possible permutations. In the Arctic for instance, the word sound *"green"* may be all that is necessary to get linguistic work done. In other areas, there may be forty shades of green.

This flexibility and truth value indeterminacy in natural language usage presents numerous paradoxes and untold difficulties for logicians. As a consequence, philosophers have come up with theories of vagueness and multivalent logics in an attempt to model natural language with notational systems that will allow for the determination of truth values for statements with vaguely used terms such as *"bald"* or *"green"*. Of course, as I wrote in Chapter Two, the distinctions humans tact with in their use of words are not precise. Nor do they need to be for the most part. Vagueness and truth value indeterminacy are logical problems, but humans are not logic machines. Speakers compensate for that vagueness and indeterminacy as best they can. There is no alternative.

Because of this vagueness, usage must often be refined. There aren't many words, other than number words such as "*three*", about which we cannot say: "*how do you define xxxx*"? Precise definition, even when requested, is difficult to deliver. How many grains of wheat does it take to make a *heap*? How many hairs must a man lose to become *bald*? How high are *tall* trees? Is that blue spruce blue or *green*? The word sounds "*heap*", "*bald*", "*tall*" and "*green*" are impossible to precisely define. In spite of that, we use these words when the linguistic task warrants their use and define them more precisely when necessary.

Vagueness for *semanticists* presents theoretical problems because it becomes impossible to give a precise meaning to words such as "*heap*", "*bald*", "*tall*", or "*green*". There seems to be no *essential* semantic content. The *meanings* for these terms must be exceptionally amorphous to account for the variations in use among speakers and occasions of use. However, if logicians and semanticists would recognize that these sounds are not symbols and have no stable independent meanings, there problems would disappear. People disagree on who is bald, what is a heap, what is tall and what is green.

The *ambiguity* of meaning is a ginormous problem for semanticists. For example, when you use the word sound "*take*", which one of the 107 meanings are you using? Within discourse, ambiguity of meaning for individual words is legend. Words have multiple and often diverse *meanings*. Take "*hot*" for instance, as in "*hot food*". Do you mean the temperature or are you referring to the level of spice? The net effect of this ambiguity of meaning for individual words within semantics is an unavoidable indeterminacy in the semantic content of larger grammatical constructions, particularly when the analysis is being done out of context on a transcript.

In addition to the ambiguity inherent in individual word sound *usage*, there are a number of other ambiguities that infect human verbal behavior. One such syntactic ambiguity is ambiguity of grouping. Willard Quine provides us with an example:

> "Another structural species of syntactical ambiguity is ambiguity of grouping. We can make sense of 'pretty little girls' camp in any of five groupings: '(pretty (little girls')) camp', '(pretty little) (girls' camp), and so on. We cope with such ambiguity by variously stressing and pausing, by inserting particles for coordination or ballast, or by rephrasing altogether (thus 'rather little camp for girls')." Quine (1960: 137)

Ambiguity is an intrinsic component of our linguistic behavior that we compensate for in various ways when we need to. For the most part, contextual congruence between speaker and hearer precludes the necessity of further elaboration by the speaker, though when we recognize ambiguity of any kind in our use of words, we have ways of compensating to clarify our goals and get the results we want. Ultimately, the speakers must be the arbiters of what they wanted to communicate and disambiguate their speech acts accordingly.

In addition to ambiguities that are noticed, there are ambiguities in many constructions that go unnoticed because discourse participants assume the most plausible interpretation of the statement. For example: "*jim gave his dog a bath yesterday and his cat last week*".

Did Jim give the cat a bath last week or did he feed him to the dog? The most plausible interpretation would depend upon what we know about Jim and the ambiguity may go unnoticed.

How we humans *use* sounds is not fixed. Fortunately, we can *use* the same word sound in many ways. We have discussed the affective, attributive and referential functional components of words along with, sarcastic uses, poetic uses and metaphorical uses et cetera. These various uses can be mixed and matched to generate the responses that the speaker has received in the past. Invariably, feedback of one sort or another tells the speaker if his or her use of words has been successful. Does the infant get the proper blanket when they ask for the green one? Later in life, adolescent children learn that being green is hip. As adults, they want to know which members of their new platoon are green.

Human speech can often be misinterpreted because of vagueness or ambiguity. Hearers only have an accurate interpretation of an utterance when they properly recognize *the use of the utterance in context*. They must recognize when an utterance is being employed humorously, sarcastically, cynically, etc. Even so, vagueness and ambiguity are natural and unavoidable effects of human speech behavior. Unique, stable, fixed, precise meanings and referents for semantic designators are pipe dreams for logicians and professors of semantics.

Problems in Syntax Theory

How do speakers sequence unrelated words together in systematic ways and make comprehensible sentences that have complex meanings? Words and phrases, as sentence constituents, are organized by speakers in a multitude of sequences to synergistically form grammatically correct sentences. *Syntax*, as a science, uses the data provided by competent native speakers to determine how they combine words and phrases into grammatically correct sentences. Syntax is said to be the study of the *rules* by which parts of speech are combined into well-formed sentences that yield holistic meanings which are more than the sum of their parts.

As a starting point, syntacticians attempt to reduce sentences to their smallest constituents or *parts of speech*. Historically, grammarians have broken down vocal behavior into words, phrases and sentences. These constituents have been further subdivided into nouns, noun phrases, verbs, verb phrases, prepositions, prepositional phrases, adjectives, adjectival phrases, determiners, etc. Using these parts of speech, well-formed sentences are deconstructed by syntacticians and analyzed in an attempt to filter out the *rules* for their production.

However, this reductionist approach to speech behavior is beset with problems. Word categorization is a case in point. In English, for example, morphology is taken to be a fairly reliable indicator of word categorization. Suffixes such as '..ion' or '...ness' (intention, repetition, quickness, neatness) are indicators that the word is a noun. Suffixes such as '...ly' (intentionally, repeatedly, quickly, neatly) indicate the word is an adverb. The suffix '...ize' is util*ize*d to convert nouns into verbs (categorize, unionize, delegitimize). There are numerous fixes (prefixes, infixes, suffixes) which give clues to what part of speech a word belongs, though none of them are foolproof. There are numerous anomalies and exceptions to morphology tests for classifying parts of speech.

Morphology often gives analysts clues as to the categorization of words, but parts of speech simply cannot be determined on the basis of morphemes which are claimed to be the smallest units of *meaning*. Nor are whole *word meanings* a criterion by which word categorization can be reliably performed. The following example is compliments of Andrew Carnie:

> "'The yinkish dripner blorked quastofically into the nindin with the pidibs.'
> Every native speaker of English will tell you that yinkish is an adjective, dripner
> is a noun, blorked is a verb..." Carnie (2007: 39)

Although Carnie was not quite correct, because illiterate English speakers would have no idea what was a noun or a verb, he concluded that parts of speech cannot be *semantically* identified because the above words are meaningless. The experts have concluded that there is overwhelming evidence that words cannot be categorized based on their putative semantic content.

Instead, the categorization of words is often based on when they appear in phrases and well-formed sentences. Consider a word such as "*very*". It is said to be an adverb as in "*very fast*", yet it can be used to modify an adjective, "*very big*". How about "*yesterday*", as in: "*i fixed the car yesterday*". It is an adverb you say; it modifies the verb. What about *this way* in: "*i fixed the car this way*". An adverbial phrase? How about *with a wrench*", as in "*i fixed the car with a wrench*". A prepositional phrase used adverbially? To make a very long syntax story short, parts of speech simply cannot be reliably determined by their position within a larger grammatical unit.

Moreover, some words defy categorization altogether within the conventional framework. Consider the utterance: "*i don't know if jill will be here but i very much hope so*" Rodney Huddleston concludes about the above use of "*so*":

> "... *so* differs from the clear members of all our primary word-classes to such an extent that it seems pointless to include it in the classification: it requires ad hoc description." Huddleston (1984: 276)

Huddleston's analysis only considers English. If other languages are taken into consideration, the precise categorization of parts of speech appears to be hopeless. Nevertheless, *parts of speech* are considered to be constituents of grammatically well-formed sentences and necessary components for explicating syntactic relations in *rule-based* speech theories

Syntacticians have developed various constituency tests to determine which parts of speech are the basic constituents of sentences. The replaceability test, the stand-alone test, the movement within a sentence test, and the coordination test where sentence constituents can be linked by a conjunction are said to be the standard rules by which parts of speech can be determined. However, regardless of which tests are used to categorize parts of speech and how they operate within English syntax, there are questions about the reliability of such tests.

Nevertheless, these parts of speech are analyzed to determine structural relations, how the constituents interact within the grammar. By modeling the structure of sentences via diagrams, syntacticians try to tease out the rules which govern the relations between the constituent parts of speech. They are not *prescribing* rules in the sense that grammarians do; they are attempting to *describe* the rules by which people form grammatically correct sentences by observing speech behavior. The underlying assumption, of course, is that human speech behavior is rule based and that parts of speech can be accurately determined and made to fit into a rule-based system.

The current theoretical backdrop for most research and writing on syntax is the previously mentioned *Generative Grammar*. The term Generative Grammar, or GG, covers other terminology as well: Transformational Grammar, Lexical-Functional Grammar and Phrase Structure Grammar. All of these theories hypothesize that sentences in any language, are generated by applying an underlying set of procedures or *rules* to parts of speech. Within any of the variations of Generative Grammar, the syntactic structures that humans routinely use are said to be generated by rules, rules that have been genetically inherited and/or rules that are acquired unconsciously by speakers from other speakers.

According to Generative Grammar theory, there are rules that can be determined from the study of *well-formed sentences* that will reveal not only the structure of syntactic relations amongst parts of speech for any given language, but will also yield a Universal Grammatical structure that provides the foundational *grammatical rules for all languages*. These well-formed sentences, which are generated by competent speakers of any individual language, provide the data to be analyzed. Within Generative Grammar these rules are referred to as phrase structure rules. They are the rules that generate the syntactic structure of phrases, phrases being anything from theoretical sentences containing an infinite number of embedded clauses to simple noun phrases such as "*the house*".

Now if one were suspicious, one might be inclined to think that syntacticians can only determine if a sentence is *well-formed* by applying grammatical rules. (remember, theorists limit their analyses to *well-formed phrases and sentences*.) In other words, if one were to be cynical, the rules that are supposedly being discovered are discovered by limiting the theory to grammatically correct sentences which conform to those rules. However, GG theorists deny that is the case. They claim that the Grammatical Judgment Task (GJT) is an intuitive yet empirically sound standard by which syntacticians are able to determine the "well-formedness" of a sentence. The GJT is a standard procedure whereby native speakers are asked to intuitively judge the "well-formedness" of sentences. Relying on such tests, syntacticians classify sentences as well-formed, ill-formed or marginal.

However, that GJT-determined standard is not as empirically rigorous as any physical science tests where the standards are measurable and universal. GJT tests, when used by individuals or groups, are fallible. There are many outlier sentences that are determined to be marginal, i.e. some native speakers judge them to be well-formed and others judge them to be ill-formed. The opinions of native speakers often diverge. Moreover, there are many perfectly well formed or grammatically correct sentences that competent mature speakers find incomprehensible. Compliments of Jean Aitchison:

> "The cat the dog the man the baby tripped up bit scratched collapsed. (The baby tripped up the man, the man bit the dog, the dog scratched the cat, the cat collapsed). This is an exceptionally difficult sentence to cope with. Some people find it impossible. But again, there is nothing tangibly wrong with it grammatically. Somehow or other, it is just too complex to be dealt with easily."
> Aitchison (1989: 204)

Conversely, speakers often agree that a sentence is ill-formed but comprehensible. They get the point, but say they would reformulate the sentence to make it grammatically correct. This would indicate a divergence between utility and "well-formedness" that might be a result of the written language and institutionalized grammar. Without the extensive efforts of language conformists, would speakers feel the need to reformulate a sentence to make it grammatically correct? In a culture without standardized grammar would speakers make the distinction between ill-formed and well-formed if comprehension and utility were sufficient? The significant point here is simply that there is a divergence between grammaticality and comprehension. Some sentences can function as intended in spite of violating rules of grammar and other grammatically correct sentences can be functionally impotent because they are incoherent.

In addition, there are borderline cases where competent mature native speakers are not sure if a sentence sounds ill-formed, inelegant or just plain unintelligible. Speakers cannot be sure if the problem is stylistic or grammatical. One example complements of James R. Hurford is: "*where is the book that the students the professor i met taught studied*" Hurford (2012: 53). Most grammarians would consider it is a grammatically correct sentence but inelegant. Most native speakers would have difficulty determining what is meant by the speaker, much less that the sentence is grammatically correct.

Not only that, the GJT can be performed on non-sense sentences where a consensus can be reached that a sentence is grammatically correct even though the sentence is-meaningless. The previous example: *"the yinkish dripner blorked quastofically into the nindin with the pidibs"* is a case in point. Literate native English speakers will converge on the "well-formedness" of this sentence based on the syntax and the word fixes. Is "well-formedness" a psychological effect or just an intuitive feeling based on habituated vocal behavior regarding the use of fixes and English syntax? At a minimum, the Grammatical Judgment Task GJT used by syntacticians has questionable credentials as a legitimate scientific procedure. Nevertheless, *GJT* is claimed to be empirically sound because it relies on a "real psychological effect".

In spite of this questionable psychological interpretation of the GJT, there generally seems to be a consensus about many grammatical constructions. Native speakers often converge on judgments about whether speech is good or bad regardless of their grammatical sophistication or educational background. Yet, these judgments about "ill-formed" vs. "well-formed" grammatical constructions do not appeal to any structural deficiencies or broken *rules*. Native speakers who make the judgments can rarely report any rule or procedure by which they made their judgment about the "well-formedness" of a sentence.

So, the next ploy of the GG theorists is to claim that the rules are *unconscious rules* and in the performance of the GJT speakers unconsciously apply the rules. However, the unconscious rules in literate cultures may be grammatical standards imposed by institutionalized linguistic practices inculcated via formal education and the written word. The GG claim about unconscious rules also presents a multitude of problems and puzzles about the use of the word sound *"rules"* and *"unconscious"*. These problems surface again and again but are rarely addressed by GG theorists. For the moment, let us say that the claims of unconscious rules being applied unconsciously to generate and judge well-formed grammatical constructions are suspect.

Would it not be more plausible to attribute the diverse syntactic regularities found in speech communities to the linguistic conditioning undergone by those who acquire the language skills? No formal grammatical education or language training is necessary to acquire the basics of speech. Untutored tribesmen and children have intuitions about basic speech behavior because they are conditioned to use normalized speech behavior. The further advantage of this behavioristic explanation is that it would not require the pernicious mentalism and psychologism so prevalent in linguistic theory. There would be no need to discuss unconscious rules being applied unconsciously, universal unconscious rules that have yet to be determined by syntacticians and UG theorists after 50+ years of research.

Aside from the theoretical problems with the GG approach to syntax, there are other practical problems that surface because of the theoretical problems just mentioned and the semantic fallacies. One practical problem evidenced in GG syntax is *the binding problem*: how anaphora, such as the word sound *"he"*, are bound to their antecedent reference. Suppose a syntactician were to analyze the utterance: *"the governor of new york says he is going to retire"*. A contemporary analysis would assume that sound *"the governor of new york"* designates a specific individual and the sound *"he"* (an anaphoric pronoun) is bound to the antecedent reference. The antecedent is said to give its meaning to the anaphor. The sound *"he"* is said to refer to the same individual as *"the governor of new york"*.

However, the use of pronouns often presents ambiguities because the antecedent reference and the binding are not revealed by the syntactic structure of the statement. In discourse for example, someone might say: *"john gave george a copy of his new video game and then he played it all night*". Exactly who does the "*he*" refer to, John or George? To which person is the anaphoric pronoun "*he*" bound? Syntacticians then use a mechanism called co-indexing to indicate co-referring expressions. If the reference of the word "*he*" is John, both "*john*" and "*he*" will have the same index (i) in their phrase structure diagrams. This leads to a fundamental precept of binding theory which posits that binding only occurs when constituents such as anaphoric pronouns are co-indexed, i.e. if both the antecedent referring expression and the anaphor refer to the same entity.

This presents a conflict, however, because co-indexing cannot be syntactically defined. To determine whether referring expressions are co-indexed and do in fact co-refer, analysts must put the statement into a context with speaker goals clearly spelled out to disambiguate the reference. Analysts must appeal to elements outside of grammar and syntax. In other words, there is no way, within the rules of generative grammar, to determine whether referring expressions with anaphoric dependency are co-indexed and co-refer. Generative grammar cannot explain anaphoric reference without appealing to elements extraneous to the grammar, viz. context, speaker conditioning, intuitions about language use etc.

There are many other practical problems with applying *rule-based* syntax to human discourse. Just as the semanticists do, syntacticians ignore segmented speech and ellipsis that are every-minute occurrences within natural human discourse, particularly among those speakers who have not been tutored in grammar. People without formal written sentences to act as templates for well-formed speech are able to communicate quite well for their purposes without any rules for well-formed phrases or sentences. They are unaware of any rules or restrictions on their speech behavior and adopt many ill-formed speech habits that are quite useful. Speech behavior need not be grammatically well formed or correct to be useful. Often that is the case.

Unfortunately, syntacticians are guilty of the same mistakes as semanticists. They analyze the written representations of grammatically correct speech and attempt to give a complete account of human speech behavior with universal rules they hope to find for the formation of such grammatically correct written sentences. They also assume that they can analyze well-formed sentences independently of context, speaker speech history, prosodic features of speech, presuppositions, etc. to determine the rules for their formation and use. They cannot, because the functional acoustic devices that humans use are not symbols or signs. Nor are there descriptive *rules* for their use.

Chapter Four

Summary & Notes

Semantics is a totally misguided effort brought about by the Greeks and their analysis of human language. As a consequence, philosophers and linguists have been laboring within a theoretical framework that cannot be reconciled with the observed speech behavior of humans. These erroneous views have led other philosophers down the garden path in many areas of philosophy, logic, science and mathematics. I have tried to give direction for future linguistic analysis in these initial chapters. The solutions for many of the puzzles in theories of language lie in the rejection of the semantic paradigm.

The origins of language in simple sounds used in tacting acts, have evolved into a complex system of sounds and symbols for those sounds. The symbols for the sounds, the written words, have produced a formalism that dictates *correct* speech behavior and de-emphasizes the functional roles of verbal utterances. This formalism engendered by writing has been given institutional status. As such, it has led theorists and researchers to a completely misguided analysis of human speech behavior. It has induced philosophers and linguists to attempt an analysis of language outside of its function within other human communication behaviors. It gave the symbols for the sounds an independent status removed from context, user speech conditioning, presuppositions etc. It enabled theorists to parse and analyze the written symbols after separating them from their source in speech behavior. Philosophers and linguists must recognize the fact that speech is functional human behavior that is generated in response to stimuli and is dependent upon the previous speech history of each speaking organism.

All areas of human intellectual pursuit are infected with the semantic virus. The symptoms are ubiquitous. As we shall see, mathematics, epistemology and physics are all contaminated by semantics and its inherent dualism. If we do not make the assumptions we ordinarily do about language and human experience, these other branches of human inquiry will become clearer. In the succeeding chapters I hope to demonstrate what effects the mischaracterization of human word sound use has in these areas. Starting with mathematics in the next chapter, I will perform my analysis from the non-semantic perspective. I will attempt to wake you from your dogmatic slumbers.

---

1. A number of books have been written about the ubiquity of metaphors and analogies in language usage. Surfaces and Essences by Douglas Hofstadter and Emmanuel Sander is one convincing case in point. It is a 500+ page compendium of the uses of analogy and metaphor in languages worldwide.

2. For a detailed discussion of natural selection pressure for the evolution of displacement in language, see Bruce Charlton, "Evolution and cognitive neuroscience of awareness, consciousness and language" at www.hedweb.com/bgcharlton/awconlang

3. "Observational" or "iterated" learning is a process by which organisms adopt useful behavior after observing similar behavior in other organisms. It is evidenced in many species. See *iterated*

learning in the Glossary.

4. I fully realize that these statements are simplified versions of appreciably more complex historical processes. Writers Daniel Nettle and Suzanne Romaine (2000: 98) make the claim that there were two great waves of change which brought about the historical success of some languages and the loss of others. "For most of the many millennia of human history, it seems likely that the world was close to linguistic equilibrium, with the number of languages being lost roughly equaling the new ones created... "Something has clearly changed, for over the last five hundred years small languages nearly everywhere have come under intense threat. The equilibrium has been broken and the forces of homogenization seem to be rampant. What has changed so much in the human environments that such a massive transition could occur? We will argue that there have in fact been two great waves of change in the human environment which have spread from their centers of origin across the globe, and have endangered most of the world's languages as they spread. One of these was the industrial revolution, which created inequities of technology, economic roles, and communications between neighboring communities which are unprecedented... "The other wave— the first wave, which made the second wave possible—is the development of agriculture... Agriculture, however, not only caused persistent waves of language disruption as farmer communities overcame hunters and gatherers, but set off the development of economic differences between human communities on a scale that had not existed before."

5. Speaking about language drift, Edward Sapir made the point in the early twentieth century: "Every one knows that language is variable. Two individuals of the same generation and locality, speaking precisely the same dialect and moving in the same social circles, are never absolutely at one in their speech habits. A minute investigation of the speech of each individual would reveal countless differences of detail – in choice of words, in sentence structure, in the relative frequency with which particular forms or combinations of words are used, in the pronunciations of particular vowels and consonants and the combination of vowels and consonants, in all those features, such as speed, stress, and tone, that give life to spoken language. In a sense they speak slightly divergent dialects of the same language rather than identically the same language." Sapir (1921:120)

6. "The "I" of *I-language* was introduced by linguist Noam Chomsky in his 1986 book <u>Knowledge of Language</u> to suggest *individual, internal* and *intentional*. The I-language approach to linguistics studies individual mental grammars, entities that are *internal* to each person." Isac and Reiss (2013:14)

7. By comparing language use to a family of games Wittgenstein helped foster the belief that language is a rule-bound activity, as are most games.

8. "And now, I think, we can say: Augustine describes the learning of human language as if the child came into a strange country and did not understand the language of the country; that is, as if it already had a language, only not this one. Or again: as if the child could already ***think***, only not yet speak. And 'think' would here mean something like 'talk to itself'." Philosophical Investigations #32. Ludwig Wittgenstein (1958a: 32) Thanks to Augustine, the translational model for child language acquisition comes to us via analogy from the process of learning a second language. When adults learn a second language they often begin by translating words from their primary language into the new language and vice versa. Supposedly, they know the meanings of the sounds in their little corner of the world and attempt to attach new sounds to the old meanings. But how could this possibly work without a starter language? If the acquisition of language by children consists of aligning a public

language with a private language of thought, when do children get the mentalese, or LOT, to which they attach the public language? Do infants come into the world with a head full of concepts, ideas, meanings, and thoughts to which they then attach the sounds? In fact, some theorists insist that they do!

9. Derek Bickerton reports that: "Without ever having been taught it explicitly, apes seem to have grasped immediately the distinction in human language between proper nouns and common nouns." Bickerton (1990: 107) They grasp the distinction because they are able to uniquely identify members of their own species. That is a prerequisite for some tacting behavior, tacting with proper nouns.

10. There are still remnants of the many non-*s* plurals in the English language before -*s* became so regularized: "When *–en* has thus become established as a plural sign, it was added analogically to words which were not originally *n* stems, e.g. ME, *caren, synnen, treen*, (OE, *cara, synna treow*), and this ending even seemed for some time destined to be the most usual plural ending in the South of England, until it was finally supplanted by *–s*, which had been the prevalent ending up North; *eyen, foen, shoen* were for a time in competition with eyes, foes, shoes, and now *–n* is only found in oxen (and children)." Jespersen (1964: 385)

11. "The phrase 'to kick the bucket,' once used literally and then metaphorically to refer to the final struggles of animals lashed by their feet to a beam called a 'bucket,' has now lost any sense of its original source." Bruce Frazer via Ortony (1979: 173)

CHAPTER 5

MATHEMATICS

Introduction

What we humans do with numbers may appear to have little relevance to my previous thesis about the semantic fallacies. However, what B. F. Skinner called "the doctrine of ideas" permeates our speech about mathematics, just as it does our speech about speech. The same dualistic representational paradigm that corrupts the current explanations for human vocal behavior corrupts the explanations for the human use of numbers. Like the non-semantic view of verbal behavior, the use of number word sounds and their derivative number symbols can be explained in behaviorist terms. There is no need or justification for couching the explanations for human mathematical skills in the usual dualistic representational terms.

In this chapter I hope to persuade you that the way you speak and think about mathematics is fundamentally misguided. It is misguided by the same assumptions that theorists make about what we humans do with word sounds and symbols. I hope to persuade you that all of mathematics, from counting to calculus, is conditioned behavior with acoustic devices. Because of the natural selection process, individual humans and whole societies have been conditioned to utilize number sounds and symbols for those sounds in very productive ways. Humans have survived and prospered because of our conditioned ability to do mathematics.

Mathematical Knowledge

"Mathematical knowledge appeared to be certain, exact, and applicable to the real world; moreover it was obtained by mere thinking, without the need of observation. Consequently, it was thought to supply an ideal, from which every-day empirical knowledge fell short. It was supposed, on the basis of mathematics, that thought is superior to sense, intuition to observation." Bertrand Russell, (1945: 34)

Mathematical knowledge, traditionally, has been considered a superior form of knowledge. In the Occident, from the Greeks on, mathematical knowledge was considered to be a body of certain and necessarily true statements. Contrary to empirical statements about the world, the truths of mathematics are not dependent upon any observations. They cannot be disproved by evidence. So, it seems that mathematical knowledge is certain and necessarily true in all possible worlds and, as such, it is superior to our empirical knowledge. How can anyone doubt that 2 + 2 = 4 is true? It is true everywhere for everyone at any time.

Nonetheless, many epistemological questions are begged when philosophers start to discuss mathematics. For example, philosopher Bertrand Russell claimed that *truth* was a logical property of empirical propositions. The psychological proposition, the thought expressed by the utterence: *the cat is on the mat* has the logical property of being true if and only if, the cat is on the mat. In some sense, it seems, the arrangement of physical objects in the world must correspond with a proposition to be true. Well then, must mathematical statements correspond with objects of some sort if they are to be called true?

The true mathematical statement expressed with the utterance *two plus two equals four* or the inscription '2+2 = 4', for instance, does not seem to correspond with anything. There are no objects referred to with those statements. Or are there? Do both the verbal and the written symbols represent mathematic objects called numbers as opposed to numerals, the symbols? Many philosophers think so. Well then, what sort of mathematical objects are these *numbers* that the *numerals* represent? More questions are begged. How do we *know* that mathematical statements are true? Is there some metaphysical reason for the certainty or necessity of all true mathematical statements? Are true mathematical statements *a priori* knowledge or just an elaborate form of bookkeeping, a coherent system of symbols and rules that happens to produce some interesting and useful results?

When we ask these questions, however, we must not assume that there is something called mathematics. We use the word sound *mathematics* in many ways. What constitutes mathematics is arguable. Knowledge, truth, number, necessity and certainty… let us not say that these are cogent clear-cut concepts, or concepts of any sort. *Knowledge*, *truth*, *number*, *necessity*, and *certainty* are acoustic devices we English speakers use in various ways. Even so, how can anyone deny that 2 + 2 = 4 is knowledge, indisputable knowledge, true in all possible worlds? How can anyone deny that such knowledge (2 + 2 = 4) is necessarily true or *a priori*?

Historical Context

"Mathematics as an organized, independent, and reasoned discipline did not exist before the classical Greeks of the period from 600 to 300 B.C. entered upon the scene. There were, however, prior civilizations in which the beginnings or rudiments of mathematics were created. Many of those primitive civilizations did not get beyond distinguishing among one, two and many; others possessed, and were able to operate with, large whole numbers. Still others achieved the recognition of numbers as abstract concepts, the adoption of special words for the individual numbers, the introduction of symbols for numbers, and even the use of a base such as ten, twenty, or five to denote a larger unit of quantity." (Morris Kline (1972: 3)

No one knows how or when humans started using numbers, though tally sticks are considered to be the earliest historical *evidence* of mathematical thinking. It is believed that early men needed a method for recording animal census. Herders wanted to keep track of the animals they owned. For each sheep in the herd, the herder could scratch a mark on a tally stick. Scratches were matched with animals. The scratches visually represented quantitative distinctions. Marking the tally sticks began a primitive number system, i.e. marks to record quantity. Not only could these herders make distinctions about the relative size of a herd, (large/small) they could tally the herd. In all likelihood, humans began their mathematical odyssey by matching marks with animals. They began by *tallying*, not *counting*.

Grouping helped the tallying process. After early men learned how to tally by means of a mark for each animal, they learned how to group the tallies to make equivalent tallies look equivalent and non-equivalent tallies look different. ///// ///// ///// //// looks different than ///// ///// ///// //. At some point, rather than using groups of the same mark to represent a large tally, some prehistoric genius said: Let's use a single symbol as a substitute for some groups of tally marks. Rather than ///// ///// /////, those three groups of tally marks could have been represented as ^ ^ ^. These herders could then reduce the number of necessary marks. For tallies that included marks for less than the five based groups, individual tally marks were simply added on: ^ ^ ^ /// (18) rather than ///// ///// ///// /// (18).

Once the grouping process matured, another ancient genius said: Let's use a symbol to represent the group of ^s. ^^^^^ could be represented by >. They ended up with a base- five number system whereby the decimal number 133 could be represented by >/>//>>>^', five groups of 25, one group of five and three individual tally marks. Of course, this system is much easier to work with when identical symbols are positioned in hierarchical order. Thus, the preferred organization in this base-five system would have been >>>>>^///. The crucial point is that in these primitive mathematical systems *grouping and positional notation* probably evolved from the basic tally stick and matching.

Subsequently, grouping and positional notation enabled the advancement of mathematics beyond the matching and tallying stage. It led to counting number symbols and calculation algorithms. The Babylonian system of number symbols, for instance, consisted of basic symbols for 1 and 10 (in our decimal notation). Combinations of these symbols were used to form decimal numbers 1 through 59. They added or subtracted by increasing or decreasing the number of symbols in their positional notation. They also developed algorithms for multiplication and division. They had a rudimentary form of algebra that was expressed verbally in geometric terms. The Babylonian equivalents of words *"length"*, *"breath"*, and *"area"* were the stated unknowns in mathematical calculations. Static geometric forms in two or three dimensions enabled the use of square roots and cube roots. The number system they used was very much tied to counting and measuring, whether it was money, land or shares in the harvest. The majority of the calculations were done for economic purposes or astronomy. The justification for their symbols and algorithms was in the results they produced.

The Egyptians were using a base-ten grouping system of numbers 5000 years ago. The groups, or powers of ten, were represented up to 1,000,000. They had single symbols representing the decimal numbers: 1, 10, 100, 1000, 10,000, 100,000, & 1,000,000. These symbols were combined, right to left, in a positional notation to form other numbers. Like the Babylonians, addition and subtraction were accomplished by inserting or removing symbols from the starting number. Computation procedures for multiplication and division were based on the addition and subtraction algorithms. Mathematical symbolism was still in a primitive state, limited to counting numbers.

In all likelihood, the Babylonians, Egyptians, and the Mayans all developed positional mathematical notation systems from the original tallying process. These positional systems became more sophisticated with the use of counting numbers and calculation procedures whereby symbols for the counting numbers were manipulated within prescribed algorithms to produce consistent, reliable results. In addition to the manipulation of number *symbols* for mathematical operations, the Russians, Chinese, Japanese, Romans, and Turks all had versions of the abacus which grouped the counts and enabled mechanical procedures that duplicated the manipulation of symbols on media.

Computations were done then, as they are now, with algorithms. Algorithms are nothing more than methods of manipulating symbols or beads in systematic ways that lead to useful results. As mathematician and author David Berlinski puts it:

> "An algorithm is a finite procedure, written in a fixed symbolic vocabulary, governed by precise steps, 1, 2, 3... whose execution requires no insight, cleverness, intuition, intelligence, or perspicuity, and that sooner or later comes to an end." Berlinski (2000: XIX)

Humans can execute algorithms with the help of a pencil or an abacus or a calculator. In all cases, algorithms are systematic finite procedures for manipulating symbols, beads, or digital electronic switches. Once learned, the execution of an algorithm "requires no insight, cleverness, intuition, intelligence or perspicuity" according to Berlinski. Even machines can execute algorithms these days. That is so because algorithms are routine symbolic procedures whether they are done by machines or humans.

There were many early algorithms developed. Various cultures developed precise steps whereby their symbols could be manipulated on a systematic basis to obtain practical results. Of course, none of these early algorithms were consistent with our current methods of manipulating symbols within the decimal system. Yet, they all provided for *rule-based routines* that moved symbols in systematic ways. They all provided precise steps for the manipulation of symbols that came to a conclusion. That conclusion at the end of the algorithm provided a result that could be confirmed. The algorithms were reliable procedural knowledge for obtaining useful mathematical results.

Morris Kline made these observations about Egyptian mathematics:

> "The rules were not expressed in symbols. The Egyptians stated the problems verbally; and their procedure in solving them was essentially what we do when we calculate according to a formula. Thus an almost literal translation of the geometrical problem of finding the volume of the frustum of a pyramid reads: 'If you are told: a truncated pyramid of 6 for the vertical height by 4 on the base, by 2 on the top. You are to square this 4, result16. You are to double, result 8. You are to square 2, result 4. You are to add the 16, and 8, and the 4, result 28. You are to take one-third of 6, result 2. You are to take 28 twice, result 56. See, it is 56. you will find it right'... No one believes that the Egyptians had a deductive structure based on sound axioms that established the correctness of their rules." Kline (1972: 20)

Take note of the numbers in the above quotation. Egyptians had not developed symbols beyond the counting numbers. They accepted the generality of numbers as evidenced by the lack of measurement units in the above quote. They realized that the numbers would come out the same no matter what the unit of measurement. They had no need to justify their numbers or algorithms philosophically because their algorithms provided practical solutions to practical problems.

The mathematical systems used by both the Babylonians and the Egyptians were based on practical needs. Counting, measuring, shapes, and formulae were inextricably bound. Numbers were used in the administration of the state apparatus. Money, land, time, and crops could all be measured and counted. With these counting numbers and measurements, Babylonians and Egyptians standardized computational procedures for utilitarian reasons. These were practical people with practical methods.

Although there is evidence of algebraic thinking, equations had not yet made an appearance. Arithmetic consisted of simple algorithmic systems with positional notation, integers, and some fractions. Mathematical problems were expressed verbally, and then done with the appropriate symbols in conformance with the established procedures. No theoretical proofs were provided. The proof was in the pyramids.

Greek contributions to mathematics and geometry were numerous and significant. There were many Greek schools of mathematics over the 1200 years from 600BC to 600AD. Most contributed to mathematical thought in one way or another. The most significant Greek contribution was the development of deductive argumentation. Starting with what were considered to be self-evident axioms, Greeks established the legitimacy of geometry and math through a series of deductive arguments. The Greeks *proved* their mathematical and geometric rules by means of argument, not practical results. Their math had to be more than useful; it had to be philosophically justified. Speaking of Aristotle, Morris Kline writes:

> "In mathematics he emphasized deductive proof as the sole basis for establishing

315

facts. For Plato, who believed that mathematical truths preexist or exist in a world independent of man, reasoning was not the guarantee of the correctness of theorems; the logical powers played only a secondary role. They made explicit, so to speak, what was already known to be true." Kline (1972: 53)

Although they had different reasons for their faith in deductive proofs, both Aristotle and Plato recognized the validity of axiomatic systems. In the process of developing their formal proofs for mathematical algorithms the Greeks divorced math from its practical origins and moved it into the theoretical realm. At that juncture, mathematics and geometry were subsumed under epistemology and logic, the searches for knowledge and truth.

The Greeks also infused mathematics with their various brands of metaphysics:

"One of the great Greek contributions to the very concept of mathematics was the conscious recognition and emphasis of the fact that mathematical entities, numbers, and geometrical figures are abstractions, ideas entertained by the mind and sharply distinguished from physical objects or pictures... geometrical thinking in all pre-Greek civilizations was definitely tied to matter. To Egyptians, for example, a line was no more than either a stretched rope or the edge of a field and a rectangle was the boundary of the field.

The recognition that mathematics deals with abstractions may with some confidence be attributed to the Pythagoreans." Kline (1972: 29)

Morris Kline goes on to chronicle the development of Greek mathematical thinking. That history blossoms during the classical period of Plato and Aristotle. For Plato, human bodies only occupied the earth for a brief period. The human souls, however, pre-existed their embodiment here on earth. It was during this pre-existence that the souls were endowed with necessarily true mathematical knowledge, *a priori knowledge* about mathematics and geometry. The Pythagoreans influenced Plato, but Plato and his successors were the philosophers who firmly enshrined numbers and geometrical shapes in their metaphysical pantheon. For Plato, numbers existed independently of the humans who used them. They were ideal forms. *Numbers* contrasted with physical *numerals, the symbols*, were entirely different entities enjoying a separate ontological status.

Aristotle differed from Plato in that he thought that numbers existed as ideas in human minds, or impressions on the soul, not as independent ideal objects. Numbers were *mental* in nature and did not exist outside of the human minds that held them. Like Plato, *numbers* enjoyed a separate ontological status. For Aristotle, these numbers were entities *existing* in the mental realm and had *numerals* to represent them in the physical realm.

Unlike the Egyptians and the Babylonians, educated Greeks looked down upon practical men with practical uses for math and geometry. Pure mathematics and geometry provided pure knowledge, knowledge that was indisputable, knowledge that was *ideal*. Greek idealism was all inclusive. Mathematics, geometry, politics, every branch of Greek philosophy was infused with Greek metaphysics. Referring to Proclus, an avowed neo-Platonist Kline says:

"Like Plato he believed that mathematics is a handmaiden to philosophy. It is propaedeutic because it clears the eyes of the soul, removing all impediments that senses place in the way of knowing universals." Kline (1972: 129)

According to most Greek philosophers, mathematics enabled the purest of thoughts. It enabled them to know universal entities. These universal *numbers* were no longer the *symbols* that were used to represent counting sounds, as they were for the Babylonians and the Egyptians; they were the mental, ideal or abstract objects represented by *numerals*. The mental, ideal or abstract nature of universal *numbers* had taken root.[1]

Additionally, the Greeks infused mathematics and geometry with a mystic character. Numerology and metaphysics took root in the same fertile Greek minds. Greek geometers took the basics of geometry from the Egyptians and expanded them dramatically and brilliantly. They had a fascination with shape and form that was not apparent in the Egyptians and Babylonians. Numbers were often depicted as geometric patterns or forms and categorized accordingly. Certain ratios and proportions were considered to be beautiful because of the shape of their geometric projections. The characterization and categorization of various numbers based on their properties became standard procedure for Greek mathematicians. Numbers were even, odd, prime, square, pentagonal, square roots, etc.

Along with the introduction of metaphysics and mysticism, the Greeks introduced more numerals. Their base-ten system eventually had symbols for decimal numbers 1-9, more unique symbols for decimal 10, 20, 30...90, and even more unique symbols for decimal 100, 200, 300...900. In addition to more numerals, the Greeks introduced various symbols to replace word sounds in the written versions of their problems. Addition was indicated by placing terms adjacent to one another. Subtraction was indicated by the use of a symbol much as we would write **'4 -2'** instead of **'subtract 2 from 4'**. This enabled them to represent mathematical problems more symbolically.

The advent of more symbols produced some insightful curiosities. Regarding the introduction of symbolism in algebra by Diophantus (the variable), Kline avers:

> "The appearance of such symbolism is of course remarkable but the use of powers higher than three is even more extraordinary. The classical Greeks could not and would not consider a product of more than three factors because such a product had no geometrical significance." Kline (1972: 139)

Although they had separated the study of geometry and mathematics, early Greek mathematics was still very much constrained by geometry. **'4^4'** made no sense to the Greeks because it could not be projected geometrically, as could **'4^3'** and **'4^2'** (a three-dimensional cube and a two-dimensional square.)

> "As we saw, Aristotle, in particular, pointed out that we must be sure that the concepts introduced are not self-contradictory; that is, they must be shown to exist. To settle this point, the Greeks, in principle at least, admitted only those concepts that were constructible. Line and circle were accepted as constructible in postulates but all other figures had to be constructed with line and circle... The Greeks failed to comprehend the infinitely large, the infinitely small, and infinite processes." Kline (1972: 176)

The Greeks, quite sensibly, refused to deal with mathematical terms they could not grasp, e.g. *"infinite"*. Mathematical terms still had to have some touchstone in observable shapes and countable or measurable quantities. The imaginative Greeks could not imagine negative numbers, irrational numbers or powers greater than three. There was no way to imagine or geometrically project the numerals **'-1, √2, 4''**. Consequently, these symbols and terms deserved no place in mathematics. Greeks tried to grasp the "numbers" represented by these strange symbols, but they could not do so.

Nevertheless, in addition to improving the symbolic notation, positional algorithms were improved under the Greeks. Numerals in between the available number symbols were written by combining the base numerals. (remember, 10, 20, 30…100, 200, 300… were represented by unique individual symbols.) The means of manipulating these symbols improved upon the Egyptian systems. Arithmetic operations were conducted somewhat like ours today. Columns of symbols were written using positional notation. They were then added, with remainders carried. The Greeks developed many new methods of conducting arithmetical operations. All of them were *rule-bound* procedures that manipulated numeric symbols in systematic ways. They were mechanical algorithms learned by rote and executed "without insight, cleverness, intuition, intelligence, or perspicuity".

By the end of the era of Greek influence, geometry, math, and algebra had become more systematized and symbolized. Arithmetic and algebra had also been separated from geometry. Thus, the appeal to geometry and practical results as proof for the validity of math and algebra no longer sufficed. Arithmetic and algebra were independent systems grounded in theory, not practical results. Basic axioms were accepted as intuitively *true*. The rest of math and algebra were *proved* by means of argument. Math and algebra had become more theoretical and less reliant upon practical applications for their justification.

The Greeks also had no doubt that mathematics and geometry provided them with new knowledge. After all, when they used math, they found out things that they had not known before. It was most certainly knowledge, knowledge of the purest kind, indisputable knowledge. Was this knowledge *a priori*, as Plato had shown by eliciting the Pythagorean theory from an untutored slave? That was the issue. Were humans born with innate mathematical knowledge that was merely brought out by teachers, as Plato believed? Instead, was this knowledge something that was learned after birth, *a posteriori*? The truths of mathematics and geometry were unquestioned, though how and when humans came to know these truths was at issue.

After the Greeks, and much like the Babylonians and Egyptians, the Romans used mathematics to solve practical problems. There were no Roman mathematical theorists. Aside from a few curiosities, Rome contributed nothing of significance to mathematical theory. The Romans developed a number system combining the Egyptian base-ten system with secondary base-five groupings. That reduced the repetitive nature of the calculation procedures to that date. The Roman mathematical system lasted for well over a millennium. Curiously, Roman numerals were used by Europeans up to the 16th century for accounting purposes. However, the superiority of the Hindu/Arabic decimal notation won over the hold-out bean counters in Europe and ultimately prevailed worldwide.

The Hindus succeeded the Greeks in furthering the development of mathematics. The Greeks had used counting numbers or natural numbers and *ratio*nal numbers, those which could be expressed as a *ratio*, ½ and ¾ for example. The Greeks had also used **'0'** as a place holder in selected applications but did not consider it *a number*. The Hindus added **'0'** as a number. The Hindus also added negative numbers about 1400 years ago. They were used to represent debts. The use of negative numbers brought about new symbols and new rules about how to manipulate these new combinations of symbols (numerals and functions) within the decimal algorithms. One such rule was the law of signs (-5 x -5 results in +25).

The Hindus, much like the Egyptians, Babylonians and Romans, were practical people. As such, the Hindus had no reticence about using irrational number symbols such as '$\sqrt{2}$'. The inability to imagine what '$\sqrt{2}$' represented was not a hindrance to using the symbol in their calculations. There were many theorists who objected to the use of irrationals just as there had been theorists who objected to the use of negatives and zero. These irrational number symbols represented no imaginable shape or conceivable quantity, though their practical value eventually won the day. Kline notes that:

> "The Hindus were less sophisticated than the Greeks in that they failed to see the logical difficulties involved in the concept of irrational numbers. Their interest in calculation caused them to overlook the philosophic distinctions, or distinctions based on principles that in Greek thought were fundamental. But in blithely applying to irrationals procedures like those used for rationals, they helped mathematics progress." Kline (1972: 186)

Zero, irrationals, and negatives were accepted by the Hindus in spite of any philosophical objections. Hindu mathematicians did not need any ideas, concepts, or independent abstract objects to pair up with these number symbols. The metaphysics didn't matter. They just needed the symbols to work.

The Arabs did yeoman's work in preserving Greek and Hindu contributions to mathematics and transferring them to Europe:

> "The significant contribution to mathematics that we owe to the Arabs was to absorb Greek and Hindu mathematics, preserve it, and ultimately, through events... transmit it to Europe." Kline (1972: 197)

Like the Hindus, the practical mindset of the Arabs precluded any further philosophizing about the nature and ontological status of *numbers* as opposed to *numerals*. Yet two divergent currents in mathematical thought were taking shape during this transitional period.

> "Two independent traditions or concepts of mathematics had now become established: on the one hand, the logical deductive body of knowledge that the Greeks established, which served the larger purpose of understanding nature; and on the other, the empirically grounded, practically oriented mathematics founded by the Egyptians and Babylonians, resuscitated by some of the Alexandrian Greeks, and extended by the Hindus and Arabs." Kline (1972: 199)

The early Greeks had melded their philosophy of mathematics with their other philosophical systems to develop a coherent body of thought, theoretical systems consistent with each other. The metaphysics of Plato and Aristotle were critical to this endeavor. However, this was not a matter of concern to the practically minded Hindus and Arabs. Greek metaphysical misgivings about the nature or the essence of numbers, as opposed to the utility of numerals, were of no concern to the Hindus and the Arabs. Hindu and Arab algebraists had no need to grasp the concepts, the ideas or the abstractions represented by irrational *numerals*. They had no need to explain what an irrational number *is*. The efficacy of zero, negatives and irrationals in their calculations justified their use.

The medieval period of European history was characterized by stagnant intellectual growth. Dogmatism, mysticism, and church authority stifled any development in science, math, or philosophy. Worldly matters were of little concern to the zealots who controlled the learning and thinking. Feudal society had stabilized into a self-contained world of religious authority and submission to that authority.

However, during the late Middle Ages the Crusades brought back the works of the Greeks from their Arab fiduciaries. Access to Greek writings began a slow revival in intellectual curiosity and inquiry. A renewed interest in mathematics was inspired by the belief that God's design principles were to be found through mathematical analysis. An ordered universe, designed by God, could be made comprehensible by understanding mathematics. To study mathematics was to look into the mind of God.

From around the 16th to 18th centuries the spread of information and expansion of education produced many mathematicians and a gradual extension of mathematical theory. Algebra became a separate field of study with broad improvements in methodology and theory. Projective geometry, probability function, and calculus were initiated and then dramatically improved. Freeing algebra from the geometric ties of the Greeks, Europeans developed the analytic approach. In the words of Morris Kline:

> "In other words, mathematicians were contributing concepts, rather than abstracting ideas from the real world... Of course the Europeans were uneasy about the new types of numbers and the calculus notions without really discerning the cause of their concern. Yet as these concepts proved more and more useful in applications, they were at first grudgingly and later passively accepted. Familiarity bred not contempt but acceptability and even naturalness. After 1700, more and more notions, further removed from nature and springing full-blown from human minds, were to enter mathematics and be accepted with fewer qualms. For the genesis of its ideas mathematics gradually turned from the sensory to the intellectual faculties." Kline (1972: 393)

The philosophical foundations for mathematics provided by the Greeks in the form of deductive proofs and geometric visualization gave way to straightforward utility. Mathematicians strung symbols together in new ways and found that these new procedures provided mathematically practical results. The original counting numbers, grounded in observable, countable objects, were superseded by new types of numbers that worked in new formulae but were not understandable in the way that counting numbers were. In spite of that, these new numbers such as $\sqrt{-1}$ provided new support for the new empirical methods of science.

Originally, mathematical thinking was thinking about practical matters and concrete objects. Basic counting numbers were manipulated within simple computation procedures to come up with sums and products. Mathematicians were functionaries employed to carry out the administration of the state. Mathematicians were not theoreticians; they utilized arithmetic and geometry for practical reasons. Counting number symbols and the algorithms to manipulate the symbols were devised as practical means of finding solutions to everyday logistical problems.

The first mathematicians counted out loud and used those counting number sounds to state problems. To state a math problem vocally, everyday quotidian word sounds were used along with basic counting number sounds. Mathematicians would say the equivalent of *"two plus two equals the unknown"* out loud to present a math problem. Mathematics was largely a vocal enterprise with only special numerals used for inscribing the number sounds. When presenting problems in the written form, graphic inscriptions for the word sounds were used along with the numerals. Mathematicians would write the equivalent of **'2 plus 2 equals the unknown'** to visually record and transmit their mathematical utterances. Math symbols were limited to counting numbers, the equivalents of decimal 1, 2, 3, 4... Those symbols could then be manipulated within the algorithms of the day.

Over millennia, special mathematical symbols gradually eliminated almost all prose in inscriptions of mathematical problems. Mathematicians would still say *"two plus two equals the unknown"*. However, they would write **'2 + 2 equals β'**. The use of symbols for operations (+, -, β etc.), including a symbol for the unknown (the variable), eliminated the need for almost all prose. Written mathematics became a uniquely symbolic enterprise utilizing its own specialized symbols to represent the statements of mathematicians. Doing mathematics was ultimately reduced to only manipulating special mathematical symbols.

The original operations of mathematics were practical applications which required nothing more than counting, measuring and simple algorithms to add and subtract. Over time, algorithms for multiplication and division were developed. Eventually, these simple calculation procedures performed with counting numbers to produce practical results led to balancing both sides of an equation. Equalizing irrational, imaginary, complex, and transcendental numbers through formal procedures became the accepted analytic method of doing mathematics.

Mathematics ceased to be a pragmatically inspired tool for calculating sums and products by using cardinal numbers and simple procedures. It became a process for balancing strange symbols on the two sides of an equation. The Arab word *"al-jabr"* (algebra) translates to *"restoring"* in English, as in restoring balance to an equation. The practical calculations of the Babylonians, Egyptians and Greeks, tied to commensurable quantities and geometric forms, had given way to the need to balance equations, even if that required the use of zeros, negatives and irrationals.

The theory and philosophy of mathematics began with the Greeks. They injected the mysticism and the metaphysics. After the Greeks, little philosophy in the field of mathematics occurred until the 1700s. Even so, there were profound shifts in the methods of mathematicians. Math had become more symbolic and further removed its origin in counting numbers. It had come into its own as a *science*. Free from counting and measuring, the symbols and procedures of math and algebra were generalized to operate independently. In fact, these rule governed procedures, these algorithms, did not require rational numbers. The symbols for variables, negatives and irrationals could be manipulated in the same manner as rational number symbols were manipulated.

Other sciences and mathematical science became inextricably bound. Advances in math produced advances in science. Calculus and coordinate geometry were powerful tools in ballistics, optics, hydro-dynamics, celestial mechanics and other branches of the new physics of Newton. Advances in science then inspired more advances in mathematics. The explanatory power of mathematics was questionable, though the predictive power was undeniable. When combined with precise measurement, mathematical equations yielded precise, accurate answers that gave clear evidence of the validity of the new math, even though the new types of numbers being used were not understood in the way that counting *numbers* were understood.

Subsequently, more symbolic algebras were developed that changed the original algebraic principles. For instance, commutative laws became non-commutative. (2 x 4 was not the same as 4 x 2 in some algebras.) Algebraists found that there was nothing sacrosanct or self-evident about the axioms they adopted, or algebra or mathematics in general. The first axioms and postulates they had developed for basic algebra were not the only options. If they wanted to propose a new axiom or postulate, they did so. They only had to remain consistent. As long as these systems were internally consistent, they could develop entirely new algebras.

Non-Euclidian geometries sprang up as well. The axioms of Euclid only held true in certain circumstances. Lobachevski and Riemann changed Euclid's second postulate that defined parallel lines and, lo and behold, they came up with different geometries, geometries that were just as *real* as Euclid's. Well, which one was *true?* As it turns out, that question is vacuous. They are internally consistent and very useful. Euclidian geometry was useful in predicting outcomes in Newtonian physics. Riemannian geometry was useful in predicting outcomes in Einstein's relativity physics. However, Riemannian geometry was not useful in quantum mechanics. Thus, it was abandoned by quantum physicists and string theorists. It did not provide the mathematical results they needed.

Mathematicians were an inventive group as it turned out. They came up with all sorts of number symbols to meet the needs of the day. Because of the law of signs, they came up with *imaginary* number symbols such as $\sqrt{-4}$. $(+2) \times (+2) = +4$ and $(-2) \times (-2) = +4$. Thus $\sqrt{-4}$ can be neither positive nor negative. It was not one of the *real* numbers (+, - or 0); it was *imaginary*. Imaginary numbers did not function like real numbers. They would not work in the normal computation methods used for real numbers, though they were still useful. Their symbols could be manipulated by other rules within the algorithms of other algebras to balance equations.

Further developments brought on transfinite mathematics, super-abstract algebra, and transcendental numbers. A very noticeable trend was apparent with each new development. It became increasingly difficult to "conceptualize" these new numbers and systems. They became more and more "abstract". Analogies, models, and explanations of all sorts seemed to fall short. Yet, the postulates, theorems, and formulae all seemed to work, and some of them proved useful in predicting real world consequences. Mathematicians had learned how to manipulate the various symbols for these mysterious numbers within their respective algorithms, but exactly what was an imaginary or a transcendental number? How could we mere mortals grasp those *concepts?*

What did these strange symbols being used to balance algebraic equations represent? The Greeks had confronted these issues 2000 years before other Europeans, and rejected symbols not tied to counting numbers or geometry. They could not imagine zero, negative numbers or irrational numbers. Neither could the Europeans, as it turned out. Although they could not imagine them, Descartes inexplicably claimed that some of them were "imaginary numbers".

> "Pascal and Barrow said that a number such as $\sqrt{3}$ can be understood only as a geometric magnitude: irrational numbers are mere symbols that had no existence independent of geometrical magnitude… Others made positive assertions that the irrational numbers were independent entities. …Descartes was willing to accept negative numbers. Pascal regarded the subtraction of 4 from 0 as utter nonsense… Descartes also rejected complex roots and coined the term 'imaginary'." Kline (1972: 252)

Philosophical storm clouds were brewing in Europe:

> "While practical interests stimulated the improvements in calculations, symbolism and the theory of equations, interest in purely mathematical problems led to renewed activity in the theory of numbers." Kline (1972: 274)

By using symbols for zero, negatives and irrationals, the Hindus had unshackled algebra from counting numbers and measurement, but they had not freed it from Greek metaphysics. Hindus and Arabs had been able to use mathematics without any metaphysical misgivings. Europeans, on the other hand, confronted the metaphysics of mathematics head on. They were unabashed dualists. Human beings had bodies and *minds*. Numerals were clearly symbols that represented mental things: number concepts, number ideas, and number abstractions, just as word symbols represented concepts, ideas and abstractions. That much was clear.

Real numbers and *rational numbers* were no problem for the European philosophers of the age. Rationalists and empiricists alike vouched for the conceptual nature of numbers. Bishop Berkeley for example, one of the leading empiricists of the eighteenth century, concluded:

> "That number is entirely the creature of the mind, even though the other qualities be allowed to exist without, will be evident to whoever considers that the same thing bears a different denomination of number as the mind views it with different respects. Thus, the same extension is one, or three, or thirty-six, according as the mind considers it with reference to a yard, a foot, or an inch." Bishop George Berkeley, The Empiricists p.155

Natural numbers, counting numbers, cardinal numbers it was clear, for most philosophers, they were ideas, concepts or abstractions created by human minds and represented by numerals.

Describing or explaining the universe with numbers such as irrationals became more commonplace as the physics of relativity changed our view of the world. Planck's constant, 'h', for instance, is .00000000000000000000000000000666... It is an approximation. It cannot be measured or quantified precisely. It can never be complete. It is an irrational number. How can it be represented in human minds? What sort of an idea, concept, or abstraction would adequately capture Planck's constant?

Michael Guillen explains the problem with irrational numbers in science:

> "Despite this preeminence of rational numbers, science does need irrational numbers. For well over a century, scientists have been taking note of a growing inventory of special quantities whose appearance in nearly every scientific theory signifies their import in the modern description of space-time. These natural constants can be seen as nature's vital statistics, and right now, every one of them is an irrational number... What this comes down to is that in merely discovering irrational numbers, mathematicians have raised a scientific possibility that cannot be settled by any imaginable measurement or series of measurements." Guillen (1983: 39)

Eventually, throughout the decimal world, symbols for incomplete numbers, such as 'h' and 'π', became commonplace. The symbol was all that was needed in an equation. These theoretical numbers were symbolized and used successfully, even though mathematicians could not quantify them precisely or comprehend them the way they grasped rational numbers. Irrational numbers may have existed in the mind of God but they couldn't be found in the minds of mathematicians. The symbols could be manipulated by those mathematicians, but they could not conceive of the numbers represented by **'h'** and **'π'**. With incomplete numbers such as these, the need for precision in the measurement was driven by the application. Approximation was good enough for practical applications.

Along the way, the metaphysics of mathematics had come into question. Most European theorists postulated that numbers were *concepts, ideas or abstractions* that were generated and sustained in human minds. They were represented by the numerals, but the numbers themselves were *mental* entities of some sort. Other European theorists suggested that numbers were objective abstract entities. Our old friend, Gottleb Frege's musings were typical:

> "It is time to get a clearer view of what we mean by our expression 'the content of a statement of number is an assertion about a concept'. In the proposition 'the number 0 belongs to the concept F', 0 is only an element in the predicate (taking the concept F to be the real subject). For this reason I have avoided calling a number such as 0 or 1 or 2 a ***property*** of a concept. Precisely because it forms only an element in what is asserted, the individual number shows itself for what it is, a self-subsistent object... in the language of everyday life number appears also in attributive constructions... So that what we have is an identity, stating that the expression 'the number of Jupiter's moons' signifies the same object as the word 'four'..." Frege (1980: 68)

The word "four" signified an *object* for Frege, just as the phrase "the number of Jupiter's moons" did. Numerals were obviously symbols. As such, they had to *sign*ify or de*sign*ate the same objects as the word and the definite description did. If "four", "4" and "the number of Jupiter's moons" all signified something, what was it that they signified? According to Frege, they signified "self-subsistent objects". These "self-subsistent objects" did not exist in the physical world they *subsisted* in another ontological realm.[2]

Frege also made a distinction that many philosophers have made: primary properties vs. secondary properties. Properties are the things which can be predicated of objects. *"the ball is red and round"*, for example. The primary properties such as color and shape are considered inherent properties, they inhere in the object. However, number is not among these properties. If number is a property, some philosophers insisted it must be a secondary property, a property that we attribute to something, as in: *"solon was wise"*. Number, like wisdom, is not an inherent property.

However, Frege, under the influence of Leibniz, offers this evidence against numbers being properties at all:

> "If it were correct to take 'one man' in the same way as 'wise man', we should expect to be able to use 'one' also as a grammatical predicate, and be able to say 'Solon was one'... In isolation, however, it seems that 'one' cannot be a predicate. This is even clearer if we take the plural. Whereas we can combine 'Solon was wise' and 'Thales was wise' into 'Solon and Thales were wise', we cannot say that 'Solon and Thales were one'. But it is hard to see why this should be impossible, if 'one' were a property both of Solon and of Thales in the same

way that 'wise' is." Frege (1980: 40)

Indeed, we English-speaking people cannot use *"one"* as a predicate. That is clear evidence that numbers are not properties like red and round, nor are they objects that exist according to Frege. They are objects that *subsist*.

Mathematicians had come full circle. Precise measurement had advanced natural philosophy, i.e. *science*, out of medieval speculation into the modern era. Now, measurement was imprecise. The old numbers made our world more understandable. The new numbers made it less understandable. What scientists had thought was a *rational* enterprise came to be dominated by *irrational* numbers. They could make predictions by using irrational numbers in the mathematical models of science, but they didn't understand them or know why they worked. The numbers and systems they used to describe and explain could not, themselves, be described or explained.

Because these numbers could not be explained, the objective *truth* of mathematics came into question. Historically, mathematics had always been considered more than a useful system. It was knowledge, knowledge of the purest kind. Mathematical truths were indisputable, necessary truths. Knowledge, truth, and certainty, virtues that philosophers had sought for millennia, were all embodied in the science of mathematics. Now, some philosophers were claiming that the alternate algebras and geometries were nothing more than self-consistent tautological systems that, at times, we humans found to be useful. They were elaborate bookkeeping systems. Mathematics was not the profound knowledge that philosophers had thought it was.

Philosophers and mathematicians then debated about whether numbers existed, at times, in human minds or subsisted in a third realm. Or were they objective abstract entities, or were they properties like red and round? Did they inhere in things like color and shape, or were they constructs that our mental faculties imposed on the world? Just what were these *numbers* that the *numerals* stood for? Philosophers and mathematicians had to stand up and be counted.

Great mathematicians weighed in on the matter from all sides. Rudy Rucker, writing about his interviews with the great theoretical mathematician Kurt Gödel, sums it up well:

> "There is one idea truly central to Gödel's thought that we discussed at some length. This is the philosophy underlying Gödel's *credo*, 'I do objective mathematics.' By this, Gödel meant that mathematical entities exist independently of the activities of mathematicians, in much the same way that the stars would be there even if there were no astronomers to look at them. For Gödel, mathematics, even the mathematics of the infinite, was essentially an empirical science.
>
> According to this standpoint, which mathematicians call **Platonism**, we do not *create* the mental objects we talk about. Instead, we *find* them, on some higher plane that the mind sees into, by a process not unlike sense perception.
>
> The philosophy of mathematics antithetical to Platonism is *formalism*, allied to positivism. According to formalism, mathematics is really just an elaborate set of rules for manipulating symbols. By applying the rules to certain 'axiomatic' strings of symbols, mathematicians go about 'proving' certain other strings of symbols to be 'theorems'.

The game of mathematics is, for some obscure reason, a *useful* game. Some strings of symbols seem to reflect certain patterns of the physical world. Not only is '2 + 2 = 4' a theorem, but two apples taken with two apples make four apples."
Rucker (1982: 181)

Like Plato, Kurt Gödel insisted that numbers were independent metaphysical objects. He was an unabashed Platonist. Frege had one foot firmly planted in both camps it seems. For Frege, numerals were symbols that we could manipulate without considering their content (formalism), yet they designate numbers which have a third (not physical or mental) ontological status (Platonism).

So… Are you a Platonist or a formalist? What sort of things are these numbers? As a thinker you must ask yourself these questions. Is there a distinction between numbers and numerals? If so, what are numbers, the things signified by the numerals? Are the numbers in your mind, in the Greek heavens, or in abstract space? As you ask these questions, keep in mind that 'number' is a symbol that represents the sound "*number*" (sound it out). The sound "*number*" (or its equivalent in Babylonian, Egyptian, Greek, Hindu, and Arabic) has had a use for over "*3000 years*" (sound it out). Those sounds can be represented by **'three thousand years'** or **'3000 years'**, the symbols. That fact is not just a curiosity.

The history of mathematics is a history of transitions: transition from counting sounds and verbal utterances to pure symbol manipulation, transition from simple calculation procedures to equational balance and transition from practical to theoretical. Over the millennia, math became more symbolic, more equational, and more theoretical.

The History of
Mathematical Symbols

Beginning about five thousand years ago, the Egyptians developed a system of mathematical symbols. The positional notations of the Egyptians required the grouping of symbols, much like our base-five system at the start of this chapter. (<<<<<^///) They had one unique symbol that took the place of decimal numeral **'10'** (two symbols). One unique symbol represented decimal numeral **'100'** (three symbols). The equivalent of the decimal symbol **'87'** took fifteen Egyptian symbols to write.

The Greek system was simpler than the Egyptian system but still required the combining of numerous symbols to represent large decimal numerals. Representing decimal **'123'** would have required six Greek symbols. The Roman numerals for **'1828'**, as every schoolboy knows, are **'MCCMXXVIII'**. All of these systems had symbols in addition to the nine counting numerals that we use in our familiar decimal notation. The efficacy of the decimal notation ultimately led to its universal adoption. In spite of the 6000+ languages in the world today, the entire planet has adopted the decimal system of numerals. Hence, it is often considered to be a "universal language".

It is a believable speculation that the only reason we use a decimal system of symbols is because we have ten *digits* on our hands. A base-twelve *duodecimal* system would be preferable because there are six factors in twelve, as opposed to the four factors in ten. Six factors in the system's base number would greatly facilitate multiplication and division. In fact, the *dozen* still has many practical applications. Butchers, bakers, and beer drinkers think a dozen is a wonderful number. It will work for 1, 2, 3, 4, 6 or 12 people who want to share equally. However, the base-ten decimal system became the norm because of its ease of use by humans who are digitally equipped to master such a system. You might say that *decimal* math is species specific. It is a people-centric earthly system, not a universal language. Now back to history.

Subsequent to the Egyptians, during the classical period, Greeks wrote numerals by using letters of the alphabet. They did not have unique symbols to be used as numerals. They distinguished numerals from letters by drawing a horizontal line over the letters, and as I mentioned earlier, the Greek mathematical work was written in prose form for the most part, with Greek letters serving dual roles. But Greeks expanded symbolism in mathematics by introducing symbols for mathematical operations in lieu of some word symbols. Rather than writing the Greek equivalent of **'subtract 10 from 33'**, the Greeks could write the equivalent of: **'33 − 10'**. (Obviously, their word sounds and the symbols for those sounds were not the ones I am using.) No further symbolism was introduced until the time of Diophantus, about 250 AD.

The critical step that Diophantus took was introducing a symbol for the unknown, a variable. He called the unknown "the number of the problem" Kline (1972: 139). Using this variable, he solved problems for indeterminate quantities. Rather than writing **'length'**, **'breadth' and 'area'** as the unknowns in mathematical statements as the Babylonians and the Egyptians had done, the Greeks began to use a symbolic variable to represent any of these unknown quantities.

As a result of this new development, balancing equations became possible. Introducing a symbol for the unknown was critical because it moved mathematics beyond numerals. It permitted the substitution of a symbol for the prose statement: **'the number of the problem'**. The Greeks could then write the equivalent of: **'33 − Δ yields 10'** rather than: **'33 − the number of the problem yields 10**'. It opened the door to algebraic thinking. It opened the door to balancing *equations* by enabling the placement of a symbol for a variable quantity anywhere in the equation. That change dramatically increased the generality and efficacy of their mathematical procedures.

Although we all use Arabic numerals today, early Arabs had limitations on their mathematical progress as a consequence of primitive symbolism. Originally, they had no number symbols whatsoever.

> "When the Arabs were still nomads, they had words for numbers but no symbols. They took over and improved the Hindu number symbols and the idea of positional notation... Like the Hindus, the Arabs worked freely with irrationals." Kline (1972: 191)

The Arabs developed the number symbols and the decimal positional notation that we use today, and unlike the Greeks, they made no distinction between numbers and numerals.

Subsequently, the Hindus and Arabs added new numbers symbols and more operational symbols to increase the efficacy of mathematics.

> "The Hindus also made some progress in algebra. They used abbreviations of words and a few symbols to describe operations... This symbolism, though not extensive, was enough to classify Hindu algebra as almost symbolic and certainly more so than Diophantus' syncopated algebra." Kline (1972: 186)

Arabs and Hindus, rather than using words in their written mathematical statements or positioning as the Babylonians, the Egyptians, and the early Greeks had done, used a mathematical symbol like **'+'**. They still *said* the equivalent of *"two plus two equals four"* when verbally stating problems, but rather than writing problems in prose, **'2 plus 2 equals 4'**, they used the mathematical symbols to record **'2 + 2 equals 4'**. (Our current equal sign was not invented until 1557 by Robert Recorde of Oxford.)

As the Hindus and the Arabs developed symbolic algebra, they found the need for negative and irrational numbers. They represented them symbolically along with the algebraic operations. Rather than write **'2 minus 3 equals negative 1'**, they could write **'2 − 3 equals -1'**. The transition from prose representations of verbal math problems to the use of specialized non-iconic, non-phonetic mathematical symbols took another step forward. The efficacy of these new mathematical symbols ultimately led to the elimination of any prose from the written statements of mathematical problems.

Many centuries later, the European Renaissance was marked by advancement in the arts, literature and astronomy, forever changing Western civilization's outlook on the order and nature of the universe. Copernicus, for example, ended the geocentric universe. Empiricism as a method of inquiry began to take root. Mathematics was an integral part of the empirical methodology. Observation, measurement and mathematics became necessary ingredients in the practice of science. Empirical evidence for any theory required measurable quantities and repeatable procedures. Scientists used *natural number* symbols extensively in the pursuit of their trade.

Algebra, however, was not bound to measurement or natural numbers. Morris Kline notes the transformation in algebra:

> "The advance in algebra that proved far more significant for its development and for analysis than the technical progress of the sixteenth century was the introduction of better symbolism. Indeed, this step made possible a science of algebra. Prior to the sixteenth century, the only man who had consciously introduced symbolism to make algebraic thinking and writing more compact and more effective was Diophantus. All other changes in notation were essentially abbreviations of normal words, rather casually introduced. In the Renaissance, the common style was still rhetorical, that is, the use of special words, abbreviations, and of course number symbols... by the end of the seventeenth century, the deliberate use of symbolism—as opposed to incidental and accidental use—and the awareness of the power and generality it confers entered mathematics." Kline (1972: 259)

The symbolism of algebra was increased dramatically in the 17th century along with the power and generality that symbolism engendered, further removing mathematics from its roots in measurement, counting, and practical applications.

Mathematical symbols were no longer limited to rationals and operators. Natural number symbols (counting number symbols) were combined with odd new symbols '$\sqrt{}$, $\sum$, -' Irrational number symbols such as '$\sqrt{2}$', and 'π' could be manipulated within the algebraic system, in spite of the fact that they are incomplete. Imaginary number symbols, such as '$\sqrt{-4}$', could be maneuvered about in algorithms just as normal counting numbers were. These new number symbols, whether they were irrational number symbols, imaginary number symbols, complex number symbols or infinitesimal number symbols provided consistent and sometimes useful results. As it turned out, the equations of algebra were valid for any number symbol or variable, no matter how far removed that symbol was from the natural counting number symbols.

Many of these new number symbols would have been anathema to the Greeks. The numbers these symbols represented were not constructible, commensurable or conceivable, yet somehow the symbols worked. There is no geometric projection for '$\sqrt{-1}, \sqrt{-4}, \sqrt{2}$ or 2^4.' What possible concepts or abstractions could be in the mind of a mathematician who uses these symbols in their calculations? Yet there they were, the number symbols '$\sqrt{-1}, \sqrt{-4}, \sqrt{2}$ and 2^4' *representing* unfathomable, ungraspable, unimaginable, inconceivable *numbers*. The Greek philosophical moorings of mathematics had to be abandoned. No longer were number symbols required to represent constructible numbers, commensurable numbers, or conceivable numbers.

Moreover, because the new algebra was freed from the geometric constraints and the deductive proofs of the Greeks, *analysis* became the guiding principle. According to Kline:

> "The classic statement of the importance of analysis was made by Lagrange in his ***Mecanique analytique***; 'We already have various treatises on Mechanics but the plan of this one is entirely new. I have set myself the problem of reducing this science (mechanics), and the art of solving the problems appertaining to it, to general formulas whose simple development gives all the equations necessary

> for the solutions of each problem... No diagrams will be found in this work. The methods which I expound in it demand neither constructions nor geometrical or mechanical reasonings, but solely algebraic (analytic) operations subjected to uniform and regular procedure." Kline (1972: 615)

No longer were mathematicians able to ground their calculations in quantitative measurement, counting, geometric forms or deductive proofs; mathematics had become pure procedure, "uniform and regular procedure". The analysis of the procedures was all that was necessary to prove the validity of solutions to algebraic problems. If the procedure conformed to the rules it was legitimate, regardless of what the symbols represented. The leap from practical math to theoretical math was then complete.

Complex numbers provided much consternation about the new number symbols being used and the "uniform and regular procedures" in which they were being used. So, exactly what was the *nature* of these complex numbers that were being used quite extensively?

> "By 1800 the mathematicians were using freely the various types of real numbers and even complex numbers, but the precise definitions of these various types of numbers were not available nor was there any logical justification of the operations with them... Hence in the 1830s the mathematicians tackled the problem of justifying the operation with literal or symbolic expressions.

> "This problem first considered by George Peacock... To justify the operation with literal expressions that could stand for negative, irrational and complex numbers he made the distinction between arithmetical algebra and symbolic algebra. The former dealt with symbols representing the positive integers and so was on solid ground. Here only operations leading to positive integers were permissible. Symbolical algebra adopts the rules of arithmetical algebra but removes the restrictions to positive integers." Kline (1972: 772)

The strange new numbers, irrationals, and complex, could not be conceived or explained. Yet, their symbolic representations produced useful results. *Symbolic algebra* had become the science of symbols, symbols totally unrelated to counting numbers, precise measurement, or geometric forms. The origins of mathematics in practical methods for arriving at sums and products had been replaced by equations with unfathomable symbols that required balance. Restoring the balance to an equation by shuffling symbols in systematic ways had become the hallmark of symbolic algebra, even though no one could imagine what many of the symbols stood for.

Along with the advanced symbolism came advancement in theory. The theory of equations produced more theorems and algorithms for manipulating the new symbols. Purely algebraic problems, i.e. those which had no immediate practical application, had become a science unto their own. Algebraic calculation procedures were routine, no matter what the symbols represented. Rule-governed algorithms for manipulating the symbols were learned and followed. The transformation from practical mathematics done with limited counting number symbols tied to imaginable geometric forms and practical applications, had moved to theoretic symbolic algebra, systematized to the point where doing it did "not require a great effort of the mind":

> "Descartes too began to see great potentialities in algebra... he sees in algebra a powerful method wherewith to carry on reasoning, particularly about abstract

and unknown quantities. In his view algebra mechanizes mathematics so that thinking and processes become simple and do not require a great effort of the mind." Kline (1972: 280)

Descartes foresaw the mechanization of mathematics. He recognized the rule-bound generality of the system and the fact that it could be mechanically encoded. Symbolic algebra did not require rational numbers or *thought*; machines could do it. The symbols, whatever they might represent, could be manipulated within routine algorithms to give symbolic answers. Mathematical word sounds and the symbols that represent those sounds provided humankind with power and reach unimaginable 2500 years before.

A Brief History of "0"

The history of "0" provides us with many powerful insights into the philosophy of mathematics. Bear in mind that our English word sound *"zero"* (sound it out) is used most often in discourse to tact with the symbol '0'. The sound *"zero"*, in turn, can be represented by the symbols 'zero' or '0' in the written form. The history of the symbol '0', the imprint on paper or the pixels on your monitor, is the subject of this section. That '0', the symbol you see, is what I will be discussing, not the sound *"zero"*, or the written representation of that sound: 'zero'.

The historical records from the earliest mathematicians show no indications of the symbol '0'. The progenitor of '0' was born approximately 500 BC. Because of confusion about the reading of their counting numbers, the Babylonians began to use two slanted cuneiform wedges impressed into their clay tablets to fill a vacant position in their positional notation. The wedges were not numbers; they were mere vacancy signs in their place value coding to enable users to properly interpret their number symbols. They said in effect: "there is no number in this column". Without the wedges, their number symbols could be construed ambiguously. The wedges had no numerical value. They were not numbers or numerals; they were placeholders. They occupied what had previously been a vacant spot between other symbols on the tablet.

The Greeks, in their metaphysical musings, made the distinction between numerals and numbers, the ideal objects or the impressions on the soul that the numerals represented. Numerals had to stand for numbers, and zero was not a *number*. There was no philosophical justification for zero, the number represented by the numeral '0'. The Greeks refused to accept any version of zero as a number for a variety of reasons. The most prominent were metaphysical. Zero, the number, must represent the void. Thus, there could be no ideal number zero in the Greek Heavens. Zero had no place in their metaphysical realm as did counting numbers: *"one, two, three"*. Nor did it have a place in the human mind as an abstraction. Zero, the *number* contra the *numeral* '0', simply did not exist. The Greeks abhorred anything resembling our modern *number* zero.

There were practical reasons for also rejecting zero the numeral. In mathematical algorithms, '0' could not be squared or tied to any geometrical figure; it was not constructible. Adding '0' to another numeral did nothing. Taking away '0' from another numeral changed nothing. Multiplication and division by '0' made no sense whatsoever. Greek notation did not use anything resembling our modern-day numeral '0'. However, they recognized its usefulness as a placeholder, and it appeared outside of their calculation procedures in the form of an omicron.

> "During the peak of ancient astronomy, Greek astronomical tables regularly employed zero; its symbol was the lowercase omicron, *o*, which looks very much like our modern-day zero, though it's probably a coincidence. (Perhaps the use of the omicron comes from the first letter of the Greek word for nothing, *ouden*.) The Greeks didn't like zero at all and used it as infrequently as possible. After

doing the calculations with Babylonian notation, Greek astronomers usually converted the numbers back into clunky Greek-style numerals—without zero."
Seif, Charles (2000: 39)

The omicron had no mathematical utility for the Greeks. It was a non-mathematical symbol that occupied a blank space in their positional notation to make sure that Greek mathematicians knew there was supposed to be a blank space there.

Of course, the lack of the symbol '**0**' and the decimal system prevented the Greeks from representing ratios in a positional notation as we do today with decimals. For example, we decimal mathematicians can express 1/100 as .01 and manipulate these decimal symbols rather than what we call fractions. However, the Greeks were limited to whole numbers and fractions, or ratios, ¼, ½, ¾…., *ratio*nal numbers. As a result, their algorithms for maneuvering their symbols were cumbersome. For many calculations they had to revert to Babylonian notation, after which they would convert the answer back to their own notation.

Alexander the Great brought the Babylonian number system, including a placeholder, to India. The limited historical evidence available suggests that Indians adopted a base-ten system with positional notation sometime around the fifth century AD.

> "Nobody knows when the Indians made the switch to a Babylonian-style place-value number system. The earliest reference to the Hindu numerals comes from a Syrian bishop who wrote, in 662, of how the Indians did calculations 'by means of nine signs.' Nine—not ten. Zero was evidently not among them. But it's hard to tell for sure… In any case, a symbol for zero—the place holder in the base-10 numbering system—was certainly in use by the ninth century. By then Indian mathematicians had already made a giant leap." Seif, Charles (2000: 67)

The giant leap Indian mathematicians had taken was symbolic, literally. They found a way to make use of a valueless symbol, a symbol that represented nothing, a symbol that took up space in a revolutionary positional notation. '**0**', the symbol, was, and still is, a symbol that enables mathematicians to avoid confusion when doing computations within positional notation math systems. It occupies a position where no counting number should be. It fills up an empty space in a binary system, a decimal system, a duodecimal system or any other positional system in which it is used.

Unencumbered by geometry or metaphysics, '**0**' became an accepted symbol used to remind decimal mathematicians that there is no counting number in that column. The Hindi word sound for the symbol '**0**' would be translated to "empty" in English. The English word sound "*zero*" comes from the Arabic "*ifr*", translated: "*empty*" or "*vacant*". In English, we should call the symbol '**0**' "*empty*", not "*zero*". The decimal symbol '**101**' should be pronounced "*one empty one*", meaning that there is no natural counting number in the tens' column; it is empty or vacant.

The actual symbol '**0**' we use these days in decimal mathematics was handed down from the Hindus to the Arabs. In 810CE, an Arab mathematician wrote a book about math and used the symbol '**0**' in his calculations. That book made its way to Europe and beyond. '**0**' became useful as a symbol in the manipulations of decimal numerals. The Greeks had recognized their equivalent omicron's functional value as a placeholder, but sensibly refused to accept it as a number because it did not function as other numbers did. Zero was mathematically inert for the

Greeks.

The Hindus, and later theorists converted the symbol '0' to number status when it suited their needs. In the West, '0' eventually became a *number* as opposed to a placeholder when mathematicians decided to define it as a number, though its function remains unchanged. It still fills up an empty column in decimal notation. The reason it has now gained the exalted *number* status is explained in a text for teaching mathematics to teachers:

> "For example, if we have defined addition only for the natural numbers and for the rational numbers which can be formed by the quotient of two natural numbers, then 3-7 is meaningless. A natural number does not exist which when added to 7 will give 3. Nor would 3-3 have any meaning, for no natural number exists for which $3 + N = 3$. It is this very fact which caused negative numbers and zero to be included in our number system. If negative numbers and zero are included in our number system, though, we then have to go back and re-define addition and multiplication for these numbers." Osborn, DeVault, Boyd, Houston (1968: 88)

However, BEWARE! Decimal math does not allow x/0. That function is undefined. How can that be if 0 is number? If we divide one number by another number, we should surely be able to come up with an answer. Surely mathematicians should be able to define x/0. In fact, mathematicians do as they please with their symbols and their word sounds. It is not what they say about their symbols that matters, it is the mathematical results that matter. The decimal symbol '0' has been redefined on an ad hoc basis so as to provide consistent results, useful results. Today it is considered to be a *number*, but that may change when the mathematical theory changes.

The symbol '0' as part of our number systems has served us well. Although today's mathematicians describe the symbol '0' in many new ways, its functional value within our decimal number system remains the same as it was hundreds of years ago. It still occupies a vacant spot in decimal notation and decimal algorithms. Additonally, need I remind you that you do not have or need a concept of zero. You need zero concepts of zero to use the symbol '0' effectively.

The History of the Word "*number*"

The use of the word sound "*number*" (or its approximation in other languages) made a significant transformation over the course of mathematical history. The Babylonians and the Egyptians used their sound, the functional equivalent of the English sound "*number*", to tact with inscriptions written on a tablet or papyrus. Numbers were the symbols that represented the counting sounds, much as we English speakers have '*2*' to represent the counting sound "*two*". There were no philosophical debates about *the nature of numbers*. There was no theoretical distinction between numbers and numerals. Numbers were the squiggles on the tablets and the papyrus.

The metaphysics of the Greeks, plus their connections between geometry and arithmetic, prevented them from accepting zero, negatives and irrationals *as numbers* even though they were aware of the symbols for those numbers. They could not project those numbers with a compass and a straight edge. They could not imagine or conceive of what these numbers could be. Zero, negatives and irrationals, as numbers, had no ontological status for the Greek philosophers. They did not exist.

Nevertheless, certain calculations produced results other than symbols for rational numbers. They produced zero, negatives, irrational and complex *symbols*. However, the Greeks, quite sensibly, refused to accept them as *numbers*.

> "Diophantus is a pure algebraist; and since algebra in his time did not recognize irrational, negative and complex numbers, he rejected equations with such solutions. It is, however, worthy of note that fractions for Diophantus are numbers, rather than just a ratio of two whole numbers… " Kline (1972: 143)

For Greek mathematicians, the use of the Greek word for "*number*" was still restricted to counting numbers and *ratios* (fractions). Those rational numbers were either the metaphysical or the mental entities. They were constructible, commensurable and conceivable by men, and they were represented by the numerals. The Hindus and the Arabs used zero, negatives, and irrationals without qualms about the metaphysical implications. Their inability to construct, measure, or imagine what these *numbers* could be was not problematic.

> "Though the mathematical work of the Hindus and Arabs was not brilliant, it did bring about some changes in the content and character of mathematics that were material for the future of the subject. Positional notation in base 10, the introduction of negative numbers, and the free use of irrationals as numbers not only extended arithmetic vastly but paved the way for a more significant algebra, an algebra in which letters and operations could apply to a far broader class of numbers." Kline (1972: 197)

For the Hindus and the Arabs, numbers were not required to be constructible, commensurable, or conceivable, because numbers were the symbols. They recognized zero, negatives, and irrationals as numbers. They could tact with those symbols with their equivalent to the word sound *"number"*. Unlike the Greeks, when using their word for *"number"*, the Hindus and Arabs were talking about the symbols, not metaphysical, mental, or abstract entities represented by the numerals.

In subsequent years, under the influence of the Greek distinction between numerals and numbers, irrational *numbers* provided much philosophical fodder and consternation for mathematicians. Rational numbers had been easy to grasp. They were intuitively accepted and used with abandon. However, irrationals were much more difficult to accept. They were imprecise numbers, the exact opposite of rational numbers. The mysterious nature of irrationals generated much theorizing. Defining irrational numbers became an occupational hazard for mathematicians.

> "It is apparent from these various approaches that the logical definition of the irrational number is rather sophisticated. Logically an irrational number is not just a single symbol or a pair of symbols, such as a ratio of two integers, but an infinite collection, such as Cantor's fundamental sequence of Dedekind's cut. The irrational number, logically defined, is an intellectual monster, and we can see why the Greeks and so many late generations of mathematicians found such numbers difficult to grasp." Kline (1972: 987)

Indeed, the use of *"number"* seemed to be changing. How could mathematicians be using the term "irrational numbers" that could not be logically defined or understood? Yet, there they were, the symbols representing these irrational numbers such as $'\sqrt{-2}'$ were right in the middle of their procedures, being juggled around as if they represented real, rational, definable numbers.

Later on, Europeans gradually accepted negatives and irrational numbers with misgivings. They then took the use of *"number"* a step further from counting and geometrical measurement:

> "Without having fully overcome their difficulties with irrational and negative numbers the Europeans added to their problems by blundering into what we now call complex numbers. They obtained these new numbers by extending the arithmetic operations of square root to whatever numbers appeared in solving quadratic equations by the usual method of completing the square. Thus Cardan, in Chapter 37 of <u>Ars Magna</u> (1545), sets up and solves the problem of dividing 10 into two parts whose product is 40. The equation is x (10-x) = 40. He obtains the roots $5 + \sqrt{-15}$ and $5 - \sqrt{-15}$ and then says, 'Putting aside the mental tortures involved,' multiply $5 + \sqrt{-15}$ and $5 - \sqrt{-15}$; the product is 25 – (-15) or 40. He then states, 'So progresses arithmetic subtlety the end of which, as is said, is as refined as it is useless.'… Cardan became further involved with complex numbers in his solution of cubic equations and formulated in practically modern form the four operations with complex numbers; but he still regarded them as useless and 'sophistic'… Descartes also rejected complex roots and coined the term 'imaginary'" Kline (1972: 253)

These "useless and sophistic" numbers later became useful. *Numbers* came to include these strange concoctions called complex numbers. Although they could not be imagined or conceived, they were bridges to solutions within the algorithms of that algebra. When complex number symbols were manipulated within the algorithms of that symbolic algebra, they led to meaningful results in spite of the "mental tortures" involved with understanding what these symbols stood for. *"complex number"* had entered the jargon of the science of mathematics. Discussing Bernoulli and Leibniz on their work toward the integration of algebraic function and transcendental function, Morris Kline reports:

> "Despite the confusion about complex numbers, neither hesitated to integrate them in this manner. Leibniz said the presence of complex numbers did no harm. John Bernoulli employed them repeatedly...
>
> "However, these results soon raised lively discussions about the nature of the logarithms of negative and complex numbers... Leibniz affirmed that the logarithms of negative numbers are nonexistent (he said imaginary), while Bernoulli sought to prove that they must be real.
>
> "By 1747 Euler had enough experience with the relationship between exponentials, logarithms, and trigonometric functions to obtain the correct facts about the logarithms of complex numbers.... He says that Leibniz's objection, if correct, shatters the foundation of all analysis, namely, that the rules and operations apply no matter what the nature of the objects to which they are applied." Kline (1972: 407)

The *nature of* mathematical objects continued to be problematic. Numbers continued their progression away from their roots in cardinal counting sounds and the symbols for those sounds toward unimaginable abstractions. Complex numbers were nothing like the original numbers, or even like negative and irrational numbers. These were completely new creatures. Nevertheless, philosophical mathematicians, much like the Greeks, said that the symbols such as $\sqrt{-15}$ *represented numbers*. The use of the word sound *"number"* and its graphic representation **'number'** had become very confusing.

The distinction between numbers and numerals continued to cause confusion amongst mathematical theorists. It produced a philosophical morass from which theorists have yet to extricate themselves. It also produced a continuing expansion of the use of the word sound *"number"* and its derivative written counterpart **'number'**. This process of expanding the use of the word sound *"number"* continues unabated, though this is not an expansion of *the concept of number*. It is simply a broader use of the acoustic device *"number"*.

"number" is a word sound that we English speakers can use in many ways. Theoreticians can make all sorts of analogies and theories about sets, groups, and elements, but the word sound *"number"* is defined by its use. Most people know perfectly well *how to* use numbers and the word sound *"number"*. They have no need for mathematical objects, mathematical abstractions, number ideas, concepts or any other mental entities to explain their use of numbers or the word sound *"number"*.

Unfortunately, most philosophers of mathematics think they do need abstract entities or mental entities to explain their use of numbers because they say that there is a distinction between numbers and numerals. They say that both the sounds *"1, 2, 19, 379 $\neq$ $\sqrt{-2}$"* (sound them out) and the inscriptions '1, 2, 19, 379 & √-2' are symbols that represent mathematical objects or mathematical abstractions. Other mathematicians say that we humans have concepts or ideas that are represented by those sounds and those symbols. Most mathematicians also say that we English-speaking humans must have a concept of number in order to use the word sound "*number*" or the word symbol **'number'**. However, they are all mistaken. You see, we humans have no concepts, ideas or abstractions, not even number concepts, ideas or abstractions. We have no need for them. But we do have many ways to employ the *sounds* "*1, 2, 19, 379 & √-2*" and the symbols '1, 2, 3, 379, √-2' as well the word sound "*number*" and the word symbol **'number'**.

Gottleb Frege spent a decade attempting to define the word "*number*". He eventually came up with a definition. He and Bertrand Russell were both attempting to define "*number*" without using any word that presupposed the use of "*number*". Frege's attempt came to naught. Russell and Alfred North Whitehead then took up the challenge and spent another decade writing Principia Mathematica, in which they claim to have defined "*number*", though that definition has not been universally accepted, and nor should it be. In fact, the word sound "*number*" is defined by mathematicians in whatever way mathematicians need to define it. The rest of us need not define it in order to use it.

A Non-semantic Proposal Mathematical Thinking

"Chimpanzees have no difficulty in determining that 2 is larger than 1, even though these two quantities differ only by one unit. However, they fail increasingly more often as one moves to larger numbers such as 2 versus 3, 3 versus 4, and so on. Similar distance and magnitude effects have been observed in a great variety of tasks and in many species, including pigeons, rats, dolphins, and apes. No animals seem to escape these laws of behavior—including, as we shall see later, *Homo sapiens*." Dehaene (1997: 26)

The ability to detect the differences of quantity in small sets is widespread within the animal kingdom. Non-counting humans and non-human animals are both able to make these distinctions. This ability is not dependent upon counting. Psychologists have termed it *"subitizing"*. This subitization seems to have universal limits among all species so endowed. The ability to subitize decreases rapidly as the size of the set increases. All animals, including humans, have an upper limit on how well they can subitize.

"But what is the nature of this limit? Are our parallel enumeration abilities really paralyzed when a set comprises more than three items? Do we necessarily have to count when this limit is reached? In fact, any adult can estimate, within a reasonable margin of uncertainty, numbers way beyond 3 or 4. The subitizing limit is therefore not an insurmountable barrier, but a mere borderline beyond which there is a universe of approximation." Dehaene (1997: 71)

That universe of approximation consists of the ability to recognize differences in magnitude amongst large sets. Both animals and humans have what Stanislas Dehaene refers to as "fuzzy counting". This, however, is not a counting process at all; it is the ability to compare approximate magnitudes. If the difference in magnitude between two sets is large enough, many species are able to detect the difference. As the difference in magnitude between two sets decreases, the ability to detect the difference decreases. For example, the difference between 9 and 19 bananas is detectable for a chimp. The difference between 18 bananas and 19 bananas is undetectable for them. Fortunately for Homo sapiens, we have learned how to count with sounds. Not only can we detect the difference between 9 and 19 bananas by comparing approximate magnitudes, we can detect the difference between 18 and 19 bananas by counting.

Matching vs. Counting

"By age 12 months all infants produce quantitative equivalence in two-object sets by reversible substituting. One half these infants also already substitute objects in three-object sets they have constructed... During the infant's second year, first order substituting that produces quantitative equivalence is expanded to single sets comprising larger numbers of objects... Thus, by age 24 months all infants compose two sets of objects in one-to-one correspondence such that the two sets are quantitatively equivalent." Gibson and Ingold (1993: 305)

The use of number sounds precedes recorded history. Consequently, the origin of numbers is lost in the fog of the past. None-the-less, philosophers of mathematics speculate that early man needed a method of recording and keeping track of animal herds. It is suggested that before the advent of tally sticks, primitive men kept track of animals by matching them with pebbles. After a night full of wolf howls, a herder could find reassurance in the fact that his bag of pebbles could still be matched with the animals in his herd. That matching process did not require the use of number sounds. Establishing a correspondence between two sets of objects does not require counting, or the counting number sounds. Well before knowing *how* to count with word sounds, humans knew *how* to match two sets of objects in a one-to-one correspondence. They still do, as reported in the epigraph for this section.

The first *evidence* of matching was tally sticks which have been recovered by archeologists. Rather than pebbles in a bag, marks on a stick provided an easy, visible method of recording herd census. As with pebbles, it is quite possible to know you have the same quantity of animals in the morning that you had the night before without knowing *how many* you have. Whatever the size of his herd last night, the herder knew that the wolves did not eat any of his sheep the previous night if the marks on a tally stick could be matched with the animals again in the morning. He could watch his sheep move by and take pebbles out of a bag or move his finger down the tally stick saying: "*sheep*", "*sheep*", "*sheep*" until he removed the last pebble or his finger reached the last tally mark on the stick. By thus establishing a one-to-one correspondence, he knew that he did not lose any sheep. *Matching* would have been very useful; it could have confirmed equivalent quantities for the shepherd without him knowing *how many* sheep he had.

Keep in mind that because of the limits of subitization, any collection larger than four or five sheep just looks like *many*, whether the lookers are primitive or mathematically sophisticated like you. ///////////////// looks pretty much like ////////////////. Of course, you could match tally marks and sheep one to one. In that way, you could determine equivalence, but you would still not know *how many* sheep you have. For humans like you, determining how many requires counting, producing a standard sequential series of sounds. You must use counting sounds to determine if groups have a cardinal number in common. In all likelihood, numbers started out as vocal devices that enabled humans to make precise quantitative comparisons.[3]

In order for the herder to know *how many* sheep he had, he must have been able to use number sounds. He must have been able to count. He had to use counting sounds, a series of distinctive utterances that enabled him to match sounds with the marks as he moved up the tally stick or picked the pebbles out of the bag. Rather than saying: "*sheep, sheep, sheep*" as the herd passed by and his finger moved up the tally stick, he could articulate: "*onka*" "*drosh*" "*tribble*"… pointing another of his fingers at the sheep as he uttered counting sounds. That primitive herder was no longer matching; he was counting by using a distinctive series of word sounds.

That herder could count: "*onka*" "*drosh*" "*tribble*"… "*nineteen*". The last sound in the sequence, the one he ended on, would tell him how many sheep he had, and by comparing *the sounds* each morning rather than pebbles or tally marks, he knew that the wolves had not eaten any sheep. That's right, in all probability numbers were first used as distinct, consistent, sequential sounds, sounds that let a herder know more than equivalence. These new vocal devices that he used told him *how many* sheep he had. Without such mastery of these number sounds, people simply cannot grasp or produce quantifier phrases. How could a non-counter possibly understand or use: "*i have nineteen sheep*"?

Shepherd Smith also knew that he was keeping up with his neighbor, Jones. Smith could do this without matching his pebbles with his neighbor Jones' pebbles. He could do this by using sounds. He could count out loud up to "*nineteen*". He could then say to his neighbor: "*i have nineteen sheep. how many do you have*"? If his neighbor said: "*i have sixteen sheep*", our herder could smile smugly and say: "*i remember having only sixteen sheep*". He finally knew how many sheep he had. And because he knew that the sound "*nineteen*" came after the sound "*sixteen*" shepherd Smith also knew he had *more* sheep than shepherd Jones.

Are some people just stupid?

> "Many primitive peoples never got beyond the recognition of 'oneness,' 'twoness,' and 'manyness.' Some primitives apparently never made the abstraction at all, for to some primitives two fish were entirely different from two coconuts and had no property in common. In fact, until the date of their extinction or absorption into other tribes and peoples, some primitives always used different word sounds to denote two fish, two coconuts, two pigs, two boys, etc." Osborn, DeVault, Boyd and Houston (1968: 10)

Obviously, these people had the ability to distinguish one thing from two things. However, the issue is not whether they "made abstractions". They would have been able to subitize the difference between two pigs and three pigs. They would have been able to make that distinction, but they saw no need to and thus, they had no sounds to tact with three pigs, three fish or three coconuts. Once again, it is not that they lacked number abstractions or number concepts. They had the ability to do the same things that you and I do. They could make the initial distinctions necessary to start counting. They could subitize.

What they and many other primitive tribes were missing was a number system based on counting sounds. They lacked procedural knowledge for the use of acoustic devices in a particular sequence to enumerate units and determine precise cardinal quantity. More than 2 or 3 of anything were just *many*. They had no ability to determine *which many*. They never saw the need to develop an ordinal series of distinct sounds that could go on indefinitely. They did not know how to count because they did not have the necessary acoustic devices. They had not learned counting *behavior*.

In summary, prehistoric humans could have recognized the difference between two things and three things; they could have subitized. They could have also made set distinctions about certain comparative magnitudes of larger sets just as other creatures could. What distinguished some prehistoric humans from other humans and animals *was their ability to count*. When they learned the counting skill, they could utter a sequential series of sounds to count and detect the difference between eighteen and nineteen things as well as the difference between two and three things. They had learned useful verbal behavior. They had learned how to use specific acoustic devices to do the work of determining cardinal quantity.

That counting process is the starting point for all mathematics. The most basic number set is cardinal numbers, the counting numbers. They answer the question: "how many" (ask yourself why you say how many rather than which many?) They enable competent users to count members of groups or sets and end that counting process on sounds that have comparative value. The symbols for the sounds, numerals, came later, much later. They were used to represent these mathematical acoustic devices, these number sounds. They were used to represent vocal counting behavior.

The Counting Sounds

Math starts with countable items. It is digital, not analog. At some point after birth each human's cognitive processes enable it to detect these countable items in the flux of experience. Trees, dogs, births, and deaths are discrete objects and events. When talking about these individuated things, we who can count are able to ask: "*how many are there*"? Interlocutors, if they have learned the counting skill, are able to tell us how many of these discrete things there are.

In many languages, the first thing infants learn about quantity when growing up is the distinction between one and many. In many languages young speakers must recognize that basic quantitative distinction to speak competently. Susan Carey writes:

> "Since the seminal work of Roger Brown (1973), the father of empirical studies of language acquisition, we have known that the first linguistic quantifiers English-learning children produce are the singular determiner 'a,' plural marking of various types (on verbs, on nouns, on pronouns), 'more' and 'some'."
> Carey (2011: 257)

That one/many (or singular/plural) distinction is repeatedly reinforced for young speakers by the verbal behavior of mature speakers who use the singular determiner "*a*" and plural marker "*s*" in English. (In fact, many languages utilize the first counting sound as an article indicating a singular subject. In effect, the word sounds "*a*" and "*one*" in the English language are the same word in many languages.)

Not surprisingly, children who learn how to speak in languages that do not mark the singular/plural distinction morphologically do not make the one/many numerical distinction as soon as those who speak in languages which do mark that distinction:

> "Peggy Li and her colleagues repeated (Barbara) Sarnecka's study with Mandarin-learning children in China and Taiwan. Mandarin is also a classifier language with virtually no singular/plural marking on nouns or verbs in the child's input, and Mandarin has only one count list. Li et al. found that Mandarin learners become "one"-knowers six to nine months later than English-learning children, in spite of evidence from other studies that they learn the numeral list at comparable ages." Carey (2011: 322)

The "count list" these researchers refer to is the sequence of counting sounds uttered by child language learners in many languages, Mandarin, Japanese, English, French... whatever. Children learn language-specific sounds for counting. However, they first learn the distinction between one and many because they can subitize and their verbal conditioning often requires them to make that distinction in order to speak competently.

Moreover, because children first learn the distinction between one and many, even English speaking children who can count will initially think that the counting sounds "*two*", "*three*", "four", "five", along with "some" and "many" are functionally equivalent; they are *all many*. They will grab a random number of objects greater than one when asked to grab two, four, six, some, or many. The distinction between two, three, four, etc. has not yet been made even though they can count. They are unable to utilize the counting sounds as mature speakers do and are unable to determine *which many* the request is for.

As previously mentioned, the distinction between countable things and measurable things is also marked in many languages. In the English language we have count nouns and mass nouns, along with concomitant articles and adjectives, to reflect this distinction, *many sheep* and *much snow*, for example. Other languages use other linguistic devices to make this distinction. Some languages, such as Igbo and Russian, do not mark this distinction at all. However, the ability to make the distinction between countable items and measurable stuff is a cognitive capacity witnessed widely in both humans and non-human animals.

Because of that ability, humans can make quantitative distinctions about countable things without mathematics. Pre-counting humans can make quantitative distinctions by subitizing or making large quantitative comparisons between large groups of things, just as other creatures do. But beyond subitizing and making relative quantitative distinctions between large groups, humans *must* be able to count with sounds in order to make precise quantitative comparisons between large groups. They *must* have a standardized series of sequentially ordered sounds. When humans learn to use counting numbers, we learn to use sounds. We learn behavior. It is *behavior* that is drilled into each of us at an early age.

After children learn to make the distinction between one and many most of them learn how to count. Those who do count do not have a unique *mental* faculty; they have a skill. They have learned a procedure. They are able to utilize a series of sounds to count. There is an observable difference in the behavior of people who know how to count and those who don't. Because they can count, they can also make precise quantitative comparisons of large sets of objects, events etc. that non-counters cannot.

For modern English speakers, "one" is the first sound in the count list. We English speakers point to objects in sequence and say "one", "two", "three", "four". We learn an infinite sequential series of sounds that we can use to count any numerable set of items. People utilize counting sounds both vocally and sub-vocally to quantify, often aided by a pointing finger. When they are done counting a set of things, they end up with a sound that they can remember. That sound indicates that they have ended the process of counting at a certain point. If they count the same set again, they will end up with the same sound, assuming that they know *how* to count correctly. They begin to use the final sound at the culmination of any counting process to tact with the exact quantity or the number of the set, *how many*.

Do these counters know that '8' & 'eight' are symbols for the sound "ate"? Not yet. Do they have a concept of the number 8? No! Are they able to abstract the number 8? No! Do they know how to use the sound "eight"? You betcha! Ask a young girl who has learned to make numeric distinctions to show you "eight" fingers. She can do it because she knows how to use the sound "eight". She knows how to behave in response to the question. The digits on her hands go up "one", "two", "three" ... "eight". She has learned counting behavior. She has the ability to make exact quantitative distinctions by counting with sounds.

Does she need the number sound "zero"? Not yet. She could count to a gazillion without the sound **"zero"**. **"zero"** is not a counting sound. Will she eventually learn the concept of 0? Of course not! Will she learn to abstract zero? No way! Will she learn to use the symbol **'0'**? Yes! The symbol **'0'** is necessary when she learns the decimal algorithms for computing. Could she do mathematics without **'0'**? Yes; just ask the Babylonians, the Egyptians and the Greeks. Does she know that **'0'** is a number? No! It will take many years of school and much philosophical jiggering for mathematicians to convince her that **'0'** is a number.

Moreover, once she has mastered the basic counting process, she will learn that there are special symbols to represent the counting sounds, plus a place holder. She will learn that in addition to phonetic representations for the counting sounds such as *"four"*, *"quatro"* and *"feir"*, there are various numerals such as **'4'**, **'////'**, **'IV'**, or **'00000100'** to represent those sounds, and she will learn that since the adoption of the Hindu-Arabic numeral system, **'4'** has been universally accepted here on earth and used in the algorithms of decimal math. It is a non-phonetic symbol, but it stands for the sound just as the written word 'four' does in English. The sounds, however, are not symbols; they are verbal behavior with the functional values of counting and tacting with exact quantitative distinctions.

The symbols **'19'** and **'nineteen'** represent the nineteenth sound we make when counting in English, *"nineteen"* (sound it out). The sound *"nineteen"* can also be represented by **'XIX'** or **'00010011'**. All of these various symbols represent the sound, nothing more and nothing less. Neither **'19'**, **'nineteen'**, **'XIX'**, nor **'00010011'** have content. There is nothing attached to the symbols, no concepts, no ideas, no abstractions. There is no need to engage in metaphysics or mentalism to explain human *behavior* with mathematical sounds or symbols.

I will ask you to perform a small task right now. Utter the first twenty decimal numbers in order. Have you done it? More than likely, you uttered the number sounds in counting order. This is the ordinality that mathematicians talk about. Is that the only order? No, it is the order you have been conditioned to use when you count. You could have said: *"20, 19, 18, 17"* … Or *"2, 1, 4, 3, 6, 5"* … They are orders. But counting order is so ingrained in you that you do not consider other orders. You likely said: *"one"*, *"two"*, *"three"*, *"four"*, the ordinality that is necessary for counting. What good would counting numbers be if you could not use them in the proper sequence and end your count on the proper number sound? And, what about all those other decimal numbers you skipped: .1, .02, .003, .0004…? Where would you fit them in the first 20 decimal numbers?

Also, when you started your recitation of the first twenty numbers, why did you start with 1? Why didn't you start counting with 0? 0 is a number now. Doesn't 0 come before 1? You could have started counting with 0, but you would be off by one every time you counted. You would end up with nine fingers and nine toes. Zero is not a counting number. It is not a *natural* number. You started counting with *"one"* because counting with sounds is conditioned behavior so ingrained in you that you do not think twice about it. If you are an English speaker, you likely began *"one, two, three"* because the utilization of this sequence of counting numbers has been drilled into your behavior.

The decimal system requires an infinite number of counting sounds *"1, 2, 3…19, 20… 30…100… 4,003,002,001"*. Remember, I am talking about the sounds, the noises coming out of a speaker's mouth. However, the decimal system only requires individual symbolic representations of the first nine counting sounds and a place holder: **'1, 2, 3, 4, 5, 6, 7, 8, 9'** and **'0'**. Although people who have been conditioned to count can go on indefinitely, it only takes these ten symbols in the decimal system to represent any of these billions and trillions of counting sounds.

A duodecimal counting system, on the other hand, would require eleven counting sounds and a placeholder if it was to be represented symbolically in a similar place-notational system. We could use our familiar decimal integer sounds of *"one"*, *"two"*... *nine"*, plus two more counting sounds *"ta"* and *"za"* which could be represented by *"V"* and *"∩"*. We could then count *"one"*, *"two... nine"*, *"ta"*, *"za"*, *"ten"*, *"eleven... nineteen"*, *"tateen"*, *"zateen"*, *"twenty"*... The counting sound "twenty" in duodecimal would be quantificationally equivalent to the counting sound *"twenty-four"* in decimal. This counting process could continue indefinitely just as our current decimal system does. These sounds could be represented symbolically as **'1, 2, 3...V, ∩, 10, 11...19, 1V, 1∩, 20'** *ad infinitum.*[4]

Is either of these counting processes true or correct or real? No! The duodecimal system would work just fine once we became comfortable with the new counting sounds and the new symbols these new number systems would require. In fact, aliens with four digits on each of their three appendages would much prefer the duodecimal counting system. The point is that counting with word sounds is a convention made with different sounds in different cultures. Those sounds are represented by standardized non-phonetic decimal number symbols. We have become habituated to the use of both the decimal sounds and the symbols. However, there is nothing sacrosanct or innate about our current human methods of counting with sounds and representing those sounds with decimal symbols.

Additionally, how do we know when someone understands counting within the decimal system? When they can count to 10? 100? 1,000? 2,467,328? There is no final exam for counting because there is no final number. Every number has a successor. A counter has learned a skill, a procedure whereby they can make noises in a systematic order, a process that can go on indefinitely. The proof is in the pudding. To prove that they can count, they must demonstrate their skill. They must display specific verbal behavior with number sounds. We know that a child knows how to count, when she is able to do it repeatedly, when she makes the sounds in the proper succession, when she performs verbally.

And what do children remember when they count? They remember the sounds and how to produce them. They practice their counting by making the sounds. They point their fingers at the Cheerios and say out loud: *"one, two, three, four"*... They learn to use culturally specific sounds. They have acquired procedural knowledge. It is a skill some of them never learn, e.g. children from primitive tribes. But, if they do learn to produce this behavior, they can eventually be taught to use mathematical algorithms to manipulate the decimal symbols that represent those sounds. What they do not remember are *concepts, ideas,* or *abstractions*!

How do you memorize important numbers, e.g. your phone number? Most of us make the sounds. We repeat them over and over, out loud, then sub-vocally using acoustic memory. When someone asks you for your phone number, you remember the sounds in sequence. There are no concepts, ideas or abstractions floating through your head to correspond to the sounds as you rattle off the number sounds. The *sounds* come out of your head, not concepts, ideas, or abstractions. You remember and reproduce vocal *behavior*.

Not surprisingly, how much you remember is affected by the sounds you use:

"Remarkably, the number of digits a person can remember depends on what language they use – Chinese uses shorter words for numbers than English, which in turn uses shorter words than Welsh, and correspondingly, under carefully controlled conditions, Chinese speakers can remember more digits than can English speakers, who in turn remember more than Welsh speakers." Marcus (2004: 126)

Why do we find this "remarkable"? We do so because we have been told that we have number concepts, ideas, and abstractions in our minds that match up with the number sounds and symbols. If that is so, how is it that Chinese-speakers can remember more concepts than Welsh speakers? How can we account for this difference?

We can account for it if we abandon the belief that number sounds have associated concepts, ideas or abstractions in our minds. The minds of Chinese-speakers do not enable them to remember more concepts or more abstractions than Welsh-speakers. Philosophers and mathematicians must come to grips with the fact that humans use and remember counting sounds with functional values, not number concepts, number ideas or number abstractions. The differences in the ability to work with numbers amongst speakers of different languages, is well documented. Most of it can be accounted for by the variations in number sound production. We should not find this remarkable.

Philosophers and mathematicians have made us believe that cardinal numbers, the numerals, stand for number concepts, number ideas or number abstractions generalized from the specific instances of numeral use. However, they make the same mistake that linguists do with word symbols. They assume that both the phonetic symbols and the numerals represent something other than the sound. *They do not*. Both the phonetic and the decimal symbols **'four'** and **'4'** represent the sound "*four*", nothing else. In English, in context, "*four*" is a sound that is used to count and tact with a quantitative distinction. Counters can say: "*four sheep*" just as they can say "*black sheep*" because they have learned tacting *behavior with number sounds*.

Furthermore, when humans developed non-phonetic numeric symbols to represent the sounds, they devised methods for manipulating the symbols. We mathematically trained people have learned *how* to manipulate Hindu-Arabic base-ten number symbols. It is rule- bound *behavior* that has been inculcated in each of us with great effort. We have the ability to use **'19'** within the computational algorithms of decimal math. We modern humans find **'19'** much easier to manipulate than **'XIX'**, though neither you, nor the Romans need concepts, ideas or abstractions to count and do mathematics. Nor does your computer need them to manipulate **'00010011'** within its binary algorithms.

When a young boy learns *how* to count, has he gained new knowledge? Yes, he has gained procedural knowledge. He has gained a skill. He knows how to do something new. He has learned useful *behavior*. He knows how to use sounds to make numerical distinctions. Must he know arithmetic to do so? No. He will gain an ability to manipulate number symbols for those sounds when he learns his arithmetic. Has he gained new concepts, ideas, or abstractions? How many has he gained? Millions of them for the millions of new numbers he can now count with? In fact, he has the same number of number concepts, number ideas, and number abstractions that he had before he learned his mathematical skill: none, nada, zero.

Number Concepts

Both human animals and non-human animals are able to subitize three objects as opposed to one object. That might lead you to believe that you and they have a concept of three. But when you are no longer able to subitize as you count large sets, do you no longer have number concepts? If you insist that you have a concept of 3, then you must have a concept of 19, 35, 432, 76937, 2471328, etc. because you can do the same things with any of these numbers that you can do with 3. You must have an infinite number of number concepts. So, what is your concept of √2? What is your concept of √-1? How does your concept of -1 differ from your concept of 1? And what is your concept of 00010011? You say you have to convert it to decimal. Why is that? Is it because your concepts are decimal, or is the conversion necessary because you have been conditioned to count and compute with decimal notation, not binary notation?

The concepts, ideas, and *abstractions* now used in explaining how we do mathematics have no explanatory force whatsoever. Debates amongst mathematicians are debates about sound and symbol use. They are debates about *behavior.* Mathematicians are constantly redefining word sounds and symbols with more subtle distinctions about how they will use them. They then condition other mathematicians to talk the same way with the sounds and manipulate the symbols the same way. They then gain intuitions about the use of their sounds and symbols to guide them in future mathematical development.

Once again, the salient point is that concepts, ideas, and abstractions are not necessary for humans, or adding machines or computers to perform mathematical calculations. They are metaphysical excrescences to mathematics that cannot be coherently explained. We humans have been taught how to use the decimal number system and we perform the calculations as mechanically as any adding machine or computer. We crunch the numbers and come up with an answer by means of inculcated behavior. You have no need for concepts that can be paired up with the number sounds *"356, 273"*, *"nineteen"*, or *"four"* (sound them out.) Neither do you need concepts to pair up with the symbols **'356,273'**, **'nineteen'** or **'four'**. You pair up the sounds with the symbols and you recognize the functional value of both because you have been conditioned to utilize them in very specific ways.

Speaking of concepts, what is your concept of infinity? You know how to use the word *"infinity"*. Mathematicians know how to use the symbol '∞', but what could the *concept of infinity* possibly be? Stephen Hawking had this to say about infinity:

> "Rather similar, seemingly absurd infinities occur in the other partial theories, but in all these cases the infinities can be canceled out by a process called renormalization. This involves canceling the infinities by introducing other infinities. Although this practice is rather dubious mathematically, it does seem to work in practice, and has been used with these theories to make predictions that agree with observations to an extraordinary degree of accuracy." Hawking (1998: 173)

Physicists can balance equations that contain '∞' symbols. Enter two '∞' symbols into the proper spots in an equation and the results prove useful. The symbol '∞' represents the word sound *"infinity"*. The graphic inscription **'infinity'** represents the sound as well. *"infinity"*, the acoustic device that English-speaking humans utter, has a precise use for mathematicians and a much less precise use for the rest of us. People learn the functional role of that device within their overall linguistic behavior and that symbol within the mathematical systems they find useful.

The speech-thinking that the sounds and symbols mathematicians use have mental or metaphysical objects paired up with them, is a result of the semantic fallacies and dualism. Unfortunately, these two erroneous assumptions about the sounds that issue from human mouths and the nature of human organisms are intrinsic elements in mathematicians' explanations of mathematics. The history of mathematics is rife with examples of the semantic fallacies and dualism. For example, mathematical historian Morris Kline discusses a letter from famed mathematician Carl Friedrich Gauss:

> "In a complete development such words as 'between' must be founded on clear concepts, which can be done, but which I have not found anywhere.' Gauss made additional criticisms of the definition of straight line and of the definition of the plane as a surface in which a line joining any two points of the plane must lie." Kline (1972: 1006)

Defining "between", "straight line", and "plane" may be possible and desirable for mathematicians, but those definitions will diverge from ordinary usage. Mathematicians must use those words more precisely because they make distinctions that most of us need not make. Ultimately, the definitions mathematicians use will depend on other words with ordinary uses, not "clear concepts".

If the primitive people mentioned previously had been shown how to count, they would have learned how to use number sounds. Their ability to subitize and make large quantitative comparisons would not have changed one whit. They could still tact with one pig and two pigs as they had done before. Though they could also tact with nineteen pigs as opposed to eighteen pigs. For them to make the distinction between 18 and 19, they would have had to count, just as we do. They would then know *how* to make that distinction and *how* to tact with it. They would have the counting skill in addition to their subitizing skill and their ability to make large quantitative comparisons. They would have gained useful verbal *behavior*.

Once they learned to represent those counting sounds with decimal symbols, they could learn how to manipulate those symbols within the rules of decimal mathematics. They would no longer be primitive. But they could still invoke occult ideas, concepts and abstractions located in their minds or consciousness or abstract space to account for their new decimal math behavior, just as sophisticated philosophers and mathematicians mistakenly do.

Tacting with Number Sounds in English

Spoken number sounds are predominately represented by two different sets of symbols in today's English-speaking world. We can use the phonetically based word symbols or the Hindu-Arabic numerals we have been trained to use. Both symbols represent the sounds and nothing more. The written symbols **'two'** and **'2'**, along with the written symbols **'too'** and **'to'**, represent the sound "*tu*" for English speakers. (Sound it out.) How do we know what to do with this single sound that is represented in many ways? Context and many presuppositions contribute to listener uptake on what the speaker is trying to do with the sound. The use of the symbols **'two'** or **'2'**, as opposed to **'too'** or **'to'** in the written form, enables us to make the distinctions when the contextual elements of speech acts are not apparent. However, the spoken sounds "*two*", "*2*", "*to*", *and* "*too*" are indistinguishable.

In the case of numbers sounds, we English speakers often use them like adjectives. When we use the spoken number words, we are doing nothing different than what we do when we use the sounds "*red*", "*round*", or "*rolling*". We are using the sounds to tact with distinctions that we are able to make when necessary. When we need to make a distinction between 18 things and 19 things, we count or calculate. Then we tact with 19 things or 18 things, just as we tact with red things, round things and rolling things. Redness is different than greenness. Roundness is different than squareness. Rolling is different than bouncing. Twoness is different than threeness. Eighteeness is different than nineteeness.

Humans are able to tact with quantitative differences with spoken numbers. This does not entail that number sounds have corresponding mental entities any more than pointing to red, round, and rolling entails that the sounds "*red*", "*round*," and "*rolling*" have corresponding mental entities in the minds of speakers. It does not entail that oneness, twoness, nineteeness, or the square-root-of-negative-oneness are ideas, concepts or abstractions. Don't take the dualist's bait. There is nothing in your mind or consciousness to correspond to the sounds "*red*", "*round*", "*19*", or "*$\sqrt{-1}$*". Nor is there anything in your mind or consciousness to correspond to the symbols for those sounds. There are, however, distinct neurological correlates for your conditioned behavior with pliers, pianos, word sounds, number sounds, and number symbols. They are in your brain, not an ethereal mind.

Mathematical Behavior

How is it that we have machines that can do math much better than we humans can? Yet, we have no machines that can carry on a conversation. So why is it that five-year-olds can speak competently, but not do math without special training? How is it that children learn to use words so easily and numbers only with much effort? Could it be that we need symbols and rules to do math but we do not need them for language acquisition and use? Could it be that the use of numeric symbols is rule-bound behavior while the use of word sounds is not rule-bound. Yes, that is precisely why we observe the discrepancy between the acquisition of math skills and the acquisition of language skills. In fact, mathematics is a rule-governed system of procedural knowledge that requires formal education to learn; language is not.

Some human cultures learned *how* to count because they found it useful; others did not learn to count. Mathematically knowledgeable people begin learning their counting skills through iterated learning, i.e. operant conditioning. Number sounds are used to count and answer the question: how many? After learning to count with number sounds, early human mathematicians developed simple non-phonetic number symbols to record the count sounds. They then devised algorithms to manipulate number symbols in many ways that proved useful. These days, we manipulate the symbol **'19'** within the algorithms of decimal mathematics just as our predecessors manipulated their special number symbols within their mathematical algorithms. All of the counting and manipulation done by mathematicians now and in the past is *rule-bound procedural behavior*.

This is true of all mathematical processes we learn: addition, subtraction, multiplication, division, algebraic equations, etc. We must learn *how* to perform algorithms; we must learn the rules. We must learn procedures. We must do exercises. We must be conditioned to behave with sounds and mathematical symbols in certain ways. You learn the decimal addition algorithm, for example, by summing up the right-most column first. Then you carry the remainder to the next column to the left, ones, tens, hundreds, etc. Is that the only method for adding decimal numbers? No! In fact, the original procedure for adding columns of numbers began with the left-most column and worked to the right. That process was more cumbersome than the current process and was thus abandoned.

So, how did you learn to multiply in the decimal system? You learned the multiplication tables by rote. You memorized the multiplication tables by uttering: *"six times six is thirty-six"*, repeatedly. Learning your multiplication tables is a matter of drills. You learned behavior, how to make noises consistently, just as you did when you learned to count. You memorized sounds so that when you see the Hindu-Arabic symbols that represent those sounds 6 x 6 = ?, you can repeat the sounds and come up with the correct answer. You can say to yourself: *"six times six is thirty-six"*.

You also learned that the sound *"thirty-six"* can be represented non-phonetically by the numeral **'36'**. You then learned:

$$36$$
$$\times\ \underline{36}$$
$$216$$
$$\underline{108}$$
$$1296$$

You learned a decimal algorithm for multiplication. You learned steps one, two, three … and where to stop. In each instance of learning, from counting to calculus, *your behavior was modified.*

However, you cannot *see* the necessity of 36 x 36 = 1296. You must have faith. You have confidence that if you have performed the algorithm correctly, it could be confirmed by counting. How could you do your math correctly and come up with the wrong count? Coming up with the correct (standard decimal) answer is performing correctly, and accurately, according to the algorithm. If you cannot count to verify your work, you verify it by "double checking it", or having someone else perform the same operation to come up with the same answer. Then you compare the symbols to *see* if your answer is correct. Soon enough, your faith in the algorithms of decimal math becomes complete.

Furthermore, you did not say: "*six times six is thirty-six today*". Nor did you say: "*six pigs times six pigs is thirty-six pigs*". Within the decimal system, six times six will always yield thirty-six, no matter when you do the multiplying, or what you are counting. Once you memorize the multiplication tables and algorithms for the manipulation of decimal symbols, sums and products are successfully arrived at, not due to any a priori or transcendental feat of cognition, but because you have been trained that way. The point is simply that the results of your mathematical calculations are correct because you have been taught to utilize the counting sounds, the symbols and the rule-bound algorithms of decimal mathematics.

Is there any necessity for 6 x 6 to be 36? No! In our previously discussed duodecimal system: 6 x 6 = 30. However, all of your rule-bound mathematical conditioning has been done with decimal notation. You are so firmly in the grip of your decimal behavior you cannot believe that 6 x 6 = 30. That could not be true! In fact, "truth" is not a useful word in mathematics. In the decimal system: 6 x 6 = 36. In a duodecimal system: 6 x 6 = 30. Neither procedure is *true*. Both are valid within their respective systems. Nevertheless, your insistence that 6 x 6 = 36 is nothing more than resolutely conditioned behavior ultimately based on the decimal counting sounds and the decimal multiplication tables you and every other mathematically trained human memorized.

Decimal math, duodecimal math, binary math, algebras and geometries are all axiomatic analytic systems. Axiomatic systems are defined as internally consistent networks of relations and operations that are based on fundamental propositions, rules, principles, or axioms which are considered primitive or self-evident. Symbols used within these systems are defined by stipulation and manipulated by rules. If we utilize the rules (are able to apply them correctly), we can determine the correctness or validity of an operation by analyzing the constituent steps to see if they conform to the rules. Have we used the algorithms properly? Is the procedure valid? Have we *behaved* correctly?

Beyond counting with sounds and multiplication tables, all of mathematics is symbol manipulation by rule. Routine procedures for maneuvering number symbols and operational symbols provide basic arithmetic algorithms. Through the years, new non-numeric mathematical symbols, symbols that represent the sound "*add*" (+), and the sound "*subtract*" (-), the sound "*equals*" (=), etc. were added to the systems. After the basic arithmetic operations were devised and perfected, algebraists learned that algebras did not even require numeric symbols. They could manipulate non-numeric variables (α, μ etc.) within their algorithms just as easily as numerals.

Even so, the *practical* manipulation of symbols within the various systems of algebra and geometry requires the use of numerals, either as quantities or measurements. Humans routinely use Hindu-Arabic numerals within decimal computation procedures to get practical results. They end up with *the count*; symbols can be related to the world by counting or measuring, i.e. counting with standard units. Otherwise, it is *pure* mathematics, theoretical math, as opposed to applied or practical math.

The story of *imaginary* numbers by George Gamov illustrates this distinction:

> "…what would be the square root of a negative number be? Have expressions such as $\sqrt{-5}$ and $\sqrt{-1}$ any meaning?
>
> "If you try to figure it out in a rational way, you will undoubtedly come to the conclusion that the above expressions make no sense at all. To quote the words of the twelfth century mathematician Brahmin Bhaskara: 'The square of a positive number, as also that of a negative number, is positive. Hence the square root of a positive number is twofold, positive and negative. There is no square root of a negative number, for a negative number is not a square.'
>
> "But mathematicians are obstinate people, and when something that seems to make no sense keeps popping up in their formulas, they will do their best to put sense into it. And the square roots of negative numbers certainly do keep popping up in all kinds of places, whether in the simple arithmetical questions that occupied mathematicians of the past, or in the twentieth century problems of unification of space and time in the frame of the theory of relativity.
>
> "…imaginary numbers soon became as unavoidable in mathematics as fractions, or radicals, and one could practically not get anywhere without using them.
>
> "…For well over two centuries after imaginary numbers broke into the domain of mathematics they remained enveloped by a veil of mystery and incredibility until finally they were given a simple geometrical interpretation by two amateur mathematicians: a Norwegian surveyor by the name of Wessel and a Parisian bookkeeper, Robert Argand." Gamov (1947: 33)

Gamov goes on to explain how the imaginary numbers became useful. These mysterious numbers could be plotted on a graph and used to depict a spatial relationship. In fact, they could be used to find hidden treasure in one of his practical applications. Although nobody could "figure out" what the square root of a negative number could *be*, it had proved useful in theoretical mathematics. Imaginary numbers had been around for centuries. Mathematicians used them with great results. However, nobody believed they were actual *numbers* until they became measurable and useful. Before that they were just "imaginary".

Many people said they understood imaginary numbers after they became useful. Yet, did they really understand $\sqrt{-1}$, or did they recognize its practical value, its utility? The point is that the transition from pure math to applied math is one which requires counting or measurement and real-world utility. Pure mathematics says nothing about the world. Applied mathematics does so because it uses counts or measurements. However, in neither case do mathematicians *understand* the numbers in the sense that they have concepts, abstractions, ideas, or mental representations to associate with the symbols. They merely manipulate symbols and come up with practical or theoretical results. The proof of their *understanding* is the *rote behavior* they can produce.

Imaginary numbers serve to make many points about mathematics. You may ask yourself in what way can $\sqrt{-1}$ be *imaginary*? I can imagine winning an Olympic gold in archery. I can imagine unicorns, the sound of a trumpet, or the taste of bacon. But I fail when I attempt to imagine $\sqrt{-1}$. Of course, I can imagine all sorts of symbols. I can close my eyes and visualize: **'$\sqrt{-1}$', '4', 'IXX', '00001010', '/////'**. What I cannot imagine are number concepts, abstractions, ideas, or mental representations that those symbols are supposed to stand for. Fortunately, imagining has nothing to do with the way humans manipulate mathematical symbols, and "imaginary" is certainly not an explanation or description of the symbol '$\sqrt{-1}$'. Imaginary numbers are used by mathematicians in opposition to real numbers. But 4, IV, 00000100 and $\sqrt{4}$ are no more real than $\sqrt{-1}$.

Nevertheless, '$\sqrt{-1}$' seems different from '-1', or '+1', or even '$\sqrt{1}$', less understandable somehow. We can make some sense of positive and negative numbers by relating them to their practical uses, e.g. checkbooks and Cartesian coordinates. The *real numbers* can be used to give us practical results. Well, it turned out that *imaginary numbers* could be used to give us practical results as well. Properly trained mathematicians are able to use the imaginary numbers in the same way that they use real numbers. What is the difference? There is none. '$\sqrt{-1}$' is no different than '-1' or '+1'. (Written numerals.)

All numbers are simply conventional symbols that can be manipulated by rule to provide theoretical and/or practical results. All those number symbols represent sounds; nothing more and nothing less. '-1' represents the sound "*negative one*". '$\sqrt{-1}$' represents "*the square root of negative one*" (sound it out—spoken numerals). If you can perform a math (most likely decimal), perform an algebra (most likely linear), or a geometry (most likely Euclidian) you have procedural knowledge. You have learned how to use number sounds and symbols for those sounds within the respective algorithms. Mathematicians have a skill that has taken three millennia to develop and years to teach each one of them. They have learned useful rule-bound conditioned behavior.

While discussing Wittgenstein's <u>Philosophical Investigations</u>, Norman Malcolm makes this observation about these mathematical rules:

> "But the question of whether one understands the rule cannot be divorced from the question of whether one will go on in that one particular way that we call 'right.' The correct use is a criterion of understanding. If you say that knowing the formula is a state of mind and that making this and that application of the formula is merely a *manifestation* of the knowledge, then you are in a difficulty: for you are postulating a mental apparatus that explains the manifestations, and so you ought to have (but do not have) a knowledge of the construction of the apparatus quite apart from what it does (#149). You would like to think that your understanding of the formula determines in advance the steps to be taken, that when you understood or meant the formula in a certain way 'your mind as

it were flew ahead and took all the steps before you physically arrived at this or that one' (#188). But how you meant it is not independent of how you use it... How he meant the formula determines his subsequent use of it, only in the sense that the latter is a criterion of how he meant it." Malcolm (1963: 101)

People, particularly mathematicians, like to say that using numbers and understanding mathematics results from having a peculiar state of mind or some esoteric cognitive ability. That is not the case. There is no need to postulate "a mental apparatus" or a "state of mind" to explain mathematical performance. Being a good mathematician is a result of good conditioning. Good mathematicians have learned *how* to manipulate symbols by rule. To determine whether or not someone understands a mathematical procedure, doubters must test their ability to perform; they must test their *behavior*. There is nothing, apart from the behavior, which we can refer to as *the understanding*. The only evidence for the purported understanding of the rules is the performance.[5]

When mathematicians are trained to use number symbols, they are nothing more than human computers. There is ample neurological evidence to support the fact that mathematical symbol manipulation is *rote behavior*.[6] Good mathematicians are good symbol mechanics and, as a side effect of their conditioning, mathematicians have what are referred to as intuitions about the use the number sounds and numeric symbols. Their *behavior* generates intuitions about the use of numeric symbols just as it generates intuitions about the use of word sounds, musical instruments, and tools.

Based on intuitions developed over long hours of working with their symbols, mathematicians like to tinker with them and synthesize new symbols and new procedures. Ultimately, they developed symbols such as '√-1' to be used within mathematical algorithms because they proved useful. However, as both Frege and Russell acknowledged, mathematicians need not be aware of the *content* of the symbols when they perform calculations.[7] In fact, there is no *content* to their symbols. For hundreds of years, the symbol '√-1' was simply moved about on paper in systematic ways that provided consistent results. At no time did it have content; nor does it now.

Also, as I briefly mentioned before, the procedures of mathematics are not *true* because they are not propositions. The algorithms of any mathematical system are valid or invalid, as are the procedures of logic. They are valid or invalid depending on whether or not you have followed the rules. 6 x 6 = 36 is not *true* because you are not making a claim. 6 x 6 = 36 is no truer than 6 x 6 = 30. One is the recordation of the multiplication procedure in a decimal system. The other is the recordation of a multiplication procedure in a duodecimal system. They are both valid, correct operations within their respective systems.

Propositions, on the other hand, are the things that we consider true or false, not mathematical algorithms or procedures. Of course, we can use numbers in propositions. We can combine the tacting use of numbers with the tacting use of other natural language words, as in: "*Kinley is 16 years old today*". That is a subject-copula-predicate proposition. It is not a mathematical procedure. I am making a precise numerical distinction and then tacting with that distinction in a proposition. That proposition can be true or false. The present point is: *truth* has unnecessarily complicated the philosophy of mathematics. I repeat: mathematical procedures are not true or false. They are valid or invalid depending on the system being used. However, mathematical symbols may be used to tact with quantitative distinctions within *propositions* which are true or false.

Nor do these symbols have any *meaning*. Decimal numbers, being symbols, are often deemed to have meanings. The symbol '3', supposedly, has a meaning, some core invariant cognitive content. That is not the case. Numbers are symbols that have uses that are operationally defined. We humans manipulate these Hindu-Arabic numbers within the algorithms of decimal arithmetic. When we know *how* to use these symbols, we know everything there is to know about them. Calculators come in many shapes and sizes, including human bodies. Doing mathematics is procedural behavior, learned by doing rigorous exercises to engrain the behavior in our muscles and brains.

Humans began their mathematical odyssey by counting with sounds. We developed number sounds that can be used to tact with distinctions we make about quantity. Those number sounds can be represented by a numeral that can be manipulated within a prescribed system, e.g. decimal notation for the most part. We can calculate with these number symbols when we utilize the correct algorithms. We can manipulate the symbols within prescribed systems to get valid results. Truth and meaning in mathematics are chimeras. The ultimate justification for these symbolic systems is their utility, and it all starts and ends with culturally transmitted *conditioned behavior*.

Unfortunately, when mathematicians try to describe what they are doing, they must use language, natural language with all the embedded mind/body distinctions, whether they are legitimate or not. The dualism in the analysis of mathematics is an artifact of Greek metaphysics and 2500 years of human speech history. The Greeks imbued mathematicians with their metaphysics and their analysis of how numbers work. Others followed suit. They are all mistaken. There is nothing mystical or supernatural about numbers or their use. Numbers are not metaphysical entities, mental entities or abstract entities; they are word sounds and symbols for those sounds: "*one, two, three ... infinity*", and '1, 2, 3, ... ∞'.

Geometries

"The axiom of Euclid's system appeared so natural and obvious that their truth seem unquestionable. In this respect, Euclid's system confirmed earlier conceptions, developed before the principles of geometry acquired the form of an ordered system. Plato, who lived a generation before Euclid, was led by the apparent self-evidence of geometrical principles to his theory of ideas; ...the axioms of geometry were regarded by him as revealed to us through the act of vision, which showed the geometrical relations as properties of ideal objects."
Reichenbach via Brody and Grandy (1971: 441)

As I have noted, there are a number of different geometries. If Euclidean geometry is true, are the other geometries false? They are all internally consistent and useful, but none of them is "self-evident". Nor are any of them true. Truth simply does not enter the equation. Declarative statements can be true or false, not geometries or mathematical systems. Yet questions about the *truth* of geometry hearken back to Euclid's plane geometry. Morris Kline explains:

"Though confidence in Euclidean geometry as the correct idealization of physical space remained unshaken from 300 BC to about 1800, one concern did occupy the mathematicians during almost all of that period. The axioms adopted by Euclid were supposed to be self-evident truths about physical space and about figures in that space. However, the parallel axiom in the form stated by Euclid was believed to be somewhat too complicated. No one really doubted its truth and yet it lacked the compelling quality of other axioms. Apparently even Euclid himself did not like his own version of the parallel axiom because he did not call upon it until he had proved all the theorems he could without it." Kline (1972: 863)

Originally, the *truth* of geometry was based on the correspondence between the Euclidean system and human perceptions of space. Most geometers thought that plane geometry revealed truths about physical space. Once the parallel axiom was questioned and alternative parallel axioms were introduced, the truth of all Euclidean geometry was called into question. Several non-Euclidean geometries demonstrated that consistency was the only mark of any legitimate branch of mathematics or geometry. *Truth* and the relation of the geometries to "physical space" were not at issue.

Theorists also debated about which geometry is *real?* Which one accurately depicts the universe? Is physical space Euclidean? All of these sorts of questions are vacuous because all geometries are self-contained axiomatic systems that, when combined with measurement, have utility. We can measure space and record those measurements with a number of systems just as we can measure temperature with a number of systems. (And as we shall see in the last chapter, the definition of "space" is problematic.) However, to ask whether plane geometry is the *true or real* geometry is like asking if Celsius is the true or real temperature. The questions should be: Does Euclidean, Reimannian or Bolyai-Lobachevskain geometry give us useful results and under what circumstances?

Unfortunately, the abuse of language leads to radically misdirected analysis in the philosophy of mathematics. In <u>The Nature of Geometry</u> Hans Reichenbach, gets caught up in the brouhaha. He introduces *Conventionalism*:

> "...introduced by Henri Poincare, according to whom geometry is a matter of convention and there is no meaning in a statement which purports to describe the geometry of the physical world." Kline (1972: 445)

Both Reichenbach and the early Poincare were misled about Euclidian geometry by the Greeks and their successors in the West because any talk about "the geometry of the physical world" dates back to the Greeks who led mathematicians to believe that geometry *described things*. As Poincare eventually concluded, all geometries are simply axiomatic systems that have uses in different arenas when combined with quantification and measurement.

The world does not have an intrinsic geometry, algebra, or number system. The ingenuity of men has produced a number of useful systems. These geometries, algebras and number systems are useful or not, depending upon the application. However, different geometries are not contending *descriptions* or *explanations* of the world. Geometries are contending systems. They describe nothing. They explain nothing. No experiment or observation can prove or disprove an algebra, a geometry or a number system. To think otherwise is to place much more importance on them than is warranted. Humans learn how to do various geometries the same way we learn to count and do arithmetic. We learn to use sounds and symbols for those sounds that can be manipulated by rule to produce useful results. We learn useful mathematical *behavior*.

Mathematical Proofs

"The construction and acceptance of the theory of divergent series is another striking example of the way in which mathematics has grown. It shows, first of all, that when a concept or technique proves to be useful even though the logic of it is confused or even nonexistent, persistent research will uncover a logical justification, which is truly an afterthought. It also demonstrates how far mathematicians have come to recognize that mathematics is man-made. The definitions of summability are not the natural notion of continually adding more and more terms, the notion which Cauchy merely rigorized; they are artificial. But they serve mathematical purposes, including even the mathematical solution of physical problems; and these are now sufficient grounds for admitting them into the domain of legitimate mathematics." Kline (1972: 1120)

Proof in mathematics, deducing theorems from other theorems, is a methodology that originated with the Greeks. It is based on deductive logic. There are canonical ways of doing things in mathematics and logic. Certain words and symbols are used in prescribed ways. The way mathematicians learn to prove their theorems is by studying how others have proved theirs, with the words and symbols of the existing canons. It is a way of life. It is learned procedural behavior. What they accept as proof is institutionalized methodology and terminology. Anything outside of these norms is considered heresy. In mathematical proofs, group thinking prevails.

This is not to say that all mathematical thinking is deductive. There is a creative process that brings forth original thinking in the field. There are many creative mathematicians who come up with conjectures. Nevertheless, they set about to *prove* their hypotheses within the canonical guidelines after coming up with the conjectures. Morris Kline reports the view of the Greeks on the matter:

"The strict deductive mathematics of Euclid and Apollonius has given rise to the impression that mathematicians create by reasoning deductively. Our review of the three hundred years of activity preceding Euclid should show that conjectures preceded proofs and that analysis preceded synthesis. In fact, the Greeks did not think much of propositions obtained by simple deduction. Results that sprung readily from a theorem the Greeks called corollaries or porisms. Such results, obtained without additional labor, were regarded by Proclus as windfalls or bonuses." Kline (1972: 99)

Conjectures in math require training in the use of mathematical terminology and symbols. Analogical or metaphorical thinking based on the intuitions created can generate novel uses. Some of these new uses are then proved deductively. However, there are some mathematical procedures that are not proven in this systematic way. Nonetheless, they prove fruitful and are accepted. Just as the Egyptians and the Babylonians accepted calculation procedures because of their utility, modern mathematicians accept procedures because of their utility. The *proof* is in the telemetry, not in deductive logic.

In fact, it has become impossible for mathematicians to understand some of the proofs they provide for their theories. A January 12, 2007 article in the Wall Street Journal reports that computers are being increasingly used to calculate proofs for mathematical theories. The writer quotes Brian Davies of Kings College in London who said: "If the goal of mathematics is understanding, computer-assisted proofs do not supply it in full measure." Later in the article, referring to a proof that could run past 10,000 pages, Davies said it: "would not be comprehensible to any single individual." The question is begged: If a proof is not comprehensible, how would anyone *know* it is a proof? Keep in mind that "*Know*" and "*proof*" are word sounds that English-speaking people use in many ways.

Mathematical Intuitionists

"None the less, metaphysical anxiety about mathematical objects like numbers seems only to increase when we reflect on the objectivity we expect of mathematical truths. Objectivity seems to require independent objects. Not only are there infinitely many primes, but also, since Euclid's proof makes no reference to living creatures, there would have been infinitely many primes even if life had never evolved. So the objects required by the truth of his theorem cannot be mental. Nor does its truth depend on the existence of this or that material thing; so it would seem that the objects required by its truth are not physical objects either. So mathematical truth seems to require the existence of objects which are neither physical nor mental but, as they are often called, abstract. This Platonism, the doctrine that there are independent abstract objects, will stick in many metaphysical craws." Hart (1996: 3)

The transition from an undifferentiated mosaic of visual sensations to the objects of perception is a well-documented phenomenon occurring in human infants. Differentiating objects from background is not an ability humans have at birth. We humans gradually develop the ability to see objects. Whatever the basis, there is a consensus that human perception changes from Hume's booming buzzing bundle of perceptions at birth to object-based perception later on. Likewise, mathematical intuitionists speculate that a similar transformation occurs in humans whereby people develop perception of "mathematical objects like numbers". This perception is a biologically based capacity of some sort not dependent upon language use or math skills. One theory among mathematicians has a human neural number-detector similar to a frog's fly detector which has been linked to neural connections.

This explanation is reminiscent of earlier intuitionist explanations:

"Thus Hugh of St. Victor held, in the twelfth century, that in addition to the *oculis carnis*, by means of which we know the physical world, and the *oculis rationis*, by means of which we know our own states of mind, there is also an *oculis contemplationis*, by means of which we know the truth of religion." Chisholm (1966: 67)

Some mathematicians have now added the *oculis numeralis* by means of which we humans know what numbers are and how to use them. They speculate that humans develop a unique perceptual tool that enables us to perceive mathematical objects in some way. This unique perception, in turn, gives us privileged intuitions about number concepts.

However, if this intuition is physiologically based, it would be evident in all humans. Clearly, untutored tribesmen have no intuitions whatsoever about numbers beyond their ability to subitize and make distinctions about magnitude by estimating that some groups are larger or smaller than others. They cannot make specific numerical distinctions beyond four or five, and they have no ability to count or perform any mathematical algorithms, not even basic addition. They intuit nothing about mathematical procedures, and, as we have seen, some make no generalizations about number as distinct from the objects (two pigs, three pigs etc.)

Nor are geometric shapes intuited by children, untutored tribesmen, or newly-sighted people. All of them take time and effort to make out the difference between squares, circles, and triangles Hart (1996: 124). Humans must learn to distinguish and categorize shapes. Without the training, humans have no intuitions about geometric figures whatsoever. However, they have the ability to develop the behavioral skills of counting and doing various maths, algebras, and geometries. Along with those skills come the intuitions about the use of number sounds, number symbols and geometric shapes. The intuitions come about because of adequate skill development; they are not a prerequisite to such training.

Intuition, whether it is linguistic or mathematical, comes with conditioning. W. W. Tait explicates:

> "...We perceive sets, for example, only when we have mastered the concept 'set', that is, have learned how to use the word 'set'. For example, it does not seem reasonable to suppose of people, before the concept of set was distinguished, that when they perceived a heap of pebbles, they also perceived a set—a different object—and simply spoke ambiguously. And, in whatever sense we may perceive numbers, it is hard to see how that can provide a foundation for the use of induction to define numerical functions, for example. The canons of proof are like canons of grammar, they are norms in our language governing the use of words like 'set', 'number', etc. What we call 'mathematical intuition', it seems to me, is not a *criterion* for correct usage. Rather, having mastered the usage, we develop feelings, schematic pictures, etc., which guide us." W. W. Tait via Hart (1996: 147)

Intuitions only come with a skill. The degree and accuracy of our intuitions is proportional to our training and skill level. Professional mathematicians have much more exacting intuitions about mathematics than laymen. Not being a mathematician, I have no intuitions whatsoever about transcendental numbers or quadratic equations. I could get them, however, by learning to manipulate transcendental numbers and quadratic equations within their respective algorithms. I could obtain intuitions by changing my behavior and, if I got those intuitions, my store of concepts, ideas, and abstractions will remain the same. It will remain the empty set.

Chapter 5

Summary & Notes

After being born into an undifferentiated miasma of sensations, we humans impose identity and structure upon the universe via our receptor organs and our brains. As a result, we humans, as well as other species, come to distinguish certain sized objects from background and recognize differences in small quantities of objects. Without any training, we learn to make the distinction between one and many (more than one). In most modern languages that basic distinction is marked in a number of ways, forcing speakers to make that distinction to speak the language effectively. In English, for instance, that difference is marked by making the singular/plural distinction, e.g. a tree vs. the trees.

Soon after we recognize objects and start making the distinction between one and many we develop the ability to subitize small sets of objects and make comparative quantitative distinctions about larger groups of objects, if the difference is large enough. No training is required. In most languages speakers are also forced to make the distinction between discrete, countable objects, such as trees, and measurable mass quantities such as snow. Their languages are marked for that distinction, e.g. many trees and much snow.

From these humble beginnings we have developed sophisticated means of making quantitative comparisons. Over the millennia we have developed number systems that use counting sounds and symbols for those sounds to provide very useful results in quantitative comparisons between discrete, countable objects. Aside from counting number sounds, humans have developed a complex series of numeric symbols that are tacted with by most English speakers with the word sound *"numbers"*. These numeric symbols represent counting sounds, whether those symbols are decimal numbers, Roman numerals, duodecimal or binary numbers. These symbols are then manipulated in rule-governed ways. There is nothing mystical or magical about that process. It is all mathematical behavior that is drilled into us with great effort.

Those of us who have undergone mathematical training know how to count and perform decimal algorithms. We have procedural skills. We gained those skills because we have been taught to perform such counting and computation procedures. What we know about numbers is their function. Just as we know nothing about the letter 'A' other than its use, we know nothing about the number '3' other than its use. When we know how to use numbers, both the sounds and the symbols, we know everything there is to know about numbers.

The use of any language is procedural behavior that results from exposure to the functional value of word sounds of others. Mathematics, on the other hand, is much more precise, rule-governed, procedural behavior acquired by learning how to count and then memorizing algorithms in which symbols are manipulated by rule. The Munduruku children learned to speak just as their parents did, without any formal training whatsoever. However, they could not count or calculate. Could the Munduruku children learn to count and tinker with decimal numbers as we do? Of course! And how many new ideas, concepts or mathematical abstractions would they need to do it? Nary a one.

Mathematicians are given to waxing philosophical at times. Ontologically oriented philosophers of mathematics who profess to contemplate the existence of numbers are under the spell of the semantic fallacies. They believe that numerals are symbols that stand for something other than the sounds *"one"*, *"two"*, *"three"*, etc. They believe that numerals must designate mathematical objects that have ontological status. These mathematical objects cannot be physical objects. They are either metaphysical objects or abstract objects. Beware! Do not allow yourself to be misled by Plato, Aristotle or Kurt Gödel. Numerals designate sounds, just as word symbols do. These sounds are used to count and talk about ways to manipulate the symbols within rule-governed algorithms that prove useful. There is no good reason to speculate about mathematical objects and the ontological status of numbers as opposed to numerals.

Nor is there any reason to believe that mathematicians have ideas, concepts or abstractions in their minds when they do mathematics. Mental entities paired with mathematical symbols such as numerals and mathematical speech about the number/numeral distinction, are impossible to square with the facts. There is no evidence for the distinction, none whatsoever. Such talk is just that, talk. That talk is generated by the same semantic fallacies that generate talk about mental entities tethered to human word use. It is bad verbal behavior which leads to totally misguided philosophical speculation and metaphysical mumbo jumbo.

Epistemologically oriented philosophers of mathematics who prefer to wonder about how we know mathematical *truths* are confused about what we do with numbers. Humans do not produce any truths with numbers. The fact that $6 \times 6 = 36$ is an idiosyncratic feature of our digitally inspired human decimal system. The fact that counting or calculating in any number system will produce consistent results should not surprise anyone. They are all tautological systems based on our ability to individuate discreet objects and quantify them by making a series of distinctive sequential sounds. We have systematized the sounds and algorithms utilizing the symbols for those sounds. Using mathematical algorithms of any kind makes no statement that could be either true or false. There are no mathematical *facts,* only valid useful algorithms in multiple systems.

---

1. When philosophers talk about certain mathematical entities, they say these entities are *abstract* because they think that such entities are not tied to the world. They can be generalized and manipulated in isolation without any practical utility. (Remember the Egyptian quote without any units of measurement.) When only number symbols are used, without any reference to specific items or measurements, the calculation procedures are rote symbol manipulation. $36 \times 36 = 1296$, though producing the correct answer seems to be a hollow accomplishment. It has no worldly consequences and is considered *abstract* as a result.

Another reason philosophers tend to say that mathematics is abstract is because the mathematical behavior we use has no spatial-temporal constraints, as does our normal speech. Decimal mathematical statements, such as $2+2 = 4$, have no locatives or tense. They are valid in all places and at all times. They have a general applicability that is not constrained by the time or the place of application, or the objects counted.

Symbolic algebraic statements have a generality even broader than arithmetic statements because they can be made without numbers. Algebraists are able to use variables or place holders which are manipulated according to formulae, e.g. $A \times A = A2$. The formulae have no practical application until mathematicians replace the variables with numbers that can be used to count and measure. The formulae are *about* nothing. Algebraists simply balance symbols in an equation. Philosophers tend to say they are more *abstract* because they are even further removed from practical application.

2. One of the modern founders of the philosophy of mathematics, Gottleb Frege, wanted to prove the truth of mathematics beginning with as few primitive concepts as possible. Those self-evident concepts would be the foundation of his arithmetic. He could then prove the validity of all of arithmetic with logic. Frege inherited his linguistic analysis and his view of numbers from Plato, Aristotle, Berkeley, Leibniz, Kant, et al. He prefaces his analysis of numbers by advising: "Never to lose sight of the distinction between concept and object." Frege (1980). The ontological divide is one premise of his analysis. There are mental things and physical things, i.e. concepts and objects.

With that in mind, let us take a look at what he wrote. He claimed that: "Number is not abstracted from things in the way that colour, weight, hardness are, nor is it a property of things in the sense that they are. But when we make a statement of number, what is that of which we assert something? ... Number is not anything physical, but nor is it anything subjective (an idea)." Frege (1980: 58)

Frege was concerned with the ontological implications of his analysis. To him, mathematical symbols and number words represent number ideas, non-physical entities. However, according to Frege, numbers were not subjective ideas. Our concepts of justice may be different, but the concept of 9 is identical for each of us. He claimed that numbers did not *exist* in physical space. Nor did they exist in human minds; He said that number ideas somehow *subsisted*.

3. Bertrand Russell claimed that: "Two equally numerous collections appear to have something in common: this something is supposed to be their cardinal number." Russell (1929: 156) If he meant that *the look* of collections is their commonality that may be true for small orderly collections. For instance: /// and ///. Yet, two jumbled up collections of random items greater than four or five do not appear to have anything other than many in common. So, to say that: "*equally numerous collections have cardinal number in common*" is not very enlightening. The present point is that to determine whether groups or sets greater than four or five have a *cardinal number* in common, we must count the group using a sequential series of sounds. We cannot readily and visually detect the sameness or commonality. We must use counting sounds to determine that they have a cardinal number in common.

4. Could we change the system and use 0 as a counting number? Sure! We could count: "zero", "one", "two", "three"... "nine". (Use your fingers, the original digits) Count them. You have nine fingers. But then we would have to designate another placeholder in our new positional notation that starts with the counting number 0. The symbol '0' could no longer be used as a vacant sign in a positional notation. We could use 'X' as a placeholder, the lack of a number, the vacant sign. In our new decimal system *'8X' would be equivalent to '90' in our current decimal system*. Alternatively, we could count: "zero", "one"... "eight", "nine", "ta" (V), "za" (∩), with 'X' as a placeholder in our new *duodecimal system*. '8X∩' would be equivalent to '9012' in our current decimal notation.

5. I am fully aware of the difficulties presented by using the words "understand" and "understanding" which are unequivocally part of the 10,000 plus English *mental* lexicon and discussed in chapter three. Nevertheless, I must use the language in which I grew up.

6. Stanislas Dehaene reports extensively on the connections between neurology and mathematical skills in <u>The Number Sense</u>. Specific mathematical behavior is affected by damage to specific areas of the brain.

7. Pernicious metaphysical musing pervades the philosophy of mathematics to this day. Yet, it is difficult to reconcile with our behavior. Even Frege recognized that: "... it is possible for a mathematician to perform quite lengthy calculations without understanding by his symbols anything intuitable, or with which we could be sensibly acquainted. And that does not mean that the symbols have no sense; we still distinguish between the symbols themselves and their content, even though it may be that the content can only be grasped by their aid." Frege (1980: 22). While he recognizes that the calculations of mathematicians are merely manipulation of symbols, he maintains that the symbols have "content". Yet he would agree that we need not be aware of this "content" when we manipulate those symbols within the algorithms of math. Just as Bertrand Russell acknowledged that we need not spend time thinking about what the symbols stand for in mathematical logic, nor do we need to think about what the mathematical symbols stand for when we do arithmetic. "This does not mean, of course, that as a tool in the handbag of thought, mathematical logic has no value, though both Russell and Whitehead have both insisted that its utility here is as a means of *not* thinking, of making manipulation of symbols a substitute for the work of thinking; so little is it necessary for the worker in this field to think of what his symbols refer to that Russell has suggested that a half-minute or so in six months would be enough." Blanshard (1962: 155)

CHAPTER VI

EPISTEMOLOGY

Introduction

We humans have claimed to *know* many things about ourselves and our world. This *knowledge* has been at the forefront of human progress. Knowledge has helped us succeed and prosper as a species. The human quest for knowledge has led us out of the caves and into the cosmos. At the same time, we humans have sacrificed, suffered and died because of various claims to knowledge. Armies have been mustered and battles have been fought because people claimed to know many things. Knowledge has been a double-edged sword. Consequently, questions about what can be considered indisputably true knowledge have plagued mankind for millennia.

Philosophical questions about knowledge abound. What is the nature of knowledge? How can we distinguish knowledge from speculation, fact from fiction? On what grounds can someone make a legitimate claim to knowledge? Is knowledge a peculiar state of awareness or cognition? Is knowledge a matter of having a true belief? How do people distinguish knowledge from belief? Did our ancestors know that the earth was the center of the Universe? Can someone know something, and yet not be able to state or demonstrate that knowledge? Such questions have confronted philosophers since antiquity. Philosophers have asked these, and many more questions within the philosophical field of *epistemology*, the study of knowledge.

Historical Context

> "The central task of epistemology is to provide a generalized critique of the grounds on which claims to knowledge are supported, by constructing a systematic account of the principles by which the truth of statements may be properly assessed, as well as of the rational of these principles." Nagel & Brandt (1965: xi)

At the outset, I should make clear a distinction that philosophers within the field of epistemology have historically made about knowledge, i.e. the difference between knowing *how* and knowing *that*. It is the difference between *procedural knowledge* and *declarative knowledge*. Procedural knowledge is not true or false. It is the knowledge of how to do something. It is having a skill, knowing a procedure. We must remember a procedure so that when we attempt to hit a tennis ball or a play a tune on a piano, we must produce the correct behavior. To say: "*i Know how*" is to say "*i Know the procedure*" or "*i can re-enact the proper behavior*". If people want to teach you the procedure, they must show you how to do it. Performers may not be able to explain or describe how they perform a procedure; they simply *know how* to do it. They must demonstrate their knowledge if pressed. They must show a doubter that they know how to play tennis or how to play the piano. The knowing is in the doing.

Moreover, many creatures can be taught *how* to do things, i.e. procedural knowledge. Humans can teach bears how to dance or parrots how to talk, for instance. Additionally, many creatures know how to do things from birth. Wildebeest calves, for example, begin running almost immediately upon birth. Human babies know how to suckle at birth. Many creatures know how to do things instinctively and need no training to perform such procedural knowledge. Theorists conclude that such procedural knowledge, or *know how* can often be genetically encoded and transmitted.

Most analytic philosophers agree that *declarative knowledge* is different from such procedural knowledge. Declarative knowledge is uniquely human because it relies on language for its expression. It is knowledge expressed with declarative statements. The fact *that* water is H_2O and *that* all bachelors are unmarried males can be declared by making the statements: "*i Know that water is H₂O*" or "*i Know that all bachelors are unmarried males*". Many logicians believed that the primary purpose of language was to assert such facts, i.e. transmit knowledge. This knowledge is not a skill or a procedure that needs to be demonstrated to doubters to prove that one has such knowledge. It is true or false and requires confirming evidence to prove its truth. It cannot be genetically encoded or transmitted. People must learn from others *that* water is H_2O and *that* all bachelors are unmarried males. They must also be able to utilize speech behavior to do so.

This knowledge is also referred to as knowledge *about* things. A chemist would know many things *about* chemical compounds and reactions. In addition to knowing the chemical composition of water she would know *that* the chemical composition of salt is NaCl and be able to declare it. Such declarative knowledge or knowledge about things has been the subject matter of analytic epistemology for centuries.

Many philosophers have argued that such declarative knowledge exists in human minds in the form of *psychological propositions*. These propositions are *the thoughts* expressed with declarative assertions. For example, someone could say "*water is h2o*" or "*agua es h2o*". Either statement is said to represent or express a language-neutral thought or a psychological proposition in the mind of the speaker. Ultimately, anything that could properly be called declarative knowledge, as opposed to procedural knowledge, could be reduced to these psychological entities, i.e. *propositions*. These mental entities were said to be translational constants and truth bearers that remained stable or consistent regardless of which language people used to express them or when they are expressed.

Other philosophers have concluded that the statements uttered by a speaker do not represent a *psychological proposition* in the mind or consciousness of the speaker. They represent abstract propositions. These *abstract propositions* are not psychological or mental entities which could vary from speaker to speaker; rather they are the semantically encoded literal meanings, the "*de dicto* readings" of declarative statements that do not rely on processes or entities in the mind of the speaker for their interpretation. They are *what the words say regardless of who the speaker is, which language they speak, and whether proposition is in the active or passive form.*

Moreover, these independent *abstract propositions* encoded in the words are the entities to be judged true or false, not the utterance of the proposition at any given time by any individual speaker. By this account, there is a speaker-neutral, time-stable, independent fact of the matter encoded in the word symbols "*water is h2o*"; a fact of the matter that is indifferent to the utterance "*water is h2o*" by any individual speaker. It is the proposition encoded in the symbols of the statement whether those symbols are uttered or written. According to many analytic philosophers, all such true declarative statements that represent true propositions of either kind constitute the totality of declarative knowledge as opposed to procedural knowledge. As a result of such theorizing, logicians and analytic philosophers began the search for *truth-stable propositions* that could provide a firm foundation for human knowledge, knowledge that could not be disputed. Moreover, if philosophers were going to discover the *nature of knowledge*, they needed to find the *nature of truth* and how to distinguish universally true propositions from mere beliefs or conjecture.

In their search for undeniably true declarative knowledge, analytic philosophers and logicians recognized different types of propositional statements, the basic atomic units which made up all of declarative knowledge. These propositional statements could be categorized and organized in such a way as to be less confusing. This process would also facilitate the development of general methodologies for determining the truth of these statements based on the categories. In that way, all human declarative knowledge could be grounded in true propositional statements based on accepted standards of truth for the various forms of such statements.

One critical division in epistemological analysis of these basic atomic units appeared early on in *analytic* philosophy. Some declarative propositional statements appeared to be true based on an *analysis* of their constituent terms. For example: "*all bachelors are unmarried males*". If someone says that all bachelors are unmarried males, we need not do a survey of bachelors to determine if the statement is true. If someone is a bachelor, he is an unmarried male by definition.

If someone claimed that he was a married bachelor he would be contradicting himself. The fact that all bachelors are unmarried males seems to be true by virtue of the meanings of the words. It is therefore an *analytic proposition*.

In the tradition of John Locke, David Hume concluded that:

> "Propositions of this kind are discoverable by mere operation of thought, without dependence on what is anywhere existent in the universe." David Hume, "An Enquiry Concerning Human Understanding" (1748)

Furthermore, these analytic propositions are not contingent upon the world being arranged a certain way. If the ideas, concepts or meanings of the words are analyzed correctly, the truth of *analytic propositions* can be ascertained without regard for any observation or evidence. Although Hume did not utilize the *analytic/synthetic* terminology in his dichotomy, he led the movement in that direction.

Conversely, *synthetic propositions* were considered to be empirical matters of fact. Philosophers could not determine the truth of a synthetic proposition by analyzing the terms. Their truth could not be determined by "mere operation of thought". The truth of synthetic propositions was dependent upon the world being arranged a particular way. For example, to determine the truth of the proposition "*all swans are white*" would require a survey of swans. Unlike analytic propositions, observation or evidence can help confirm or refute synthetic propositions. The sighting of one black swan, for example, would disprove the claim that "*all swans are white*". Moreover, contrary to analytic propositions, the negation of a synthetic proposition is not self contradictory: "*no swans are white*". Whereas "*no bachelors are unmarried males*" is self contradictory.

Immanuel Kant was exceptionally influential in philosophy. During the 18th century he introduced "analytic/synthetic" terminology and explained the dichotomy in terms of the "explicative" or "expansive" content of what he called "judgments":

> "***On the Distinction between Analytical and Synthetical Judgments in General.***
> – The peculiarity of its sources demands that metaphysical knowledge must consist of nothing but *a priori* judgments. But whatever their origin or their logical form, there is a distinction in judgments, as to their content, according to which they are either merely ***explicative***, adding nothing to the content of knowledge, or ***expansive***, increasing the given knowledge. The former may be called ***analytical***, the latter ***synthetical***, judgments.
>
> "Analytical judgments express nothing in the predicate but what has been already actually thought in the concept of the subject, though not so distinctly or with the same (full) consciousness. When I say: 'All bodies are extended,' I have not amplified in the least my concept of body, but have only analyzed it, as extension was really thought to belong to that concept before the judgment was made, though it was not expressed. This judgment is therefore analytical. On the contrary, this judgment, 'All bodies have weight,' contains in its predicate something not actually thought in the universal concept of body; it amplifies my knowledge by adding something to my concept, and must therefore be called synthetical." Kant (1783: 14)

With the blessing of Kant et al., one epistemological demarcation had been drawn for future analytic philosophers and logicians. *Synthetical judgments* were those which added something to our store of knowledge. For example, "*all swans are white*", if true, expands our knowledge. "*all bachelors are unmarried males*", on the contrary, does not expand our knowledge. According to Kant, it merely explicates what is obvious to anyone who fully understands the terms "*bachelor*", "*unmarried*" and "*male*". It is true by virtue of the ideas, concepts, or meanings of the terms and adds nothing to what we already know. It is merely explicative. It is an *analytical judgment*.

Philosophers also tried to account for other phenomena by further dividing declarative propositions into *a priori* and *a posteriori*. That fault line was inspired by a distinction made between what humans learned from experience and what we could know independently of experience in the world. Many philosophers claimed that some things are known by humans prior to birth. They were innate ideas. Some of these philosophers had postulated a pre-existence for human souls during which time we humans acquire this *a priori* knowledge. In the <u>Meno</u> for example, Socrates had coaxed the Pythagorean theory from a slave boy untutored in geometry. According to Socrates, that knowledge was in him *prior* to his birth. It was *a priori knowledge* known independently of any experience in the world.

Furthermore, it was only such *a priori* knowledge that was necessarily true because it was not learned via the senses. It was not contingent upon the world being arranged a certain way; no empirical evidence could disprove it. *A priori* knowledge could not be otherwise. It could not be doubted. One such a priori declarative knowledge claim, it is said, is the statement: "*every event has a cause*". It is *a priori* knowledge, necessarily true and known independently of any experience.

Conversely, *a posteriori* knowledge is derived from experience. The ultimate source of *a posteriori* propositional claims, such as "*all swans are white*", are human interactions with the world. People come to know these facts by observation or evidence. Future observation or evidence provided by the senses can disprove these a posteriori claims as was the case when black swans were discovered in Australia. There could also be other worlds where things are different, e.g. a planet where all swans are speckled. Consequently, such *a posteriori* claims are not held to be *necessarily* true, as are a priori claims. They are *contingent*, contingent upon certain states of affairs in the Universe. That being the case, philosophers could not be as confident about the truth of a posteriori propositions as they could about *a priori* propositions.

A posteriori knowledge was also suspect because it was based on evidence provided by notoriously limited and unreliable human senses. For instance, the fact that germs spread disease was unknown for most of human history because humans could not observe germs. Furthermore, everyone knows that our senses deceive us at times. People are subject to hallucinations, phantom leg pain, optical illusions and other faulty perceptions. All of these phenomena provided more reasons to be less confident about a posteriori knowledge claims, because they are based on limited and unreliable human sense perception and are not *necessarily* true. They just happen to be true as far as we know at this time.

Many *a posteriori* knowledge claims are also inductive generalizations. For example, the claim that the sun will come up in the east tomorrow is based on our experience. It is a posteriori knowledge, derived from experience and based on inductive reasoning. It is *probable* that the sun will come up in the east tomorrow based all previous experience, but it is not certain or logically necessary. We can imagine the earth reversing its rotation and the sun coming up in the west tomorrow. That is not logically impossible or inconceivable, just highly unlikely given our current knowledge of astronomy and physics. In consequence, some philosophers are inclined to say that such inductive *a posteriori* claims are merely well-founded *beliefs* based on our previous experience, not certain knowledge.

You might think that the *a priori/a posteriori* distinction is just another version of the analytic/synthetic distinction because neither a priori propositions nor analytic propositions can be confirmed or refuted by evidence. Conversely, *a posteriori* propositions, like synthetic propositions, can be confirmed or refuted by further evidence or observation. They are both contingent and depend upon the arrangement of things in the world for determining their truth value. However, the *a posteriori/a priori* distinction is an etiological distinction, a distinction about the cause or source of our knowledge, how we come to know such things, i.e. through experience or independently of experience.

The *analytic/synthetic* distinction *was not* an etiological one. This distinction concerned the nature of knowledge claims and their method of verification. Declarative *analytic* statements could be verified by analysis of the constituent terms, by "mere operation of thought". However, to verify declarative *synthetic* statements one had to appeal to something other than the constituent terms. The veracity of synthetic propositional statements could only be confirmed or refuted by observation or evidence. How we come to know such things is not at issue in the analytic/synthetic dichotomy.

A further divide in epistemology was opened by the *rationalists* and the *empiricists*. The rationalists claimed that the means of producing certain knowledge was *reason*. Only reasoning could determine the undeniable truth of propositions, not evidence of any kind. For instance, humans claimed to know that the earth was the center of the universe for most of recorded history. That claim to knowledge was based on human experience, evidence provided by the senses. Yet, that "knowledge" turned out to be false. We could just as well be wrong about many of our current claims to knowledge. Consequently the rationalists argued that the only way to determine the indubitable truth of any proposition is by reasoning from true first principles or other incontrovertible truths. We must start with what we know for certain, then, by means of *rational* argument, reason to a certain conclusions. As the Greeks had shown, this was the case with all indisputable mathematical and geometric knowledge. The rationalists said these disciplines provided the models for all legitimate claims to rational knowledge.

Empiricists, on the other hand, claimed that all knowledge came from experience. According to them, we had to observe things in order to make any claims to knowledge. Our knowledge of the world came to us through our senses. Prior to experience in the world, human minds are blank slates, *tabula rasa*. The ultimate grounding for our knowledge must be observation according to the empiricists. We had to make observations of nature and draw conclusions based on the evidence of our senses. The empiricists said human experience was the basis for any legitimate claims to knowledge no matter how tenuous that experiential knowledge might be.

Our old friend Emmanuel Kant claimed that rationalists and the empiricists were both wrong. He conjoined these two competing theories of knowledge. In the <u>Critique of Pure Reason</u> (1781) he attempted to synthesize rationalism with empiricism. He claimed that all legitimate claims to knowledge were derived from experience combined with reason. According to Kant, declarative "judgments" were a synthesis of the evidence provided by experience and the reasoning ability of the human mind.

At any rate, the epistemological debate within the Western analytic tradition of philosophy had been circumscribed. Elemental, true atomic propositions constituted all of our declarative knowledge. It was up to philosophers to describe the origins of such knowledge, the nature of such knowledge and the means for determining the truth of such knowledge claims. Debates about the categorization of declarative propositional knowledge kept philosophers busy for centuries. Philosophers wanted to know if various declarative knowledge claims were analytic, synthetic, a priori, a posteriori, certain, necessary, contingent and so forth.

Over the years, this categorization of declarative propositional statements engendered novel combinations to explain the nature and source of various problematic statements. Kant, for example, came up with "synthetic *a priori* knowledge" to explain the truth of the statement: *"every event has a cause"*. He claimed that this statement is necessarily true, but *not analytic* because the concept of cause is not contained in the concept of event. This claim is not just "explicative"; it is "expansive". Thus it must be *synthetic*. Yet every human knows this with certainty, he claimed. It must be *a priori* knowledge, something necessarily true, but not *analytic*. It is knowledge expressed in a *synthetic a priori* "judgment".

Centuries later, Saul Kripke came up with necessary *a posteriori* to buttress his theory of "rigid designators" and "natural kinds" (<u>Naming and Necessity</u> via Ludlow: 609). This necessary a posteriori propositional knowledge is gained by means of observation or evidence, and it is necessarily true in all possible worlds. He claimed that the assertion *"water is h2o"*, for instance, is something humans have learned through experience and yet it cannot be doubted. Hence, this propositional knowledge *is a posteriori and necessarily true.*

In all cases, according to these philosophers, we humans had the ability to know things that other creatures could not know because we had words to represent or encode the propositions. *True propositions*, either the thoughts we expressed or the speaker-neutral, semantically encoded abstract type, constituted the totality of knowledge we passed from person to person and generation to generation via language, any language, in both the oral and the written form. These declarative statements that represented or encoded these propositions could be examined and parsed by various means to determine their truth.

Truth by that time had become a contentious matter in analytic epistemology because declarative propositional statements included both *beliefs and knowledge.* Most people would agree that for us to *know* anything, it has to be true. If someone claims to *know* something that turns out to be false, we conclude that he or she, in fact, did not know it. Knowledge, as opposed to mere belief, had to consist of propositional statements that were *true* with certainty for all people, at all times, in all places.

In the pursuit of such indubitable propositional statements philosophers and logicians began the search for *eternal sentences*. Eternal sentences were those that, supposedly, had no temporal or contextual dependence. These sentences had to be true regardless of who uttered them or when they were uttered. They were eternally true in all possible worlds. No one could contest the truth of *"water is h2o"*, for example. That statement is true regardless of who states it or when and where they state it. It is considered to be an *eternal sentence*, true now and forever.

This entire philosophical enterprise was directed toward melding empiricism with logic to yield a coherent system of scientific facts expressed with words that was impervious to criticism.

Eternal sentences would comprise a body of knowledge that was indisputable. The philosophical foundations of science were at stake. Willard Quine explained:

> "The primary distinction of eternal sentences is that they are the repository of truth itself, and so of all science. Insofar as a sentence can be said to be true, and not just true now or in this mouth, it is an eternal sentence." Quine (1960: 227)

Eternal sentences such as "*water is h2o*" were indisputable facts which held true for eternity. The fact that their truth extended into the everlasting future enabled scientists to make predictions about chemical reactions and a multitude of other scientific claims. All of science was to be composed of such indisputable eternal sentences, scientific facts that were *true* for all people at all times.

The epistemological trail had taken philosophers to truth's doorstep. Philosophers needed to determine the *nature of truth*. They wanted to explore the *concept of truth*. They wanted to know the *meaning* of the word sound "*truth*". Theories for truth were proffered. Bertrand Russell, for instance, contributed the *correspondence theory of truth* whereby true propositions required correspondence with things outside of the believer's mind:

> "Thus a belief is true when there is a corresponding fact, and is false when there is no corresponding fact.
> "It will be seen that minds do not create truth or falsehood. They create beliefs, but when once the beliefs are created, the mind cannot make them true or false, except in the special case where they concern future things which are within the power of the person believing, such as catching trains. What makes a belief true is a fact, and this fact does not (except in exceptional cases) in any way involve the mind of the person who has the belief." Russell (1912: 90)

For Russell at this time, as well as the early Wittgenstein, the world was comprised of *facts*. Both Russell and Wittgenstein needed these independent facts to fill out their logical theories. Within most analytic philosophy, it was argued that declarative knowledge and facts were not dependent upon people who may have such knowledge and facts.

One argument, for example, asserts that the knowledge that the earth revolves around the sun was true even before anybody knew that fact, and, after a future plague wipes out the human population on earth, it will still be a fact that the earth revolves around the sun. It remains a fact about our solar system regardless of the existence of any humans who can state and record such facts. "A fact" used in this way is often synonymous with "a state-of-affairs in the world". The truth of certain propositions, according to Russell and the early Wittgenstein was dependent upon their *correspondence* with such facts (states-of-affairs). Of course, the *nature of facts*, the *concept of fact* and *the meaning of "fact"* then became contentious issues in analytic philosophy and theory of logic.

Regardless of what and where facts were, for Russell, facts had to correspond to the proposition. If a proposition did not correspond to the fact, it could not be true. The nature of truth, the concept of truth and the meaning of "*truth*" had been established for Russell. However, Russell's correspondence theory of truth could not meet the objections of its critics. For instance, how do we know that $2 + 2 = 4$, or that all bachelors are unmarried males? These propositions need not *correspond* to anything existing independently in the world. We can ascertain the truth of these propositions by "mere operation of thought". Problems also arose with interpretations of "correspondence". What does it mean for one thing to *correspond* to another thing?

An alternative *coherence theory of truth* suggested that as long as propositions were consistent with accepted knowledge, they were true. This was more in line with the rationalists' thinking. If propositions do not conflict with established facts, they are true by virtue of their consistency with those other facts. This theory is sometimes referred to as "epistemological holism". A. C. Ewing's objection to the coherence theory, one among many, was that coherence is a matter of degree. Hence, propositions could be more or less true. However, for most theorists this would not do. Truth, in keeping with Aristotle's logic, was not a matter of degree. Propositions were either true or false. The middle ground was excluded. The facts that composed the edifice of knowledge could not be somewhat true or sometimes true. They had to be entirely true for everyone at any time to be considered indisputable facts.

A third *performatory theory of truth* was offered by P. F. Strawson and J. L. Austin. These analytic philosophers wanted to focus on language and how we use the word sound "*truth*". It was the job of philosophers to determine the meaning of "*truth*" through linguistic analysis, i.e. by observing human verbal performances with that word. How was that word used by competent English speakers? That trend is still apparent today as philosophers continue to argue about the *nature* of truth, the *concept* of truth and the *meaning* of "*truth*" in various discourse settings. It was part of a trend toward philosophical analysis of human speech behavior in context that continues today.

More theories for *truth* were put forth by numerous philosophers. The criteria for the truth of propositions were variously: correspondence, coherence, convention, performatory, intuition, pragmatism, self-evidence, authority et al. Was *truth* a property of sentences or was it a property of the psychological proposition represented by the sentence? Or was *truth* a property of a speaker neutral independent fact encoded by the literal meaning of a sentence? What is the meaning of *truth*? How can *truth* be defined? How could philosophers analyze the *concept of truth*? The questions and contradictions were abundant. Yet, philosophers needed to agree on truth before they could agree on what constituted *knowledge*. The nature of *truth* remained a mystery, and as a result, so did the nature of knowledge.

The search for incontrovertible truth also led to formal logic and truth tables. Aristotelian logic needed refinement. According to the bivalent logic of Aristotle, propositions were either true or false. Aristotle adopted his logic from Plato. It was all or nothing. The middle ground was excluded. As Peter Hylton points out:

> "By contrast with the idealist talk of degrees of truth or reality, Platonic Atomism adopts a straightforward and absolute attitude towards these notions: either a proposition is true or it is false. The idea that it might have some intermediate status, that it might be true for certain purposes but not for others, that it might be true from one point of view or stage of thought but false from others – these ideas with which Moore and Russell have, after their rejection of Idealism, no sympathy whatsoever." Hylton (1990: 112)

Many analytic philosophers were logicians, schooled in the bivalent logic of Aristotle. Propositions were either true or false. Yet dreamy idealist philosophers insisted that not all propositions were true or false. Some were partially or somewhat true, and certainly, they said, some propositions were *meaningful* even if their truth or falsehood could not be determined.

Leading logicians and analytic philosophers would have no part of that thinking. The rejection of meaningful indeterminate propositions was part of the ongoing refutation of idealism started by Kant and continued by G.E. Moore and Bertrand Russell. Russell and the later *logical positivists* recognized three categories of statements: true, false and substantively meaningless. Russell (1940: 216) Substantive, meaningful propositional statements had to be either true or false. Absolute truth as the standard for knowledge had to be maintained. How could we claim to know anything that is sorta, kinda, rather true? A fuzzy relative truth could not be countenanced. The positivists maintained that statements which were neither positively true nor false were cognitively insignificant, nonsense to their way of thinking.

Moreover, some positivists said *the truth* of any meaningful statement had to be *verifiable*. Anything less was to be considered either false or nonsense. When people make assertions *to know* that such and such is the case, they may be challenged. These claims to declarative knowledge must be verifiable, if they are to qualify as true knowledge, not mere beliefs or substantively meaningless, uninformative speculation. Empirical claims are true based on the data, *verifiable* data. Alternative versions of the *verification criterion* were also proposed: the *testability criterion* for example, or Karl Popper's *falsifiability criterion*. The positivists said that in all cases, true declarative claims to knowledge had, somehow, to be subject to *verification, testability* or *falsifiability*.

Of course, positivists were hoisted by their own petards because any of the criteria they proposed as criteria for substantive meaningful statements did not meet those very criteria. It is impossible to verify, test or falsify the claim that all substantively meaningful propositions must be verifiable, testable or falsifiable. Moreover, it is quite clear that most general scientific claims fail to meet the verification, testability or falsification claim criteria. For instance, how could scientists verify, test or falsify the claim that *all whales are mammals*? That statement is nothing more than inductive conjecture based on the evidence so far. There may be non-mammalian whales lurking in the deep somewhere. And if it is true by definition, it is trivial.

Analytic philosophers also concluded that if they were to be clear about their knowledge, they needed precise forms of deduction and inference. A logical calculus was needed, one with explicit procedures and symbolic in form. This would formalize the syllogisms of Aristotle which had provided the backbone of reasoned argument for the preceding two millennia. Consequently, formal symbolic logics were developed to provide the laws of reasoning. These notational systems were language-neutral, rule- bound procedures. Logical notations were utilized to show the form of sound reasoning. Logics provided the means of reasoning from first principles or basic verified empirical propositions to valid conclusions that would extend human knowledge, indisputable verifiable knowledge.

As we have seen, the quest for knowledge and truth had led analytic philosophers up the epistemological path to declarative propositional statements which represented psychological propositions in the minds of speakers or speaker-neutral independent facts encoded in the word symbols. These elemental units of knowledge, these bearers of truth, had become the focus of philosophical speculation. What was the nature of these propositions and facts? How could they be analyzed? What constituted a fact? What was the difference between facts and mere speculation? How could logicians determine the truth of any proposition?

Well, it would seem that if one is to determine the *truth* of declarative propositional statements, one must know the *meanings* of the words in that statement. Analytic philosophers said that if a speaker knows the meaning of "*bachelor*" and "*unmarried male*", the meaning and truth of "*all bachelors are unmarried males*" becomes obvious. Clarifying the meanings of "*bachelor*", "*unmarried*" and "*male*" would be the necessary first step. As a result, meaning took center stage in analytic philosophy. Meanings became the subjects of heated debate. How could philosophers determine the meanings of words? What did the word "*meaning*" mean? They needed to explore the concept of meaning.

Of course, core invariant *word meanings* were critical to epistemologists' goals. Variability in *word meanings* would result in variability in truth values in propositional statements made with them. The truth of a statement could not depend on what was going on in the speaker's head, e.g. idiolectic speaker meanings. For the truth value of a statement to be stable from speaker to speaker every time it was spoken, the meanings of the words had to be stable and consistent. It was the fixed lexical or *literal meanings* encoded in the symbols that would yield a stable truth. These stable consistent abstract meanings carried by the symbols would provide the indisputable knowledge regardless of any mental machinations by the speakers who uttered them.

The traditional semantic view, of course, held that declarative statements represented, designated or encoded a speaker-neutral literal/lexical meaning, the semantic content of the statement that was stable across all users and all incidents of use. If the stable semantic content encoded by the word symbols was precisely determined, the truth of many propositions could be determined through analysis of those universal fixed literal/lexical meanings. Many philosophers hypothesized that these stable meanings designated by the word symbols must be analyzed if they were to determine stable truth values for declarative propositional statements. They wrote tomes about the meanings of the word sounds: "*mind*", "*knowledge*", "*truth*", "*facts*", "*certainty*" and "*necessity*".

For others, the investigation of the meanings of declarative propositional statements was reduced to *conceptual* inquiry. Philosophers needed to clarify the concepts that composed the psychological proposition. The concepts of "truth", "fact", "meaning", and "concept" itself had to be clarified. Detailed analysis of words symbols and their associated concepts dominated analytic philosophy for decades. Philosophers, logicians and linguists became embroiled in debates about the concepts designated by, encoded in, or represented by words. They wrote more tomes about the *concepts* of "mind", "knowledge", "truth", "facts", "certainty" and "necessity".

The debates about the nature of knowledge, how we humans can know anything, what constitutes knowledge, what knowledge is certain, necessary, contingent, *a priori, a posteriori* and so forth, befuddled philosophers for centuries. These debates then produced terminological debates and criticisms of various philosophical positions based on criticisms of the language used in stating those positions. Yet, the most critical assumption about language, the semantic paradigm, was rarely questioned.

The semantic paradigm of representational human speech behavior and its reliance upon concepts, ideas and propositions in the minds of speakers along with universal stable lexical or literal meanings and referents encoded in the symbols, remain with us today. The search for indisputable criteria by which all of humanity could agree on what we accept as a warranted claim to knowledge has no end in sight. The *concepts* of "knowledge", "truth", "fact", "certainty" and "necessity" have yet to be clarified. The *meanings* of "*knowledge*", "*truth*", "*fact*", "*certainty*" and *"necessity"* are proving to be as elusive as the meanings of *"beauty"* and *"goodness"*. Philosophers, in spite of all the analysis, are more confused than ever about the nature of knowledge, truth and meaning.

These confusions will not end if the analysis continues under the semantic paradigm. All of these conundrums are a result of a mistaken assumption that spoken words are symbols that stand for, represent, denote, refer to, or designate something else. If philosophers would accept the fact that humans employ acoustic devices that have functional values when utilized in context by speakers conditioned through (S-R-R), the conundrums would disappear. Historically, the analysis of propositions and the nature of knowledge, truth and meaning broke down because of the failure of philosophers to properly recognize what we humans do with sounds. They all fell victim to the semantic fallacies.

A Non-semantic Proposal

Most declarative propositional knowledge claims are currently considered to be a unique form of knowledge because the claims are said to be composed of symbols that encode stable semantic content, i.e. lexical or literal meanings. This premise that the word symbols encode unchanging speaker-neutral, time and context-indifferent meanings and referents is a matter of epistemological dogma in analytic philosophy. Hence, the knowledge and facts encoded by those word symbols, in the form of declarative propositional statements, also become speaker-neutral and constant through time and context. It is an error in reasoning that has resulted in untold confusion and controversy.

Of course, preliterate humans claimed to know that something was the case by stating it. They stated their knowledge with word sounds in the form of declarative speech acts. They behaved with functional acoustic devices in predictable conditioned ways utilizing the languages they grew up in. The oral tradition of passing down such declarative knowledge from one generation to the next is still prevalent in some cultures. However, in most modern cultures, people have come to record such speech declarations and pass them down via the written word, thus enabling philosophers to give knowledge and facts an independent status, independent of the humans who state such knowledge and facts.

However, this argument should be thoroughly discredited because, even if the source of a written knowledge or fact claim cannot be determined or if it is universally accepted as true, such a claim still had its origin in someone's idiolectic speech behavior. As such, the claim is not stable across speaker boundaries, changing contexts or occasions of use. It does not stand for, represent, signify, designate, denote, refer to or encode independent speaker-neutral semantic content. It is a form of verbal behavior that takes place in context with myriad presuppositions and unavoidable idiosyncrasies. Additionally, based on the analysis of human verbal behavior in Chapter Two, we have seen that the word sound *"Knowledge"* is not the name of something. The word sounds *"Know"*, *"Knowledge"* and *"fact"* do not represent ideas, concepts or thoughts. Nor do they have speaker neutral meanings; they have no lexical meanings, literal meanings or semantic content. They are not signs, symbols or semantic designators. They are functional behavior that is completely context dependent and variably inculcated in speakers by means S-R-R conditioning.

As we humans learn *how* to speak we learn to *how* to utilize sounds. These phonetic units then become the devices we humans use to speech-think. Ultimately we can do our speech-thinking sub-vocally if we so desire. In fact, when we humans produce declarative claims to knowledge, silently or aloud, we are combining the idiosyncratic functional value of word sounds within an incredibly complex background of culturally specific presuppositions and contemporaneous encyclopedic knowledge. These sounds are used in individualized ways based on the conditioning of the speaker or writer *precluding the possibility of stable speaker-neutral independent knowledge and facts.* The present point is that knowing *how to use* these acoustic devices is the *sine qua non* for making claims to knowledge and thinking about our knowledge. All of that speaking and thinking is unavoidably idiosyncratic.

So, if we take a closer look at how we English-speaking humans use these acoustic devices in making declarative claims to knowledge it may prove to be helpful in finding out what humans *know*. Our investigation will ultimately take us to the propositional form of verbal behavior, the atomic units of epistemological claims in analytic philosophy. However, we must constantly remind ourselves that the word sounds that humans use to produce declarative propositional knowledge claims have no encoded semantic content, semantic correlates or semantic features; they have no literal meanings, lexical meanings or meanings of any kind. They are functional verbal behavior that can be represented by a variety of written symbols. If you are willing to acknowledge that these sounds are acoustic devices used in various ways, not symbols, signs or semantic designators with stable speaker-neutral independent meanings, you will have taken the necessary first step in your epistemological recovery program.

The Uses of the Words
"Know" and *"Knowledge"*

"In general, where present sensible facts are concerned at any rate, there is some sense in which we can know them without using words. We may notice that we are hot or cold, or that there is thunder or lightning and if we proceed to state in words what we have noticed, we merely register what we already know. I am not maintaining that this pre-verbal stage always exists, unless we mean by 'knowing' an experience, no more than that we have the experience; but I do maintain that such pre-verbal knowledge is very common." Russell (1940: 58)

Of course there are many uses for the word sounds *"know"* and *"knowledge"*. One such use recognizes a *pre-verbal* awareness that Bertrand Russell describes in the above epigraph. We humans can certainly say that we *know* when we are cold even though we may not declare it at that time. Indeed, this is a very common use of the word sound *"know"*. Both humans and non-human animals are said to have this extra-verbal knowledge that they do not express. Animals of most species, including humans, are constantly reorienting themselves in time and space based on this knowledge of their surroundings.[1]

We English speakers also use the word *"know"* to make claims regarding our skills and abilities. We say: *"she knows how to play piano"*, or *"he knows how to play chess"*. We might even say: *"my dog knows how to speak"*. Typically, when we use the words *"know how"*, the proof is in the pudding. If you or your dog *know how* to do something, you would counter my skepticism by showing me that you or your dog can, in fact, do it. As a result, *"know how"* can be used colloquially in the same way that word sound *"skill"* can. Knowing *how* is being able to perform or knowing the procedures for performing. It is procedural knowledge. The ultimate test of for skeptics is demonstrating such skills.

"know" is an exceptionally flexible word sound. Not so curiously, we are inclined to use it to describe the dispositional states, innate behavior and conditioned behavior of various organisms. Your pet beagle may know not to bite people. Salmon know when to swim upstream. Some bears know how to dance. Various organisms know how and when to perform actions. As we move down the phylogenetic scale we are less inclined to make these knowledge claims about various simpler organisms such as amoeba. When we move out of the organic world, upon reflection, we are very unlikely to attribute knowledge. Yet some folks are willing to concede that calculators do know how to add.

Would you be inclined to say that mosquitoes know not to bite you because of the repellant on your arm? Would you say that sunflowers know how to track the sun? Does the calculator know how to add and subtract? The point is simply that we normally associate knowing and knowledge with mental capacity, cognitive ability or, at a minimum, sentience. Our speech conditioning normally places knowledge on the *mental* side of the ontological register. As such, we English speakers are reluctant to attribute knowledge to organisms on the lower end of the phylogenetic scale or inanimate objects and artifacts. In the Western world our linguistic conditioning makes it quite clear that humans know a great deal and rocks know nothing.

In between those poles we English speakers are often unsure how to use the sound "*know*". However, we give other speakers the benefit of the doubt, particularly when we are sympathetic to their goals. For instance: "*my pet snake knows not to eat your pet gerbil*". Making that statement is much easier than giving a comprehensive history of the conditioning a pet python has been through, his innate response mechanisms and the current state of their digestive tract. By using "*know*" this way a speaker is not making any claims about the mental capacity of their snake. They are trying to assuage their friend's anxiety (not to mention the gerbil's) over the fate of their beloved gerbil.

"*smart*" is a related word that has become less restrictive. People debate the relative smartness of presidential candidates, dogs, pigs, digital toys etc. The use of "*smart*" has expanded into the inanimate realm. We now have smart phones, appliances and cars, but they are not intelligent. They really don't know anything. The use of "*know*" is inching in that direction too, as cars know how to park autonomously. We will have smart cars and appliances that *know-how* to do things, but they will not *know-that* anything is the case. They will not be able to declare their knowledge. They will not be able to produce declarative, propositional claims on their own. They won't be "that" smart.

Another way we English speakers use the word "*know*" is to make a claim about our acquaintance with an object, event or distinction that we make. (This is not to be confused with Bertrand Russell's distinction between knowledge by acquaintance and knowledge by description.) We can do this because we can refer to or direct attention to things. We can say: "*i know joe snow donuts red pain*", in other words, I am acquainted with Joe, snow, donuts, red and pain. This use of the word "*know*" could be interpreted as: "*i have met joe experienced pain eaten donuts played in the snow*" etc. The claim is that the speaker has an acquaintance with or has some unspecified knowledge about the subject.

When someone makes this sort of claim to knowledge, skeptics cannot test the veracity of this experiential claim by comparing it to some standard. Although a skeptic may disagree, they cannot say that the claim is not factually true. They might say: "*you really don't know joe snow red pain*". They might ask for proof by requesting relevant history of the claimant's experience, but they would need more information to make it a testable claim. They would say: "*what about joe*" or "*when did you meet joe*" or "*what color is joe's hair*".

The claim could also be rephrased: "*i know how to use the words 'snow' 'donuts' 'red'*". The claim is made with words and is about the claimant's use of the words. The proof of the claim is in the doing. Leaving aside the phenomenological issues, the question is simply: can the claimant use the word sounds in the way others in their speech community use them. They must pass a test. They must demonstrate their ability to use the words competently. Do they use the word sound "*red*" when they point to a green sweater? Do they use the word "*donut*" when they point to a muffin? Do they use the word "*snow*" when they point to glare ice? If they do, we might justifiably conclude that they don't really know red, donuts or snow.

This use for the sound "*know*" can also be interpreted to be a claim about the subject and an as-yet undeclared predicate. When someone says: "*i know snow*", for example, it could be interpreted as: "*i know that snow is _____*" (white, flaky, cold, etc.). It is a claim that the speaker can make the correct taxonomies and identity connections with the subject, or that they understand the relationship between the use of the word "*snow*" and the use of the words which describe the characteristics of snow, or that they can identify snow within a certain system, e.g. "*snow is h2o*". If asked, they could do the proper connecting; they could make other claims or assertions correctly. Paraphrased, it can be construed as: "*i know things about snow*". In any case, this is another of the many uses for the English word sound "*know*".

We also can and do use "*know*" to emphasize the strength of a claim. Someone might say: "*i know that there are guardian angels*". It is not just a belief or an article of faith. In this instance "*know*" is used as an instrument of rhetorical force. You might well be justified in asking the claimant how they "*know*" that fact. After a civil debate you would conclude that the claimant was merely trying to move their claim from belief status to knowledge status and thereby convince you to hold the same belief. The point is, "*know*" is often used to convince the listener that a belief is more than just speculation: it is a warranted belief based on some sort of evidence or conviction. It is true knowledge.

So too with so-called introspective claims to know, e.g. "*i know that i am feeling pain*". That is another use of the word "*Know*". How would that differ from "*i believe i am feeling pain*"? Is the pain different, or is my use of "*know*" or "*pain*" different? We could use "know'" this way to possibly emphasize our feeling of pain. But why would anyone say: "*i do not know that i am feeling pain*". Then again, maybe someone is trying to say that they are merely uncomfortable. At what point does the discomfort turn into pain, and the pain into agony? How does one know they are in pain, and not discomfort or agony?

A person also might say: "*i know it but i just can't say it*". What is the *it* that they claim to know? If *it* is not a claim about having a skill or ability, what could a private inexpressible claim of knowledge be? They may feel or sense something, a premonition of sorts. Suppose you have such a feeling. You might think that you knew something that others did not, but you would have no way of knowing if anyone else knew it unless you could ask. How could you do that if you could not put it into words?

The consequential point being made in this section is that people use the word sound "*know*" in many and often inexplicable ways. No doubt there are many uses of the sound "*know*" in addition to those mentioned. This is not a comprehensive attempt to cover them all, but rather an attempt to show that there are many and varied uses for the word sounds "*know*" and "*knowledge*".

The Structure of Propositions

As we have seen, the uses of the sounds *"know"* and *"knowledge"* are many. The use most critical to epistemology is the declarative claim to propositional knowledge. In these declarative *know-that* claims, a linguistic formula follows the *"i know that"* claim. Such claims to know must be declarable: *"i know that all swans are white"* or *"i know that all bachelors are unmarried males"*, or *"i know that some bears can dance"*. What we humans claim to know is necessarily linguistic if we make know-that declarative propositional claims. Of course the *"i know that"* is optional. In any case, the knowledge itself must be structured with word sounds, such as *"all swans are white"*, *"all bachelors are unmarried males"*, or *"some bears can dance"*. The knowledge we are claiming is expressed in the form of verbal behavior, either silently or aloud. Word sounds or their derivative symbols must be used to produce these declarative propositional knowledge claims. They are speech acts.

Declarative propositional knowledge claims of this sort, as well as beliefs, are structural. However, as argued in Chapter Two, *the proposition is the verbal beha*vior, not some underlying psychological entity represented by the behavior or an independent speaker-neutral, abstract entity encoded in the behavior. The proposition is the declaration. These declarative propositional statements are the fundamental atoms of knowledge. They are the basic units of epistemological investigation within analytic philosophy. Yet, without our linguistic skills, we humans would be unable to produce this declarative knowledge. We must *know-how* to utilize language-specific word sounds within a language-specific syntax. We must have behavioral skills to produce these claims.

This propositional speech behavior is directed. In making these declarative claims of knowledge, speakers *tact with* something and make a claim *about* it. Speakers have the ability to *tact with* things by means of sounds. They often fix their target by engaging in verbal *tacting acts*. These *tacting acts*, if performed adequately, give declarative propositional claims their "aboutness". If the speaker has succeeded in their tacting task, the hearers will know what they are talking about. The subject of the claim will have been established. The focal point for the speaker will be shared by the listeners by virtue of the speaker's successful tact. However, as previously discussed, it is *the act* of tacting that gives utterances their "aboutness", not the verbal instruments used in its performance.

This tacting, the most elemental behavior we perform in a declarative propositional claim to knowledge, establishes the subject of the claim. Please recall the previous discussion about what we do with words in Chapter Two. Acoustic devices such as *"my gerbil"* can be used as instruments to tact with the subject in a declarative propositional claim to knowledge. By utilizing these devices speakers engage in tacting acts to establish the subjects of their propositional knowledge claims. They say things like: *"my gerbil is fearless"*.

Of course, we could point to a dog with a finger and say: *"is black"*, or *"that is black"*.

We can introduce the subject of discourse in many ways, but ordinarily, we use verbal devices or the written derivatives in context to point to the subject, e.g. "*my gerbil*", "*joe*" or "*the universitys basketball team*". We utilize our verbal skills. A competent hearer recognizes what the speaker is *doing*. They recognize the tacting behavior. They recognize the functional value of an acoustic device being used in context. If the hearers properly interpret the tacting behavior of the speaker their attention is properly focused, the subject of discussion is established for discourse participants.

If the hearer cannot follow the speaker's tacting behavior, they would be inclined to ask: "what are you referring to". This is often the case when a speaker's tacting is not sufficiently effective to establish a subject of discussion. The hearer says: "*joe who*", or "*which basketball team mens or womens*". The hearer does not know what the speaker is tacting with through the use of sounds "*joe*" or "*the universitys basketball team*". The hearer does not recognize what the speaker's claim is *about*? The referring act lacks specificity. The point is simply that, in many instances, speakers are not successful in focusing the hearer's attention on the correct subject of discourse.

When humans *write* declarative propositional claims we record these tacts. Literate people can use those symbols for those sounds and recognize the tacting action. Literate people recognize the writer's behavior and follow their direction. In either case, both spoken and written propositions need successful tacts to establish the subject of the declarative propositional claim. Readers and listeners must focus their attention where the writer or speaker wants it to go.

The subject of conversation with which speakers' tact need not exist, be real or imaginable. Speakers can tact with mysterious *inferred* entities, such as cherubs, souls, numbers, psychic forces, centers of gravity, dark matter, ideas and abstractions. Speakers infer entities they have been conditioned to infer. It can be something as foolish as a round square, a wavicle or the concept of justice. The point here is that we can make claims about hypothetical entities. Someone can say: "*archangels give orders to the cherubs*", or "*in humans, the concept of two is universal*". Claims to knowledge are most often made with word sounds or number sounds because phonetic units *are used* to tact, but that referring act makes no existential claim.

In addition to the referring use of acoustic devices, the formula we use for making factual claims to knowledge in English often contain the connector "*is*" or a tensed version of it. (In an equivalent Russian claim there is no "*is*". Word order provides the same function.) As this author pointed out in Chapter Two, "is" has *no meaning*. There is *no concept of 'is'*. "*is*" has become the obligatory connector in much English speech behavior, joining the subject of discussion to other things. "*is*", or one of its tensed offspring, does its connecting duty in a declarative propositional statement.

The English word sound "*is*", of course, has more than one functional value. The sound "*is*" also has a function similar to an '=' sign in mathematics. With declarative utterances, speakers can perform identity claims with the copula "*is*". They make identity claims with the subject-equal-subject formula, e.g. "*clark kent is superman*". A predicate is not present in these declarative propositional statements of identity. Speakers point to two subjects and connect the subjects in an identity claim. These two different "meanings" for the English word sound "*is*" was a "disgrace" which Lord Russell thought he corrected with his system of logic.

In one such use of an English propositional statement, the speech act synthesizes a taxonomy or classification of the subject of the sentence. The behavior produces a connection. The proposition *predicates*. Speakers often perform predication with the subject-predicate syntactic formula, e.g. "*my dog is white*". The connecting is a process; it is useful, functional, verbal behavior. This predication is possible because of the sorting process humans engaged in at an early age. As discussed in Chapter Two, classifying objects is a preverbal process observed in infant humans and other non-human animals. [2].

There are other variations of the referring and connecting formula we witness in declarative speech behavior. Another use of the spoken word "*is*" is to position objects and events in our spatial-temporal framework. We tact with states of affairs. We say that "*the window is between the floor and the ceiling*", or that "*world war two was before the cold war*". This form of knowledge is expressed through the use of a three-, four-, or five-part proposition. There are multiple objects or events in a spatial or time relationship. We say: "*x is* (above, below, near, before, after, etc.) *y*". We also express comparative/relational knowledge this way. We say: "*beer is different than ale*" or "*family are more important than friends*", or "*my garage is cleaner than yours*".

All of these declarative propositional statements are vulnerable to multiple interpretations. There simply are no stable *meanings* that are carried by the individual words to be rooted out so to speak, and combined to form a solitary literal meaning for a declarative propositional claim. People disagree: "*no, the window is in the wall, not between the floor and the ceiling*". "*the cold war started during world war two*". Who do you consider family? Who are friends? Does ale not come in a beer bottle? What makes a garage cleaner than another garage? All declarative propositional claims are subject to multiple interpretations because they are all S-R-R conditioned behavior and that conditioning varies with each speech-producing person.

When we humans hear a propositional speech act, we recognize the claim formula because of our conditioning. We hear the language-specific word sounds and determine what the speaker is talking about and connecting. Language-specific syntax is one clue among many that leads us to the proper connection. The upshot is that we understand what the speaker is doing most of the time. However, it is easy to get confused because there are so many elements we can misinterpret. But we have no choice because we English speakers must state our claims to knowledge with the verbal implements our English language provides. And neither the words nor the syntactic formulas we employ to produce propositional behavior give us all the information necessary to interpret the claims.

For example, what appear to be simple declarative claims often turn out to be stipulative definitions because the formula for offering such definitions and for making the claims is the same. If a speaker says: "*water is h2o*", they may be saying that they will use "*water*" and "*h2o*" in the same way; that they are synonymous. In this use of the claim, it could be construed as a stipulative definition. Alternatively, they could be making a predication, e.g. water is H_2O within a certain system, chemistry in this case. They could also be making an identity claim, e.g. water and H_2O are the same substance and have all the same features or properties. In addition there can be various implicatures or "intended meanings" for "*water is h2o*"", e.g. inducing someone to drink the H_2O in the beaker.

Any sense of comprehension or understanding on the listener's part comes from recognizing the functional value of the sounds in many contexts, and up-taking speaker presuppositions and the proper contextual elements. Only by such recognition can speakers determine what other speakers are *doing*, what their message is. They must recognize whether the speaker is predicating, making an identity claim, implying a request etc. If they are competent mature speakers they make the correct uptakes and construe the speech act in the same way that the speaker did. Like all other declarative claims, the utterance "*water is h2o*" can be used to perform a number of tasks.

We humans store our declarative propositional knowledge (know-that) internally the same way we store our non-propositional procedural knowledge (know-how), in neurological connections. There are no great controversies when theorists explain how people remember how to manipulate pliers or how to play the piano, often generating novel behavior. Remembering small units of such behavior and producing novel combinations in response to stimuli is a result of conditioned muscle movement and the combinatorial capacity of the human brain. Declarative propositional knowledge is no different, unless we make dualist assumptions about minds and bodies. When we recall knowledge claims, we recall behavior. We perform our speech acts with word sounds either vocally or sub-vocally. We behave in ways which have been previously reinforced.

Remembering declarative propositional knowledge is having the ability to state it, having the ability to use the proper word sounds, having the ability to perform verbally. In <u>Memory</u>, A. J. Ayer makes the point:

> "And here the point is not that the word 'remember' is used dispositionally, so that one can properly be said to remember things that one is not actually thinking of. It is that when such dispositions are actualized, their actualization consists in nothing more than giving a successful performance. In this sense, to remember a fact is simply to be able to state it. The power displayed in its exercise; and such exercises need not be accompanied by anything that one would be even tempted to call a memory-experience." Nagel and Brandt (1965: 488)

There is nothing in addition to the speech behavior that we need to remember when we remember declarative knowledge or facts. We must recall the behavior and produce it. That does not mean that we must produce the sound. We can suppress the sound.

No doubt we retain much knowledge that we are not immediately aware of. We remember how to play the piano or ride a bicycle for a considerable time. So too, we retain our declarative knowledge when we are not immediately aware of it. But we do not retain sentences of mentalese in our heads to retrieve and express. Speakers remember *how* to perform verbally. Knowledge claimants must be able to say or write: "*water is h2o*" in their chosen language. People must have the ability to reproduce specific verbal behavior, silently or aloud if they claim to remember knowledge.

In fact, all of human knowledge, including declarative knowledge, is *know-how*. Declarative knowledge claims are functional behavior with language-specific devices. To know a fact is to know how to behave verbally, to know a procedure. When we humans understand *how* to successfully perform propositions we know everything there is to know about propositions. We know behavior. Our ability to state propositions is a result of our ability to recognize the functional behavioral value of sounds. It is a skill. In the final analysis, *knowing that is knowing how. All knowledge is procedural knowledge.*

Some might counter that declarative knowledge requires more than procedural knowledge. They might claim that speech requires unique mental correlates with the words: concepts, ideas, propositions, speaker meanings, mental representations, notions etc., and that these mental correlates are somehow retained in memory and recalled prior to or contemporaneously with the propositional speech behavior. However, if one does not start the analysis with semantic assumptions, one will not conclude that *mental* correlates are required for word production any more than one would require mental correlates for each specific hand movement in playing a sonata or unlocking your front door with a key. Speech behavior is no different than other behaviors in this regard, unless you *assume* that speech is a representational, symbolic activity.

In the linguistic world of Plato, he needed ideal forms to match up with the word symbols. Aristotle needed "impressions on the soul". John Locke needed "internal conceptions". Today's semanticists need concepts, ideas, propositions, speaker meanings, mental representations, notions, etc. in the speaker's head or abstract speaker neutral meanings encoded in the word symbols. Yet, without semantics there is no need to infer any of these non-physical entities represented by the sounds or encoded in the sounds.

Ultimately, propositions are verbal behavior produced by human beings using the word sound skills they have been conditioned to use. When humans state a proposition, they are not expressing or representing *mental or psychological* entities in their *minds*. Nor are they using symbols that designate independent, semantically-stable knowledge and facts. They are making connections by utilizing word sounds whose functional values have been incorporated into their communication behavior repertoire and can be produced when speakers are properly stimulated.

These verbal performances constitute the knowledge claims in any culture. Internally, people store this knowledge by means of neurological connections, the same as other functional behaviors that humans can produce. In addition, people are able to capture and externally store these performances in a durable fashion by recording their verbal behavior with symbols. Competent speakers can thus transmit this knowledge behavior across oceans and across generations to other similarly conditioned humans. In the final analysis, the knowledge that humans can retain within their bodies, record with symbols and transmit to others is a functional verbal *behavior*. Theorists must learn to talk about it as such.

Analytic/Synthetic

"Like Hume, I divide all genuine propositions into two classes: those which, in his terminology, concern 'relation of ideas,' and those which concern 'matters of fact.' The former class comprises the *a priori* propositions of logic and pure mathematics, and these I allow to be necessary and certain only because they are analytic. That is, I maintain that the reason why these propositions cannot be confuted in experience is that they do not make any assertion about the empirical world, but simply record our determination to use symbols in a certain fashion. Propositions concerning empirical matters of fact, on the other hand, I hold to be hypotheses, which can be probable but never certain. And in giving an account of the method of their validation I claim also to have explained the nature of truth." A. J. Ayer (1952: 31)

As discussed earlier, the division of declarative propositional statements into analytic and synthetic has been around in one form or another since the beginning of analytic philosophy. Philosophy in much of the West had become, in the words of A. J. Ayer, "an analytic rather than a speculative enquiry" A.J. Ayer (1959: 3). Other propositional dichotomies had also been made: a priori vs. a posteriori, necessary vs. contingent, certain vs. probable. The history of analytic epistemology abounds with analyses of propositional statements, slicing and dicing them in various and diverse ways, all in a vain attempt to find indubitable, unassailable, indisputable *knowledge*, the Holy Grail for philosophers. The most prominent and enduring of these epistemological dichotomies has been the *analytic/synthetic* distinction.

David Hume's analysis in 1748 got the ball rolling. In Hume's world, *thoughts, ideas, and concepts* held sway. Mind/body substance dualism, along with the symbolic status of words, was received wisdom of the day. Words were believed to *represent* mental entities, the thoughts, ideas, and concepts in human minds. In the dualistic mindset of Hume, it was not the word symbols that philosophers were comparing in *analytic propositions*, they were comparing the thoughts, ideas, and concepts that were represented by or encoded in the words. To analytic philosophers such as Hume, the statement "*all bachelors are unmarried males*" clearly represented a thought whose truth depends upon the relation of the ideas or concepts of "bachelor", "unmarried" and "males".

Also previously discussed, Hume distinguished analytic propositions, those whose truth could be determined by mere "operation of thought", from *synthetic propositions* whose truth was contingent upon observations of the world. For example, the propositional thought represented by the utterance "*all swans are white*" had swans, the birds, as the referents of the sound symbol "*swans*" (in a semantic analysis). The truth of that proposition could not be determined by analyzing the concept or the idea of swans. One had to investigate swans, the creatures designated by the word symbol "*swans*".

Clearly, the two statements were different in character and should be analyzed differently to determine their truth value. For centuries, it had been a matter of epistemological dogma that this analytic/synthetic distinction could be made and utilized to determine the truth of propositions. Analytic philosophers routinely made the distinction between synthetic propositions which were "empirical matters of fact", and analytic propositions which were not "empirical matters of fact". The analytic/synthetic distinction birthed by Hume and christened by Kant has been a staple of analytic philosophy for at least two hundred years.[3]

Some philosophers, such as A. J. Ayer who is quoted in the epigraph for this section, suggested that the only pure analytic statements were those of logic and mathematics. True statements made in either field are said to be *necessarily true* with *certainty*, and thus *a priori*, because there is no disagreement about the use of logical and mathematical symbols and no evidence can disprove these statements.

Empirical propositional knowledge claims made with natural language, on the other hand, are not universally true, certain, or necessary; they are merely hypothesis about the world. They may be contingently true, but they can never be completely confirmed or verified. Further observations may disprove them. Thus, they are not necessarily true, analytic, or *a priori*.

Historically, these propositions concerning empirical matters of fact were subject to all the vagaries of linguistic usage. As a result, some philosophers began to focus on language. They began saying that declarative knowledge claims, other than those of logic and pure mathematics, were true, not because of the relationship of ideas or concepts, but because of our conventions of linguistic usage, e.g. "*all bachelors are unmarried males*". That presented a problem. How could logicians *positively* know the truth of "*all bachelors are unmarried males*" based on mere linguistic *conventions* which are subject to change and misinterpretation? As Brand Blanchard put it: "To say that a proposition is necessary is to say that the state of things it asserts could not be otherwise, and hence that there are no possible alternatives to it. To say that it is conventional is to say that there *are* possible alternatives to it." Blanshard (1962: 267)

Russell, Ayer and the positivists were part of a larger movement toward an *ideal logical language*. The analytic/synthetic dichotomy manifested itself in the quest for that language as the *logical/descriptive* distinction. The logical operators, e.g. '→', are merely cogs in the machinery which manipulates the symbolic variables within the algorithms of symbolic logic. Once the logical operations were defined and formalized it became clear that many natural language debates were based on poor logic. The form of the arguments was faulty. Symbolic logic showed philosophers the correct algorithms with which to make valid arguments.

Logicians such as Russell ran into problems, however, with the *descriptive* functions in their logics because they could not replace logical variables with "single symbols which always have a definite and unique meaning" Russell (via Wittgenstein's Tractatus, p.8). Ayer recognized that the analytic, and to his mind "*a priori* propositions of logic and pure math", had no *descriptive* content because they contained no acts of reference; they said nothing about the world. Symbolic logic is a language without vocabulary; it has syntax only. No descriptive statement could be made with symbolic logic and pure math because their symbols did not designate anything in the world (within the semantic paradigm).

All of the logicians attempts to produce certain and necessarily true natural language propositions that could yield incontrovertible knowledge *about* the world, stalled because the terms used to produce descriptive content were subject to interpretation. Their attempts to combine a logical system with a fool proof system of meaning and reference (descriptive content) failed. Russell claimed in the introduction to Wittgenstein's <u>Tractatus</u> that: "A logically perfect language has rules of syntax which prevent nonsense, and has single symbols which always have a definite and unique meanings". When Russell could not produce unambiguous reference with natural language words he was forced to conclude that the demonstratives such as *"this"* and *"that"* were the only words that could be used in his logical language to refer unambiguously. He claimed that: "The only words one does use as names in the logical sense are words like 'this' or 'that'." Russell (1918: 29)

Their incorrect analysis of word use sent Russell, Wittgenstein, Ayer and the logical positivists on a wild goose chase during the first half of the 20th century. Speaker-neutral, independent *facts* signified, denoted, designated, or referred to by declarative propositional statements gradually gained special status. For Russell, at that time, true propositional statements were symbols that *denoted* facts.

Facts could not "be understood as a species of object". Nor were they in the mind of the speaker. There had to be an independent fact of the matter when someone made a propositional claim, e.g. *"all swans are white"*. Yet, explaining these *facts* became exceedingly difficult. The *concept* of fact and the *meaning* of "fact" became a matter of much concern. The assumptions about the symbolic status of words and the independent status of knowledge and facts led to myriad misguided explanations for *the nature of* knowledge, truth and facts.

The early Wittgenstein needed a world of facts to correspond to his true atomic propositions in his logic and his picture theory of language and thought. The first two entries in the <u>Tractatus</u> are:

I   The world is everything that is the case.
I.I   The world is the totality of facts, not of things.
Wittgenstein (1922:v31)

However, Wittgenstein's world of facts in the <u>Tractatus</u> gives way to silence in <u>Philosophical Investigations</u>.[4] Russell's attempt to explain facts was futile. These ill-advised posits of speaker-neutral independent facts that they required for their theories of knowledge became metaphysical monstrosities. Their attempts to explain independent, speaker-neutral facts that corresponded to declarative propositional statements all failed. Once again, language misled philosophers, i.e. they use the word *"fact"* in lieu of "state-of-affairs". States-of-affairs are not true or false, but declarative propositional claims about them are. States-of-affairs just are. They are out there in the universe, with or without creatures who speak about them, unlike facts which are produced by humans with the ability to speak.

The world is not made up of *facts* as Russell and the early Wittgenstein claimed. Facts are not out in the world waiting to be discovered. (J. L. Austin commented that "…when a detective says 'Let's look at the facts' he doesn't crawl round the carpet, but proceeds to utter a string of statements: we even talk of 'stating the facts' ") via 'Truth' in Nagel & Brandt (1965: 170). Facts are declarative propositional speech acts which are true. English-speaking humans say: *"the fact that"* and follow that utterance with a declarative statement such as *"all swans are white"*. Moreover, these facts are not mind dependent; they are dependent upon humans being conditioned to use word sounds to tact and predicate. Without the human ability to utilize sounds, there are no facts. A world without human speech is a world without facts; states of affairs yes, facts no.

Moreover, in stating empirical facts, natural language word sounds must be employed to make statements *about* the world through *acts of reference*. Only listeners who have roughly the same ability to use the word sounds in context will recognize what the speaker is doing and duplicate their verbal behavior, most often silently. Consequently natural language propositions cannot be isolated logically or semantically. They cannot be analyzed outside of a use and a user. There are no speaker-neutral, objective, independent *facts* that correspond to declarative propositional statements. Natural language propositions are ineluctably idiosyncratic and dependent upon a multitude of presuppositions and other contextual elements for correct listener uptake of the constituent acts of reference.

Along with the nature of facts, the distinction between analytic propositions and synthetic propositions remains, even today, a hotly debated subject. In the early1950s, Willard Quine investigated the analytic/synthetic distinction and persuasively argued that it was ill founded. His classic work showed that analyticity, synonymity, and definition were inextricably tangled and that:

> "But, for all it's a priori reasonableness, a boundary between analytic and synthetic statements has not been drawn. That there is such a distinction to be drawn at all is an unempirical dogma of empiricists, a metaphysical article of faith." Quine (2001: 55)

Indeed, the analytic/synthetic distinction has been a dogma of analytic philosophy since the time of Hume. However, analytic philosophers have been unable to extricate themselves from that dogma, because of another dogma. That other dogma is the belief that words are symbols that have stable, consistent meanings and referents. In spite of that unacknowledged dogmatism, Quine's analysis drew much attention to the difficulties in making the analytic/synthetic distinction.

Nevertheless, competent speakers seem to think that some linguistic statements are necessarily true by means of analysis, with no evidence or observation necessary. We say that some statements are *truisms*. We are told that "*all bachelors are unmarried males*" is true by *definition*. However, we must bear in mind that definitions are *descriptive* reports based on observed human speech behavior. Analysts should say that human linguistic intuitions conditioned through S-R-R by means of a lifetime of verbal behavior inform competent English speakers that a statement is a "truism". Competent speakers, because of their habitual verbal behavior, develop intuitions that some statements are necessarily true and certain (*a priori* in some circles; see below).

In spite of that, interpretations for apparent truisms can and do vary. For example, the author has been advised that the Pope is an unmarried male. Yet he is not really a bachelor! Are male infants *really* bachelors? Well, *adult* males! Adults of what age? 15, 16, 18, 21? How about widowers? If you are a logician, you may say that "*all bachelors are unmarried males*" does not assert that all unmarried males are bachelors. You are correct, of course. Nevertheless, the use of "*bachelor*" is not precise. For some folks, the Pope is not a bachelor. For others he is. The relevant point is: epistemologists must realize that they are analyzing conditioned speech behavior that varies and produces varied intuitions about what is true and what is false.

It is always possible to debate the use of word sounds. Even proper names, such as "*salem*" or "*neil armstrong*", can be construed differently. There will always be an element of inference when people use acoustic devices and their derivative symbols. Ordinary language does not provide us with precise, rigid, consistent and universal functional values for these devices. Therefore, parties to an exchange can agree to knowledge claims based on a congruence of word usage. Others may not agree. There is no "truth of the matter" or "fact of the matter" when *the matter* must be expressed with a natural language. If the matter is expressed with words, truth is always dependent upon agreement about word usage.

In summary, the traditional distinction between analytic and synthetic propositions was based on the false premises that words were symbols that had stable, consistent, semantic content and stable referents in the world. That assumption is mistaken. In the final analysis, when people make declarative propositional claims, they propose. The proposition is the verbal behavior that is produced as a result of the speech history of the organism and the stimuli inducing the organism to produce the tacts, silently or aloud. That propositional claim can be interpreted in different ways. There simply is no speaker-neutral independent fact of the matter which can be unequivocally captured in a declarative, propositional statement. So, the analytic/synthetic distinction must be abandoned along with the semantic fallacies which helped produce it.

A Priori /A Posteriori

"The same conclusion is drawn from the Meno as in the Phaedo, that knowledge is brought by the soul from a previous existence… Only the sort of knowledge that is called *a priori*—especially logic and mathematics—can be possibly supposed to exist in every one independently of experience. In fact, this is the only sort of knowledge (apart from mystic insight) that Plato admits to be really knowledge." Russell (1945: 139)

In addition to the Analytic/Synthetic distinction, analytic philosophers have traditionally dichotomized knowledge along the *a priori/a posteriori* fault line. It was originally a fundamental epistemological version of the nature/nurture controversy, i.e. what knowledge are we humans born with and what knowledge is learned after birth. According to Plato, *a priori* knowledge is brought from a previous existence and said to be necessarily true, true with certainty, true in all possible worlds independent of any human experience or evidence. Plato demonstrated through Socrates in the Meno that indisputable geometric knowledge could be coaxed from an untutored slave. Therefore, it must be *a priori* knowledge, innate knowledge, knowledge acquired *prior* to the birth of that slave and any experience during the earthly incarnation of his soul.

However, in the modern era, the *a priori* distinction has morphed. It is no longer associated with the metaphysical excesses of Platonic theory. Today's thinkers claim that some truths are known to us with certainty. They are necessary truths that cannot be confirmed or confuted by any evidence or observation. They will be *necessarily true* in all cases for all eternity. Thus, they are considered to be a priori. In fact the terms "*necessary truth*" and "*a priori truth*" are used interchangeably these days, with the statements of logic and pure math being prototypical: (2 + 2 = 4). Certain non-analytic statements such as: "*one cannot be in two different places at the same time*" are also considered to be *necessarily* true by some philosophers and, thus, *a priori*.

On the contrary, the knowledge that the Sun is the center of the solar system, for example, is considered *a posteriori* knowledge, *post* birth. We are not born with this sort of knowledge. This knowledge about the solar system is ultimately grounded in the senses; it comes to us through our collective worldly experience. It is also *contingent* upon the world being organized a certain way. It is ultimately based on observation or evidence about the world and can be refuted by future observations or evidence. Consequently, unlike *a priori* knowledge, *a posteriori* knowledge claims are not certain or necessary: they are contingent or conditional. They just happen to be true, to the best of our knowledge, right now.

Not only are these *a posteriori* claims to knowledge contingent, many are so because they are inductive generalizations. Most of modern-day science claims, for instance, are just such generalizations. For example, the claim that all whales are mammals is a contingent claim based on the evidence so far, here on earth. Every whale in the universe thus far observed has proven to be a mammal. However, not all whales have been observed. The Universe may hold non-mammalian whales. Many such *a posteriori* knowledge claims are contingent inductive generalizations, *not certain or necessarily true* in all possible worlds.

Furthermore, many a posteriori knowledge claims are based on notoriously unreliable human sense perception. Human senses deceive us at times, e.g. hallucinations and phantom limb pain. Humans often have perceptions that lead them to the wrong conclusions. Not only are human sense receptors unreliable, they are limited. Our human sense receptors are just not up to the job of observing the entities that many scientists discuss these days: germs, viruses, molecules, electrons and so on. Consequently, a posteriori knowledge gained by means of human sense experience can be questioned on the grounds that our senses do not always perceive things correctly, if at all. All things considered, a posteriori knowledge gained by means of observation and evidence is not *necessarily true*. However, it is fair to say it is all *contingently true* based on the limited evidence so far.

Use caution, my friend, because all of this sophistry is unwarranted. It is founded on a mistaken assumption about the use of word sounds. We humans *do* need worldly experience to make *any* declarative claim to propositional knowledge. Analytic, synthetic, *a priori*, *a posterior*, however you want to slice and dice declarative propositional knowledge claims, without the ability to produce and utilize language, we humans would produce as many of these knowledge claims as our pets do, none.

Of course, humans, as well as other creatures, are born with some procedural knowledge. We know how to cry, suckle, etc. Such *a priori* knowledge is genetically transmitted. Beyond that, we humans have the innate capacity to respond to our environment with our bodies. We follow objects with our eyes and then follow others' eyes as they gaze at objects, eventually tacting with our fingers.[5] Ultimately, most of us learn how to tact and connect with spoken words. These are *a posteriori* skills necessary to produce *declarative propositional* knowledge. They are skills we learn through stimulus, response and reinforcement, the interaction of our bodies with the environment in a social milieu.

Propositional knowledge claims are actions, verbal behavior, that take place in time and space. We humans devote an incredible amount of time and effort passing on this declarative propositional knowledge to succeeding generations. We often say these propositional acts are independent *facts* because they can be recorded in a durable written form and claimed to be independent of any speaker. This is an error. No matter how these epistemological debates are framed, making knowledge claims and talking about them requires language skills, language skills that are *a posteriori*, learned behavior that is inescapably idiosyncratic.

Statements made exclusively with decimal numbers have consistently created problems in logic and epistemology because they are thought to express universal, certain and necessary truths and are therefore *a priori*. However, those statements can only be made because of the earth-wide acceptance of the decimal system. Amongst humans, there is no idiosyncrasy or indeterminacy in the *use* of this decimal system; it is not controversial. Thus, we get agreement on the "universality", certainty and necessity of mathematical statements. It should also be noted that these mathematical statements are not propositions in spite of the fact that they are often considered to be true or false. They are simply statements about the procedures of decimal mathematics, *valid or invalid*.

Of course, we decimally skilled humans can also use numbers in *linguistic propositions*, e.g. "*cameron is 12 years old today*". The counting sound "*12*" can be employed to tact with a distinction we decimal-using humans make about cardinal quantity, just as we can tact with distinctions about color or shape. We must learn to make most of these distinctions about quantity by learning *how* to count. The numerals which represent the counting sounds can then be manipulated within the algorithms of decimal mathematics after much operant conditioning. However, the consequential point here is that mathematical statements, such as "2 + 2 = 4", are not propositions, much less *a priori* propositions. They are not *about* anything. They are recordings of decimal algorithms with no subject matter, and utilizing those algorithms is behavior learned through experience.

The vital point of all this is that the traditional *a priori/a posteriori* distinction is not legitimate because the making of any claim to any declarative propositional knowledge or mathematical knowledge requires the use of the language skills that humans have learned by means of S-R-R conditioning after birth. Whatever necessity we might give to any statement is a result of our firmly conditioned verbal behavior with sounds and symbols for those sounds.

Rationalism/Empiricism

"Rationalism: Any philosophy magnifying the role played by unaided reason, in the acquisition and justification of knowledge. The preference for reason over sense experience as a source of knowledge began with the Eleatics, and played a central role in Platonism. Its most significant modern development was in the 17th century belief that the paradigm of knowledge was the non-sensory intellectual intuition that God would have into the workings of all things, and that human beings taste in their acquaintance with mathematics." The Oxford Dictionary of Philosophy p.318.

"The fundamental tenet of modern empiricism is the view that all non-analytic knowledge is based on experience. Let us call this thesis the principle of empiricism." (Carl Gustav Hempel via Nagel and Brandt (1965: 17)

Over the years, the *a priori/a posteriori* divide was evidenced in another philosophical dichotomy. Philosophers had staked out positions or been categorized by other philosophers as *rationalists* or *empiricists*. Although the distinction is not clear cut and many philosophers have elements of both schools in their writings, most rationalists started with a belief in God and insisted that God placed certain knowledge in the minds of men. Such knowledge was innate and intuitive. It was *a priori*, certain and necessarily true. Mathematics and geometry were the prototypes for such knowledge, but not exhaustive. Beginning with such *a priori* knowledge, *rational* men could reason to conclusions about the nature of God, man, and the universe. The purest form of knowledge could be obtained by means of *pure reason*, beginning with *a priori knowledge* as a foundation.[6]

On the other hand, *empiricists* insisted that, outside of mathematics, geometry and pure logic, all knowledge was based on the evidence of the senses. The entire edifice of science is based on observation and inductive generalizations. The claim that the earth revolves around the sun, for instance, has been confirmed repeatedly by many observational techniques. In spite of the fact that such empirical claims were not *a priori*, certain or necessarily true in all possible worlds, they had proven their usefulness. They were contingent truths about our world, but legitimate claims to knowledge nonetheless. Empiricists would rely on the evidence of their senses for their knowledge claims, not pure reason.

Eventually, the search for unassailable knowledge led Western theorists away from pre-enlightenment *truth*, revealed in religious manuscripts and church doctrine, toward a naturalist view of a detached truth, detached from divinity or the viewer. Observation of the natural world replaced the authority of the scriptures. For example, the heliocentric solar system became gospel, regardless of any interpretation of the bible. Observation replaced dogmatism. Truth was to be found through experience. An objective truth, available to all and supported by the evidence of the senses, became the standard for secular scholars. *Empiricism* was in ascendance and rationalism was in decline.

The empiricist's program included a refinement of language because language had become the primary obstacle to establishing a philosophical foundation for indisputable empirical knowledge. Empiricists needed to clarify terminology and eliminate any disputes about the truth of their observational claims. Unfortunately, the indeterminacy of meaning and reference presented roadblocks in the drive toward truth from experience. The truth of empirical statements often seemed to depend on the meanings of the words which were often found to be subjective. Yet the crux of an empirical account of the world was to reduce the egocentricity of empirical assertions to a minimum.

Thus, at that time, philosophical empiricism became a program to expunge any bias or subjectivity from observational methods and terminology. Empirical terms had to be defined with precision and accuracy beyond dispute. So the empiricists began a systematic program to define scientific terms such as *"force"*, *"matter"*, *"mass"*, *"energy"* etc. They ultimately came to the conclusion that most such scientific terms were defined in terms of each other, *"mass"* and *"matter"* for instance. Attempts to define them precisely often led to infinite regresses. Yet, the starting point for committed empiricists had to be observational terms without regressive definitions.

Some suggested that foundational words had to be defined ostensively. That is, the word *"red"* was to be defined by pointing to a red thing and saying: *"that is red"*. However, such *ostensive definitions* were severely limited. How can anyone point to the *seeing* that would allow an ostensive definition of *"see"* in *"see that red spot"*? Or, how can someone point to *"the energy"* going through the power lines? A great many terms used to make empirical claims cannot be reduced to the ostensively-defined terms allowed by these theorists.

Another possibility was *operationism*. Scientific terms were given officially sanctioned operational definitions. By conducting an operation of some type, scientific terms gained measurable value. The term *"hard"*, for instance, was quantified by a standard operation that consisted of measurable pressure being placed on a standard metallic point which is then dragged across a surface for a measurable distance. Such an operational definition quantified and standardized the term, unlike the ordinary use of the word *"hard"* which had been based on human sensory experience. Yet, what possible measurement or test could be used to precisely define the word *"spot"* in *"hard spot"*? Defining *"spot"* with the precision necessary for the empiricist's theories became problematic.

The empiricist's dream of incontestable empirical knowledge based on incontestable declarative statements composed of words with incontestable meanings and referents failed. Of course, the reason it failed is because the empiricists began their quest with an inaccurate philosophical foundation for language. They began their analysis thinking that word sounds are symbols that have stable, consistent meanings and referents paired with them. However, word sounds have no *meanings or referents*; they have uses, many uses, and any word's uses are not based on definitions, ostensive, operational or otherwise. It is the other way round.

Grounding science in observation and quantification is a worthwhile goal, as is rational thinking. By quantifying observational terms as much as possible, science can reduce the inevitable egocentricity of natural language terms and make foundational claims for rational debate, though ultimately, the value of scientific statements lays in their utility, not in their definitions. Empirical claims are put to the test. Their success or failure determines whether or not they become accepted science without regard for their philosophical foundation or their terminological purity. E=MC^2 works, no matter how you define the word sounds *"energy"*, *"mass"*, *"speed"*, and *"light"*, or justify that claim philosophically.   As Wilfrid Sellars explained:

> "For empirical knowledge, like its sophisticated extension, science, is rational, not because it has a ***foundation*** but because it is a self-correcting enterprise which can put any claim in jeopardy, though not all at once." Sellars (1997: 70)

Empiricism as a philosophical foundation for science is unnecessary. Success is necessary. Defining the word sounds *"space"*, *"time"*, *"force"*, *"matter"*, *"mass"*, and *"energy"* as we shall see, is no more precise than defining "virtue", "piety" and "courage".   However, once these terms are reduced to numbers in an equation, they have proven to be useful. Ask no more of them.

The Misuses of the Words: "*truth*", "*logic*" and "*certainty*"

The remarks in this section must be prefaced with the author's standard proviso: the word sounds "*truth*", "*logic*" and "*certainty*" are neither signs nor symbols. The philosophical use of these terms has been refined over the years and many distinctions have been made. Some of them have been useful, some have not. In spite of this refinement, the word sounds "*truth*", "*logic*" and "*certainty*" are still used with abandon by many theorists and it is often assumed that they have consistent *meanings*. Not only do they not have consistent meanings, they have no meanings at all. There is no semantic content for these word sounds or their derivative symbols, not even essential meanings. Neither do they designate stable semantic referents. Nor do these word sounds represent ideas, concepts or "notions".

For starters, "*truth*" is a sound that has many, many uses. The sound "*truth*" is not the name of something. **'Truth'** with a capital T is not out in the world somewhere to be found. That is the sort of sophomoric banality that clutters the literature of New Age and Pop philosophy. Neither is truth a primitive notion or clearly recognized idea of some sort. Nor is there any good reason to believe, as Lord Russell did, that truth is a fundamental concept to which we must appeal in order to ground our epistemology. Accurately recognizing what we humans do with word sounds such as "*truth*", is a necessary first step in recognizing the limitations of epistemology and logic. With that in mind, the author will attempt to make some salient points about the use of the word sounds "*truth*", "*logic*" and "*certainty*" in the field of epistemology.

These word sounds have played a pivotal role in epistemology as a result of analytic philosophers and logicians incessantly searching for declarative propositional statements that were *true* with *certainty*. Propositions had become the basic epistemological units of analysis. Legitimate claims to knowledge had to be based on incontrovertibly true propositions, it was said. Without such positively true propositions, all the claims to knowledge were to be considered mere *beliefs*, some warranted, some not.

This quest for propositions that were true with certainty became the bugaboo for logical positivists during the first half of the 20th century. A.J. Ayers assessment was fairly typical of the work being done by analytic philosophers at that time:

> "The quest for certainty has played a considerable part in the history of philosophy... Sometimes the word 'certain' is used as a synonym for 'necessary' or for 'a priori'. It is said, for example, that no empirical statements are certain, and what is meant by this is that they are not necessary in the way that a priori statements are, that they can be denied without self-contradiction. Accordingly, some philosophers take a priori statements as their ideal. They wish, like Leibniz,

to put all true statements on a level with those of formal logic or pure mathematics; or, like the existentialists, they attach a tragic significance to the fact that this cannot be done. But it is perverse to see tragedy in what could not conceivably be otherwise; and the fact that all empirical statements are contingent, that even when true they can be denied without self-contradiction, is itself a matter of necessity. If empirical statements had the formal validity which makes the truths of logic unassailable they could not do the work that we expect of them; they would not be descriptive of anything that happens. In demanding for empirical statements the safeguard of logical necessity, these philosophers have failed to see that they would rob them of their factual content. Ayer (1956: 41)

Ayer clearly recognized that "unassailable" truth, logical necessity and certainty could not come from empirical statements. He realized that all empirical statements were contingent. They were contingent because their truth depended upon the world being arranged in a certain way, and unlike the statements of formal logic or pure mathematics, empirical statements can be denied without self-contradiction. (Not all whales are mammals, as opposed to: not all bachelors are single.) Consequently, he believed that only the statements of formal logic and pure mathematics provided logically necessary and certain truths, but that we ought not to demand that standard for empirical claims of knowledge.

Unfortunately, Ayer also believed that the word sounds "*truth*", "*logic*" and "*certainty*" represented mental entities and had semantic content. He had fallen victim to the semantic fallacies, as did all other analytic philosophers and logicians when they assessed "the nature of" truth, logic and certainty. In contrast, let's take a *non-semantic* look at some of the issues that analytic philosophers such as Ayer confronted over the last century.

In the traditional rendition of declarative propositional statements, most logicians and analytic epistemologists assume that any such written statement or verbal utterance encodes a stable, universal, speaker-neutral *proposition*. It is this speaker-neutral independent proposition that is true or false, said the logicians, not the utterance or the writing of that statement, on any occasion. The truth of a proposition had to be invariant with regard to speakers and the incident of its use. This is standard logical theory grounded in standard semantic theory. The theoretical foundations of both propositional logic and predicate logic are grounded in linguistic theory which hypothesizes a universal truth-stable independent proposition encoded or represented by the symbols.

Not only is this theoretical semantic underpinning of modern propositional logic faulty, the bivalent logic of contemporary theorists is also faulty. The true/false bivalent Aristotelian logic was a byproduct of the Greek views of language and mathematics. Morris Kline reports on the mathematical origins of Aristotle's logic:

"A major achievement of Aristotle was the founding of the science of logic. In producing correct laws of mathematical reasoning the Greeks had laid the groundwork for logic, but it took Aristotle to codify and systematize these laws into a separate discipline. Aristotle's writings make it abundantly clear that he derived logic from mathematics. His basic principles of logic—the law of contradiction, which asserts that a proposition cannot be both true and false, and the law of the excluded middle, which maintains that a proposition must be either true or false—are the heart of the indirect method of mathematical proof. Further, Aristotle used mathematical examples taken from contemporary texts to illustrate his principles of reasoning." Kline (1972: 53)

The Greek view of numbers provided for no indeterminacy. There were no negative, incommensurate or irrational numbers within their mathematics. The truth of mathematical statements, in the view of the Greeks, was determinate and precise. There was no intermediate ground. That mathematical precision carried over to their logic. There would be no indeterminacy in Aristotle's logic. There would be no middle ground in which a linguistic statement could be relatively true or somewhat true. True and false were the options; the middle was excluded.

However, as philosopher John Hospers points out:

> "The law of the Excluded Middle does not say that there is no middle ground between opposites (hot and cold), for of course there is. It only says that there is no middle ground between a term and its *negative* (hot and not-hot). Wherever you draw the boundary-line between hot and not-hot, there is no middle ground between them—the law, true to its name, excludes any such middle ground: any temperature that isn't hot is not hot, but of course the not-hot includes both lukewarm and cold." Hospers (1967: 214-15)

Of course the problem is drawing the boundary-line. Any such line is subjective at best, and totally arbitrary at worst.

As a result, applying Aristotelian bivalent logic to all linguistic propositions is difficult, if not impossible. Bertrand Russell acknowledged the problem with Aristotle's law of the excluded middle and attributed it the vagueness of symbols in 1923. Kosco (1993: 92) By 1940 he had concluded that *truth* was a "fundamental concept" necessary for his epistemology. "I conclude that 'truth' is the fundamental concept, and that 'knowledge' must be defined in terms of 'truth,' not vice versa," Russell (1940: 23). Yet the law of the excluded middle did not apply to his correspondence theory of truth, the fourth in his view of the competing theories at that time:

> "In recent philosophy we may distinguish four main types of theory as to 'truth' or as to its replacement by some concept which is thought preferable... For my part, I adhere firmly to this last theory. It has, however, two forms, between which the decision is not easy. In one form, the basic propositions must be derived from experience, and therefore propositions which cannot be suitably related to experience are neither true nor false. In the other form, the basic propositions need not be related to experience, but only to 'fact,' though if they are not related to experience they cannot be known. Thus, the two forms of the correspondence theory differ as to the relation of 'truth' to 'knowledge... I shall assume that 'truth' is to be defined by correspondence, and examine the two forms of this theory, according as 'experience' or 'fact' is taken as that with which truth must correspond. I will call these two theories the 'epistemological' and the 'logical' theory respectively... That is to say, the law of the excluded middle is true in the logical theory, but not in the epistemological theory. This is the most important difference between them." Russell (1940: 363)

Russell clearly recognized the limitations of the law of the excluded middle within epistemology. Aristotle's bivalent logic with the law of the excluded middle is not reflected in the human use of natural language propositions that are the foundational units of analytic epistemology. The fuzzy definitions and idiosyncrasy inherent in the employment of words by different individuals does not permit the strict application of bivalent logic to propositional speech activity.[7]

To account for these vagaries of natural language usage and to salvage the bivalent logic, theoretical logicians postulated a *language-neutral proposition*. "Logic deals not with verbal or sentential utterances but with propositions, Russell (1940: 69). "Thus in determining truth or falsehood, it is the proposition that is relevant," Russell (1940:98). The *proposition*, as mentioned previously, was considered to be a psychological entity by Russell, or an abstract entity by others. To them, both verbal utterances and written statements signified another thing, a theoretical truth-stable proposition of one sort or another.

By that time, the manipulation of natural language propositions had become much too cumbersome for logicians. Natural language propositions had become obstacles in the development of logical calculation procedures. Consequently they were abandoned in favor of symbolic, variable notation:

> "Originally logic was conceived of as a tool to study the logical properties of natural language. By translating arguments in natural language into propositional calculus one hoped to obtain the arguments in a more perspicuous form, where it would be easier to see whether they were valid. However, the translation turned out to be difficult; natural language with its vagueness and ambiguity had to be transferred into a somewhat arbitrarily chosen unambiguous system of formal representation. Since such a system was considered a great advantage in other respects, logic became increasingly estranged from the study of natural language." Allwood, Andersson and Osten (1977: 29)

Symbolic logics use variables, as do algebras and geometries. Symbolic statements, (those using variables, whether they are within the disciplines of logic or mathematics,) make no claims and cannot be judged to be true or false. The variables are place holders that occupy a spot in the formula where the contents are unknown or unspecified. Theorists can manipulate the symbolic variables, by rule, and obtain a resulting symbolic answer that proves the *validity* of the operation. However, when using variables, symbolic mathematics, algebras, geometries, and logics, are sterile, indifferent to the world. As long as they are internally consistent or coherent, their operations will yield correct results, *valid* results within their respective algorithms, not *true* results. Truth and falsity only appear when speakers utilize natural words or numbers in referring acts within a declarative proposition.

The distinction between *validity and truth* is often conflated in epistemology and everyday language. Deborah J. Bennett makes the point:

> "In formal logic, we carefully distinguish between 'truth' and 'validity,' but in everyday reasoning we are not aware of this distinction. We confuse truth with validity or justifiability. We fall into Henle's categories of 'refusing to grasp the logical task' and the 'introduction of outside knowledge'." Bennett, D (2004: 184)

Logicians themselves have contributed mightily to the confusion. Propositional logic provides a system to determine valid or invalid deductions, inferences and implications. Logicians have come up with *truth tables* to classify the outcomes of their calculation procedures. In fact, truth tables tell you if your propositional calculations are valid or not. The truth of any conclusion is dependent upon the truth of the premises and the validity of the calculation. Logicians cannot determine the truth of any individual proposition by means of logical calculus; they can only determine the validity of their calculations. Truth is irrelevant in logical calculations.

The following would be a *valid* logical calculation:

> P: All men are stupid.   (all x are p)
> P: Socrates was a man.   (z is an x)
> C: Socrates was stupid.   (z is p)

However, the conclusion is not true. Although the calculation is valid, it is not a sound argument because of a false premise. The point is that propositional logic alone cannot provide us with *truth*. The validity of the calculation is the only result proved by logic. Parties to the exchange must agree on the truth of any premises to arrive at a true conclusion by means of a valid calculus. For example, if someone begins a logically valid operation with what are agreed to be true premises, a true conclusion will be the result. We see this again in Aristotelian syllogisms:

> P: All men are mortal.   (all x are p)
> P: Socrates is a man.   (z is an x)
> C: Socrates is mortal.   (z is p)

If we agree that the premises are true and the calculation is valid, the conclusion will be true. The argument would be considered a *sound* argument. Logic has also provided a symbolic system of calculus whereby we have no need to agree on the truth of premises:

> P: All x are p.
> P: z is an x.
> C: z is p.

Variables are used in the premises. The premises make no claims that can be true or false. The variables used will not yield any truth, agreed or otherwise because no claim is being made. Nothing is being said *about* anything. Yet, this symbolic form of logical calculus will show us the validity of our reasoning.[8]

Truth enters the picture when conditioned human speech enters the picture. Ordinarily, we humans produce propositions, such as: "*socrates was stupid*", "*all swans are white*" or "*mary is rich*" by engaging in referring acts with functional acoustic devices. We can then *agree* to the truth or falsity of a propositional claim, e.g. two parties can agree that all swans are white. They must recognize the functional value of the sounds, the context etc. to come to agreement as to the truth of that claim. However, logic is not a factor in that decision because logic can only provide the validity of a logical calculation procedure.

Conversely, a proposition (the proposing act) cannot be *valid*. Any single proposition conducted with words can be *agreed to,* but it cannot produce validity, truth, certainty or logical necessity. While you and the author may agree that a statement is true or certain, someone else might interpret the statement differently. Word use is personal behavior shaped by each person's speech history. The use of the sound "*stupid*" varies considerably with speakers. Are those swans white or cream colored? How much money makes a person rich? There is always stimulus variability, contextual considerations and personal speech history factors that determine the use of word sounds by an individual in any incident of use. There can always be differences about speaker definitions for the word sounds: "*stupid*", "*white*", "*rich*", or any other word sound.

You might think that certain words have polar opposites which would make them more amenable to bivalent logic, antonyms such as male/female, alive/dead, open/shut. They may be more amenable, but are not foolproof. There are *always cases* where folks cannot determine if something is male or female, alive or dead, open or shut. Word usage is unavoidably imprecise. The author's intuitions about word sound use, based on years of conditioning, are different than yours. With the use of ordinary language we simply cannot cordon off neat clear-cut *meanings* or *concepts* that exclude the fuzzy middle ground, not even essential core meanings.

As Wittgenstein pointed out in <u>Philosophical Investigations</u>, there are no essential core meanings for words. Examples: some activities are clearly games; others are not. Other activities may be on the fuzzy edges, "*it depends on your definition of game*". Some things are furniture, some are not, while some, well, "*it depends on your definition of furniture*". 65-year-olds consider 30-year-olds young; 10-year-olds do not. The employment of word sounds has fuzzy regularities produced by years of speech history, but, inevitably, each user has a different history of learning and a different perspective that determines their use of word sounds. If someone states propositions such as: "*language is a game*", or "*bean bag chairs are furniture*", or "*you are old*" there is no *fact of the matter.* Given the tenuous nature of referring acts and the fuzzy edges of human word use, we can only obtain agreement from the hearer or reader when we propose a declarative knowledge claim.

Some logicians have developed multivalent *fuzzy logic* systems to account for the variability in natural language usage and the fact that declarative statements often occupy the middle ground. The vagueness that Russell and other bivalent logicians attribute to words is accounted for by using fuzzy sets. In these fuzzy systems words are weighted with relative values or degrees of determinacy. The words "*young*" and "*old*" can be plotted on a graph where 40 years of age is approximately the age where young and old lines intersect. At the ages of 1 through 25 people are generally considered young. At the ages of 65 and beyond people are generally considered old. In between there is a fuzzy set curve that quantifies the degree of youth or old age. By quantifying the fuzzy degrees of old and young these fuzzy logicians are able to approximate human reasoning much more closely than bivalent Aristotelian logic.

Contradiction also assumes an invariant core meaning for words and bivalent logic. However, even the same word can be used in context for the opposite effect. We native-English speakers say: "*hold fast*" and "*run fast*". The uses of the utterances "*he had a bad scare*" and "*he had a good scare*" are the same. "*fat chance*" and "*slim chance*" can be used to do precisely the same work for an English speaker. The utterance "*thats history*" has opposite uses in Europe and America. In America it is used to say that something is no longer relevant. In Europe it is used to say that something is relevant, historically relevant. The point is: people employ word sounds in imprecise, divergent and often seemingly contradictory ways. So, proving a logical contradiction is often difficult because the uses of so many terms have fuzzy edges and multiple interpretations.

The doctrine of epistemological atomism and its propositional logic offspring can be used to refine our thinking. We can break down complex assertions into basic propositions. However, in ordinary conversation we rarely need to. We get agreement without doing so. There is no need for us to find a *truth value*. Scientists, logicians and philosophers can only hope for agreement based on the consistent functional value of word sounds used with consistent presuppositions and stable context amongst discourse participants. Once agreement on the truth of the premises' is reached, valid reasoning will provide true conclusions.

The attempt by logicians to compress natural language into a bivalent logical calculus is futile. The discrepancy between bivalent logic and natural language is strikingly apparent. For instance, in their quest for the truth value that supposedly lies within the proposition, logicians have conveniently eliminated verb tenses from their analyses, making propositions less contextually dependent. Logician Willard Quine does so thusly:

> "Our ordinary language shows a tiresome bias in its treatment of time. Relations of date are exalted grammatically as relations of position, weight, and color are not. This bias is itself an inelegance, or breach of theoretical simplicity. Moreover, the form that it takes—that of requiring that every verb form show a tense—is peculiarly productive of needless complications, since it demands lip service to time even when it is farthest from our thoughts. Hence in fashioning canonical notations it is usual to drop tense distinctions." Quine (1960: 170)

Although cultural idiosyncrasies are revealed in different languages, time, as perceived, is a critical distinction for most speakers. Positioning an event or action in time is a crucial need in our linguistic endeavors. We English speakers find the following constructions useful: "*john is home john was home john would have been home john will be home john had been home*" etc. Most logicians find them to be a nuisance. So they exclude them from their logical domain and their linguistic analysis. (Some have tried to develop tense logics.)

As another example of the discrepancies between logic and actual speech behavior, predicate logic is incapable of capturing the use of *proportional quantifiers* such as "*most*", "*some*", "*several*", "*few*" and "*many*". *Proportional quantifiers* are contrasted with cardinal quantifiers. Cardinal quantifiers are then explained in terms of set theory. However, it is impossible to account for proportional quantifiers with set theory. Yet, these English word sounds clearly have uses. Those *uses* are obviously idiolectic and entirely context driven. Thus, logically determining the *truth* of any assertions utilizing proportional quantifiers is impossible.

The fuzzy uses for word sounds have given logicians fits. Bivalent logicians simply cannot replicate human speech-thinking with their logical algorithms. So they stipulate definitions that vary from conventional usage for many words used in their logical calculations. For example, the proportional quantifier "*some*" has a different interpretation in practical use as opposed to logical calculations:

> "To a logician, 'some' always means at least one and possibly all… 'Some' in common life, often means both *not-none* and *not-all*; in logic, only *not-none*."

Bennet (2004: 64 & 72)

Logicians must stipulate many definitions because their logical calculations do not reflect the human use of word sounds and never will.

A practical example of the difference between a logical interpretation of human speech and the practical interpretation might be a scenario where a man purchases three books and says to his spouse: "*i bought a book*". Logically he is correct. He did buy *a book*, but the implication is clearly misleading his spouse. The point is, we simply do not use language as logicians would wish us to and our argumentation and reasoning with natural language will not conform to bivalent Aristotelian logic. Determining the truth of *any* assertion by speaker-neutral logical analysis is impossible. It is just more obvious when proportional quantifiers are used.

Indeed, much of our faulty reasoning in human affairs is due to our variability in word use. Truth evaluative statements require the use of natural language, which is dependent upon each speaker's idiolectic word use and many elements of context. The word sound interpretation process may vary even when the reasoning process is valid. How we use words and how we reason are two different processes. They are interrelated, but as Deborah J. Bennett put it:

> "Any theory of logical reasoning needs to distinguish between the subject's interpretation process and the subject's evaluation process in reasoning."
> Bennett (2004: 107)

Of course logicians can stipulate definitions for the words used in propositions. Once they do, they can draw all sorts of conclusions through logical calculations. That is what scientists do as well. Scientists stipulate definitions and quantify measurements against accepted standards. Philosophers, linguists, teachers and truck drivers do not have that luxury. They cannot eliminate the egocentricity and ambiguity inherent in natural language usage. Thus they can never arrive at a speaker neutral independent "truth of the matter".

To this day, logicians and truth-conditional semanticists search for the truth value of declarative propositional statements. They think that they can extract a speaker-neutral, independent *proposition* from the symbols. They believe that there is an invariant literal/lexical meaning in a declarative propositional statement: something that is said directly by the symbols and will yield a bivalent truth value. They think that there is a *de dicto* reading of sentences, both the spoken and the written symbols. They are mistaken. They have been misled by the conventional semantic view of language. There simply are no *de dicto* readings, literal meanings or independent speaker-neutral propositions for these theorists to analyze.

The word sounds "*truth*", "*logic*" and "*certainty*" are often used to give proposals an authoritative ring, but because of what we humans do with word sounds, declarative propositional claims of knowledge are always subject to interpretation. When theorists search for the truth content or truth value in a natural language statement they search in vain for at least two reasons. They assume that there is a *lexical/literal meaning* for the statement *and*, that meaning can be subjected to bivalent logical analysis. There is no good reason to believe either assumption. Ultimately, true statements are a matter of consensus, consensus on what we do with words.

Another point should be made about logic. So-called "inductive logic" differs from deductive logic in that it does not entail or guarantee conclusions. "Inductive logic" only provides varying degrees of support for an argument, based on the evidence. It is based on probability. It is *reasonable* not logical. Many empirical knowledge claims are a result of such inductive reasoning. They can be disproved by counter examples, disconfirming evidence. The claim that the sun will come up in the east tomorrow is not necessary or certain, only inductively reasoned, based on all of our prior experience with the sunrises. The point is that some arguments are logical, some are reasonable and some are neither.

A final word about possible worlds is in order here. Possible worlds are heuristic devices used to make the distinction between nomological possibility and logical possibility.[9] Nomologically possible events or conditions are those which comport with the known laws of nature in this universe. Possible world scenarios allow for different laws of nature. For example, gravity could be inversely proportional to the *cube* of the distance between bodies in another universe rather than inversely proportional to the square of the distance. We can conceive of such a universe being nomologically distinct. Nevertheless, the laws of logic would remain. One can ask what makes the laws of logic unassailable. But to argue that point would require the use of the laws of logic. Ultimately, the skeptic must see and accept the laws of logic as self-evident and universally valid. If someone does not, he cannot logically argue his case.

The Misuses of the Word Sounds
"belief", "Knowledge" and "fact"

The word sound "belief" has been used extensively in analytic epistemology because belief claims and declarative propositional knowledge claims have the same linguistic form. We can say: "i believe that all swans are white" just as well as: "i Know that all swans are white". We SAE-speaking people make many claims about what we believe and what we know. However, what the difference is between believing something and knowing something has generated an abundance of philosophical wrangling.

Within much analytic epistemology in the 20th century, believing and knowing were considered to be forms of transient consciousness, *propositional attitudes*. They were different psychological attitudes of knowing or believing in speakers that were directed at propositions: "i know or believe that all swans are white". The knowing and believing were described as cognitive relations between the speaker and the proposition represented by the utterance, relations between the speaker and the thought being expressed. Speakers were said to have a mental, psychological or cognitive attitude of belief or knowledge toward these psychological propositions, i.e. *propositional attitudes*.[10]

Many modern physicalists attempt to deny that knowledge and beliefs are states of transient consciousness, cognitive relations or propositional attitudes. They claim that knowledge and beliefs are nothing more than *dispositions* to behave in certain ways. Unfortunately, the multiple uses of the word sound "disposition" markedly confuse the debate. One definition attributes dispositions to inanimate objects: "physical inclination or tendency: the disposition of ice to melt when heated." (Random House Dictionary 1970: 414). Another definition of "disposition" includes a use that places dispositions firmly on the mental side of the ontological ledger: "the prevailing tendency of one's spirits, mental outlook or mood." (Ibid).

Without a doubt, humans and other creatures are disposed to do many things based on heredity and behavioral history of each organism. Both have dispositions to behave in many ways that have nothing to do with knowledge or beliefs. For instance, this author doesn't use his right hand predominantly because he *knows or believes* he is right-handed. He is just disposed to use his right hand most often for one-handed tasks. We humans have dispositions to walk, eat, and drive in our own unique ways. As our dictionaries inform us, many such dispositions are considered to be simple tendencies or inclinations for inanimate objects, humans and other creatures to react in a certain way when they are exposed to certain contingencies in their environment. They are considered to be "*physical* inclinations or tendencies", like the ice cube's disposition to melt when exposed to heat.

Yet, other human dispositions are said to be based on *mental* attitudes of belief or knowledge. For example, if this author has the belief or knowledge that beer is in the fridge, he will be disposed to behave in certain ways, e.g. go to the fridge for a beer or tell someone else that there is beer in the fridge. The disposition to produce such behaviors is commonly said to depend on the mental beliefs and knowledge retained in memory and brought to mind or consciousness at times. The philosophical question is whether beliefs and knowledge, as dispositions, can be both mental and physical in nature. Do both types exist, as our English speech about them would indicate? The pertinent question for physicalists is: are humans endowed with, or do they develop unobservable *mental or psychological* attitudes in the form of knowledge and beliefs which guide their observable behavior or are they like the ice cube with purely physical dispositions?

From the non-semantic point of view, there is no justification for making mental/physical distinctions about dispositions. The fact that the author can perform declarative propositional statements with varying degrees of certitude does not entail that he is carrying psychological or cognitive attitudes of belief and knowledge in his mind or consciousness. The author's disposition to behave verbally in certain ways is no different than his disposition to behave non-verbally. He has dispositions to put speech sounds in a certain order to perform various tasks. Such behavior has nothing to do with "the prevailing tendency of one's spirits, mental outlook or mood". It is a result of S-R-R neural connections.

All speaking humans have a disposition to produce certain verbal behavior in response to stimuli. That behavior is often in the form of a proposition. It is a result of the previous conditioning of the organism. To say that you have knowledge or beliefs is to say that you have a disposition or inclination to put language specific words together in a certain way if you are given the proper stimuli. That disposition comes with other behavioral dispositions. If the door on the bathroom swings in, you will have a disposition to say: *the bathroom door swings in*. You will also have a disposition to push on the door from the outside rather than pulling on it. In neither case do these dispositions entail that you are carrying cognitive attitudes of belief or knowledge toward a mental proposition that you are toting around in your head.

Without dualism and its semantic accomplice, these mental or psychological attitudes are just historical oddities brought about by the ontological musings of philosophers. Philosophers are the culprits who have concluded that we humans have cognitive relations of belief or knowledge toward psychological propositions, that we have "propositional attitudes". Unfortunately this dogma of psychological attitudes of belief or knowledge toward mental propositions retained in human minds has since been institutionalized in English speech behavior.

We *say* that beliefs and knowledge are the *reasons* for our behavior, as opposed to our dead ancestors, demons, the alignment of the planets, etc. However, the disposition to make these claims about beliefs and knowledge are entirely misguided by our English speech behavior. We SAE-speaking people talk about our verbal behavior this way because of the language habits we have been inculcated with, language habits that have dualism and semantics baked into the cake. Let us eliminate our disposition to speak about our speech in dualistic terms. Knowledge, beliefs, propositions, propositional attitudes, and all the rest of the habitués of human minds or consciousness are dualistic fictions that have no place in serious linguistics, science, or philosophy.

At this point, another point must be made about the abuse of the word sounds *beliefs*, *knowledge* and *facts* by epistemologists. There are an infinite number of declarative assertions that humans can create with language. A person could say: *i believe there is a stoplight on the corner of broadway and main street*, or *i know there is a stoplight at washington and main street*", or "*it is a fact that there is a stoplight on the corner of first and main*". Humans place objects and events in space and time relative to other objects and events. This provides them with the ability to create an infinite number of linguistic assertions about these states of affairs.

Unfortunately, philosophers have done an enormous disservice and created an incredible morass of philosophical literature by saying that any of these propositional statements can be interpreted as "properties". Consider for example: "*the light had the property of being green at 12:31 pm*" or "*the light had the property of being located at broadway and main street*". Obviously, this creates an infinite number of properties for philosophers who use this ploy. However, it is plainly absurd to talk about properties in this way and it leads to endless confusion. It is philosophical mumbo jumbo of the highest order. Like "*reality*" and "*truth*" the word sound "*properties*" is hideously abused by non-philosophers and philosophers alike

An alternative way of talking about "properties" is to say that humans detect differences and similarities just as non-human creatures do. On the basis of those differences and similarities they make distinctions based on their needs as individuals and cultures. Humans make distinctions about color, shape, size, location, time, duration, quantity, and so on. They then make distinctions about these distinctions. They then tact with them and connect them with word sounds. They create facts. That is what makes humans exceptional.

"What it's like" Knowledge

As an epistemic argument (the ontological argument was discussed in Chapter 3), many epistemologists like to say that congenitally color-blind people cannot *know what it's like* to see red because they have had no red qualia, i.e. no sensations of red. These *absent qualia* are used as a justification for claims that certain people do not *know* certain things that other people know. To present the point another way, because we humans cannot see ultraviolet radiation these philosophers are suggesting that we are missing some knowledge about ultraviolet radiation. (Some creatures, e.g. bees, can sense ultraviolet radiation.)

Of course, all *facts* about ultraviolet radiation consist in the ability to produce declarative propositional knowledge, e.g. "*i know that ultraviolet radiation is...*" Consequently, if a person is able to use language proficiently, they would be able to know everything there is to know *about* ultraviolet radiation. They can *know that* ultraviolet occupies a certain portion of the EM spectrum, *know that* ultraviolet can be refracted, reflected, and used in chemical analysis. They can know everything that other people *know about* ultraviolet because they *know how* to use word sounds. Yet, they cannot *know what it's like* to see ultraviolet radiation. Bees can.

This "what it's like" knowledge is a recent innovation for epistemologists. It is new and unique because it is neither procedural knowledge (know how) nor declarative knowledge (know that). Knowing what it's like to see red, for example, is not a skill or procedure that can be practiced or performed, as can alternative procedural knowledge. Nor can knowing what it's like to see red be judged true or false, as can declarative knowledge claims. Thus through this use of the phrase "*what its like*" epistemologists seem to have created a new form of knowledge outside of the traditional procedural/declarative knowledge partition, i.e. *what it's like knowledge*.

The upshot is that the use of the word sound "*knowledge*" this way opens up a whole new can of epistemological worms. Of course there is no reason philosophers can't create new forms of knowledge but, in this case, this author would propose that this absent qualia argument is just another linguistic contortion being used as a rhetorical device. If we do accept this new category of knowledge it would seem that bats, bees, sharks and other creatures of all sorts have knowledge that humans will never have and some people will have knowledge that other people will never have no matter what they do. Would it not make more sense to keep knowledge claims within the traditional procedural/declarative framework and say that sensations are species specific?

Chapter VI

Summary & Notes

Down through history, philosophers have searched for indisputable knowledge. Disputes about what can be known to be true with certainty have fueled heated debates and many distinctions about various types of knowledge claims. However, all of these debates and distinctions have been misguided because they have presupposed the semantic fallacies and their concomitant mind/body dualism. If we dispense with these false assumptions about human verbal behavior, knowledge claims in the form of propositions can be seen for what they are, a form of verbal behavior with acoustic devices that produces neural connections in hearers who have the same language skills.

Making these claims to knowledge requires linguistic skills humans learn at an early age, skills that can produce approximately equivalent behavior in similarly skilled individuals. It is behavior that humans learn through iterated learning. Epistemologists must ultimately acknowledge that they are not analyzing concepts, ideas or propositions in the mind or consciousness of a speaker when they analyze declarative propositional statements. Nor are they analyzing context invariant lexical or literal meanings encoded in the symbols. They are analyzing conditioned verbal behavior in a declarative propositional format which can be used in many ways.

Propositions are not only the smallest units of a dualist's epistemology; they are the smallest units of a behaviorist's epistemology. Propositional knowledge claims are verbal behavior used to propose connections between the people, objects, actions, events and kind-sortals that humans can recognize and tact with by means of acoustic devices. However, these *know that* declarative propositional claims are no different than *know how* procedural claims of knowledge. Speakers must perform muscle movements based on neural connections; how to make the sounds and what to do with them in response to various stimuli. Speakers must *know how* to tact with word sounds and how to perform a proposition within their linguistic community if they are to claim to *know that* something is the case.

Although these speech acts are normalized within speech communities they are not *rule governed*. They are very simple procedures whereby humans can pair up people, objects, etc. they recognize. We humans remember how to form the sounds and what to do with them in various contexts under the influence of various stimuli. People who are similarly skilled because of their iterated language learning will recognize the referring acts and the connection being made in a propositional speech act performed by a speaker. They will follow the speaker's lead, making similar connections between the objects, events, actions and kind-sortals he is tacting with, i.e. "my dog is black".

The *truth* of any declarative propositional statement made with natural language is entirely dependent upon the parties agreeing, either implicitly or explicitly, to use the words in the same way. That may be difficult though, because with word sounds, humans work in a fuzzy world of approximation, perspective and interpretation. When people use natural language in a declarative knowledge claim, the inherent imprecision of word use creates the indeterminacy that frustrates the attempts of logicians and linguists to find their absolute truth, certainty and logical necessity. Yet people need natural language acoustic devices to tact. People need these word sounds to say anything *about* the world.

A written declarative knowledge claim is merely a recording of the use of a propositional speech act by someone at sometime in response to stimuli. When we do record verbal behavior by means of writing we have not created independent speaker neutral facts that are true or false regardless of the context, the presuppositions and the writer's history of verbal behavior. There are no speaker neutral independent facts carried by word symbols. To think otherwise is to head up the primrose path of Plato, Aristotle, Augustine, Hume, Locke, Leibniz, Kant, Russell, Frege, Ayer, Wittgenstein, Kripke, et al.

The availability of a surfeit of functional acoustic devices is the hallmark of educated people. But what each one of them does with the devices is a matter of conditioning that differs from person to person. How English speakers use "know" and "knowledge" will never be totally consistent. Nevertheless, delineating and refining their uses for educated people is a worthwhile enterprise. Epistemology, ultimately, can be a subject of empirical investigation. It is a matter of investigating how people utilize word sounds and then delimiting their use within other empirical investigations.

---

1. "In 2014 the neuroscientist John O'Keefe won a Nobel prize for showing that mammals have 'place cells' in their brains – an inner mapping system that helps them find their way in the physical world." Susan Pinker, The Wall Street Journal, 10/24/15.

2. Humans sort through their experiences as presented by their receptor organs and make kind-sortals. This sorting process is often influenced by conditioned reinforcement in their culture, making the sorting process culturally specific. Some people sort green into forty classes or *sorts*. Others have one *sort* of green.

3. A third category of paradoxical propositions has been added by some philosophers, e.g. "All bachelors are married". However, in doing so, they have unnecessarily complicated things because these paradoxical propositions are still analytic. That is, they are known to be false "by mere operation of thought" just as all true analytic statements are.

4. His picture theory of language fell by the wayside too: "It is our failure to recognize this fact about language, Wittgenstein contends, that has led us to mistakenly assume that we can make use of language as a tool for furthering our understanding of the mental world. We mistakenly assume that because we have words such as 'thought,' or 'reading,'or 'understanding,' there must exist structures or processes which we then rely upon for orienting our investigations of the mental world. But if 'thought,' 'reading,' and 'understanding,' as well as any seemingly more precise scientific terms we happen to coin, merely constitute a set of meaningless verbal tools, lacking in any consistent application, which we manipulate in multiple and highly variable ways in talking about the mental world—in playing that aspect of our language game—then we certainly cannot reliably make use of them as analytic tools for investigating that world. This is not to imply that, according to Wittgenstein, there is no mental world, no level of cognition separate from language, nor that language might not exert an important influence on that world, but only that we cannot make use of the words our language provides as keys to an understanding of that world. Unfortunately, however, we have no other means at our disposal; and, thus, any understanding of the mental world and, therefore, its relationship to language lies beyond the limits which the very nature of language places on our

cognitive capacities. For Wittgenstein, then, the question of whether or not language shapes thought makes sense to ask, but it is impossible to answer." Bloom (1981: 8-9)

5. There is a great deal of research that has been done regarding "joint attentional" behaviors that arise as part of the development of social cognition in infants. Such as: "Carpenter, Nagell, and Tomasello (1998) followed longitudinally the emergence of nine different "joint attentional" behaviors, along with the emergence of linguistic skill, in infants from 9 to 15 months of age. The joint attentional behaviors included both those in which the infant followed into the adult's behavior or attention (e.g., gaze following, imitation of actions on objects) and those in which the infant directed the adult's attention via such actions as pointing and showing. Language comprehension and production were also assessed. The relevant findings were as follows: (1) All nine of the nonlinguistic joint attentional behaviors emerged in individuals as a group (mostly within a three to four month time window). (2) These behaviors emerged in a predictable order: first, behaviors that involved the infant checking what the adult was attending; next, those in which the infant followed adult attention to outside objects and events. (3) There was a very strong correlation between infants' ability to engage in joint attentional activities with their mothers and the emergence of language comprehension and production." Gentner and Goldin-Meadow (2003: 49)

6. Einstein was a prototypical rationalist in that he relied upon pure thought to develop his theories. He did no experiments. When experimental evidence confuted his thinking, e.g. quantum mechanics, he dismissed it.

7. Contemporary truth conditional semantics suffers from the same defects of bivalent Aristotelian logic. This view posits that as long as our *meanings* are clear, statements are either true or false. They cannot be of indeterminate status or middle ground. This TCS analysis fails to account for the ubiquitous personal and fuzzy applications for word sounds in context.

8. Logicians have come up with various ways to *show* the logic of propositional calculus. One of the most ingenious and widely used visual representations of propositional logic is the system of Leibniz/Euler circles. These diagrams can *show* the form of a logical calculus. In the visual form Aristotelian syllogisms become more perspicuous. This geometry of propositions lends credence to the bivalent logic of Aristotle where precise delineation is required and the fuzzy middle is nowhere to be seen. With these diagrams we can also see why Kant introduced the word "containment" into propositional analysis. We can say that Leibniz/Euler diagrams graphically represent the containment distinction.

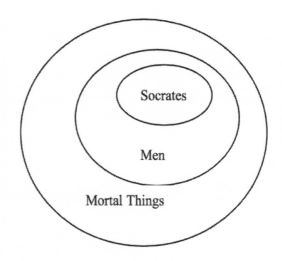

9. This distinction between nomologically possible and logically possible is the same as Russell's epistemic vs. logical truth distinction. For instance, it is an epistemic truth (based on our knowledge) that the Earth will not leave its orbit around the Sun unless it is acted upon by an outside force. The natural laws of motion developed by Newton and confirmed by centuries of observation have gained the status of *laws* because they predict what we invariably see. However, these natural laws do not preclude the *logical* possibility of a universe in which these laws do not hold. They are not logically necessary. We can imagine another world where gravity is inversely proportional to *the cube* of the distance between relevant bodies rather than the square of the distance.

It should also be noted that these natural laws are referred to as *descriptive* laws vs. *prescriptive* laws, the legal statutes or moral laws which *prescribe* legal or moral behavior. Descriptive laws *describe* the way the world is arranged, not the way that humans ought to behave.

10. Russell had reservations about the psychological nature of these propositional attitudes as early as 1918: "What sort of name shall we give to verbs like "believe" and "wish" and so forth? I should be inclined to call them "propositional verbs". This is merely a suggested name for convenience, because they are verbs which have the form of relating an object to a proposition. As I have been explaining, that is not what they really do, but it is convenient to call them propositional verbs. Of course you might call them "attitudes", but I should not like that because it is a psychological term, and although all the instances in our experience are psychological, there is no reason to suppose that all the verbs I am talking of are psychological." Russell (1918: 60)

CHAPTER 00000111

THE UNIVERSE

Introduction

What is "the nature of the Universe"? Of what does the Universe consist? These questions, it would appear to many, have straightforward answers. Yet they are questions that have befuddled and beguiled philosophers since antiquity. At first glance, the answers seem apparent. The Universe consists of stuff: birds, trees, coffee cups, stars, planets, human beings et cetera. These things *exist*. These are all things that we humans somehow sense or perceive. These are physical things, substantial things, material things, i.e. things composed of *matter*.

In addition to things composed of matter, physicists have told us that there are forces of *energy*. Various forms of energy are observed and measured: electromagnetic energy, kinetic energy, potential energy, etc. Currently, we are told by physicists that the Universe is composed of matter and energy in various manifestations and that matter and energy are interrelated; both matter and energy can be transformed into each other. Although earlier philosophers did not reach such conclusions, contemporary *physicists* have told us that the universe consists of matter and energy, *physical* things. That is the nature of the Universe.

Contemporary physicists also tell us that there are numerous interactions between these forces of energy and matter which follow *laws*, e.g. the universal law of gravitation. Physicists have discovered and described many physical laws, laws that tell us what we can expect when matter and energy, in their various manifestations, interact. Without non-physical spirits, souls, minds or divine entities interfering in physicist's equations, they have informed us that the Universe is incredibly intricate yet an ultimately predictable law-governed clockwork machine.

However, during the last century physicists suggested that the laws which govern the interaction of subatomic particles were not always predictable, not even in principle. For most practical purposes, the laws of physics still worked. On the basis of such laws, we humans could go on producing nuclear power plants and space shuttles. We could go on with our research on sub-atomic particles and space exploration. But at the quantum level of discrimination, the predictability, the models, the analogies and the language broke down. At the quantum level of the new physics, words such as *"matter"*, *"energy"* and *"law"* simply did not apply. They could not be used to describe or explain what the physicists observed at that level of discrimination.

So what is the nature of the Universe? Of what does the Universe consist? Philosophers and physicists continue to speculate, much the same as the ancient Greeks did. They not only speculate about the nature of the Universe, they speculate about the nature of matter and energy, things that make up the physical Universe.

Historical Context

"In all history, nothing is so surprising or so difficult to account for as the sudden rise of civilization in Greece. Much of what makes civilization had already existed for thousands of years in Egypt and Mesopotamia, and had spread thence to neighbouring countries. But certain elements had been lacking until the Greeks supplied them. What they had achieved in art and literature is familiar to everybody, but what they did in the purely intellectual realm is even more exceptional. They invented mathematics and science and philosophy; they first wrote history as opposed to mere annals; they speculated freely about the nature of the world and the ends of life, without being bound by the fetters of any inherited orthodoxy. What occurred was so astonishing that, until very recent times, men were content to gape and talk mystically about the Greek genius."
Bertrand Russell (1945: 3)

We can go back to the Greeks, once again, to understand the history of *matter* in Western civilization. The ancient Greeks believed that the non-celestial world was made up of four basic elements: earth, fire, water and air. In the fifth century BCE Leucippus wondered if water was composed of small particles that flowed like particles of sand on the beach, both forming the shape of the containers that held them. He believed the continuity of *materials* such as water, air or silver was actually an illusion. All matter was particulate in nature, discontinuous, and discrete particles. We should be able to identify and count the particles of air, water, or silver just as we could identify and count particles of sand.

His pupil, Democritus, thought that there must be a limit to the divisibility of these particles, and even though they were undetectable to the human eye, these particles formed the identity of substances. They were what gave different materials the characteristics that were observed. For these particles to maintain their identity as matter and not become pure form there had to be some point at which they were indivisible. Those indivisible particles would be "*atomos*", the smallest particles of air, water, or any other basic material that could maintain the characteristics and identity of the material from which they came. (The Greek sound "*atomos*" could be used as we who speak English would use "*without parts*".)

The phenomenon of diffusion in gases and liquids, and the interpenetration of solids, also led some of these Greek thinkers to the conclusion that these smallest of particles of matter, these atomos, could be combined with other such particles to form different composite materials. However, ultimately, there had to be basic particles that maintained their individual characteristics and could not be split. They would constitute the elemental particles of matter, atomos.

Underpinning the speculation about the nature of matter was the belief that the universe consisted of two realms. For some Greeks, the *material* realm contained the basic elements of earth, fire, water and air which exist here on earth, physical things. Within this material realm, these physical entities had sensable properties. We humans could see, touch and feel these physical elements. Natural philosophy for them was the study of physical things, sensable things, substantive things, material things, things composed of matter, things that *exist* here in our Universe.

Conversely, for the Platonists and many other schools, some entities were not physical, sensable, substantial or material. Non-natural philosophy, or *metaphysics* , had a vocabulary and subject matter all of its own; "'meta' coming from the Greek, defined as 'after,' 'along with,' 'beyond,' 'among,' 'behind,' used in the formation of compound words... " (Random House Dictionary 1970: 900). Souls, numbers, and ideal forms were the currency of metaphysics. These metaphysical entities were immaterial and did not exist here on earth; they existed in the *ideal* realm.

For Platonists, the Universe was bifurcated. Their dualism was quite clear about what things were located where. Material objects were only the physical counterparts of the metaphysical ideal forms. For example, because of the imperfections in any actual triangle that might be drawn here on earth, the ideal triangle, the perfect triangle, was an ideal form, a *metaphysical* entity that did not exist here on earth. Clearly, the Universe consisted of physical things and metaphysical things thought the Platonists. Of course, there were variations on this theme. But, through the years philosophers continued to juxtapose physical things with metaphysical things of one sort or another.

The development of Western civilization saw changes in beliefs about the nature of the physical Universe. During the enlightenment Western thinkers began to draw a picture of a physical Universe consisting of space, time, matter, and forces. Metaphysics was relegated to the church. With this intellectual backdrop, scholars could provide utilitarian explanations for the nature of the Universe.

These intellectual developments produced the scientific method. Natural science became more than a division of philosophy; it became a process, a methodology. Observation, experiment, measurement and verification were essential elements of the new natural science. Space, time, matter and forces could be measured in standard units. Formulae were then developed to predict the outcomes of interactions between matter and forces within a fixed background of unlimited space and time.

As physics matured, many new descriptive laws were discovered. The laws described and predicted the interactions of matter and various forces. The quantifiable interactions of matter and forces within a background of absolute space and time were the only components necessary to predict the outcomes in the material Universe. Physical phenomenon had physical causes and physical effects. The new science of physics gradually depicted a *causally closed* physical Universe with law abiding processes that gave predictable results. These new laws of physics did not allow for any non-physical causes such as divine intervention or evil spirits; only physical causes had physical effects.

As science progressed and discoveries continued, the physical Universe was found to operate on principles that men could understand and employ to control their environment. Physics and chemistry flourished as men began to appreciate the laws of nature. The movement of heavenly bodies, as well as earthly bodies, became entirely predictable when scientists applied these new laws of physics. Chemicals reacted quite predictably once the chemical laws were understood.

Physics and chemistry proved to be exceptionally reliable predictors within a law-governed, causally closed, physical Universe.

Ex hypothesis, physicists were supposed to concern themselves with *physical* phenomenon. Physical phenomena are those that humans can observe and measure. In the mechanistic Universe of Newton, space, time, matter, and forces could all be defined, measured and quantified. Speculation about matters outside of these physical phenomena was considered *metaphysics*. And although metaphysical speculation lingered on in some circles, the physical scientists were determined to restrict their investigations to space, time, matter and forces, the physical realm, things that were observable, things that existed.

Yet, in spite of the causally closed Universe depicted by physicists, few people doubted that human beings, as causal agents exercising their free will, could have effects on the physical world. Humans, through the use of their mental faculties, could be causal agents within the gigantic clockwork physical Universe. People with *mental* states and processes caused things to happen in the *physical* world. Yet no one could explain how. The physical sciences were painting a picture of a causally closed Universe governed by laws that allowed for no mind/body interaction. But it was obvious to most people that humans were in fact causal agents. By virtue of knowledge, beliefs, intentions, and personal will power (mental states and processes) people could control their future by acting upon their environment. Ergo, the *physical universe* was not causally closed.

To this day, the mind/body distinction is maintained as the psychological/physical distinction within contemporary science. The physical world is subject to investigation by physical scientists and the mental world is subject to investigation by psychologists. However, this new science of psychology cannot be reduced to physical laws. Psychological phenomena have laws of their own, mysterious laws that are described and explained with the new psychological terminology: the subconscious, obsessive compulsive, paranoia, manic-depressive and so on. An entire industry has grown to deal with psychological science as opposed to physical science. The study of psychology became part of the standard curriculum in education. Yet no one could explain how human mental machinations produced changes in the physical world.

While physical scientists and psychological scientists strictly proscribed their separate methods, models and terminology, philosophers continued to quibble about the ultimate nature of the Universe. Was it physical or mental? During the enlightenment, Western philosophers divided along a major fault line: *idealism vs. realism*. The *idealists* were persuaded by the arguments of Bishop George Berkeley made in 1710:

> "Their *esse* is *percipi*, nor is it possible they should have any existence out of the minds or thinking things which perceive them… in a word, all those bodies which compose the mighty frame of the world, have not any subsistence without a mind, that their *being* is to be perceived or known… " (The Empiricists p. 152)

The idealist's view (solipsism in its most severe form[1]) that we cannot prove the existence of the material world, was the crux of their philosophy. *Ideas*, thoughts, concepts, imaginings and sensations perceived by a mind were all humans could indubitably know. These items populated the internal mental world. They were not physical things. They were *ideal* things perceived by and *existing* in human minds.

The idealists and realists continue the debate to this day. The universe we humans perceive must exist in some form: mental, physical or perhaps both. In any case, *physicists* concluded that they would not indulge in such philosophical speculation. They would restrict themselves to observable data, the Newtonian world of space, time, matter and forces. The methodology and the results were important, not the philosophical speculation. Real world physics produced obvious practical results.

Then again, maybe the universe of physicists is not so real. Today, the desire to find the ultimate constituents of matter, particles that maintain their material identity, has turned into a pipe dream. As physicists divided matter into smaller and smaller particles, particles become something other than particles. Matter becomes something other than matter. In fact the words *"matter"*, *"identity"* and *"particle"* have become otiose in the world of sub-atomic physics. As the renowned physicist Erwin Schrodinger put it:

> "Democritus and all who followed in his path up to the end of the nineteenth century, thought they had never traced the effect of an individual atom (and probably did not hope ever to be able to), were yet convinced that the atoms *are* individuals, identifiable, small bodies just like the coarse palpable objects in our environment. It seems almost ludicrous that precisely in the same years or decades which let us succeed in tracing single, individual atoms and particles, and that in various ways we have yet been compelled to dismiss the idea that such a particle is an individual entity which in principle retains its 'sameness' forever." Young (1965: 121)

The smallest *particles* of matter, those Greek atomos, can, as it turns out, be subdivided. Those smaller particles can be subdivided into smaller particles, and those particles can be subdivided into smaller particles, well, sort of particles. As physicists have discovered, *"particle"*, *"space"*, *"time"*, *"matter"*, *"energy"*; all the terminology of classical physics becomes inadequate to explain the phenomena that they observe or extrapolate in the physics of relativity and quantum theory. Those terms cannot be *used* in contemporary sub-atomic physics.

Moreover, it seems that contemporary theory in physics has no connection to common sense or experimental data. Some people have concluded that it is not *science* at all. String theory, the predominant area of research in physics over the past forty years, has provided no testable hypotheses. It has not produced one single prediction that could be confirmed or denied by experiment. Smolin (2006:128). The theory consists of background dependent mathematical formulae and crude drawings of strings and loops. So, what are these strings made of? They are not material objects like strands of thread or particles of sand. They are not particulate. They are the ultimate constituents of matter according to the theory, the material that makes up material objects. Yet they do not appear to be material:

> "Strings, like their namesakes, in everyday experience, are one-dimensional extended objects. They have only length. Strings in string theory move through a background of spacetime. Ripples on the string are interpreted as particles." Hawking (2001: 52)

So now you understand that particles are composed of "strings... one-dimensional extended objects", much like a line in geometry, things that occupy space, but only one dimension of space. They have no width, only length and they ripple. Do you understand? These things are nothing like what the author can understand. It is possible to imagine a string, a particle and a line on a blackboard, but impossible to imagine one dimensional extended objects or a zero-dimensional point particle in a four dimensional spacetime background. To *imag*ine something it must have at least two dimensions in space and endure through time. These strings are unlike anything one can conjure up or understand.

Contemporary physicists also talk about eleven different dimensions of space. How can space be more than three or four dimensions? Steven Hawking, in spite of his valiant attempt to make sense of contemporary physics, finally admits:

> "I must say that personally, I have been reluctant to believe in extra dimensions. But as a positivist, the question 'Do extra dimensions really exist?' has no meaning. All one can ask is whether mathematical models with extra dimensions provide a good description of the universe." Hawking (2001: 54)

How can a mathematical model be a description of the universe? Normally we describe things with words based on the characteristics of sensable objects. We describe their shape, size, color, density and so forth. Unless they are being used to measure or count, how can mathematical symbols *describe* anything? And more to the point here, how can the universe have "extra dimensions"?

After trying to explicate string theory's eleven dimensions, Brian Greene, another contemporary physicist/writer admits:

> "... earlier work of Horowitz and Strominger, which showed that to persons such as ourselves who are directly cognizant only of three extended spatial dimensions, the three-brane 'smeared' around the three dimensional sphere will set up a gravitational field that looks like that of a black hole. This is **not** obvious and becomes clear only from a detailed study of the equations governing branes." Greene (1999: 330)

For persons such as the author, there is nothing *imag*inable, much less obvious, about branes, one-dimensional strings and the eleven dimensional-spacetime of string theory. The basic constituents of the universe seem to be indescribable, unimaginable things, things that show up in equations but cannot be described or imagined. They do not appear to be anything like the good old subatomic *particles* we learned about in elementary chemistry: protons, neutrons, and electrons.

In contemporary physics, *forces* are out too. How can gravity or electromagnetic forces act upon distant bodies without any apparent nexus? There is no spatial contiguity or medium of transmission for these forces. Gravity is said to be a distortion in a force field. Statements by physicists about force fields are subjunctive claims: *if* they were to do X, Y would happen. They observe and measure input and output; they do not observe the phenomena that they are discussing: Force fields, branes, strings, point particles, are all unobservable posits.

The space and time background of Newtonian physics has gone by the wayside too. Newton's law of universal gravitation within a fixed background of absolute space and time is inadequate to explain or describe the observations of contemporary physicists. As Steven Hawking puts it: "Gravitation is just an expression of the fact that *spacetime* is curved," Hawking (2001:18). Space and time are no longer separate background constructs. The word sounds *"space"* and *"time"* are no longer useful in physics. *"spacetime"*, however, is a useful word in contemporary physics.

Traditional ways of talking about the universe are no longer adequate to the task. Old words, models and analogies cannot satisfactorily describe or explain the hypothesized phenomena and their theoretical underpinnings. Physics was the science of the physical world. Physicists had talked about matter, forces, space, and time: things we mortals could understand, physical things. But, what is *physical* about force fields, branes, strings, point particles, or eleven dimensional spacetime? These strange concoctions are not substantive, material, physical things. The things that today's physicists are attempting to describe and explain are more like the things the ancient meta-physicians speculated about: immaterial things, insubstantial things, things without physical dimensions. The physicists have become heretics; they seem to be dabbling in *metaphysics*.

A Non-semantic Proposal
The Metaphysics of Physics

The study of what *exists* or what has *being* has been dubbed "ontology". According to many Western philosophers, ontology must provide an inventory of what there *is*, i.e. what *exists*. The ancients clearly had entities that existed in separate realms, the physical and the metaphysical. Their metaphysical realm often had theological overtones. For example, heaven was a location outside of the material world where various non-physical deities and spirits were located, as opposed to the physical entities here on earth. Many such theologies provided for the existence of entities in other non-physical worlds and for thousands of years, these beliefs fashioned much human speech about these non-physical entities enjoying another mode of existence, not a physical existence.

However, in the post-modern world, these theological renditions of metaphysical entities are rejected by many, if not most serious thinkers. Although many sophisticated individuals reject the belief that there are divine agents and forces controlling the physical universe, they continue to talk freely about human minds that interact with the physical universe. Humans clearly have minds full of thoughts, concepts, ideas, knowledge, beliefs, and intentions that enable them to interact with their physical environment, and these conscious minds are *real*; they *exist*. Yet, these minds full of mental entities and processes are clearly not physical things; they enjoy an alternate mode of existence say many well-informed people.

Ontologically speaking, there have always been two realms of some sort. In the post-modern era, minds and bodies still have separate ontological statuses or "modes of existence". In consequence, the English-speaking world has physical terminology and mental terminology that enable us to talk about entities in either ontological realm. Accordingly, we say that thoughts, ideas, concepts and intentions *exist* in our minds or consciousness, while space, time, matter, and the forces of energy *exist* in the physical world.

Regrettably, this pernicious mental/physical dualism pervades the language of physicists as much as it does our everyday discourse. Many of the problems physicists encounter when they attempt to explain their science are a result of using languages and the derivative thought processes that have evolved within the historic two-world ontology. English-speaking physicists discuss the *ideas, concepts and notions* of "*spacetime*", "*matter*", and "*energy*" as if there were *mental* correlates for these word sounds existing in their minds or consciousnesses. They also discuss *mental intentions, beliefs and knowledge* being the causes of human behavior. Yet, all this verbal behavior regarding metaphysical entities in the minds of men has no empirical evidence to support it and is a direct contradiction to their hypothesis that the Universe is causally closed.

Likewise, physicists are no longer hypothesizing about *physical* phenomena in any traditional sense. Point particles, wavicles, branes, one-dimensional strings etc. are all heuristic metaphors and models trying to make the unimaginable somehow imaginable. However, these objects of inquiry and speculation by physicists are not sensable, substantial, material, *physical objects*. They are not things that can be sensed or imagined in any way. So even if physicists use their heuristic metaphors and models, their current theories are still not grounded in classical physical phenomena and terminology that most of us can relate to. They are hypotheses grounded in unimaginable, incomprehensible posits that cannot be intelligibly explained by the physicists themselves.

Contemporary philosopher Daniel C. Dennett provides a useful "gedankenexperiment" to illuminate a number of points:

> "Imagine that we visited another planet and found that the scientists there had a rather charming theory: Every physical thing had a soul inside it, and every soul loves every other soul. This being so, things tend to move toward each other, impelled by the love of their internal souls for each other. We can suppose, moreover, that these scientists had worked out quite accurate systems of soul-placement so that, having determined the precise location in physical space of an item's soul, they could answer questions about its stability ('It will fall over because its soul is so high.'), about vibration ('If you put a counterbalancing object on the side of that drive wheel, with a rather large soul, it will smooth out the wobble.'), and about many more technical topics.
>
> "That we tell them, of course, is that they have hit upon the concept of center of gravity (or more accurately, a center of mass), and are just treating it a bit too ceremoniously. We tell them that they can go right on talking and thinking the way they were – all they have to give up is a bit of unnecessary metaphysical baggage. There is a simpler, more austere (and much more satisfying) interpretation of the very facts they use their soul-physics to understand. They ask us: Are there souls? Well, sure, we reply – only they're abstracta, mathematical abstractions rather than nuggets of mysterious stuff. They're exquisitely useful fictions. It is as if every object attracted every other object by concentrating all its gravitational oomph in a single point – and it's vastly easier to calculate the behavior of systems using this principled fiction than it would be to descend to the grubby details---every point attracting every other point."
> Dennett (1991: 367)

As Dennett explains, "the center of gravity" is a term used by physicists to refer to a theoretical location required by their theory of gravitation. Physicists cannot show you a center of gravity or observe it in any way. There is nothing at the center of gravity to indicate that it is, in fact, the center of gravity. It is merely a calculation. It shows up in their formulae as a number. Although they do not have a "concept of the center of gravity", good physicists know how and when to use the phrase *"the center of gravity"* or *"a center of mass"*. It enables physicists to talk about the formulae in which certain coordinates appear. It is an "exquisitely useful fiction".

We must also note that if physicists were to substitute the word sound *"soul"* for *"center of gravity"*, nothing of practical value would be lost. *"soul"* would give us every bit as much predictive power as *"center of gravity"*. Physicists could locate the soul just as they now locate the center of gravity. They could say that they located the soul of a space capsule and determined its trajectory. Their calculations and predictions would not change one whit. The word sound *"love"* could be used instead of *"gravity"* with the same results. They could measure the love force as they now measure the gravitational force.

"well, you say the words soul and love have so many theological or psychological connotations". This, my learned friends, is not so. Words do not have connotations; they have uses. Your uses for all of these word sounds are restricted by your previous usage. Your previous verbal behavior informs you that *"soul"* and *"love"* are not *physical* terms and cannot be used in this context. However, the soul and love explanations, while not satisfying to us because of our linguistic conditioning, would enable us to predict outcomes every bit as well as the center of gravity explanation. We accept the physicist's center of gravity explanation only because it coincides with other *physical* explanations made with the language of physicists. Thus our linguistic conditioning allows that usage.

Even more important, is Dennett booting souls out the front door while "abstracta", as more acceptable non-physical entities, come in the back door? The theology is gone, but the metaphysics is not. *Abstracta*, wherever they exist, cannot be observed, measured or reduced to physical terms. *Souls* with their theological baggage and *concepts* with their mentalistic baggage have been replaced by other non-physical entities without such baggage it seems, *abstracta*. These simpler, more austere fictions may seem more satisfying, but they are metaphysical fictions none the less. Dualism lives on.

On the other hand, if Dennett is willing to concede that the phrase *"center of gravity"* can be used as an acoustic device to tact with a number in a formula that physicists calculate, he may have stumbled upon the elimination of metaphysics in physics. If he is willing to admit that we humans build a repertoire of sounds starting with the *use* of the sounds *"center"*, *"of"*, and *"gravity"* there is no need to speculate about the concepts and ideas in the mind of the speaker or *abstracta* in abstract space.

We humans accumulate uses for word sounds and build a linguistic arsenal as a consequence of observational learning. We use *"center"*, *"of"*, and *"gravity"* to tact with a useful fiction we have created by means of our language skills. Some of these terms have been operationally defined; others have not. Some can be quantified; others cannot. However, theorizing about the *existence* of the center of gravity makes no more sense than speculation about the *existence* of souls. Let us not put too much ontological credence in such musings. Our linguistic behavior is not a reliable source of evidence for what *exists* in the universe.

The Use of the Word *"space"*

> "The notion of the existence of empty space was first advanced by the atomist Leucippus. With this idea he undid a web of tangled thought as unwieldy as the Gordian knot, in the process providing for a mechanistic view of the world that is free of obvious contradictions. Atoms move in empty space; and that is all there is: the space the atoms occupy is filled, and the rest remains empty space. The changes we observe in the world do not imply changes in the atoms. They move, but they carry all the qualities of true existence as defined by the Eleatics – eternal, unchanging, immutable." Genz (1999: 61)

The Greek philosopher Leucippus proposed the existence of empty space. After all, something had to remain when you removed material objects from a space, viz. empty space and that empty space had to *exist*. Others disagreed. Greeks argued about the *existence* of space 2500 years ago. Western intellectual giants continued to argue about it many years later:

> "The two concepts of space considered by Aristotle also determined the philosophies of his disciples Thophrastus and Strato. The former defined space via ***the positioning qualities of the world of bodies***; the latter assumed space to be ***the container of all bodily objects***... Two millennia after Aristotle, Leibniz and English philosopher Samuel Clarke, the latter inspired by Newton, squabbled bitterly... over these ideas." Genz, (1999:85)

Leibniz and Clarke never did resolve their squabble. Nor has anyone else resolved the debate. For many philosophers and physicists the question remains: does space exist?

The space of Leucippus and Newton comes naturally to us English speakers. Space is a void without limits, stretching to infinity in three dimensions. Space is what is occupied by objects. When we remove the objects the space remains. That empty space has a location. It is where the object formerly was. Even when we think of nothing existing, English speech-thinking is in a context of space. No-thing existing simply means that objects are not present. However, the space is still there, void of objects. The empty space still exists. Why do we think this way?

Because the words we English speakers use require us to think this way. This is how English-speaking humans have been conditioned to use the word sound *"space"*. Generally, the sound *"space"* is used to point to an area not occupied by objects, as in *"empty space between the lines"*. When we use the word in this way, we are not concerned about the nature or the essence of space. We are not concerned about whether space is absolute, curved, finite, or infinite. We are not concerned about the concept of space or whether space exists. We are getting work done with those words. Nevertheless, in doing so, we create intuitions about how we can and cannot think with the word sound *"space"*.

The original word sound *"space"* was use to tact with the empty area between two objects. When philosophers and physicists joined the action, *"space"* was co-opted for sundry purposes. We can now use it to tact with the space between our ears, logical space, outer space, inner space, virtual space, curved space, infinite space, phase space, abstract space and so forth. In each incident of use the speaker has presuppositions, a history of verbal conditioning and a context. These factors dictate their future speech and thinking about space.

How do contemporary physicists explain *"space"*? There is none in modern physics, at least none that you would recognize. That's right; there is no empty space in physics today. Gone is the empty container of space. What was empty space was found to have energy density. In fact, there is no non-empty space either. Space is no longer the container for bodily objects, force fields or energy. Space simply no longer exists. *"space"* is no longer a useful word sound for physicists doing cutting-edge physics. The infinite space and time backgrounds for Newtonian physics have gone by the wayside. *"space"* and *"time"* are not useful words for contemporary physicists. However, *"spacetime"* is a useful word. Spacetime is background for the distortions that appear to us as things in space and time. Space and time are simply different measurements for the same thing, *spacetime*.

Within the realm of physics, what are philosophers and physicists trying to do with this word sound *"space"*? If they are attempting to change your notion of space, they will fail. You have no notion of space. If they are trying to capture the nature or the essence of space, they will fail again. There is no nature or essence of space. They may succeed in changing our use of the word in certain circumstances, but the traditional uses will remain. We English-speaking humans will continue to use *"space"* to tact with the space between the lines. This language behavior will continue to shape our intuitions about the word's use, allowing us to say and think: *"what is beyond the edges of the universe"* *"what occupies that space"*. This speech behavior will also continue constraining our ability to speak or think about a limited spacetime continuum in which spacetime is curved and finite.

The Use of the Word "*time*"

> "If one takes the positivist position, as I do, one cannot say what time actually is. All one can do is describe what has been found to be a very good mathematical model for time and say what predictions it makes." Hawking (2001: 31)

It may give you comfort to know that if you speak English you think like Isaac Newton. Space and time are absolute for you if you live in the English-speaking world. When you ask: "*what time is it*", given the appropriate adjustments for time zones, you can come up with a measurement in *universal* time, e.g. 2:01 PM CST, July 6, 3019 CE. That configuration is used to refer to a point on an infinite timeline stretching to *eternity* in both directions. In Newton's world, time was absolute, universal, and eternal.

That time is not personal. That time is not something we can alter to suit our needs or measure subjectively. In the English-speaking world, time is impersonal and objective. Time is not in me or you; time is out there, speaker neutral, universal, and absolute by most reckoning. We all agree on how much time we have in a day or a year. We all agree that we have a limited amount of time here on earth. Although your personal experiences of time may be different, there is a *real* time or an *actual* time. That time would be there even if there were no people to perceive it. That time is an eternal and stable background element in Newtonian physics, just as space is.

In Occidental culture, time is measured in sidereal (measured by the stars) seconds, minutes, days, and years. We have digitized time. "*mississippi one, mississippi two*". Time does not fluctuate in our Western world. Time moves on, tick, tick tick….at a steady pace, the movement of the planets and the stars tell us so. Time was moving before you were born and will continue after you are gone. Time is out there, steady, constant, irreversible and endless.

However, what happened before the beginning of time and what will happen after the end of time? Although we are able to ask these questions, they baffle us because we view time as infinite, marching endlessly in both directions? In English it is always possible to use the words "*before*" and "*after*" when we speak about time. As a result of such speech behavior, as Benjamin Whorf recognized, we SAE speakers speak and think about time the way we do and have the intuitions about time that we have. Our speech behavior provides us with a Newtonian world of infinite space and time as background for the objects and events we witness.

However, different cultures with different languages may measure and experience time differently. Occidental measurement of time as a neutral impersonal flow independent of the observer is not a universal methodology. There are different frames of reference. The Hopi, for example, have a tenseless language and they categorize their time experience differently than Westerners with our language roots in the Indo-European, Greek and Latin cultures. Benjamin Whorf describes it:

"What surprises most is to find that various grand generalizations of the Western world, such as time, velocity, and matter, are not essential to the construction of a consistent picture of the universe. The psychic experiences that we class under these headings are, of course, not destroyed; rather, categories derived from other kinds of experiences take over the rulership of the cosmology and seem to function just as well. Hopi may be called a timeless language. It recognizes psychological time, which is much like Bergson's 'duration,' but this 'time' is quite unlike the mathematical time, T, used by our physicists. Among the peculiar properties of Hopi time are that it varies with each observer, does not permit of simultaneity, and has zero dimensions; i.e., it cannot be given a number greater than one." Whorf (1956: 216)

The Hopi did not talk about time as do SAE speakers. They did not measure time in standard, consistent impersonal units. They had no clocks and no need for them. They did not have a speaker-neutral, measured, universal time as we do. That in turn, resulted in much different speaking and thinking about time and much different intuitions about time for them. Of course the Hopi would have been able to make the same distinctions that we SAE speakers make about time, but they did not do so in their language. We find it useful to position events within a speaker-neutral background of universal time; the Hopi did not.

Because of our verbal behavior, we English speakers also speak and think about space and time as distinct and separable phenomena stretching to infinity. However, there is no background of infinite space *and* time in relativity physics. Relativity has substituted a four-dimensional spacetime manifold for three dimensions of space and one dimension of time in Newtonian physics and our speech behavior. Measurements of space and time are completely interchangeable within the physics of relativity. They are measurements for the same thing, i.e. *spacetime*. However, because of our conflicting conditioned verbal behavior about space *and* time, we SAE speakers find it very difficult to understand and accept spacetime.

Of course, relativity states that $E=MC^2$. The "C" (from the Latin 'celeritas' or 'speed') in $E=MC^2$ stands for the speed of light though that is a misnomer from the standpoint of relativity theory. "C" is simply a limit which cannot be exceeded when comparing standard, stable *Newtonian measurements* within a background of fixed universal space and time. In classical physics, we must remind ourselves, speed is a *relative change of position in space over time* as perceived and measured by an observer in a specific inertial frame of reference. The crucial point being: "C" is a comparative relation between two measurements, not a fixed, single measurement of one phenomenon. It compares a stable measurement (distance) in Newtonian space to a stable measurement of Newtonian *time*, expressed as *300,000km/s*.

However, in relativity physics the distinction between space and time cannot be made. Therefore, independent measurements of space and time cannot be made. They are the same thing and that is why the Newtonian measurement of one necessarily affects the Newtonian measurement of the other. As a result, a measurement for speed simply cannot be made in the physics of relativity. Nor can the term "speed" be defined.

Moreover, because the use of the term "acceleration" depends on the prior use of "speed" the word sound "acceleration" becomes useless in relativity as well. As Jonathan Powers explains:

"The reason why the velocity of light is an unsurpassable limit is not that things 'become too massive to move any faster' – as if the amount of matter in them were increasing – but simply that there is no way of adding velocities together so that you can reach it. In classical physics, 'constant acceleration' meant 'equal increases in speed in equal times', but in relativity theory as the speed increases so does the time dilation effect. The consequence is that the classical concept of acceleration collapses, and a new formula is needed for the addition of velocities. This formula is so contrived that if you add any velocity to the velocity of light the result is the velocity of light – hence its invariance." Powers (1982: 98)

With all due respect to Mr. Powers, there is no "concept of acceleration". However, as previously stated, relativity theory does not distinguish space from time. Hence one cannot determine speed or acceleration without reverting to Newtonian measurements which make that distinction. Yet, the precise measurement of Newtonian time (in small enough chunks) shrinks as the precise measurement of distance in Newtonian space (in large enough chunks) increases, always yielding the same result for speed: 300,000km/s; hence the invariance of C and the "speed limit".

As a side note, Western cultures developed clocks and eventually synchronized the clocks around the world to provide a universal time as measured by consistent changes in mechanical devices. The devices created the impersonal, standardized time measurement system we have become accustomed to and speak of accordingly. The late nineteenth century political battles over time synchronization from town to town and the technology that enabled it got Einstein thinking about *simultaneity*. How could anyone determine that two events occurred simultaneously, i.e. *at the same time*? The inability to ever determine if two distant clocks were perfectly synchronized led him to the conclusion that determining the simultaneity of events was impossible. That realization ultimately led to his theory of special relativity.

At any rate, modern-day physicists are no different than you and me. They ask what time it is and leave home on time to get to work on time. They talk about their office space and lab space. They then attempt to explain and describe their mathematical models with the English language. They fail because the English language they use shapes their thinking about space and time. "*space*" and "*time*" will always be useful word sounds for English-speaking physicists, but not when they discuss the physics of relativity. At some point their uses for the word sounds "*space*", "*time*", "*speed*", and "*acceleration*" simply become ineffective in the relativity frame of reference.

When physicists say that "*time*" is no longer a useful concept, they are intending to say that the distinction between time *and* space is no longer useful or even possible within the physics of relativity. However, that does not alter their quotidian discourse about time. They still find that it is worth making the distinction between time *and* space that their language dictates. As a consequence, English-speaking humans will continue to have intuitions about time *and* space that are inconsistent with relativity theory. They will continue to find it useful to measure time and space as they have done for millennia, thousands of years, or thousands of earth revolutions around the sun.

Picture a cotton sheet stretched out in two dimensions with a bowling ball placed in the center. The distortion in the sheet is like a warping of spacetime. Got the picture? Have you got the concept of spacetime? No, you haven't. Rest assured you will never get a concept of spacetime. Nevertheless, if you become an English-speaking physicist you must be able to competently use the word sound "*spacetime*" and its derivative symbol **'spacetime'**. Perhaps pictures of bowling balls distorting flat sheets will help you do so.

The three dimensions of Newtonian space and the one dimension of time are distinctions we English speaking humans impose on the universe. They are not intrinsic to the universe. They are not absolute, infinite, objective, real, or substantial. They do not exist. They are the universal background constructs that Newtonian mechanics and the SAE languages require. We have different word sounds to tact with separate distinctions about space *and* time. We also have different measurements for them. We perceive and tact with objects and events in three-dimensional space *and* time, the infinite space and time we impose on the universe by means of our receptor organs and our language.

The Use of the Word "*matter*"

"The first crack in the materialistic front appeared with the discovery of radioactivity where matter was seen to be disintegrating before our eyes into light and energy. This discovery was followed by Einstein's theory that matter and energy are different manifestations of the same thing. And, simultaneously, the unraveling of various aspects of atomic structure led to the strange conclusion that both matter and energy could be described as either particles or waves, depending on the circumstances under which they were studied. Finally, it was suggested that even particles can be presented as configurations of confined waves. Waves of what? Physics has not answered that question. Some scientists believe that they are not waves of anything but are just shapes." Young (1965: 69-70)

The history of the English word sound "*matter*" is enlightening. That history informs us on the evolution of human sound use as well as the development of modern physics. "*matter*" in discussions about physics is a relatively recent high-tech innovation. The word's origins were much more pedestrian. The English sound "*matter*" comes from "*mater*", meaning mother in Latin. Matter is the mother substance. "*matter*" was used to point to *mater*ial things, things humans could somehow sense, things they could touch and see, things that *existed* here on Mother Earth as opposed to heaven. Matter occupied *space* and endured through *time*. Our predecessors used the word sound "*matter*" in what appeared to be a straightforward way. But, all that talk was not so clear. When scientific thinkers attempted to define "*matter*", it became an impossible task.

The speculation about matter probably began with the Greeks who had the time and the inclination for such speculation, although they obviously did not use the English word sound "*matter*". Greek philosophers thought of matter quite differently than we moderns do. Take Platonic Idealism for instance:

"Plato attributes actual existence not to matter as such, but to the structural plan of matter, to its form, its idea... " Genz (1999: 26)

Werner Heisenberg characterized Aristotle's matter in the following way:

"Aristotle's matter is certainly not a given substance such as, say, water or air; also it is not just simply space. Rather it is an indeterminate physical substrate which contains the faculty to assume some given form, and thus to enter into physical reality." Genz (1999: 27)

Aristotle's matter was different than Plato's matter and Newton's matter was different than

Einstein's matter, while your matter is different from Heisenberg's matter.

Throughout history, because of pervasive influence of dualism in SAE speech, the contradistinction between *material* things and im*material* things has been quite confused. As a rule, most uses of the word sounds "*material*" and "*matter*" seemed to revolve around the use of "*existence*". As we know, for materialists, something must be substantial or material to exist, not insubstantial or immaterial. For strict *materialists*, demons, angels and ghosts do not exist. Yet spacetime, point particles and one-dimensional strings exist. Are we clear about existence now? Do you now know what "existence" *means*? Of course you don't. Neither the sound "*existence*", nor the word symbol **'existence'**, has a meaning! Nor does the word sound "*matter*".

In fact, nothing was ever clear about *existence* or *matter*. In spite of that, scientists had continued the quest for the ultimate constituents of matter. Atomic theory advanced spectacularly in the late 19th and early 20th centuries. By then, physicists had come full circle. The fundamental particles that existed inside of the atoms, the smallest units of matter, were less than particulate. They were less than matter. The great physicist Erwin Schrodinger, referring to atoms and molecules, wrote:

> "The **new** idea is that what is permanent in these ultimate particles or small aggregates is their shape and organization. The habit of everyday language deceives us and seems to require, whenever we hear the word 'shape' or 'form' pronounced, that it must be the shape or form of **something**, that a material substratum is required to take on a shape. Scientifically this habit goes back to Aristotle, his **causa materialis** and **causa formalis**. But when you come to the ultimate particles constituting matter, there seems to be no point in thinking of them again as some material. They are, as it were, **pure shape**, nothing but shape; what turns up again and again in successive observations is this shape, not an individual speck of material." Young (1965: 123)

As it turned out, the fundamental particles of matter were not material. When physicists began to dissect matter, the matter disappeared. The word sound "*matter*", although useful for some people, had become useless for subatomic physicists. Matter vs. non-matter was not a distinction they could make.

"*matter*" and "*space*" have often been juxtaposed in our verbal behavior. Space, as part of the background for Newton, is filled with matter that endures through time. Matter, space, time, and forces were the starting points for Newton. After two millennia of confusing talk and speculation about matter, Isaac Newton took the word "*matter*" and used it to define *mass*. Jonathan Powers writes:

> "For Newton the most important characteristic of a fundamental particle was its 'mass', which he defined as its 'quantity of matter'. He stated that the measure of the mass of a body is equal to the product of its density and its volume. However, since density is defined as 'mass per unit volume' this is evidently circular... Some critics, in consequence, have argued that Newton's concept of 'quantity of matter' is metaphysical and scientifically superfluous." Powers (1982: 34)

Of course, Newton had no concepts of mass, matter, or anything else. However, Newton needed to nail down a measurable quantity to use in his calculations. The term *"matter"* was too generic to label this number. He tweaked the word sound *"matter"* and came up with *"mass"*, using *"matter"* as a starting point, assuming that everyone knew what matter was. As a matter of fact, they did not. Matter was never clearly understood. In fact, all definitions of matter and mass were and are, arguably inadequate and imprecise. Even so, measurement of these things within Newtonian physics, along with predictable results in their practical application, made them supremely utilitarian and thus proved. *"mass"* had entered the language of physics with questionable philosophical credentials but real world results.

Later on physicists defined *"matter"* with some specificity:

> "Using the principle of measurement, physics defines matter in terms of the property called *mass*. Mass is measured by weighing the object or by finding the amount of effort required to produce a given change in its motion. Matter is defined as *that which has mass when it is at rest*. This definition does not explain what matter is but it does give us a way of measuring how much of it there is. It also draws a clear distinction between matter and non-matter. Perhaps this is what Bertrand Russell meant when he said that matter is merely 'what satisfies the equations of physics.'" Young (1965: 6)

Are we clear now on what matter is? Physicists claim that matter is "that which has mass at rest" and according to Newton, mass is a "quantity of matter". That sounds suspiciously circular. But wait a minute, physicists tell us nothing is at rest. Everything is hurtling through the cosmos at great velocity. "Mass at rest"?

In addition, the astro-physicists have now decoupled mass from matter:

> "John Archibald Wheeler, who coined the term 'black hole,' refers to them as disembodied mass—mass without matter." Ferris (1997: 85)

How can that be? If mass is defined in terms of matter or vice versa, how can mass be non-material or matter be non-massive? If mass and matter are decoupled, what could possibly be the meanings of these word sounds *"matter"* and *"mass"*? Physicists use these words all the time when they discuss physics. The physicists must have meanings for the word sounds *"matter"* and *"mass"*. They must understand the concepts of matter and mass. Sadly, they do not.

Do not allow yourself to say that the sounds *"matter"* and *"mass"* have meanings, ideas, concepts, or "notions" tethered to them. These metaphysical excrescences are not required for speakers to utilize these sounds or their derivative symbols. These word sounds have functional values depending upon presuppositions, the incident of use, speaker history, and so on. The word sounds *"mass"* and *"matter"* can be used by speakers within certain contexts. Yet, they represent no concepts and have no meanings, regardless of what linguists tell you. These words do, however, enable physicists to state things such as: *"energy is equal to mass times the speed of light squared"* and plug numbers into a formula that is useful.

The Use of the Words
"cause" and *"force"*

"From the time our knowledge of Greek civilization and culture begins to be reasonably definite and specific, that is, from about 600 B.C., we find among the intellectuals a totally new attitude toward nature: rational, critical, and secular. Mythology was discarded, as was the belief that the gods manipulate man and the physical world according to their whims. The new doctrine holds that nature is orderly and functions invariably according to plan." Kline (1972: 146)

The term *"physical cause"* is critical to the physical world view propounded by Occidental philosophers since the Greeks. In most of the Western world, events do not happen randomly, spontaneously, or at the whim of the gods. A predictable law-governed universe requires physical causes, followed by physical effects. Every physical event has a physical cause. Without physical causes, the underpinnings of an orderly predictable physical world disappear. That being the case, the word sound *"cause"* often comes up in any debates about scientific explanations. This opens up the Pandora's Box of *cause*.

Eighteenth century British philosopher David Hume famously analyzed *cause* by viewing a billiard game. He repeatedly witnessed one ball striking another ball. Then he saw the second ball move. Hume said that all he *saw* was the constant conjunction of events in succession. He witnessed one event repeatedly followed by another event when they were temporally and spatially contiguous. However, he did not witness *a cause*. From this he concluded that cause was an inference that may or may not be justified.

We must remember that in Hume's time, people thought that there were many *forces* at work in the world: mechanical forces, life forces, cosmic forces, supernatural forces, and more. There were many non-physical forces that animated sentient creatures, mysterious life forces, and animal spirits. There were also unobservable magical forces and divine forces that caused events to happen. However, in the nascent world of physics, only physical forces caused events to happen. These forces were clearly observable. People could see the effects of wind and water on their windmills and waterwheels. They concluded, quite sensibly, that the pushing and pulling *caused* physical objects to change position.

However, earlier in the century, Newton had declared that an apple fell from a tree because of the *force* of gravity. That was revolutionary, because he inferred a new kind of force. All physical forces, up to that time, were imagined as the pushing and pulling of bodies interacting with each other in a mechanistic fashion. Yet, the universal *force* of gravitation, according to Newton, was not a mechanical force. From all appearances, gravity required no direct contact between the physical objects under its influence. It operated at a distance without any intervening medium. Newton could see the effects of this new force, but the force itself was not apparent in any way. Yet, it was part of the fundamental glue that held the universe together. The *universal force* of gravity *caused* the earth to revolve around the sun and *caused* the apple to fall from the tree.

Moreover, the force of gravity did not move as other physical forces such as wind and water did. According to Newton, the force of gravity was ubiquitous and instantaneous. In Newton's universe, if the sun exploded, we Earthlings would recognize it even before the eight minute interval it would take for the electromagnetic radiation from the explosion to reach Earth. The gravitational impact would be felt immediately, and the Earth would leave its solar orbit. As the Earth's human inhabitants sailed spaceship Earth off into the cosmos away from the remains of the sun, the visual report of the exploding sun would eventually catch up to us.

Newton went to his grave searching for the medium that instantaneously transmitted the force of gravity across the cosmos. In spite of his failed search, this mysterious new force of gravity was ultimately accepted because it was extremely utilitarian. Gravitational *force* is a type of *cause* in physics that has satisfying explanatory power because it is used in formulae to accurately predict outcomes.

The word sound "*force*" was also prominent in pre-quantum subatomic physics. There were other forces at work: the weak force and the strong force within atoms. These forces were much like gravity. These forces acted at a distance, albeit a minute distance, and required no intervening medium to transmit them. Nor could anyone observe these forces, only their effects. The physicists just inferred that forces were at work holding sub-atomic particles together. These unobservable forces, as witnessed at Hiroshima, had incredible power as measured by previous standards.

However, "*force*" is not a popular word in today's quantum physics discussions. The origins and quotidian use of the word might confuse people into thinking that there is some kind of physical connection necessary for sub-atomic particles to have an effect on other particles. However, at that level of discrimination, interactions cannot be explained by the use of the word sound "*force*". In quantum physics today, *forces* are not even inferred. Nor are *causes* inferred. At the quantum level of discrimination, forces, temporal, and causal asymmetries are not apparent. Things just happen.

Steeped in Platonism and the semiotic analysis of language though he was, Bertrand Russell succinctly makes the point about the use of the word sound "*force*" in contemporary physics:

> "There are some respects in which the concepts of modern theoretical physics differ from those of the Newtonian system. To begin with, the conception of 'force,' which is prominent in the seventeenth century, has been found to be superfluous. 'Force,' in Newton, is the cause of change of motion, whether in magnitude or direction. The notion of cause is regarded as important, and force is conceived imaginatively as the sort of thing that we experience when we push or pull... Gradually it was found that all the equations could be written down without bringing in forces. What was observable was a certain relation between acceleration and configuration; to say that this relation was brought about by the intermediary of 'force' was to add nothing to our knowledge." Russell (1945: 539)

With all due respect to Bertrand Russell, what has changed in contemporary physics is not the "conception of 'force'". The use of the sound "*force*" and its written derivative '**force**' has changed. Verbal behavior, and the thinking done thereby, have changed. For theoretical physicists the word sound "*force*" has become otiose.

Others of us still have many uses for the sound "*force*" along with the written version. In the mechanistic Newtonian world all physical processes are interrelated by forces which cause things to happen. For example, contemporary chaos theory gives us the "butterfly effect" in which a small perturbation in one part of the world causes an effect in another part of the world. A butterfly flaps its wing somewhere and that action results in physical forces which ultimately cause a hurricane in another part of the world. Of course, that butterfly wing flap coincides with a great number of other causes to influence the creation of a hurricane. It was not the only cause.

In such cases, when philosophers say that there is more than one cause for an event, they say it was "overdetermined". Rarely does any event have just one cause. Any good lawyer can tell you that. What was the cause of today's plane crash? The plane crashed *because* the widget failed, *because* it had not been built properly, *because* it had not been designed properly, *because* it had not been tested adequately, *because* an old machine was being used in the test. Additionally, the widget failed *because* the pilot had to use an evasive maneuver, *because* the air control tower received a poor signal *because* the weather was very bad that day, because the solar radiation that day was very high, *because* there were high levels of sun spot activity, and so on, all the way back to the Big Bang.

So, what *caused* the plane to crash? Human error? Mechanical failure? Weather? Solar activity? The Big Bang? An act of God? What are you trying to prove? Your choice of *the cause* from the confluence of preceding events in the causal trail will depend upon your goals and your weltanschauung. Some people will accept impersonal mechanistic forces acting upon each other, purely physical causes in a causally closed universe. Others will accept nothing less than human or divine motivations; somebody somewhere is behind the curtain pulling the levers. People will pick and choose different causes for the same event depending upon their needs and their background beliefs.

The interconnectedness of the Universe, as we modern English-speaking humans envision it, provides for innumerable physical causes and effects. The causal chain (more accurately, the causal tree because there is no simple linear relation) extends, unbroken, back to the Big Bang. Any effect is dependent upon a substantial number of preceding causes. When people point to *the* single cause of any event, they are simply pointing at the juncture in the causal tree where they decide to stop their analysis based on what they, and others, will accept as an explanation.

Within the realm of human behavior at the societal level, humans often decide to stop the analysis of *cause* when we are able to establish moral or legal culpability, or credit, as the case may be, by whatever standards we decide to use. We play the blame game. Consider crime. Some would suggest that criminal behavior is the result of poor parenting. Perhaps we should put the criminal's parents in jail if they are the cause of crime. Another analysis can eliminate personal responsibility by saying that environmental factors, e.g. poverty, cause crime. Thus, if we eliminate poverty, we will eliminate crime. Others might hold the perpetrators personally responsible for their criminal act regardless of their parents or economic background. No claim is necessarily true or false. It just depends on where you want to assign the blame based on a whole host of factors. Those decisions are usually based on inculcated standards: cultural, legal, conventional, moral, religious, etc.

The important point is that we *decide* what causes are, based on our background beliefs, our need to maintain social order, and a coherent view of the universe. These needs vary. Hence, the causes of any event can vary considerably based on different standards.   Sociologists and politicians have great fun with their causes and effects, pointing to all manner of causes for the perceived problems of society. So, when someone uses the sound *"cause"*, ask yourself what part of that speaker's life history conditioned them to use *"cause"* in that way. What part of their cultural background and speech history induced them to pick out *one* spot in the confluence of events preceding the event which it caused?

Causation has provided rich fodder for philosophers since antiquity. Cause has spawned an entire industry which employs battalions of philosophers, scientists, lawyers, preachers, poets, and politicians. Academics and laymen alike weigh in on the subject of causation. They talk about root causes, proximate causes, causal laws, causal relations, and causal concepts. Yet, few of them agree on just what a cause *is*. Are causal relations directly perceived? Is causation like a number, a primitive, non-reducible indefinable *notion*? Is cause an innate *concept*?[2] Unfortunately they are all misled by the semantic fallacies. We English-speaking humans use the sound *"cause"* in many ways. Cause is not an idea, a concept, a notion, or a mental representation. It is a word sound used to tact with junctures in the cascade of events leading up to other events as witnessed by humans.

What Hume detected and tried to explain was the *inference* of cause by means of our verbal behavior. English speakers think that all events have causes *because* they constantly use the word sound *"because"* to connect events. Because of our persistent verbal behavior with the word sound *"because"*, we English-speakers insist that every event has a cause. *"because"* provides the glue that holds our universe together in a predictable confluence of events. We SEA speakers infer causal connections between events to draw a picture of an orderly, law-governed, predictable universe with various *forces* causing things to happen. As is the case with space and time, *cause* is imposed on the flux of our experience by our verbal behavior. SAE-speaking humans observe constant conjunction, temporal succession and spatial contiguity within a Newtonian universe and infer causes and forces because they repeatedly use the word sound *"because"*.

Of course, in conformance with our dualistic speech behavior in EA cultures, people nowadays accept the *psychological* explanations for mind/body interactions as the cause of human behavior. (1000 years ago they did not.) Psychological terms can be used to explain the causes of human behavior within the contemporary EA mind/body paradigm. For instance, your body gets up and goes to the refrigerator *because* you believe there is beer in the refrigerator. Yet, how do these mental beliefs about the world produce physical actions? We return once again to our well-worn mind/ body interaction conundrums. How do beliefs and desires *cause* changes in physical things, the neurons of your brain and, thence, the movement of your leg? Perhaps we should be more circumspect about our use of the word *"cause"* *because* we seem to be very confused about it.

Empirical research, fortuitously, can provide us with some insights on our use of the word *"cause"*. Initially, human infants do not recognize causes. The world is a just a flux of random events. Things just happen. But, gradually, they learn about causes:

> "Consider the development of tool construction and use. As early as age six months infants consistently generate simple first-order causal functions or dependencies. On the one hand, infants construct and replicate effects that are direct functions of causes while observing the effects. For instance, one object, such as a block, is used as a tool with which to push another dependent object

several times in succession while looking at the dependent object moving. On the other hand, infants anticipate and predict causal effects. For instance, they accurately use one object as a tool to block, stop, and trap another object that is moving in front of them." Gibson and Ingold (1993: 305-306)

Infant humans "anticipate" and "predict" nothing. This is the way adult humans within the ancient SAE dualist mind/body paradigm try to explain the behavior of infants. Infants react to external stimuli in their environment. Some behavior is reinforced. Infants then acquire a conditioned response that is generalized. The recognition that their actions *cause* effects is a not a leap of cognition for the infant; it is a conditioned response to stimuli that is repeatedly reinforced. Infants then learn to speak and think that events are caused *because* their caregivers persistently use the sound "*because*". When infants repeatedly ask "*why*", their caregivers repeatedly respond with "*because*", inferring a causal connection between two events.

Some analysts are inclined to say that infants acquire a concept of cause to which they later attach the sound "*cause*" in English speaking cultures. Bunkum! Children have no concept of cause, nor do they get one. The human use of the sound "*cause*" is not dependent upon concepts; it is dependent upon S-R-R conditioning and the intuitions that conditioning engenders. In mature English-speakers, the persistent conditioned use of the sound "*because*" gives language learners the intuition that everything has a cause *because* we English speakers can always use the word sound "*because*" and *because* we can and persistently do tact with something as the cause of an event.

All processes, including the flow of the universe, unfold as a tree of events, connected to one another, connected by *causes*. So say many humans.

> "As for the idea of strict causality, not only does science, after all these years, suddenly find it an unnecessary concept, it even demonstrates that according to quantum theory strict causality is fundamentally and intrinsically undemonstrable… ". *"The only object of theoretical physics is to calculate results that can be compared with experiment, and it is quite unnecessary that any satisfying description of the whole course of the phenomena should be given."* Hoffman (1959: 179)

The quote is from Banish Hoffman, an Einstein collaborator. The bold portion is from mathematician Paul Dirac. However, they are both mistaken. *Cause* is not an idea or a concept; nor has it ever been one. It is a useful word sound though *because* it makes much of our speech and thinking useful.

444

The Use of the Word "*energy*"

"The word *energy* is surprisingly new, and can only be traced in its modern sense to the mid 1800s. It wasn't that people before then had not recognized that there were different powers around – the crackling of static electricity, or the billowing gust of wind that snaps out a sail. It's just that they were thought of as unrelated things. There was no overarching notion of 'energy' within which all these diverse events could fit." Bodanis (2000: 11)

Long before the word sound "*energy*" became vogue, the world had many *forces*. Early civilizations recognized mechanical forces, life forces, cosmic forces, divine forces, and demonic forces: natural and supernatural forces of many sorts. But, gradually, as Greek philosophers came to view the Universe as an orderly predictable system, the *forces* of nature began to take on a more modern interpretation.

Aristotle's physics had separated the celestial forces from the terrestrial forces. That view held sway for nearly two millennia. After Copernicus showed that the solar system was heliocentric, it fell upon Newton to describe the natural laws of motion, combining these two types of forces into one system, a system which did not differentiate between forces on earth and forces in the celestial world. Newton said the same force that caused an apple to fall from a tree caused the earth to revolve around the sun. His *forces* could be measured and used to predict outcomes, from the trajectory of cannon balls to the trajectory of the planets. However, the contemporary use of "*energy*" had still not begun. Newton had defined mass but had no equivalent of modern *energy* to go with his mass.[3] Mass, *force*, and acceleration in a background of infinite *space and time* were all that were necessary to describe the mechanical universe in Newton's classical physics.

"*energy*" is a word sound that became popular within the past two hundred years. As the years wore on, *energy* began to appear in many guises: chemical energy, frictional energy, heat energy, kinetic energy, potential energy, electromagnetic energy, nuclear energy, and so forth. The physicists used this word very effectively by measuring and calculating the energy in various physical, chemical, and nuclear reactions. A number pointed to with the sound "*energy*" was needed to balance all the equations. But if you ask physicists what their *notion of energy* is, you will not get an intelligible answer. That is because they have no notion of energy.

The Use of the Words
"physical objects"

"In a scientific sense, we know that objects are nothing but slow events, some slower than others. Meson are extremely fast events, existing apparently for less than a millionth of a second; adult mayflies are slower events, living for only a day; and we humans are objects that will with luck exist for as much as a hundred years, making us even slower events... Where we humans naturally draw a line between objects and events is entirely relative to our size, our lifespan and life rhythms, and our perceptual mechanisms (and to a limited extent to our particular cultures). There is no absolutely non-relative fact of the matter distinguishing objects from events." Hurford (2007: 158)

It has been common practice in philosophical discussions, from the most sophisticated to the most mundane, to talk about *physical objects*. Physical objects are asserted to be material things that we humans sense, somehow. Some physical objects are detectable only by sophisticated means. They are contrasted with immaterial things which are not detectable by humans, no matter how sophisticated the equipment or techniques. Physical objects are extended in space and endure through time, whereas non-physical objects (minds, thoughts, concepts, etc.) are not extended in space, although they endure through time. Physical objects are material, made up of matter. They are substantial. Physical objects exist. Non-physical objects, although they are immaterial and insubstantial, are said to enjoy a "separate mode of existence". This is how English-speaking philosophers often speak about physical objects and their counterparts in the non-physical realm.

First and foremost, we must keep in mind that our human receptor organs and our neurological networks are not reliable sources for making claims about what exists. (recall the earlier mention of germs not being discovered until relatively recently.) Paul M. Churchland succinctly makes this point about physical objects *existing*:

"Our eyes evolved to exploit a narrow window of EM transparency in the earth's indiosyncratic atmosphere and oceans. Nothing of ontological importance need correspond to what makes our rods and cones sing." Churchland via Chalmers (2002: 364)

Of course the same argument can be made concerning our other receptor organs. Human sensations are simply too limited and too unreliable to be the only sources of data supporting existential claims about physical objects.

Moreover, it is an accepted fact about the world that whatever physical objects humans ultimately might agree to, are not observed at birth. When they are born, infants perceive nothing more than a kaleidoscope of sensations. They do not come into a world of physical objects. They enter a world of indiscriminate sensory input. The process of synthesizing that input into physical objects is a neurological process carried out by human receptor organs and their brains as they mature over time. Their cognitive apparatus puts its spatial-temporal stamp on that input and organizes it in a coherent fashion, discriminating some physical objects from background.

However, the neural processes that congeal the sensory data provided by human receptor organs into physical objects are not foolproof. Optical illusions are evidence that seeing, for instance, is interpretive. People can see the same image two different ways as in Wittgenstein's infamous rabbit/duck drawing. Or, they see an Escher drawing and get confused. The "simple seeing" of infants comes back to adults at times when they cannot discriminate physical objects in a confused visual field. They cannot see the ten rabbits hidden in the picture. The simple point is that the ability to recognize physical objects, however they are defined, is an imperfect neurological process even in mature adults.

Furthermore, psychologists have shown that infants do not realize that the physical objects they perceive continue to exist when they are beyond the infant's immediate perception. That changes. Most children by about age two are aware that previously sensed physical objects will be someplace, even though they do not perceive the objects at that moment. They become conditioned to expect things to persist. This world of physical objects persisting through time is a necessary but insufficient precondition for much mature competent human speech behavior. It is also very much a non-trivial artifact of that vocal behavior and other interactions between human organisms and their environment. English-speaking people learn that *physical objects exist*. More accurately, they learn how to use the words "*physical*", "*objects*" and "*exist*".

In the process of learning how to use the equivalents of these terms within different languages, wide variations in their use leads to wide variations about what constitutes a physical object. Not every language makes the same distinctions about physical objects that English speakers do. The differentiation between a physical object and an event, for instance, can be radically different, as Benjamin Whorf demonstrated with the Hopi and the Nootka cultures where waves, flames and houses were viewed as events. The physical objects and/or events of our experience are imposed by humans on the world no less than are the Newtonian absolute space and absolute time background for those physical objects and/or events. Physical objects and/or events are not intrinsically distinct constituents of the universe. The distinction between what exists and what happens often depends upon what language we grow up in.

Moreover, there is an implicit assumption in the use of the terms "*physical objects*" and "*physical events*" by English speakers that there are *non-physical* objects and events as well. These non-physical objects and events cannot be sensed by humans. They are not extended in physical space, although, curiously, they do persist through time and sometimes interact with physical objects and events. Some occupy the heavens: angels, souls and saints. Many are said to occupy a non-physical space: virtual space, abstract space, meta-space, or private space. Others are mental objects and processes occurring in the mind or consciousness. Objects and events come in at least two varieties for most English-speakers, physical and non-physical.

The present point is simply that much of human SAE speech-thinking about *physical objects* existing is based on our historic speech behavior, and the way SAE-speaking cultures objectify the universe is one of many possibilities. To non-SAE speaking people a tree may be an event lasting about 100 years as opposed to a physical object. Even an SAE-speaking botanist can view a tree as an ever-changing agglomeration of cells. To a theoretical physicist it can be a contiguous group of vibrating strings or a systematic modification of a field. To the author and many others it is a physical object. There is no fact of the matter.

That does not mean that physical objects are somehow illusory or unreal. It does mean that the way English-speaking philosophers ordinarily talk about physical objects existing is not a universal or necessary way of speaking and thinking about things. To say that a tree is a physical object that exists is a convenience based on our human perception and our conditioned SAE verbal behavior. As infants begin to speak, they make the same distinctions their parents do because of this verbal behavior. However, these distinctions have no ontological significance whatsoever; they vary from culture to culture and language to language.

Moreover, the physical objects and/or events, along with the space and time we English-speaking humans talk about, are interdependent. Our verbal behavior about physical objects, occurring events, space and time, all rely on each other for support. It is a coherent weltanschauung that has served us well for millennia. It is a worldview, however, that cannot be supported by the new physics of relativity. Willard Quine has characterized physical objects from the perspective of contemporary physics:

> "Physical objects, conceived thus four-dimensionally in space-time, are not to be distinguished from events or, in the concrete sense of the term, processes. Each comprises simply the content, however heterogeneous, of some portion of space-time, however disconnected and gerrymandered." Quine (1960: 171)

Modern subatomic physics tells us that the physical objects which we experience in space and time are manifestations of constituents which are not physical objects in space and time. These constituents have no sensable properties, nothing that we humans are able to discriminate with our senses. "Particles" such as bosons, mesons, gluons, quarks, photons, or gravitons are colorless, odorless, shapeless, tasteless, unsensable things. Whatever these things are, they cannot be distinguished from events. They are spacetime habitués floating in and out of existence.

Physicists can only hypothesize their existence and observe them indirectly. That is, they describe a hypothetical model; then they test the model and verify *the existence* of the model constituents by observing the effects they presumably produce. The Wilson cloud chamber, for instance, displays the track someone predicts. Hence, the model must be accurate and a "particle exists". Physicists see something in time and space. From that they infer the *existence* of something spaceless and timeless. As a result, there is a huge disconnect between the particles of physicists and physical objects we English-speaking humans experience and talk about.

In physics, the tiniest of *physical objects*, subatomic particles, have been subdivided into quarks, gluons, and one-dimensional strings. Then, invariably, when physicists talk about their trade and become philosophical, they bandy about the phrase *"physical objects"* as if it had some literal meaning. Of course, it does not. It still has some *uses*, but all of us must be aware of the ontological and epistemological limitations of its uses. When talking about particle physics, it has no use. When talking about ontology, it has no use either. Fortunately, the term *"physical object"* is not necessary in physics or philosophy. *"physical objects"*, *"see"*, *"real"*, *"actual"*, and *"true"* have uses for children, untutored tribesman, and theologians, but not for theoretical physicists or philosophers.

The realist vs. anti-realist debate in philosophy of science is a manifestation of the varied use of the sounds *physical object*, *see*, *real*, *actual*, *true*, et al. Scientists have been arguing about the ontological status of theoretical objects for centuries. Ever since the invention of the microscope, they have disagreed about whether the physical objects they see are *real*. With the advent of more sophisticated instruments such as electron microscopes, "we could use any property of light that interacts with a specimen in order to study the structure of the specimen. Indeed, we could use any property of any kind of wave at all," Hacking via Brody and Grandy (1971: 36). Electron microscopes are used to study the structure of molecules, for example. Philosophers began to say that scientists were no longer *seeing physical objects*. At some point, it seems, scientists must say that they are no longer observing *real, actual, true* objects.

Throughout our discussion about physics we must remember that people are conditioned to use sounds such as *physical object*, *space*, *time*, *matter*, and *energy* in many ways. However, these word sounds have no application in much of contemporary physics. They are *useless*. These words only make sense within certain contexts. To ask how much space is occupied by a one-dimensional string is fatuous. To ask if muons are real or if space exists is equally foolhardy. The point is: be careful how you use terms when you talk. Using the terms *space*, *time*, *matter*, *energy*, *cause*, *force*, and *physical object* may lead you where you do not want to go.

As it turns out, theologians and philosophers created supernatural entities out of linguistic gossamer. From the so-called physical objects that humans perceive in space enduring through time they inferred objects just like them only not physical. They created souls, spirits, selves and minds, non-material entities that do not occupy space, yet they endure through time and mysteriously interact with material objects which do occupy space. Gilbert Ryle clearly recognized the source of the trouble in "Descartes Myth". Referring to Descartes and his res cogitans (thinking substance) Ryle said:

> "…he tried to avert disaster by describing minds in what was merely an obverse vocabulary. The workings of minds had to be described by the mere negatives of the specific descriptions given to bodies; they are not in space, they are not motions, they are not modifications of matter, they are not accessible to public observation. Minds are not bits of clockwork, they are just bits of not-clockwork." Ryle via Chalmers (2002: 36)

Our English speech leads us to believe there is a universe of physical objects enduring through time and occupying space. Philosophers and psychologists then posit a world of *non-physical objects* not occupying space but enduring through time; they are just like clockwork only composed of bits of not-clockwork.[4]

Over the years, accommodating these *non-physical objects* within a Universe of *physical objects* has become more and more difficult as philosophical physicalism has gained traction. The interactions between heavenly habitués and earth, for instance, have become exceedingly rare. Sightings of the divinities are now greeted with skepticism. Angels, leprechauns, souls, and spirits may not be accepted as legitimate non-physical objects for many, but oddly, minds and consciousness still are. People routinely talk about human minds or human consciousness full of thoughts, ideas, concepts, intentions, etc. The non-physical conscious self with non-physical intentions, beliefs, and knowledge does non-physical thinking to maneuver the physical human body. These explanations are perfectly plausible for most people because they are so firmly ensconced in our verbal behavior. They cause little concern except for philosophers of the mind who wonder about mind/body interaction and the *existence* of intentions, thoughts, beliefs and knowledge in non-physical minds or consciousness. So mind/body dualism lives on in our SAE speech behavior and every cognitive domain that depends upon SAE speaking and thinking.

The Use of the Word *"imagine"*

"Heisenberg had hoped to play safe by playing ostrich. He had rejected all mental images and offered no unproved pictures of what might be going on within the atom, for it was such pictures, he felt, that had caused the Bohr theory's downfall. Dirac, too, began by renouncing pictorial imagery." Hoffman (1959: 141)

The word sound *"imagine"* is used quite haphazardly by English speakers. As we now know, it has no meaning. It has multiple and varied uses. To *imag*ine something is often to create an *image* in the mind's eye, ear, nose, or tongue as the case may be. I can imagine evergreen trees, the sound of a violin, the smell of charcoal, the taste of chocolate etc. I can also imagine composites of things I have experienced, e.g. unicorns, an up-tempo star-spangled banner, and blackberry pie. Yet, there are things that cannot be imagined things people have not experienced. People cannot imagine the color of infrared light or the sound of a dog whistle. Our imaginations are limited.

Indeed, because we cannot imagine many of the constructs of modern physicists their explanations are less than compelling. Willard V.O. Quine explicates that process well:

"Thus in the physics of light, with its notorious mixed metaphor of wave and particle, the physicist's understanding of what he is talking about must depend almost wholly on context: on knowing when to use various sentences which speak jointly of photons and of observed phenomena of light. Such sentences are like cantilever constructions, anchored in what they say are familiar objects at the near end and supporting the recondite objects at the far end. Explanations become oddly reciprocal: photons are posited to help explain the phenomena, and it is those phenomena and the theory concerning them that explain what the physicist is driving at in his talk of photons.

"One tends to imagine that when someone propounds a theory concerning some sort of objects, our understanding of what he is saying will have two phases: first we must understand what the objects are, and second we must understand what the theory says about them… In the case of wavicles there is virtually no significant separation; our coming to understand what the objects are is for the most part just our mastery of what the theory says about them. We do not learn first what to talk about and then what to say about it." Quine (1960: 15)

From the standpoint of extraterrestrials observing human physicists, *understanding* the constructs of physics consists in *saying* the proper things about them and doing certain mathematical calculations proficiently. The talk becomes more and more recondite and more distant from our commonsense intuitions created by our quotidian speech behavior. We can imagine particles and waves, and we know how to use these words. Yet, we cannot imagine what a *wavicle* could be. The only *evidence* for an *understanding* of wavicles consists in being able to talk about them proficiently and perform certain mathematical calculations.

Nevertheless, physicists have a desire to imagine and explain these mysterious objects that they talk about. They fail. Human imagination, based on human sensations and ordinary language, simply falls short. Words such as *"dark"*, *"matter"*, *"energy"*, *"existence"*, *"physical object"*, etc., simply will not work to make these hypothetical constructs imaginable. Physicists will still use models, metaphors, and analogies to describe and explain their constructs but that will not make these new objects more imaginable. The heuristic imagery may be helpful, but it will never adequately describe or explain what is, at its core, unimaginable.[5]

Furthermore, it is worth repeating that when physicists talk about these unimaginable objects, none of them have acquired new *concepts*. What they have acquired are new word sound uses. Just as they learn how to use *"center of gravity"* by starting with *"center"* and *"gravity"* and combining their functional values. They can then tact with inferred, yet unimaginable constructs: dark matter, p-branes, non-extended point particles, wavicles and one-dimensional strings in eleven-dimensional spacetime. However, when they do so, they have no concepts to associate with them. They have simply learned arcane verbal behavior which is encoded in their neurons.

The Use of the Word "*explanation*"

> "Descartes with his vortices, his hooked atoms, and the like explained everything and calculated nothing; Newton, with the inverse square of gravitation, calculated everything and explained nothing." Rene Thom via Nancy Cartwright (1972: 65)

Explanation as a philosophical issue has been around since Aristotle. Lately it has become more contentious in the philosophy of science. When is something explained? What is an adequate explanation? Various theories and models have been developed, yet no model is acceptable to everyone. The debate continues. To give you a flavor of the debate, this is a quote from Peter Achinstein:

> "A model of explanation is a set of necessary and sufficient conditions that determine whether the explanans correctly explains the explanandum." via Brody and Grandy (1989: 200)

The response from many was that birth is a necessary and sufficient condition for a death, but it does not explain the death. Also, you may well have noted that Atchinstein's explanation of a model of explanation says that an explanation must "correctly explain". Now that clears things up!

Scientists and philosophers of science have been trying to promote various models of explanation for years. There was the Deductive-Nomological model, the Inductive-Statistical model, the Essential Property model, et al. Sadly, the debaters think they are talking about the *meaning* of "*explanation*", or the *concept* of explanation and all its attendant concepts: "*cause*", "*truth*", "*essential properties*" etc. While all these discussions helped expose the linguistic source of the debate, they failed to resolve the debate because, as we now know, these word sounds do not have stable lexical meanings, referents, concepts, or "notions". While it may be helpful to refine our use of these words in various contexts, no one will ever find universally acceptable *explanations* because the use of the sound "explain" will vary, as it always has.

How do we use "*explain*" today? What constitutes an adequate explanation? These questions bring to mind the author's father's refusal to believe the explanation that market forces were to blame for the rise in gas prices. For him, the only acceptable explanation was somebody, somewhere, somehow manipulating prices, some shady characters in a smoke-filled room, motivated by greed, deciding they wanted to increase the price. Any explanation short of cabal-like shenanigans of evil profiteers was simply unacceptable. The point is, people accept explanations when they coincide with their preconceived beliefs about the how the Universe and the people in it function.

What would constitute an adequate explanation for anyone depends on many cultural, educational, philosophical, and personal factors. In addition, there are many conversational clues that dictate appropriate or satisfactory explanations within specific contexts. H.P. Grice and John Searle outlined some of these "Conversational Implicatures" in the 1970's. Suffice it to say that the study of human conversation is in its infancy. However, the basic point Grice and Searle made is that conversation is a skill that requires much more than a technical command of a language. It requires familiarity with appropriate responses for each conversational setting, including what would be an acceptable explanation in varying circumstances.

As is the case with all human speech activity, requests for explanations are entirely context dependent. For example, if you drive to work on a regular basis and a coworker repeatedly asks you: "*why did you drive to work today*" you have little idea what would be an explanation. Your response would likely be a question. "*was i supposed to hitch-hike*" or more likely: "*what on earth are you getting at*". If your wife asks you the same question after taking the bus to work because her car is in the shop, you know perfectly well what an adequate explanation would be. There is none.

From an EA scientific point of view, many adequate explanations have changed over the years. For example, the pre-Darwinian explanation for plants following the sun was couched in intentional terms. Plants followed the track of the sun because they *wanted* to survive, and they *intended* to do so by following the track of the sun. That explanation has been supplanted by a functional/mechanical explanation that has gained acceptance in the post-modern era. The plant secretes hormones etc. Because of this, it follows the sun and survives. A purely physical natural selection process drives the survival of each plant and each botanical species within the functional/mechanical natural selection explanatory paradigm. Consequently, for most well-educated people the anthropomorphic intentional explanation has been eliminated within the botanical realm. There are no intentions, purposes or desires required in the functional/mechanical explanation of plant behavior and survival. However, that has only been considered an adequate explanation for a few hundred years in the West.

Within a philosophical setting, what individuals accept as an adequate explanation varies with the individuals, their circumstances and their background beliefs. For example, evolution is generally accepted by scientists as an explanation of the development of the human species. They are a minority in a world of fundamentalist Christians, Jews, and Muslims who accept other explanations for the appearance of human beings on this planet. The pertinent point of all this is simply to say that explanations vary as much today as they have always done. Nevertheless, some consensus on the adequacy of an explanation must ultimately be grounded in its coherence with other explanations and the data to be explained. *For the author's purposes here, evolution, the functional/mechanical paradigm and S-R-R conditioning explain all matters at issue in this book.*

The use of the sounds "*truth*", "*correctness*" and "*accuracy*" come into play here as well. Explanations are not true, correct, or accurate. They are simply *accepted* or not, *ex post facto*. Voodoo, astrology, and Freudian analysis are often accepted as explanations for human behavior. They provide acceptable answers to those who have some non-traditional beliefs about the world and how it works. To think that any explanation is true, accurate or correct, results from the belief that other explanations you accept are true, accurate, or correct and this one is consistent with those others. The point is; anyone who claims to have a *true, accurate or correct* explanation of any sort is simply saying that it is *acceptable* to them.

More to the point, here, what humans accept as an adequate explanation changes with their culture *and their language*. If they insist that there is something intrinsically *mental* in their experience that distinguishes humans from mechanistic plants, no explanation short of a *mental* explanation for human behavior will suffice. However, intellectually sophisticated people will not make that assumption. The mind/body dichotomy is an ancient artifact provided by philosophers and inculcated in many language users by virtue of their linguistic upbringing. Given enough empirical data and a change in their linguistic behavior, the functional/mechanical explanation will be adequate to explain human behavior as well as the behavior of sunflowers.

Moreover, in our talk about explanations, let us not be fooled by Greek writings about *the nature or the essence of anything*. This talk is metaphysical hocus pocus of the highest caliber, yet hocus pocus none the less. Scientists are rightfully reluctant to talk about the nature or essence of anything. Philosophers have not shown such restraint. In 1996, Paul Churchland reviews the philosophical arguments concerning the *ultimate nature* of light in "The Rediscovery of Light":

> "Why should mutually-inducing electric and magnetic fields (for example) oscillating at a million billion Hertz and propagating at 300,000 km/sec ever give rise to the intrinsic feature of *luminance*? After all, we can easily imagine a universe that is filled with oscillating EM fields propagating back and forth all over the place, a universe that is nonetheless utterly *dark*, because it is devoid of the additional feature of luminance. We need to know how, when, and why oscillating EM fields cause the ontologically distinct feature of intrinsic luminance. Until we understand that mysterious causal relation, we shall never understand the ground and real nature of light." Churchland via Chalmers (2002: 364)

Within the physicist's model, light is electromagnetic radiation within the visible spectrum consisting of all colors, etc. That is an adequate explanation of light *for a physicist*. The scientific explanation of light gives us some very utilitarian methods of measuring and manipulating light, though it is not the only way of *explaining* light. A graphic artist or a religious fundamentalist may not agree. Even within the scientific community there are experts who disagree.

Anti-reductionists, for instance, assert that the nature of light is not reducible to physicist's models of electromagnetic radiation. *Explanations* of waves and/or particles cannot possibly explain the "real nature of light". However, the problem is that Churchland and the others start with the wrong assumption, i.e. there is *a nature of light*. Light can be described and explained in many ways. None of them can capture the nature of light because there is none. This sort of musing is straight out of the Greek essentialism playbook. The point is simply that there is no essential nature of light. Nor are there any essential meanings that accompany the use of the sounds: *"light"*, *"explain"*, or *"explanation"*. Nor are there any explanations that will reveal *the nature of light*.

In this instance, the question should be: what are the many ways in which English- speaking humans use the word sound *"light"*? In response to what stimuli? In what circumstances? The sounds *"explanation"* and *"light"* refer to nothing. They are sounds and derivative symbols that have many and varied uses that are totally context dependent. We *"flip a light switch light a fire light up the scoreboard"* and *"take up a light load"*. We have *"sunlight"*, *"black light"*, *"artificial light"*, *"light waves"*, *"light particles"*, and on and on. In addition to sunlight we have sunshine. What is the ultimate nature of *"shine"*?

To wrap this section up, let me suggest that the ex post facto need for explanations allows for the variability in them. After the fact, we can have a multitude of explanations consistent with what is being explained. Post-dictability opens the explanatory door to voodoo, astrology, and Freudian psychoanalysis. However, pre-dictability slams that door shut. Most of us accept scientific explanations because they not only provide the answer to *why* something *did happen*, but help us predict *where and when it will happen again*. Thus, predictability ought to be the gold standard of acceptability for any explanations. Nevertheless, acceptable explanations for any phenomenon will vary from person to person, as they always have.

The Use of the Word "*describe*"

"Explain something… to give an account of something by giving details of its characteristics." Encarta Dictionary online.

As always, we must be aware of the fact that "*describe*" is a sound we English speakers use in response to various stimuli at various times under various circumstances. The sound refers to nothing. It represents nothing. It has no literal/lexical meaning. Speakers use the sound quite idiosyncratically because how people go about describing anything is not clearly *prescribed*.

At the novice level, the process of *describing* consists of verbal tacting acts which enable young speakers to tact with objects and their characteristics. Ordinarily, to describe something requires words such as "*green*", "*stinky*", "*wet*", "*hard*", or "*loud*", words based on human sense perceptions of what are sometimes called "properties". We learn to use these sounds as youngsters when we discriminate sensable characteristics of objects. We engage in verbal tacting behavior when any given characteristic is made relevant by stimuli. We have other words such as "*round*", "*below*", "*before*", "*big*", and "*three*" which we developed to describe our experiences. If you eliminate these word sounds, descriptions seem less than adequate. E=MC^2 for example, does not seem to describe anything.

However, with language, humans can carve up the world differently. Different groups of people find needs for different descriptions. For instance, within the portion of the EM spectrum detectable to most humans, we sort the spectrum in many ways. Nowadays, a local paint store can produce thousands of colors of paint. One can choose from clean pink, cornsilk gold, gelato, frosted apricot, and so and so forth. The visible spectrum has not changed. Human perception has not changed. What has changed from your grandmother's day, are the distinctions we make about color. We make more and more distinctions using more and more words to more accurately *describe* things. You can now say that the bedroom is a "*clean pink*". However, we must keep in mind that the word sounds we use to describe are in no way an intrinsically necessary or essential part of nature, or even an essential part of human culture. The distinctions we tact with to describe things are filtered through our senses, our cultures, and our word histories. Other people may make other distinctions.

The relevant point here is that we must have the ability and the need to make distinctions. When we do, we will use words to tact with those distinctions. That is how we *describe* things. However, we cannot understand distinctions that are not grounded in human perceptions in the same way that we understand those that are. Modern physics makes many distinctions that are necessary for their constructs, yet many of those distinctions cannot be related to human sensory experience. We have no way of sensing, imagining, explaining or describing mass points, one-dimensional strings, gluons or Bose-Einstein condensate. They are beyond human sensory abilities and our imaginative abilities. Even so, we can talk about them and just as we can talk about infrared light. We just can't sense, imagine or describe them in the way we normally sense, imagine, and describe things.

Modern day physicists say that mathematical equations are adequate to describe the Universe. But are they? They have *predictive* power, no doubt, but the *descriptive* force of mathematical equations used by physicists is suspect at best. Physicists get predictability and utility. They get results. What more of a description do we want? We want one that uses the words the way we have always used them. But we will not get that. Physicists will be unable to fulfill our wish, no matter how hard they try. There are no words that can *describe* mass points, one-dimensional strings, gluons or Bose-Einstein condensate the way we can describe *the soft red fragrant sweet strawberry*. Nevertheless, physicists talk about these constructs and perform mathematical calculations that are very useful in their practical application.

There are a number of other points to be made about the process of *describing*. *red*, *sweet*, *fragrant*, *loud* and *painful* are sounds we use to describe by tacting with these features based on our human sense receptors. However, we cannot describe red, sweet, fragrant, loud, and painful; we have no tools to do so. We describe things with words that result from our sensations, but we cannot describe the sensations. The red, the sweet, the stink, the loud, and the pain are simply indescribable. We can tact with these characteristics with sounds, but we cannot describe them. We cannot pull ourselves up by our bootstraps. These are the foundational word sounds used to tact with distinctions that humans are able to discern with their receptor organs. These foundational words are used to do the describing, but we cannot describe the sensations they are based on.

Scientific description, however, can often be made totally independent of any human sensory experience. The philosophy of science has dubbed the method of officially defining terms used in science as "operationism". Scientific terms have officially sanctioned operational definitions. By conducting an operation of some sort, scientific terms gain measurable value. They are quantified. The use of the term *hard*, for instance, is quantified by a standard operation that consists of measurable pressure being placed on a standard metallic point which is then dragged across a surface for a measurable length. This produces a scale of relative hardness for the subject materials. Such operational definitions quantify and standardize the term, unlike the ordinary use of the word *hard*, which is based on idiosyncratic human sensory experience.

Because of operationism, or some other basic conditioning process, people without the foundational sensory experiences are able to use some basic sensation words. The above process, for instance, could define the sound *hard* for someone who has no tactile sensations. We could tell them that *hard* is the opposite of *soft* on a relative scale of penetrability. We might say that *hard* is used to describe dense material that cannot be easily penetrated and let them see material being penetrated, and other material that is impenetrable. After operationally defining *hard* and using it in context, repeatedly, a learning speaker would be fully able to use the word, although they could not distinguish hard things from soft things the way normally sensitized humans do. They could use the word sound *hard* effectively in a description, and if someone else used the word sound *hard* they would adapt its use.

This, in turn, leads to misunderstanding about the use of *understanding*. Understanding hardness is not some peculiar psychological or mental state. Like understanding the number 19, understanding hardness is having the ability to perform verbally. In physics, if people can talk the talk and do the math, they understand. If they can talk like a physicist and solve the equations, they understand. They may not be able to *imagine, explain,* or *describe* what they speak of, yet they *understand*. They have the skills. They can talk the talk and do the math. They know *how* to perform these tasks and it proves useful because they can predict consequences with their calculations. Yet, there is nothing undergirding the mathematical performance or the speech which can be described as *the understanding.*[6]

A word is in order here about what has been called the "phenomenological fallacy" in science and philosophy of science. This is said to be the mistaken idea that the descriptions or appearances of things as perceived by humans are *the actual state of affairs*. However, English-speaking people must accept that how they describe things is based on their limited perception and their verbal behavior which is couched in the classical constructs of space, time, matter, and energy. How they perceive the world and talk about it is the actual state of affairs, *for them*. Aliens, as well as other humans, might perceive and speak about completely different states of affairs. Their sense *phenomena* could be different.

In the final analysis, how we *describe* is not a consistent or foolproof undertaking. Scientists must acknowledge that there are many competing descriptions of the Universe. The acceptance of any description as adequate and complete is ultimately dependent upon its utility. If people find their descriptions useful, they will accept them. There is no fact of the matter. There is no actual state of affairs or nature of the Universe. There is no true, accurate, or correct *description* of the Universe. Live with it.

The Use of the Word "*certainty*"

"Quantum mechanics is different. By 1928 or so, many of the mathematical formulas and rules of quantum mechanics had been put in place and, ever since, it has been used to make the most precise and successful numerical predictions in the history of science. But in a real sense those who use quantum mechanics find themselves following rules and formulas laid down by the 'founding fathers' of the theory—calculational procedures that are straightforward to carry out—without really understanding *why* the procedures work or *what* they really mean." Greene, Brian (1999: 87)

"*certainty*" is a much-used word in philosophy and science. That word has various uses in various contexts. Within the field of logic, for example, logicians can reach certain conclusions by starting with certain premises and proceeding logically to certain conclusions. Scientists, on the other hand, cannot reach logically certain conclusions about the world because they cannot construct logically certain premises. As any thoroughgoing empiricist must acknowledge, scientific "laws" (i.e. the law of universal gravitation) are *probable* by virtue of inductive reasoning; they are not certain. There may be other worlds with other laws of gravitation.

Nevertheless, it has become commonplace to say that the "laws of nature" hold true with certainty. And because the "laws of nature" were considered universally true, the Universe was considered to be a giant, deterministic, clocklike machine in classical physics. In classical Newtonian mechanics, if a given set of measurable circumstances obtained, it was claimed that the future could be predicted with certainty. In principle, if the position and the momentum of every particle in the Universe could be determined, the entire future of the Universe could be predicted. Of course, as a practical matter, this could never be done. Nevertheless, it was believed that, *in principle*, the future of the Universe was entirely predictable within classical Newtonian physics because the laws of nature were true with *certainty*.

Because of this belief, there was great consternation in the scientific and philosophical communities when Werner Heisenberg developed matrix mechanics for quantum theory. Heisenberg threw a monkey wrench into that clockwork Universe, when he introduced what has been called "the uncertainty principle". Because of his work, it was determined that the law-like certainty of the mechanistic universe is lost in sub-atomic physics. At the quantum level of discrimination, the results of particle interactions were unpredictable. They were *uncertain*.

Yet, this use of "*uncertainty*" is a bit misleading. Gino Segre explains:

"*Uncertainty principle* may be an unfortunate name since it suggests that, with some decisiveness, one could do better. Sometimes, rarely, 'indeterminacy' is used in technical discussions, but the awkward-sounding 'unknowability' or 'impossibility' is closer to the principle's true meaning. What Heisenberg

460

showed was that if one accepts quantum mechanics validity, certain types of measurements are impossible. Classically, one can simultaneously specify the position of a particle and its momentum; quantum mechanics says one cannot. The best one can do is a measurement for which the unknown part of the position measurement times the unknown part of the momentum measurement equals Planck's constant." Segre (2007: 150)

In fact, Heisenberg demonstrated that parts of the clockwork Universe were immeasurable at times. At the quantum level of discrimination, the position and momentum of "a particle" cannot be simultaneously measured. Consequently, physicists cannot even, *in principle*, determine the results of an interaction in quantum physics. Physical determinism at this level of discrimination was not even theoretically possible. Physicists could no longer predict the consequences of what were considered to be mechanical processes, because they could no longer measure or quantify all of the input.

Because of this incapacity, the output of some interactions is unknowable until after the fact. Based on the laws of large numbers, theorists could still determine outputs, but only as probabilities. Timothy Ferris makes the point this way:

> "Central to quantum physics is Heisenberg's indeterminacy principle. We recall that owing to Heisenberg indeterminacy, certain information about subatomic systems can be obtained only at the cost of remaining ignorant about other information. If, for instance, we ascertain the exact position of an electron, we lose information about its momentum, and vice versa. Indeterminacy mandates that quantum calculations incorporate probabilities." Ferris (1997: 254)

As we can see from both Segre's and Ferris's insights, *"indeterminacy"* is a more appropriate term for where Heisenberg's theories lead physicists. The normal macroscopic rules of engagement for particles and forces interacting causally in space and time are not detectable at the quantum level. Causes cannot be distinguished from effects. In fact, the asymmetry of causes producing effects can be questioned. There may be some effects that happen before their causes. Both temporal and causal asymmetries are not always detectable at the quantum level of discrimination where an indifferent Universe makes no such distinctions. Things just happen and there is no way to predict what will happen next. Radioactive decay confirmed the *indeterminacy* of particle physics. There was no way to predict which atom would emit radioactivity, or when it would.

Accompanying the transition from Newton's clockwork universe to the world of quantum theory was the transition from mechanical models to pure mathematical formulae. The use of pictorial representations of physical objects in space and enduring through time to explain and describe the interactions of the particles of particle physics became obsolete. Interactions these days are neither explained nor described with mechanical models; they are simply *expressed* in the form of equations. No mechanical models can depict the interactions. Images will not suffice. Metaphors and analogies are ubiquitous yet inadequate explanations and descriptions in modern physics.

In physics, confidence in calculations has replaced the evidence of our senses. In fact, a new word has recently been coined to refer to the new paradigm in physics, *"physmatics"*. The line between physics and mathematics has been blurred. The new physics can only be done with sophisticated mathematical formulae. Models, metaphors, and mastery of the mother tongue will not provide an adequate account of the new physics. In spite of all the popular books written about the latest speculation in physics, words and pictures cannot provide comprehension, much less mastery, of the subject. One must be able to talk the talk and do the math.

The Language of Physmatics

"When I took my first physics course, I was confronted with quite a bit of new terminology all at once: energy, momentum, acceleration, mass and the like. As should be no surprise to anyone who noted the failure of the positivists to define theoretical terms in observation language, I never learned any definitions of these new terms in terms I already knew. Rather, what I learned was how to use the new terminology—I learned certain relations among the new terms themselves (e.g. the relation between force and mass, neither of which can be defined in old terms), some relations between the new terms and old terms, and most importantly, how to generate the right numbers in answers to questions posed in the new terminology." Ned Block (1986: 419)

We have seen that language enables humans to perform tacting acts with sounds, although the sounds themselves tact with nothing. That begs the question: When physmatists use the word sounds *"energy"*, *"momentum"*, *"acceleration"*, *"mass"* and the like, to what are *they* referring? What are *they* tacting with? These word sounds were invented or commandeered from common parlance and given tentative, stipulative definitions. Energy, momentum, acceleration, mass etc. could then be quantified and used to predict outcomes by means of standard mathematical formulae, formulae that could be talked about with these newly defined terms.

However, these definitions that physmatists have for the words do not square with normal usage and the resulting intuitions and common sense beliefs we English speakers have about space, time, matter, energy, etc. based on years of verbal conditioning with those word sounds outside of physmatics. The functional value of these sounds has diverged for physmatists and laymen. That is because, although phsymatists cannot explain, describe, or even imagine what they are talking about, they can refer to these constructs with words, *and measure them*. In the process, physmatists have vastly expanded on a tradition of inferring unobservable, inexplicable, indescribable, unimaginable entities within science, and then talking about them.

Scientific theories abound with non-observational theoretical terms: *"electrons"*, *"valence"*, *"symmetry"*, *"spin"*, *"charm"*, etc. These terms have come to be used, in context, after being explained or defined with other more basic terms, e.g. *"particle"*, *"balance"*, *"force"* etc. As an example, the word sound *"symmetry"* has taken center stage in the particle zoo of contemporary quantum physics. *"symmetry"* was a quite ordinary word often used to describe a visual relationship observed between objects in three- dimensional space. There were rotational symmetries, mirror symmetries, translational symmetries – all spatial symmetries, distinctions humans could see and tact with using the sound *"symmetry"*. Timothy Ferris takes over here:

"…researchers often invoke abstract spaces to solve particular problems… So the physicist makes an abstract, three dimensional 'space,' the axes of which represent charge, mass, and spin. An electron if transformed into a positron is said to be symmetrical along the axes of mass and spin – since these remain the same – but asymmetrical with respect to charge, which inverts when the particle is transformed. This example may not be very edifying insofar as understanding electrons is concerned, but it is meant to broaden our conception of symmetry, by demonstrating that symmetry need not have anything to do with geometrical shapes in ordinary space. In this broader sense we can move beyond appearances, and define symmetry as representing *a quantity that remains unchanged through a transformation...*

"The word *invariance* is shorthand for 'a quantity that remains unchanged.' To understand invariance is to see why symmetry is the central theme of physics. The laws of nature express symmetries because symmetries identify invariances. The law of conservation of energy, for instance, describes a quantity ('energy') that remains unchanged (is conserved) through such transformations as a steam engine's doing work or a star's burning its way toward its red-giant stage. The special theory of relativity exposes several invariances, notably the equivalence of mass and energy (e = mc^2). Ferris (1986: 207)

The transformation Ferris describes here is the transformation of a word's functional value. At one point "*symmetry*" was *used* to tact with a distinction humans could make about things we could *see*. Physmatists redefined it so that it could be used to point to invariance in their equations. These days, symmetry and invariance are watchwords for physmatists. However, physmatists have not broadened their "conception of symmetry". They have found another use for the sound, one totally unrelated to visual imagery or human sensations. It can now be used by properly trained physmatists to tact with any quantity that remains unchanged through transformation.

Exhibit two: physmatists can imagine a particle spinning. They can visualize the rotational symmetry of that particle spinning. From this they say that electrons have spin and symmetry. However, electrons are not actually *particles* and they do not actually *spin*, much less have a rotational *symmetry*. A spinning particle is a heuristic device. Phymatists infer the existence of an unobservable, unimaginable, inexplicable, and indescribable "particle". Physmatists then quantify the *spin* of this entity and say that it is invariant and symmetrical. They use these measurements in their formulae and come up with useful answers. They have developed a new use for the sounds "*spin*" and "*symmetry*" based on metaphorical thinking.

Other visual analogies in physmatics are also less than compelling. When physmatists say that a photon has both wave and particle characteristics, that is for our heuristic convenience. There is nothing wavy or particulate about a photon. In fact, according to the latest physmatics, when distortions in a field move away from us (or we move away from them, because it makes no difference in relativity theory) and the distance of the movement over time from our inertial frame of reference reaches C, humans perceive the distortion as energy. If distortions in the field are stable relative to us, we perceive mass. Distortions in a field? What happened to the waves and particles? They were never there to begin with. Despite this, those words sounds enabled physmatists to heuristically talk about photons and depict them as having the characteristics of both waves and particles.

This is one reason why modern physics seems somehow detached. The uses of words such as "*spin*", "*symmetry*" "*particle*", and "*wave*" are not what we are accustomed to. Those words have been commandeered from ordinary usage and redefined. Well, who said the physmatists could do that? We liked these words just the way they were. We knew how to use them. Now these physmatists have bungled up perfectly good words. Fear not, all of us can still use them the old way. They work quite well for original purposes. Unfortunately, the physmatists are attempting to do things that they cannot do with these words. They are attempting to imagine, explain and describe entities that are beyond the ability of humans to imagine, explain or describe, because they are nothing like what we humans experience.

The world of subatomic particles, the standard model, no longer has *particles and forces*. Today, fields, vectors, Higgs Bosons, masspoints and one-dimensional strings are the *objects* of physical investigation. Old words and distinctions are inadequate to the task of modern physics. The uses for words such as "*particle*", "*matter*", "*energy*", "*time*", "*location*", "*space*", simply break down. They can no longer capture or in any intuitive sense give us an appreciation for what the phenomena physmatists postulate *are*. We enter a realm where our language cannot do the work we want it to do. The numbers go into the formula and numbers come out. How or why cannot be imagined, explained, or described.

The latest speculation in scientific circles suggests that the Universe is composed of only 5% matter and energy. 72% of the universe is said to be dark energy and the remaining 23% dark matter, neither of which interact with us. They enjoy a parallel existence. Nor are the unperceived *dark energy* or *dark matter* associated with any particles or waves. Supposedly, we humans only perceive the 5% of what the universe consists, ordinary matter (atoms) and energy. The balance is unperceived, but thought to exist based on indirect evidence, e.g. gravitational lensing (bending rays of light). That is, the physmatists' calculations do not correspond to their observations. They assume that there must be hypothetical entities of some sort to account for the anomalies in their calculations. Hence, they posit something to complete the theory. However, they have not observed anything other than the effects of these hypothetical entities on their equations.

The word "*dark*" in lieu of "*unperceived*" lends a certain mystique to the speculation. Yet, it hides (excuse the pun) the profound metaphysical implications of such theories. If the theories are correct, there is no way to imagine "*dark*" anything. We may, in fact, measure it indirectly to confirm its *existence*. However, human cognitive skills, shaped by our perception and our language, will never be adequate for the task of imagining, explaining or describing dark matter and dark energy with images, models, analogies or examples. Pictures and words will not do this work. We are locked in our Newtonian world of *physical objects* interacting by means of the various *forces of energy* in a background of *space and time*.

However, maybe you can find a wormhole to an alternative universe in a black hole where your doppelganger exists as anti-matter! They may understand dark energy and dark matter! Do not take the colorful language of modern physics too seriously. Just like you, physmatists are limited by their perception, their imagination and their language. They are just a little better at math.

The Abuse of the Word "*reality*"

For some writers, *the nature of reality* is a serious philosophical matter. They ask: What is the nature of reality? (reality has been cleverly juxtaposed with un-reality by some!) That was one formulation of the ontological question: What exists? What really exists? What is real? These age-old questions about reality hinge on the limitations and fallibility of human perception. Some things are only appearances: hallucinations, optical illusions, etc. They are not *real*. Well then, how do we know when our perceptions are real? How can we be sure that any perceptions are veridical? How can we know what *exists*? We cannot rely on our senses. We must doubt them all. Truck drivers, teachers, philosophers, and physicists talk about *reality* this way.

The word sound "*reality*" is bandied about with aplomb by speakers of all sorts, as if they knew exactly what they were talking about. People of all stripes confront *the nature of reality* and talk about *their individual reality*, or even worse, their "realities." Of course, philosophers have no one else but themselves to blame for this. The "*nature of reality*" and other such pious nonsense are pieces of the philosophical jargon that have filtered down to the hoi polloi. Nebulous as all this chatter is, we must not be fooled by our use of these word sounds. If we change "*real*" into "*reality*", adjective to noun, we cannot assume we are talking about something, something called reality.

Philosopher J.L. Austin performed the initial analysis of the use of the English word "*real*":

> "'Real' is an absolutely *normal* word, with nothing new-fangled or technical or highly specialized about it. It is, that is to say, already firmly established in, and very frequently used in, the ordinary language we all use every day. Thus *in this sense* it is a word which has a fixed meaning, and so can't, any more that can any other word which is firmly established, be fooled around with *ad lib*." Austin (1962a: 62)

So sayeth J. L. Austin. While his semantic philosophy of language forced him to erroneously conclude that words have "fixed meanings", he still recognized one functional role of "real" in the English language. He goes on:

> "Lastly, 'real' also belongs to a large and important family of words that we may call *adjuster-words* – words, that is, by the use of which other words are adjusted to meet the innumerable and unforeseeable demands of the world upon language… ('Like' is *the* great adjuster-word, or, alternatively put, the main flexibility-device by whose aid, in spite of the limited scope of our vocabulary, we can always avoid being left completely speechless.) And then, having said of this animal that it's *like* a pig, we may proceed with the remark, 'But it isn't a *real* pig'… " Austin (1962a: 73)

More importantly, and for our purposes here, Austin points out that the word sound *"real"* is an acoustic device that only functions in a background environment. *"real"* only makes sense if it is opposed to something else. For instance, by saying *"it isnt a real pig"* does the speaker mean it is a mechanical pig, a stuffed animal, a piggy bank, a decoy pig, an animated pig, an imaginary pig? Additionally, to oppose real pigs with unreal pigs is just as fatuous as opposing reality with unreality. We don't know what to make of it.

People who talk about "unreal pigs" or "unreality" are merely abusing a perfectly good word. A thoughtful person is likely to say: *"what are you talking about if it oinks like a pig smells like a pig eats like a pig and looks like a pig it must be a pig"*. Then someone insists: "but it is not a real pig". We are left incredulous. Exactly what is required for something to be a real pig? The point is: be careful how you use that word! "real", in the appropriate context, is useful, but do not expect more of it than it can deliver.

The Use of the Word "*life*"

"There is no clear boundary between living and nonliving things, from this perspective… The very fact that the boundary between life and nonlife is blurred (and where to draw the boundary is a subject for discussion), is, though, an important discovery. It helps make clear that there is nothing unusual about life in the context of the way the Universe works." John Gribbin (2004: 247)

Planet Earth, home to some 7.8 billion humans, has a rather confused history of late. *Life*, and more particularly, human life has been breathed into us by God, handed down to us by the Great Spirit, arrived from other galaxies, etc. The debate amongst scientists, philosophers and theologians about life and its origins is a never-ending carnival of theories and explanations that involve tortured arguments and grand metaphysical pronouncements of many flavors. Yet, a thorough analysis of the uses of the word sound "*life*" has not been forthcoming. That should be the starting point for all of them. While the author does not intend to provide that comprehensive analysis of the use of the English word sound "*life*", or its functional equivalents in other languages, a cursory look is called for at this time.

One would hope that by this point you have come to appreciate the emphasis of this book. It is a book about behavior, the linguistic behavior of humans about their linguistic behavior, and the ramifications thereof. For English speakers, the sound "*life*" is a part of that behavior. We all know by now that the word sound "*life*" does not refer to anything. Nor does "*life*" have a meaning, much less an essential meaning. Make no mistake; there is no concept of life. But what is life? That is a foolish question engendered by the semantic fallacy which would lead you to believe that there is something *called life*. There is not. Nevertheless, we can ask what it is to which English-speaking people often tact with the sound "*life*".

No doubt the use of the word sound "*life*", or its approximate equivalent in languages other than modern English, preceded the use of symbols. (The word "approximate" is used here because there will be many nuances and varying usage from language to language.) Because some things move around or change shape, humans began to refer to them as "*live*". People then inferred that there was an élan vital inside these live things, something called *life*. This very basic distinction between animate things and inanimate things is a helpful distinction that mankind makes to enhance their chances of survival. Its importance in many cultures is reflected in a mandatory noun class (gender) marker for this distinction.[7,8]

In every culture some things were considered living; others were considered non-living. However, the distinction has never been clear cut. People used that distinction on an *ad hoc* basis. To this day there are circumstances when we English speakers do not know if we should use the word "*life*" or not. The criteria for life are not fixed, even within the scientific community. There are competing scientific definitions of life. What standards should we apply in a determination that something is alive? Growth, mobility, self-replication? Are viruses living organisms or not? It depends on whom you ask. Are clouds alive? It depends on whom you ask? There are disagreements because the criteria for determining the living from the non-living are not agreed upon.

Most English-speaking people are quite indiscriminate in their use of the word *"life"*. Once again, this is not because they have a nebulous *concept* or *notion* of life; it is because their history of uses for the sound *"life"* does not give them a clearly demarcated boundary between when they can use the word and when they cannot use it. They don't know if a virus is alive or not because the criteria for life are in dispute. However, humans are alive for various lengths of time. That we do know.

In addition, human life is precious and worth saving. We make heroic efforts and spend an inordinate amount of money trying to save lives. *Saving lives* is used to justify everything from universal health care to atom bombs. However, rather than debating the morality of *saving lives*, theologians and ethicists ought to study language to recognize what they are doing. The issue of *life* in moral and theological circles is a Gordian knot brought on by faulty linguistic analysis. The distinction between life and non-life forms is not an intrinsic division in the natural world. Scientists, philosophers, and theologians cannot agree on a definition for *"life"*, much less *"human life"*. The point being: the use of the sound *"life"* has practical value but no precise application. Because of that fact, much science and philosophy has reached the point where the word *"life"* has outlived its usefulness.

Ultimately, this is a problem we must solve we by *deciding* what the criteria for life are. This is a prescriptive solution. We cannot have a descriptive solution, primarily because that is the problem. Our uses of the word *"life"* have become wildly inconsistent. We must clarify our uses of other words that we use to explain life and agree on criteria by which we will determine what is alive and what is not.

Even so, there seems to be a general consensus that some humans are alive at any given time. At a later time, they become not alive, they become dead. (Of course, there still seems to be a preponderance of living people that believe they will be alive again after death. I have seen no reliable surveys of formerly dead people to support this belief.) The question this poses is: What do humans and other living organisms lose when they become dead? What do you lose when you lose your life? The history of human death provides us with a fascinating study of word use, metaphysics, and cultural adaptation.

Once upon a time mirrors were held over the mouth to determine if someone had died. It was said that they *"gave up the ghost"* because they had no breath. To this day, many humans bury corpses on sacred ground instead of burning them so they can, at some future date, arise from the dead. Humans have sent the dearly departed to the after-life with food, clothing, and servants. Customs and rituals surrounding human death abound, most of them assuming a life after death of some sort. All of these practices and beliefs required elaborate metaphysical systems as justification. In all of them, the assumption was that the sound *"life"* must refer to something that humans have and whatever it is, it can go on in some form after the death of the body.

The more important question from the standpoint of a scientist is: How can the growth, mobility, and self replication of living organisms be accounted for within the scientific paradigm of a causally closed physical universe? Framed in its simplest terms, how can an ordered state (the human body) result from a disordered state? This process would defy the law of entropy which states that all systems move toward a less orderly state and, in the process, dissipate energy consistent with the second law of thermodynamics. Eventually the system reaches equilibrium when the entropy in the system is maximized.

However, theorists have shown that under the right circumstances, this entropic process can be reversed. Complexity and self-organization can come from simplicity and chaos. Recent studies on chaos theory have demonstrated that life, as some physicists define it, could have evolved from non-life, animate organisms from inanimate matter. Life can indeed emerge from non-life. The mystery of life has been de-mystified for many physicists. As Timothy Ferris put it:

> "... the universe is not exclusively engaged in shambling down an entropic slag heap but has also, in some times and places, articulated itself into fascinating antientropic entities like binary pulsars and mathematicians. We employ the term 'evolution' to describe the racheting mechanism by virtue of which this has happened." Ferris (1997: 202)

The philosophical issues surrounding life and human life await a thoroughgoing linguistic analysis and subsequent decisions made by each of us. Yet, if you start your analysis with the belief that words are labels for things or that you have a concept of life, you are doomed to failure. So, PLEASE, do not ask: *what is the meaning of life*. That is a question posed by children, untutored tribesmen, and the residents of asylums.

Chapter 00000111
Summary & Notes

As astrophysicist David Lindley put it: "Nowadays most physicists who are reared in the Anglo-Saxon style, steer clear of Plato and Kant, and are belligerently uninterested in what philosophers make of their theories," Lindley (2007: 209). Scientists, like historians, engage in what Stephen Davies calls "willful obtuseness," Davies (2003: 128). They turn their backs on the philosophical issues. As pragmatic scientists, they focus on results. They massage numbers in their formulae and get utilitarian results. However, the philosophical issues will not go away unless they recognize the functional value of their speech behavior and the concomitant common-sense intuitions it produces. This chapter was a beginner's exercise in analyzing such speech behavior in science.

Conversely, philosophers have a tendency to ignore science. They develop positions based on reasoned argument using words as they have traditionally used them. Strategies and tactics are employed to persuade skeptics of the soundness of their arguments. They punch and counter-punch without presenting any empirical evidence, relying on guile and imagination to construct counter examples and counter arguments. Today's philosophers have high-minded debates about all matter of philosophical issues, totally oblivious to the science of linguistic behavior. That available science points to a totally faulty premise in all of their arguments, i.e. words are symbols.

All of the empirical evidence indicates that human languages consist of S-R-R conditioned behavior with sounds. That behavior, in turn, shapes human thinking. English-speaking humans perceive and talk about a world of physical objects and forces in a background of space and time, a Newtonian world. As we investigate the mysteries of the Universe, we are no longer in that world. When we attempt to go beyond the limits of our perception and the linguistic behavior we inherited, we find mysteries. We can develop new linguistic behavior to make predictions about the relativistic Universe, but we cannot comprehend it in the way we comprehend the Newtonian Universe because we cannot explain it or describe or imagine it the way we explain, describe and imagine a Newtonian Universe.

Although our perception and our linguistic behavior limit our comprehension of the modern physics, physmatists can still talk about non-extended point particles, dark matter and quarks. They can say many things about non-extended point particles, dark matter and quarks, but they cannot imagine, explain, or describe what these things are. They have a knowledge that language can provide by using the sounds *"nonextended point particles"*, *"dark matter"*, and *"quarks"* in their conversations. They can infer their existence and say things about them. They can also use mathematical processes to predict outcomes when they use numbers and symbols that they can point to with the sounds "non-extended point particles, dark matter" and "quarks". However, they will never be able to imagine, explain, or describe what they are talking about.

Like Heisenberg, Pauli, and Dirac, modern physmatists struggle with the imagery and the language of physics. Analogies, metaphors, models, and word sounds will fail them when they try to describe things outside of our English language's Newtonian spatial-temporal world. Physmatists must develop new words with new uses. Those words will not be able to do the work the traditional language has done in describing and explaining phenomena. The Universe is what it is, describable and explainable in many ways, yet at some levels of discrimination, not describable or explainable in the way that we have traditionally described and explained it. We should not expect that our linguistic skills will be adequate for that task.

In spite of the presented arguments and the lack of any empirical evidence supporting mental entities and processes, you might think that the *concepts* of space, time, matter, energy, force and cause are intuitive or primitive and indefinable. But keep in mind that you have no need for *concepts* outside of the semiotic analysis of language and dualism. Nor do you have a need for an *essence* or *nature* of the word sounds *"matter"*, *"space"*, *"time"*, *"energy"*, *"cause"*, *"certainty"*, *"imagine"*, *"physical object"*, *"life"*, *"reality"*, *"explain"*, *"describe"*, or any other word sound. Yet if you insist that these sounds are symbols, you have a problem. You will get caught up in a fanciful world of thoughts, ideas, concepts, meanings, essences, minds, and consciousness, and you will find no way out. You will fall victim to the semantic fallacies and dualism.

There are no meanings or concepts that these word sounds represent or designate. Your intuitions about the use of these word sounds are simply the inclinations to use sounds in a certain way, the way you have been conditioned through S-R-R to use them. They are useful word sounds. However, do not think that there must *be* something to which they refer and represent, or that there must *be* something to which you refer when you use these words. They are sounds that have a variety of uses, for a variety of people, at a variety of times, in a variety of contexts. Physmatists now use these words in ways that are far removed from their origins. Nevertheless, linguistic analysis is worthwhile because it reveals the limits of language. It exposes the folly of trying to explain the constructs of subatomic physics

How useful are these word sounds and their derivative symbols in physmatics? They are very useful if physmatists define them in terms of measurements and use them to make predictions. If they use these words to point to specific measurable quantities that can be used in the calculation procedures of physmatics to produce useful results, their use is warranted. In contrast, philosophical speculation about space, time, matter, energy, or the *nature of the universe* is unwarranted. People who use these word sounds in that way are asking these words to do more than they can do.

If physmatists were to claim they could teach you physmatics, how would they know that you *understood* physmatics? You would have to do the math and talk the talk. If you speak like a physmatist and manipulate the physmatists' symbols competently, you *understand* physmatics. The *understanding* is in the performing. You must *behave* like a physmatist.

When scientists debate the nature of reality or about what exists, they are engaged in debates about behavior, their verbal behavior. Debates about the nature of reality, existence, space, time, matter, energy, life and the Universe are also debates about how they want to use the word sounds: *"reality"*, *"existence"*, *"space"*, *"time"*, *"matter"*, *"energy"*, *"life"* and *"the Universe"*. They are not discussing concepts and ideas; there are none. If a scientist can use these word sounds effectively in the appropriate scientific contexts, they understand their use. There is nothing more to understand.

---

1. The "brain in a vat" argument is a modern-day version of the solipsist argument. It goes something like this: "How do you know that your brain has not been removed from your head and

placed in a vat of nutrients by unscrupulous super scientists who are simulating the environment by means of electrodes implanted in your brain? Your reason for believing you inhabit the ordinary world is that your experience has a certain consistent pattern, but that pattern could in principle be produced artificially, simply by mimicking the sensory inputs you receive. It might all be one giant hallucination." McGinn (1999: 34)

2. Kant believed that human experience is asymmetrical. *Cause*, he believed, requires a temporal order, a constant conjunction of events in the correct order. Causes are followed by their effects. We English speakers cannot imagine otherwise. Causal asymmetry and temporal asymmetry are fundamental constraints upon our cognitive abilities. That is why Kant and so many other theorists claim that causation is a fundamental innate concept. To him: "The concept of cause accordingly is a pure concept of the understanding, which is totally disparate from all possible perception and only serves to determine the representation subsumed under it, with respect to judging in general, and so to make a universally valid judgment possible." Kant (1783: 48). For Kant, "the concept of cause" was a necessary category that governs our experience.

3. According to David Lindley: "Today heat and energy are viewed almost self-evidently as the same kind of thing, but at the beginning of the nineteenth century they were regarded quite differently. Energy meant specifically the idea of energy invented a century and half earlier by Isaac Newton; it was the quantity possessed by solid bodies in motion. A flying cannonball had a lot of energy, a falling snowflake had little. Heat, on the other hand, was mysterious. It was thought of as a sort of substance, perhaps an invisible fluid that could be transferred from one body to another but could also be created apparently out of nothing, as when a drill bit bores into metal. Was the heat fluid released from the pores of the metal's structure by abrasion?" Lindley (1993: 30)

4. Not surprisingly, the process works in reverse for many philosophers. Rather than immaterial souls, spirits, selves, etc. without any physical attributes – composed of bits of not-clockwork – zombies are theoretical posits with all the physical attributes and behaviors of ordinary people, but with no inner life. They are indistinguishable from normal people but are not conscious. They have the observable bits of clockwork, but none of the unobservable bits of not-clockwork. However, philosophical zombies are no more plausible than souls, spirits, selves etc. Theorists can stipulate whatever they wish. But that does make their theoretical posits comprehensible much less plausible. So, without dualism, it makes no more sense to say that the behavior of a zombie is the same as a human's yet minus the consciousness than to say souls, spirits and selves are functionally the same as conscious humans, only minus the physical bodies.

5. Indeed, the imagery problem in physics spills over into the cognitive and neural sciences, albeit for totally different reasons. The scientists and philosophers in these fields engage in what some have called boxology. They try to depict our *mental machinery*. They draw up diagrams of boxes, rectangles, parallelograms, triangles, etc. and create connecting lines between the forms that are supposed to represent different functional aspects of cognition, memory, language, etc. This may give them a better appreciation of the relations amongst functions of the *mind*, as they perceive them in their *mental* world. But they have yet to show any such relationships in the physiology of the brain. The mental models do not match the machinery of the brain. The language of these speculators is replete with spatial analogies of higher and lower levels of this and that, areas where thoughts, memories, concepts, and mental functions are located. However, if they ever locate anything in our brains, it will not be thoughts, memories, concepts, or mental functions. They could locate the NCCs of these inferred

mental entities and functions, but they cannot, in principle, locate these non-corporeal mental things. They cannot do mind surgery because they cannot observe minds. Our current English word usage will not allow that because our conditioned linguistic behavior puts things in that behavior's own boxes, labeled *mental and physical*. Psychology can never be reduced to physics because our intuitions, as a result of English verbal behavior, will not allow it.

6. As previously mentioned, the use of the term "*understanding*" for many English speakers implies some sort of special mental state that "stands under" or supports the observed mathematical or speech behavior. However, this is just one more example of the dualism so firmly embedded in our speech behavior. There is nothing supporting or backing up the mathematical behavior with the algorithms of decimal math. It is all rote behavior resulting from much practice. Successful performance is the only evidence of the understanding.

7. Noun class or gender systems vary dramatically from English in the 6,000-plus languages still in existence. A number of languages have the animate/inanimate distinction as part of their noun class or gender system. All nouns are marked for this distinction. That is, all words classified as nouns must be either animate or inanimate. According to the man who wrote the book on gender, Greville Corbett: "First, the systematic presentation of linguistic data from many different languages may help to broaden a discussion which has tended to centre on English. It will show how divisions into animate and inanimate, or human and non-human, function in language exactly as does the division into female and male." Corbett (1991: 3)

8. James R. Hurford explains the distinction between "biological motion" and "animacy" in SAE-speaking cultures and its interrelationship with language: "'Biological motion' is a label attached to a kind of motion typical of an animal; it is distinct from trees waving in the wind, rocks tumbling down a cliff, waves in the sea, or eddies in a stream. Recognizing biological motion is not just a matter of certain sensors being excited. There has to be a quite complex calculation of the temporal and spatial relations among the moving parts. In many animals, including humans, a disposition to recognize biological motion is hardwired: there no question of learning a concept of biological motion; we recognize it instinctively without training... Two parallel literatures deal with essentially the same topic, under headings of 'biological motion' or 'animacy'...

Biological motion and animacy differ in degree of abstraction. Biological motion involves an immediate perceptual (possibly multimodal) response to an experience, whereas animacy reflects a more permanent and less perception-dependent judgment. A sleeping dog is animate, but (except for dream twitches) does not exhibit biological motion. Animacy is a generalization from biological motion. Anything which *could* exhibit biological motion, though it may be inert at the time of referring to it, is credited with animacy. Animacy is *potential* biological motion...

Biological motion and its more abstract derivative, animacy, impinge strongly on linguistic structure, in at least three ways. Firstly, many human languages discriminate grammatically between words denoting animate objects. The animacy feature is deep seated in semantic universals. Many noun classification systems use the category of animate things... Secondly, there is also, of course, a very strong tendency for words denoting biological motion to be verbs... A third connection between biological motion and linguistic structure is seen in the theta-role (or participant role) labeled 'Agent'. Many theories postulate a level of linguistic structure in which the objects or persons involved in some event are labeled with terms indicating their manner of participation in the event..." (The bold words are by Hurford.) Hurford (2007: 41)

Hermeneutic circle:

The problems in the process of interpretation that arise
when one element, for instance in a text, can only be understood in
terms of the meanings of others or of the whole text, yet understanding
these other elements, or the whole text, in turn presupposes understanding
of the original element. Each can only be understood in the light of the
others. Similarly, we may hold that the past can only be understood in the
light of the present, and the present can only be understood in the light of
the past.

The phenomenon has preoccupied German thinkers from
Schleiermacher and Dilthey through to Heidegger and Gadamer.
In Anglo-American philosophy a similar problem arises from the holism
of meaning, but is not generally felt to pose a fundamental difficulty:
as Wittgenstein said: light dawns gradually over the whole.
Oxford Dictionary of Philosophy.

Book Summary

Words still mystify us. They do because our common-sense beliefs about words have been brought about by thousands of years of misguided philosophical speculation about human languages. That speculation has, in turn, been incorporated in our speech about our speech. The most pernicious of these speculations about words and language, when viewed under the empirical microscope, offer no explanatory force whatsoever. It is wildly speculative metaphysical musing that has come to be accepted as unquestioned fact.

Because of this entirely misguided philosophy of language, the puzzles and the enigmas remain. They remain not only in philosophy of language, but in the philosophies of mathematics, epistemology and science. It is high time to dispense with that misguided semantic premise and eliminate the mind/body dualism necessary for its success. Theorists must begin to view human speech as the S-R-R conditioned behavior that it is.

The preceding chapters have attempted to point the way to a new non-semantic perspective on the human use of word sounds which eliminates the age-old conundrums about language. There is every reason to pursue this course of action and abandon the semantic paradigm, as difficult as that may be. Properly analyzed from a non-semantic perspective, humankind may finally obtain an accurate framework from which to successfully analyze the human use of sounds and resolve the puzzles and enigmas in all areas of intellectual inquiry that result from our mistaken beliefs about ourselves and our verbal behavior.

Index of Names

Nettle, Daniel, 306

Newton, Isaac, 16, 226, 321-322, 418, 424-426, 431-443, 445, 447, 453, 460-461, 465, 471, 473

Ojemann, George, 266-267

Ortony, Andrew, 30, 290, 307

Osborn, Roger, 334, 341

Osten, Dahl, 42, 405

Papineau, David, 176, 232

Paul, Saint, 150

Pauli, Wolfgang, 471

Peacock, George, 330

Pinker, Steven, 16, 32-34, 113, 120, 142, 144-145, 170, 231, 260, 269

Pinker, Susan, 416

Plato, 7-8, 11, 15, 18, 36, 48, 52 59, 103, 113-115, 125, 137, 149-150, 162, 164, 179, 200, 207-208, 227, 231, 237, 244, 252, 255, 270, 272, 275, 277, 316, 318-319, 326, 357, 364-365, 377, 390, 396, 416, 437, 471,

Poincare, Henry, 358

Popper, Karl, 378

Powers, Jonathan, 434-435, 438

Price H.H., 109, 114-117, 125-126

Prince, 281

Putnam, Hilary, 70, 106, 109, 146, 169, 218, 264

Quine, Willard V. O., 42, 69-70, 72, 264, 294, 297-298, 376, 394, 408, 448, 451

Reddy, Michael, 30, 72

Reichenbach, Hans, 357-356

Reiss, Charles, 259, 306

Rodman, Robert, 39, 136, 282, 285-286

Romaine, Suzanne, 306

Rucker, Rudy, 325-326

Rumelhart, David, 290

Russell, Bertrand, 7, 12, 14-15, 18-19, 26, 42-43, 48-49, 67, 91, 94, 96-97, 113-115, 123-124, 129, 133, 141-142, 149-150, 200-201, 207-208, 227, 231, 237, 270, 274-276, 312, 338, 355, 365-366, 376-378, 383-384, 387, 392-393, 396, 404-405, 407, 416, 418, 422, 439, 441

Ryle, Gilbert, 8, 10-11, 18-20, 26, 97, 103, 109, 149, 151, 161, 175-176, 178, 227, 449

Sander, Emmanuel, 127, 139, 245, 291, 305

Sapir, Edwin, 15, 117, 120, 126, 306

Schlick, Morris, 42

Schrodinger, Erwin, 425, 438

Searle, John, 23, 25, 27-30, 85, 101, 113, 172, 176-177, 182-184, 187, 189, 224, 232, 233-235, 260-261, 275, 454

Segre, Gino, 460-461

Seif, Charles, 333

Sellars, Wilfred, 401

Shapiro, Lawrence, 230

Glossary

Abbreviations used in this Glossary are: The Oxford Dictionary of Philosophy (ODP), The Oxford Concise Dictionary of Linguistics (OCDL), The Cambridge Encyclopedia of Language, second edition (CEL)

<u>Abductive reasoning</u>: "…it extrapolates backward to infer the hypothesis that gives the most plausible explanation of all known facts. Koch, Christof (2019: 12)

<u>Absent qualia argument</u>: pp.166, 343 203, 414

<u>Abstracting</u>: p.125

<u>Ambiguous</u>: Having two or more meanings. Defined as a property of sentences or utterances: I filled the pen is thus ambiguous, as a whole, in that *the pen* might refer to a writing instrument or to an enclosure for animals. Most accounts distinguish **lexical ambiguity**, due as in this example to the different meanings of lexical units, from **grammatical** or **syntactic** ambiguity. For the latter compare e.g. *I like good food and wine,* where good could relate syntactically to either *food* alone or to both *food and wine*: what is liked would correspondingly be good food and any wine whatever, or good food and wine that is also good.

Many linguists will talk of ambiguity only when it can be seen as in these examples, as inherent in a language system. It can thus be defined as a property of sentences, independent of the contexts in which they are uttered on specific occasions. Other linguists will distinguish semantic ambiguity, as ambiguity inherent in a language, from pragmatic ambiguity. But what exactly is inherent in a language is as problematic here as elsewhere. (OCL: 17) pp. 246-248, 297

<u>Analogy</u>: "A respect in which one thing is similar to another. The analogical extension of terms is the way in which a term covers similar things: people, bottles, and rivers have mouths. Shops, boxes, verdicts, ports, strings of a violin, questions, roads, and books may all be open, but in analogical senses. Analogy butts upon literal meaning, but also upon metaphor, and thus forms a perplexing phenomenon in the philosophy of language. Arguing by analogy is arguing that since things are alike in some way, they will probably be alike in others. Its famous uses in philosophy include the argument to design and the argument by analogy to the existence of other minds: if you behave like me, and I have such and such mental states when I so behave, then by analogy you probably do too. But: 'How can I generalize the one case so irresponsibly?' (Wittgenstein). In medieval philosophy an important question was whether we can make statements about God only by analogy." (ODP:14) pp.171, 251, 291, 306

<u>Analytic philosophy</u>: The philosophy that takes the process of analysis to be central to philosophical method and progress. The common idea of analytic philosophers was that the surface form of a language may conceal hidden logical structure, and may mislead us as to that structure. This could be revealed by a process that would itself solve philosophical problems, or alternatively show them to be offspring of the delusive surface forms of ordinary language. Confidence in the method of analysis was fostered by the early successes of Frege and Russell in reducing mathematics to logic, and by the insights afforded by the theory of definite descriptions. The practitioners of analytic philosophy also included Moore and Carnap. (ODP: 14) pp. I, 11,

Analytic/synthetic: A contrast originally introduced by Kant between types of proposition. An analytic proposition is one where the concept of the predicate 'is contained in' the concept of the subject. 'All brothers are male' is an example. A synthetic proposition is one where this is not so, and which is therefore apt for providing substantial information. Kant's definition is only preliminary, in that not all propositions are of subject predicate form, and the notion of 'containment is left metaphorical. But his goal of defining a class of propositions that are importantly trivial can be pursued in ways drawing on modern logic. Thus we might define a proposition to be analytic if it has the form of a tautology, or valid formula of elementary logic, or can be represented as having that form by substitution of synonyms for synonyms. For example, if we substitute 'male and sibling' for brother, then 'all brothers are male ' is of the form 'all things that are F and G are F' and this is a valid formula of the predicate calculus.

The point of Kant's division is that we might not be too disturbed, philosophically, if everything that can be known *a priori* is analytic: analytic truths are so trivial as barely to count as knowledge at all. But if we can know synthetic propositions *a priori* the question of how such knowledge is possible becomes urgent. Part of the programme of logical positivism was to show that all *a priori* propositions are, at bottom, analytic. The entire distinction was queried in one of the most famous papers of modern philosophy, Quine's 'Two Dogmas of Empiricism' (1950), which attacks the idea that we have a reasonable criterion for synonymy, on which definition depends. (ODP: 15) pp.391-395

Animacy & biological motion: p. 474

A priori/a posteriori: A contrast first between propositions. A proposition is knowable a priori if it can be known without experience of the specific course of events in the actual world. It may, however, be allowed that some experience is required to acquire the concepts involved in an a priori proposition. Something is knowable only *a posteriori* if it cannot be known *a priori*. The distinction gives one of the fundamental problem areas of epistemology. The category of a priori propositions is highly controversial, since it is not clear how pure thought, unaided by experience can give rise to any knowledge at all, and it has always been a concern of empiricism to deny that it can. The two great areas in which it seems to do so are logic and mathematics, so empiricists have commonly tried to show either that these are not areas of real, substantive knowledge, or that in spite of appearances the knowledge that we have in these areas is actually dependent on experience. The former line tries to show that all *a priori* propositions are in some sense trivial, or analytic, or matters of notation or conventions of language. The latter approach is particularly associated with Quine, who denies any significant split between propositions traditionally thought of as a priori, and other deeply entrenched beliefs that occur in our overall view of the world.

Another contested category is that of a priori concepts, supposed to be concepts that cannot be 'derived' from experience, but which are presupposed in any mode of thought about the world: time, substance, causation, number, and the self are candidates. The need for such concepts, and the nature of the substantive *a priori* knowledge to which they give rise, is the central concern of Kant's *Critique of Pure Reason* (ODP: 21) p. 396

Anaphora: pp. 38, 303

Appearances vs. reality: pp. 199-202, 440, 459, 466

Artificial intelligence: pp. 233, 124, 169

Aristotle's Essentialism: pp. 66, 455

Aristotelian logic: pp. 377, 403, 407, 409, 417

Assertion, statement, sentence, utterance: forms of verbal behavior which are often claimed to represent underlying propositions.

Autoclitics: "The term autoclitic is intended to suggest behavior which is based upon or depends upon other verbal behavior." There are descriptive autoclitics, qualifying autoclitics, quantifying autoclitics, relational autoclitics, manipulative autoclitics et al. (Skinner 1957: 315 & chapter 12) pp. 130, 132, 133, 245, 246

Blindsight: p. 229

Bose-Einstein condensate: Asimov, Isaac, Understanding Physics pg. 248: The photon has a spin of 1 and the Graviton a spin of 2. These particles, and all others possessing integral spin, including a number of atomic nuclei, behave according to Bose-Einstein statistics, worked out by Einstein and by Indian physicist Satyendra Nath Bose (1924-25). Such particles are bosons, and the exclusion principle does not hold for them. p. 457

Butterfly effect: p. 442

Cartesian dualism: The view that mind and body are two separate substances; the self is as it happens associated with a particular body, but is self-subsistent, and capable of independent existence. (ODP: 56) p. 50, 113, chapter 3

Categorematic/syncategorematic: pg. 100

Cause: pp. 439-444, 119, 154, 161, 162, 186, 187, 194, 206, 238, 245, 374, 375, 423, 428

Causal gap: pp. 168, 174

Certainty: pp. 460-462, 402-409, 312, 325, 375, 396

Chaining: pp. 265, 266

Chaos theory: Historically, the contrast is between chaos, or the unordered, unformed, undifferentiated beginnings of things, and the comos, which is the ordered universe. The concept is thus implicit in early Greek cosmogony. In modern science, chaotic systems are ones in which an arbitrarily small difference in the initial conditions can produce arbitrarily large differences in later states… The possibility of such systems forces a distinction between thinking of a system as deterministic and thinking of it as completely predictable in principle. Chaotic systems can be deterministic, but not predictable, for however accurate a measurement of the state at a time, a variation smaller than any it can detect may be responsible for a difference in the eventual outcome. (ODP: 61) p. 442

Clitic: A form that resembles a word that cannot stand on its own as a normal utterance because it is structurally dependent on a neighboring word. (CEL: 423)

Common ground: Shared intersubjective context, broadly construed. p. 75

Definitions: pp. 66-67

Denoting phrases: pp. 95-96

Diexis, dietic: pp. 39, 282-284

Direct or naïve realism: p. 201

Displacement: It is possible to talk about events remote in space and time from the situation of the speaker (unlike most animal cries, which reflect immediate environmental stimuli). (CEL: 401) pp. 69, 253, 305

Displaced speech: Speech referring to objects etc. which are not part of its immediate setting in space and time. Characteristic of communication in man, but not demonstrated in any other species; hence displacement has been included in accounts of design features. (OCDL: 110) pp. 88-92

Dyadic: p. 87

Duodecimal math: p. 327

Dualism: Any view that postulates two kinds of thing in some domain is dualistic; contrasting views according to which there is only one kind of thing are monistic. The most famous example of the contrast is mind-body dualism, contrasted with monism in the form either of idealism (only mind) or more often physicalism (only body or matter). (ODP: 110) pp. 9, 60, 103, 110-113, 137-138, chapter 3

Eliminativists: The view that the terms in which we think of some area are sufficiently infected with error for it to be better to abandon them than to continue to try to give coherent theories of their use. Eliminativism should be distinguished from scepticism, which claims that we cannot know the truth about some area; eliminativism claims rather that there is no truth there to be known, in the terms with which we currently think. An eliminativist about theology simply counsels abandoning the terms or discourse of theology, and that will include abandoning worries about the extent of theological knowledge. Eliminativists in the philosophy of mind counsel abandoning the whole network of terms mind, consciousness, self, qualia that usher in the problem of mind and body. Sometimes the argument for doing this is that we should wait for a supposed future understanding of ourselves, based on cognitive science and better than any our current mental descriptions provide; sometimes it is supposed that physicalism shows that no mental descriptions of ourselves could possibly be true. (ODP: 116) pp. 169-173, 238

Emergentism: p. 169

Emotional meanings: pp. 96-97

Empirical criterion of meaning: pp. 42-43

Empiricism: Any of a range of doctrines in philosophy which hold that knowledge is derived from sense experience. Traditionally opposed to nativism. (OCDL: 122) pp. 399-401

Encyclopedic knowledge: pp. 76-77

Energy: pp. 421, 445

Entification: p. 92

Entropy: A property of a closed thermodynamic system (i.e. one considered in terms interchanges of heat and other forms of energy) corresponding to the degree to which the particles of the system are randomly arranged. Entropy is a measure of the disorder in the system. The second law of thermodynamics states that entropy always increases. (ODP: 121) pp. 469-470

Epiphenomenalism: The view that some feature of a situation arises in virtue of others, but itself has no causal powers. In the philosophy of mind this means that while there exist mental events, states of consciousness, and experiences, they have themselves no causal powers, and produce no effect on the physical world. The analogy sometimes used is that of the whistle on the engine, that makes the sound (corresponding to experience), but the sound (corresponding to the experience), but plays no part in making the machinery move. Epiphenominalism is a drastic solution to the major difficulty of reconciling the existence of mind with the fact that according to physics itself only physical event can cause another physical event. An epiphenominalist may accept one-way causation, whereby physical events produce mental events, or may prefer some kind of parallelism, avoiding causation either between mind and body or between body and mind. A major problem for epiphenomenalism is that if mental events have no causal relationships it is not clear that they can be objects of memory, or even awareness. (ODP: 122) p. 171

Epistemic: Having to do with epistemology or the theory of knowledge.

Epistemological holism: p. 377

Epistemology: pp. 12, 43, 129, chapter VI

Erosion in language: the progressive reduction of the phonetic forms of words by sound change. 'Eroded' words are often replaced: thus a classic study by Gillieron showed how the forms derived from Latin *apis* 'bee', when reduced by sound changes in French to monosyllable, were widely replaced by longer forms derived by suffixation (*French* abeille <diminutive *api-culu*) or by others. (OCDL: 127) p. 254

Essentialists: pp. 65--66

Eternal sentences: p. 375

Etiological: The study of causes, causation or causality. p. 374

Euphemism: Word etc. used in place of one avoided as e.g. offensive, indecent, or alarming. E.g. the word 'girl' used of prostitutes in place of the specific word for "prostitute". (OCDL: 129) p. 289

Explanation: p. 453

Explanatory gap: p. 168

Extensions and intensions: p. 178

<u>Extreme nativists or radical innatists</u>: Theorists who posit a complete or near complete LOT or mentalese which is part of the native endowment of all fully functional infants and allows them to dress up their LOT in a surface language. In effect, the learning of a native natural language is simply a matter of learning a second language, LOT being the first. p.32

<u>Extended consciousness</u>: p. 230

<u>Facts</u>: Wittgenstein wrote that the world was the totality of facts, not of things. But although facts have the nice solid ring about them that opposes them to such things as values and theories, they prove to be slippery items out of which to build anything. Facts seem to be shaped just like sentences: it is a fact that dogs bark and stones sink... The last well-known systematic philosophy of facts was the <u>Tractatus Logico-Philosophicus</u> of Wittgenstein, which depended heavily on a conception of atomic or basic facts, conceived as logically simple, independent structures in a logical space. But Wittgenstein repudiated the metaphysic in his later work. (ODP: 134) pp. 393-394

<u>Falsifiability</u>: The property of a statement or theory that it is capable of being refuted by experience. In the philosophy of science of Popper falsifiability is the great merit of genuine scientific theory, as opposed to *unfalsifiable pseudo-science, notably psycho-analysis* and *historical materialism*. Popper's idea was that it could be a positive virtue in a scientific theory that is bold, conjectural, and goes way beyond the evidence, but that it had to be capable of facing possible refutation. If each and every way things turn out is compatible with the theory, then it is no longer a scientific theory, but, for instance, an ideology or article of faith. (ODP: 135)   pp. 315-316

<u>Family of resemblances</u>: p. 17

<u>Feature dualism</u>: pp. 176-177

<u>Figurative meanings</u>: pp. 40, 289, 291

<u>Folk psychology</u>: Originally a disparaging term, now widely used, for the process of attributing thoughts, beliefs, intentions, and meanings to each other (the 'folk' referred to include such masters of human understanding as Shakespeare and Tolstoy, as well as the rest of us.) The term arises from unease that ordinary processes of attribution do not seem 'scientific', and the categories they use fit with difficulty into the categories of physical science. Often the term invites contrast with a supposed future when there will be a science whose terms will quite eclipse the categories with which we normally describe each other, perhaps by being more comprehensive, less vague, and better matched to scientific understanding of ourselves. (ODP: 141) pp. 137, 138, 150, 152, 162, 181, 183, 185, 194, 209, 213, 217, 239, 240

<u>Force</u>: pp. 440-442

<u>FOXP-2, the language gene</u>: p.268

<u>Frame</u>: pp. 30, 67, 106, 173, 196, 198, 250-251, 254, 433, 435, 464

<u>Frame semantics</u>: Treatment of meaning developed by Charles J. Fillmore since the 1970s, emphasizing in particular the ways in which words change their meanings with the frame of reference in which they are used. Thus *set* has one meaning in a frame one might distinguish as

that of 'tennis', in which it is related variously to those of *game, serve, love*, etc.; but another e.g. in a frame in which one might talk of a complete set of crockery. *Serve* has a meaning in a frame one might describe as 'eating in a restaurant', in relation to *waiter, course*, etc., which again is different from its meaning in the frame of 'tennis'; and so on. (OCDL: 147) pp. 20, 106

Free will: The problem is to reconcile our everyday consciousness of ourselves as agents, with the best view of what science tells us that we are. Determinism is one part of the problem. It may be defined as the doctrine that every event has a cause. More precisely, for any event e, there will be some antecedent state of nature, N, and a law of nature, L, such that given L, N will be followed by e. But if this is true of every event, it is true of events such as my doing something or choosing to do something. So my choosing or doing something is fixed by some antecedent state N and the laws. Since determinism is universal these in turn are fixed, and so backwards to events for which I am clearly not responsible (events before my birth, for example). So no events can be voluntary or free, where that means that they come about purely because of my willing them when I could have done otherwise. If determinism is true, then there will be antecedent states and laws already determining such events; how then can I truly be said to be their author, or be responsible for them? (ODP: 147) pp.153, 160, 164, 177, 188, 224-225, 226, 227, 237-238

Functional devices: pp. 20, 40, 56, 59, 62, 64-65, 67, 81-445

Functional holism: p. 20

Functional/mechanical explanation: pp. 184, 217, 454-455

Fuzzy logic: pp. 124-125, 263, 407

Generative grammar: See universal generative grammar below.

Gordian knot: A complicated problem.

Grammatical or structural meaning: Any aspect of meaning described as part of the syntax and morphology of a language as distinct from its lexicon. Thus especially the meanings of constructions and inflections, or of words when described similarly. Such words include, in particular, ones belonging to closed rather that open classes, or those seen as marking a syntactic unit. Thus *he* has a grammatical meaning in opposition to other members of a closed class of personal pronouns; *if* as the marker e.g. of an indirect question *I asked if they were coming*. (OCDL: 165) p. 256

Gravity: pp. 387, 410, 426-441

Graphology: A study of the written forms of language modeled on phonology as the study of their sound systems. (OCDL: 166) p.56

Heterophenomenology: pp. 173, 249

Holism, holistic: Any doctrine emphasizing the priority of the whole over its parts. In the philosophy of language, this becomes the claim that the meaning of an individual word or sentence can only be understood in terms of its relations to an indefinitely larger body of language, such as a whole theory, or even a whole language or form of life. In the philosophy of mind, a mental state similarly may be identified only in terms of its relations with others. Moderate holism may allow that other things besides these relationships also count; extreme holism would hold that the network of relationships is all we have. A holistic view of science holds that the experience only confirms or disconfirms large bodies of doctrine, impinging at the edges, and leaving some leeway over the adjustments that it requires. (ODP: 177) p. 20

Holophrases: A sentence or utterance consisting of a single word. Especially of single word utterances by children at an early stage in their development of language: called accordingly the holophrastic stage. (OCDL: 177) p. 81

Holophrastic: See above Holophrases.

Homunculus: A small person. A bad idea in the philosophy of mind to explain a person's agency, or intelligence, or experience, as if there were a smaller agent, or intelligent thing, or experiencing subject 'inside the head'. But homuncular functionalism decomposes complex functions into simpler ones, thereby avoiding the obvious regress. (ODP: 178) p. 152

Hopi: an indigenous tribe of Native Americans who lived in the American southwest and were studied extensively by Benjamin Whorf in the early 20th century. pp. 15, 16, 120, 140, 433, 434, 466

I-language: Chomsky's term from the mid-1980s for the knowledge of a language system as internalized (hence in Part 'I') as a system in the minds of speakers. Opposed to E-language as 'external language'. pp. 259, 306

Idealism: Any doctrine holding that reality is fundamentally mental in nature. The boundaries of such a doctrine are not firmly drawn: for example, the traditional Christian view that God is a sustaining cause, possessing greater reality than his creation, might just be classified as a form of idealism. Leibniz's doctrine that the simple substances out of which all else is made are themselves perceiving and appetitive beings (monads), and that space and time are relations among these things, is another early version. Major forms of idealism include subjective idealism, or the position better called immaterialism and associated with Berkeley, according to which to exist is to be perceived, transcendental idealism, and absolute idealism. Idealism is opposed to the naturalistic belief that mind is itself to be exhaustively understood as a product of natural processes. The most common modern manifestation of idealism is the view that we 'create' the world we inhabit by employing mind-dependent linguistic and social categories. The difficulty is to give a literal form to this view that does not conflict with the obvious fact that we do not create worlds, but find ourselves in one. (ODP: 184) pp. 138, 200-201, 316, 378, 424, 437

Identity theory: p. 172

Idiolect: An idiolect is a personal dialect. It is regarded as important in the philosophy of mind and language not to think of a public, shared language as simply a number of coincident idiolects, but rather as something prior, from which idiolects are derivative. (ODP: 215) pp. 32, 45, 46, 110

Idioms: A set expression in which two or more words are syntactically related, but with a meaning like that of a single lexical unit: e.g. 'spill the beans' in *Someone has spilled the beans about the bank raid*, or 'put one's foot in it' in *her husband can never make a speech without putting his foot in it.*' (OCDL: 182) pp. 66, 81, 82, 132, 292, 295

Intentionality: The directedness or 'aboutness' of many, if not all, conscious states. The term was used by the scholastics, but revived in the 19th century by Brentano. Our beliefs, thoughts, wishes, dreams, and desires are about things. Equally the words we use to express these beliefs and other mental states are about things. The problem of intentionality is that of understanding the relation obtaining between a mental state, or its expression, and the things it is about. A number of peculiarities attend this relation. (ODP: 196) p.182

Introspection: Looking into one's own mind, to find what one thinks and feels. The idea that this process is rather like that of perception, only turned inwards, *is rejected by most current philosophers of mind.* (ODP: 197) (My italics) pp. 31, 151, 153,177, 222-225, 229

Irony: Originally of a 'figure of speech in which one thing is said but the opposite is meant: e.g. *'that's just what I needed!'* said as the tool one is using comes apart in one's hands. Usage in pragmatics or linguistics generally tends to reflect this, but others are also current, as in literary studies especially. (OCDL: 202) pp. 70, 78, 289

Iterated learning: (Also referred to as "observational learning") Iterated learning is a process in which an individual acquires a behavior by observing a similar behavior in another individual who acquired it the same way.

Spoken (or signed) language is an outcome of iterated learning. Although in some circumstances aspects of language may be explicitly taught, acquired from a written form, or arise from deliberate invention, almost all the features of the languages we speak are a result of iterated learning. Models of this process demonstrate that, over repeated episodes of transmission, behaviors transmitted by iterated learning tend to become 1) easier to learn, and 2) increasingly structured. Note that this process is cumulative and is not considered to arise from explicit intentions of the individuals involved. Rather, this type of cultural evolution is an "invisible hand" process leading to phenomena that are a result of human action but are not intentional artifacts. (Kirby, Cornish and Smith) PNAS 8/5/2008 /vol. 105/no 31/. pp. 257, 260, 262-263, 305

Lexemes: "So far in this section, we have used the term 'word' to discuss semantic units, and this is the traditional use. People readily talk about the 'meaning of words'. However, if we wish to enquire precisely into semantic matters, this term will not do, and an alternative must be found. There are three main reasons.

1. The term *word* is used in ways that obscure the study of meaning. The forms *walk, walks, walking,* and *walked* could all be called 'different words'; yet from a semantic point of view, they are all variants of the same underlying unit, 'walk'. If the variants are referred to as 'words', though, what should the underlying unit be called? It would not be particularly clear to say that 'these four words are different forms of the same word'.

2. The term word is useless for the study of idioms, which are also units of meaning. A much-used example is *kick the bucket* (='die'). Here we have a single unit of meaning, which happens to consist of three words. Again, it would hardly be clear to talk of this unit as a 'word', if we then go on to say that this word consists of three words.

3. The term word has in any case been appropriated for use elsewhere in linguistic study—in the field of grammar, where it does sterling service at the junction between syntax and morphology.

For such reasons, most linguists prefer to talk about the basic units of semantic analysis with fresh terminology, and both *lexeme* and *lexical item* are in common use. We may now avoid the lack of clarity referred to above, and say that the 'lexeme' WALK occurs in several variant forms— The 'words' *walk, walks*, etc. Similarly we can say that the 'lexeme' KICK THE BUCKET contains three 'words'; and so on. It is lexemes that are usually listed as headwords in a dictionary. Accordingly, we shall put this term to use in the remaining parts of this section. (CEL: 104) pp. 61, 69, 81,82, 293

Lexemes reflect a grammatical holism where each traditional grammatical unit does not have a unique or separate meaning. The lexeme, no matter how many words are in it, functions as a single unit of speech.

Literal meanings: Variously of the meaning or other expression as determined solely by the separate words etc. of which it is composed, or of what is said, as opposed to what is implied or implicated, in a given context. (OCDL: 228) Contrasted with figurative meanings. pp. 5, 13, 26-30, 34, 36, 40, 46, 70, 289-290, 296, 371, 379, 409

Logical positivism: Also known as logical empiricism and scientific empiricism; the ideas and attitude towards philosophy associated with the Vienna circle. This group was founded by Morris Schlick in 1924, and in effect ended with his death in 1936 and the dispersal of Austrian intellectuals at that time… The central interest of the Vienna circle was the unity of science and the correct delineation of scientific method. The idea was that this would act as a final solvent of the disputes of metaphysicians. The task of constructive philosophy became that of analyzing the structure of scientific theory and language. The movement can be seen as a development of older empiricist and sensationalist doctrines in the light first of a better understanding of the methodology of empirical science and secondly of the dramatically increased power of formal logic to permit the definition of abstractions and to describe the structures of permissible inferences... The most characteristic doctrine of logical positivism was the verification principle or denial of literal or cognitive meaning to any statement that is not verifiable; the meaning of a statement is its method of verification... (ODP: 223) pp. 14, 15, 27, 42-43, 99, 201, 378, 393, 402

Logical connectives: p. 45

Mass: pp. 400, 438-445

Matter: pp. 363-365, 437-439

Meanings: pp. 5-8, 10, 12, 14-41, 42-47, 55-60, 61-69, 70-72, 73-84

Meat based mentalism: p. 170

Mechanical/functional paradigm: p. 184

Mereological fallacy: p. 170

Mentalese or LOT (language of thought): pp. 12, 105, 210, 307

Mentalism: pp. 9, 22, 138, 303

Meta-language: pp. 3, 31

Metaphor: 1. Figure of speech in which a word or expression normally used of one kind of object, action etc. is extended to another. This may lead to **metaphoric change** in meaning: thus what is now the normal sense of 'lousy' in origin a metaphorical extension from the sense 'full of lice'.
2. Extended by George Lakoff in the 1980s to refer to a general pattern in which one domain is systemically conceived and spoken of in terms of another. E.g. terms directly applicable to war, as one domain, are systemically applied to that of courtship: *She was besieged by suitors, I have lost count of her conquests, and so on.* (OCDL:242) pp. 6, 30, 40, 82, 101, 132, 160, 198, 235, 244, 251, 252, 254, 271, 289-291, 295, 428, 461

Metaphysics: Originally a title for those books of Aristotle that came after *Physics*, the term is now applied to any enquiry that raises questions about reality that lie beyond or behind those capable of being tackled by the methods of science. Naturally, an immediately contested issue is whether there are any such questions or whether any text of metaphysics should in Hume's words, be 'committed to the flames, for it can contain nothing but sophistry and illusion' (Enquiry Concerning Human Understanding, Bk. xii, Pt. 3). The traditional examples will include questions of mind and body, substance and accident, events, causation, and categories for things that exist (ontology). The permanent complaint about metaphysics is that in so far as there are real questions in these areas, ordinary scientific method forms the only possible approach to them. Hostility to metaphysics was one of the banners of logical positivism, and survives in a different way in the scientific naturalism of writers such as Quine. Metaphysics, then, tends to become concerned more with the presuppositions of scientific thought, or of thought in general, although, here too, any suggestion that there is one timeless way in which thought has to be conducted meets sharp opposition. A useful distinction is drawn by Strawson, between descriptive metaphysics, which contents itself with describing the basic framework of concepts with which thought is (perhaps at a time) conducted, as opposed to revisionary metaphysics, which aims for a criticism and revision of some hapless way of thought. Although the possibility of revisionary metaphysics may be doubted, it continues to the present time: eliminativism in the philosophy of mind and postmodern disenchantment with objectivity and truth are conspicuous examples. (ODP: 240) pp. 423, 8, 9, 11, 22, 103, 113, 137, 162, 164, 238, 240, 271, 316, 321, 323, 324, 356, 427, 428-430, 469

Metonym: Figure of speech in which a word or expression normally or strictly used of one thing is used of something physically or otherwise associated with it e.g. *the Pentagon* (strictly a building) when used of the military inhabiting it. This may lead to metonymic change of meaning: e.g. the sense of bureau changed successively from 'cloth used to cover desks': first to 'desk' itself, then to agency etc. (working from a desk). (OCDL: 243) pp. 6, 101, 289

Mind/body dualism: pp. 11, 21, 102, 106, 110, 113, 136, 137, 149, 161, 175, 199, 208, 231, 260, 450, 476

Modal terms: p. 45

Morphology: The study of the grammatical structure of words and the categories realized by them. Thus a morphological analysis will divide *girls* into *girl* and *-s*, which realizes 'plural'; singer into *sing* and *-er*, which marks it as a noun referring to an agent.
A category is 'morphological' if it is realized within words. Thus morphological case is case as realized by different elements within nouns or words of other classes, as opposed to an abstract case which might be realized differently or not at all. A morphological causative is a causative form of a verb as opposed to a causative construction, and so on. pp. 38, 61, 143, 261, 285-288

Munduruku tribesmen: pp. 51-52

Mysterians: pp. 173-174

Naming and descriptions: pp. 272-281

NASA: p. 210

Naïve realism: p. 201

Nativism: The theory that specific properties of the mind are inherited, not acquired. Hence especially, in linguistics, of Chomsky's theory of the development of language in children from genetically inherited principles of Universal Grammar. Empiricism is the philosophical doctrine traditionally opposed to nativism. (OCDL: 258) pp. 16, 33

Non-teleological: pp. 186-192, 241, 242

Noun phrases: pp. 15, 301

Object language: pp. 3, 91

Observational learning: See: Iterated learning.

Ontogeny: Biologists' term for the origin and development of an individual organism. The ontogeny of language is therefore its development in children, as opposed to its 'phylogeny' which is its evolution in our species. 'Ontogenetic' is similarly opposed to 'phylogenetic'. (OCDL: 278) pp. 68, 140, 148, 163, 89

Ontology: Derived from the Greek word for being, but a 17th-century coinage for the branch of metaphysics that concerns itself with what exists. Apart from the ontological argument itself there have existed many *a priori* arguments that the world must contain things of one kind or another: simple things, unextended things, eternal substances, necessary beings, and so on... (ODP: 269) pp. 428, 151, 168, 181, 207, 448

Operants: pp. 21, 123, 192, 217

Operant conditioning: pp. 21, 110, 192, 197, 219, 246, 261, 262, 270, 398

Parallelism: In the philosophy of mind, the difficulty of seeing how mind and body can interact suggests that we ought instead to think of them as two systems running in parallel. When I stub my toe, this does not cause the pain, but there is a harmony between the mental and the physical (perhaps due to God) that ensures that there will be simultaneous pain; when I form an intention and then act, the same benevolence insures that my action is appropriate to my intention. The theory has never been wildly popular, and in its application to the mind-body problem many philosophers would say that it was the result of misconceived Cartesian dualism. (ODP: 267) pp. 164, 171

Performative utterances: pp. 25-27

Phenomena: pp. 74, 23, 70, 82, 103, 120, 138, 150, 162, 172-174, 199-208, 263, 268, 373, 424-427, 434, 459, 465, 471

Phenomenal dualism: pp. 164, 199

Phenomenalism: The philosophy of perception that elaborates the idea that, in the words of J.S. Mill, 'objects are the permanent possibilities of sensation'. To inhabit a world of independent, external objects is, on this view, to be the subject of actual and possible orderly experiences. Espoused by Russell, the view issued in a programme of translating talk about physical objects and their locations into talk about possible experiences. (ODP: 284) p.150

Phenomenological fallacy: p. 459

Phonetics: pp. 5, 271

Phylogeny: Biologists' term for the evolution of a species or other group of organisms. Theories of the phylogeny of language are similarly theories about what is traditionally called the 'origin of language'. Thence 'phylogenetic': compare ontogeny; ontogenetic. (OCDL: 303)   pp. 48, 68,166, 246, 383

Physical objects: pp, 199-206, 312, 316, 361, 428, 440, 446-450, 452, 461, 465

Physmatics: pp. 461, 463-465, 471

Planck's constant: p. 323

Platonists: p. 423

Polysemy: pp. 67, 76

Possible worlds: Any state in which the world could be: a proposition, e.g. as expressed by a sentence, may accordingly be true in some 'possible worlds' and false in others. pp. 410, 133, 218, 276, 277, 312, 375, 396, 399

Possible World Semantics: An alternative appellation for Truth Conditional Semantics. In Possible world semantics or Truth Conditional Semantics theorists can imagine and describe a world which is fundamentally different from our world. One in which the "laws" of nature are different. Philosophers use these possible worlds to propose different outcomes for contingent truths that obtain in our world. For example, oceans in another possible world could be full of a liquid which appears to be water in every respect but whose chemical makeup is not H_2O. We can imagine these possible worlds which would produce different veracity outcomes for the same proposition. p. 43

Pragmatics: pp. 5, 6, 17, 18, 25-27, 31-36, 39, 46, 70, 86, 250, 280, 282, 289

Predication: To predicate something of a subject or subjects is to describe it or them as having some property or as standing in some relation. A temptation is to think of a predicate as itself the name of a property or universal, in which case a sentence seems to be no more than a string of names, a list rather than the expression of a proposition. (ODP: 299) pp. 132, 146, 388, 415

Presuppositions: pp. 28, 32, 33, 44, 45, 57, 59, 66, 67, 75-80, 95, 96, 106, 110, 137, 234, 256, 276, 279, 280, 284, 291, 294, 381, 394, 408, 416, 432

Principle of linguistic relativity: The claim made by Benjamin Whorf and Edwin Sapir who asserted that some languages (most notably Hopi) influenced the thinking of their speakers to such an extent that they have profound differences in the way they see the world compared to SAE (standard average European) speakers. pp. 16, 119,121, 126, 127, 144, 204

Procedural knowledge: pp. 370, 315, 341, 346, 347, 351, 354, 371, 383, 389, 390, 397

Property or feature dualists: pp. 176, 177, 164

Proportional quantifiers: pp. 45, 106, 408

Propositions: Language neutral claims that are mental or "abstract" in nature and can be represented or expressed in any number of languages or in active or passive forms in addition to different wording such as "Steel is heavier than wood" and "wood is lighter than steel." All are said to express or represent the same underlying propositions in a LOT (language of thought) or "mentalese", or an abstract entity encoded in the symbols. pp. 12-15, 19, 20, 22, 25, 27, 41-43, 60, 99-102, 106, 113, 124, 129-135, 213, 216, 352, 355, 371, 372-379, 386-390, 391-395, 396-398, 402, 405-409

Propositional attitudes: pp. 213, 214, 216, 245, 411, 418,

Prosody: pp. 68, 83, 84, 95, 97, 98, 130, 133, 271,

Quantificational adverbs: p. 46

Quantum mechanics: pp. 322, 417, 460

Radical pragmaticists: pp. 33, 34

Rationalism/empiricism: pp. 399-401

Realism/anti-realism: The standard opposition between those who affirm, and those who deny, the real existence of some kind of thing, or some kind of fact or state of affairs. Almost any area of discourse may be the focus if this dispute: the external world, the past and future, other minds, mathematical objects, possibilities, universals, and moral or aesthetic properties are examples. (ODP: 319)

Reality: pp. 16, 199, 200--203, 466, 467

Recursive: (Operation, rule that can reapply to a form or construction that is itself partly or wholly derived by it. Thus, by a rule of syntax, a noun phrase (NP) can include a modifying prepositional phrase (PP): ...This in turn includes a noun phrase... that in turn can include a further prepositional phrase); and so on.
In this construction both 'noun phrase' and 'prepositional phrase' are recursive categories. The pattern in general is 'recursion'. (OCL: 335) pp. 84, 264-266

Reductionism: A reductionist holds that the facts or entities apparently needed to make true statements of some area of discourse are dispensable in favour of some other facts or entities. Reductionism is one solution to the problem of the relationship between different sciences. Thus one might advocate reducing biology to chemistry, supposing that no distinctive biological facts exist, or chemistry to physics, supposing that no distinctive chemical facts exist. Reductionist positions in philosophy include the belief that mental descriptions are made true purely by facts about behaviour (behaviourism), that statements about the external world are made true by facts about the structure of experience. (ODP: 322) pp. 5, 20, 202

Reference: pp. 14, 15, 17-19, 27, 28, 39, 40, 59, 60, 85, 86, 93-101, 132, 139, 140, 142, 178, 195, 196, 250, 251, 254, 274, 276, 277, 279, 303, 392-394, 433-435

Representation: pp. 6, 7, 9, 11, 32, 34, 55, 56, 59, 61, 74, 78, 79, 97, 102-113, 131, 142, 143, 156, 175, 202, 212, 260, 270, 311, 330, 345, 379, 390, 417

Representational theory of perception: p. 202

Representative realism: p. 200

Rules for speech: pp. 5, 6, 24, 28, 29, 39, 62, 73, 140, 226, 260, 261-288, 300-304, 318

Saccadic gaps/stream of consciousness: p. 228

SAE languages: p. 6

Scope ambiguity: p. 44

Second law of thermodynamics: See Entropy above.

Semantics: Chapter One

Semantic properties, features and facts: p. 65

Sense data or qualia: Literally, that which is given by the senses. But in response to the question of what exactly is so given, sense data theories posit private showings in the consciousness of the subject. In the case of vision this would be a kind of inner picture show which itself only indirectly represents aspects of the external world... (ODP: 347) Also   pp.150, 199-208

Solipsism: The belief that only oneself and one's experience exists. Solipsism is the extreme consequence of believing that knowledge must be founded on inner, personal states of experience, and then failing to find a bridge whereby they can inform us of anything beyond themselves. Solipsism of the present moment extends its scepticism even to one's own past states, so that all that is left is me, now. Russell reports meeting someone who claimed that she was a solipsist, and was surprised that more people were not so as well. (ODP: 356) Also p. 424

Space: pp. 16, 32, 88-92, 94, 96, 149, 152, 199, 200, 203, 214, 253, 326, 357, 422-427, 430-432

Speech acts: pp. 25-30, 56, 87, 91, 99, 133, 189, 194, 257, 284, 296, 381, 386, 393, 415

Speaker meaning: pp. 28, 32, 33-37, 107, 110, 111-114, 123, 156, 194, 195, 274, 379

State consciousness: pp. 165, 213, 220, 222

Stimulus-Response-Reinforcement (S-R-R): pp. 21, 28, 122, 186

Subitize: p. 339-343

Supervenience: Term introduced by Hare to describe the way that ethical properties relate to other psychological and natural properties of things. Properties of one kind, f, supervene upon those of another kind, G.
   The notion is exploited in many areas: for example, biological properties plausibly supervene upon chemical ones; mental properties upon physical ones; dispositional properties and powers upon categorical ones, and so on. One promise the notion holds out is that by its means we can understand the relation of such different layers of description without attempting a reduction of the one area to the other. The value of this promise depends on how well we understand the supervenience relation itself. (ODP: 368) p. 172

Symmetry: pp. 463-465

Synesthesia: p. 205

Synonymy: The relation between two lexical units with a shared meaning. 'Absolute' synonyms, if they exist, have meanings identical in all respects and in all contexts. 'Partial' synonyms have meanings identical in some contexts, or identical only in that replacing one with the other does not change the truth conditions of a specific sentence. Thus *paper* is a partial synonym of *article*: compare *I got my paper published, I got my article published*. But their synonymy is not absolute: e.g. *paper*, but not *article*, can also be used to refer to a newspaper. (OCDL: 395)

Syntax: The study of relations established in a grammar between words and other units that make up a sentence.

Usually distinguished from morphology. E.g. in the phrase *these books*, the relations between the words belongs to syntax: thus *these* modifies or is a determiner of *books*; it comes before it, they agree in respect of number. The internal structure of the words belongs to morphology: thus *books* and *these* are each plural, *books* has the ending -*s*. Also distinguished widely from semantics. Thus the order of *these* and *books* is seen as belonging to syntax, as does the rule which for excludes *this books* or *these book*. But anything to do with the meaning of the phrase (that *these* is a dietic element, that it qualifies *books*, that the expression is used to refer to more than one book) belongs to semantics. Distinguished finally, in itself or as part of grammar, from the lexicon: thus the role of *these* in relation to books belongs to syntax, but the properties of book as an individual unit belong to an individual lexical entry.

The term itself is univocal: where detailed definitions vary they reflect varying theories of the structure or nature of language generally. (OCDL: 396) pp. 5, 39, 41, 62-65, 81, 134, 137, 255, 256, 261, 263, 300-304, 392

Tact: pp. 132, 139, 195-198, 202, 205-208, 217, 256, 270, 278, 281, 284, 350, 397, 457, 458

Teleological: (GK., *telos*, End) The study of the ends or purposes of things. The idea that there is such a thing as the end or purpose of life is prominent in the Aristotelian view of nature (and ethics), and then in the Christian tradition. The theory of evolution through natural selection allows speculation about the function for which particular things are adapted, and so permits assertions about the purpose an adaptation serves, without any commitment to the idea of a designer who put it there for a purpose, and without the unscientific belief that the future utility of a feature somehow brings about its existence by a kind of backward causation. (ODP: 374) p. 241

Testability: The capacity of a theory to yield predictions that can be tested, thereby either refuting the theory, or, more controversially, confirming it. (ODP: 374) p. 315

Theory of mind: pp. 158-160, 190, 191, 239, 40

Thorndike's law of effect: p. 241

Time: pp. 6, 16, 58, 77, 88, 120, 127, 141, 145, 149, 151, 243, 253, 255, 269, 282, 283, 291, 364, 376, 408, 423-426, 432-436, 448, 449, 463, 472

Tone languages: One in which phonological units within words are distinguished by a distinct tone or sequence of tones: e.g. Chinese. Typically of those in which tones are assigned to separate syllables; thence, more generally, of ones in which most syllables are so distinguished, or most units of the lexicon, or in which contrasting pitches on accented syllables have some lexical or morphological role. Thus, at the limit, Norwegian is also conventionally called a 'tone language'.

(OCDL: 409) pp. 65, 123

Validity/truth: pp. 316, 318, 321, 330, 352, 365, 405-407, 461

Veridical: Truthful. A veridical perception is one that represents things as they are, contrasted with an illusory or even delusory one that does not. (ODP: 392) pp. 205, 221, 466

Verification criterion: The principle central to Logical Positivism, according to which the meaning of a statement is its method of verification. Sentences apparently expressing propositions that admit of no verification (such as those of metaphysics and theology) are in consequence meaningless, or at least fail to put forward theses with cognitive meaning, capable of truth or falsity. The principle requires confidence that we know what a verification consists in, and tended to coexist with a fairly simple conception of each thought as answerable to individual experiences. To avoid undue simplification the principle moved from requiring a strong or conclusive verification as the condition of meaning, to admitting indirect and inconclusive verification. However, more complex and holistic conceptions of language and its relation to the world suggest a more flexible set of possible relations, with sentences that are individually not verifiable nevertheless having a use in an overall network of beliefs or theory that itself answers to experience. (ODP: 392) pp. 172, 174, 374, 378, 423

Weltanschauung: Ger., a general world view; and overarching philosophy. pp. 225, 442, 448

Selected Bibliography

Aitchison, Jean, 1987, <u>Words in the Mind</u>, Malden, MA, Blackwell Publishing

Aitchison, Jean, 1989, <u>The Articulate Mammal</u>, London, UK, Routledge

Aitchison, Jean, 1992, <u>Linguistics</u>, London, UK, Hodder Headline Plc.

Aitchison, Jean, 1996, <u>The Seeds of Speech</u>, Cambridge, UK, Cambridge University Press

Aitchison, Jean, 2010, <u>Aitchison's Linguistics</u>, Seventh Edition, USA, McGraw-Hill

Allwood, Jens, Andersson, Lars-Gunnar, and Osten, Dahl, 1977, <u>Logic in Linguistics</u>, Cambridge, UK, Cambridge University Press

Austin, John L., 1962a, <u>Sense and Sensibilia</u>, London, Oxford University Press

Austin, J.L., 1962b, <u>How to Do Things with Words</u>, Cambridge, MA, Harvard

Ayer, Alfred Jules, 1952, <u>Language, Truth and Logic</u>, New York, Dover Publications

Ayer, Alfred Jules, 1956, <u>The Problem of Knowledge</u>, Baltimore, Penguin Books

Ayer, Alfred Jules, 1959, <u>Logical Positivism</u>, New York, The Free Press

Ayer, Alfred Jules, 1982, <u>Philosophy in the Twentieth Century</u>, New York, Random House

Asimov, Isaac, 1966, <u>Understanding Physics</u>, Dorset Press

Azimov, Isaac, 1976, <u>Azimov on Physics</u>, New York, Avon Books

Baggini, Julian and Fosl, Peter S., 2010, <u>The Philosophers Tool Kit</u>, Second Edition, Chichester, West Sussex, UK, Wiley-Blackwell

Baker, Mark C. and Goetz, Stewart, 2011, <u>The Soul Hypothesis</u>, London, Bloomsbury

Baugh, Albert C. and Cable, Thomas, 1993, <u>A History of the English Language</u>, Fourth Edition, Englewood Cliffs, NJ, Prentice Hall

Baum, William M., 2005, <u>Understanding Behaviorism</u>, Second edition, Blackwell Publishing, Malden, MA

Beaney, Michael, 1997, <u>The Frege Reader</u>, Malden, MA, Blackwell Publishers Inc.

Bennett, Deborah J., 2004, <u>Logic Made Easy</u>, New York, W. W. Norton & Company

Bennett, Maxwell; Dennett, Daniel; Hacker Peter; Robinson, Daniel; Searle John, 2007, Neuroscience and Philosophy, New York, Columbia University Press

Bergman, Gustav, 1954, The Metaphysics of Logical Positivism, New York, Longmans, Green and Co.

Berlinski, David, 2000, The Advent of the Algorithm, New York, Harcourt, Inc.

Bickerton, Derek, 1990, Language & Species, Chicago, The University of Chicago Press

Bickerton, Derek, 1995, Language and Human Behavior, Seattle, WA, University of Washington Press

Bickerton, Derek, 2009, Adam's Tongue, New York, Hill and Wang

Blackburn, Simon, 1994, The Oxford Dictionary of Philosophy, Second Edition, Oxford, Oxford University Press

Blandshard, Brand, 1962, Reason and Analysis, La Salle, IL, Open Court Publishing

Bloom, Alfred, 1981, The Linguistic Shaping of Thought, Hillsdale, NJ, Lawrence Erlbaum Associates, Inc.

Bloom, Paul and Kiel, Frank C., 2001, Mind and Language, Vol. 16 No. 4, September

Blum, Susan D., 2013, Making Sense of Language, Oxford, Oxford University Press

Boaz, Franz, 1939, Race, Language and Culture, Read Books Ltd.

Bodanis, David, 2000, $E=mc^2$, New York, Berkeley Books

Boroditsky, Lera via Gentner, Dedre and Goldin-Meadow, 2003, Language In Mind, The MIT Press, Cambridge, Massachusetts

Bourke, Vernon J., 1964, The Essential Augustine, Indianapolis, IN, Hackett Publishing

Bova, Ben, 2001, The Story of Light, Naperville, IL, Sourcebooks, Inc.

Bowerman, M. & Choi, S. (2001). Shaping meanings for language: Universal and language specific in the acquisition of spatial semantic categories. In M. Bowerman & S.C. Levinson (Eds.) The origins of children's spatial semantic categories: Language acquisition and conceptual development. Cambridge, UK: Cambridge University Press.

Braddon-Mitchell, David, and Jackson, Frank, 1996, Philosophy of Mind and Cognition, Malden, MA, Blackwell Publishers Inc.

Brody, Baruch A., and Grandy, Richard E., 1971, Readings in the Philosophy of Science, Second Edition, Englewood Cliffs, NJ, Prentice Hall, Inc.

Brown, Gillian and Yule, George, 1983, Discourse Analysis, Cambridge, Cambridge Univ. Press

Brown, Roger, 1958, <u>Words and Things</u>, New York, The Free Press

Calvin, William H., 1996, <u>How Brains Think</u>, New York, Basic Books

Campbell, Lyle, 2000, <u>Historical Linguistics</u>, Cambridge, MA, The MIT Press

Carey, Susan, 2011, <u>The Origin of Concepts</u>, Oxford, UK, Oxford University Press

Carnie, Andrew, 2007, <u>Syntax</u>, Second Edition, Malden, MA, Blackwell Publishing

Carrol, John B., 2011, <u>Language, Thought and Reality</u>, Cambridge MA, MIT Press

Carston, Robyn, 2002, <u>Thoughts and Utterances</u>, Malden, MA, Blackwell Publishers Inc.

Caton, Charles E., 1970, <u>Philosophy and Ordinary Language</u>, Chicago, University of Illinois Press

Chalmers, David J., 2002, <u>Philosophy of Mind</u>, New York, Oxford University Press

Crystal, David, 2005, <u>How Language Works</u>, New York, The Overlook Press

Chisholm, Roderick M., 1966, <u>Theory of Knowledge</u>, Englewood Cliffs, NJ, Prentice Hall Inc.

Chomsky, Noam, 1966, <u>Cartesian Linguistics: A Chapter in the History of Rationalist Thought</u>, New York, Harper & Row

Chomsky, Noam, 1975, <u>Reflections on Language</u>, New York, Pantheon Books

Chomsky, Noam, 2006, <u>Language and Mind</u>, Cambridge UK, Cambridge University Press

Christiansen, Morten and Kirby, Simon, 2003, <u>Language Evolution</u>, Oxford, Oxford University Press

Comrie, Bernard, 1985, <u>Tense</u>, Cambridge, UK, Cambridge University Press

Corballis, Michael C., 2002, <u>From Hand to Mouth</u>, Princeton, NJ, Princeton University Press

Corbett, Greville, 1991, <u>Gender</u>, Cambridge, UK, Cambridge University Press

Coulmas, Florian, 1989, <u>The Writing Systems of the World</u>, Oxford, Basil Blackwell Ltd.

Crick, Francis, 1994, <u>The Astonishing Hypothesis The Scientific Search for the Soul</u>, New York, Macmillan Publishing Company

Cruse, Alan, 2015, <u>Meaning in Language</u>, Second Edition, Oxford UK, Oxford University Press

Crystal, David, 1997, <u>The Cambridge Encyclopedia of Language</u>, Second Edition, Cambridge UK, Cambridge University Press

Crystal, David, 2005, <u>How Language Works</u>, The Overlook Press, New York

Damasio, Antonio R., 1994, <u>Descartes Error</u>, New York, Harper Collins Publishers Inc.

Damasio, Antonio, 1999, <u>The Feeling of What Happens</u>, New York, Harcourt Inc.

Darwin, Charles, 1859, <u>The Origin of Species</u>, New York, Random House, Alfred A. Knopf, Everyman's Library, Fourth printing, Copyright 2003.

Davies, Stephen, 2003, <u>Empiricism and History</u>, Hampshire, UK, Palgrave Macmillan

Deacon, Terrence W., 1997, <u>The Symbolic Species</u>, New York, W. W. Norton & Co.

Dehaene, Stanislaus, 1997, <u>The Number Sense</u>, Oxford, Oxford University Press

Dennett, Daniel C., 1987, <u>The Intentional Stance</u>, Cambridge, MA, The MIT Press

Dennett, Daniel C., 1991, <u>Consciousness Explained</u>, Boston, Little, Brown and Company

Dennett, Daniel C., 2005, <u>Sweet Dreams</u>, Cambridge, MA, The MIT Press

Dennett, Daniel C., 2013, <u>Intuition Pumps</u>, New York, W.W. Norton & Company

Dessalles, Jean-Louis, 2007 English Translation, <u>Why We Talk</u>, New York, Oxford University Press

Deutscher, Guy, 2005, <u>The Unfolding of Language</u>, New York, Henry Holt & Company

Deutscher, Guy, 2010, <u>Through the Language Glass</u>, New York, Metropolitan Books, Henry Holt and Company, LLC

Dixon, R.M.W., 2016, <u>Are Some Languages Better Than Others</u>, Oxford, Oxford University Press

Edelman, Gerald M., 1989, <u>The Remembered Present</u>, New York, Basic Books

Everett, Daniel L., 2012, <u>Language the Cultural Tool</u>, New York, Vintage Books

Feigl, Herbert, 1958, <u>The "Mental" and the "Physical"</u>, Minneapolis, MN, University of Minnesota Press

Ferreira, Pedro G., 2014, <u>The Perfect Theory</u>, New York, Houghton Mifflin Harcourt Publishing Company

Ferris, Timothy, 1997, <u>The Whole Shebang</u>, New York, Simon and Schuster

Fogelin, Robert J., 1976, <u>Wittgenstein</u>, Second Edition, New York, Routledge

Fodor, Jerry A., 1987, <u>Psychosemantics</u>, Cambridge, MA, The MIT Press

Frege, Gottlob, 1980, The Foundations of Arithmetic, Translated by J. L. Austin, Second Revised Edition, Evanston, IL, Northwestern University Press

Fromkin, Victoria and Rodman, Robert, 1998, An Introduction to Language, Sixth Edition, New York, Harcourt Brace College Publishers

Gamow, George, 1947, One Two Three…Infinity, New York, Viking Press

Gentner, Dedre and Goldin-Meadow, Susan, 2003, Language In Mind, Cambridge, MIT Press

Genz, Henning, 1999, Nothingness, Translated by Karin Heusch, Reading, MA, Perseus Books

Gertler, Brie, and Shapiro, Lawrence, 2007, Arguing About the Mind, New York, Routledge

Gibson, Kathleen R., and Ingold, Tim, 1993, Tools, Language and Cognition in Human Development, Cambridge, Great Britain, Cambridge University Press

Glick, Thomas F. and Kohn, David, 1996, Charles Darwin On Evolution, Indianapolis, IN, Hackett Publishing

Goldstein, Rebecca, 2005, Incompleteness, New York, W. W. Norton & Company Inc.

Gould, James L., and Carol Grant, 2007, Animal Architects, New York, Basic Books

Graziano, Michael, S. A. 2019, Rethinking Consciousness, New York, W. W. Norton & Company Inc.

Greene, Brian, 1999, The Elegant Universe, New York, Vintage Books

Gribbin, John, 2004, Deep Simplicity, New York, Random House Publishing

Guillen, Michael, 1983, Bridges to Infinity, Los Angeles, CA, Jeremy P. Tarcher, Inc.

Hart, W. D., 1996, The Philosophy of Mathematics, Oxford, Oxford University Press

Harris, Annaka, 2019, Conscious, New York, Harper Collins Publishers

Harris, Randy Allen, 1993, The Linguistics Wars, Oxford, Oxford University Press,

Hawking, Steven, 2001, The Universe in a Nutshell, New York, Bantam Books

Hawking, Steven, 1998, A Brief History of Time, New York, Bantam Books

Hayakawa, S. I., 1940, Language in Thought and Action, NY, Harcourt Brace Jovanovich Inc.

Herrnstein, Richard J. and Murray, Charles, 1996, The Bell Curve, New York, Free Press Paperbacks

Himmelfarb, Gertrude, 1959, Darwin and the Darwinian Revolution, Chicago, IL, Elephant Paperbacks

Hinzen, Wolfram and Sheehan, Michelle, 2013, <u>The Philosophy of Universal Grammar</u>, Oxford, Oxford University Press

Hoffman, Banish, 1959, <u>The Strange Story of the Quantum</u>, New York, Dover Publications

Hofstadter, Douglas & Sander, Emmanuel, 2013, <u>Surfaces and Essences</u>, New York, Basic Books

Horwich, Paul, 1998, <u>Meaning</u>, Oxford, UK, Oxford University Press

Hospers, John, 1953, <u>An Introduction to Philosophical Analysis</u>, Second edition, Englewood Cliffs, NJ, Prentice Hall, Inc.

Hospers, John, 1988, <u>An Introduction to Philosophical Analysis</u>, Third edition, Englewood Cliffs, NJ, Prentice Hall, Inc.

Hook, Sidney, 1969, <u>Language and Philosophy</u>, New York, New York University Press

Hook, Sidney, 1960, <u>Dimensions of Mind</u>, London, Collier-MacMillan

Huddleston, Rodney, 1984, <u>Introduction to the Grammar of English</u>, Cambridge, UK, Cambridge University Press

Hurford, James R., 2007, <u>The Origins of Meaning</u>, Oxford, UK, Oxford University Press

Hurford, James R., 2012, <u>The Origins of Grammar</u>, Oxford, UK, Oxford University Press

Hylton, Peter, 1990, <u>Russell, Idealism and the Emergence of Analytic Philosophy</u>, Oxford, UK, Clarendon Press

Isac, Daniela and Reiss, Charles, 2013, <u>I Language</u>, Oxford, Oxford University Press

Jackendoff, Ray, 1983, <u>Semantics and Cognition</u>, Cambridge, MA, The MIT Press

Jesperson, Otto, 1921, <u>Language Its Nature, Development and Origin</u>, New York, W.W. Norton & Company Inc.

Kant, Immanuel, 1781, <u>Critique of Pure Reason</u>, Translated by Norman Kemp Smith, 1965, New York, Macmillan & Co.

Kant, Immanuel, 1783, <u>Prolegomena to Any Future Metaphysics</u>, Indianapolis, IN, Bobbs-Merrill Company, Inc., Copyright 1950

Karplus, Robert, 1970, <u>Physics and Man</u>, New York, W.A. Benjamin, Inc.

Kearns, Kate, 2000, <u>Semantics</u>, Hampshire, UK, Palgrave Macmillan

Kline, Morris, 1972, <u>Mathematical Thought from Ancient to Modern Times</u>, Volumes 1, 2 & 3, Oxford, UK, Oxford University Press

Koch, Christof, 2019, <u>The Feeling of Life Itself</u>, Cambridge, MA, The MIT Press

Kosko, Bart, 1993, <u>Fuzzy Thinking</u>, New York, Hyperion

Kuhn, Thomas S., 1970, <u>The Structure of Scientific Revolutions</u>, Second Edition, Chicago, University of Chicago Press

Langacker, Ronald W., 2008, <u>Cognitive Grammar</u>, Oxford, UK, Oxford University Press

Levi, Albert William, 1966, <u>Philosophy and the Modern World</u>, Bloomington, Indiana University Press

Levinson, Stephen C., 1983, <u>Pragmatics</u>, Cambridge, Cambridge University Press

Levinson, Stephen C., 2003, <u>Language and Mind: Let's get the Issues Straight</u>!

Lightfoot, David and Westergaard, Marit, 2007, <u>Language Acquisition and Language Change : Inter-relationships, Journal Compilation</u>, Blackwell Publishing Ltd

Lindley, David, 1993, <u>The End of Physics</u>, New York, BasicBooks

Lindley, David, 2007, <u>Uncertainty</u>, New York, Doubleday

Ludlow, Peter, 1997, <u>Readings in the Philosophy of Language</u>, Cambridge, MA, The MIT Press

Macdonald, G.F., <u>Perception and Identity</u>, 1970, London, The Macmillan Press, LTD

Malcolm, Norman, 1963, <u>Knowledge and Certainty</u>, Englewood Cliffs, NJ, Prentice Hall

Marcus, Gary, 2004, <u>The Birth of the Mind</u>, New York, Basic Books

Martinich, A.P., 1985, <u>The Philosophy of Language,</u> Oxford, Oxford University Press

Mathews, P.H., 2014, <u>The Oxford Dictionary of Philosophy</u>, Oxford, Oxford University Press

McGinn, Colin, 1999, <u>The Mysterious Flame</u>, New York, Basic Books

McGinn, Colin, 2004, <u>Mindsight</u>, Cambridge, MA, Harvard University Press

McGinn, Colin, 2015, <u>Philosophy of Language</u>, Cambridge MA, MIT Press

Miller, Charles D., and Heesen, Vern E., 1973, <u>Mathematical Ideas</u>, Glenview, IL, Scott, Foresman and Company

Moore, G.E., 1953, <u>Some Main Problems of Philosophy</u>, New York, Collier Books

Myers, Gerald E., 1969, <u>Self</u>, New York, Western Publishing Company Inc.

Nagel, Ernest and Brandt, Richard B., 1965, <u>Meaning and Knowledge</u>, New York, Harcourt, Brace & World Inc.

Nettle, Daniel and Romaine, Suzanne, 2000, <u>Vanishing Voices</u>, New York, Oxford University Press

Ortony, Andrew, 1979, <u>Metaphor and Thought</u>, New York, Cambridge University Press

Osborn, DeVault, Boyd, Houston 1968, <u>Understanding the Number System</u>, Columbus, Ohio, Charles E. Merrill Publishing Company

Papineau, David, 2002, <u>Thinking about Consciousness</u>, Oxford, Clarendon Press

Parkinson, G.H.R., 1968, <u>The Theory of Meaning</u>, Oxford, Oxford University Press

Penrose, Roger, 1989, <u>The Emperor's New Mind</u>, Oxford, Oxford University Press

Pinker, Steven, 2003, <u>The Blank Slate</u>, New York, Penguin Books

Pinker, Steven, 1997, <u>How the Mind Works</u>, New York, W. W. Norton & Company

Pinker, Steven, 1995, <u>The Language Instinct</u>, New York, Harper Collins Publishers Inc.

Pinker, Steven, 2007, <u>The Stuff of Thought</u>, New York, Penguin Group

Pinker, Steven, 1999, <u>Words and Rules</u>, New York, Basic Books

<u>Great Dialogues of Plato</u>, 1956, Translated by W. H. D. Rouse, New York, The New American Library

Powers, Jonathan, 1982, <u>Philosophy and the New Physics</u>, New York, Methuen & Co.

Price, H.H., 1953, <u>Thinking and Experience</u>, London, Hutchinson House

Putman, Hilary, 1975, <u>Mind, Language and Reality</u>, Cambridge, Cambridge University Press

Quine, W. V. O., 1974, <u>The Roots of Reference</u>, LaSalle, IL, Open Court Publishing

Quine, W. V. O., 1960, <u>Word and Object</u>, Cambridge, MA, The M.I.T. Press

Rothstein, Edward, 1995, <u>Emblems of Mind</u>, New York, Avon Books

Rucker, Rudy, 1982, <u>Infinity and the Mind</u>, New York, Bantam Books

Russell, Bertrand, 1912, <u>The Problems of Philosophy</u>, 2004 edition published by Barnes and Noble Inc., New York

Russell, Bertrand, 1918, <u>The Philosophy of Logical Atomism</u>, First Indian Reprint, 2010, Oxon, Ox, Routledge

Russell, Bertrand, 1929, <u>Mysticism and Logic</u>, New York, W. W. Norton & Company

Russell, Bertrand, 1940, <u>An Inquiry into Meaning & Truth</u>, New York, W. W. Norton

Russell, Bertrand, 1945, <u>A History of Western Philosophy</u>, New York, Simon & Schuster

Ryle, Gilbert, 1949, <u>The Concept of Mind</u>, London, Hutchinson & Company, Ltd.

Ryle, Gilbert, 1957, <u>Theory of Meaning</u>

Sapir, Edward, 1921, <u>Language an Introduction to the Study of Speech</u>, Dover Publications, Inc., Mineola, NY, 2004

Searle, John, 1969, <u>Speech Acts</u>, Cambridge, UK, Cambridge University Press

Searle, John, 1992, <u>The Rediscovery of Mind</u>, Cambridge, MA, The MIT Press

Searle, John, 2002, <u>Consciousness and Language</u>, Cambridge, UK, Cambridge University Press

Searle, John, 2004, <u>Mind, A Brief Introduction, Oxford, Oxford University Press</u>

Seif, Charles, 2000, <u>Zero The Biography of a Dangerous Idea</u>, New York, Penguin Putnam Inc.

Segre, Gino, 2007, <u>Faust in Copenhagen</u>, New York, Penguin Group

Sellars, Wilfrid, 1997, <u>Empiricism and the Philosophy of Mind</u>, Cambridge, MA, Harvard

Skinner, B. F., 1953, <u>Science and Human Behavior</u>, New York, The Free Press

Skinner, B. F., 1957, <u>Verbal Behavior</u>, Englewood Cliffs, NJ, Prentice-Hall Inc.

Skinner, B. F., 1969, <u>Contingencies of Reinforcement</u>, Englewood Cliffs, NJ, Prentice-Hall Inc.

Skinner, B. F., 1971, <u>Beyond Freedom and Dignity</u>, New York, Bantam Books

Skinner, B. F., 1974, <u>About Behaviorism</u>, New York, Vintage Books

Smolin, Lee, 2006, <u>The Trouble with Physics</u>, Houghton Mifflin Company, New York

Sosa, Ernest, and Tooley, Michael, 1993, <u>Causation</u>, Oxford, Oxford University Press

Stainton, Robert J., 2006, <u>Words and Thoughts</u>, Oxford, Clarendon Press

Strawson, P. F., 1959, <u>Individuals</u>, Garden City, NY, Anchor Books

Taylor, Kenneth, 1998, <u>Truth and Meaning</u>, Oxford, UK, Blackwell Publishers Ltd.

Thompson, Evan, 2007, <u>Mind in Life</u>, Cambridge, MA, Harvard University Press

Tomasello, Michael, 2003, <u>Constructing a Language</u>, Cambridge, MA, Harvard University Press

Tomasello, Michael, and Slobin, Dan Isaac, 2005, <u>Beyond Nature-Nuture</u>, Mahwah, NJ, Lawrence Erlbaum Associates Inc.

Tomasello, Michael, 2008, <u>Origins of Human Communication</u>, Cambridge, MA, The MIT Press

Toulmin, Stephen, and Goodfield, June, 1965, <u>The Discovery of Time</u>, Chicago, IL, The University of Chicago Press

Velarde-Mayol, Victor, 2000, <u>On Brentano</u>, Belmont, CA, Wadsworth/Thompson Learning, Inc.

Vigotsky, L. S., 1962, <u>Thought and Language</u>, Cambridge, MA, The MIT Press

Watson, John B., 1919, <u>Psychology from the Standpoint of a Behaviorist</u>, Philadelphia, PA, J. B. Lippincott Company

Warner, Rex, 1958, <u>The Greek Philosophers</u>, New York, The New American Library

Whitehead, Alfred N., 1965, <u>A Philosopher Looks at Science</u>, Philosophical Library Inc.

Whorf, Benjamin Lee, 1956, <u>Language Thought and Reality</u>, Copyright 1956, MIT, printed by Martino Publishing, Mansfield, CT

Wilson, Deidre and Sperber, Dan, 2012, <u>Meaning and Relevance</u>, Cambridge, UK, Cambridge University Press

Wittgenstein, Ludwig, 1988, <u>Tractatus Logico-Philosophicus</u>, Translated by C.K Ogden, London, Rutledge & Kegan Paul Ltd.

Wittgenstein, Ludwig, 1958b, <u>The Blue and Brown Books</u>, Malden, MA, Blackwell Publishing Ltd.

Wittgenstein, Ludwig, 1958a, <u>Philosophical Investigations</u>, Third edition translated by G.E.M. Anscombe, Basil Blackwell & Mott, Ltd.

Young, Louise B., 1965, <u>The Mystery of Matter</u>, New York, Oxford University Press

Ziff, Paul, 1960, <u>Semantic Analysis</u>, Ithaca NY, Cornell University Press

<u>The Empiricists</u>, 1961, New York, Doubleday

<u>The Rationalists</u>, 1974, New York, Anchor Books

A Word from the Author

I have had a love for analytic philosophy since I was first introduced to it as a young man attending the University of Wisconsin many years ago. At that point, career concerns forced me to focus on money-making options rather than pursue a career in academia. In spite of my career choices I continued to read and write philosophy.

After retiring in 2001 I returned to school as an independent scholar, taking classes at UW Madison and UT Austin. This book was begun in 2006 as an attempt to synthesize what I had learned independently with what I was learning in the classroom, and produce a coherent Weltanschauung. I believe that I have done so. However, you will be the ultimate judge of my success. We may agree or disagree upon many things in this book. In either case, I trust that your experience reading it will prove to be a worthwhile endeavor.

R.J. Mott Jr., August 2020
www.soundingoutsemantics.com

Cover photos:
1. B.F. Skinner
2. Benjamin Whorf
3. Nicholaus Copernicous
4. Isaac Newton
5. Charles Darwin
6. Bertrand Russell
7. Albert Einstein
8. Ludwig Wittgenstein
9. Michael Reddy
10. David Hume
11. John Locke
12. William Baum
13. John Searle
14. Michael Tomasello
15. Antonio Damasio
16. John Langshaw Austin
17. Daniel Dennett
18. Gerald Myers
19. Gilbert Ryle
20. Plato